# A Man from Héric

## The Life and Work of Paul Tessier, M.D.
## Father of Craniofacial Surgery

### Volume I

# A Man from Héric

**The Life and Work of Paul Tessier, M.D.**
**Father of Craniofacial Surgery**

S. Anthony Wolfe, M.D.

ISBN 978-1-257-78215-4

I have not been able to determine who actually took the picture of Dr. Tessier with the skulls (a Franceschetti, an Apert, and a cleft lip and palate). Carlo Cavina of Bologna, Italy. Carlo is a friend of many years and one of Dr. Tessier's favorite trainees. He obtained a copy of the Tessier picture from Dr. Tessier and juxtaposed it with Caravaggio's "St. Jerome" (which hangs in the Cathedral of La Valetta in Malta). (Courtesy Mme. Mireille Tessier and the Bishopry of Malta.)

***If you are interested in purchasing several videos of Dr. Tessier compiled on a DVD of his work as well as the English Translation of his book (1976), kindly contact my Secretary, Donna Aloni, at donna@wolfemarshall.com. There is a nominal fee for the DVD of $25.00 to cover the costs of shipping and handling.***

# Preface

June 5, 2009. There is quiet, with some birdsong. *Les moineaux (*small birds of whatever variety) flit like little Vs from treetop to treetop. The wind rustles through the large, old oak trees, and the leaves of the hedge along the *grand*e *allée,* the gravel driveway, flutter quietly.

It is a soft day with the freshness of spring, and a few small, white clouds slowly make their way across the pale, gray-blue sky.

I am in Héric, a small town about a half hour's drive inland from Nantes, in Brittany, at the birthplace of Paul Tessier. I am sitting on the front porch step of the house in which he was born, *Bonne Hygié.* You might call it a small chateau, with a high peaked slate roof, and chimneys. A walk down the *grande alleé* brings you to the gate. To the right, the road goes on to Blain and, as usual, there is no traffic. To the left, the road takes you through the small village of Héric, with only a few locales (a florist, a stationer, and an elementary school), and then another hundred feet or so, to the Church of Héric and its cemetery.

Paul Tessier died on June 5, 2008, in Paris, one year ago today. He is buried here, in the family plot of his maternal grandfather, Auguste Clergeau. To the left of the plot are the Tessiers and, on the right, the Clergeaux.

Paul Tessier's contributions to the field of surgery are legendary and rank him among the several greatest surgeons of all time, of any specialty. He was a dreamer and could change his dreams into daring, iconoclastic innovations that were spectacularly successful. The entire specialty of craniofacial surgery was his single-handed creation; and, because of his work, countless patients the world over with serious facial malformations due to birth defects, trauma, or tumors, have received treatment that would not have been otherwise possible. Some of the results that he obtained decades ago still far exceed anything the current generation of plastic surgeons are capable of (and that certainly includes myself).

I will examine what his contributions to surgery were and how he came to make them. Some of the descriptions of the procedures themselves may seem a bit technical, but it is the job of a surgeon to be able to explain an operation in simple enough terms that the patient, a layperson, will understand. The DVD in the envelope at the back of this book has several video clips of Dr. Tessier, a large compendium of his work (put together for the *Honoris Causa* meeting held in his honor in London in 2006), and an English translation of a book he wrote in 1976 almost all by himself, even though he insisted on giving his coauthors equal listing.

I will also look at other aspects of his life—his trips to Africa for elephant hunting, for example. These trips were approached with the same careful, methodical analysis, and the same thoroughness and self–criticism that he applied to surgery, the design of surgical instruments, the renovation of *Bonne Hygié,* the rating of meals and wines that he consumed in various restaurants, and virtually everything else in his life.

I am enormously grateful to many of those who knew and worked with Paul Tessier for providing their remembrances. And, particularly, to Paul Tessier himself, who, in the last decade of his life, gave me free access to all of his records and reminiscences. His wife Mireille has been of inestimable help and generosity as well, and this book would not have been possible without her help and constant support. Jean Francois Tulasne, Dr. Tessier's associate for many years, has done his best to help me decipher some of Dr. Tessier's acronyms, with which his writing is filled.

Over the years that I knew Paul Tessier (I first watched him operate in Chicago in 1971), I suppose I have been like a Boswell to his modern-day Samuel Johnson trying to understand what he did in surgery so that I and others might reproduce it. Also, I sought to get to know this remarkable man gradually as I became better acquainted with him. I have tried as much as possible to have it be his story and to be the Boswell in the background, merely; but, alas, this must, to a certain extent, be my own story as well.

Whatever successes I have had as a surgeon I attribute to what I learned from Dr. Tessier over the years, and I hope have passed on to several generations of plastic surgery residents and fellows.

The French have a word, *terroir,* which loosely translates to *terrain* or *ground.* The term is generally used to describe those properties of a certain *Grand Cru* wine, which come from the soil in which the grapes are grown. Paul Tessier's *terroir* is Brittany, the land in which he was born into a family of wine merchants, the land he returned to throughout his life, the land he loved, and the land in which he is buried. Like a Petrus or a Chateau Margaux or a Romanéé Conti that draws its character from the soil that nourished its grapes, Paul Tessier's character and essence came from his beloved Brittany.

The story of Paul Tessier begins here, in Héric, and will end here.

# Table of Contents


Chapter 1. Geneology and Childhood Years ........ 1
Chapter 2. Going into medicine and training in Nantes ........ 35
Chapter 3. Post-war: off to Paris ........ 47
Chapter 4. First steps into Craniofacial Surgery ........ 79
Chapter 5. Further development of the field ........ 107
Chapter 6. Problems at Foch ........ 113
Chapter 7. Applications of Craniofacial Surgery to other conditions ........ 119
Chapter 8. The SFO (French Society of Ophthalmology) Report ........ 139
Chapter 9. The Tessier Classification of Facial Clefts ........ 141
Chapter 10. Mise au Point of Craniofacial Surgery ........ 147
Chapter 11. *Secteur "T"* ........ 197
Chapter 12. Cousteau ........ 215
Chapter 13. Stock Cars ........ 217
Chapter 14. International Meeting Rome 1967 ........ 219
Chapter 15. Mireille ........ 237
Chapter 16. Paris in 1974 ........ 245
Chapter 17. Training with Tessier ........ 261
Chapter 18. US Trips ........ 265
Chapter 19. The Tessier Consultation ........ 271
Chapter 20. Trips to Miami ........ 277
Chapter 21. Brazil ........ 281
Chapter 22. Iran/Iraq ........ 289
Chapter 23. $60^{th}$ birthday ........ 299
Chapter 24. JIVAROS ........ 303
Chapter 25. Maltreatment in the US and elsewhere ........ 359
Chapter 26. The Artists ........ 367
Chapter 27. Instruments ........ 377
Chapter 28. $70^{th}$ birthday ........ 383
Chapter 29. Lebanon ........ 385

Chapter 30. Le Grand 26 ........ 401
Chapter 31. SAPP ........ 403
Chapter 32. Solange ........ 409
Chapter 33. Kudos ........ 411
Chapter 34. Val de Grace ........ 415
Chapter 35. A trip to Cuba ........ 421
Chapter 36. Tour de Bretagne ........ 435
Chapter 37. Open Heart surgery ........ 441
Chapter 38. Légion d'Honneur ........ 443
Chapter 39. Honoris Causa ........ 449
Chapter 40. A Year of Suffering ........ 457
Chapter 41. Final Events ........ 465
Chapter 42. Funeral ........ 471
Chapter 43. Memorial Mass ........ 473

# Chapter 1

## Genealogy and Childhood Years

Tessier is not an uncommon name in Brittany. The name may derive from workers who dealt with fabrics or "tissues," washing their linen in the waters of the Loire, and then spinning and weaving it. Paul Tessier wrote that his family still had a spinning wheel when he was a child, which he saw being used by his maternal grandmother Bodin. Besides weavers, other Tessiers were sailors and wine merchants. He wrote that, in 1794, "Tessiers witnessed the slaughter of thousands of Vendeéns, who [for their religious beliefs] were slaughtered by the "Armies of the Republic," a French butchery worthy of the Soviets at Katyn or the Ruandans in 1995 … I can still remember recitals by my grandmother, who was born only 60 years after the atrocities. That was the apotheosis of atrocities and the triumph of monsters, cloaked behind revolutionary liberty and fraternity … and the mass drowning of people in their own blood. In two years, there were as many tortured, hung, decapitated, burnt, skewered, and drowned at Nantes as in four centuries of Cathares, Albigeois, Huguenots, Red Bonnets, and False Prophets."

During the French revolution, the Revolutionary Commune and the *sans culottes* ordered that all religious orders be dissolved and monasteries closed. Churches were vandalized and priests who refused to swear allegiance to the new government were executed. When the population in Brittany refused to give up their Catholic Religion, General Turreau was sent in with his army, and people in towns in the Vendée and Brittany were slaughtered. It has been estimated that up to 30 percent of the entire population were killed, often after rape and butchery. Paul Tessier was never a fan of the French revolution (he said that he considered flying the Bourbon flag with its golden fleur-de-lys on a white background outside his apartment on Avenue Kléber during the bicentennial celebrations of the French revolution).

The Bretons have traditionally considered themselves separate from the rest of France, and they have great pride in their own identity. Recall that when General Charles de Gaulle gave his famous "Vive le Quebec Libre!" speech in Montreal in 1967, bumper stickers almost immediately appeared in Brittany announcing "Vive la Bretagne Libre!"

As far as the Bodins of Héric, he was not able to trace back their lineage more than a few generations. His great, great-grandfather lived in Le Pavé in a little thatched-roof cottage, but he worked in the village as a blacksmith, making plows and hoes and shoeing horses. Grandfather Clergeau built him a little house with a forge, where Tessier wrote, "I saw sparks fly under his hammer."

He writes, "From Herbraie in Vertou came the Clergeau. Great grandfather was a marine carpenter at Portillon, at the mouth of the Sèvre and the Loire, in Nantes. There were seven children, and the little farm of 3 or 4 hectares could not feed 9 mouths or even 5 or 6 families. Four or five of the boys therefore left home early to find work."

*"Our grandfather Auguste was a hard worker, and he had known poverty, real poverty, and he wanted to assure well-being and security to his family by his own work. He succeeded in building a small wine business, developing it, and making it prosper. On both sides of the road to Blain there were the following:*

- *The 4 hectares of the (new) house, its stores, pressing shed, arbors, stables, two enclosed gardens, a wood burning oven for baking bread, a large chicken house, and a large brick rabbit hutch. All according to his plans.*
- *The 5 hectares of Bonne Hygié for his children with the pond, the large meadow, the little wood, and the 'large garden.'*

- *The 3 hectares of the 'Croppe,' 300 meters away on the dirt road, now gravel."*

Grandfather Clergeau was the patriarch of the family, and purchased Bonne Hygié from the Planchenault family, who in turn had purchased it from the Logereau family , who had built it in 1850. Auguste Clergeau's wholesale wine business prospered, and he expanded his farm to the other side of the road to Blain where he built another house for family members.

Ernest Tessier, Paul's father, was from Couéron, and also worked in the wine business. He had finished his military service in 1911, but was recalled to the 17th Regiment of the Infantry Unit of Vannes. He left for Belgium in 1914, where he was wounded after fifteen days on the front, taken prisoner by the Germans, and hospitalized at Arras. A woman who was visiting her own wounded husband met him and sent a letter to Tessier's mother, Solange, saying that her husband was still alive. In 1915, he was sent to Switzerland, though not allowed to return to France during the course of the War. In order that the Tessier wine business did not go downhill, Solange managed the enterprise with one old worker who had not been subject to mobilization. She delivered the wine in a charette, a light horse-drawn buggy.

Solange, his wife, accompanied by her sister, Mathilde, were permitted to visit Ernest in Vevay, Switzerland. (Mathilde died young of Addison's disease of tubercular origin.) Paul Tessier was conceived in Switzerland during one of these visits, and thanks to his birth in Héric, his father was repatriated from Switzerland in 1917. The wine business of the Tessier family in Couéron went downhill, since Ernest Tessier had difficulty walking and was never the same after his war injuries. The Tessier wine business was liquidated, and Ernest moved in with his father-in-law at Bonne Hygié and began working in the Clergeau wine wholesale business, which was quite successful.

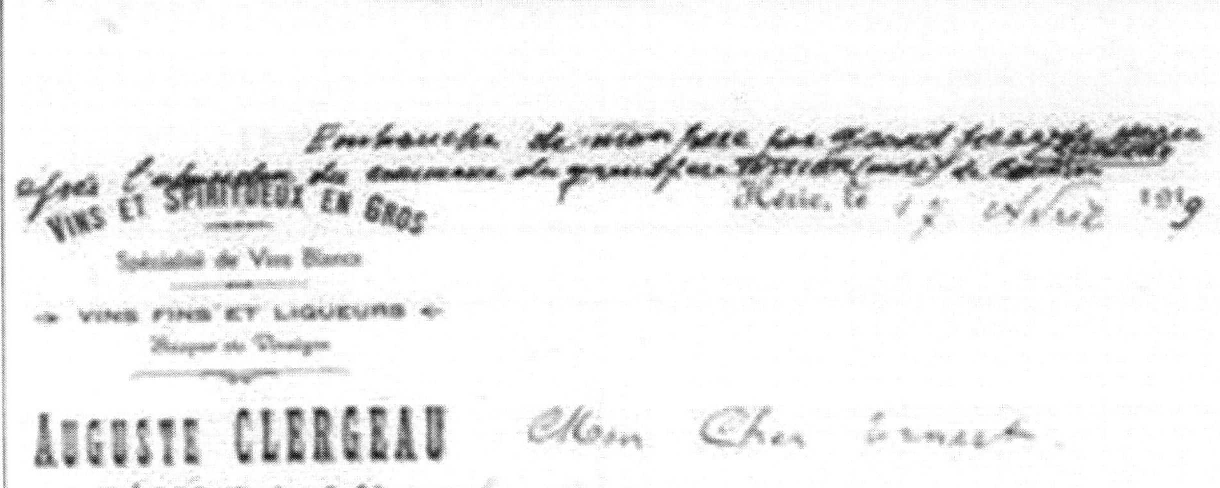

Embauche de mon père par Grand père Clergeau

VINS ET SPIRITUEUX EN GROS

Spécialité de Vins Blancs

VINS FINS ET LIQUEURS

AUGUSTE CLERGEAU

HÉRIC (Loire-Inf.)

Héric, le 17 Avril 1919

Mon Cher Ernest.

D'après nos conditions convenues et faites entre nous, il est entendu que vous rentrez à la maison pour représenter ma clientèle — moyennant les appointements mensuels de trois cents francs —

Plus les commissions suivantes deux francs pour trente et vingt bouteilles & fillettes. la bouteille considérée comme litre et la fillette comme demi litre —

Deux francs pour cent sur vins fins & liqueurs de marques

Deux francs cinquante pour cent sur les alcools compris Cognac. Rhum & Liqueurs (Deux francs par tête de ...)

Cinq francs pour cent sur les vinaigres —

Vingt cinq centimes par bouteilles de champagne et vins mousseux —

Il est entendu que ces ~~sommes~~ votre commission pour cent attribuées du ~~tant pour cent tant~~ sur les marchandises vendues par vous même & ... c'est à dire le montant des ... bonbonnes & bouteilles n'est pas compté dans la remise de ~~tant pour cent~~ votre commission

Les frais de voyages sont à ma charge et le cheval et la voiture doivent être fournis par moi —

Le nombre des communes à visiter sera déterminé par nous. et combien elles devront être visitées par an selon leur importance et distance.

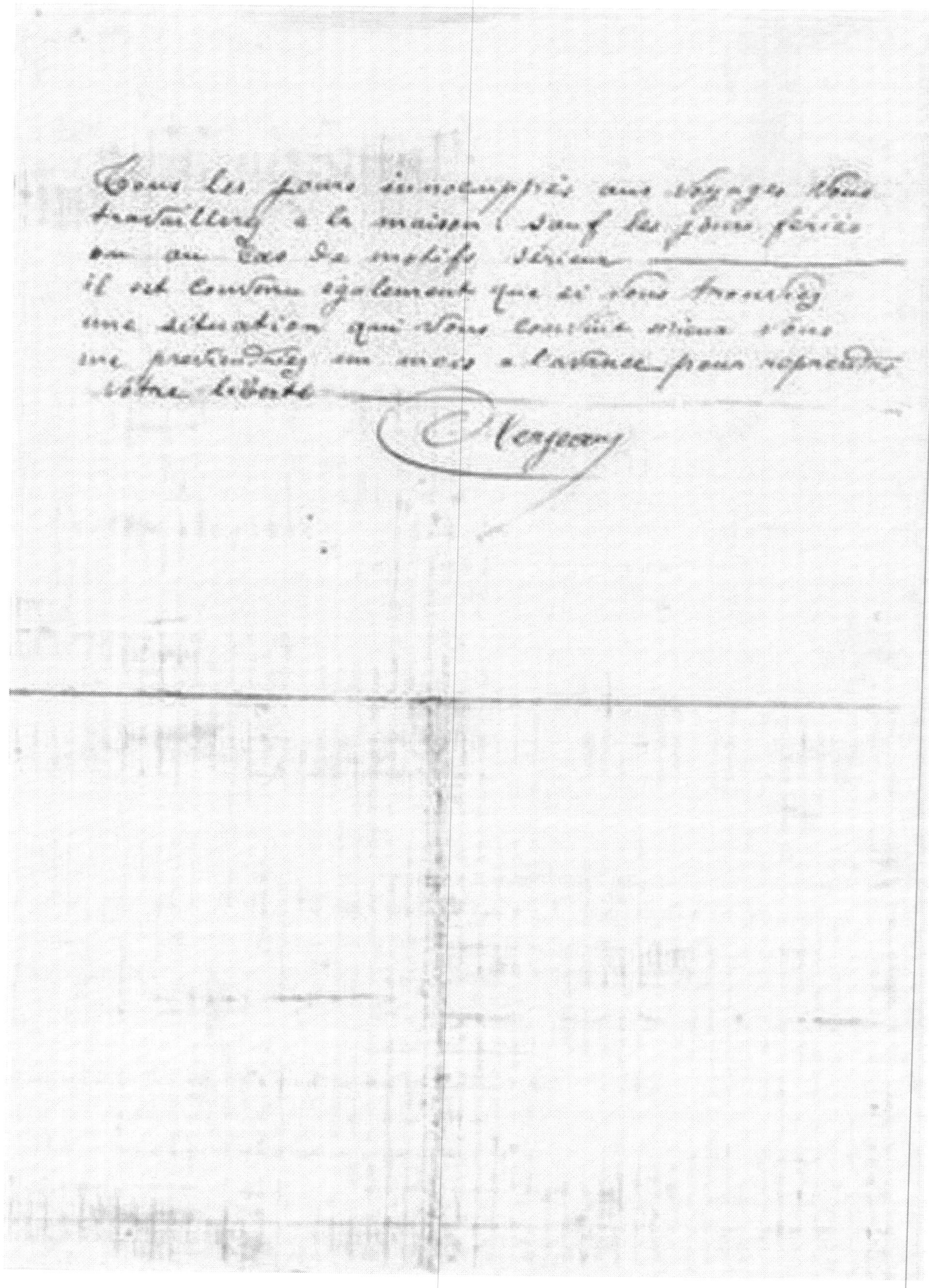

Tous les jours inoccupés aux voyages vous
travaillerez à la maison sauf les jours fériés
ou au cas de motifs sérieux
il est convenu également que si vous trouviez
une situation qui vous convienne mieux vous
me préviendrez un mois à l'avance pour reprendre
votre liberté

Clergeau

*Fig. 1.1 Letter of agreement between Auguste Clergeau and his son-in-law, Ernest Tessier. (See Translation, Appendices/Family/Héric.)*

To visit his paternal grandmother in Couéron, there were no direct connections. Young Paul, aged five to six, would go north from Héric on top of a stagecoach, then *in* the stagecoach, then on a train to Nantes, then on a river boat (an abeille or "bee") to his grandmother's house on the Loire in Couéron.

In 1920, when Tessier was three, his mother developed pulmonary tuberculosis and had to be isolated. Solange and Paul were sent to live across the street, and his mother was treated by rest, since at the time there were no sanatoriums.

Of this period of his life we know fairly little, but we can surmise what his daily activities must have been. He played with his sister and cousins and other children from the neighborhood. He was living on a working farm, essentially, with chickens, horses, cattle, goats, rabbits (angoras, raised for their wool), beehives, different kinds of fruit trees, a large kitchen garden, and all of the nearby activity of a busy wholesale wine business. He was out in the fields most of the time, had a .22 rifle with which he hunted birds, spent time fishing, and enjoyed frolicking with the family dogs.

Paul went to parochial grade school in Héric, and, at age twelve, he left for the College St. Louis in St. Nazaire, where he became a boarder. To get there, he would go to Blain in a horse-drawn carriage with his mother or an employee of the wine business and then take the train to St. Nazaire (three hours to go 160 km).

Here he found himself quite behind in everything except Latin, and he worked very hard. In February, he became ill with a hemolytic streptococcal abscess of his thigh. He was hospitalized at the infirmary of the College of St. Louis. His mother came, with the surgeon Poussie, who placed four drains in his enormously swollen leg. A call was placed to Hôpital St. Vincent (a children's hospital) in Paris for an antiserum to be used against a streptococcal infection. He returned to Héric, occupying a room on the ground floor, and Dr. Gachillard came to do the daily dressings (hydrophilic cotton and irrigations with Dakin's solution). He returned to school by Easter, but he had a relapse and missed three months of school.

The summers he spent at Héric, in the fields and forests, and on boats on the Loire. There were frequent trips to the nearby beach at La Baule, where years later he rented a house and eventually bought an apartment overlooking the beach.

Auguste Clergeau, his grandfather, who, in his later years, was plagued by a debilitating polyarthritic condition and lived on the ground floor of the house since he could not climb the stairs, died in 1929 The family, who had been among the most well off in the community (Auguste was the first in Héric to have an automobile, a telephone, and electricity in his house), fell into somewhat impoverished circumstances.

Paul's older sister, Solange, had gone into nursing, and Paul considered a number of careers. His first choice was to go into the navy to have a maritime career, but this became impossible after he had a stormy first bout ("primo") of tuberculosis. Other considerations were becoming an agriculturalist or a forest agent, since he liked the countryside, or a veterinarian, since he had spent a good bit of time tagging along with the veterinarian who treated their animals. His mother, perhaps because of her long illness, proposed medicine. Paul felt that the studies would be too long and costly, but his parents insisted. He finished his bacalaureat in Nantes, sometimes going the 25 km in each direction by bicycle.

*Fig. 1.2 Héric is about 20 km north of Nantes and Blain is another 10 km to the west of Héric.*

*Fig. 1.3 The road out of Héric to Blain will lead you past Bonne Hygié.*

*Fig. 1.4 Postcard of Heric, ca. 1900, showing the view from the "park" of Bonne Hygié.*
*The church of Héric is seen in the background.*

*Fig. 1.5 Condition of Bonne Hygie in the late 1980s after a decade of being uninhabited; Solange, his sister, was in a nursing home much of this time, unable to look after the management of the family home.*

*Fig. 1.6 During repairs that began after Solange's death, and after an old tree threatened the roof repairs following a major storm.*

*Fig. 1.7 Bonne Hygié. June 2009, after its complete rehabilitation. The driveway (grande allée) runs off to the left, to the road to Blain.*

*Fig. 1.8 View of house with road to Blain on the left.Paul Tessier was born in the room on the second floor, the upper left window of the side of house facing us.*

*Fig. 1.9 View of driveway (grande allée) passing in front of the house. Greenhouse is just visible.*

*Fig. 1.10 Interior of the Greenhouse, 2009.*

*Fig. 1.11 The pond. Inlet on the left was where washing was done.*

*Fig. 1.12 Two large oaks; the one on the left Tessier said his mother planted at the time of his birth.*

*Fig. 1.13 Current shed, which used to be a wine warehouse.*

*Fig. 1.14 House on the other side of the road to Blain built by Auguste Clergeau to house other family members. Paul and his sister, Solange, lived here during the time that his mother was in isolation with tuberculosis.*

*Fig. 1.15 Auguste Clergeau, maternal grandfather.*

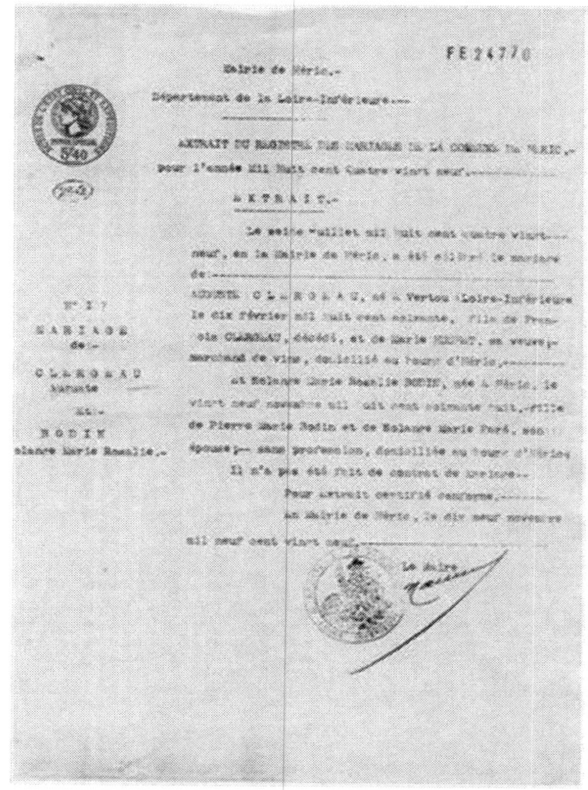

FE 24770

Mairie de Héric.-

Département de la Loire-Inférieure.-

EXTRAIT DU REGISTRE DES MARIAGES DE LA COMMUNE DE HERIC,-
pour l'année Mil huit cent quatre vingt neuf.-

EXTRAIT.-

Le seize juillet mil huit cent quatre vingt-neuf, en la Mairie de Héric, a été célébré le mariage de:-

AUGUSTE CLERGEAU, né à Vertou (Loire-Inférieure) le dix février mil huit cent soixante, fils de François CLERGEAU, décédé, et de Marie [illegible], sa veuve, marchand de vins, domicilié au bourg d'Héric,-

et Solange Marie Rosalie BODIN, née à Héric, le vingt neuf novembre mil huit cent soixante huit, fille de Pierre Marie Bodin et de Solange Marie Paré, son épouse, sans profession, domiciliée au bourg d'Héric.

Il n'a pas été fait de contrat de mariage.-

Pour extrait certifié conforme,-

En Mairie de Héric, le dix neuf novembre mil neuf cent vingt neuf.-

Le Maire

N° 17

MARIAGE de:-

CLERGEAU Auguste

et:-

BODIN Solange Marie Rosalie.-

*Fig. 1.16 Marriage certificate of Tessier's maternal grandparents, August Clergeau and Solange Bodin, 1889.*

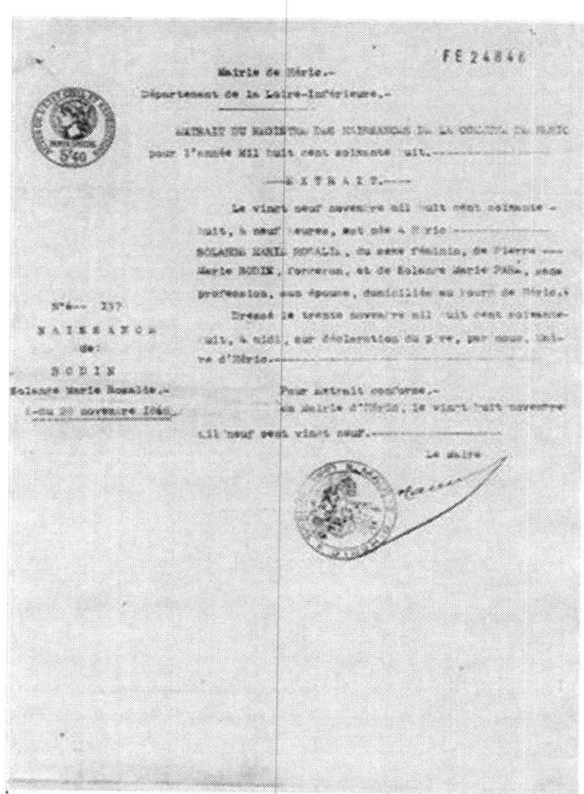

FE 24846

Mairie de Héric.-

Département de la Loire-Inférieure.-

EXTRAIT DU REGISTRE DES NAISSANCES DE LA COMMUNE DE HERIC
pour l'année Mil huit cent soixante huit.-

EXTRAIT.-

Le vingt neuf novembre mil huit cent soixante-huit, à neuf heures, est née à Héric SOLANGE MARIE ROSALIE, du sexe féminin, de Pierre Marie BODIN, forgeron, et de Solange Marie PARÉ, sans profession, son épouse, domiciliés au bourg de Héric.

Dressé le trente novembre mil huit cent soixante-huit, à midi, sur déclaration du père, par nous, Maire d'Héric.-

Pour extrait conforme,-

En Mairie d'Héric, le vingt huit novembre mil neuf cent vingt neuf.-

Le Maire

N°-- 137

NAISSANCE de:

BODIN Solange Marie Rosalie.-

[illegible] du 29 novembre 1868.

*Fig. 1.17 Birth certificate of Tessier's maternal grandmother, Solange Bodin, whose father, Pierre, is listed as a Blacksmith, her mother was Solange Paré.*

*Fig. 1.18 Solange Clergeau (née Bodin), Tessier's maternal grandmother.*

*Fig. 1.19 Auguste and Solange Clergeau, arm-in-arm in the front row, with Tessier and his sister, Solange, behind. ca. 1937.*

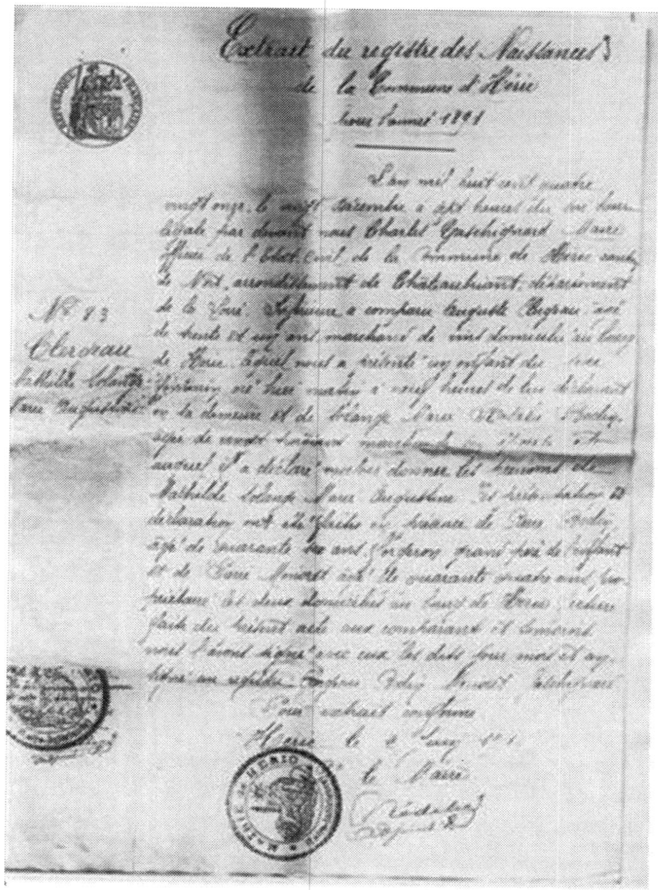

Extrait du registre des Naissances
de la Commune d'Héric

*Fig. 1.20 Birth certificate of Solange Clergeau, Tessier's mother, 1891.*

*Fig. 1.21 Ernest Tessier and Solange Clergeau on their wedding day, 1913*
*Note that they are on the grande allée, in front of the same hedge shown in Fig. 1.9 above. The original Greenhouse is visible.*

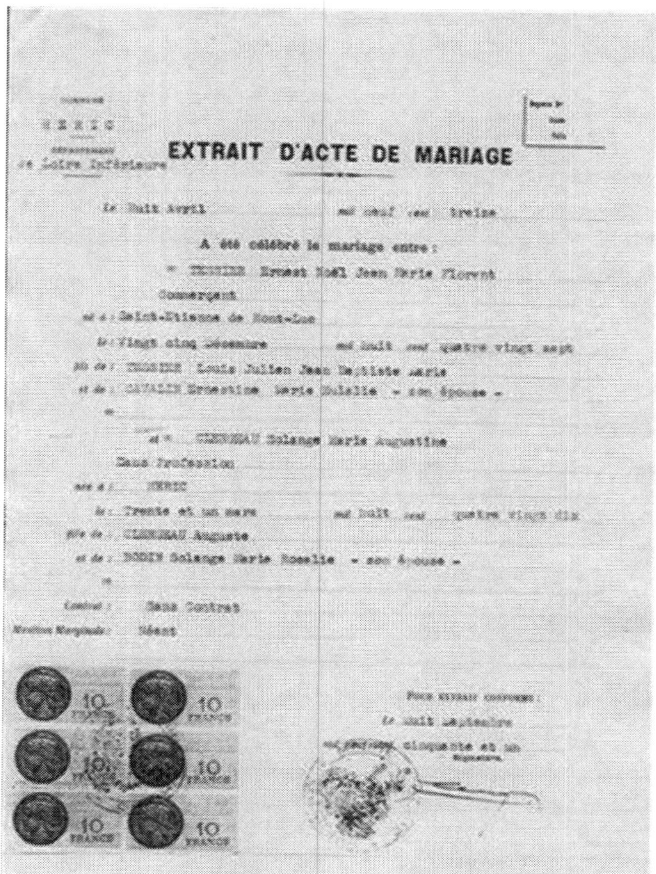
HERIC

Loire Inférieure

EXTRAIT D'ACTE DE MARIAGE

Le Huit Avril mil neuf cent treize

A été célébré le mariage entre :

TESSIER Ernest Noël Jean Marie Florent

Commerçant

né à : Saint-Etienne de Mont-Luc

le : Vingt cinq Décembre mil huit cent quatre vingt sept

fils de : TESSIER Louis Julien Jean Baptiste Marie

et de : CAVALIN Ernestine Marie Eulalie - son épouse -

et CLERGEAU Solange Marie Augustine

Sans Profession

née à : HERIC

le : Trente et un mars mil huit cent quatre vingt dix

fille de : CLERGEAU Auguste

et de : BODIN Solange Marie Rosalie - son épouse -

Contrat : Sans Contrat

Mention Marginale : Néant

Pour extrait conforme :

Le huit Septembre

mil neuf cent cinquante et un

Fig. 1.22 Marriage certificate of Tessier's parents, 1913.

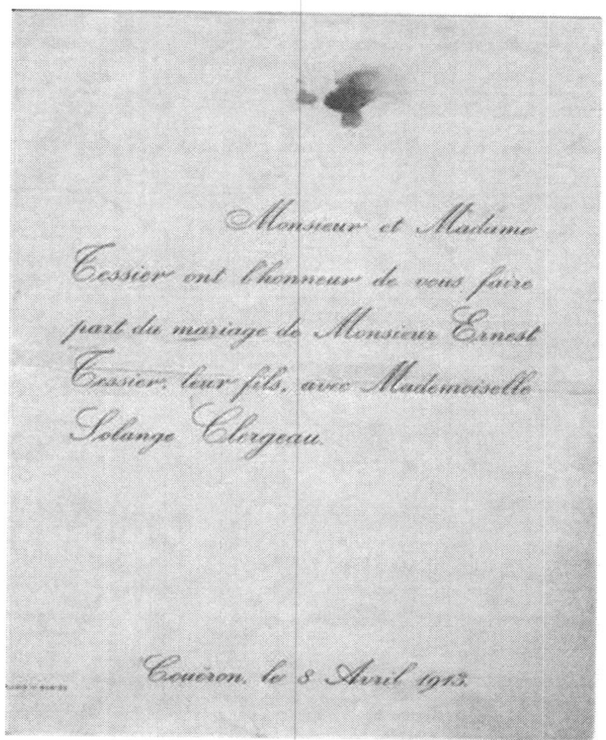
Monsieur et Madame Tessier ont l'honneur de vous faire part du mariage de Monsieur Ernest Tessier, leur fils, avec Mademoiselle Solange Clergeau.

Couëron, le 8 Avril 1913.

Fig. 1.23 Invitation to the marriage of their son sent by Ernest Tessier's parents.

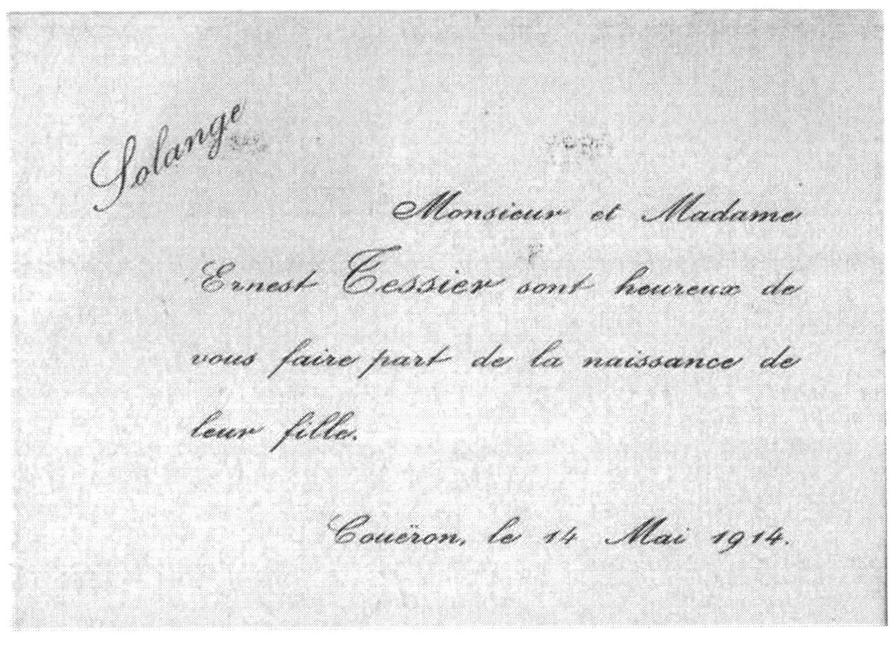

Solange

Monsieur et Madame

Ernest Tessier sont heureux de

vous faire part de la naissance de

leur fille.

Couëron, le 14 Mai 1914.

*Fig. 1.24 Birth announcement of Tessier's elder sister, Solange, 1914.*

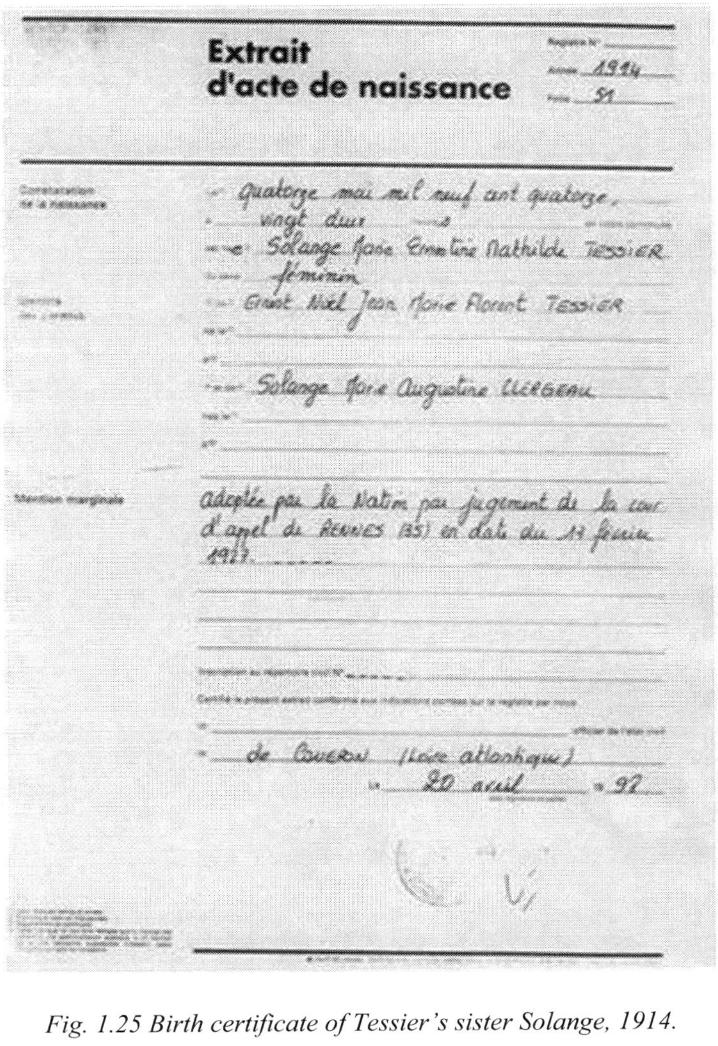

**Extrait**
**d'acte de naissance**

Année 1914
Acte 51

quatorze mai mil neuf cent quatorze,
vingt deux
Solange Marie Ernestine Mathilde TESSIER
féminin
Ernest Noël Jean Marie Florent TESSIER

Solange Marie Augustine CLERGEAU

Mention marginale

adoptée par la Nation par jugement de la cour d'appel de RENNES (35) en date du 17 février 1917. -----

de Couëron (Loire atlantique)
le 20 avril 92

*Fig. 1.25 Birth certificate of Tessier's sister Solange, 1914.*

*Fig. 1.26 Ernest Tessier, in WWI military attire.*

*Fig. 1.27 Ernest Tessier, second from the left in the second row, before being wounded and captured by the Germans, 1914.*

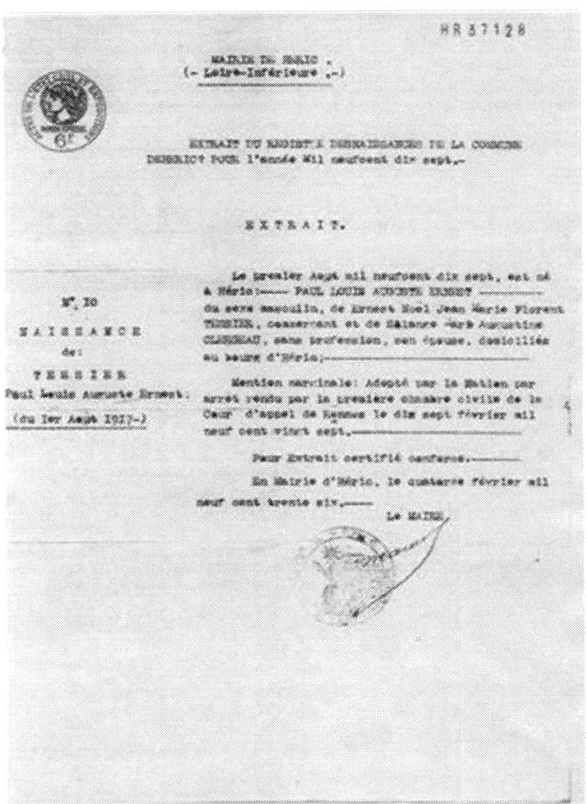

HR 37128

MAIRIE D'HÉRIC .
(– Loire-Inférieure .–)

EXTRAIT [illegible] DE LA COMMUNE [illegible] POUR l'année Mil neufcent dix sept.–

EXTRAIT.

N°. [illegible]

NAISSANCE
de:
TESSIER
Paul Louis Auguste Ernest.
(du 1er Août 1917.–)

Le premier Août mil neufcent dix sept, est né à Héric:—— PAUL LOUIS AUGUSTE ERNEST —— du sexe masculin, de Ernest Noel Jean Marie Florent TESSIER, [illegible] et de [illegible] Marie Augustine [illegible], sans profession, son épouse, domiciliés au bourg d'Héric;——

Mention marginale: Adopté par la Nation par arrêt rendu par la première chambre civile de la Cour d'appel de Rennes le dix sept février mil neuf cent vingt sept.——

Pour Extrait certifié conforme.——

En Mairie d'Héric, le quatorze février mil neuf cent trente six.——

Le MAIRE,

*Fig. 1.28 Birth certificate of Paul Louis Auguste Ernest Tessier, August 1, 1917.*

*Fig. 1.29 Mother Solange and young Paul, 1918.*

*Fig. 1.30 Solange and Paul Tessier, ca. 1920.*
*His delicate grip of the pail and shovel is perhaps an indication of his future manual abilities.*

*Fig. 1.31 Paul Tessier on his tricycle in front of his maternal grandfather, Auguste Clergeau, ca. 1921.*

*Fig. 1.32 Paul and Solange, ca. 1922.*

VOUS QUI L'AVEZ CONNUE ET AIMÉE

SOUVENEZ-VOUS DANS VOS PRIÈRES

DE

**Mathilde CLERGEAU**

*Pieusement endormie dans la paix du Seigneur*

*le 13 Octobre 1922*

A L'AGE DE 30 ANS

Elle a gardé la patience, la gaité, la résignation dans sa longue maladie.

Elle a passé ne laissant dans la vie que le souvenir du bonheur qu'elle a donné aux siens.

Seigneur, vous nous l'aviez donnée pour faire notre bonheur, vous nous la demandez, nous vous la rendons sans murmurer, mais le cœur brisé de douleur. *(Saint Ephrem.)*

DERNIÈRES PAROLES A SA FAMILLE:

Je ne vous vois plus. Je ne vous entends plus, mais je vous aime tant. Toutes mes souffrances, mon Dieu, je vous les offre pour leur bonheur à tous. Je fais le sacrifice de ma vie pour que vous soyez tous heureux, tous bienheureux, adieu.

Mon Dieu, que votre volonté soit faite Ma petite sœur Thérèse de l'Enfant Jésus, priez pour moi.

Lanoë-Mareau, Libraire, Nantes.

*Fig. 1.33 Death notice of Mathilde Clergeau, Tessier's aunt, who had accompanied his mother to Switzerland. She died of tuberculosis at age thirty.*

*Fig. 1.34 Tessier at First Communion, ca. 1927.*

SOUVENEZ-VOUS DANS VOS PRIÈRES

DE L'AME DE

**Monsieur Auguste CLERGEAU**

*Rappelé à Dieu le 23 Février 1929*

Le plus long jour a son déclin, le labeur le plus dur a son terme, la douleur la plus amère sera suivie d'une consolation éternelle. *(Père Faber.)*

La croix porte au ciel ceux qu'elle a soutenus sur la terre. *(Psaumes.)*

Il sut s'oublier et penser aux autres et aux siens.

Daignez ô mon Dieu ne pas séparer dans le ciel ceux qui se sont tant aimés sur la terre.

*Doux Seigneur Jésus, donnez-lui le repos éternel !*
(300 j. d'ind.)

Librairie Libaros, Nantes.

*Fig. 1.35 Death notice of Auguste Clergeau, 1929.*

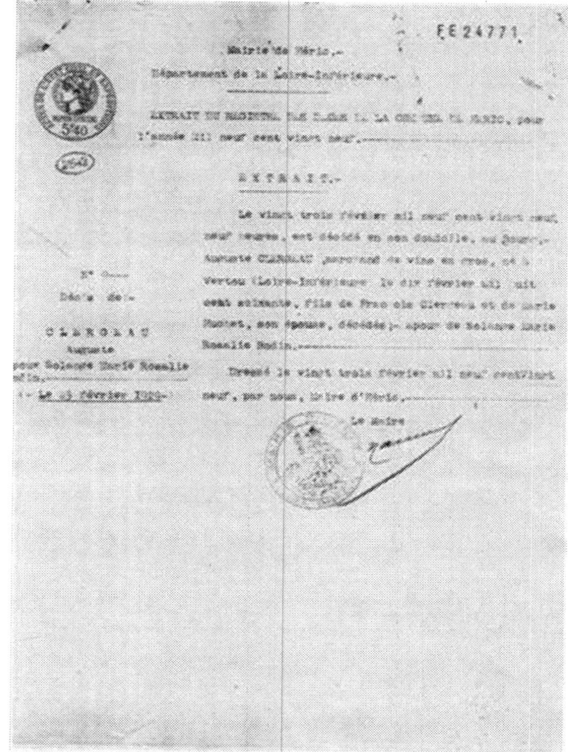

EE 24771

Mairie de Héric.-

Département de la Loire-Inférieure.-

EXTRAIT.-

Le Maire

*Fig. 1.36 Death certificate of Auguste Clergeau, son of Francois Clergeau and Marie Huchet.*

*Fig. 1.37 Secondary school with the Holy Fathers, Héric. Tessier is the third from the left in the second row. ca. 1930. Fourth from the left in the last row is Henri Toscer, older brother of the mother of Joël Cornet, son of his medical school classmate and friend, Ernest Cornet. Toscer was killed in 1942 when his boat was sunk in the Mediterranean.*

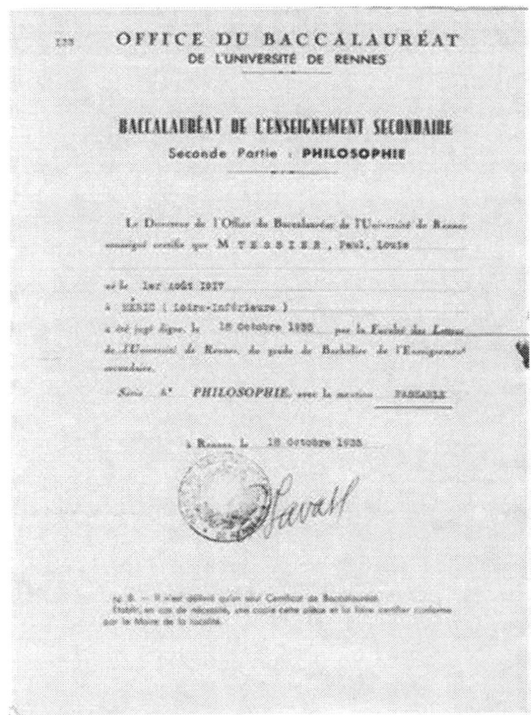

OFFICE DU BACCALAURÉAT
DE L'UNIVERSITÉ DE RENNES

BACCALAURÉAT DE L'ENSEIGNEMENT SECONDAIRE
Seconde Partie : PHILOSOPHIE

Le Directeur de l'Office du Baccalauréat de l'Université de Rennes soussigné certifie que M TESSIER, Paul, Louis

né le 1er août 1917
à HÉRIC ( Loire-Inférieure )
a été jugé digne, le 18 Octobre 1935 par la Faculté des Lettres de l'Université de Rennes, du grade de Bachelier de l'Enseignement secondaire.

Série A' PHILOSOPHIE, avec la mention PASSABLE

à Rennes, le 18 Octobre 1935

[illegible]

*Fig. 1.38 Secondary school diploma, 1935.*

*Fig. 1.39 1931. College de St. Nazaire. Tessier is to the far right in the second row (the only one in long trousers).*

*Fig. 1.40 Tessier fishing, ca. 1932.*

*Fig. 1.41 Tessier on a fishing yawl on the Loire, ca. 1933.*

*Fig. 1.42 With cousins in La Baule, ca. 1933.*

*Fig. 1.43 Ca. 1933, while at College in St. Nazaire.*

*Fig. 1.44 Tessier with his father, mother (Solange), sister (Solange), and the cat, ca. 1934.*

*Fig. 1.45 Sister, Solange; grandmother, Solange; and Tessier. Ca. 1935.*

*Fig. 1.46 The young photographer and admirers, ca. 1935.*

*Fig. 1.47 Tessier; grandmother, Solange; sister, Solange. Ca. 1936.*

SOUVENEZ-VOUS DANS VOS PRIÈRES

de

Madame Auguste CLERGEAU

Rappelée à Dieu le 8 Juillet 1955

à l'âge de 87 ans.

---

Tout le monde l'aimait parce qu'elle ne sut jamais que s'oublier pour penser aux autres.

Elle aimait le labeur incessant, «qui travaille prie» disait-elle.

*Fig. 1.48 Death notice of maternal grandmother, 1955.*

# Chapter 2

## Going into medicine and training in Nantes

Paul Tessier entered medical school in Nantes in 1936, and during his first year he continued to live at home in Héric to avoid paying for a room (since the situation of his parents was quite modest at this time). He commuted the 25 km to Nantes either in a car (he paid a monthly rate) or, in the spring months, by bicycle. For his second year in medicine, he lived in Nantes with friends of his parents (Geffroy).

His first rotation in general medicine was with Professor Duverget, who he recalled could be a bit cranky, and then he had a surgical rotation with Professor Picard, who he felt was a good teacher and spoke well. Every opportunity Paul had, he would go to the consultation of Professor Sebillaud, who was an exceptional clinician and could spend an hour talking with a patient.

There was another surgical rotation with Professor Lerta, who did what was then called general surgery—since, at that time, there was no thoracic surgery (except for thoracoplasties) and no vascular surgery.

When he took his externship during his second year, he functioned as an intern at Pen-brou, a sanatorium located 80 km from Nantes. Every week there was a visit from a surgeon, and there was one operative day per week. The pathology included Pott's disease, tuberculous coxarthroses, renal tuberculosis, and tuberculous abscesses. On the operative day, there were frequent iliac bone grafts and lots of plaster casts of all sorts.

At about this time during his training, he saw a cleft lip repair performed, and this generated a strong interest in plastic surgery.

He began his internship on September 1, 1939, and, after a month, there was a general mobilization and a recall to Nantes. Here, mobile military hospitals were formed (*ambulances militarie*, similar to a M.A.S.H. unit in the U.S. Army), and the students were called up as student officer reserves (*élèves officiers de reserve,* or E.O.R.).

The active-duty doctors came from the military hospitals (Lyon had Déjette; Bordeau had La Marine; and Paris had Val de Grace), and the others were from the E.O.R. They were all brought together in an old chocolate factory in Doulon, to the east of Nantes. Here, there were efforts to inculcate them with military discipline, the use of mortars and rifles, and, particularly, to subject them to long marches on foot in ill-fitting uniforms and terrible shoes.

Paul was mobilized into the French Army in 1938, as were all young Frenchmen. The war started, the Germans came sweeping down, and he and several friends (Robert Toussaint, a dentist; Robert Duloquin; and M. Brousseau, a pharmacist) prepared Toussaint's car, a Peugeot cabriolet, and were preparing to drive it to Spain. They parked inside the gates of *Hôtel Dieu* hospital , as they normally did so that the car would be safe. But in the morning, the guard had closed the gates (the Germans were going to arrive from Angers), and he would not let them out, in spite of an effort to bribe him. They were thus de facto prisoners, and when the Germans arrived in Nantes, the 16th, 17th, and 18th of June, 1940, they were transferred to the Broussais Hospital (the French military hospital) where they again were essentially prisoners. Paul at this point became ill: he had fever and diarrhea for eight days. Tessier was transferred to a small German military hospital near the park in Nantes, where he was moribund, febrile, and comatose for several days, and neither the French or German military doctors could make a diagnosis. Tessier contacted his uncle, and his mother came. He asked his mother to ask the German *Kommandant* whether she could bring his old professor of medicine by for a consultation. Permission was granted, the professor came, and he immediately diagnosed typhoid fever.

As Tessier told the story, a French military doctor and the German *Kommandant* were with Tessier's mother around his bed when the nurse announced the arrival of the professor, who remained just inside the door (about two meters away), and looked at him for about ten seconds without saying anything. At this precise moment, Tessier realized that he had made the diagnosis. The professor turned towards his colleagues, approached Tessier, took his pulse, looked at the temperature chart, palpated and ausculted with his stethoscope rapidly, and then exchanged a few words with his colleagues. He listened to the presentation of one of them politely, and then asked, "Of course, you have ordered a serological test?" This question fell like a bomb. There was silence. Tessier understood that the diagnosis was typhoid.

While waiting for the serological test, his high temperature (41 degrees Celsius.) was treated by wrapping him in towels and cold baths. There was no other treatment, and the risks were intestinal perforation and myocarditis.

After forty-eight hours, the fever broke and, after several further visits from his mother, he went to Héric to recuperate, his weight having fallen from 80 kg to 58 kg. The official report of the Medical Commission evaluating him for return to service was paratyphoid B, with signs of myocarditis.

After recuperation he found a place in the hospital at St. Nazaire. This being a major Nazi submarine base, however, there were daily bombings by the English at night. Tessier said that this was a beautiful scene: anti-aircraft searchlights lighting up the clouds and magnificent tracer rounds making superb fireworks, particularly when a plane was struck. One night, he was sleeping well--he had already gone down several times to the air raid shelter in a nearby retirement home, and this time didn't want to go—despite an increasingly loud roar (a storm?). After fifteen to twenty minutes of this noise, he woke up and noticed that there were no more panes in the windows. He looked across the debris and saw that the maternity hospital fifty meters away had disappeared. He went down to the on-call room and his three colleagues were very surprised to see him, believing him dead.

He returned to his hospital work in Nantes as an intern in 1943, and this time there were daytime bombardments by the American 8th Air Force. (Clark Gable was one of the pilots on these missions.)

One of the worst was on Thursday, September 16, 1943. He and a friend were in the on-call room at the hospital when there came the drone of approaching bombers and the shrill sound of air raid sirens. They debated where to take cover. The friend said that he thought the safest place would be the deep crater in the courtyard where a previous bomb had fallen, saying that it would be unheard of for another bomb to fall in exactly the same spot. Tessier decided that they would be safer inside, and they covered themselves with mattresses. A deafening blast came from close by, where another bomb had fallen precisely into the same crater. Tessier had escaped death a second time.

A number of his fellow interns did not, however, and the *Hôtel Dieu* in Nantes was totally destroyed by the bombings.

Since he had nowhere to work in Nantes, Tessier went to Paris (by foot, bicycle, and train) to continue his training.

*Fig. 2.1 Tessier as medical student, ca. 1937.*

*Fig. 2.2 With fellow house officers, ca. 1937 (Tessier is in the center).*

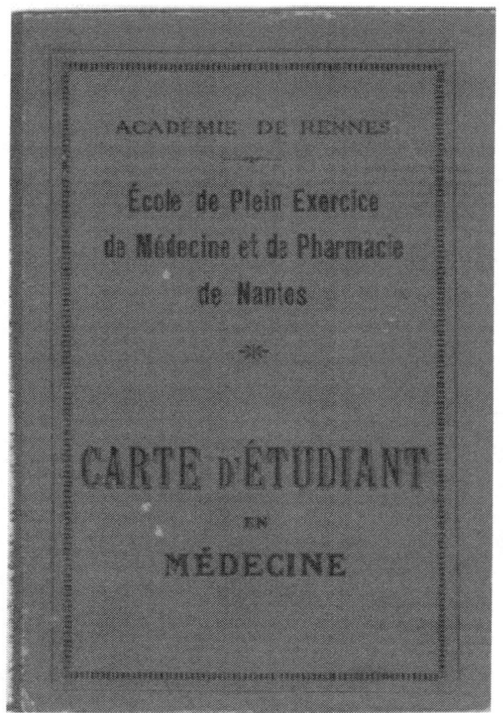
ACADÉMIE DE RENNES

École de Plein Exercice
de Médecine et de Pharmacie
de Nantes

CARTE D'ÉTUDIANT
EN
MÉDECINE

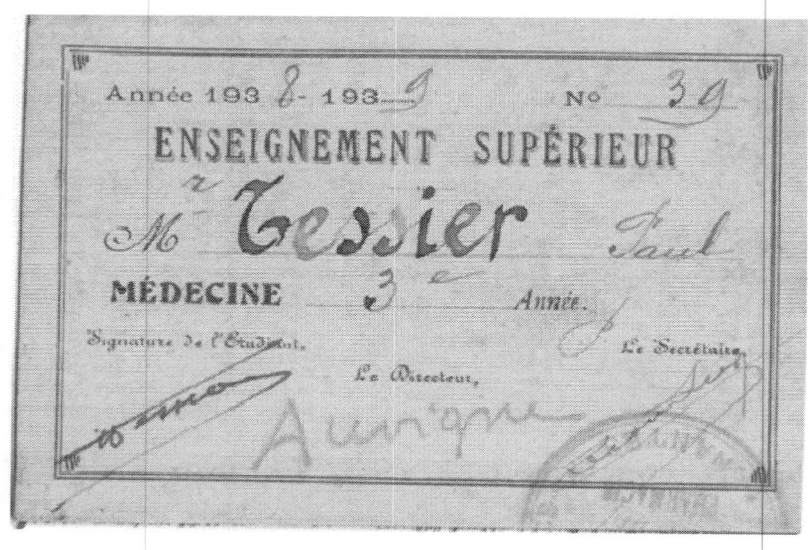
Année 1938-1939 N° 39

ENSEIGNEMENT SUPÉRIEUR

M^r Tessier Paul

MÉDECINE 3^e Année.

Signature de l'Étudiant. Le Secrétaire,

Le Directeur,

*Fig. 2.3 Card as 3rd year medical student, 1938.*

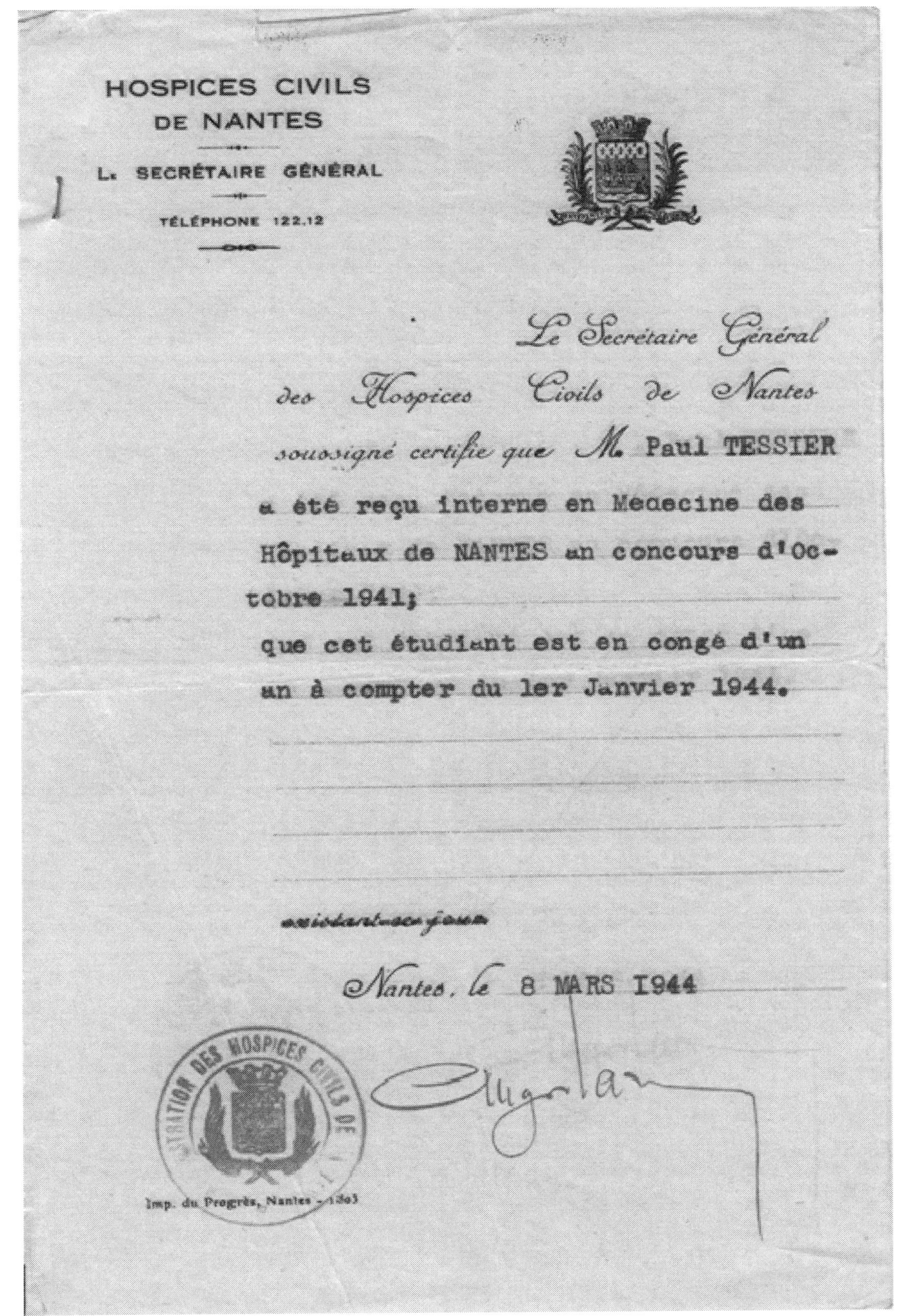
HOSPICES CIVILS
DE NANTES

LE SECRÉTAIRE GÉNÉRAL

TÉLÉPHONE 122.12

Le Secrétaire Général
des Hospices Civils de Nantes
soussigné certifie que M. Paul TESSIER
a été reçu interne en Medecine des
Hôpitaux de NANTES au concours d'Octobre 1941;
que cet étudiant est en congé d'un
an à compter du 1er Janvier 1944.

~~existant ce jour~~

Nantes, le 8 MARS 1944

ADMINISTRATION DES HOSPICES CIVILS DE ...

Imp. du Progrès, Nantes - 1303

*Fig. 2.4 Document stating that Tessier had been accepted as an intern in 1941 and was "on leave" after January 1944 (there no longer being a hospital in Nantes).*

*Fig. 2.5 Paul Tessier (on the left) in Cadet Uniform as a sanitary engineer, ca. 1938.*

*Fig. 2.6 Paul Tessier now in the uniform of an officer, E.O.R. (élève officier de reserves or student reserve officer), 1940.*

*Fig. 2.7 Tessier in uniform, age twenty-three, 1940.*

Kreiskommandantur 504 Chateaubriant,den 17.April 1941

Tgb.Nr. 318

An
A Tessier, Paul

in Héric
à Loire Inf.

Sie haben sich zukünftig einmal in jedem Monat im Geschäftszimmer
Vous avez à l'avenir à vous présenter une fois par mois au bureau

der Kreiskommandantur in Chateaubriant zu melden.Ausweispapiere
de la Kreiskommandantur de Chateaubriant. Les piéces d'identité

sind stets hier vorzulegen. Ausserdem melden Sie sich wöchentlich
sont à présenter.En outre vous aurez à vous présenter une fois par

einmal bei der nächsten Standortkommandantur bezw. falls diese
semaine à la Standortkommandantur la plus proche et pour le cas

über 10 km. entfernt liegt, bei Jhrem Bürgermeister. Erstmalige
où celle-çi est éloignés de plus de 10 km à la mairie de votre

Meldung hier zwischen dem 20. u. 25. April 1941.
commune.Premir pointage ici entre le 20 et le 25.avril 1941.

Der Kreiskommandant

Hauptmann u. Kommandant.

*Fig. 2.8 Letter from the German Kommandant telling Paul Tessier that, because of curfew violations, he would in the future have to present himself once a month at the German headquarters in Chateaubriand and once a week at the nearest sub-Kommandentur.*

~~RÉPUBLIQUE FRANÇAISE.~~
République ~~ETAT FRANÇAIS~~ Française

Diplôme de Docteur en Médecine.

Le Ministre de l'Éducation nationale,

Vu le Certificat d'aptitude au grade de Docteur en Médecine accordé le 27 octobre 1943 par les Professeurs et Agrégés de la Faculté de Médecine de Paris, Académie de Paris, à M. Tessier Paul Louis Auguste Ernest né à Hérie, département de la Loire Infre, le 1er août 1917,

Vu l'approbation donnée à ce Certificat par le Recteur de ladite Académie;

Ratifiant le susdit Certificat,

Donne par les présentes à M. Tessier le Diplôme de Docteur en Médecine, pour en jouir avec les droits et prérogatives qui y sont attachés par les lois, décrets et règlements.

Fait à Paris, sous le Sceau du Ministère de l'Éducation nationale, le 2 NOVE 1944

Le Ministre de l'Éducation nationale,

Signé: René CAPITANT

Le Directeur de l'Enseignement supérieur,

Délivré par le Recteur de l'Académie de PARIS le 21 NOV. 1944

Fig. 2.9 Medical school diploma. The document, issued during the German occupation, has "République Française" crossed out and "Etat Français" (the term used by the Germans) stamped on it. This, in turn, has been crossed out, and the rightful name of the country has been restored in red ink.

Fig. 2.10 His sister, Solange, working as a nurse. Ca. 1943, Nantes.

*Fig. 2.11 Hospital staff, Hôtel Dieu, Nantes, ca. 1943. Paul Tessier is in the last row, on the far right. This was before the complete destruction of the hospital by American bombings. To the left of Tessier is his friend Ernest Cornet. To Tessier's right is Michel Verge, who became an obstetrician in Saint Nazaire and La Baule.*

*Fig. 2.12 Tessier in Nantes, 1943, before the bombings.*

*Fig. 2.13 Ernest Cornet, Paul Tessier's classmate at Nantes and lifelong friend, became a cardiothoracic surgeon. His son, Joël, has provided much information about Tessier's early days in Nantes.*

Académie
de
Rennes

École de plein exercice de Médecine
et de Pharmacie de Nantes

Nantes, le Ier Mars 1944.

Le Secrétaire de l'Ecole
certifie que Monsieur TESSIER Paul
né le Ier Août 1917 à HERIC (L.Inf.)
a été nommé , par arrêté rectoral en
date du 14 Décembre 1942, aide d'Anatomie et Préparateur de Médecine légale, pour l'année scolaire 1942-1943.

Le Secrétaire,

ECOLE DE PLEIN EXERCICE DE MEDECINE ET DE PHARMACIE NANTES

Monsieur

*Fig. 2.14 Appointment of Tessier as "Assistant in Anatomy and Lecturer in Legal Medicine," for the school year 1942–43 (although it was issued in 1944).*

# Chapter 3

## Postwar: - Paris

Having moved to Paris from Nantes in 1943 because of the destruction of the hospital in Nantes by Allied bombings, Tessier took up his training again. At that time in France (and elsewhere), surgical training was much less formal than it is now. There was no such thing as a formal training course in plastic surgery with a subsequent examination for board certification as now exists in the United States and Europe. One simply found a job in the service of a well-known surgeon and learned on the job.

Tessier received his medical degree from the Faculty of Medicine Paris in 1943. He then went on to work in a military hospital in Paris, Croix Rouge (Red Cross), with Maurice Virenque, a maxillofacial surgeon who had written a book with a dental colleague titled *Prothèse, Chirurgie Cranio-Maxillo-Faciale Surgery* in 1918 on his experiences in treating the injured from World War I. The service was then moved to Hôpital Foch where Virenque headed a maxillofacial surgery service, and Tessier went with him to work as an assistant. He also worked as an assistant to M. Aubry, an E.N.T., (Ear, Nose and Throat) Surgeon at Hôpital Puteaux, between 1944–46.

The teacher that he felt he gained the most from, however, was Georges Huc (1887–64), a pediatric orthopedist. Huc had trained after the World War I with Morestin, the father of French plastic surgery (who stimulated Harold Gillies to become a plastic surgeon), and Ombredanne, who made many contributions to cleft lip and palate surgery. Tessier worked with Georges Huc at Hôpital Saint Joseph from 1945–50, and after that he joined the staff there as a plastic surgeon.

Now that he was certain that he wanted to become a plastic surgeon, Tessier took six trips of one to two months duration between 1946 and 1950 to Great Britain where he crossed paths with Ralph Millard and Hugo Obwegeser, who during that time were both with Harold Gillies. Tessier visited Gillies, Rainsford Mowlem, and John Barron and spent the most time with Archibald McIndoe.

This is the best way to learn plastic surgery—by watching the very best surgeons operate. Unfortunately, this is not the way plastic surgery is taught in the United States today. A trainee is usually confined to one hospital complex where he is taught by a "professor" who, in some cases, simply does not know how to operate. And the whole "educational" process is surveilled by an agency, accountable to no one, that seems more concerned with the minutiae of recordkeeping, filling out forms, and being sure that the trainee does not exceed an eighty-hour work week than establishing that the young surgeon has actually learned how to operate. Craniofacial surgery would never have come to be if Paul Tessier had not been able to learn as he saw fit.

In 1951, Tessier took his first trip to the United States, and stayed for five months where he visited Jerome Webster in New York, Sterling Bunnell in San Francisco, James Barrett Brown and others of his service in St. Louis, and various surgeons in Los Angeles. Subsequent trips took him to Ralph Millard in Miami and both Mario Gonzales-Ulloa and Fernando Ortiz-Monasterio in Mexico City. (These two had been in a state of long-standing war and had not spoken for many years. Tessier related that after he had spent a few days with Fernando, the two finally got on the phone to arrange his delivery to a "neutral" location where Mario would pick him up.)

When he returned to France, he had essentially made the grand tour of plastic surgery, having seen every major plastic surgeon in world at work.

When he was in Nantes as a medical student, he became good friends with Gabrielle Sourdille and Francois Hervouët, both of whom were prominent ophthalmologists, and his collaboration with them continued. Tessier was named as a consultant on the ophthalmology service in Nantes between 1947–75 and the ophthalmology service in Lille from 1957–73. Several times a year he would go to Nantes and Lilles to operate, largely on orbital and eyelid cases.

I asked Tessier when he had done his first bone graft to the orbit, and he said it had been fairly soon after the war that he did a dozen or so, and under *local* anesthesia because good general anesthesia was unavailable. He had performed a retro-orbital block, where the anesthetic needle passes behind the globe to infiltrate anesthetic solution, a procedure done by ophthalmologists that very few plastic surgeons would feel comfortable doing.

In 1973, Tessier had several patients with oro-ocular clefts (#3 and #4 in the Tessier classification) scheduled in Nantes and invited Joe Murray of Boston, Linton Whitaker of Philadelphia, and a few others to come with him. Unfortunately, there was a railroad strike on at that time (not an unusual occurrence in France), so Tessier chartered an air taxi to fly them down.

In 1975, I went with Tessier on one of the trips to Nantes to operate at the Clinque Sourdille. I have no recollection of the cases that were done, but I do recall that we drove back to Paris and stopped at a restaurant he liked for lunch. He ordered a *steak au poivre* and enjoyed it so much that he ordered a second one. The Clinique Sourdille had been founded by Gilbert Sourdille, a professor of ophthalmology at Nantes, whose son, Gabriel-Pierre Sourdille (1901–56), went on to become a world-renowned ophthalmologist himself. Paul Tessier was certainly exposed to Gabriele Sourdille during his own training in Nantes, and a close connection was formed with ophthalmologists throughout France that continued throughout his career.

The following is from Gabriele Sourdille's obituary, published in the *British Journal of Ophthalmology* (1956, 40, 702–704,):

> As a surgeon, he was swift, gentle and dexterous, capable of doing a dozen major operations, including corneal grafts, sclera resections, and cataract extractions without evincing fatigue. His routine examinations would often continue until 10 or 11 o'clock at night. He has been know to drive himself through the night from Paris in the midst of the French Society meeting, get through a mass of operative and consulting work, and then drive back to Paris in time for the rest of the congress, still smiling and full of energy.

This could easily be a description of the work habits of Paul Tessier as well, and one can conjecture that he had Sourdille as a role model. Tessier's good friend Hervouët, with whom he had developed an operation for eyelid ptosis, continued to run the Clinique after Gabrile Sourdille's untimely death.

There had been a very unfortunate event at Clinique Sourdille in the late 1970s. A young woman Tessier had operated on (a rhinoplasty under local anesthesia) returned to the floor after the operation. The events were unclear, but apparently she received a double dose of pain medication without Tessier's knowledge, aspirated, and died. Under French law, criminal charges rather than a civil lawsuit can be leveled. This put Tessier and the Clinique into antagonistic positions. Tessier asserted that the patient had been under the clinic's care, and the clinic maintained that the responsibility was the surgeon's. A trial did take place in Nantes and charges were dropped against both parties. Unfortunately, because of this event, Tessier did not operate in Nantes any further.

Tessier went to Hôpital Foch with Virenque in 1944, and worked on his maxillofacial service. Virenque died ( a suicide, reportedly), and in 1946 Tessier became Chief of the Department of Plastic Surgery and Burns.

The first paper that Paul Tessier wrote appeared in 1948, and was a review of the treatment of burns.

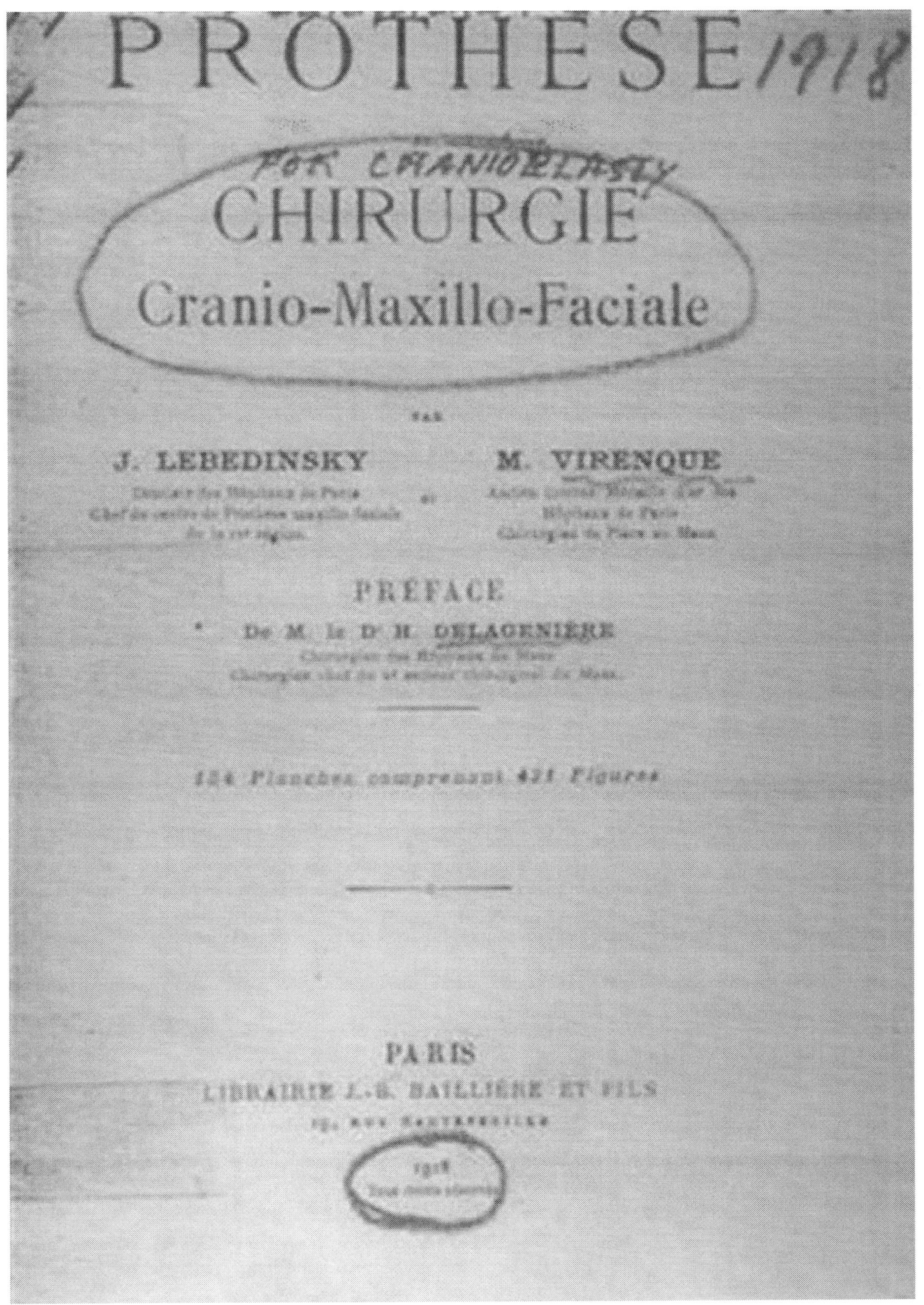

PROTHESE 1918

FOR CRANIOPLASTY

CHIRURGIE

Cranio-Maxillo-Faciale

PAR

J. LEBEDINSKY et M. VIRENQUE

PRÉFACE

De M. le Dr H. DELAGENIÈRE

124 Planches comprenant 431 Figures

PARIS

LIBRAIRIE J.-B. BAILLIÈRE ET FILS

19, RUE HAUTEFEUILLE

1918

*Fig. 3.1 The frontispiece of a book written in 1918 by Tessier's teacher, Virenque. Tessier has written on the page, "For Cranioplasty," since it contained one of the first references to using autogenous bone grafts (osteoperiosteal from the tibia, pioneered by Delagenière) for the reconstruction of skull defects.*

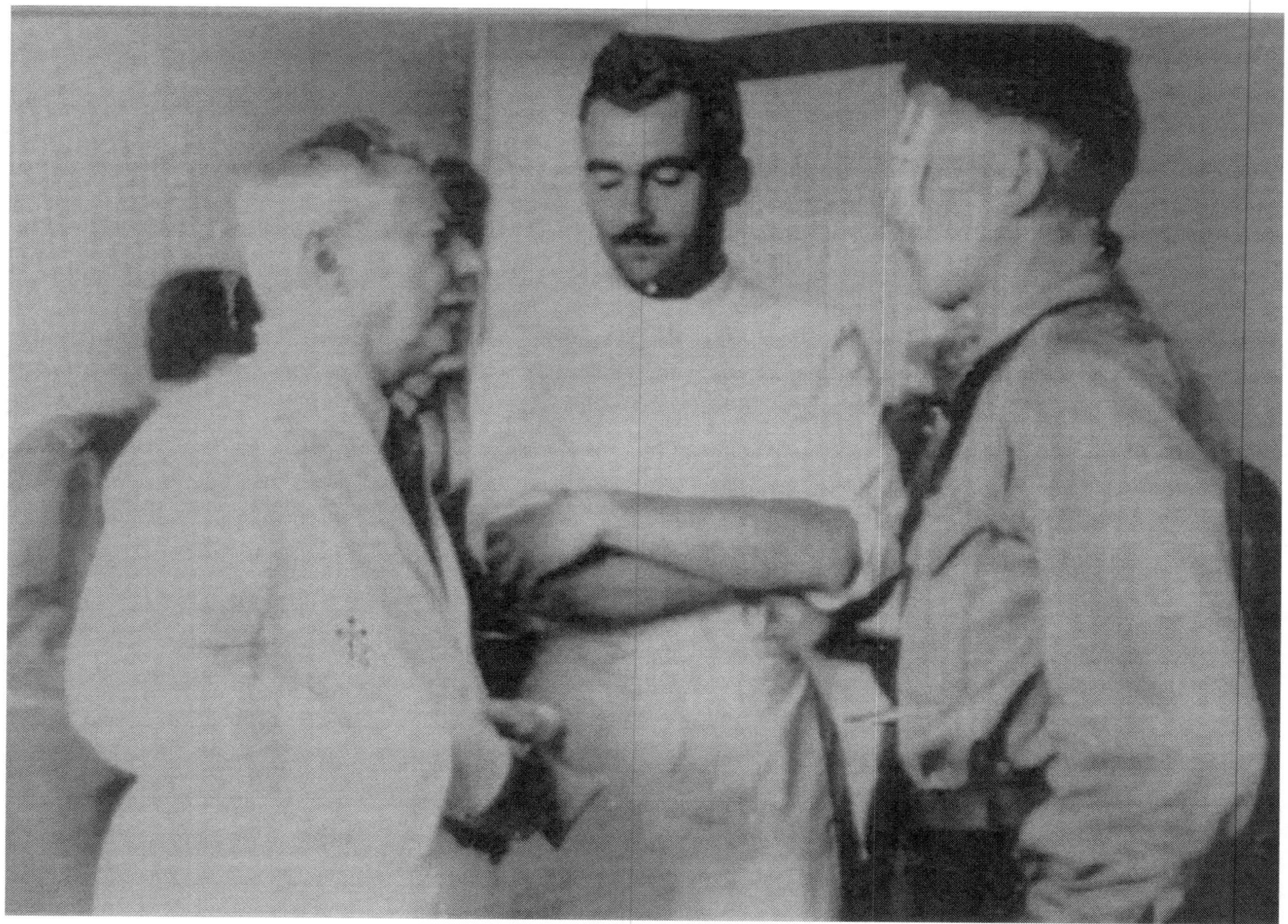

*Fig. 3.2 Maurice Virenque and Paul Tessier, 1945, Paris, examining a wounded soldier (the brother of Jacques Dautrey, a superb maxillofacial surgeon who collaborated with Tessier at Foch, even though he was on the Service of Ginestet, before he moved to Nancy, France, to practice).*

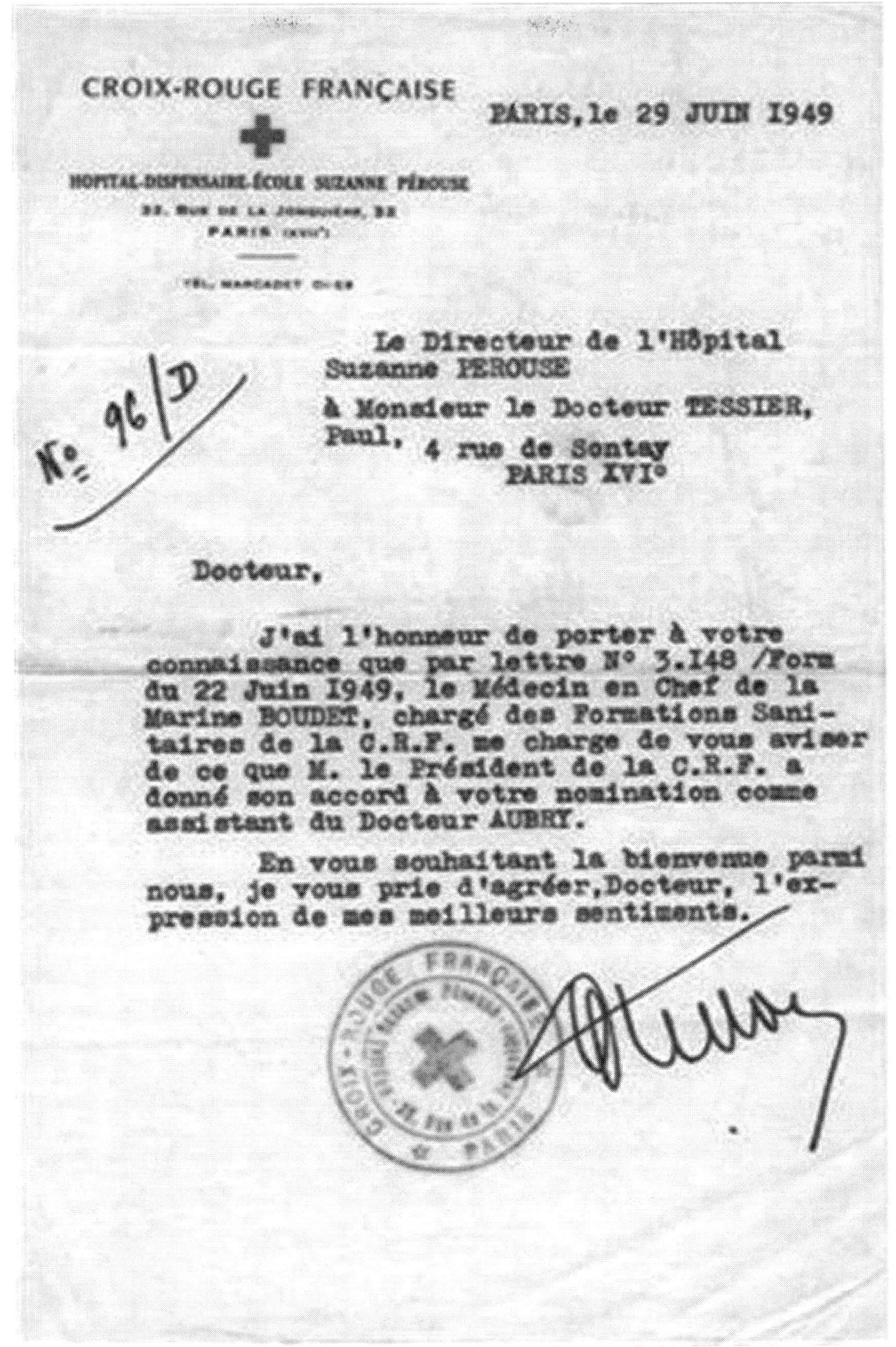

CROIX-ROUGE FRANÇAISE

HOPITAL-DISPENSAIRE-ÉCOLE SUZANNE PÉROUSE

PARIS, le 29 JUIN 1949

N° 96/D

Le Directeur de l'Hôpital
Suzanne PEROUSE
à Monsieur le Docteur TESSIER,
Paul, 4 rue de Sontay
PARIS XVI°

Docteur,

J'ai l'honneur de porter à votre connaissance que par lettre N° 3.148 /Form du 22 Juin 1949, le Médecin en Chef de la Marine BOUDET, chargé des Formations Sanitaires de la C.R.F. me charge de vous aviser de ce que M. le Président de la C.R.F. a donné son accord à votre nomination comme assistant du Docteur AUBRY.

En vous souhaitant la bienvenue parmi nous, je vous prie d'agréer, Docteur, l'expression de mes meilleurs sentiments.

Aubry

*Fig. 3.3 Document naming Tessier assistant to Doctor Aubry, an otolaryngologist.*

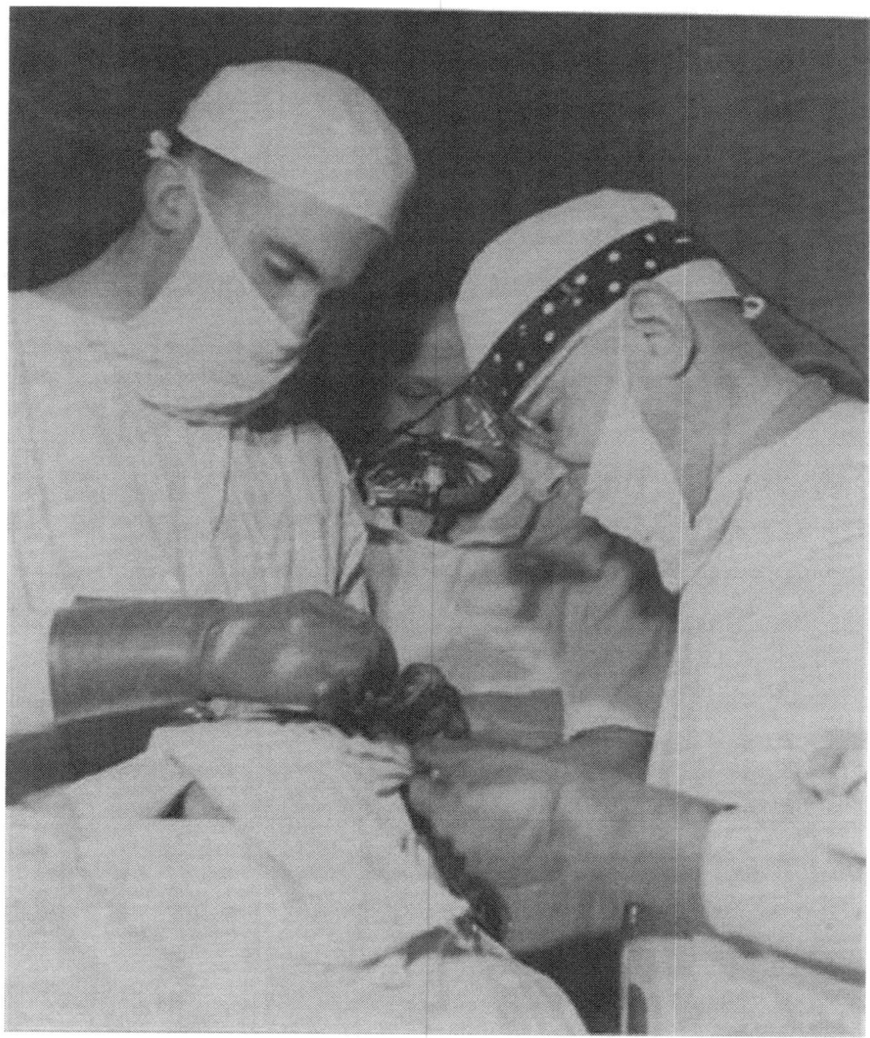

*Fig. 3.4 Georges Huc, pediatric surgeon and orthopedist, on the left, watching Tessier operate with Aubry, ca. 1946. Tessier felt that of all of the people who had trained him, he owed the most to Huc. Huc was born in Martinique, and his training had been with Morestin (also from Martinique), and Ombredanne, at l'Hôpital des Enfants-Malades.*

RM

Le CONSEIL NATIONAL de l'ORDRE des MEDECINS,

Vu la requête présentée par le Docteur Paul TESSIER, demeurant à Paris, 4 rue de Sontay, ladite requête tendant à l'annulation d'une décision par laquelle le Conseil départemental de la Seine de l'Ordre des Médecins, après avis de la commission régionale de qualification en chirurgie de Paris, lui a refusé le droit de faire état de la qualité de médecin spécialiste qualifié en chirurgie;

Vu les autres pièces produites et jointes au dossier;

Vu les lois et règlements régissant la profession médicale notamment l'article 11 du décret du 27 juin 1947 portant Code de déontologie médicale et l'arrêté du 6 octobre 1949 modifié par l'arrêté du 31 janvier 1952, pris en application de l'article 11 sus-visé;

Après avis de la commission nationale d'appel de qualification en chirurgie qui a entendu le Docteur TESSIER en ses explications;

APRES EN AVOIR DELIBERE,

Considérant qu'il résulte des pièces du dossier que le Docteur TESSIER a rempli les fonctions d'interne des hôpitaux de Nantes de 1941 à 1944 dans les services du Pr PICHAT et du Dr GAUDIN (chirurgie générale), des Prs AUVIGNE (urologie) et DUREAU (orthopédie et chirurgie infantile); qu'il a ensuite, de 1944 à 1946, /été assistant du Dr VIRENQUE au centre maxillo-facial de la région de Paris (hôpital Marie Lannelongue) et, de 1945 à 1948, a fait fonction d'assistant du Dr HUC à l'hôpital St Joseph, où depuis 1948 il est attaché de chirurgie plastique;

Que par suite, le Docteur TESSIER remplit les conditions requises pour faire état de la qualité de médecin spécialiste qualifié en chirurgie.

D E C I D E :

Art. 1er.- La décision du Conseil départemental de la Seine de l'Ordre des Médecins est annulée.

Art. 2.- Le Docteur TESSIER est autorisé à faire état de la qualité de médecin spécialiste qualifié en chirurgie.

Art. 3.- La présente décision sera notifiée au Docteur TESSIER et au Conseil départemental de la Seine de l'Ordre des Médecins.

Ainsi prononcé par le Conseil National dans sa séance du 16-1-1953 par : M. le Dr DEGUIGNAND Vice-Président, président; M. le Conseiller d'Etat BLONDEL; M. le Pr AUVIGNE, M. le Dr BARDON, M. le Pr BAUDOUIN, MM les Drs BODSON, CAFFORT, CARLOTTI, CHENE, COULET, J.R. DEBRAY, DESGUINES DUHAMEL, M. DURAND, GRASSET, LAFFITTE, LAGNY, MM. les Prs LEGRAND, VIDAL M. le Dr VILLEY.

Par délégation du VICE PRESIDENT,
Le SECRETAIRE GENERAL, membre du Conseil,

Dr J.R. DEBRAY.

*Fig. 3.5 1950 document of the Advisory Council of the Medical Board, granting Tessier's qualification in surgery, which had originally been turned down due to lack of documentation.*

PREFECTURE DE LA SEINE

DIRECTION des AFFAIRES
DEPARTEMENTALES & GENERALES

Sous-Direction des Communes
Personnel Communal

Le PREFET de la SEINE,

Vu l'article 26 de l'acte dit loi du 31 Décembre 1941,
Vu le règlement d'administration publique en date du 17 Avril 1943 pris pour l'application de ladite loi et notamment l'article 110,
Vu la délibération de la commission administrative de l'Hôpital intercommunal de Créteil en date du 29 Mai 1951, portant nomination de médecins attachés,
Vu l'avis favorable du Conseil de l'Ordre Départemental des médecins de la Seine et de la Chambre Syndicale des médecins de la Seine concernant les désignations de cette nature.
Vu l'avis favorable de M. le Ministre de la Santé Publique et de la Population,
Vu l'avis favorable donné le 28 Juin 1951 par M. le Directeur Départemental de la Santé,

ARRETE :

ARTICLE 1er - Les praticiens dont les noms suivent sont nommés à l'Hôpital Intercommunal de Créteil :

..........................................................................

M. le Docteur TESSIER Paul, domicilié rue Sontai à Paris, est nommé dans les fonctions d'attaché de chirurgie auto-plastique.

..........................................................................

ARTICLE 2 - Les intéressés sont nommés, à compter du 29 Mai 1951, pour une durée d'un an qui pourra être tacitement reconduite.

ARTICLE 3 - Le Directeur des Affaires Départementales & Générales et le Président de la Commission Administrative de l'Hôpital intercommunal de Créteil sont chargés, chacun en ce qui le concerne, de l'exécution du présent arrêté.

Pour copie conforme :
Le chef du Bureau du Personnel Communal
signé : [illegible]

Paris, le 6 Juillet 1951
P. le PREFET de la SEINE,
et par délégation
Le Secrétaire Général de la Seine :
Richard POUZET

Pour copie certifiée conforme,
Le Directeur,

*Fig. 3.6 1951 document stating that Paul Tessier was named as a trainee in plastic surgery (chirurgie auto-plastique).*

*Fig. 3.7 Meeting of the French Society of Plastic Surgery, 1954. Tessier is in the third row back, in the aisle.*

There was another Maxillofacial Service at Foch, headed by, Médecin General Gustave Ginestet, who held a high rank in the Army Medical Corps. After Virenque's death Tessier found himself somewhat isolated. In a letter dated March 14, 1962, Ginestet said to Tessier, "There cannot be two services of maxillo-facial surgery in the same Institution, and I demand that you from this moment stop "competing" with us. It is a question of ethics and simple courtesy."

CENTRE
MÉDICO-CHIRURGICAL FOCH
40, RUE WORTH A SURESNES (SEINE)
TÉL. : LONGCHAMP 19-00

SURESNES, LE 14 mars 1962

N/RÉF. JS/SM/62
à rappeler dans toute correspondance

Docteur TESSIER

Mon cher Confrère,

J'ai bien reçu votre lettre du 13.

En ce qui concerne votre opéré, Monsieur BODET, mes assistants pourront procéder aux extractions nécessaires et à la prothèse, à la condition que les frais soient pris en charge par la Sécurité Sociale. Quant aux soins dentaires, il ne saurait en être question, car pour les malades de mon service même, on ne les assure pas, par manque de temps, de personnel et de locaux.

Renseignements pris, votre malade relève de la chirurgie maxillo-faciale, par conséquent de mon service. J'accepte donc exceptionnellement de faire faire le travail que vous demandez.

Ce genre de patient doit être opéré chez nous : mes assistants travaillent très bien et ne demandent qu'à travailler. Il ne peut pas y avoir deux services de chirurgie maxillo-faciale dans le même établissement, et je vous demande de vous abstenir dorénavant de nous "concurrencer." C'est une question de déontologie et de courtoisie simple.

Croyez, mon cher Confrère, à mes bons sentiments.

Docteur GINESTET
Chef de Service de
Chirurgie Maxillo-Faciale
et de Stomatologie

*Fig. 3.8 Letter to Tessier from Ginestet, dated March 14, 1962. Ginestet informs Tessier that "There cannot be two services of maxilla-facial surgery in the same Institution, and I demand that you from this moment stop 'competing' with us. It is a question of ethics and simple courtesy."*

And in another letter dated April 27, 1962, he reiterates this demand, saying, "As concerns you, I had you return to the Institution where you have been put in charge of the Burn Service. Being part-time, you can do as you wish elsewhere, maxillo-facial surgery included if that pleases you; but here you are going beyond your competence ... there cannot be two services of maxillo-facial surgery here. Besides, you should not be treating members of the Military, for whom arrangements have been made between the Army and my Service. You know that I have always proven to have great tolerance and I hope that there will be no further difficulties between us ... Docteur G. Ginestet."

*Fig. 3.9 Médecin Général Gustave Ginestet*
*(See complete translation in Appendices/Foch)*

There is no copy of any response from Tessier to Ginestet, and he seems to have just ignored him and continued doing maxillo-facial surgery. So well, in fact, that Gustave Ginestet ended up being one of the great philistines of all time in the face of the enormous contributions that were coming regularly from a surgeon who was "going beyond his competence." And when the French Society of Maxillofacial Surgery was founded in 1973,Paul Tessier was elected as its first president.

In 1949, Jacqueline Auriol, a famous aviatrix of the time and daughter-in-law of Vincent Auriol, who was President of France, was the passenger in an airplane that was forced to crash land on the Seine. She sustained a badly impacted Le Fort 3 fracture. Due to her prominent position, the best known facial surgeons of Paris were asked to see her (one of whom, known for his rhinoplasties, actually suggested a rhinoplasty!).. Madame Auriol was hospitalized at Foch, on the Service of Ginestet, and apparently he had no idea how to deal with her floating midface. Someone told the family that they should have Tessier see the patient. Not able to avoid this request, Ginestet begrudgingly asked for the consultation. Tessier saw Madame Auriol and told the family that she would require proper reduction with bone grafting in order to have the fracture consolidate in a proper position. Ginestet, although he was not competent to do the surgery himself, was, however, able to prevent Tessier from doing it. Ginestet arranged to have her sent to

New York, where she was operated on by John Marquis Converse. Converse had had training with Sir Harold Gillies and later with Varastad Kazanjian in Boston, and he knew what to do.

Tessier had met Converse in 1946 at Foch, before he left France. Converse's father, an American, was the director of The American Hospital of Paris, and Converse had gone to secondary school and medical school in France and spoke perfect French. After leaving Alger in 1943, Converse came to work at Foch on the service of Merle d'Aubigné, an orthopedist, and met Tessier in 1946. Tessier even handled a few burn cases with Converse, using a Padgett dermatome that he had smuggled in from England on the advice of Archibald McIndoe. Converse, when he was a resident at Foch, also assisted Thierry de Martel, a leading neurosurgeon who, unfortunately, shot himself when the Germans entered Paris in 1940.

In gratitude to Converse, the Auriol family gave a large donation, which helped establish The Institute of Reconstructive Plastic Surgery at New York University.

There was an offshoot of Ginestet's petty nature and jealousy: he forebade the dental laboratory at Foch, which was under his control, to provide any assistance to Tessier. Tessier once told me that this was what led him to develop the methods of interlocking bone fixation that he used in many of his procedures to provide internal stability. It is ironic that Ginestet, not being able to see beyond his bureaucratic fiefdom, was there at Foch at the same time that some of the greatest advances in the history of maxillofacial and craniofacial surgery were being developed. Fortunately, try as he might, he was not able to prevent them.

*Fig. 3.10 Paul Tessier was married in Paris, in 1946, to Micheline "Mic" Poulain.*

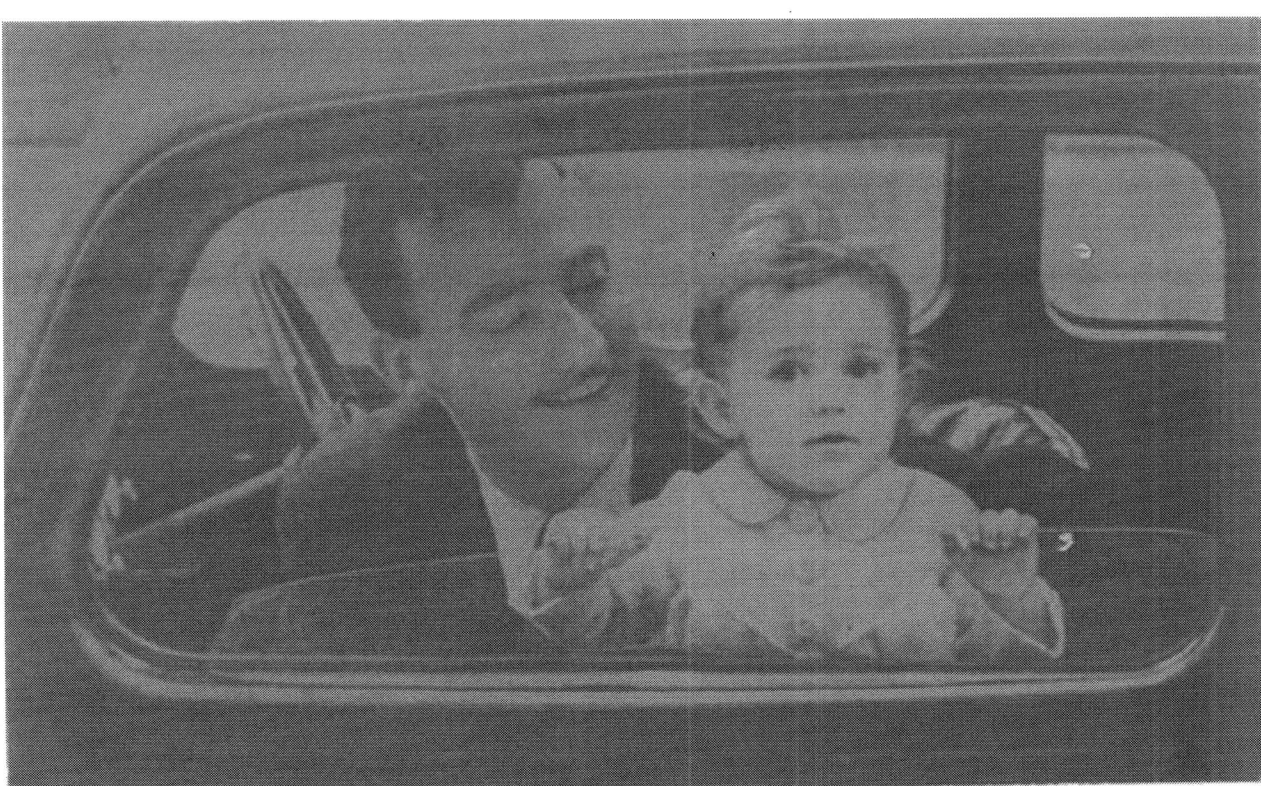

*Fig. 3.11 Tessier with his daughter Claude, born 1947, ca. 1948.*

*Fig. 3.12 Paul Tessier, at a family reunion, can be seen in the last row, fourth from the left. "Mic" is to his right, ca. 1948.*

*Fig. 3.13 Paul; first wife Mic; and sister, Solange, ca. 1948.*

*Fig. 3.14 With daughter Claude, ca. 1949.*

*Fig. 3.15 Claude's First Communion, ca. 1954. They are sitting in front of Bonne Hygie, in Héric.*

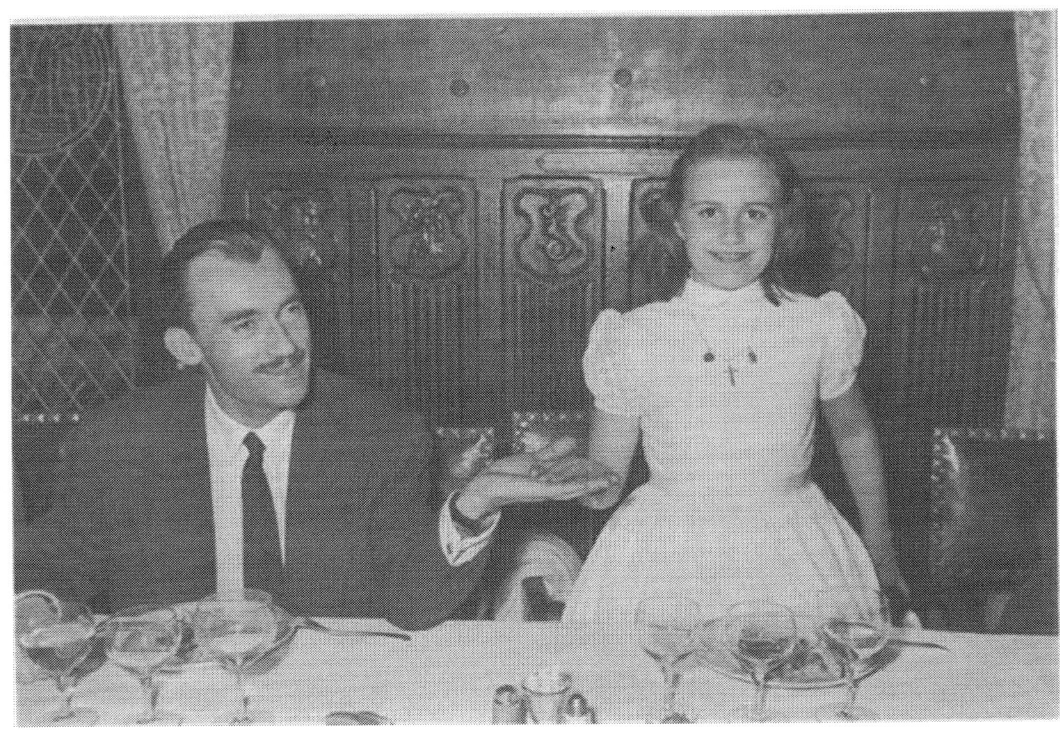

*Fig. 3.16 Claude's First Communion, ca. 1954.*

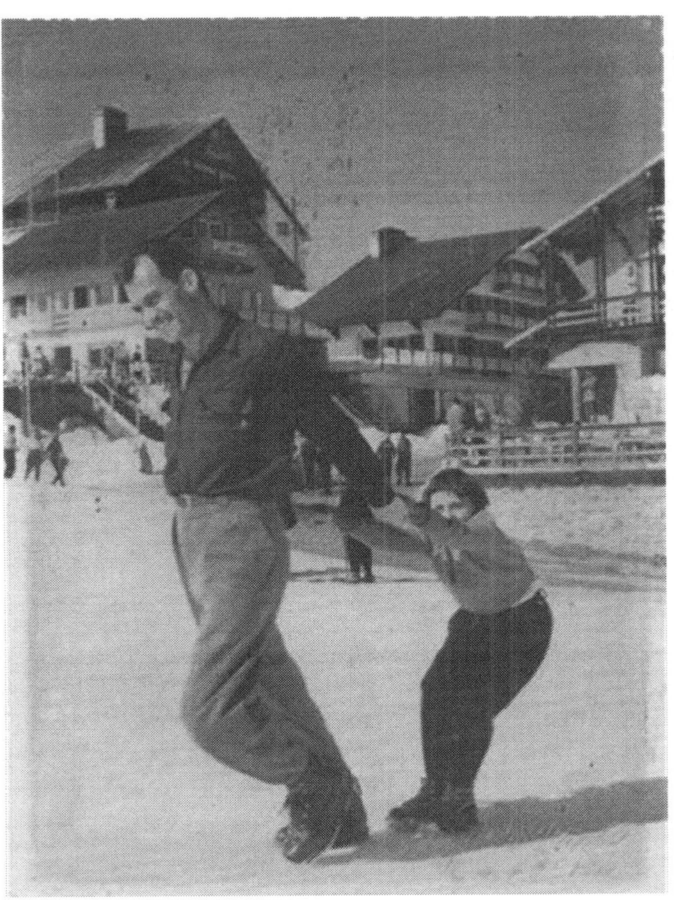

*Fig. 3.17 1955, skiing with Claude.*

*A l'occasion des Entretiens sur la Chirurgie Plastique des Paupières et de l'Orbite. Centre FOCH, 11-15 Mars 1963.*

LE DOCTEUR ET MADAME PAUL TESSIER

VOUS PRIENT DE LEUR FAIRE L'HONNEUR D'ASSISTER A LA RÉCEPTION QU'ILS DONNERONT LE MERCREDI 13 MARS 1963, A 19 HEURES.

6, RUE LAURENT-PICHAT, PARIS-XVI° R. S. V. P.

*Fig. 3.18 Invitation to Tessier's home for a reception, 1963, following his first course at Foch on Orbit and Eyelid Surgery.*

The first teaching course that Tessier put together was in March of 1963. It was called "Conversations on the Plastic Surgery of the Eyelids and Orbit," and lasted five days. It shows the continuing close relationship that he had with ophthalmologists. On the 13th of March, the Tessiers had a reception for the participants at their home on Rue Laurent-Pichat. (Rue Laurent-Pichat is just off of Avenue Foch, only a few blocks from Avenue Klébèr where Tessier would next live.)

He divorced after 18 years and had a difficult relationship with his daughter, who got pregnant and left the family. She then had two other children.

One cannot know from afar the details of a marriage, nor what caused its breakup. This is relevant material only in that, during this painful period of his personal life, he was able to turn to surgery and completely immerse himself in it

> In the late 1960s, Tessier took a lease on a large second floor space at 26, Avenue Klébèr. Jacqueline, his housekeeper of many years, oversaw the renovations and got him and his cocker spaniel, Max, moved into the new space, which had a small residence attached to the larger space that would serve as his office. During his years as a bachelor, many of the children of his friends from Nantes stayed with Tessier in his new dwelling. For two years, Joël Cornet, the son of his friend and medical school classmate, Eugène Cornet, stayed with Tessier while finishing his law studies. France Schiltz, a niece of "Fafa" (François) Hervouët also stayed with him.
>
> Jacqueline "ruled" the household, where Tessier only came to eat and sleep. It was important for him to have clean and pressed shirts, shaving soap, good tea, and grated carrots for Max, who loved them. Jacqueline had *carte blanche* to run the household, and she did a good job. The evening meal, Joël reports, which was around 10 or 11 p.m., was always impeccable.
>
> In any event, by 1963 Paul Tessier had a well-deserved reputation in France as an extraordinarily good reconstructive surgeon in the treatment of burns, maxillofacial injuries, and other areas of plastic surgery, including aesthetic surgery.
>
> His training had been in many different areas: ophthalmology, otolaryngology, pediatric orthopedics, and maxillofacial surgery. He had taken many trips to England to see the masters

of the specialty of plastic surgery there (Gillies, McIndoe, Mowlem, Barron) and, in 1951, took his five-month trip to the United States, where he visited almost every major center. He had the tools to put it all together. And he did.

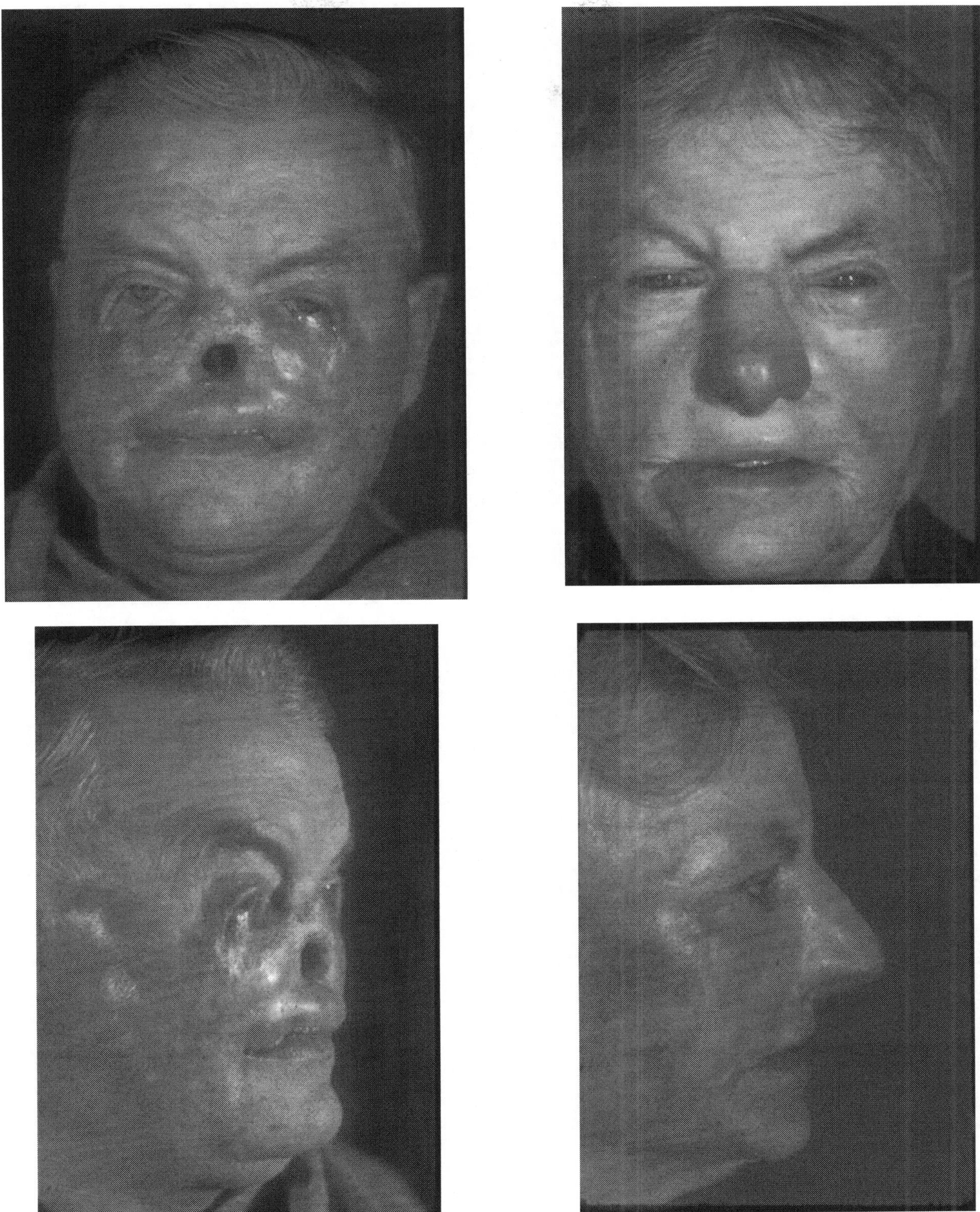

*Fig. 3.19 Burn reconstruction by Tessier done in the early 1960s.*
*Superb eyelid reconstructions and nasal reconstruction with a forehead flap and iliac bone graft.*

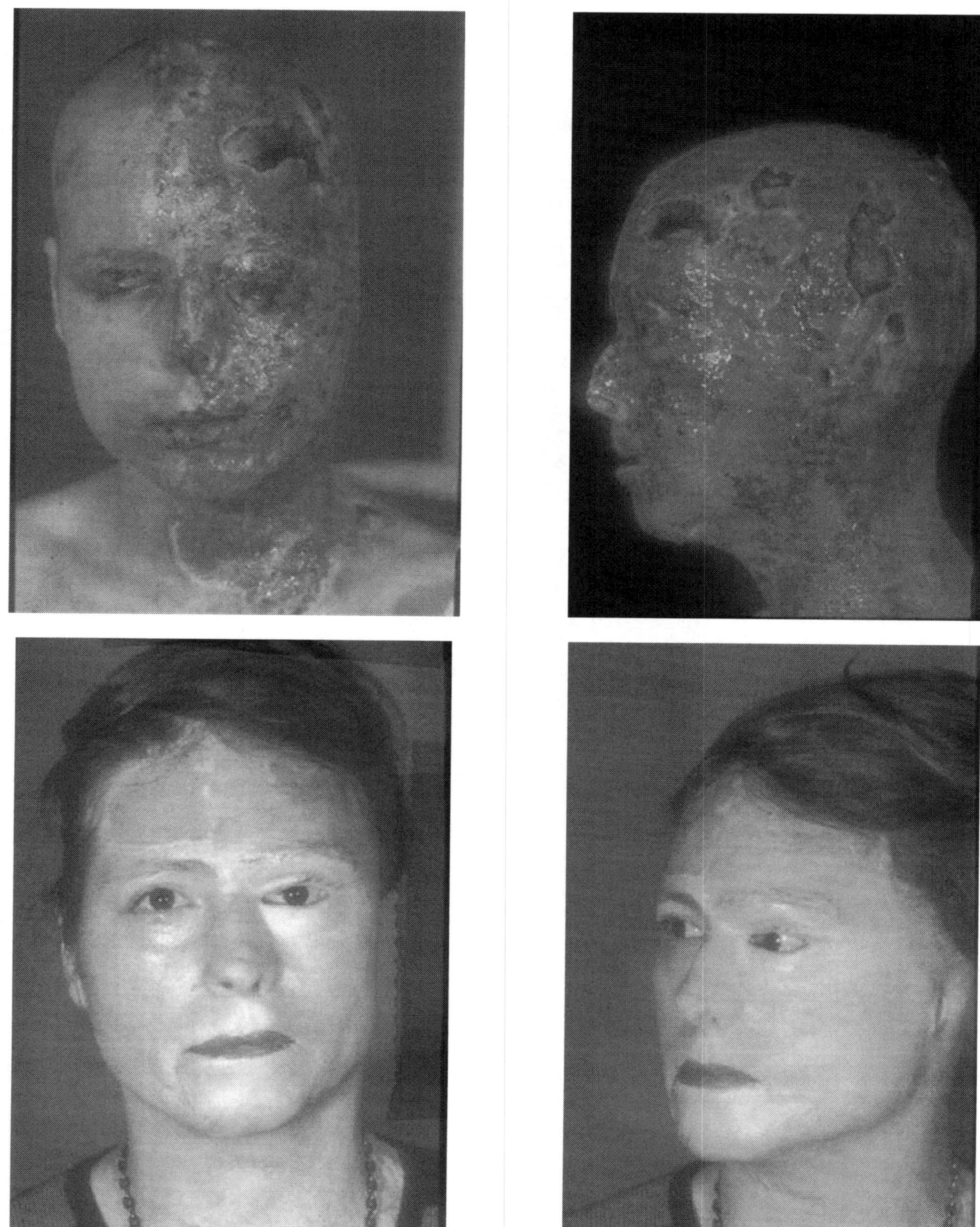

*Fig. 3.20 Another burn reconstruction performed in the 1960s by Paul Tessier. The right forehead has been used to make the nose, and full-thickness grafts have been used to reconstruct the cheek and neck. The eyebrow has been reconstructed, by graft from the other eyebrow, and the eyelid reconstruction is staggeringly good. There are even eyelash grafts, something rarely attempted in 2009, almost fifty years later after these grafts were performed.*

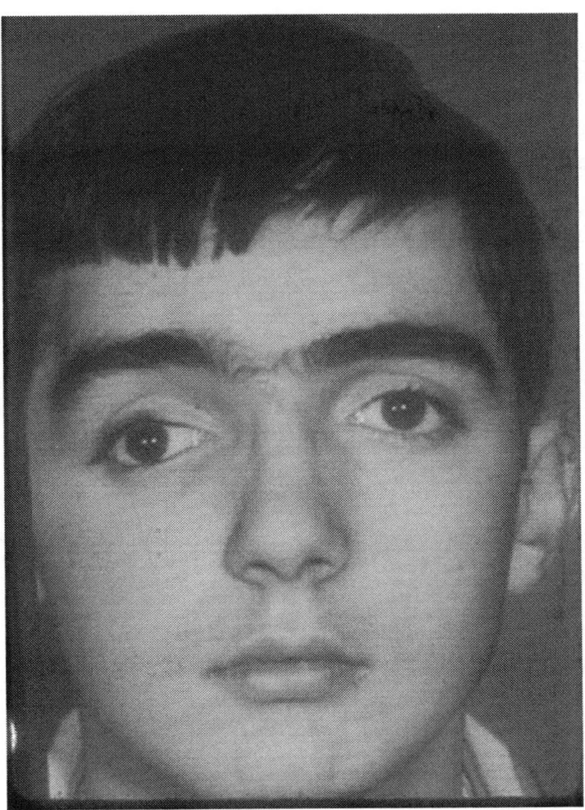

*Fig. 3.21 Patient with a displaced zygomatic fracture, enophthalmos, and hypoglobus (eyeball sunken into the maxillary sinus)*

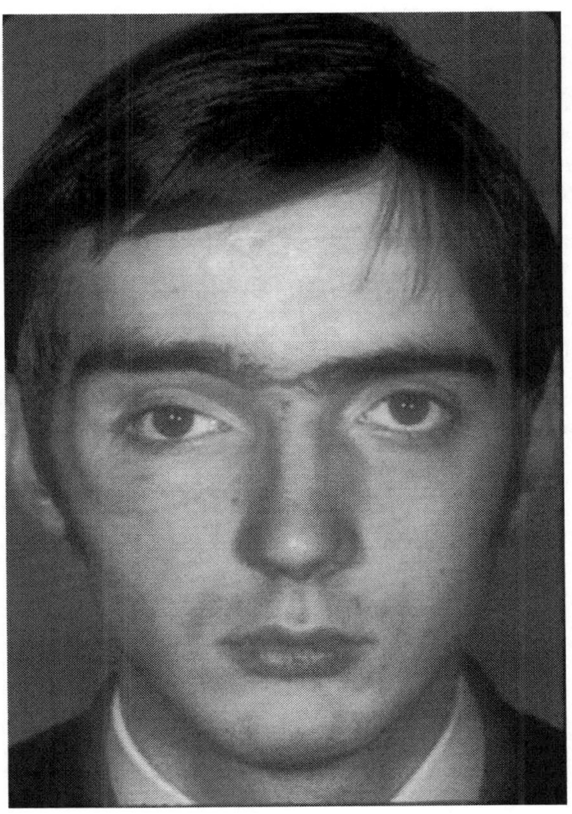

*Fig. 3.26 Final result. This case was slightly undercorrected; but, in subsequent cases, Tessier gets it right on the money.*

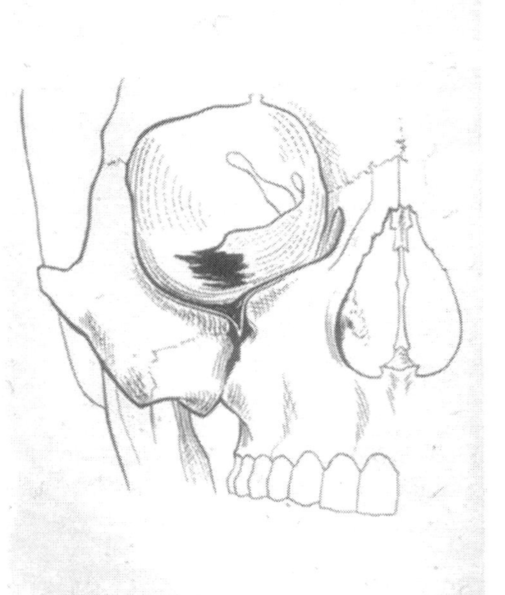

*Fig. 3.22 Francine Gourdin's drawing that shows the displaced zygoma.*

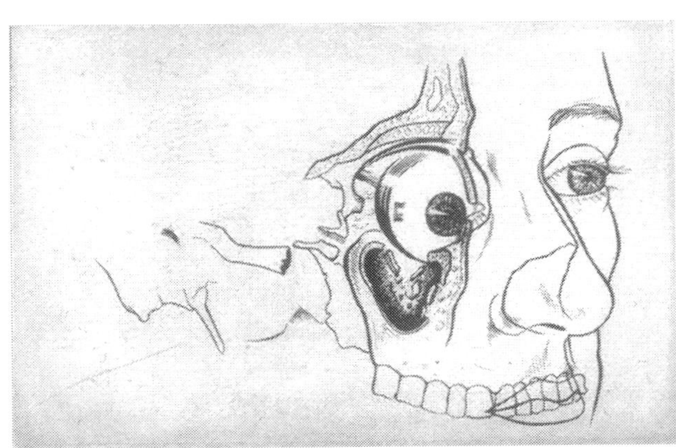

*Fig. 3.23 With the zygoma removed, one can better appreciate the defect of the orbital floor.*

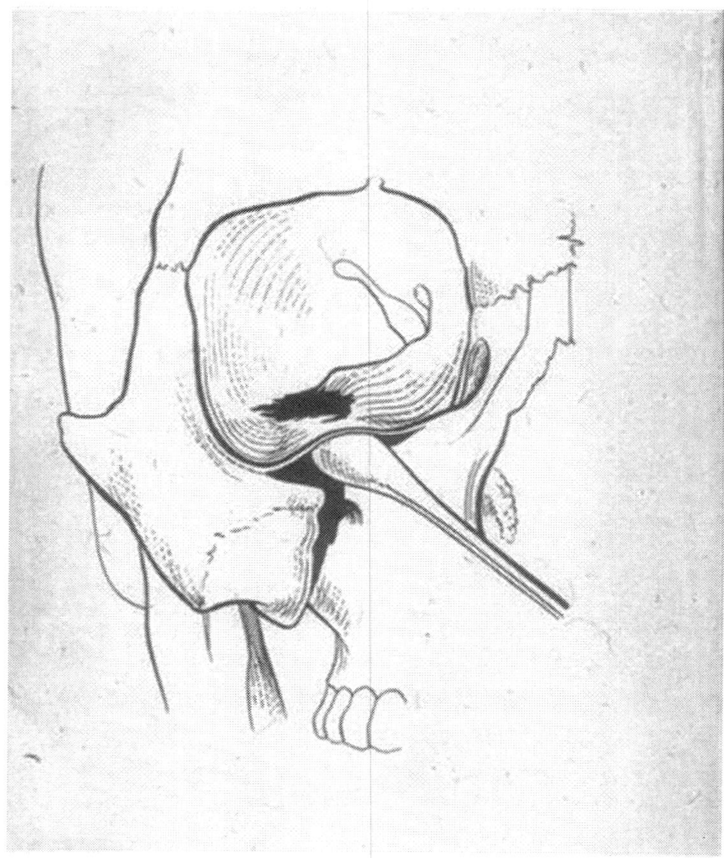

*Fig. 3.24 Subperiosteal dissection of the orbital floor.*

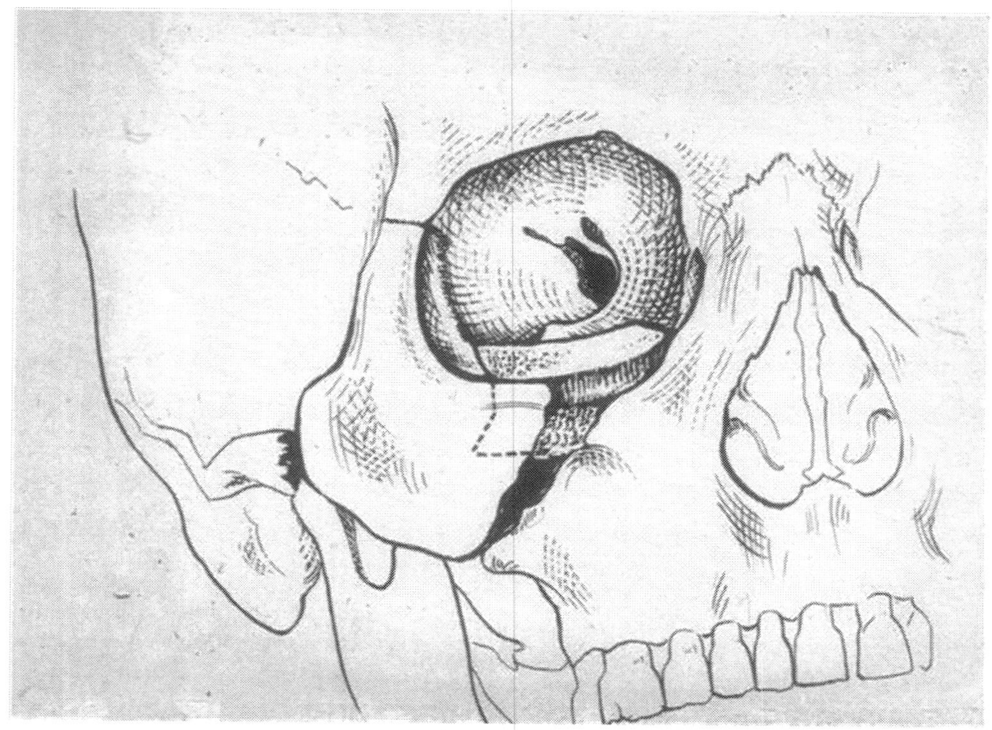

*Fig. 3.25 After refracture and repositioning of the zygoma and iliac bone grafts.*

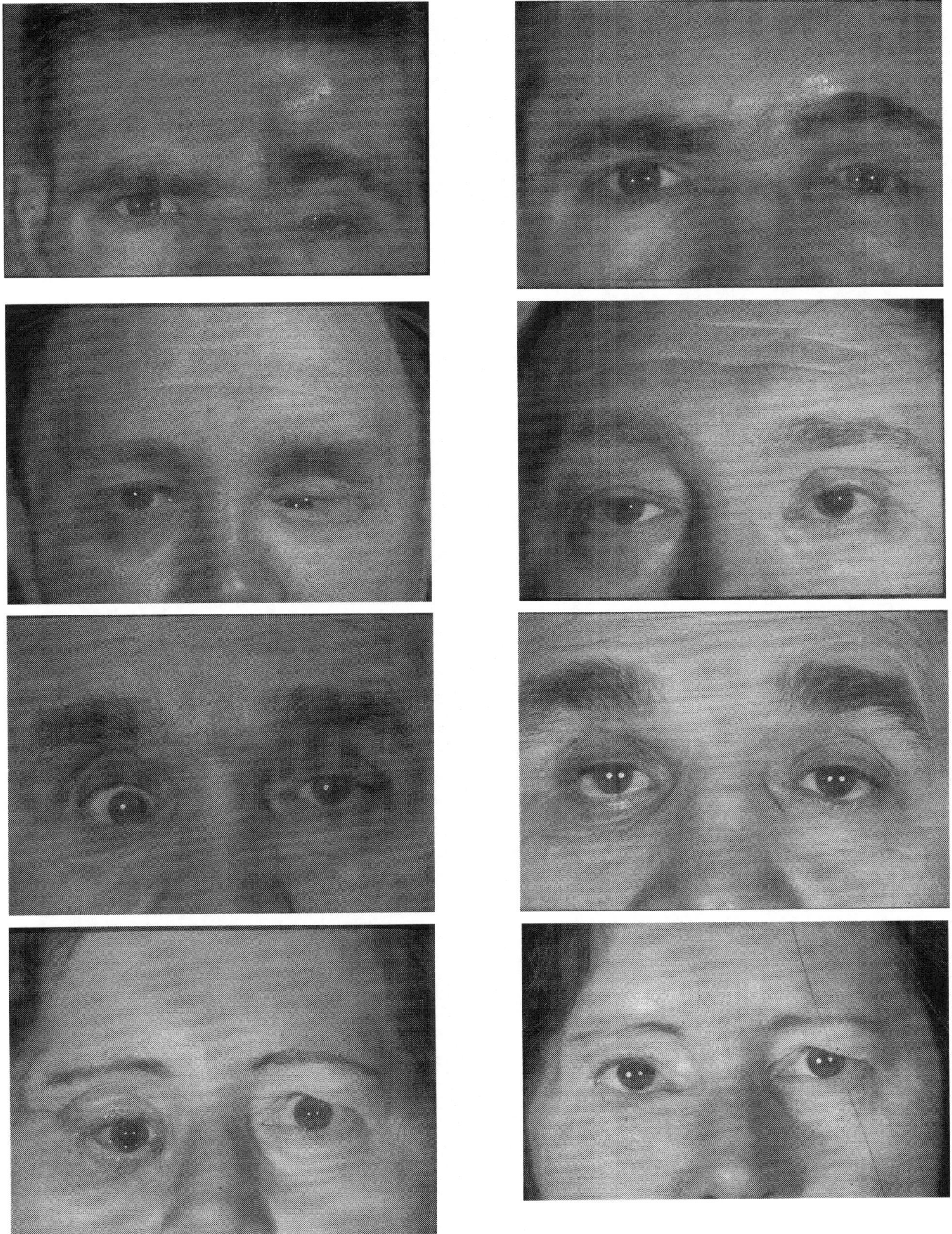

*Fig. 3.27 The above cases are all patients with severe enophthalmos, corrected by Dr. Tessier in the 1950s and 60s.*

The drawings appeared in a French publication "Extrait des Bulletins et Mèmoires de la Société Française d'Ophthalmologie," 1960, pp. 257-285, entitled "Diplopies Post-Traumatiques et Greffes Osseuses" (Post-Traumatic Diplopia and Bone Grafts), authored by P. Tessier, M. Woillez, M. Lekieffre, and R. Asseman (all ophthalmological colleagues). This work was certainly unknown to most American ophthalmologists and plastic surgeons.

In a later publication, with Woillez (Extrait des Bulletins de la Société Française d'Ophthalmologie, 1967, pp. 598-599), Tessier responded to several questions after his presentation: (see Fig. 3.22-3.25)

"I thank Woillez for having presented our joint work so well, and Sourdille for having showered him with laurels.

In sum, two questions have been asked us:

—the question of delay

—how to interpret the 'blow out' [a term proposed by Jack Converse and Byron Smith]

On the question of delay, it is very difficult to be dogmatic. It is not always the diplopia, it is not always the duction test, it is not always the extent of the bony defects shown on an x-ray which provide an urgency to the operation. It is more the concordance of these symptoms and also the importance of the enophthalmia which lead one to operate. An important enophthalmia signifies the incarceration of orbital tissues, in general into the maxillary sinus. If it is paired with a positive duction test of the inferior rectur muscle, the diplopia has little chance of improving. The same goes for major orbital fractures. It is for them that the delays should be shortened, but it is also in this group that there are the greatest number of traps. In effect, the reduction of a multiply comminuted malar bone increases the defects of the floor and calls for a bone graft, even at the primary operation.

As for the 'blow out,' one must distinguish between a word, a mechanism, lesions, and a treatment. The *word* 'blow-out' signifies that the walls of the orbit have been displaced by the effect of a blow, an internal increase in pressure. The coiners of this term spelled out carefully that the term applied only to ruptures of the walls, excluding fractures involving the framework, the orbital rims. However, as to the *mechanism,* one cannot say as a rule that an eye can sustain without major lesion a direct blow, where the increases in pressure, the contre-coups, fracture only the floor or the medial wall. The bendings of the orbital framework also enter into the discussion As concerns the *lesions* which I have noted in performing 250 operations for post-traumatic diplopia, in only 3 cases did I encounter a fracture of the floor without a fracture of the orbital rim, and these three cases were children. When one realizes how easy it is to bend the bone of a child, one can doubt not only the reality of the 'blow-out,' but the authenticity of a large number of cases labeled as 'blow-outs.' From the mental image of a word and a mechanism, where there is yet no proof, one has gone on to recreate an entire pathology which is already know; this is abusive. In any case, the *treatment* remains the same, it is necessary to disincarcerate the orbital tissue in the sinus and do a bone graft if the sinus cavity is open, and sometimes an implant, if it is not."

Tessier was regularly performing primary bone grafting of orbital fractures in the 1950s and 1960s, and it would be at least another decade before this would be done by only a few surgeons in the United States. Even to this day, it seems radical to some, and many surgeons use only alloplastic (artificial) materials, most likely because they lack the training and skill to work with bone. Tessier's rationale for a primary bone graft was to *prevent* the development of late enophthalmos.

He demonstrated that this was possible.

Established post-traumatic enophthalmos, once present, was widely felt to be uncorrectable in the United States, well into the 1970s. The reason given for this assessment was that there was (presumptively) loss of orbital fat, and (presumptively) there was contraction and scarring that prevented the globe from moving forward. What Tessier had done was to dissect the orbit more widely in a strictly subperiosteal level, return all of the orbital contents to the orbital cavity, and reconstruct the missing portions of the orbit with bone grafts. The French ophthalmology community knew that he could do this, and referred him large numbers of patients. But, because his work was not published in English, the English-speaking world remained ignorant. The cases shown above were all done in the 1950s and 60s, and it was on the basis of this enormous experience in orbital surgery that Tessier was able to develop craniofacial surgery.

His area of greatest comfort was in the orbit, and he once referred to himself as *'le refaisseur dé orbites,"* the orbit maker.

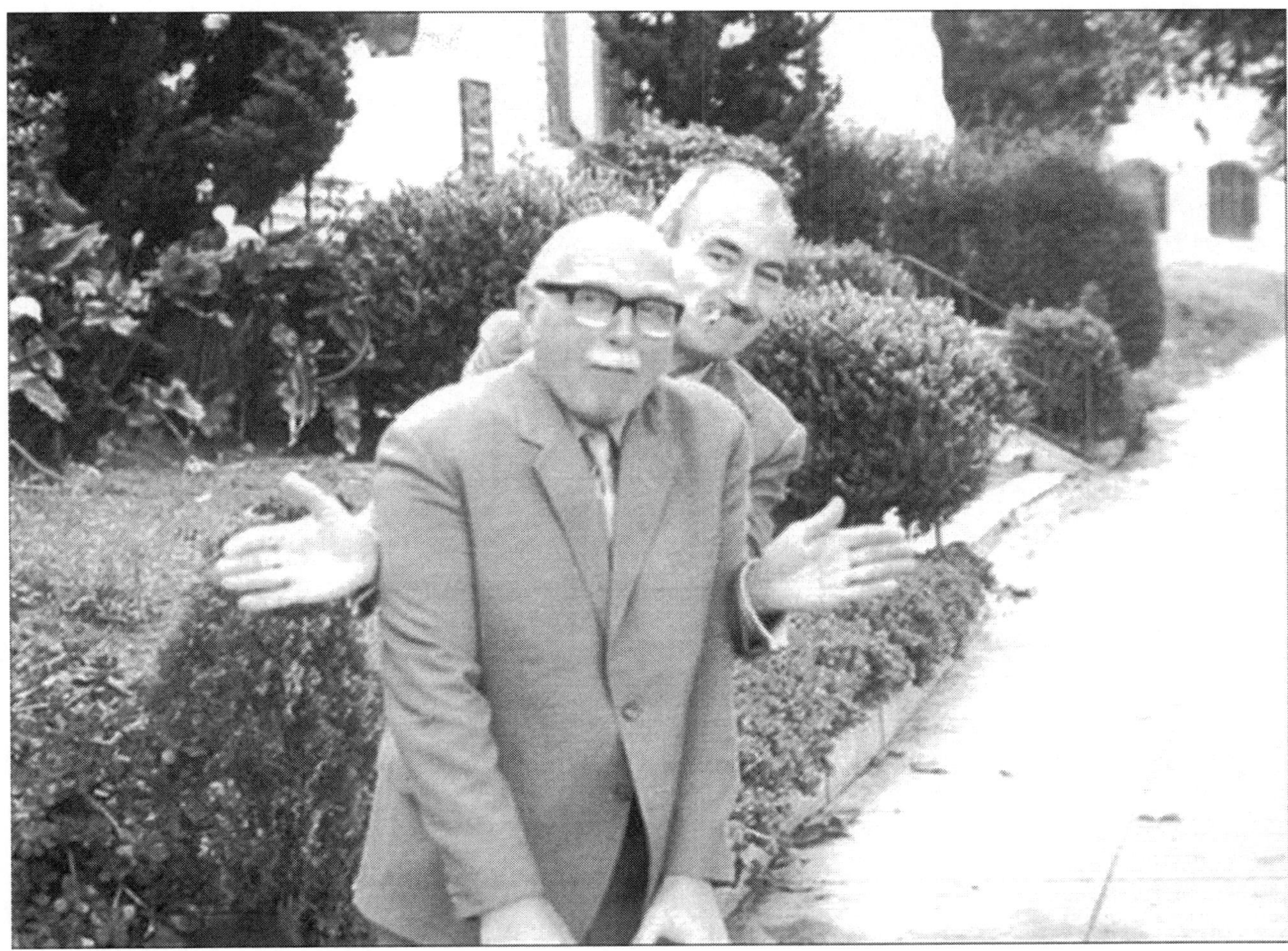

*Fig. 3.28 Paul Tessier demonstrating the correction of enophthalmos, with Jack Mustardé as the eyeball.*

This picture was taken in Los Angeles in the mid-1970s, at a meeting on orbital surgery hosted by UCLA. Jack Mustardé, the Scottish ophthalmologist and plastic surgeon who trained with Sir Harold Gillies, had made the statement that post-traumatic enophthalmos was uncorrectable. Tessier had jokingly stood behind Mustardé as shown here and said, "No Jack, it is easy; you just get the walls correct and the eye comes forward," and he said this he gently brought his arms together and pushed him forward. When Henry Kawamato and I went to pick them up at their hotel in Brentwood the following morning, I asked them to recreate that moment and took a picture. (This photo was later given to Henry Kawamoto to use in a paper he published in *Plastic and Reconstructive Surgery* on the correction of enophthalmos.)

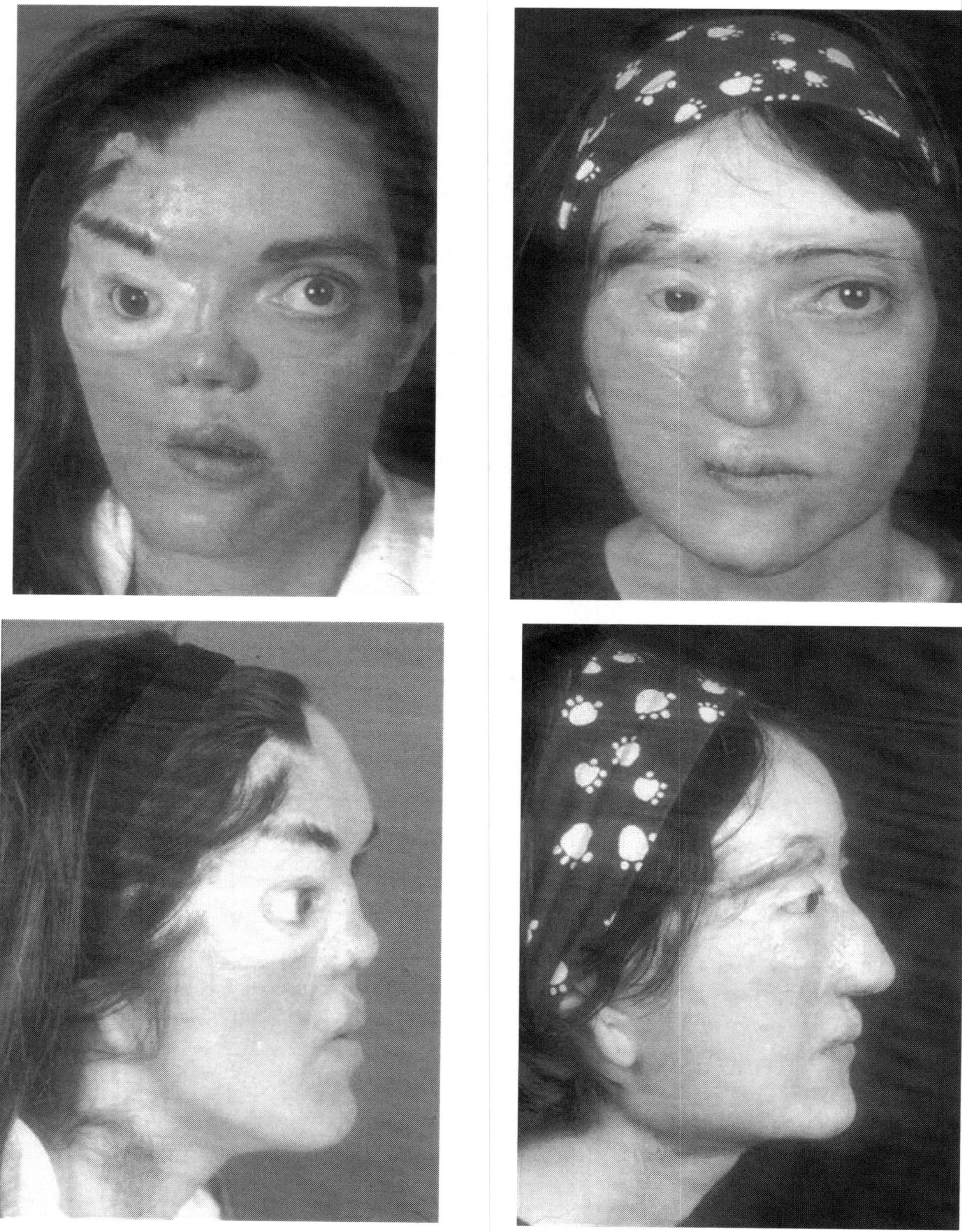

*Fig. 3.29. Here Tessier has made a proper eye socket on the right to house an eye prosthesis, done medial and lateral canthopexies, reconstructed the nose with a forehead flap and iliac bone graft, created a zygomatic arch on the right, sidejunked the previous eyebrow graft and replaced it with one taken from the left, and done two jaw surgeries with extensive bone grafting of the right. Early 1970s.*

The fusion of his abilities as a nasal and orbit/eyelid surgeon, incorporating jaw surgery, is evident in this extraordinary result.

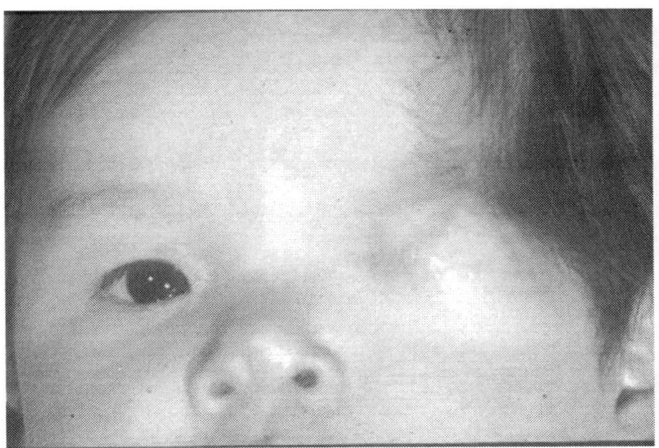
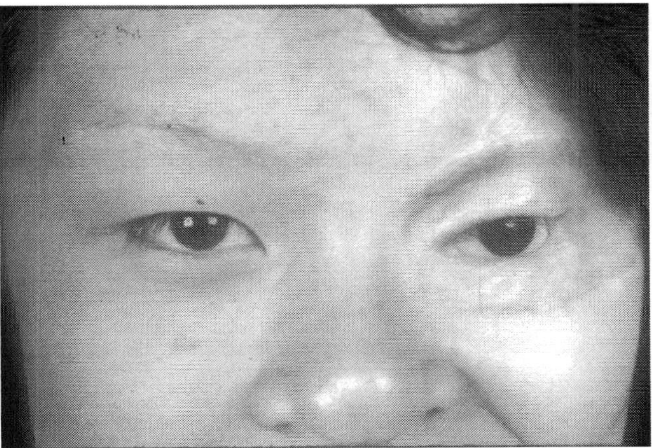

*Fig. 3.30. Creation of eyelids, eye socket, and eyebrow in a patient with ablepharria. There are no results in the medical literature that are nearly as good.*

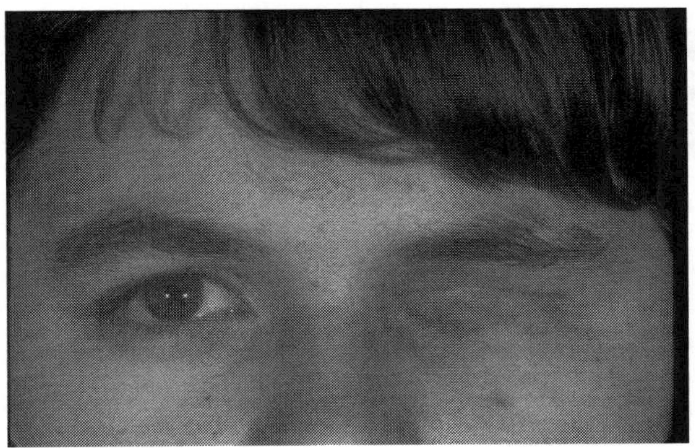
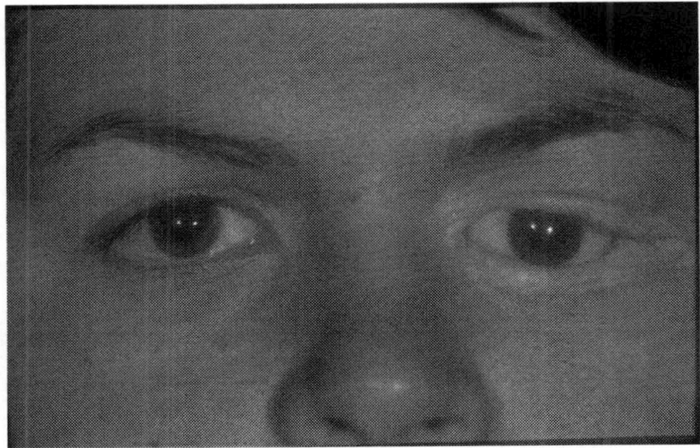

*Fig. 3.31 Reconstruction of both eyelids, and a socket to accept a prosthesis. There are even eyelash grafts! Superb result.*

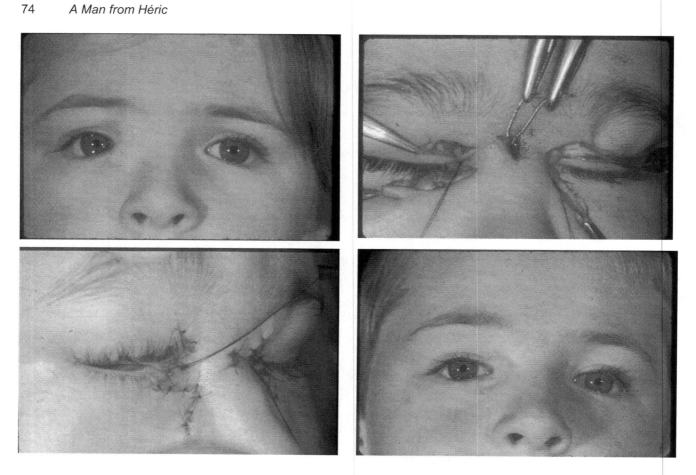

*Fig. 3.32 Child with asymmetric blepharophimosis.*
*Transnasal medial canthopexies and multiple z-plasties of Tessier's design.*

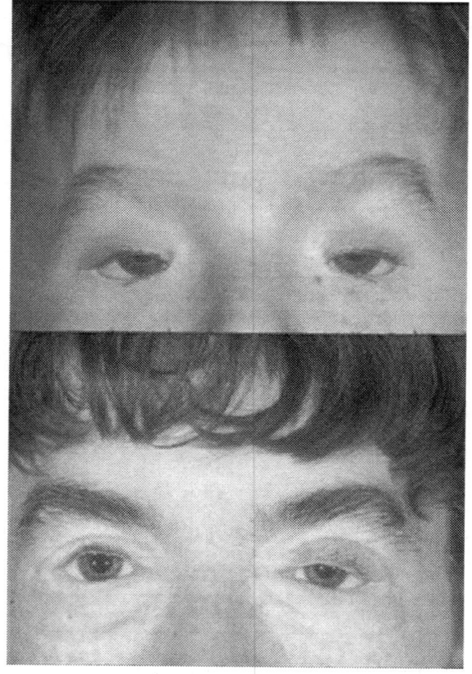

*Fig. 3.33 More severe form of blepharophimosis, with full-thickness skin grafts for lower eyelids, medial cantopexies, and ptosis correction.*

Eyelid reconstructions in burned patients and sequelae of orbital fractures were referred to Tessier by his ophthalmologist colleagues, and his results in these areas were outstanding. Congenital eyelid malformations were also referred, such as blepharophimosis, a condition seen more commonly in Celtish people (which is why the largest series was that of Tessier, the Bretons being Celts largely and Jack Mustardé's Scottish patients similarly being Celts. Blepharophimosis, where the eyelids are short, ptotic, with a poorly developed lateral canthus and telecanthus, is a difficult condition to obtain a good result. The cases Tessier was doing in the 1960s remain the best I have seen (and, like most of his work, remained unpublished).

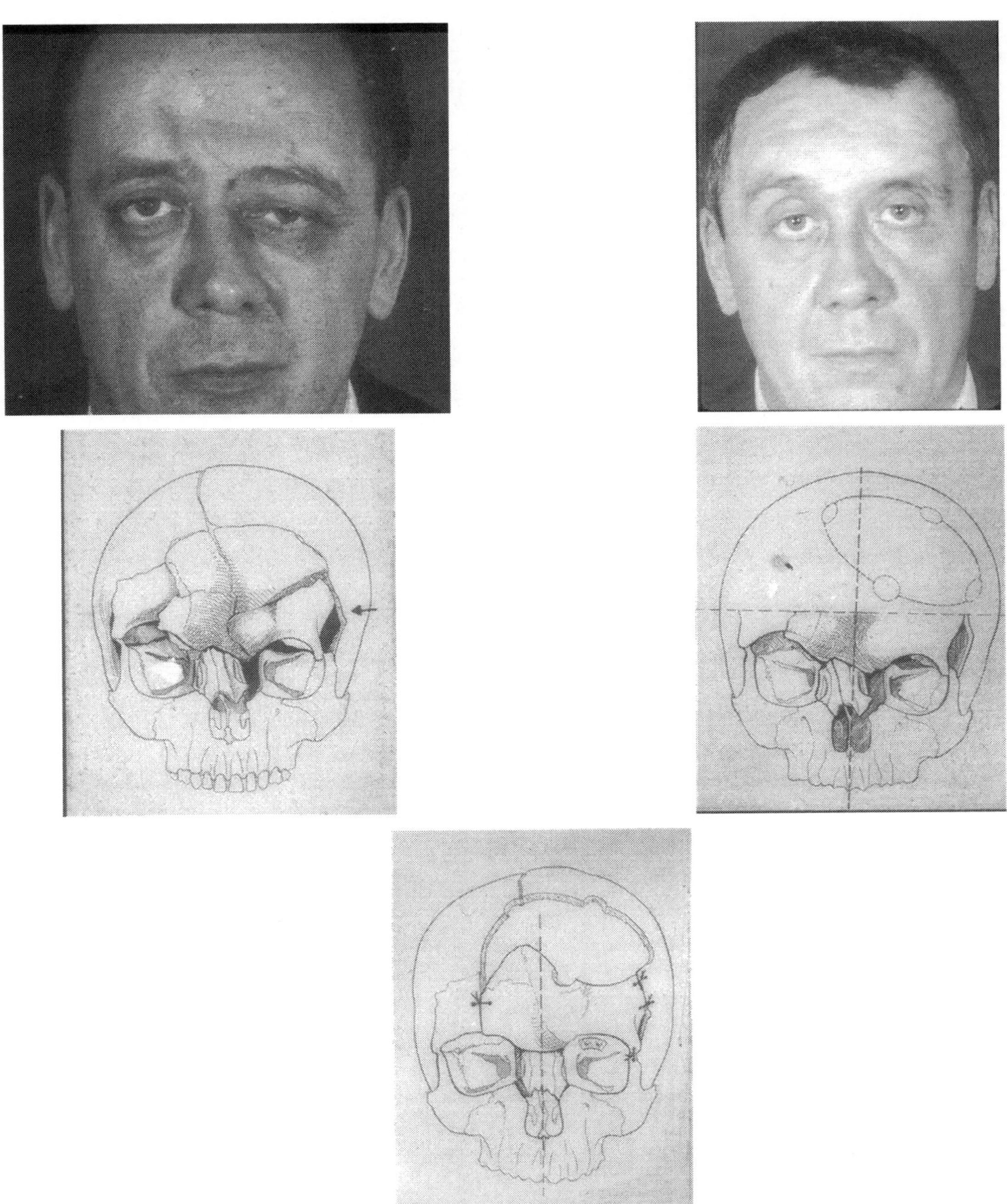

*Fig. 3.34 Another patient from the late 1960s with a complex displaced orbito-frontal fracture. Francine Gourdin's drawings show beautifully how the use of the transcranial approach enabled Tessier to properly reposition the displaced segments.*

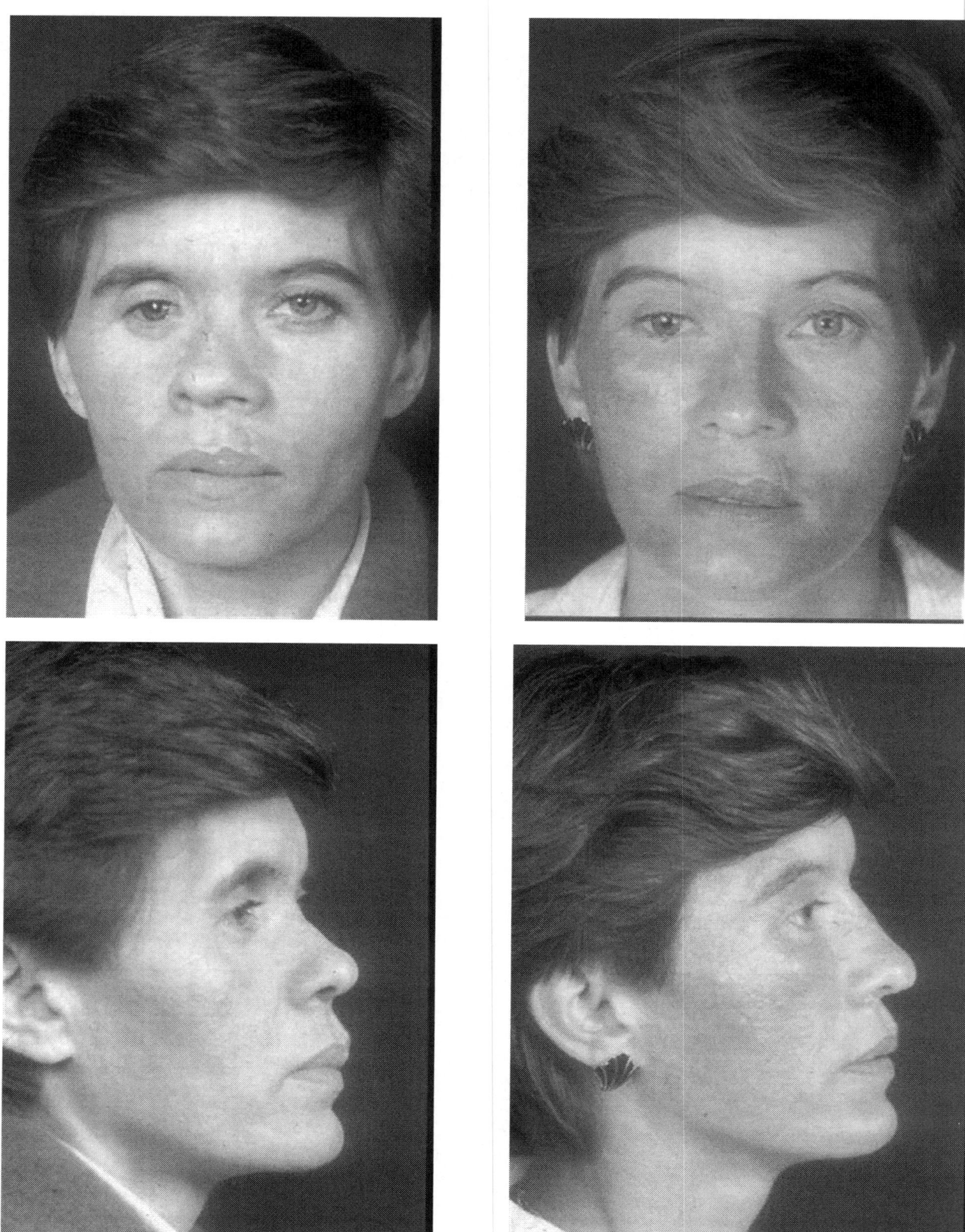

*Fig. 3.35 Putting his increasing number of tricks together, Tessier corrected the enophthalmos, repositioned the right cheekbone, placed the medial canthus in the proper position with a trans-nasal medial canthopexy, and straightened and lengthened the nose with osteotomies and an iliac bone graft. All of these were techniques that he had developed on his own.*

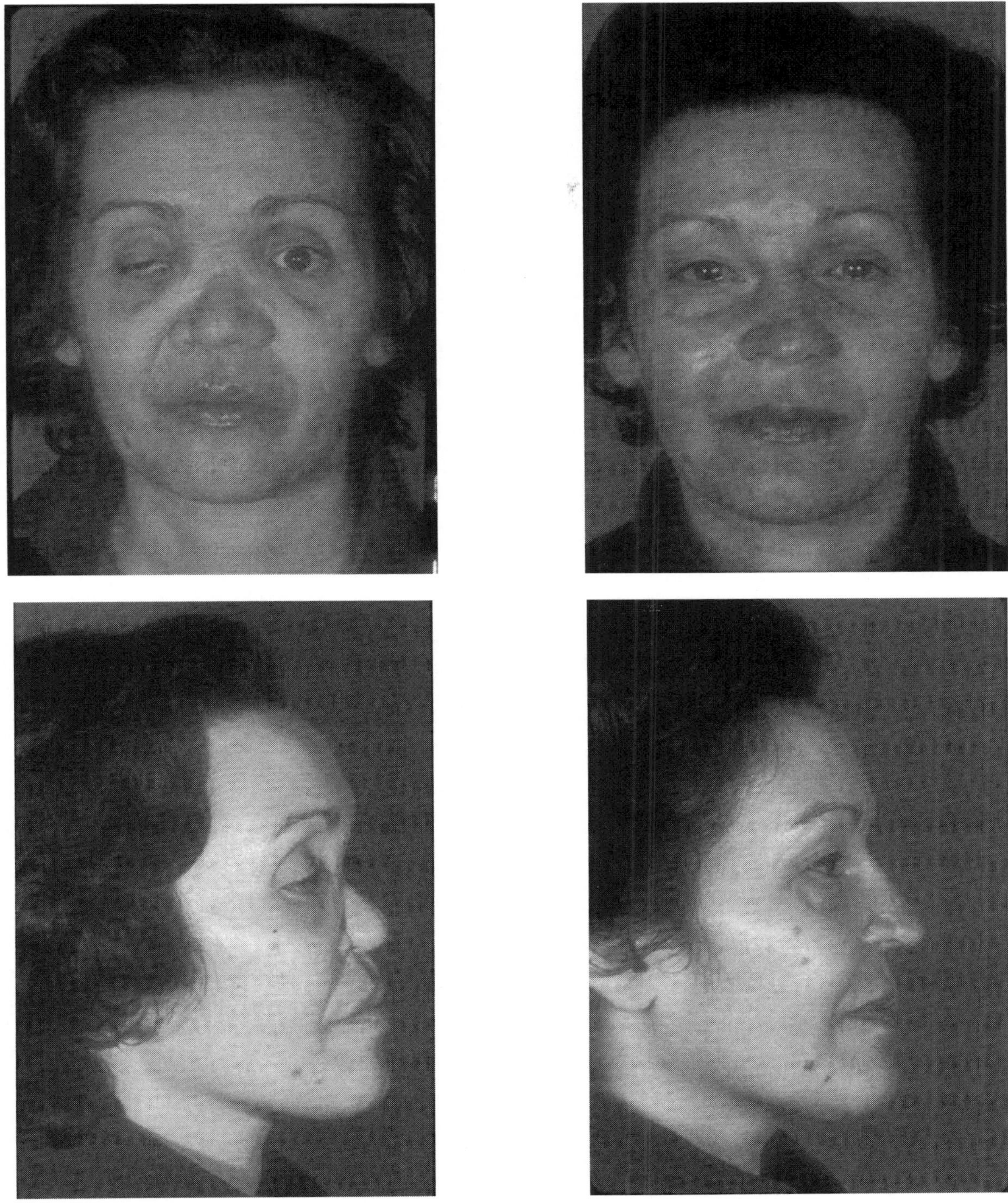

*Fig. 3.36 Another post-traumatic case where the enophthalmos and telecanthus were corrected along with substantial nasal lengthening with an iliac bone graft.*

These results established Tessier as one of—if not the—best orbito-maxillary surgeons in the world (although, at this time, little was known of him outside of France). He had become a master at working with bone, orbital and eyelid deformities, nasal reconstruction, and the correction of jaw deformities. He was comfortable using the transcranial approach when it was indicated.

The synthesis of his techniques and their further evolution would soon bring him to the world's attention.

# Chapter 4

## First steps into Craniofacial Surgery

In 1958, a mother brought in her son, in his twenties, to Paul Tessier's clinic at Hôpital Foch. The man had a severe form of Crouzon's disease: bulging, proptotic eyes due to underdevelopment of the orbital cavities, retrusion of the midface, and a severe underbite. Tessier said that, at the time, he was not even really certain of the diagnosis, but told the mother to come back in a few months, after he had had time to think about it for awhile. He recalled that he had seen a similar case with Sir Harold Gillies in England, but that the outcome in that case had not been entirely successful due to significant relapse. In fact, Gillies is said to have told his trainees, "Never do that operation" according to Hugo Obwegeser. Obwegeser, however, later saw a letter from Gillies to the father of a patient with Apert's disease in Switzerland that indicated Gillies intended to repeat the procedure on the patient in question. Tessier did some reading and realized that his patient, Maurice Anquetil, had Crouzon 's disease.

Tessier then went to the Muséè de l'Homme in Paris and found that they had the skull of a patient with Crouzon's disease. He had models made of this skull and devised a new operation, differing from the Gillies procedure in several important aspects.

After a day's work, he took the train to Nantes with his scrub nurse, Micheline Huguenin, to work on fresh cadavers, and then he took the latest train back to Paris. Cadavers were accessible to him in the medical school in Nantes (since he still had the title of instructor in anatomy there), whereas in Paris he had no academic position. After doing the operation several times on fresh cadavers (where the anatomy was clearly not the same as in a Crouzon patient), he contacted the mother and said that he was ready.

This was the first successful case of midface advancement at the Le Fort III level because Tessier used bone grafting, which prevented the relapse that Gillies's case had experienced. Tessier had problems with the stabilization of the midface. He initially used a plaster headcap with outriggers since that was what was current treatment entailed, but this didn't work, so he went to instrument maker, D. Simal, and had an innovative metal head frame (diadem) fabricated.

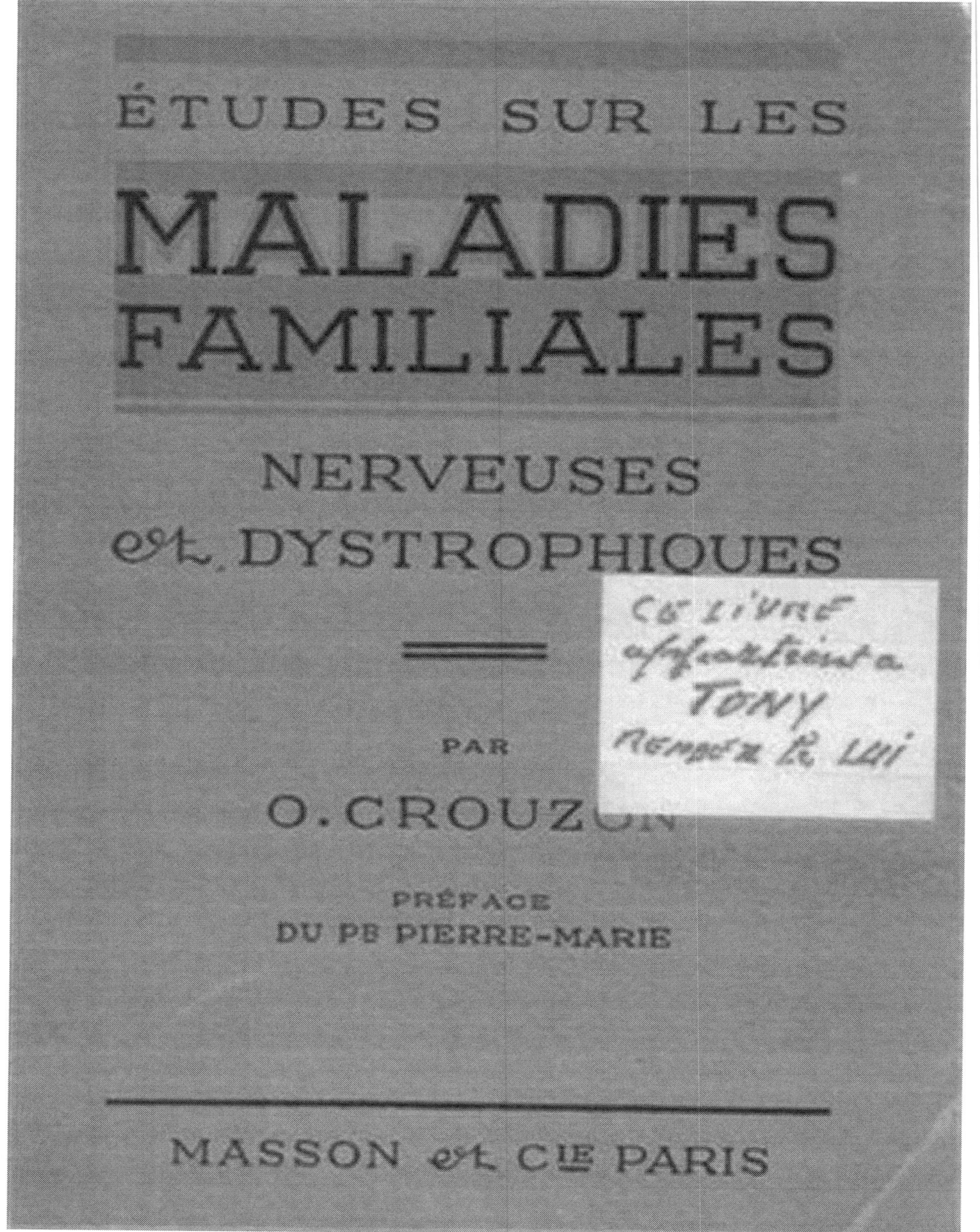

ÉTUDES SUR LES

MALADIES FAMILIALES

NERVEUSES

et DYSTROPHIQUES

PAR

O. CROUZON

PRÉFACE

DU Pr PIERRE-MARIE

MASSON et Cie PARIS



*Fig. 4.1 1929 book by Octave Crouzon, which gave the first description of the syndrome which bears his name. I found this book in the catalogue of an "antiquarian book" merchant, bought it for several hundred dollars, and gave it to Dr. Tessier. He initially refused the gift, saying that I should keep it. I insisted that it was a present, and he finally accepted it. After his death, I was cataloguing his library for Mireille, and I found the book with a little, yellow Post-it attached. It read, "Ce livre appartient a Tony. Remettez le lui," This book belongs to Tony. Return it to him..*

Il n'en faut cependant pas plus pour porter le diagnostic de *dysostose crânio-faciale* ; la malade présente, d'ailleurs, un tel « air de famille » avec le jeune Roger W..., antérieurement présenté ici le 10 mai 1912, que nous pensons tout d'abord avoir affaire à la mère de ce sujet.

Par ailleurs, il n'existe, chez Mlle Ap..., aucune autre malformation : l'ossature du corps, la musculature oculaire sont normales ; on note simplement la fréquence des céphalées, un degré appréciable de myopie, une intelligence un peu fruste.

Fig. 72. — Mlle Ap... Dysostose crânio-faciale

La *radiographie* a confirmé — bien que le syndrome radiologique typique soit ici incomplet — l'existence d'une dysostose crânio-faciale. La table externe de la voûte crânienne ne semble pas amincie, mais la table interne est extrêmement irrégulière, et le crâne présente un aspect feuilleté avec zones claires et sombres alternantes. *Le* massif facial, les os du nez, l'ethmoïde donnent une image floue où l'on ne retrouve pas trace de l'architecture normale. On remarque encore le prognathisme du maxillaire inférieur, l'augmentation de volume de la selle turcique dans tous ses diamètres, l'amincissement des apophyses clinoïdes postérieures et l'existence d'un éperon occipital anormalement saillant.

Cette dysostose remonte, comme il *est* de règle, aux premiers jours de la vie. Mais, fait curieux, elle semble constituer chez Mlle Ap... un *cas isolé, ni héréditaire, ni familial* : la mère et la sœur de la

*Fig. 4.2 Adult patient presented in Crouzon's book with the midface retrusion, exorbitism, and pseudo-prognathism characteristic of the syndrome. This was the first use of the term "cranio-facial dysostosis."*

## Midface

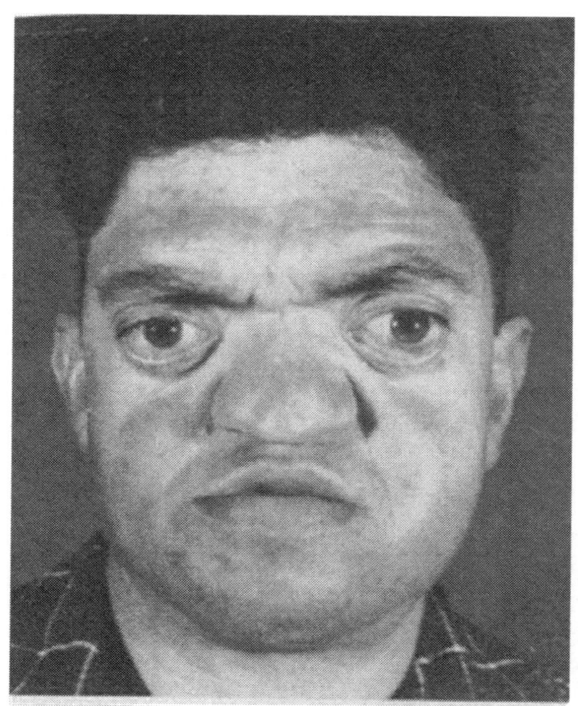
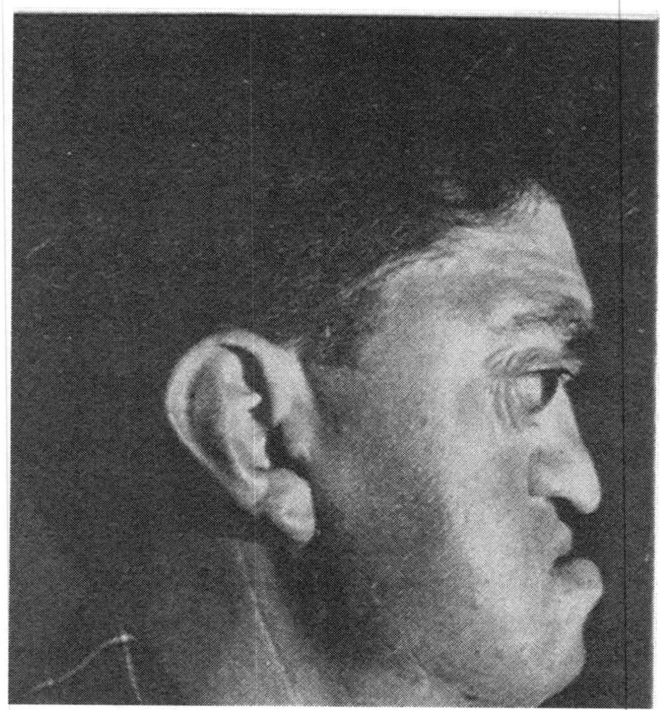

*Fig. 4.3 Maurice Anquetil, on Jan. 9, 1958. Severe midface retrusion, proptosis, and pseudo-prognathism.*

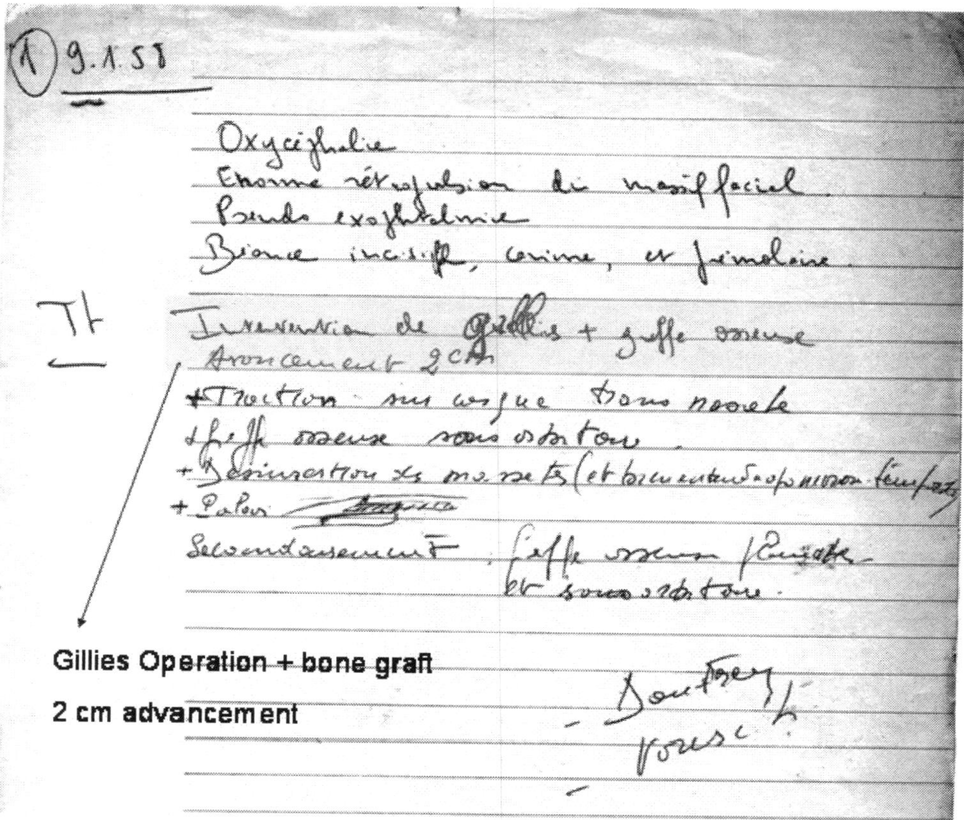

(1) 9.1.58

Oxycéphalie
Énorme rétropulsion du massif facial.
Pseudo exophtalmie
Béance incisive, canine, et prémolaire.

Intervention de Gillies + greffe osseuse
Avancement 2 cm
+ Traction sur casque trans nasale
+ greffe osseuse sous orbitaire.

Secondairement greffe osseuse [illegible] et sous orbitaire.



*Fig. 4.4 Tessier's consultation note:*

Oxycephaly

Enormous retrusion of the midface

Pseudo exophthalmia

Anterior crossbite, canines and premolars

Treatment: Operation of Gillies + bone graft

Advancement 2 cm.

+ traction from a plaster head frame to a transnasal wire

+ infraorbital bone graft

+ disinsertion of the masseter (and even extended over the temporal muscle)

+ Palate

Secondarily, bone graft of floor and infraorbital region

—Dautrey—Vourc'h

With this one brief note, one could say that craniofacial surgery was born. Tessier had realized that Gillies case had failed because of lack of a bone graft, so his procedure included multiple bone grafts. At the bottom of the page, he says to involve Dautrey and Vorsc'h. This is the Jacques Dautrey whose brother was being examined in Chapter 3 by Virenque and Tessier. Although he was on Ginestet's service and ostensibly forbidden to provide Tessier any assistance, he was a good friend of Tessier's and was consulted nevertheless. Dautrey does not seem to have been present at the operation, and the assistant was Jean Delbet, one of the plastic surgical staff. Vourc'h was the chief of anesthesiology.

[In later years, when Tessier was leaving town, he always advised his trainees/visitors to go to Nancy to see Dautrey operate. Dautrey would set up a "wet clinic" several times a year, where he would bring in a number of pre- and post-op patients to be seen, and then he would go through his surgical repertoire, which, although limited, he performed superbly. He would do a sagittal splitting of the mandible, for either set-back or advancement; a type of "z-plasty" of the zygomatic arch that he developed for patients with chronic dislocation of the mandible (the Dautrey procedure); modeling of the mandibular condyle for TM joint problems; and a posterior impaction of the upper molars to close an open bite.]

*Fig. 4.5 Jacques Dautrey*

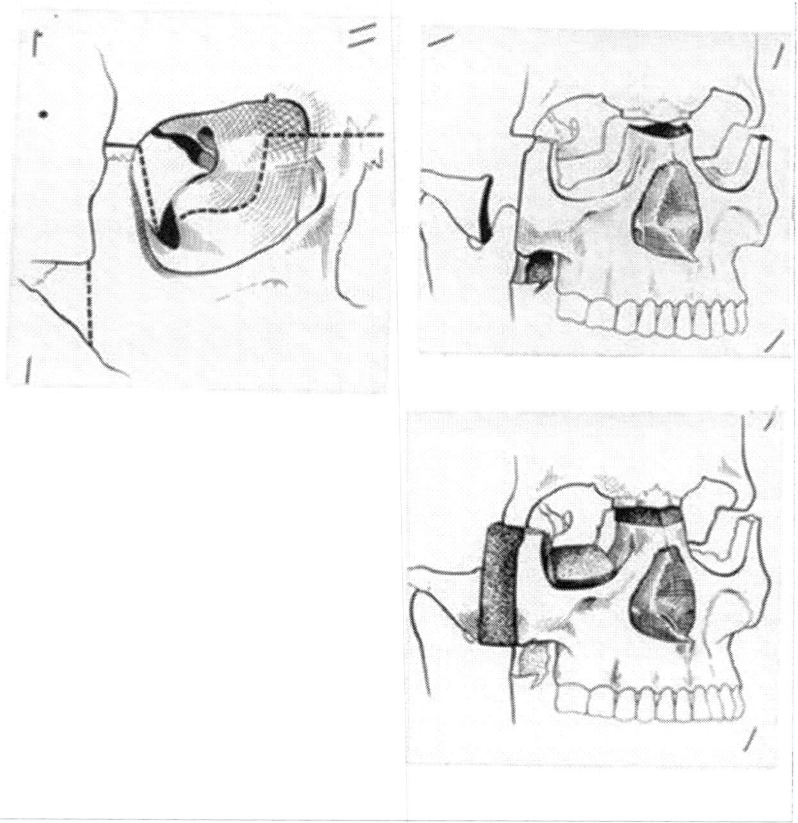

*Fig. 4.6 Francine Gourdin's drawing of Tessier's first Le Fort 3-type osteotomy. The bone grafts are indicated by dark stipple.*

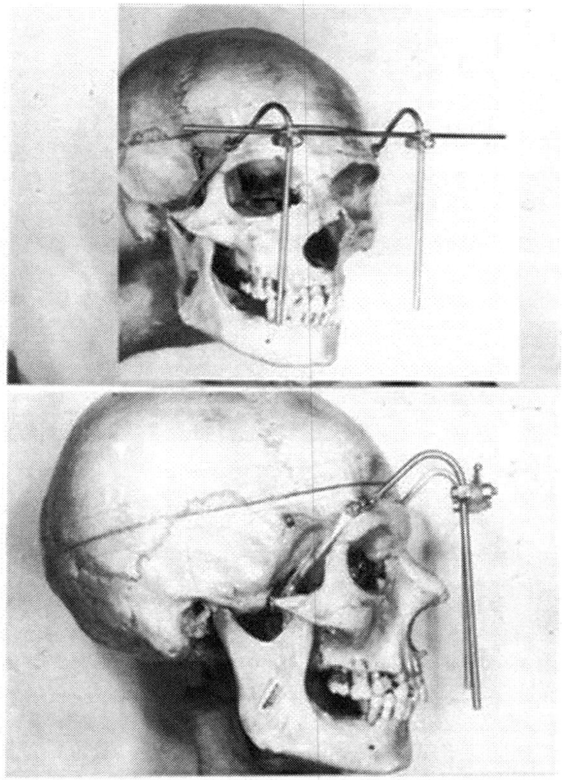

*Fig. 4.7 Diadem that Tessier had made by the instrument company, D. Simal, to maintain a forward pull on the midface.*

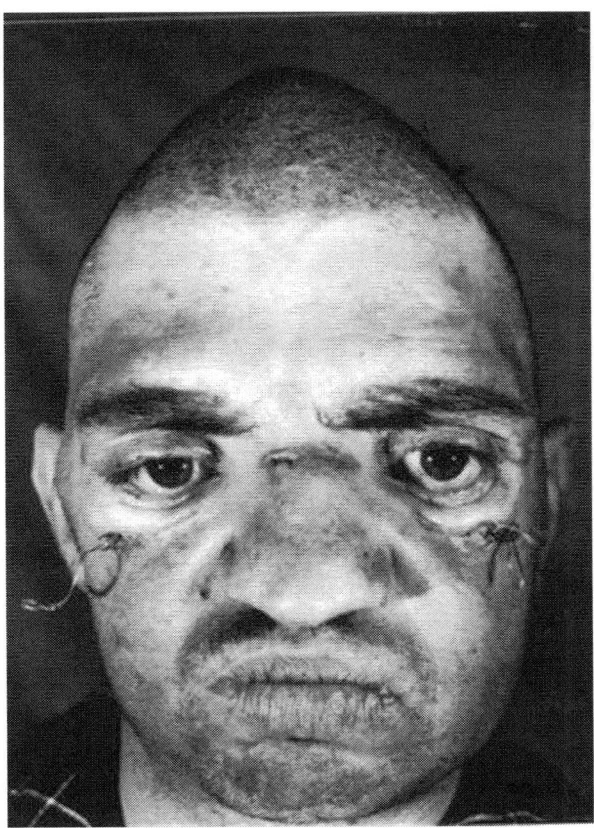

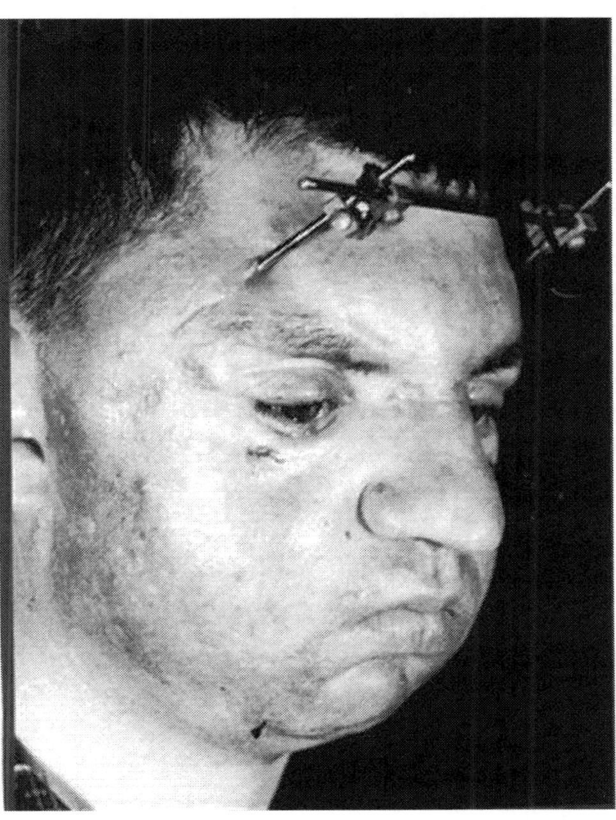

*Fig. 4.8 Wires led from the vertical limbs of the diadem to wires from the malar bones.*

Nom : ANQUETIL        Sexe : M    Lieu : FOCH

Date : 26.2.1958

<u>CRO.</u>

I – Voie d'abord palatine et interptérygo maxillaire D et G.

a) Incision en U ouvert en AR
Le branche transversale du U est à 2 cm en AV du bord postérieur du palais.

Rugination du palais.

Ostéotomie (burin large à nez) palatine transversale à 5 m/m en AV du bord postérieur du palais. Elle doit donc se situer dans la suture maxillo palatine. Elle va d'un trou palatin à l'autre.

b) Les branches sagittales du U contournent en dedans le trou palatin et en AR l'arcade dentaire.

Ostéotomie interptérygo maxillaire (burins larges et courbes: rugines "dites américaines" sigmoides)

Cette ostéotomie atteint 2 cm de profondeur et se dirige franchement en dehors.

<u>Difficultés, Dangers, Critiques.</u>

- Le fibro muqueuse palatine flotte en drapeau.
- Epargner la palatine postérieure dont les anastomoses avec la palatine antérieure sont une sécurité pour le maxillaire supérieur.
- Toutefois, dans ce cas on sectionne ses branches destinées au voile dt cette section peut devenir responsable d'une nécrose du lambeau palatin.
- Epargner la palatine dans son trajet vertical au cours de l'ostéotomie (rester postérieur)

Obtenir une ouverture suffisante de la bouche. L'écarteur de Bott n'est pas valable (rétrogénie)

2 – Voie d'abord zygomatique D et G.

Incision oblique de 10 m/m en B et en AR sur le versant postérie de la pommette.

*Fig. 4.9 Operative note of M. Anquetil, February 26, 1958. The surgical approaches are described, as well as an osteotomy between the posterior portion of the maxilla and the pterygoid plate of the sphenoid bone.*

He underlines the difficulties and dangers, and provides self-criticism.

Difficultés - Dangers.

L'angulaire.

Le peu d'écartement latéral possible.

Les ethmoïdales antérieures (hémostase à la cire)

La poulie du G.O.

Le L.P.S. à ne pas désinsérer.

Le dôme du sac à récliner en bas.

La lame criblée.

7 - Ostéotomie de la cloison.

Par l'ostéotomie fronto-nasale introduire l'ostéotome de Stille de 20 cm/m et faisant levier - provoquer un diastasis F.N.

Ciseaux coudés sur le plat.
Sectionner la cloison jusqu'à l'épine nasale postérieure

8 - Mobilisation.

Retirer le packing nasal et buccal.

Aspirer - Bouche et nez.

Pince de Wolsheim protégée de caoutchouc dans chaque narine et sur le palais.

Mobiliser - tirer dans tous les sens pour faire céder les parties molles.

Hypercorriger.

Difficultés - Dangers.

Le masseter, l'aponévrose temporale.

Les parties molles.

Les pédicules vasculaires et nerveux élongués.

La fracture inter-maxillo-malaire difficile à éviter.

Faut-il embrocher transversalement d'un malaire à l'autre à travers un bordinférieur de l'orbite bien fragile ? Et le sac lacrymal !

..

*Fig. 4.10 Further mention of difficulties and dangers: the angular vessel, the lack of retraction possible through small incisions, the anterior ethmoidal vessels, the pulley of the superior oblique muscle, the lower eyelid (risk of disinserting it), the lacrimal sac (risk of inferior displacement, the cribriform plate.*
*He has carefully thought out beforehand every element of this operation.*

8) Formation d'un lambeau tubulé sous-claviculaire gauche, destiné à fermer la communication oro-nasale.

9) La réduction est maintenue par un blocage inter-maxillaire assuré par les gouttières et les tractions d'abord élastiques puis par fils d'acier.

(K 80 + 40/2)

*Fig. 4.11 There was a complication: an oro-nasal fistula occurred after a tear of the palatal mucosa,and it was repaired with a tube pedicle passed through the cheek.*

(8)

M. ANQUETIL

Consultation 23.12.1958

La contention est excellente. L'hypercorrection manifeste. Il existe un excellent engrainement. La consolidation parait très avancée. On supprime la contention par fils d'acier.

*Fig. 4.12 Note from December 23, 1958: "The healing is excellent, and there is overcorrection. There is an excellent occlusion. The consolidation seems very advanced. The interdental wires are removed [after 10 months of intermaxillary fixation!!!]."*

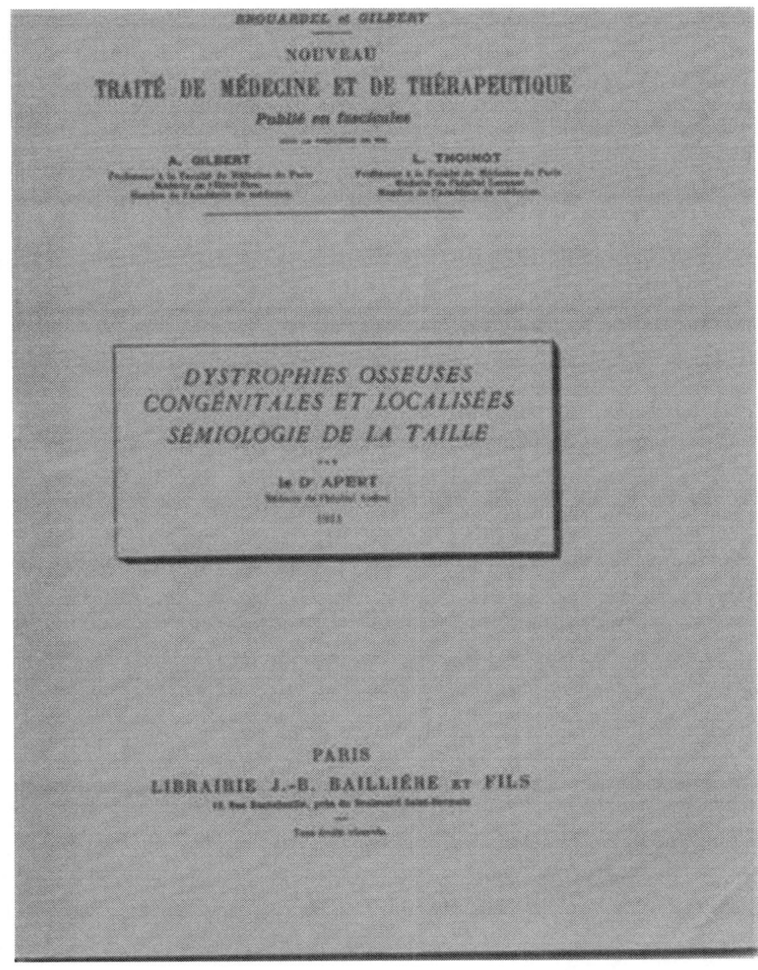

BROUARDEL et GILBERT

NOUVEAU

TRAITÉ DE MÉDECINE ET DE THÉRAPEUTIQUE

Publié en fascicules

A. GILBERT

L. THOINOT

DYSTROPHIES OSSEUSES CONGÉNITALES ET LOCALISÉES

SÉMIOLOGIE DE LA TAILLE

le Dr APERT

PARIS

LIBRAIRIE J.-B. BAILLIÈRE ET FILS

*Fig. 4.13 First description by Apert of the condition that bears his name, also known as acrocephalo syndactyly. There is a facial deformity similar to the Crouzon, but the patients also have webbing of the fingers and toes.*

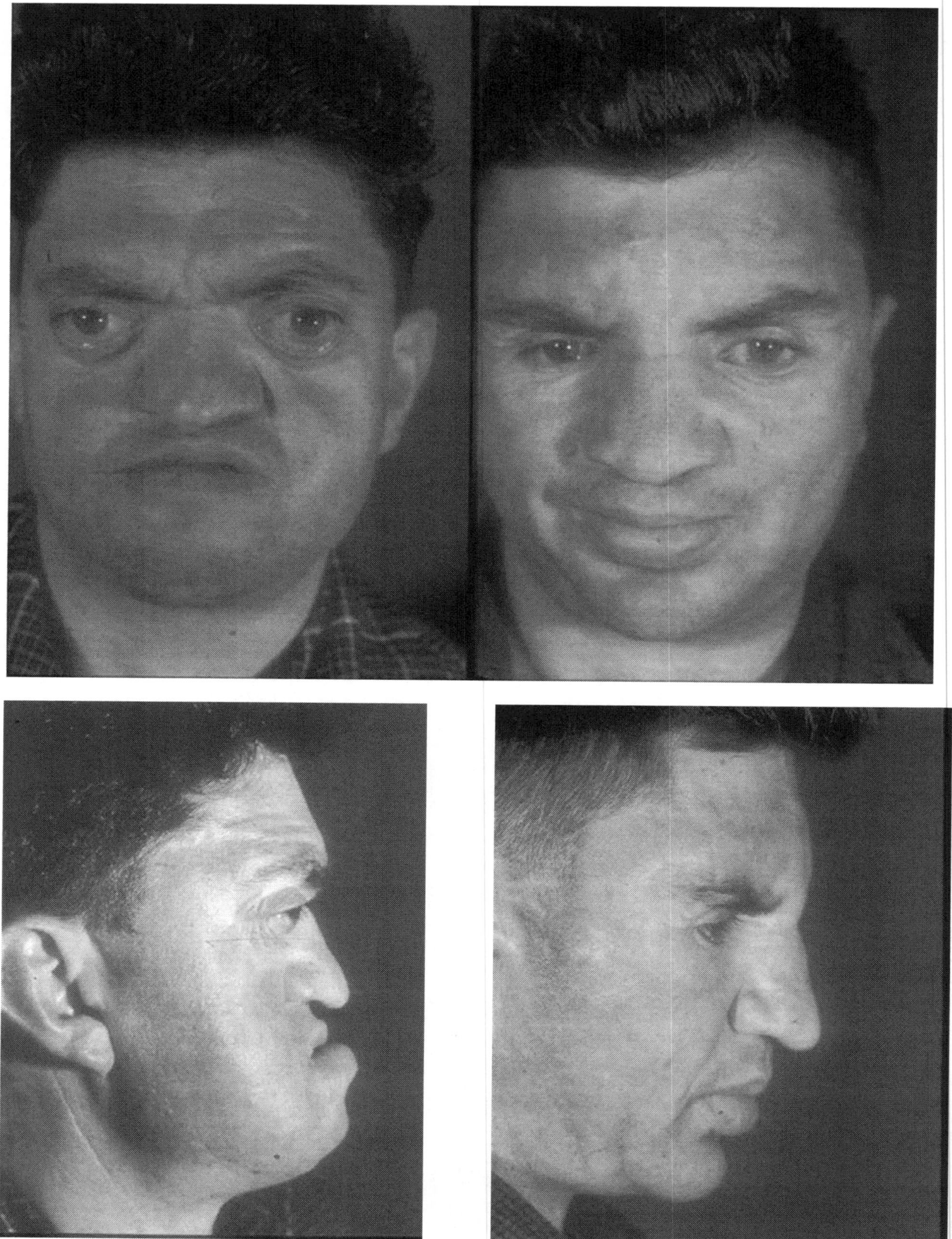

*Fig. 4.14 Result obtained for M. Anquetil, following a final genioplasty. This is a difficult case, even by today's standards, and the result is stunning in that it was the first case ever done with this method.*

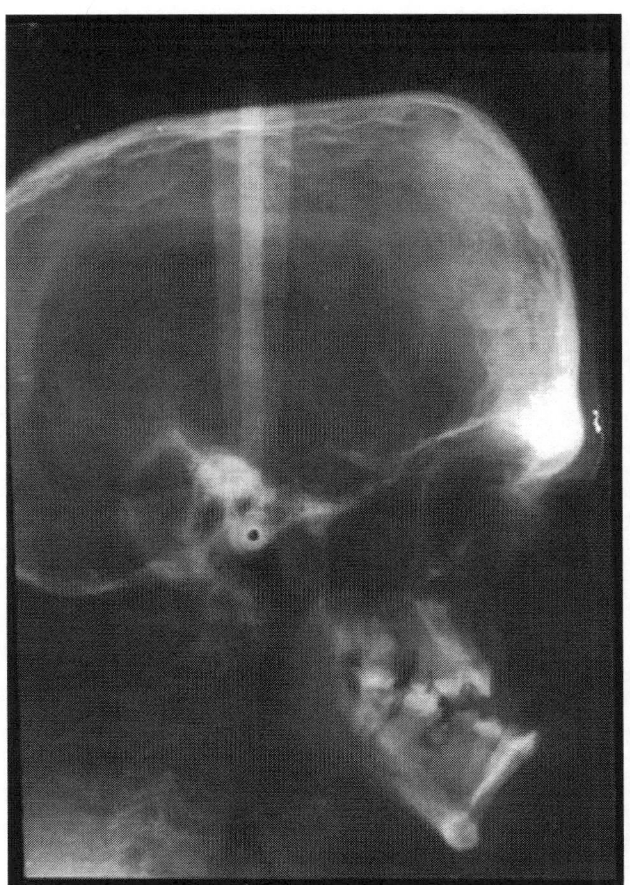

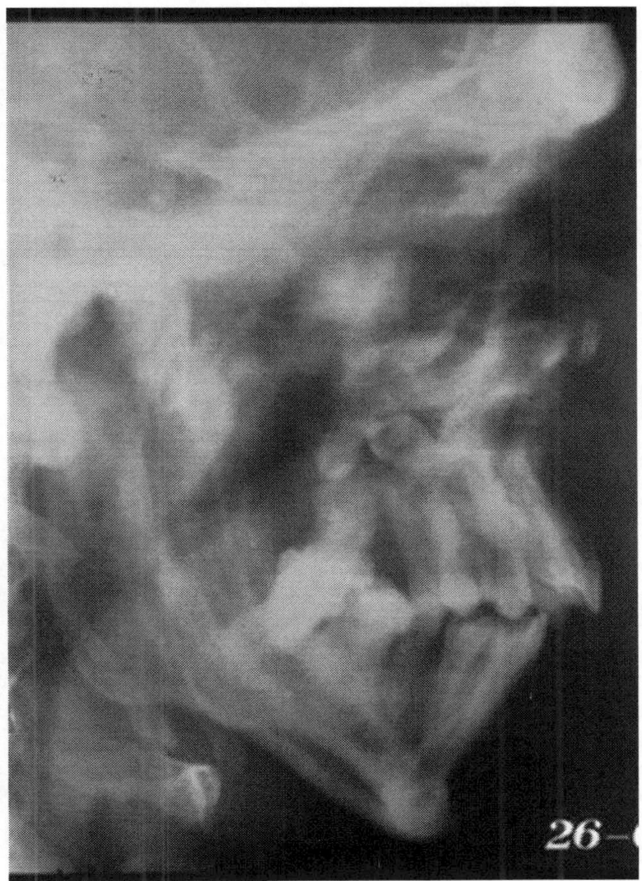


*Fig. 4.15 Before and after radiographs of Anquetil. Very few craniofacial surgeons of 2009 would be able to obtain this result by a straightforward advancement; almost all would use distraction osteogenesis.*

(Anquetil's mother called Dr. Tessier fifteen years later and told him that her son had died in his sleep. She thanked him for everything he had done.)

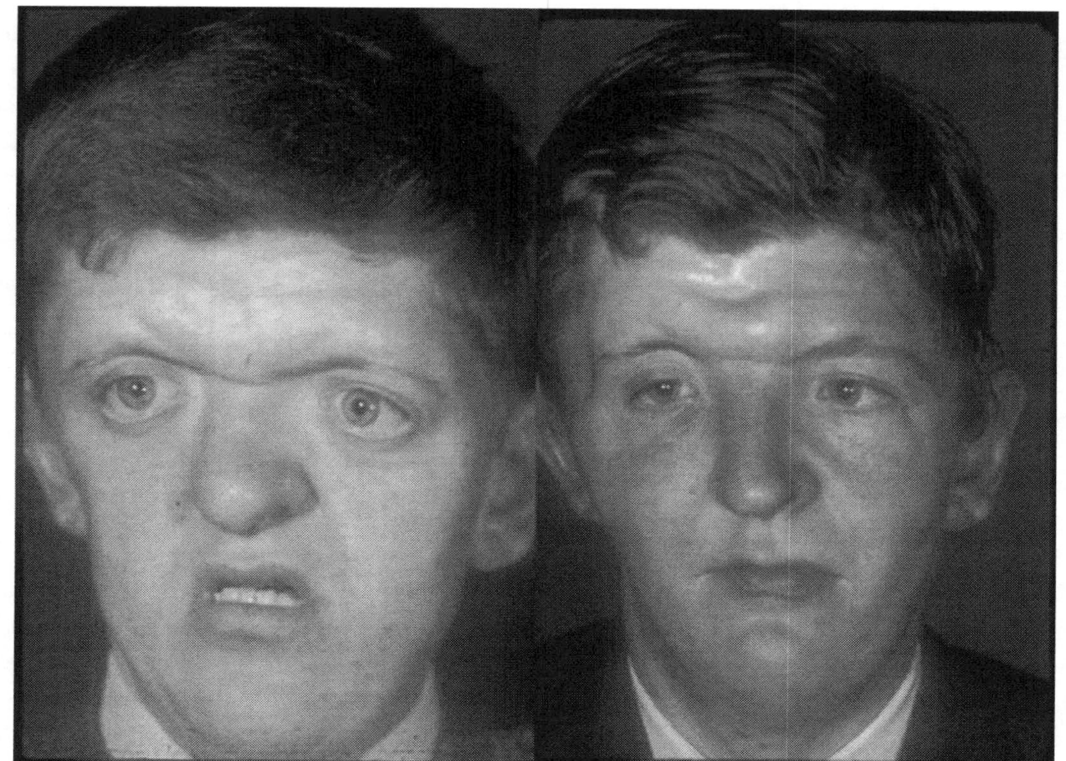

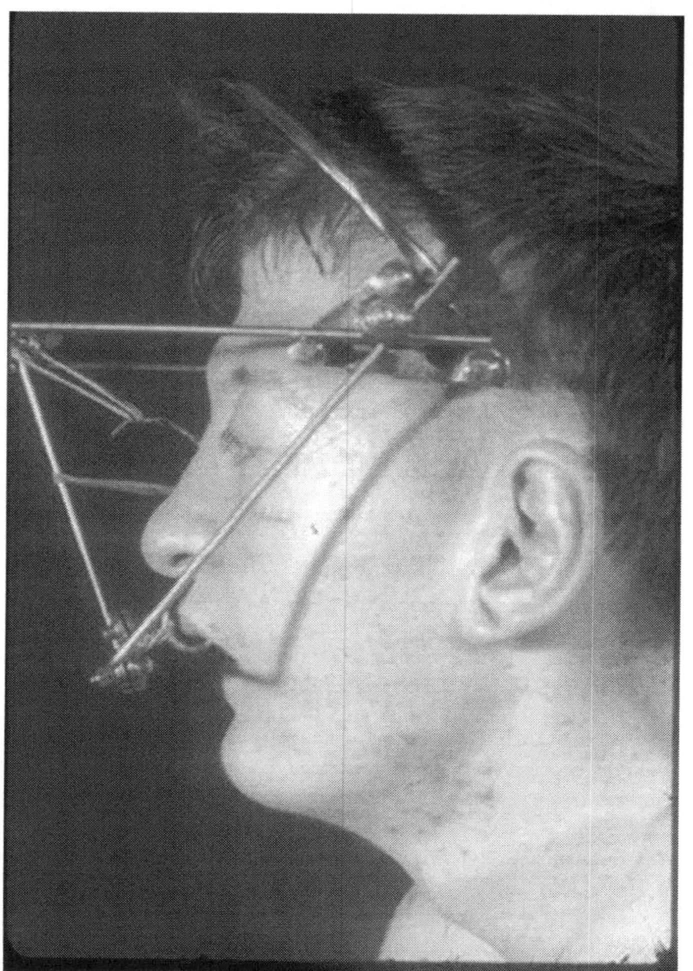

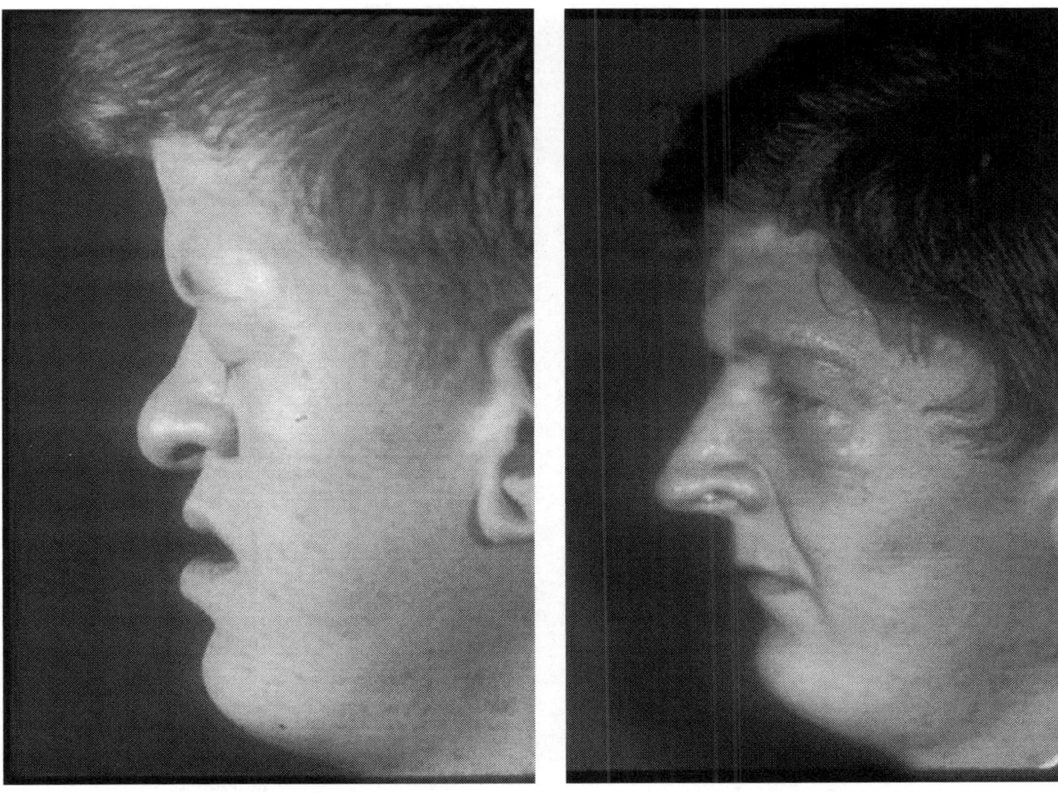

*Fig. 4.16 Patient with Apert's syndrome treated by the same method of Le Fort III-type osteotomy. Nasal bone graft also performed.*

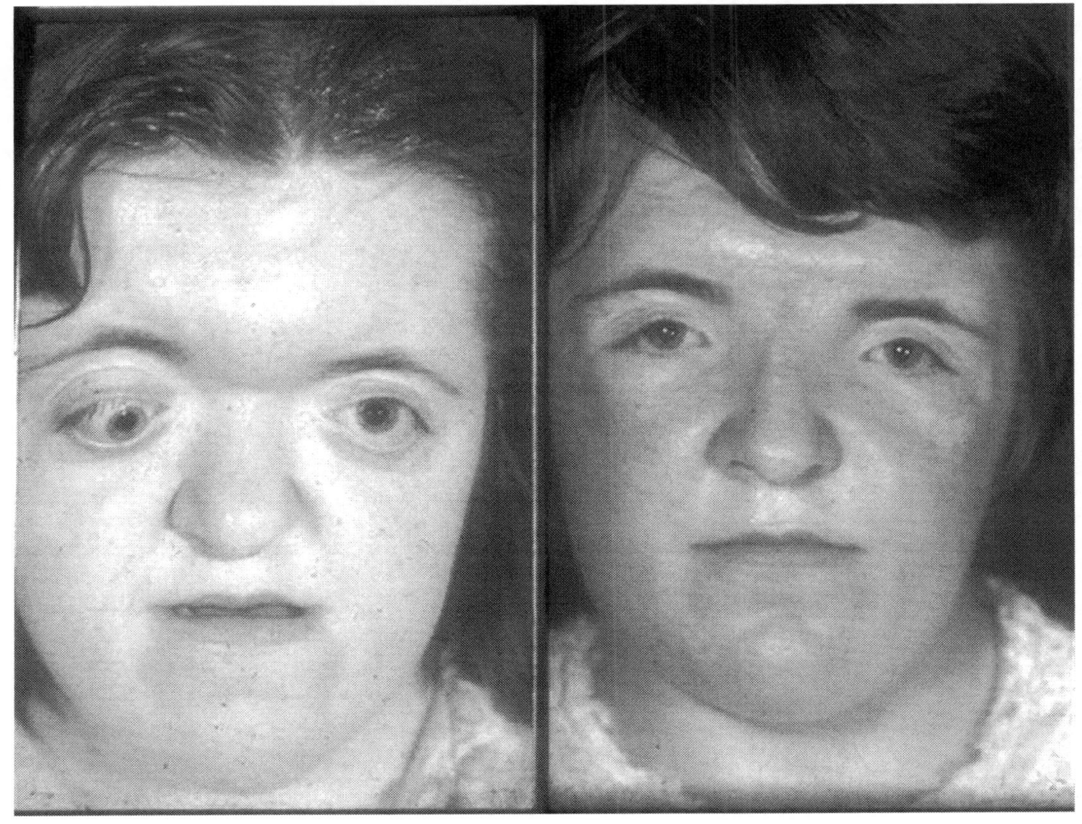

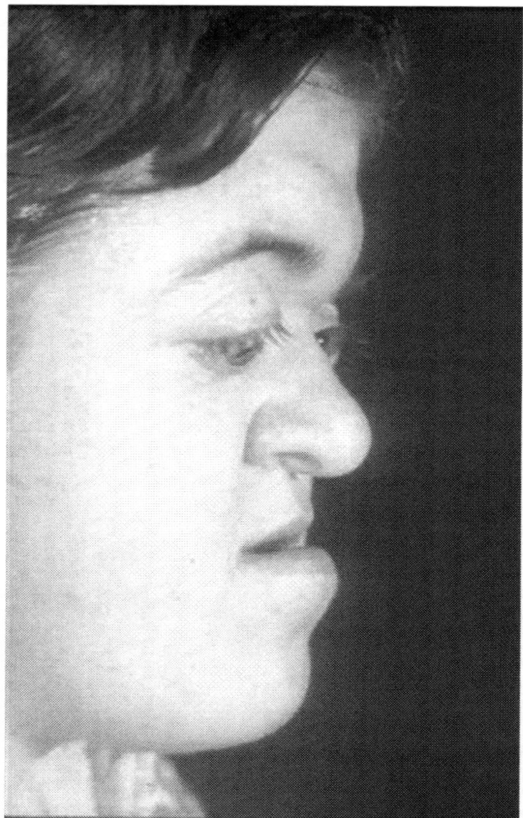

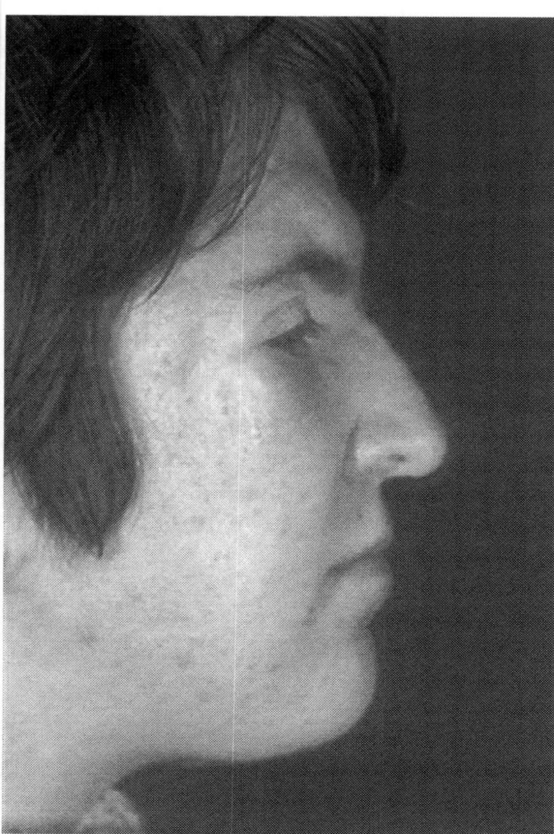

*Fig. 4.17. Another patient with Apert's syndrome. Simply enlarging the right orbital cavity to a normal shape has corrected the strabismus. By this case, Tessier had progressed to doing almost the entire operation through a coronal incision (behind the hairline) and an intraoral incision. Both cases done in the late 1960s.*

Aesthetic surgery. Paul Tessier was an exceptional aesthetic surgeon due to his technical abilities and innate sense of what constituted a beautiful face. In 1968 (*Extrait de la Gazette Médicale de France*, No. 28, November 1968), he was the guest editor of a 111-page supplement on aesthetic surgery. Although probably 90 percent of the many cases shown were his, his collaborators, Jean-Paul Delbet, Michel Lekieffre, and Jacques Pastoriza, were listed as coauthors. The results shown are outstanding.

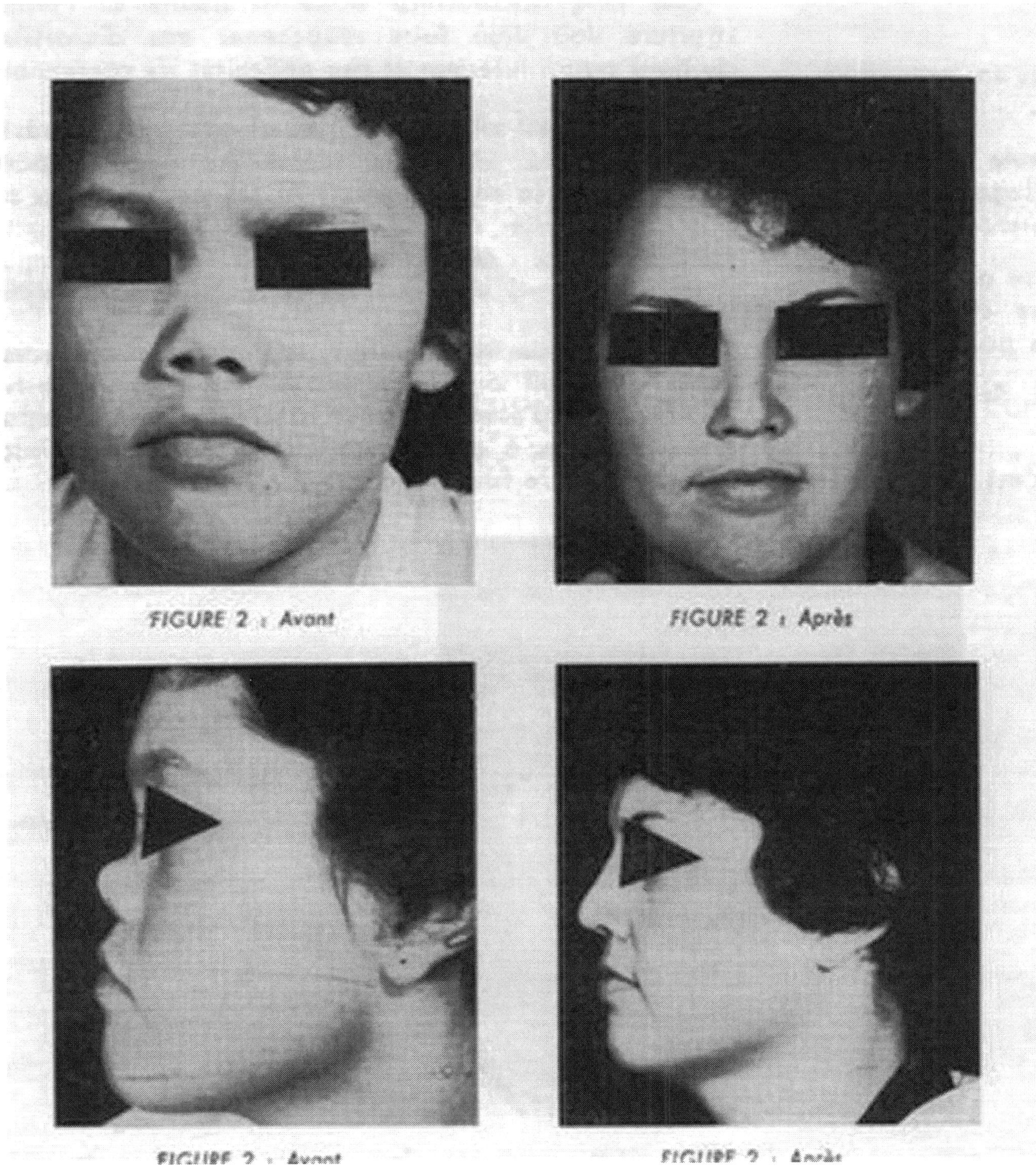


*Fig. 4.19 Septal abscess with saddle nose. Iliac bone graft.*

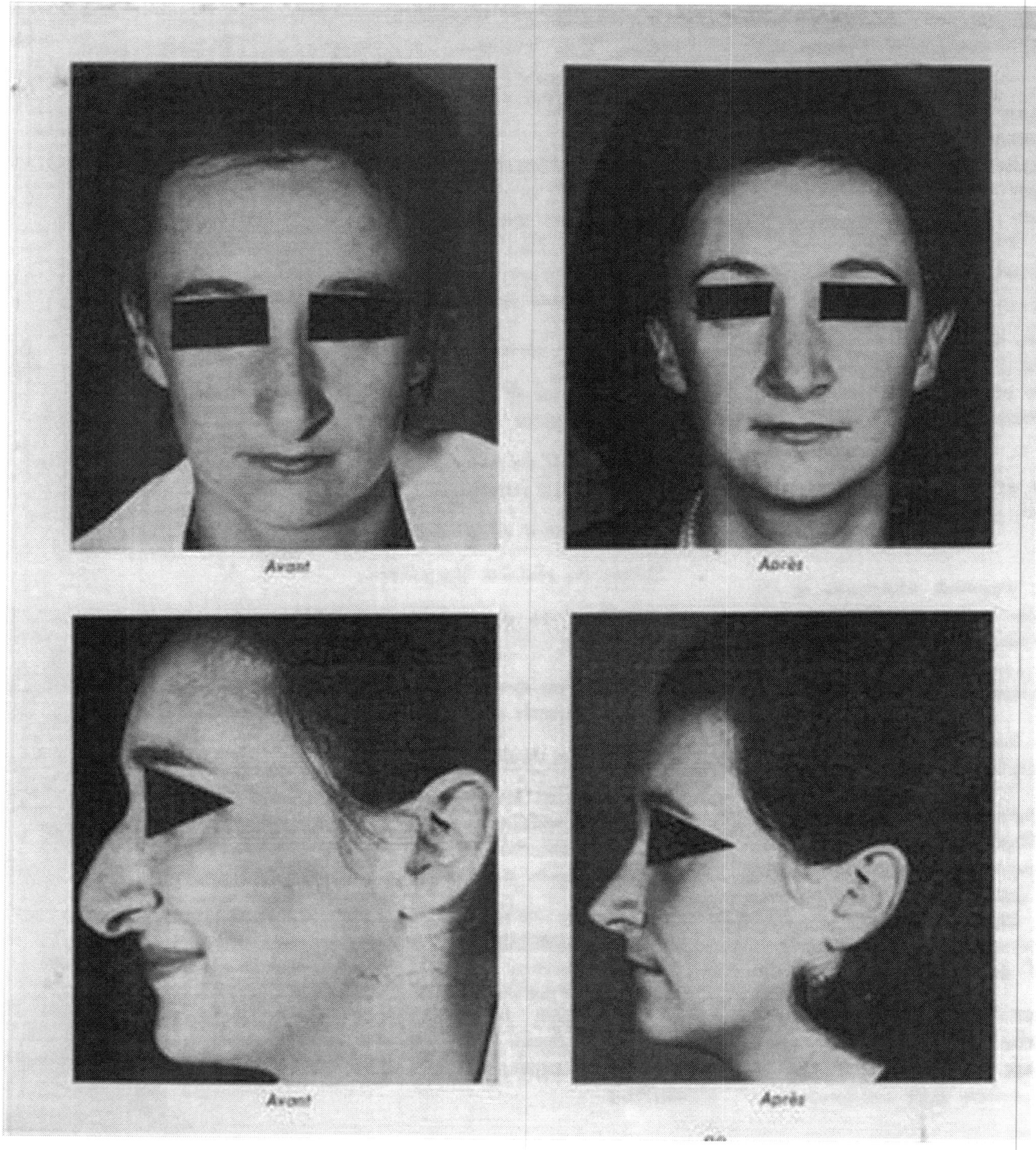


*Fig. 4.20 Reduction of a gigantic nose.*

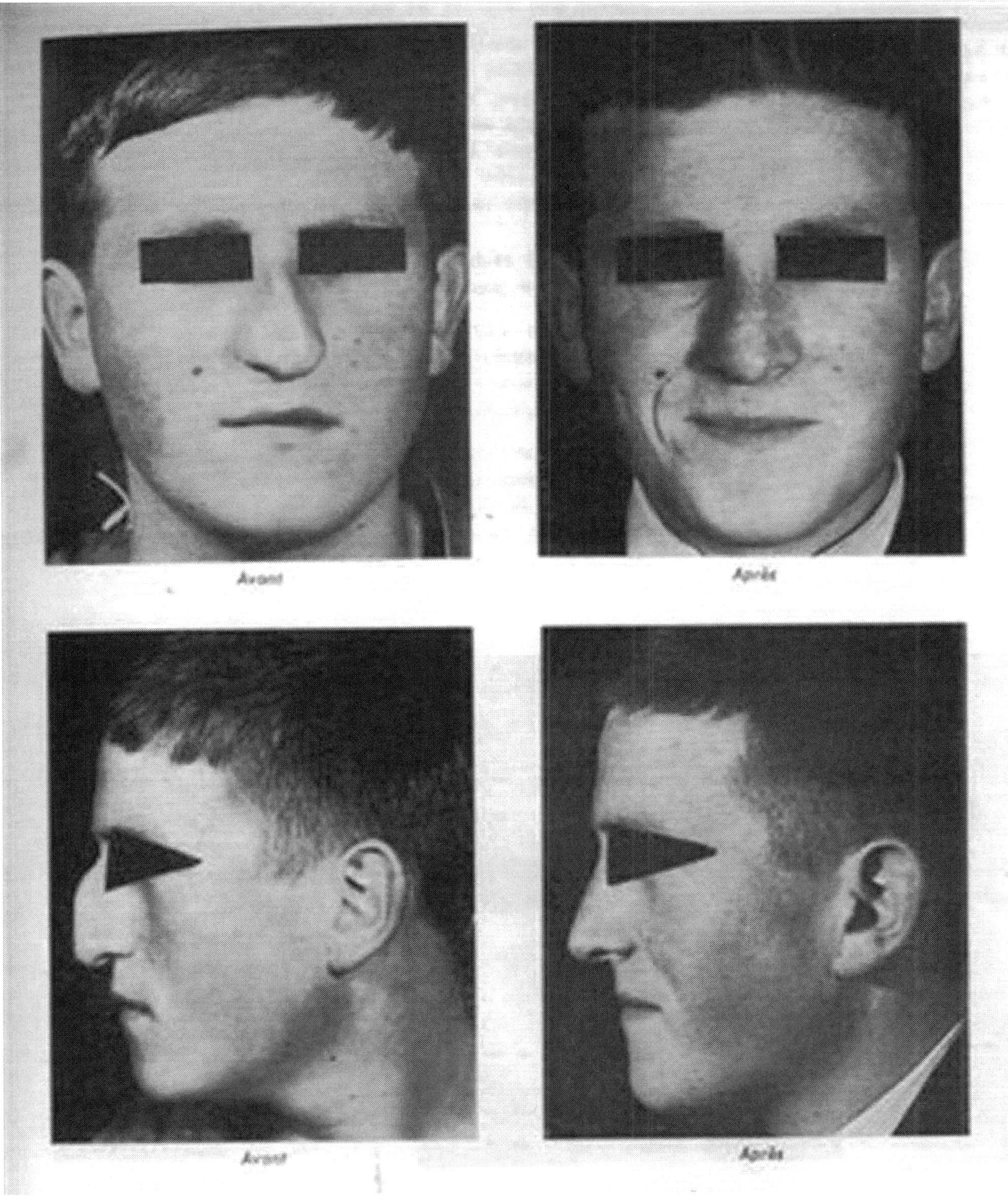


*Fig. 4.21 Straightening of a severely deviated nose.*

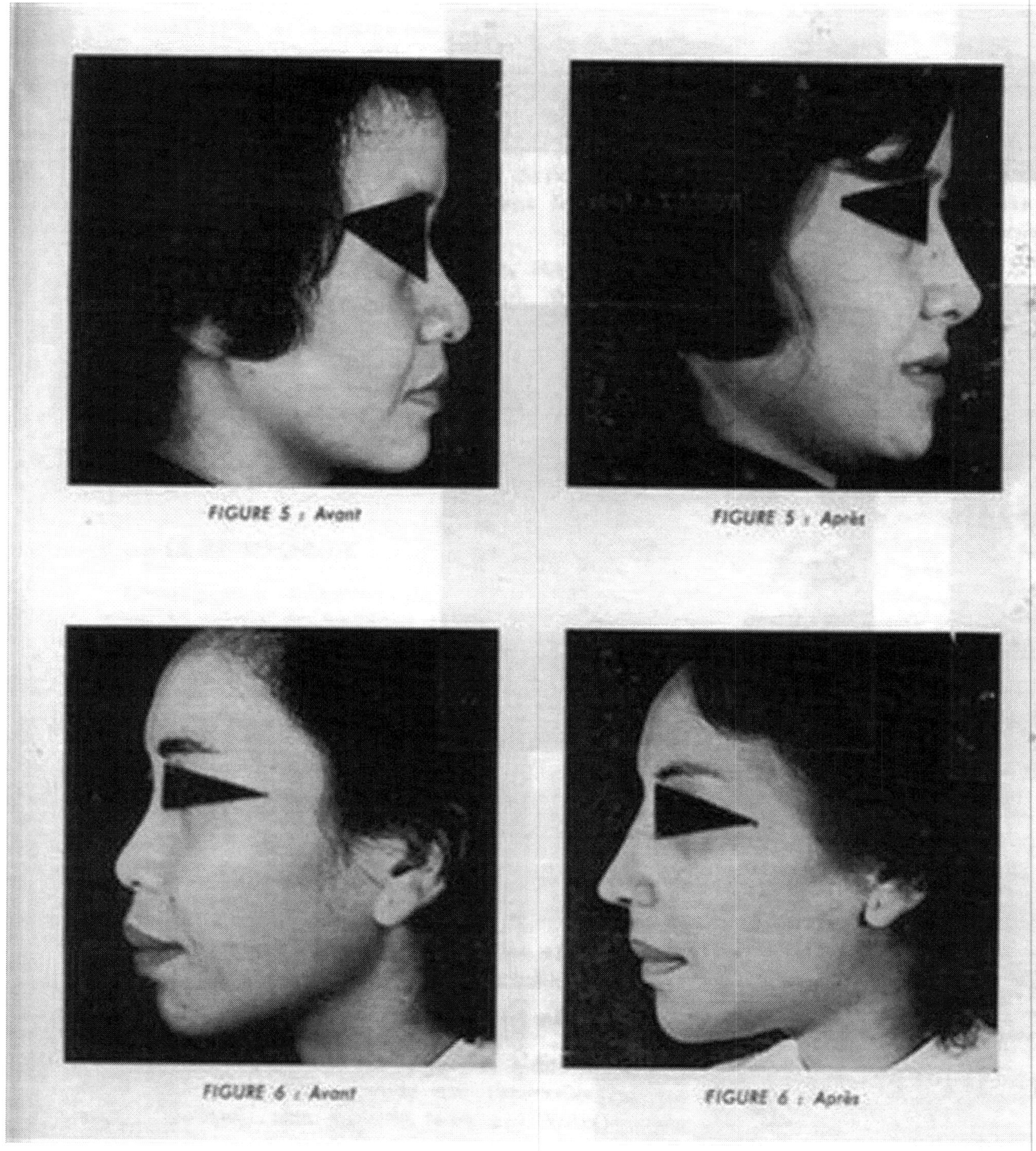


*Fig.4.22 Asiatic noses. Septal cartilage grafts. Nasal lengthening.*

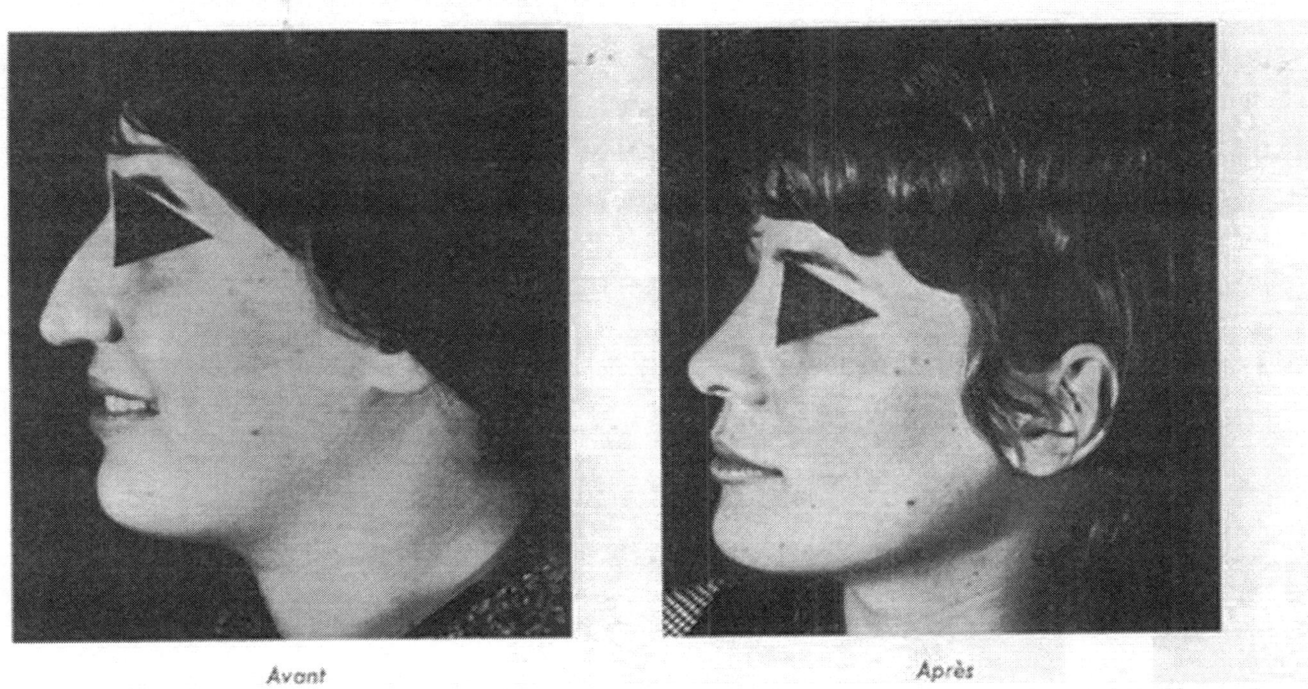


*Fig. 4.23 A purely "aesthetic" nose. Rome, 1967*

With these results, it is evident that Paul Tessier was an excellent aesthetic surgeon. In the 1960s, he could have easily chosen to do nothing but aesthetic surgery, as many surgeons who were skillful reconstructive surgeons in the early days of their career decided to do.

**Rome, 1967**.

Tessier had presented his work in France (Montpellier, 1966) on the Le Fort 3, intracranial correction of hypertelorism, and correction of oro-ocular clefts, but his work remained unknown in the English-speaking world. His presentation at the International Society of Plastic and Reconstructive Surgery in Rome in September, 1967 changed this. This was a "seismic" event, and dozens of plastic surgeons went back to the United States, Canada, Mexico, South America, Scandinavian and elsewhere with an extreme interest in and enthusiasm about what they had seen. Because he was being bombarded with requests from potential visitors, Tessier put together several teaching sessions, which he entitled C.H.O.C.–I (*Chirurgie Orbito Cranial*, or Orbito Cranial Surgery) and C.H.O.C.–II.

CHOC–I lasted a week and entailed twenty hours of clinical discussion and forty hours of surgery. The sixteen invitees included P. Petit (a French pediatric surgeon); Gerard Guiot (a French neurosurgeon and Tessier's collaborator at Foch); Oudard; Roger Mouly (a French plastic surgeon and associate of Claude Dufourmentel at Hôpital St. Louis); G. Vourc'h (head of anesthesiology at Foch); Blair Rogers (John Converse's associate at NYU); J. Mustardé (a Scottish ophthalmologist/plastic surgeon trained by Gillies); H. Obwegeser (a maxillofacial surgeon from Zürich, also trained by Gillies); and K. Schuchardt (a German maxillofacial surgeon). Tessier's colleagues from Foch who helped with the meeting were Jean Paul Delbet, Jacques Pastoriza, and Françoise Leymarie, who had just become Tessier's intern after a vacancy in the one available spot suddenly came up.

*Fig.4.24 CHOC–I. Foch, December, 1967.Hugo Obwegeser, Roger Mouly, Blair Rogers, Karl Schuchardt, Jack Mustardé are here with Françoise Leymarie (later Firmin) appearing over his shoulder alongside Tessier.*

*Fig. 4.25 Blair Rogers, Karl Schuchardt, and Jack Mustardé. Tessier sitting.*

*Fig. 4.26 Françoise Leymarie (now Firmin), who was Tessier's intern at the time of CHOC–I; Patrick Derome, neurosurgeon, standing; Louis Merville to the right.*

C.H.O.C.–II took place in 1969, and there were sixty invited participants. Among them were Jack Converse, Tom Cronin, Karl Erick Hogeman, Bengt Johanson, Fernando Ortiz-Monasterio, and others.

Suresnes, 14 October 1969

PERSONAL INVITATION

Dear Sir,

One week of work on the SURGICAL TREATMENT OF ORBITAL, CRANIAL and CRANIO-FACIAL MALFORMATIONS will take place in Paris, from Monday 24 November until Saturday, 29 November 1969.

The meetings will take place at Hôpital FOCH in Suresnes (Hautes de Seine) from 8:30 am until 7 pm.

The subjects to be dealt with are:

Hypertelorism

Craniofacial osteotomies

Intercraniofacial sub-ethromoidal osteotomies

The cranio-facial dysostoses (Crouzon and Apert)

Total osteotomies of the midface

Orbito-cranial trauma

Orbito-cranial tumors (hyperostosing meningiomas)

Critiques will be made by specialists, in general from outside Hôpital FOCH: neurosurgeons, anesthesiologists and intensivists, ophthalmologists, rhinologists, stomatologists and pediatric surgeons.

Several cases will have been operated upon three weeks prior to the CONVERSATIONS, and the participants can therefore examine the post-operative course.

Several patients operated upon much earlier will be invited to the consultation of Monday, 24 November, but the fact that they are coming from areas far from Paris means that not all of them may be able to make it.

Each day there will be an operation on the condition discussed that morning or the day before.

In principle, the following will be operated upon:

2 or 3 hypertelorisms

1 or 2 Crouzons

1 orbito-cranial trauma case

1 hyperostosing meningioma

Saturday the 29th will be reserved for discussions and the examination of the patients operated upon between the 24th and the 28th. We think we will be able to present about 40 patients and, with documents, the provisional or definitive results on 40 others.

The presentations and debates will take place in French and English.

The objectives of this week of work are therefore:

— to show the work that has been accomplished

— to elicit criticisms on:

- The basic principles
- The interpretation we have made of certain malformations
- The results

— to discuss the cases which will be presented

— to show the surgical procedures on 5 to 7 particularly difficult cases.

— to try to establish the operative indications, as they seem to arise from the first 100 cases operated upon.

We thank all of the participants for the help which they bring with their comments and their criticisms.

To those who accept this invitation before the 27th of October, there will be sent—before the 3rd of November:

— the exact time table of these CONVERSATIONS.

— the list of participants

Please let us know as soon as possible your decision.

With our best wishes,

Dr. Paul TESSIER

Dr. Gérard GUIOT

The services of NEURO-SURGERY and PLASTIC SURGERY of Hôpital FOCH have pursued, in common, over the past six years, original work on craniofacial surgery. This has two aspects: a constant facial one: orbital, nasal or maxillary, and the other frequent: cranial.

The NEURO-SURGERY service is interested in the treatment of:

— malformations (encephalocoeles)

— tumors of the anterior cranial base (hyperostosing meningiomas)

— post-traumatic [CSF] rhinorrhea

— finally, in the preparation for osteotomies and craniofacial resections (hypertelorism)

The service of PLASTIC SURGERY is oriented in particular towards the treatment of:

- hypertelorisms(resections—craniofacial osteotomies)
- hypertelorisms of moderate extent (resections—intercraniofacial sub-ethmoidal osteotomies)
- facial dysmorphias (orbital, nasal and maxillary), Crouzons and Aperts
- post-traumatic deformities of craniofacial disjunctions (total and sub-total osteotomies of the midface)
- sequelae of orbital or orbito-cranial trauma
- retromaxillisms, either essential, or secondary to maxillary clefts
- orbito-facial clefts (colobomas)

**ENTRETIENS SUR LA CHIRURGIE PLASTIQUE**
**CHIRURGIE CRANIO-FACIALE**

Centre Médico-Chirurgical FOCH
92-SURESNES
TÉL. : [illegible]

Docteurs Paul TESSIER et Gérard GUIOT

Suresnes, le 14 OCTOBRE 1969

<u>INVITATION PERSONNELLE</u>

Cher Monsieur,

Une semaine de travail sur le TRAITEMENT CHIRURGICAL DES MALFORMATIONS ORBITO-CRANIENNES et CRANIO-FACIALES aura lieu à PARIS, du lundi 24 Novembre au Samedi 29 Novembre 1969.

Les réunions se tiendront à l'HOPITAL FOCH à SURESNES (Hts de Seine) de 8 h 30 à 19 heures.

Les <u>points traités</u> seront :

L'hypertélorisme

Ostéotomies craniofaciales
Ostéotomies intercraniofaciales sous-ethmoïdiennes

Les dysostoses cranio-faciales (Crouzon et Apert)

Ostéotomies totales du massif facial

Les traumatismes orbito-craniens

Les tumeurs orbito-craniennes (méningiomes hyperostosants)

Les <u>critiques</u> seront faites par des spécialistes, en général étrangers à l'Hopital FOCH : neurochirurgiens, anesthésiste et réanimateur, ophtalmologistes, rhinologistes, stomatologistes et de chirurgie infantile.

Plusieurs cas auront été opérés les 3 semaines précédant les ENTRETIENS, les participants pourront donc examiner les suites opératoires.

Plusieurs anciens opérés seront convoqués à la <u>consultation</u> du lundi matin 24 Novembre, mais leur éloignement de Paris ne permet pas d'assurer qu'ils seront tous présents.

Chaque jour aura lieu une intervention sur le problème discuté le matin même ou la veille.

En principe <u>seront opérés</u> :

2 ou 3 hypertélorismes
1 ou 2 maladies de Crouzon
1 traumatisme orbito-cranien
1 méningiome hyperostosant

- 2 -

Le samedi 29 sera réservé aux discussions et à l'examen des malades opérés entre le 24 et le 28. Nous pensons donc être en mesure de présenter environ 40 malades et, sur documents, les résultats provisoires ou définitifs de 40 autres.

Les exposés et les débats auront lieu en français et en anglais.

Les objectifs de cette semaine de travail sont donc :

- de faire le point sur le travail accompli
- de susciter des critiques, sur :
  . les idées de base
  . l'interprétation que nous avons faite de certaines malformations
  . les résultats
- de discuter sur les cas qui seront présentés
- de montrer l'exécution de 5 à 7 cas particulièrement ardus.
- de tenter de préciser les indications opératoires, telles qu'elles semblent se dégager des 100 premiers cas opérés.

Nous remercions tous les participants de l'aide que nous apporteront leurs exposés et leurs critiques.

A ceux qui accepteront cette invitation avant le 27 Octobre, il sera envoyé - avant le 3 Novembre :

- les précisions sur l'emploi du temps de ces ENTRETIENS
- la liste des participants.

Veuillez avoir l'obligeance de me faire connaître au plus tôt votre décision.

Croyez, cher Monsieur, à l'assurance de nos sentiments les meilleurs.

Dr Paul TESSIER

Dr Gérard GUIOT.

Les services de NEURO-CHIRURGIE et de CHIRURGIE PLASTIQUE de l'Hôpital FOCH ont poursuivi en commun, depuis 6 ans, un travail original sur la chirurgie craniofaciale. Elle présente deux aspects : l'un facial constant : orbitaire, nasal ou maxillaire, l'autre fréquent : crânien.

Le Service de NEURO-CHIRURGIE s'est intéressé au traitement :

- des malformations (encéphalocèles)
- des tumeurs de l'étage antérieur de la base du crâne (méningiome hyperostosant)
- des rhinorrhées post-traumatiques
- enfin, à la préparation aux résections ostéotomies craniofaciales (hypertélorismes)

Le Service de CHIRURGIE PLASTIQUE s'est orienté en particulier vers le traitement :

- des hypertélorismes (résections - ostéotomies craniofaciales)
- des hypertélorismes d'importance moyenne (résections - ostéotomies intercraniofaciales sous-ethmoïdiennes)
- des dysmorphies faciales (orbitaires, nasales et maxillaires), des maladies de Crouzon et d'Apert.
- des déformations post-traumatiques des disjonctions craniofaciales (ostéotomies totales et sub-totales du massif facial)
- des séquelles de traumatismes orbitaires ou orbito-craniens.
- des rétro-maxillies soit essentielles, soit secondaires aux fentes maxillaires.
- des fentes orbito-faciales - (colobomas)

*Fig. 4.27 Personal Invitation by Tessier and Guiot to C.H.O.C.- II., in French , with English translation.*

One could not have designed a better teaching program for a new and exciting branch of surgery. The originators themselves present their work, with live surgery, and showed almost all of their previous patients at various stages after their surgery. Participants were asked to criticize, and ask questions. In 2010, this type of Meeting is rare indeed.

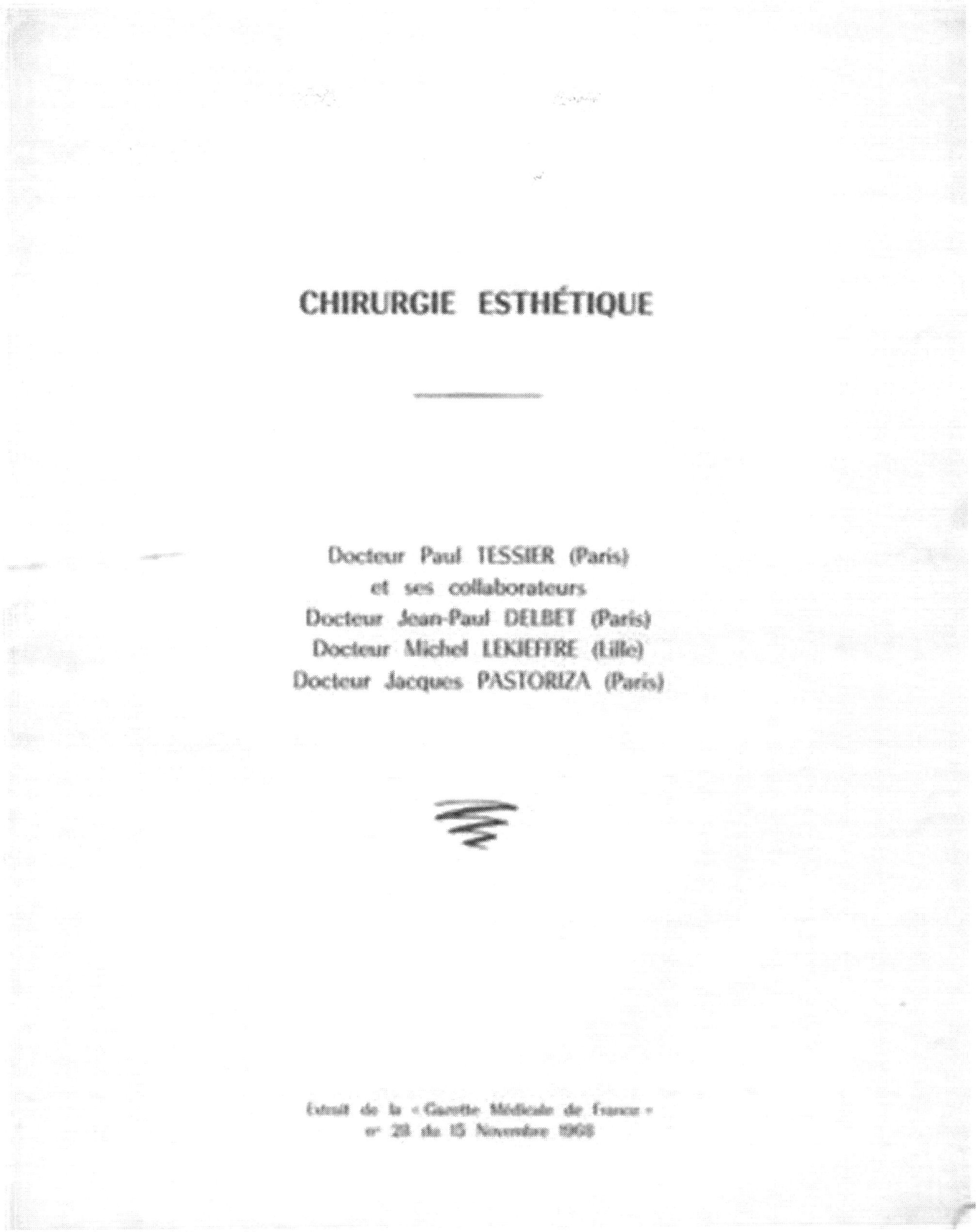

# CHIRURGIE ESTHÉTIQUE

Docteur Paul TESSIER (Paris)
et ses collaborateurs
Docteur Jean-Paul DELBET (Paris)
Docteur Michel LEKIEFFRE (Lille)
Docteur Jacques PASTORIZA (Paris)

Extrait de la « Gazette Médicale de France »
n° 28 du 15 Novembre 1968

*Fig. 4.18 Reprint of the Gazette Médicale de France, a Journal for general circulation, devoted to aesthetic surgery. Delbet and Pastoriza were Tessier's assistants at Foch, and Lekieffre was an ophthalmologist friend from Lille. Almost all of the cases shown were Tessier's.*

# Chapter 5

## Further Development of the field. The first Intracranial case (Bernadette Le Roy)

Tessier had worked with neurosurgeons, Gerard Guiot in particular, on the reconstruction of the orbital roof after the excision of sphenoid ridge meningiomas. After seeing a particularly monstrous case of orbital hypertelorism (Fig. 5.2), Tessier realized that there was no way that the deformity could be corrected without using an intracranial approach. He asked Guiot if he would be willing to operate with him. (It was absolutely taboo at that time for a neurosurgeon to transgress the cranial base and open up the cranial cavity to exposure from the midface and nose). Guiot thought for a minute, looking up at the ceiling, and then replied *Pourquoi Pas?* (This was also the name of Charcot's son's sailboat, with which he explored the North Pole). *Pourquoi Pas?*—Why Not?—has become the motto of The International Society of Craniofacial Surgery and is on their logo.

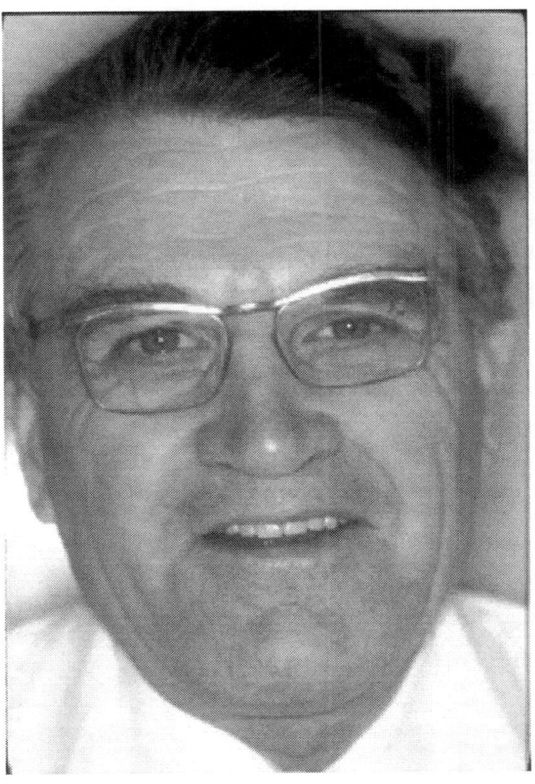

*Fig. 5.1 Gérard Guiot, Neurosurgeon of Hôpital Foch, without whom craniofacial surgery would not have gotten started.*

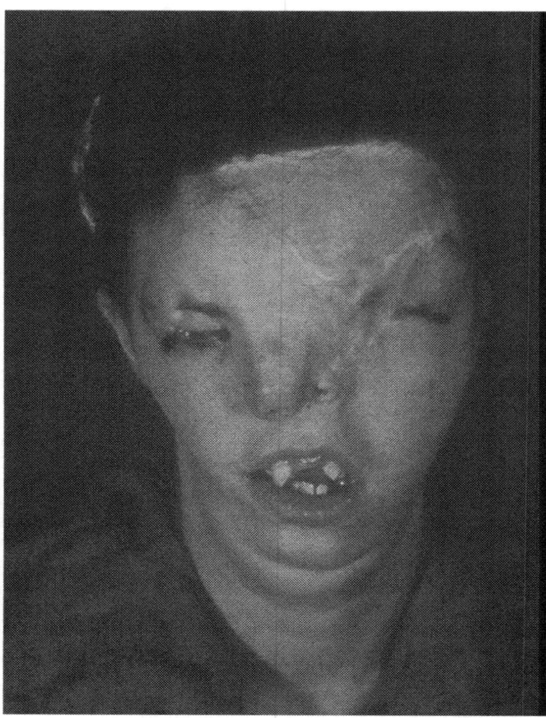

*Fig. 5.2. Mlle. Bernadette LeRoy, from Lille, as first seen in consultation by Dr. Tessier She was referred by his ophthalmologist friend, Lekieffre.*

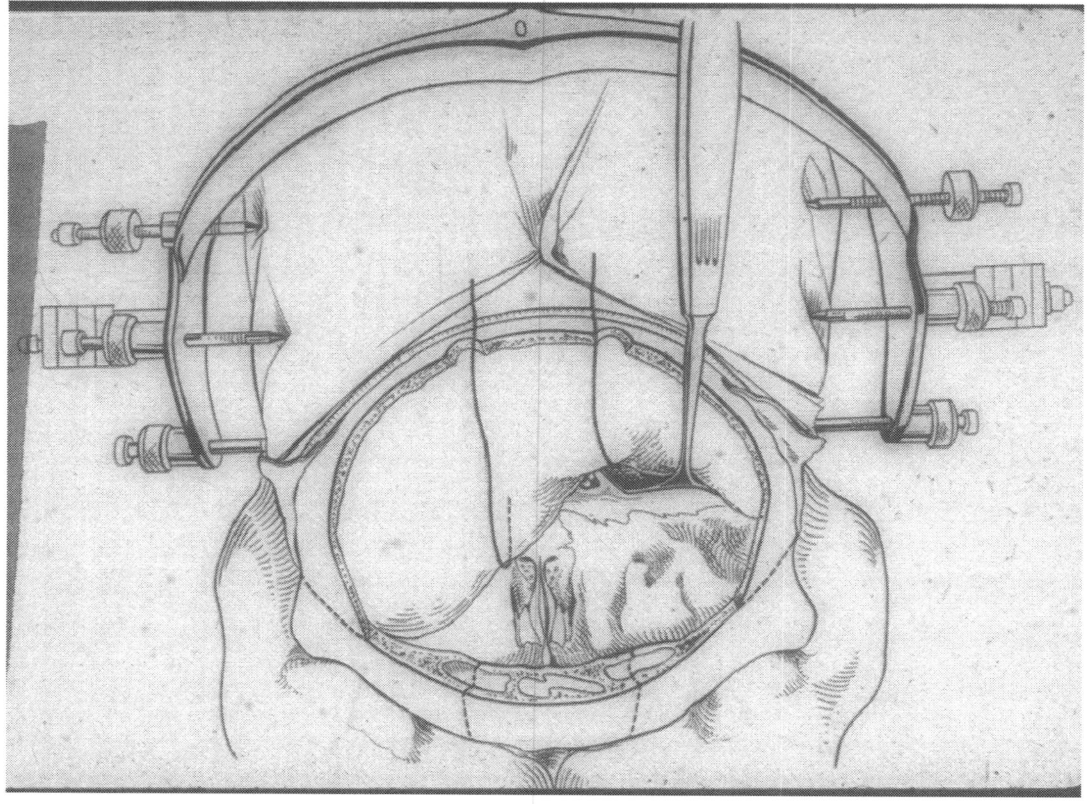

*Fig. 5.3 Francine Gourdin's anatomically precise drawing, done with Tessier's direction, showing a preliminary dissection of the anterior cranial base and placement of a large dermal graft from the abdomen. Guiot and Tessier decided to do this months ahead of the major craniofacial operation to seal off the dura completely and prevent spinal fluid leakage.*

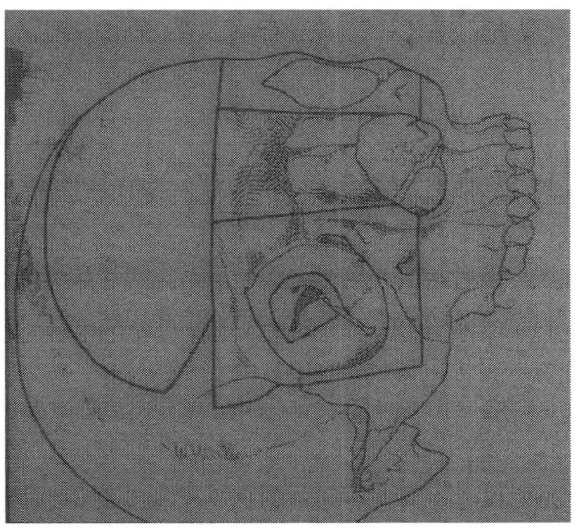

*Fig. 5.4. Showing Tessier's conception of "box" osteotomies resulting in segments which, when moved, would move the "effective orbit" and the eye, but not the optic nerve.*

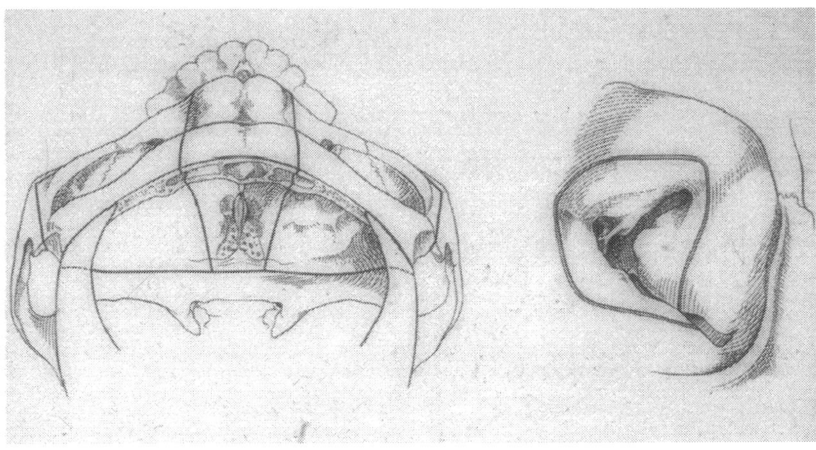

*Fig. 5.5 Tessier's conception of circumferential internal orbital osteomies and removal of a central ethmoidal segment to permit correction of orbital hypertelorism.*

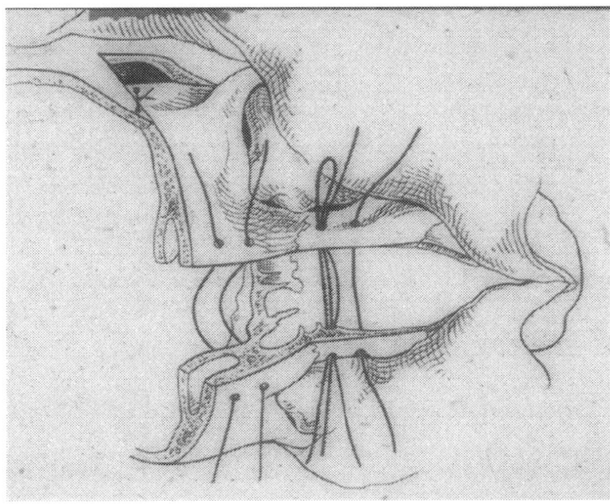

*Fig. 5.6 Wires are being used to bring the two orbital boxes to the midline, and a looped wire is passed for medial canthopexies.*

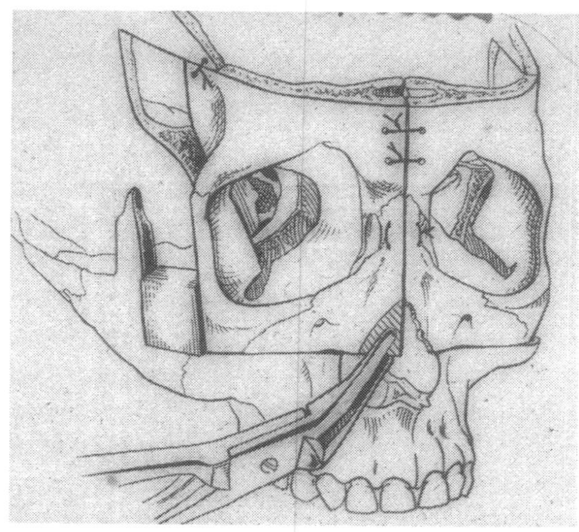

Fig. 5.7 Removing bone to prevent impingement on the nasal airway.

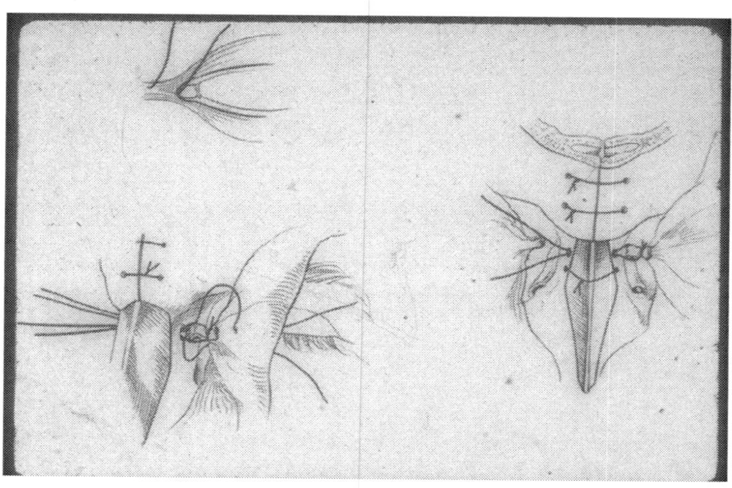

Fig. 5.8 Details of transnasal medial canthopexy and fixation of nasal bone graft.

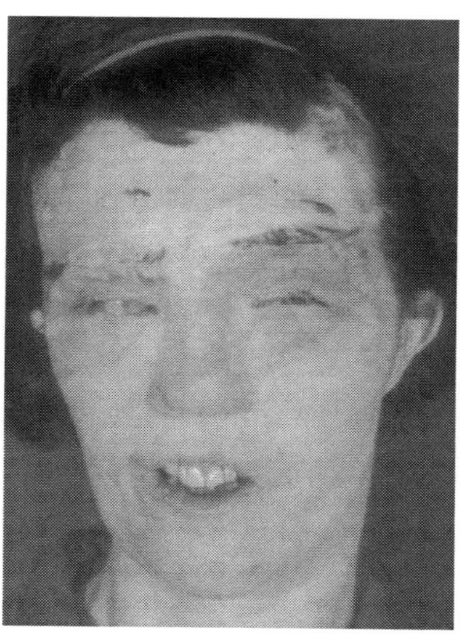

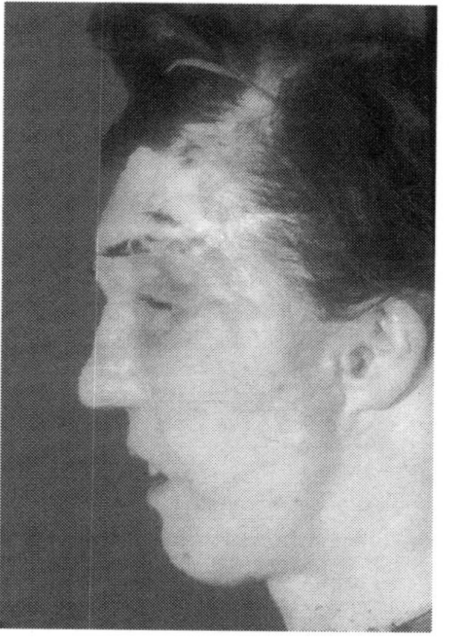

Fig. 5.9 For the first case ever performed of transcranial correction of wide orbital hypertelorism, this is an extraordinarily good result. It is doubtful that any craniofacial surgeon currently in practice could do nearly as well.

The slides of Mlle. Le Roy before she had her first surgical procedure performed in Lille were given to me by Philippe Pellerin, a plastic surgeon of Lille. The removal of the hair-bearing area of her forehead and the replacement of it with a skin graft provided little aesthetic improvement and complicated Dr. Tessier's subsequent task considerably.

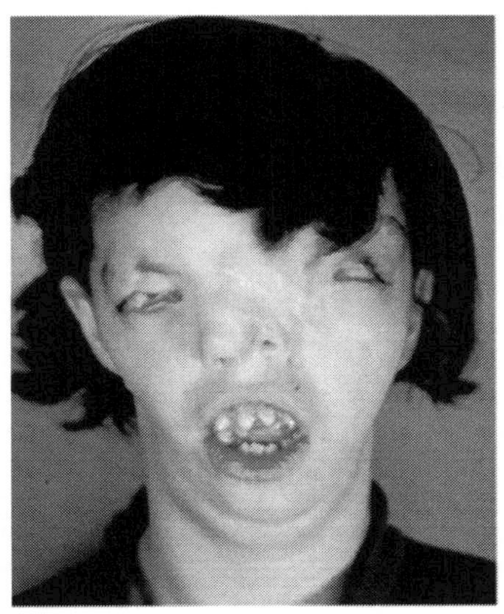

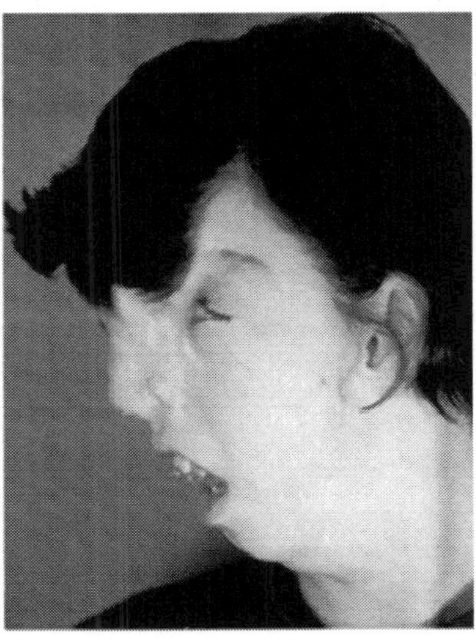

*Fig. 5.10 Patient B.L. before surgery in Lille, early 1960s.*

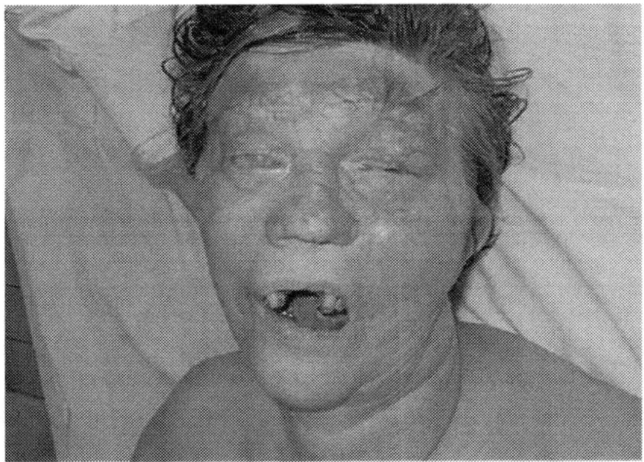

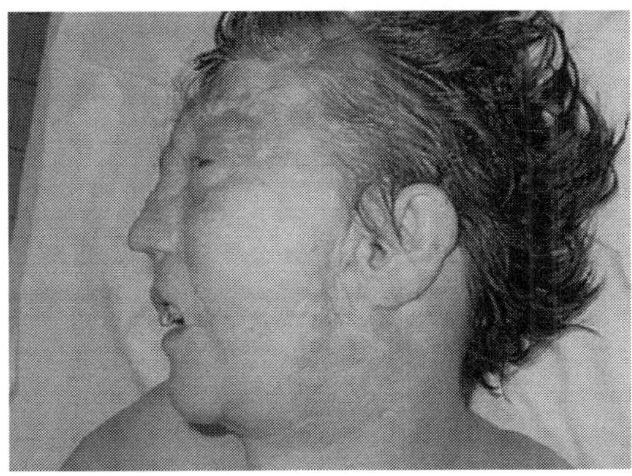

*Fig. 5.11 Dr. Pellerin also provided me with recent pictures of B. Le Roy when she was admitted to the hospital in Lille with a scald burn on her leg. She is shown without her denture, but for the first case of transcranial correction of orbital hypertelorism, her result (including nasal reconstruction, canthopexies, and maxillary osteotomies) has held up exceedingly well. The scarring of her right cornea had occurred before she became Dr. Tessier's patient.*

Although the first case of a successful Le Fort III-type osteotomy in Anquetil in 1958 had been a major, pioneering leap in the history of craniofacial surgery. The case of B. LeRoy and the planned use of the intracranial approach to correct a major facial deformity really mark the true beginning of the specialty of craniofacial surgery.

# Chapter 6

## Problems at Hôpital Foch.

Hôpital Foch has an interesting history. In 1926, Bernard Flursheim, an American citizen, and Justin Godart, a former Minister of Health in France, began to raise money to build an institution, modeled after "what existed in Boston" (probably referring to the Peter Bent Brigham Hospital, which had just opened with Harvey Cushing as its first chief of surgery) devoted to the care of the middle classes.

Hôpital Foch was built between 1932 and 1937, and it originally consisted of 350 beds and a nursing school. American contributions, particularly from Winaretta Singer (heiress to a sewing machine fortune who later became the Princess Edmond de Polignac) and Consuelo Vanderbilt (once married to the Duke of Marlborough and later to Colonel Jacques Balsan) were instrumental in getting it built. (It had a unique position in Paris in that it was a private hospital with its own board, and it was not state-owned, as were all of the other, larger hospitals. As such, Foch was not a part of the officially-sanctioned Paris system of teaching hospitals, the *Hôpitaux de Paris*. Nevertheless, it was an important research institution, and pioneering work in organ transplantation and neurosurgery was carried out there. Currently, the hospital has grown to 890 beds. At its beginning, it was directed by La Fondation médicale Franco-américan du Mont Valérian (Fondation Maréchal FOCH), then requisitioned by the French army, then by the Germans, then by the French National Railroads System after the war, and, in 1996, control again reverted to the Franco-American Foch foundation.

Further up the hill from Foch is the American Military Cemetery of Mont Valérian, where 1541 American soldiers from World War I are buried, along with 24 (unknown) American soldiers killed in World War II.

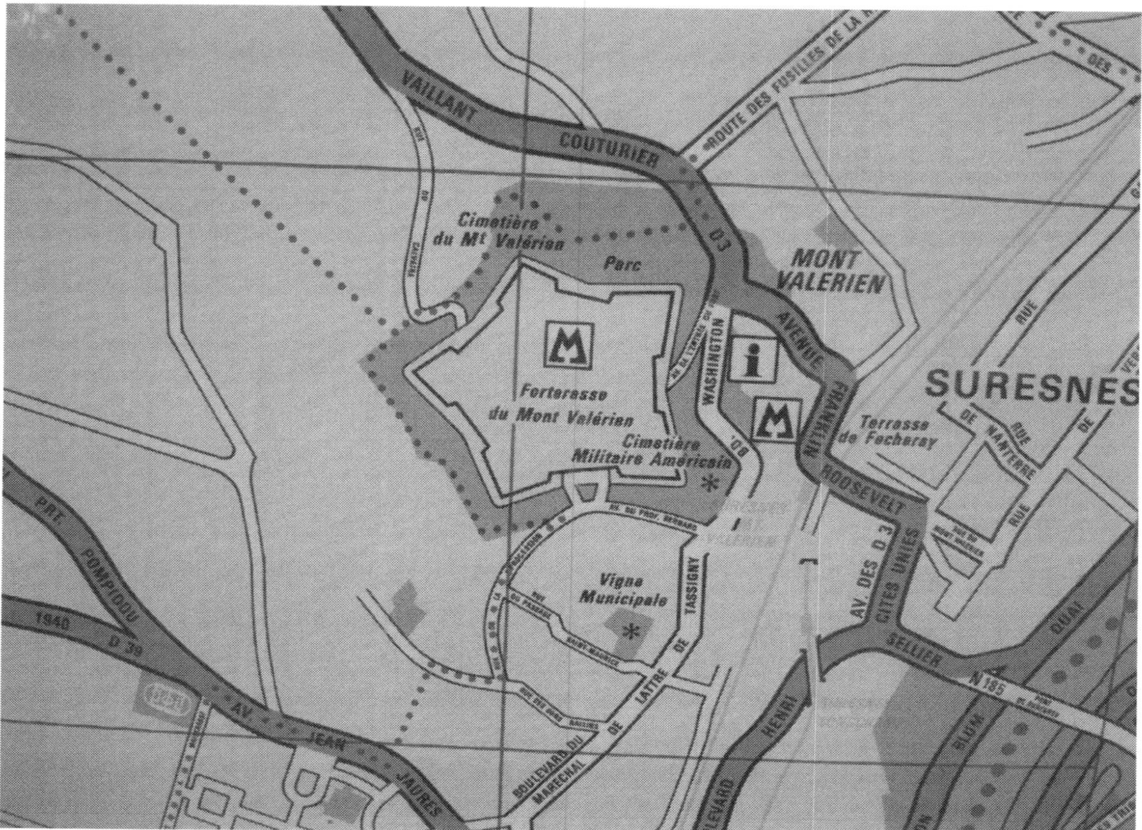


*Fig. 6.1 Hôpital Foch is located between the American Military Cemetery and the Seine, near the asterix.*

*Fig. 6.2 The American Military Cemetery at Mont Valérian.*

As mentioned earlier, in 1944, Tessier came with Maurice Virenque when his maxillofacial surgery service was relocated to Foch. Tessier was made head of the department of plastic surgery and burns in 1946, and in 1949, Virenque, Tessier's mentor, died. This left Tessier in charge of the service, but politically outgunned by Ginestet, who ran the other maxillofacial surgery service, and who tried to prevent Tessier from doing any maxillofacial surgery at Foch. In 1958, Tessier performed the first Le Fort 3-type osteotomy at Foch, and over the next decade the amount of major craniofacial surgery performed left Ginestet far outclassed and sputtering in the dust.

Tessier also staged a number of teaching courses at Foch for ophthalmologists and other surgeons in 1963 and 1965, and then held the two C.H.O.C.–II "juries" there in 1967 and 1973 to pass judgement on the future of craniofacial surgery. Foch Hospital had become by then the acknowledged world center of cutting edge collaboration between neurosurgeons in the new specialty of craniofacial surgery.

Nevertheless, things were not going smoothly at Foch. In a note dated January 25, 1973, *("Mon Conseil d'Administration me fout a La Porte")*, (My Administration Kicks Me Out—see Appendices /Foch), Tessier reports on his meeting with the Hospital administrators, when he was told that he would no longer be the chief of the service. They first congratulated him on the general good quality of his service and his now almost complete monopoly of orbito-palpebral surgery, and his very good reputation in the service in France and abroad. The reason for being asked to step down was, in essence, that Tessier had become *too* successful. His expenditures for teaching, making films, and research programs were deemed excessive. They noted, "We are not a Faculty of Medicine."

Tessier continued to operate at Foch once a week, tending to a small clinic in the morning and then beginning whatever case or cases he would be doing at around noon, often ending at 11 p.m. or later. This was the case for the decade from 1973 to 1983, when he formally sent a letter to the director of the hospital stating that he would be ceasing his activities there after thirty-seven years of service. After he left, the plastic surgery service was run by Gilbert Ozun and Jean-Paul Delbet, who had been his junior staff members. (Darina Krastinova, who had worked with Dr. Tessier when he was still active at Foch, runs the service now and, although she continues the tradition of the service with a strong interest in orbital and eyelid surgery, very little major transcranial craniofacial surgery is now performed at Foch. Most is performed at Necker/Enfants Malades by Eric Arnaud, Daniel Marchac's junior staff member).

A correspondence occurred in 1974 between Professor Vourc'h, the head of anesthesia, and Tessier. The basis of the anesthesiologist's lament was that Tessier was working too much and staying too late. This was placing too much of a stress on the anesthesia and nursing staffs. Tessier responded with a long list of patients who had had problems because of poor airway control on whom he had to perform emergency tracheostomies. (See Appendixes/Foch.)

In his letter of resignation to the director in 1983, Tessier wrote, "Can one imagine a situation more paradoxical than the following: The Service which, today, has the greatest experience in the world in facial and craniofacial malformations cannot even operate upon a simple cleft lip, without this being brought up for question. We have not therefore operated on cleft lips for more than 10 years … like my friend Rougerie [a neurosurgeon], I had the greatest difficulty in getting the Anesthesia and Intensive Care services to accept craniofacial surgery in infants."

This inability to be able to operate on infants and young children in a top-notch facility was one of Tessier's greatest regrets over the years. He would regularly operate on younger children when abroad, particularly in the United States, but in Paris he was compelled to treat them at Clinique Bélvédere, which was even more poorly equipped to care for them than Foch. Madame Deleague, a pediatric anesthesiologist would come for the younger cases, and the post-operative "intensive care unit" consisted of having a surgical resident spend the night at the patient's bedside.

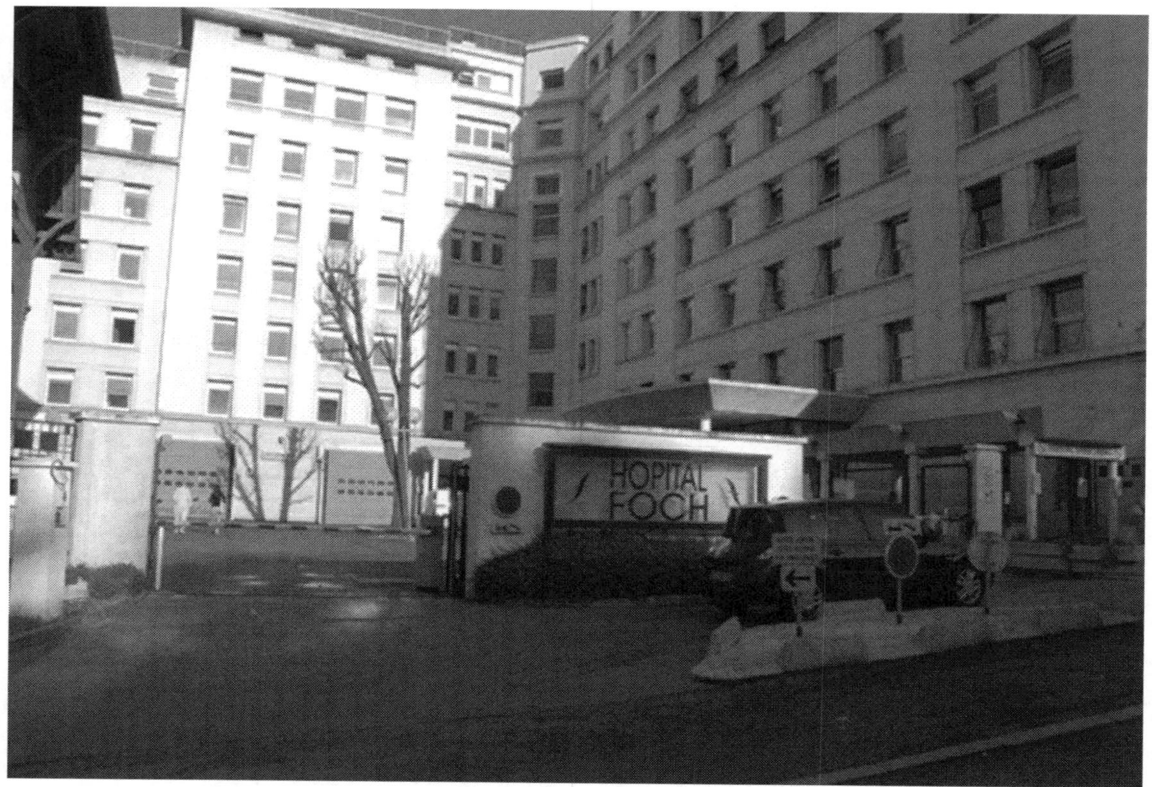


*Fig. 6.3 Hôpital Foch in 2009.*

*Fig. 6.4 The Pavillon Balsan is on the left, originally located in the park of the estate of Worth, the great coutourier, and it has been preserved.*

Dr. Tessier had also maintained a private practice outside of Foch, operating primarily in a number of private clinics in Paris: Clinique d'Alleray, in the 15th Arrondisesement, where he saw patients before he had office space in town (in the late 50s and early 60s); Clinique Val d'Or; Clinique du Trocodéro, up until 1968; Clinique Marignan, near the avenue Montaigne, where he did some aesthetic surgery before 1967; and Clinique Belvédère. Private Clinics in France co-exist alongside the state-run hospitals. They are smaller and generally much more efficient, but it was—and still would be—unusual for major intracranial surgery to be done in a private clinic.

After 1969, Tessier operated only at Belvédère, operating at Foch only one afternoon a week after he held a small clinic to see patients. (See Chapter 16, Paris in 1974.) He came to an arrangement with the Belvédère administration that allowed him to do as much surgery as he liked—and of any kind—as long as he provided all of the personnel and instrumentation.

# Chapter 7

## Application of craniofacial principles and techniques to other conditions.

Treacher Collins was an English ophthalmologist who gave one of the early descriptions of the syndrome that came to bear his name. Due to an autosomal dominant gene, children with this condition look remarkably alike. They have deficient or absent cheekbones, clefts of the lower eyelids, small lower jaws with retrusive chins, and ear malformations. Europeans tend to add the name of Franceschetti, who also gave one of the early descriptions of the condition (and in some instances, also Zwallen and Klein).

Treacher Collins Franceschetti (TCF) syndrome, with its deficiencies of the facial skeleton and orbit and abnormalities of the eyelids, was an ideal condition for Paul Tessier to put his skills to use as a corrector of abnormalities of the facial skeleton and orbit, and allowed him to use his extensive experience with eyelid reconstruction.

He first focused on correction of the orbital and zygomatic defects and the eyelid abnormalities. This was a different kind of condition than the craniofacial dysostoses of Crouzon and Apert, and the orbital dystopias, such as hypertelorism, where creation of a normal facial skeleton could be provided by moving existing structures into anatomically proper positions. In TCF, the structures were absent, and had to be built from scratch. Dr. Tessier did this initially by trimming away overgrown portions of the upper orbit and constructing a cheekbone and zygomatic arch out of split rib grafts. He then corrected the cleft of the lower eyelid and put the lateral canthus into a proper position. There was some resorption of these bone grafts and, often, the bone grafting would need to be repeated. When Dr. Tessier began using cranial bone for the construction, a technique he developed in the early 1980s, he noticed that that there was significantly less resorption. Nevertheless, he felt that TCF was one of the most challenging conditions in craniofacial surgery, largely due to the fact that there was such s significant deficiency of bone. He felt that understanding and correcting the skeletal deformity, as in all other craniofacial conditions, was the key to developing effective surgical procedures. In the mid-1970s, Sam Pruzansky presented Dr. Tessier with a model of a TCF skull that he had arranged to have made using the regular x-rays of the time as guides. Dr. Tessier was ecstatic with the gift. With the development of 3-D CAT scans and the ability to make stereolithogramatic facsimiles, a model of the skeletal abnormality of every patient became easy to obtain.

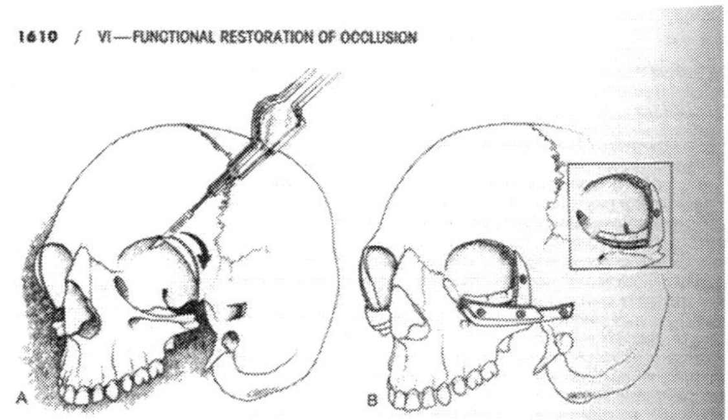


*Fig. 7.1 Drawings of the initial Tessier technique for the correction of the orbital and zygomatic abnormalities of the Treacher Collins Franceschetti syndrome.*
*The overhanging portion of the upper lateral temporal bone is trimmed away, and a lateral orbital wall and zygomatic arch are constructed of bone grafts. The lateral canthus is then elevated and fixed to the newly created lateral orbital rim. Further bone grafts are placed in the orbit to obdurate the enlarged inferior orbital fissure.*

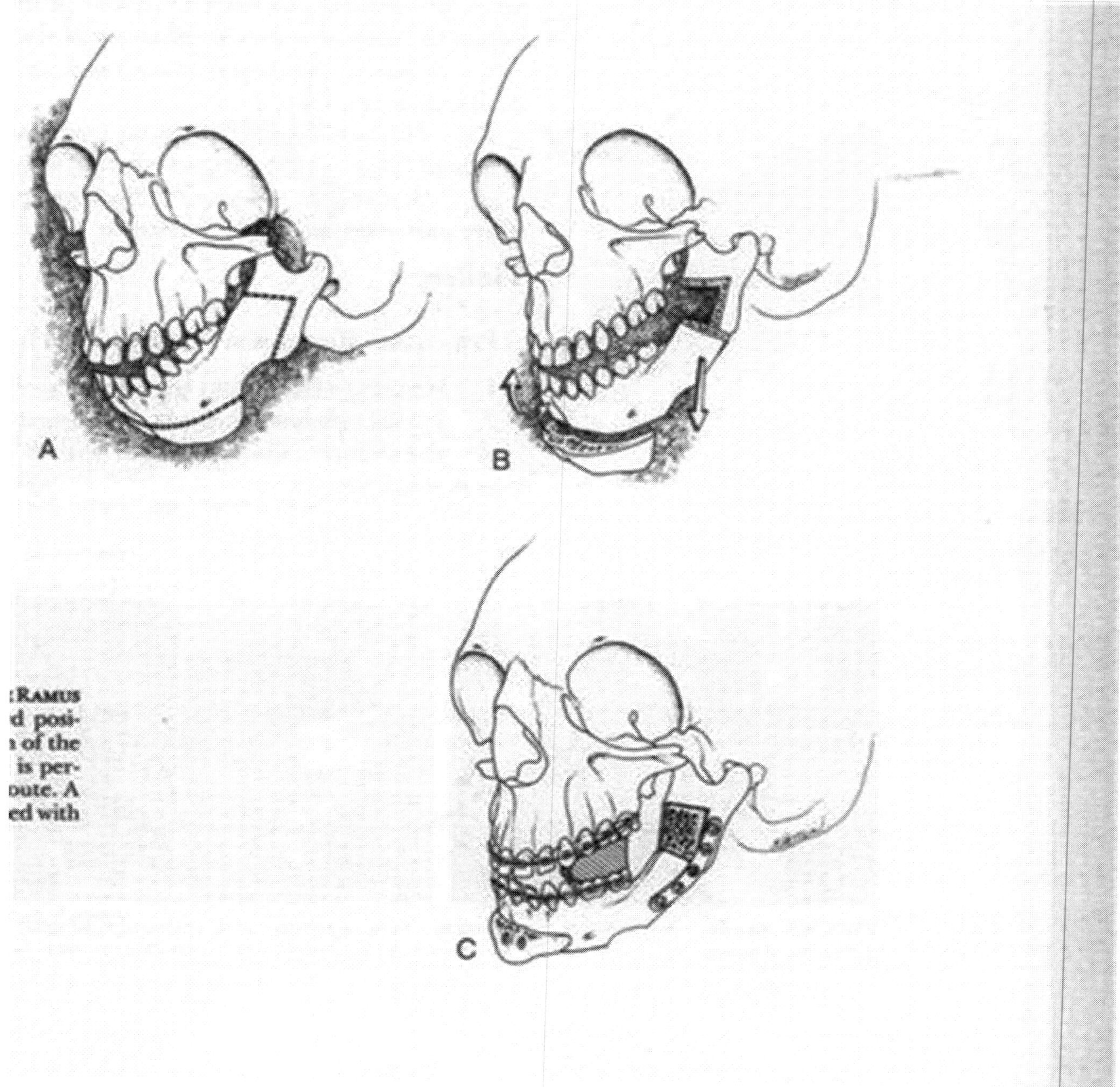


*Fig. 7.2 TCF syndrome is also characterized by a very short ascending mandibular ramus and short posterior maxillary height, sometimes also associated with posterior choanal atresia (where there is a constricted opening of the back of the nasal airway into the pharynx). The initial procedures involved lengthening the ramus with an interpositional bone graft and a jumping genioplasty where the chin is simultaneously shortened and advanced.*

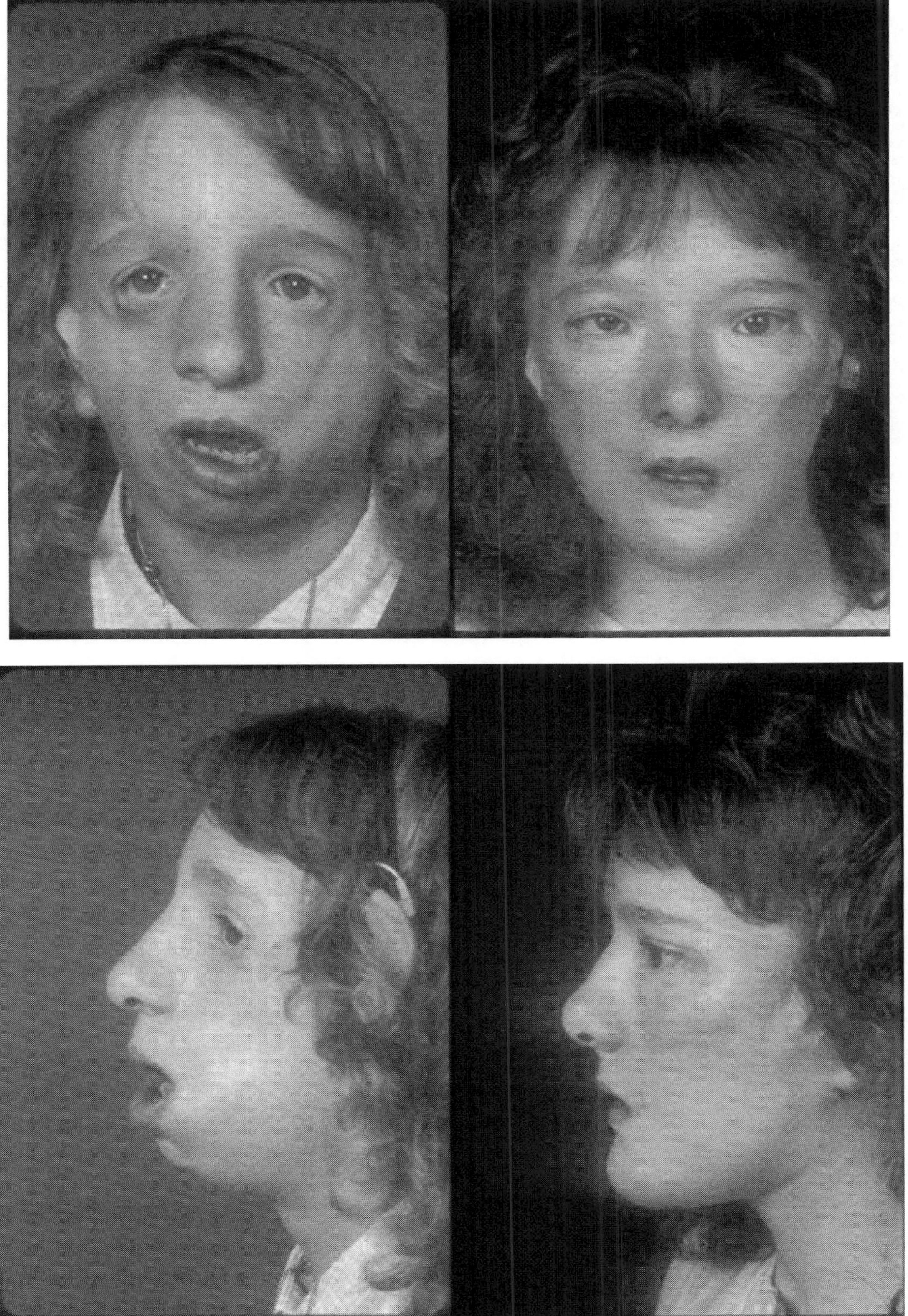

*Fig. 7.3 Patient with a fairly severe case of TCF syndrome treated by Dr. Tessier with his original technique of zygomatic construction with several sessions of bone grafting and lengthening of the mandible and genioplasty. Here he has resorted to large full-thickness skin grafts to correct the lower eyelid deformity, something that he did to perfection due to his experience with burned eyelids.*

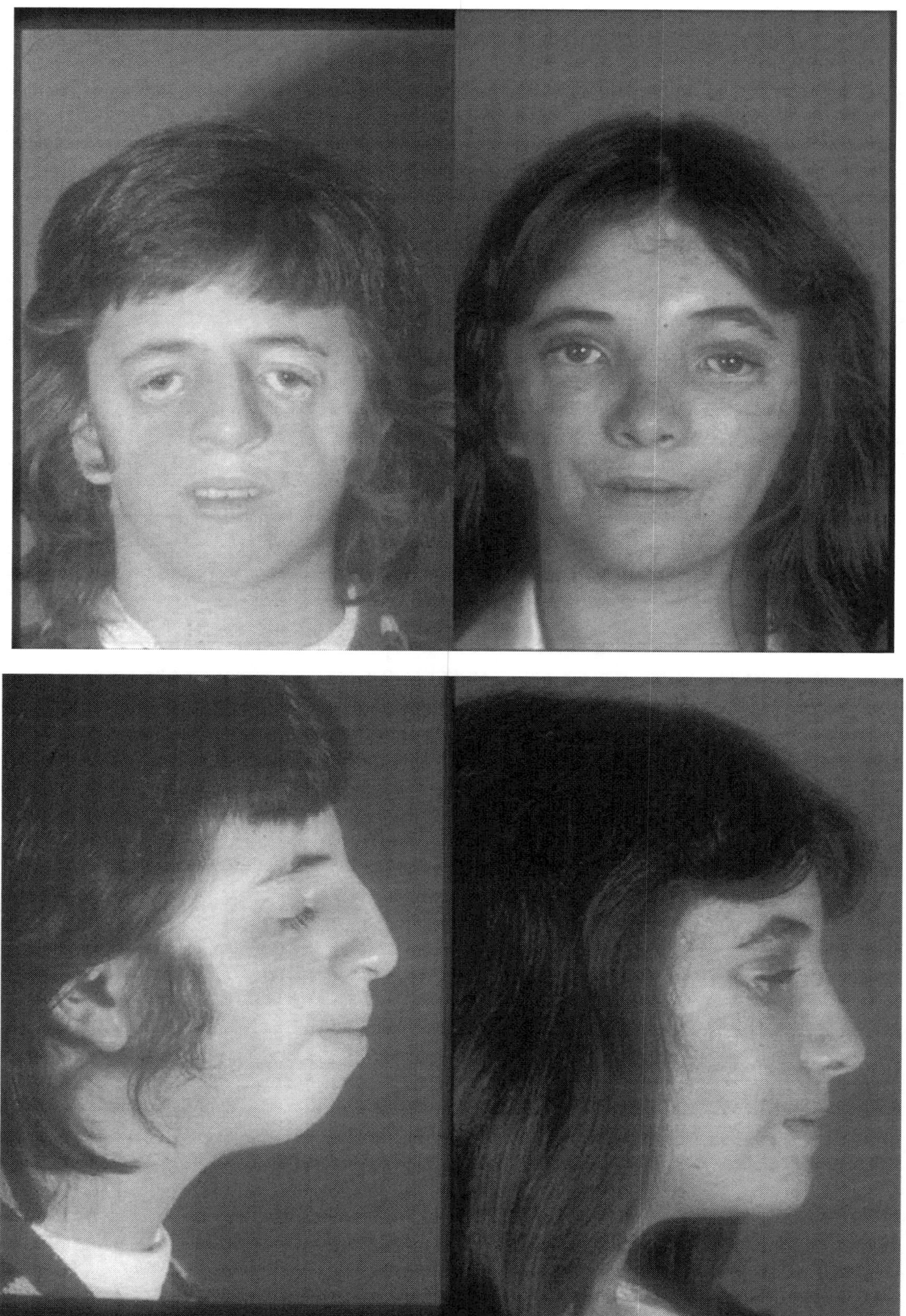

*Fig. 7.4 Another TCF patient treated with the original technique of zygomatic construction, genioplasty, and rhinoplasty. The lower eyelid clefts and lateral canthal repositioning were accomplished in this case by transposing flaps of skin and muscle from the upper eyelids to the area between the lower eyelid and the cheek.*

Dr. Tessier realized that his initial approach to the TCF deformity did not correct all of the skeletal abnormalities, so he went on to develop what he called the "Integral" procedure, which separates the face from the skull with a Le Fort II-type osteotomy, and rotates it in a way that the posterior maxillary height is lengthened. Here, split cranial bone taken from the parietal area is used for the zygomatic construction. The mandible, of course, needs to be lengthened at the same time to allow the posterior maxilla to become lengthened. (Drawings courtesy of Jean Francois Tulasne, co-author with Dr. Tessier of a chapter on TCF, which appeared in Volume 2, Modern Practice in Orthognathic and Reconstructive Surgery, Edited by William Bell, W.B. Saunders Co.)

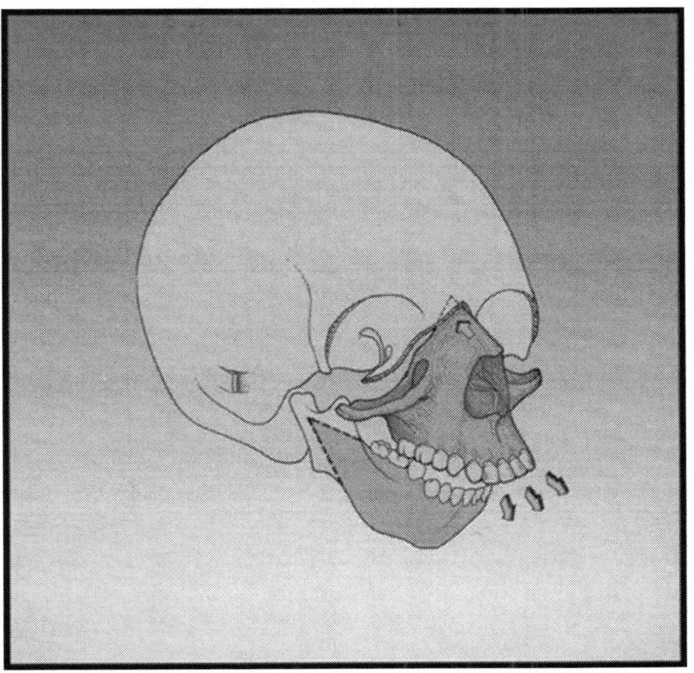

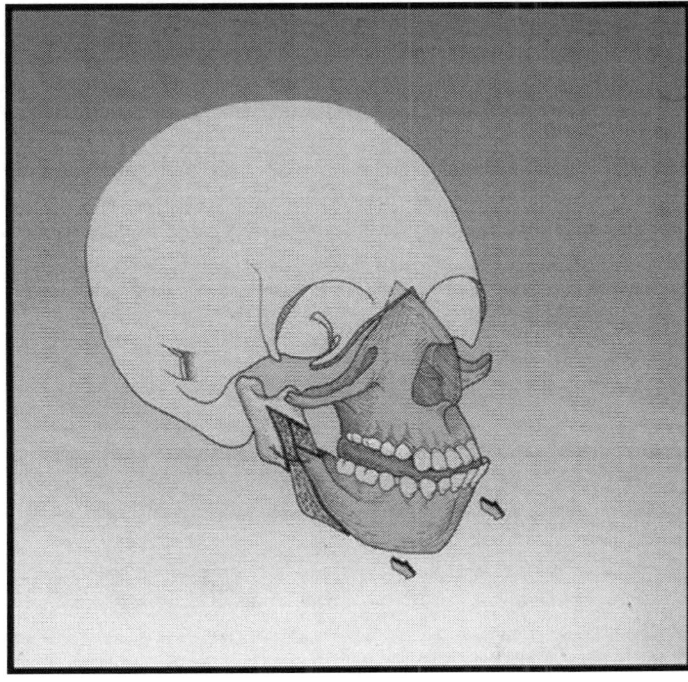

*Fig. 7.5 The "Integral" procedure in one stage.*

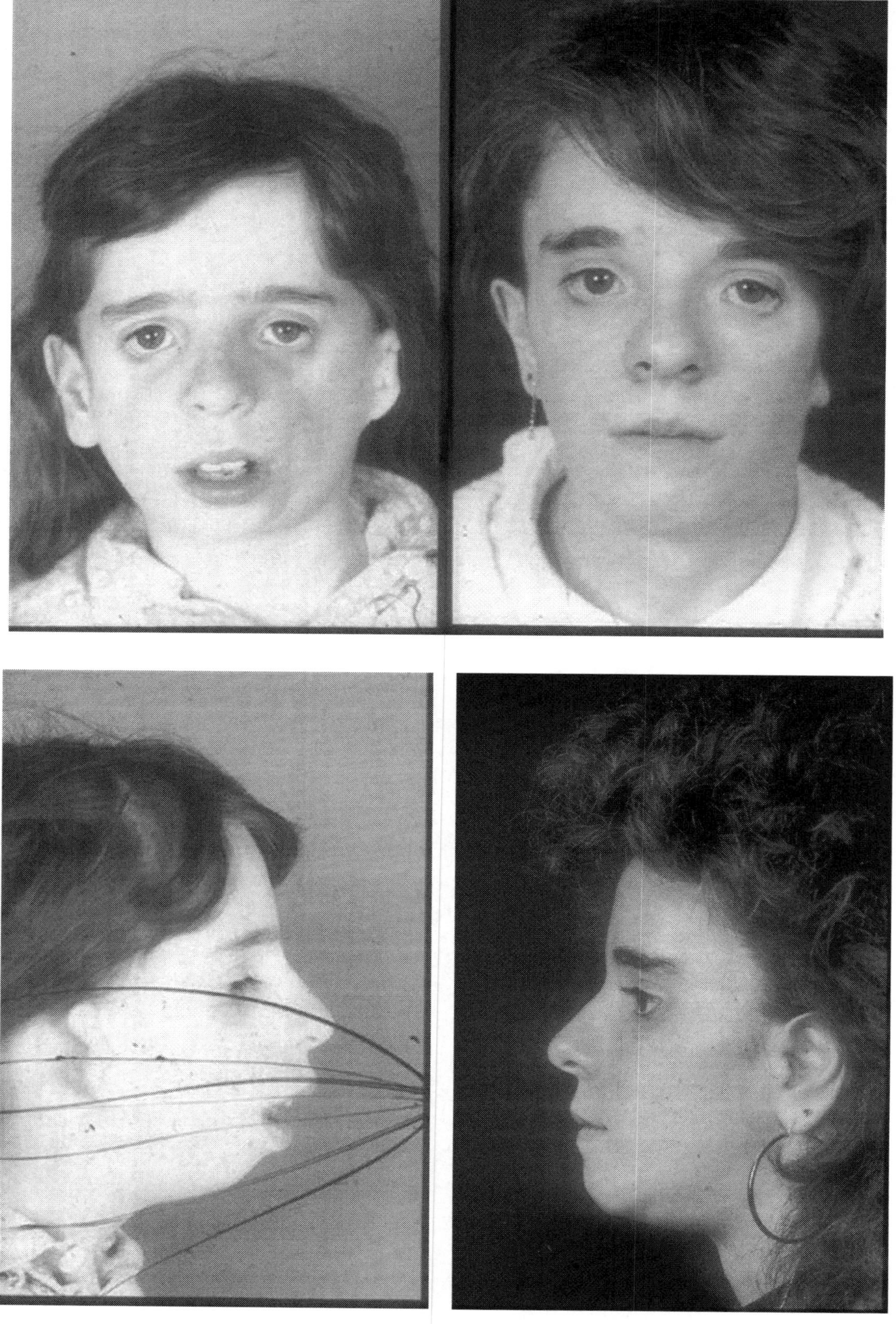

*Fig. 7.6 TCF patient treated with the "Integral" technique, which simultaneously corrected all of the skeletal abnormalities. (The normal-appearing ear in the post-operative photo is a prosthetic one; this was taken before Dr. Tessier began sending all patients requiring ear reconstructions to Françoise Firmin.)*

Hemifacial microsomia is a commonly encountered birth defect which can occur as a bilateral condition and be confused with the TCF syndrome. (Patients with unilateral or bilateral facial microsomia can be distinguished from TCF by the fact that their lower eyelids are perfectly normal, and TCF patients will not have lashes on the medial two thirds of the lower eyelid. The location of the genetic abnormality in TCF has also been identified.)

Shown below is a patient with right hemifacial microsomia. Dr. Tessier shifted the midface with a Le Fort II-type osteotomy which also straightened the nose, and the mandibular deformity was corrected by constructing a right ramus, temporomandibular joint, and zygomatic arch, performing an osteotomy of the left ramus, and a genioplasty. A fat-dermal graft and flap transposition at the corner of the mouth on the right were necessary to provide final facial symmetry and the cant of the oral commissure.

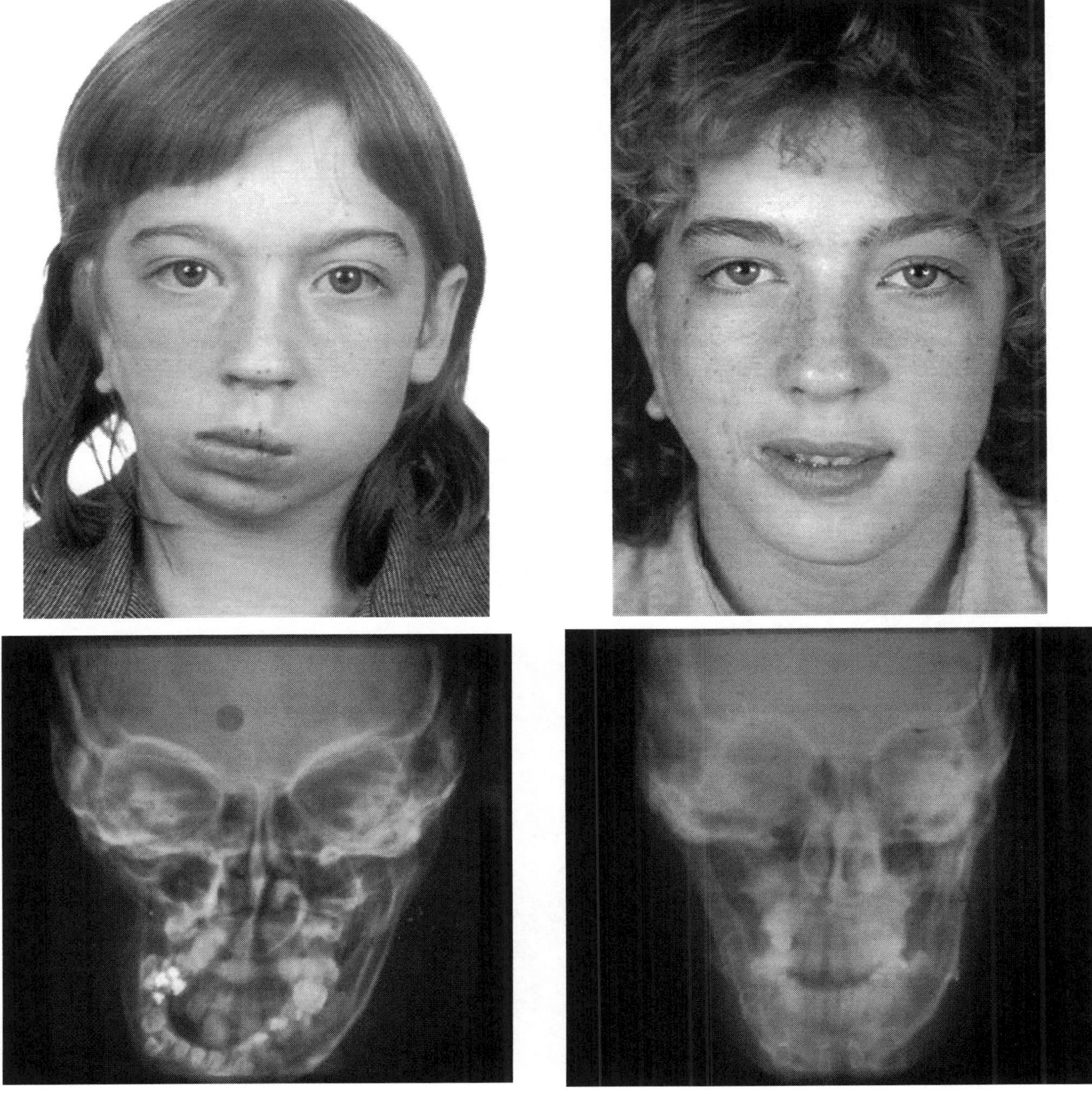

*Fig. 7.7 Hemifacial microsomia patient treated by Dr. Tessier, obtaining almost complete symmetry.*

Dr. Tessier's ability as an orbital surgeon and master of the transcranial approach made possible the complete removal of craniofacial tumors, which would have previously been unresectable, and simultaneous facial reconstruction. I recall the child shown below, who came to Paris from Recife, Brazil. He was operated on at Foch in conjunction with Guiot's successor, Patrick Derome. Many of the techniques for removing previously inaccessible tumors of the cranial base were developed at Foch because of the collaboration of Tessier and Derome. In some cases, Tessier would separate the face from the skull simply to give Derome access to remove tumors through the posterior pharynx.

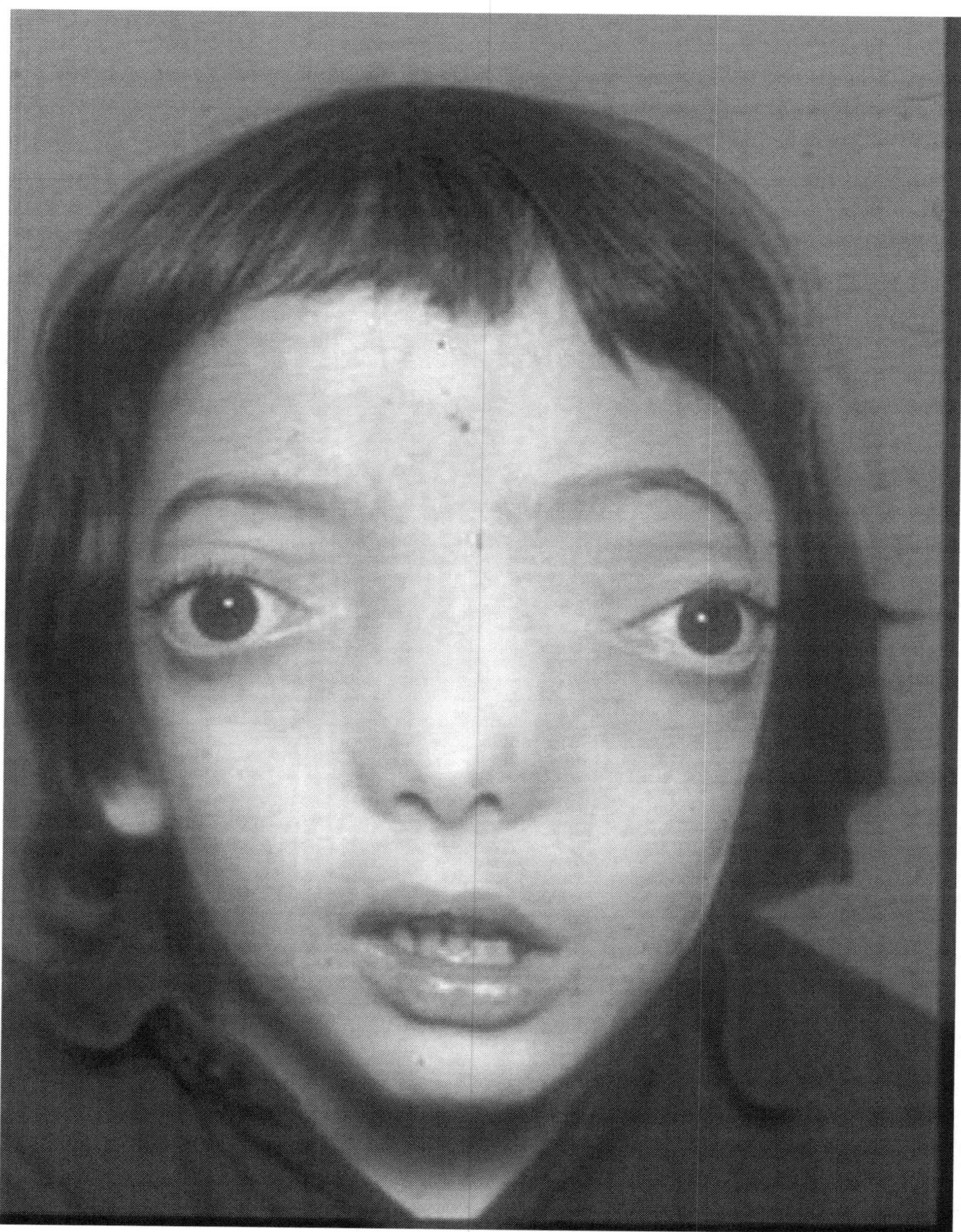

*Fig. 7.8 Child with extensive fibrous dysplasia of the ethmoidal interorbital space and anterior cranial base.*

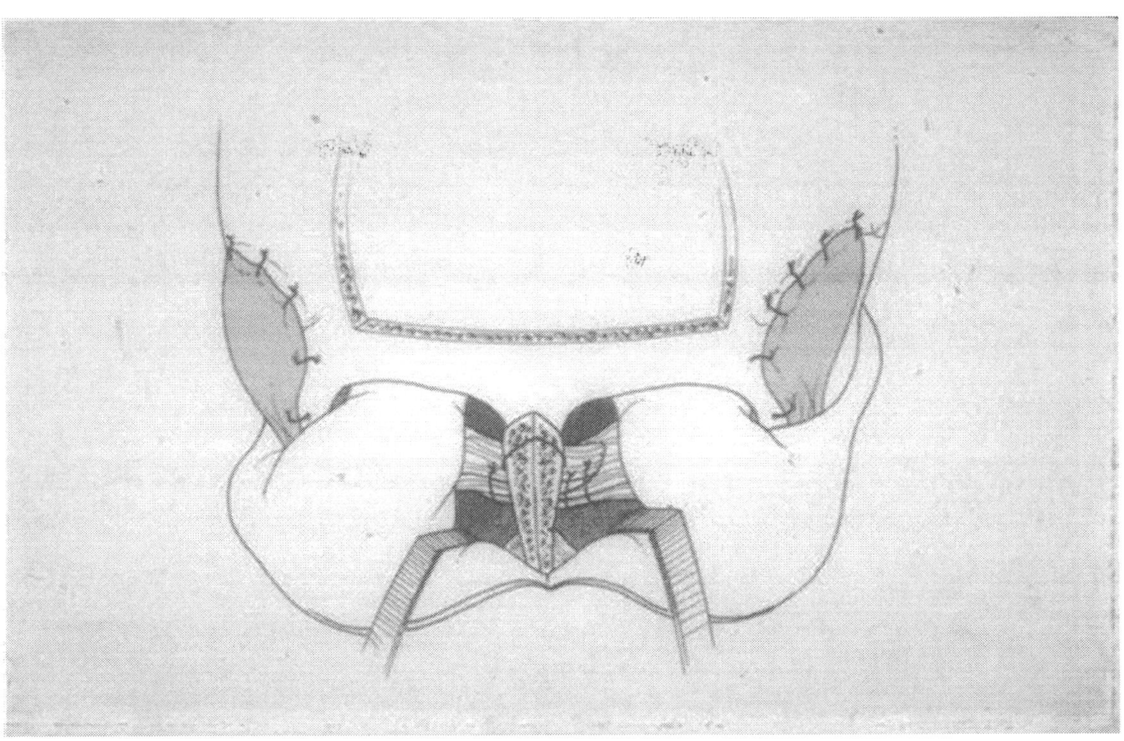

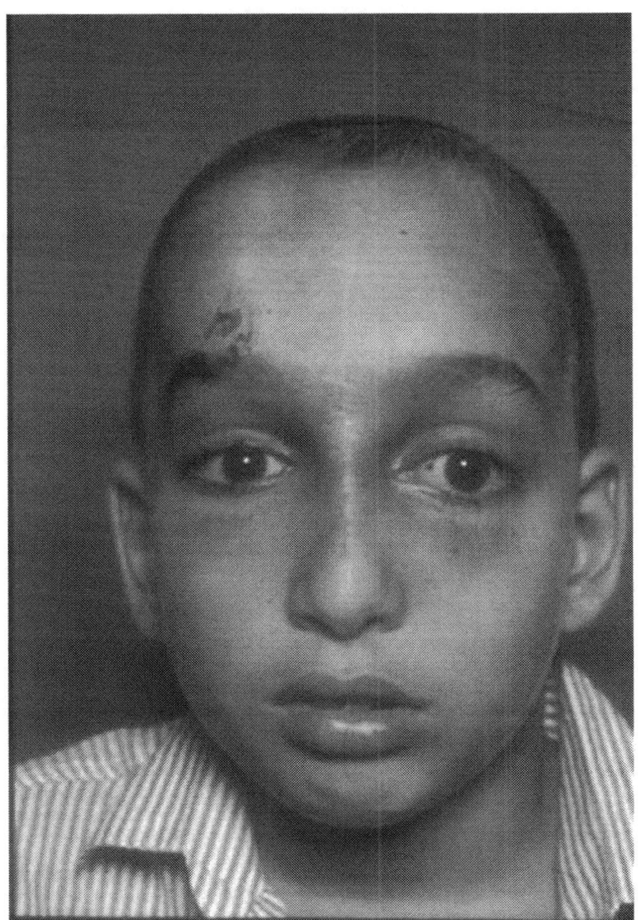

*Fig. 7.13 The final result: superb, with preservation of vision. Dr. Tessier did not hesitate to use a midline forehead and nasal incision, although it might have been possible to avoid that.*

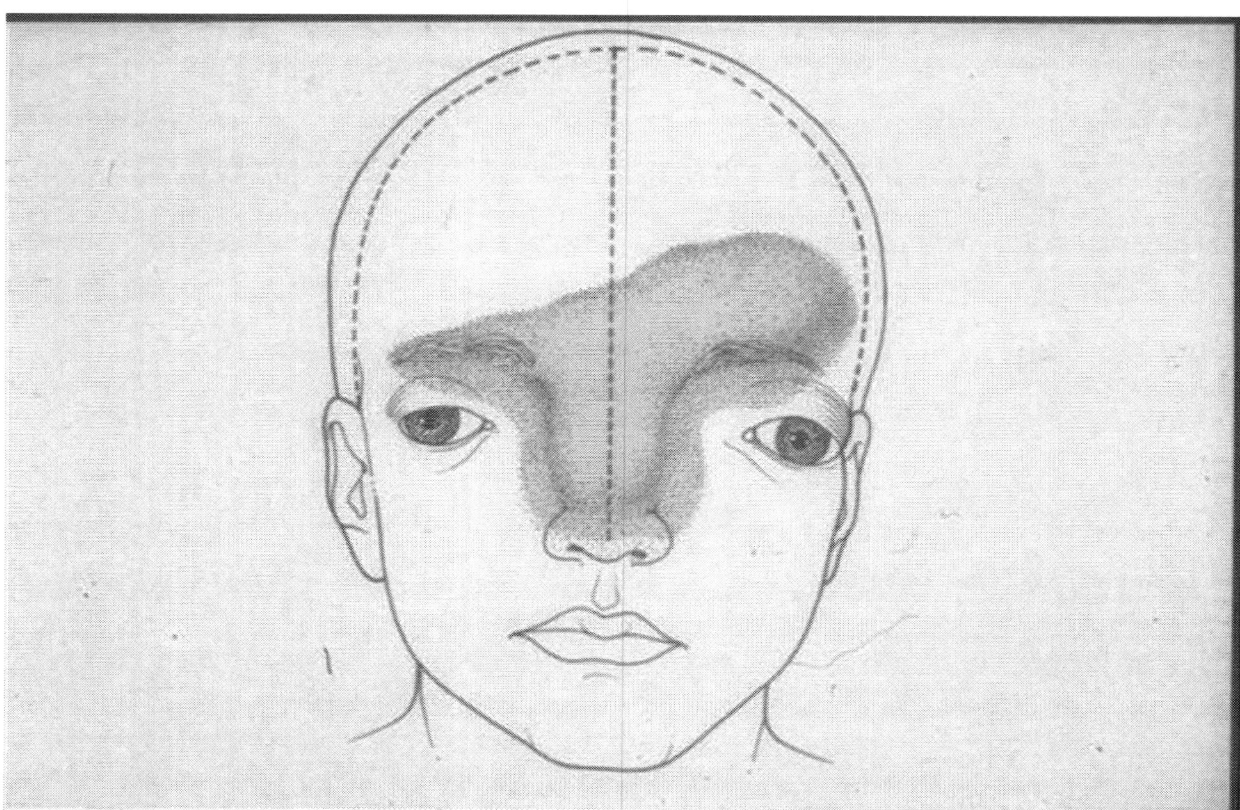

*Fig. 7.9 Drawing showing the extent of the tumor.*

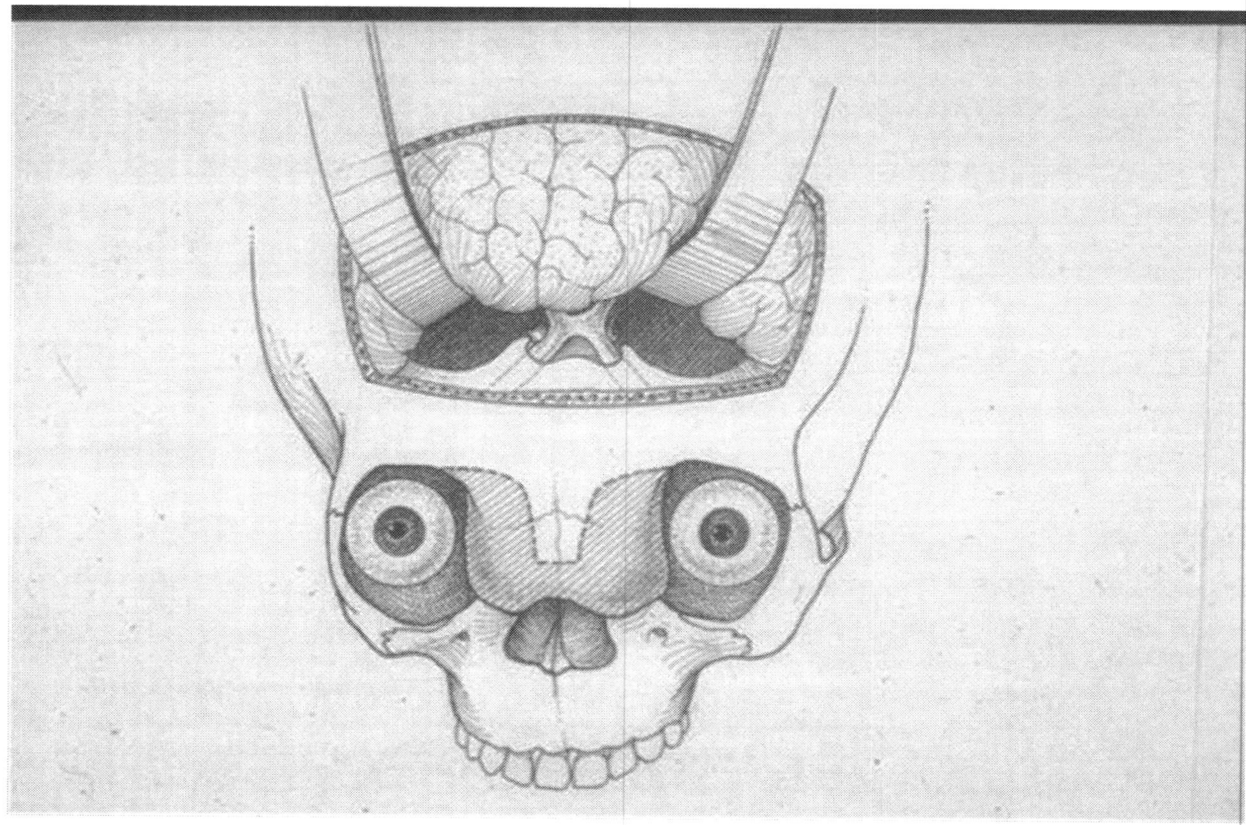

*Fig. 7.10 After retraction of the frontal lobes and exposure of the optic chiasm.*

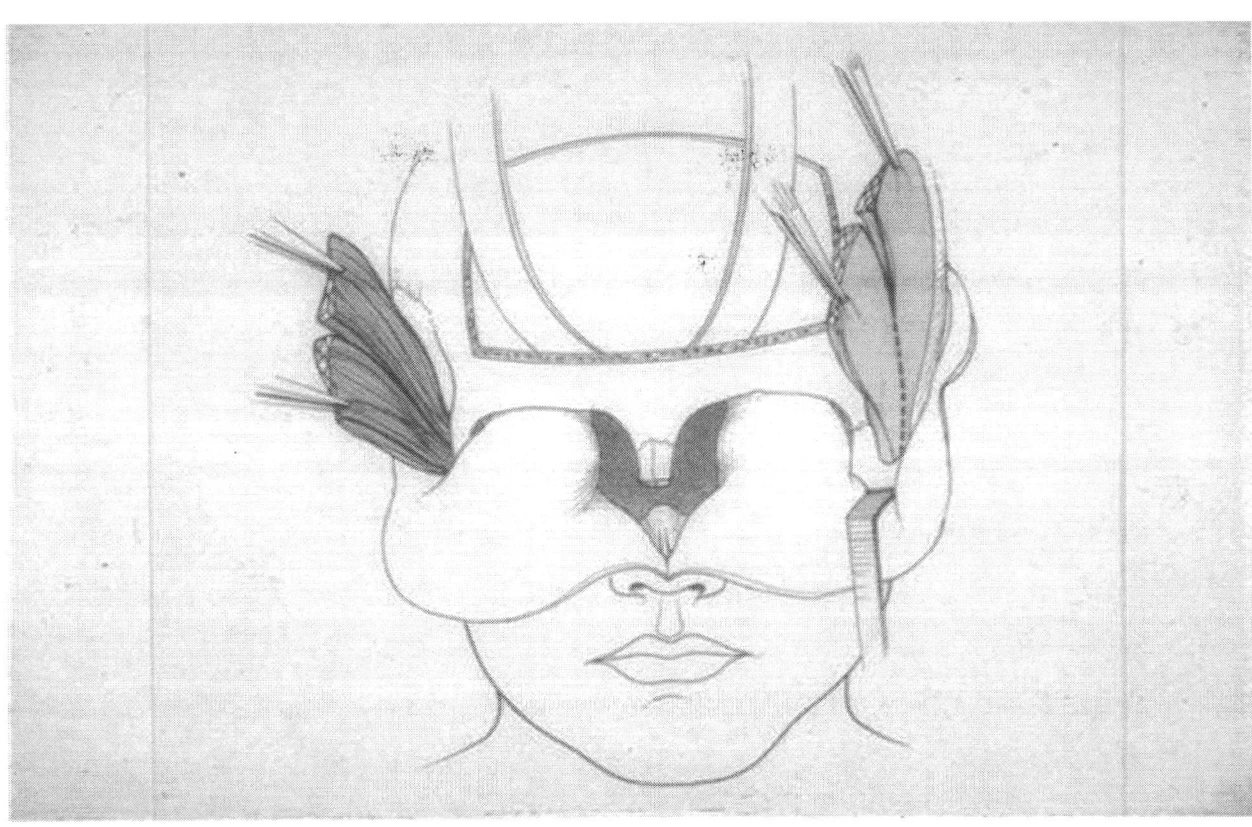

*Fig. 7.11 After completely removing the tumor and unroofing the optic nerves, mobilizing the temporal muscles, and splitting of the temporal muscles into two halves (one to be transposed across the anterior cranial base beneath the globes, and the other to be advanced to the lateral orbital rim to prevent a temporal deformity).*

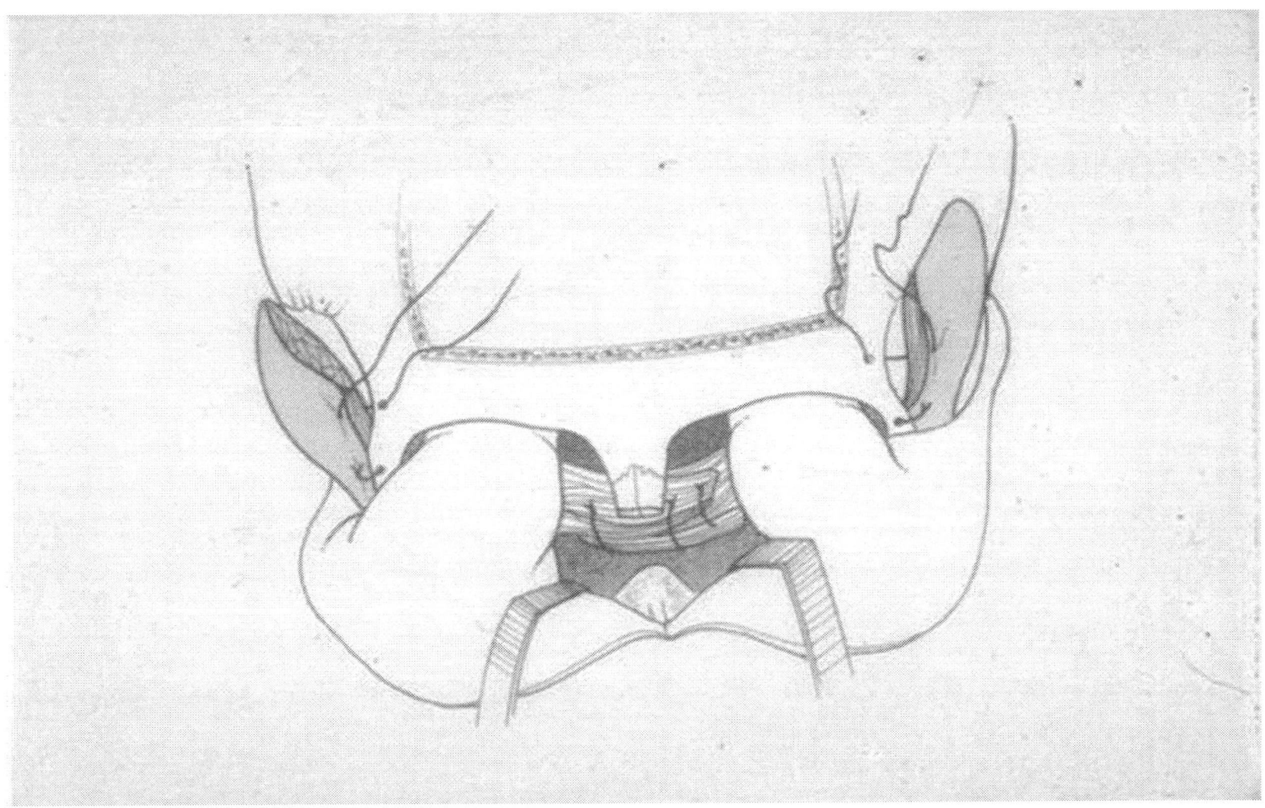

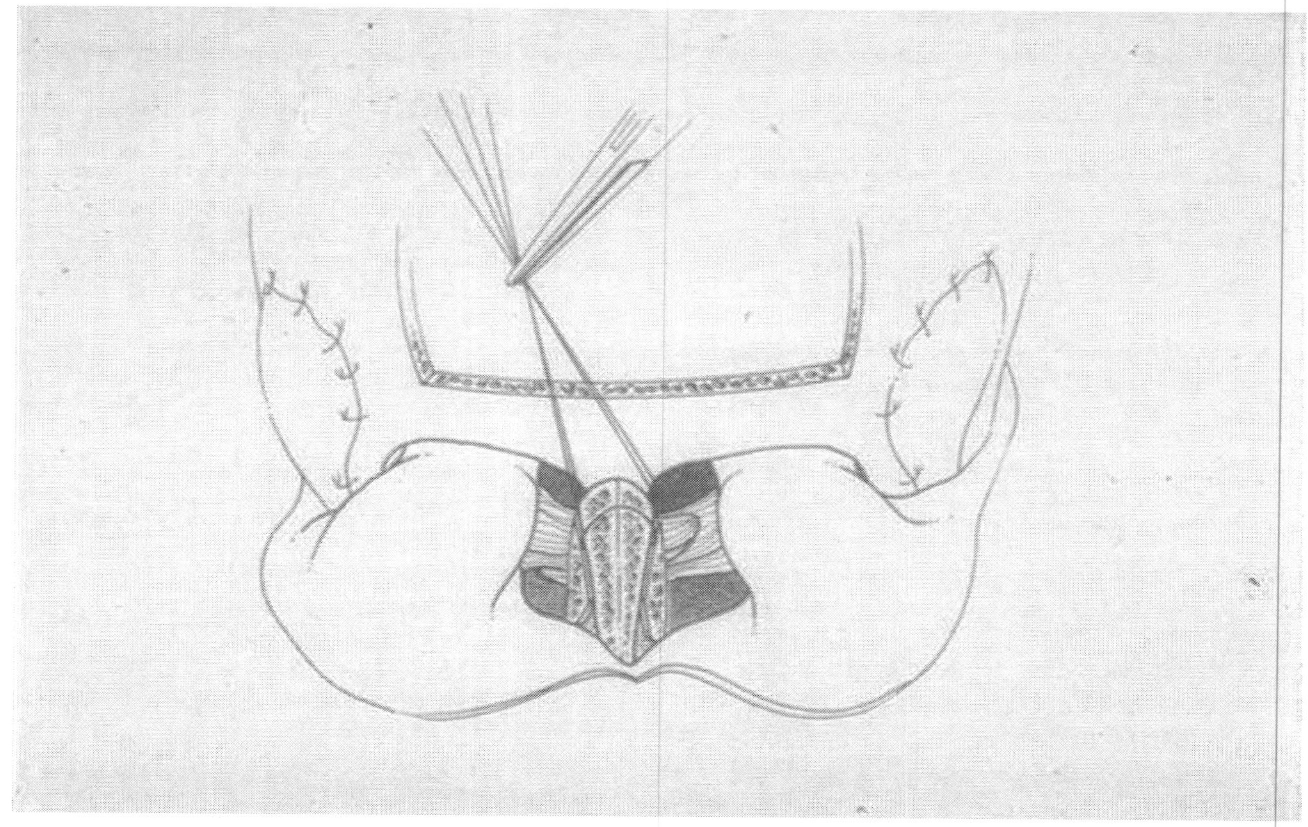

*Fig. 7.12 After suturing the temporal muscles together to separate the cranial base from the pharynx and performing medial canthopexies over the nasal and orbital bone grafts.*

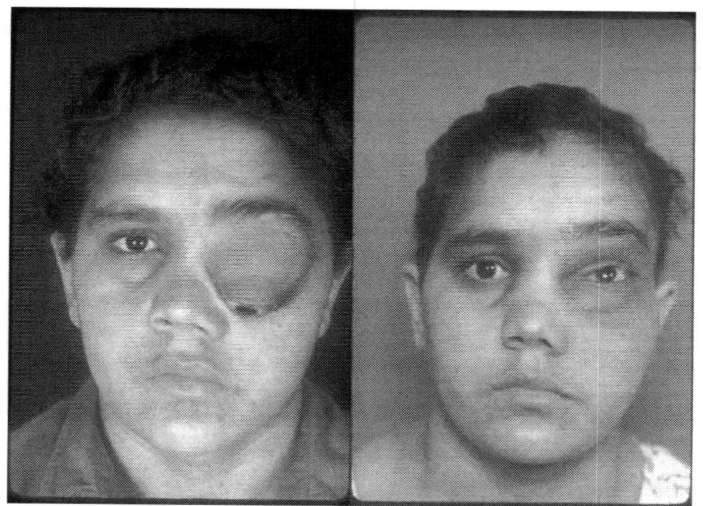

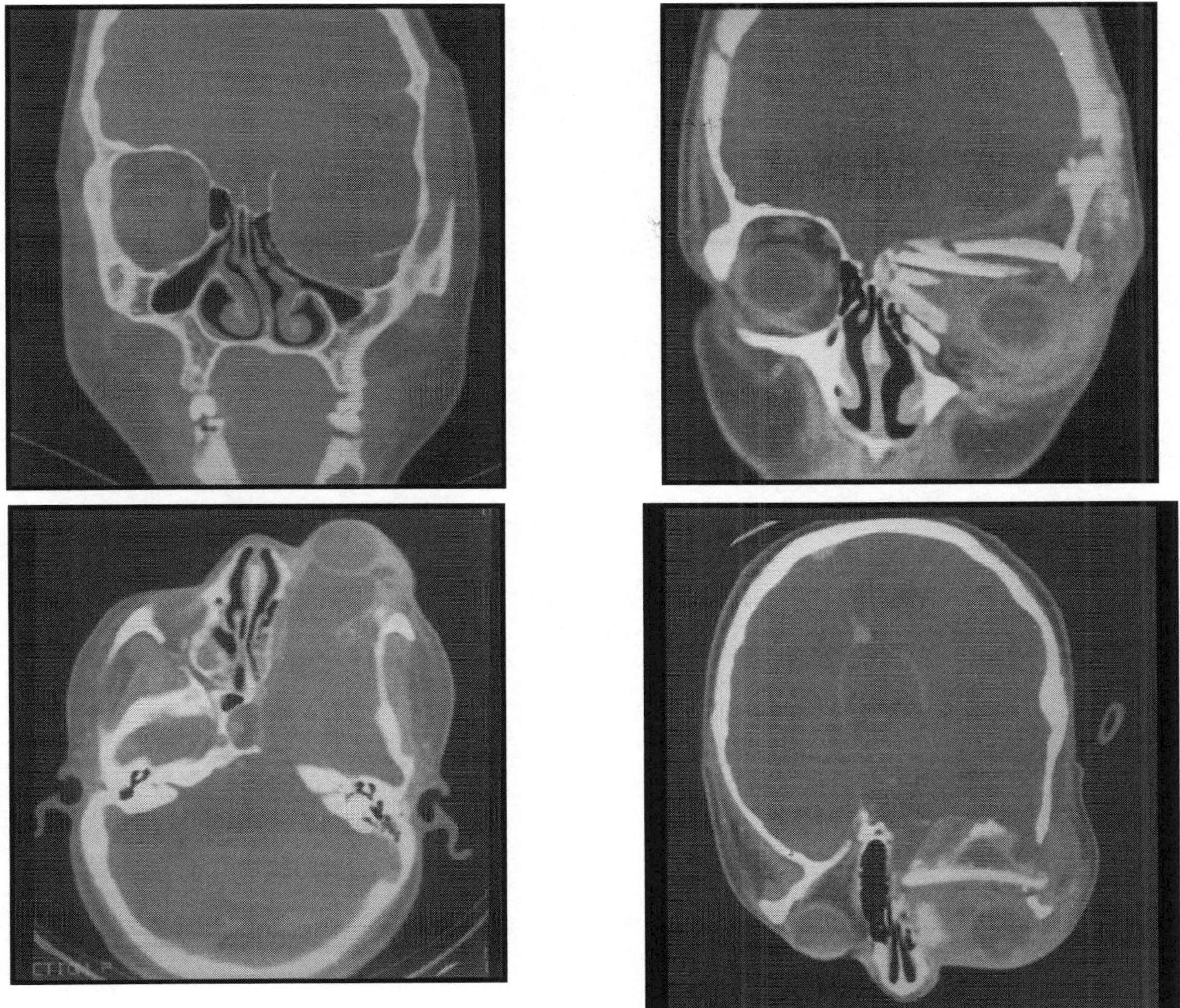

*Fig. 7.14 Patient with orbitopalpebral neurofibromatosis (von Recklinghausen's disease). The large plexiform neurofibroma has eroded through the entire orbital roof into the anterior cranial fossa. Tessier has placed massive bone grafts to separate the orbit from the cranial cavity, radically resected the eyelids, performed medial and lateral canthopexies, and preserved the eye (a prosthetic cover shell was placed over it).*

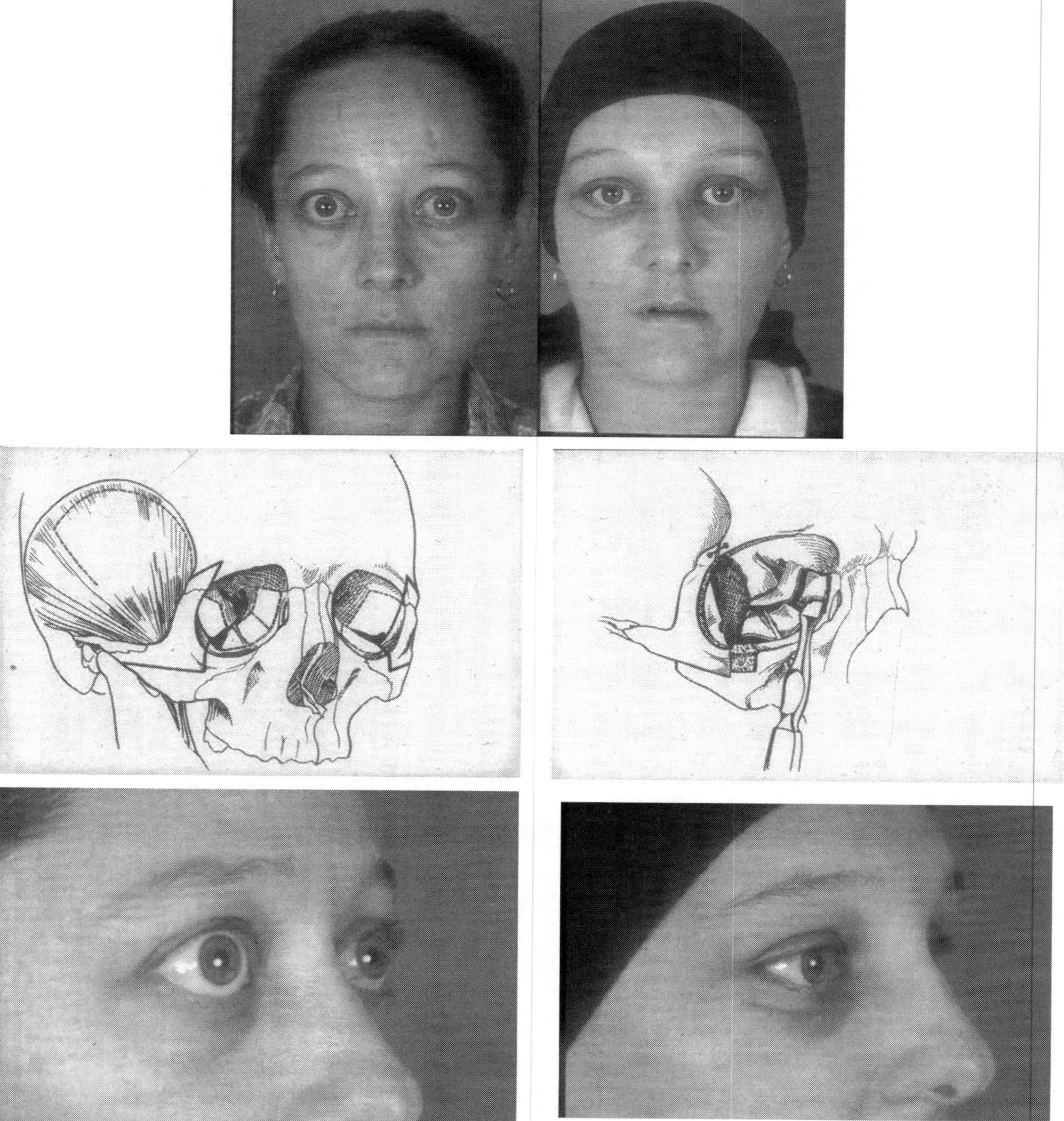

*Fig. 7.15 Patient with Grave's disease (Europeans often use the term Basedow's disease), or dysthyroid exophthalmopathy, after a three-wall orbital expansion developed by Tessier. He is applying his experience in correcting post-traumatic enophthalmos in reverse.*

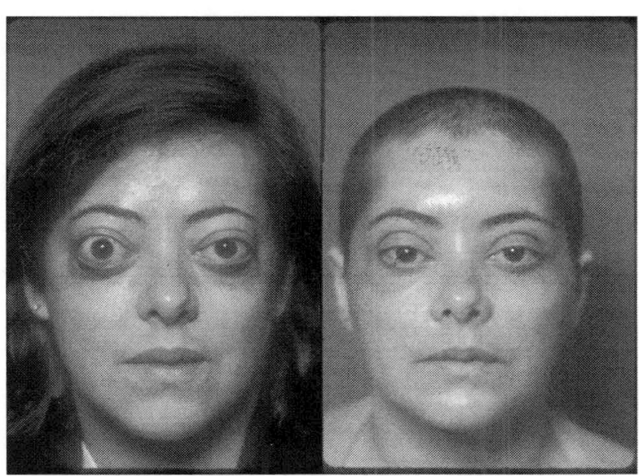

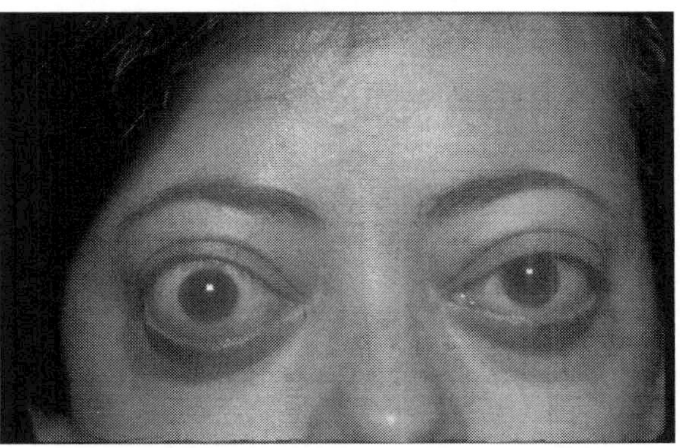

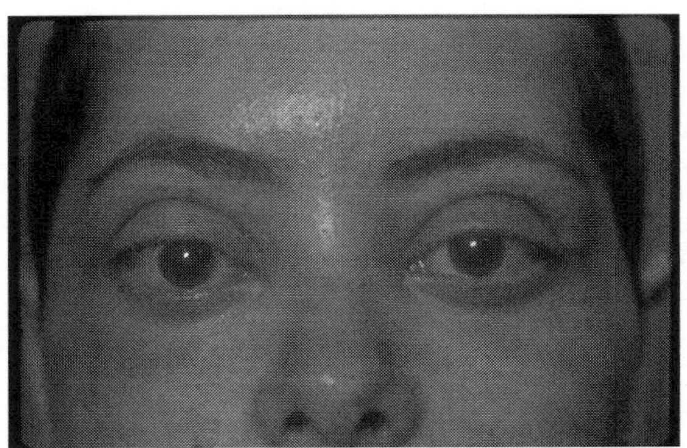

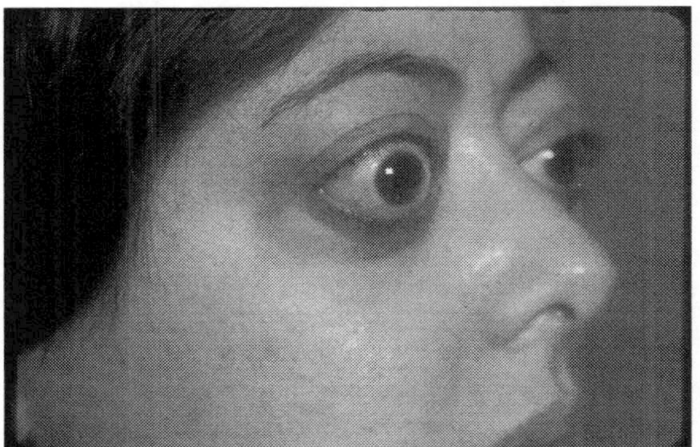

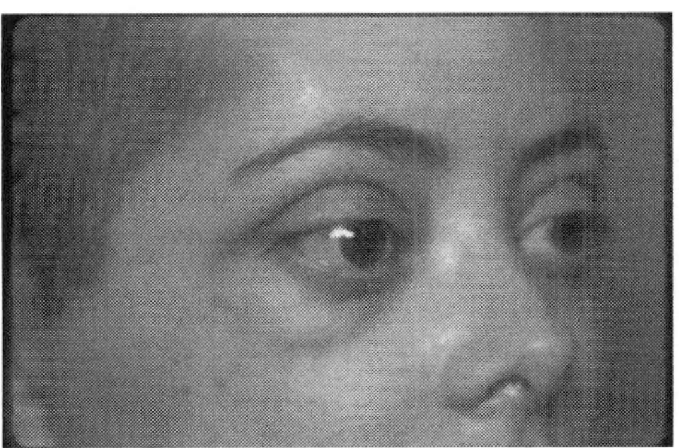

*Fig. 7.16 Another patient with dysthyroid exophthalmopathy corrected with a Le Fort III-type osteotomy coupled with a Le Fort I; the whole midface was moved forward as he would do for a patient with Crouzon's disease, and then the maxilla was cut again just above the roots of the teeth (and that portion was moved back to preserve dental occlusion). Dr. Tessier felt that this was a more effective way of expanding orbital volume than the three-wall expansion.*

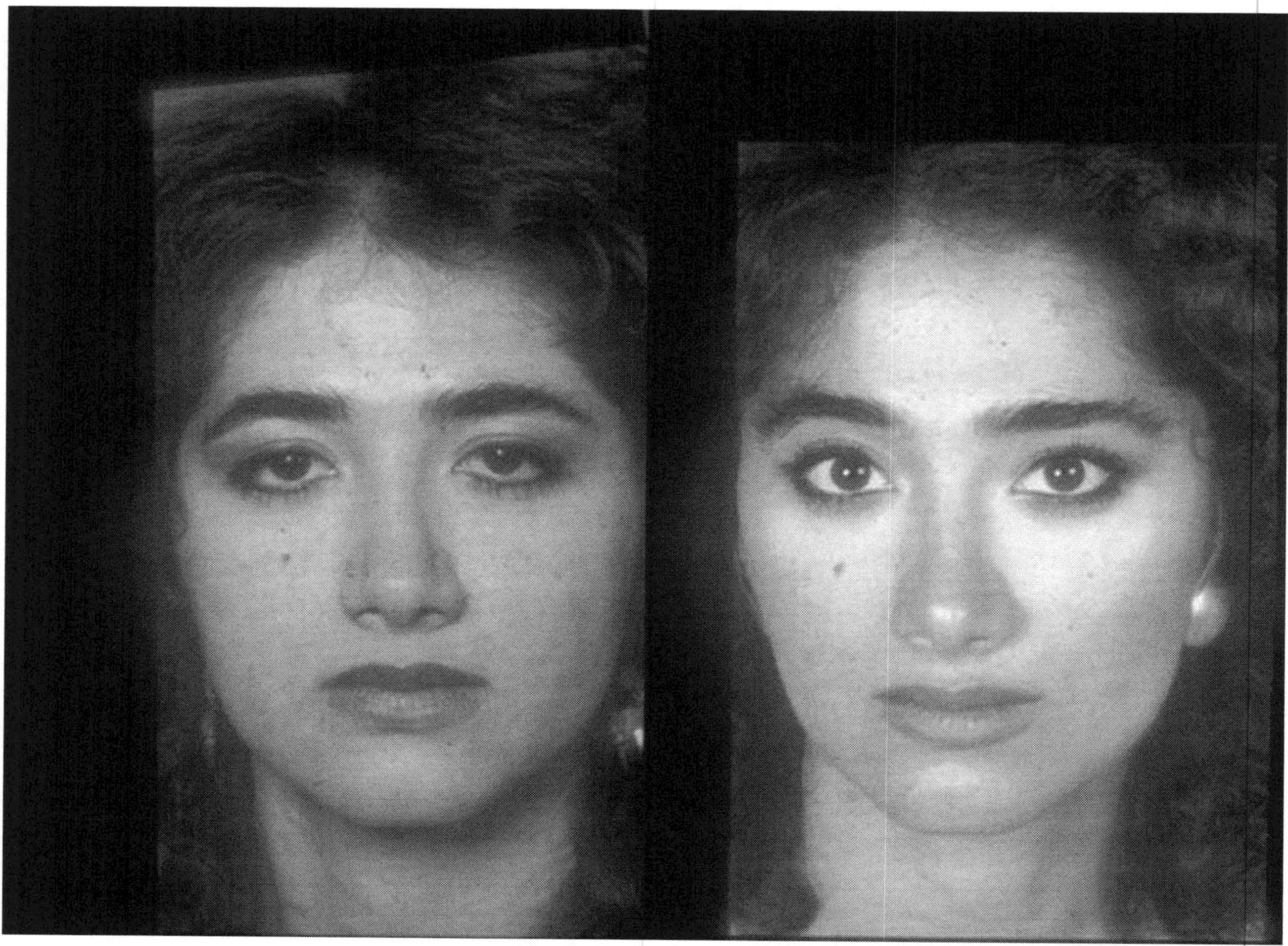

*Fig. 7.17 Young patient treated with the "mask lift."*

Dr. Tessier's experience with craniofacial surgery, and his uncanny ability to control the relationships between the globe, the orbit, and the lateral canthus led him to develop what he called the "mask lift" (also referred to by some as the "subperiosteal facelift"). Here, a rather plain and somewhat haggard young woman is changed into a beauty by performing a procedure through a coronal incision that elevated the brows, increased the prominence of the eyes by removing some of the lateral orbital rim, placed bone grafts over the zygoma, and elevated the lateral canthus. Merri Scheitlin's drawings show the orbit as seen from above, and they show how bone is removed to behind the equator of the globe.

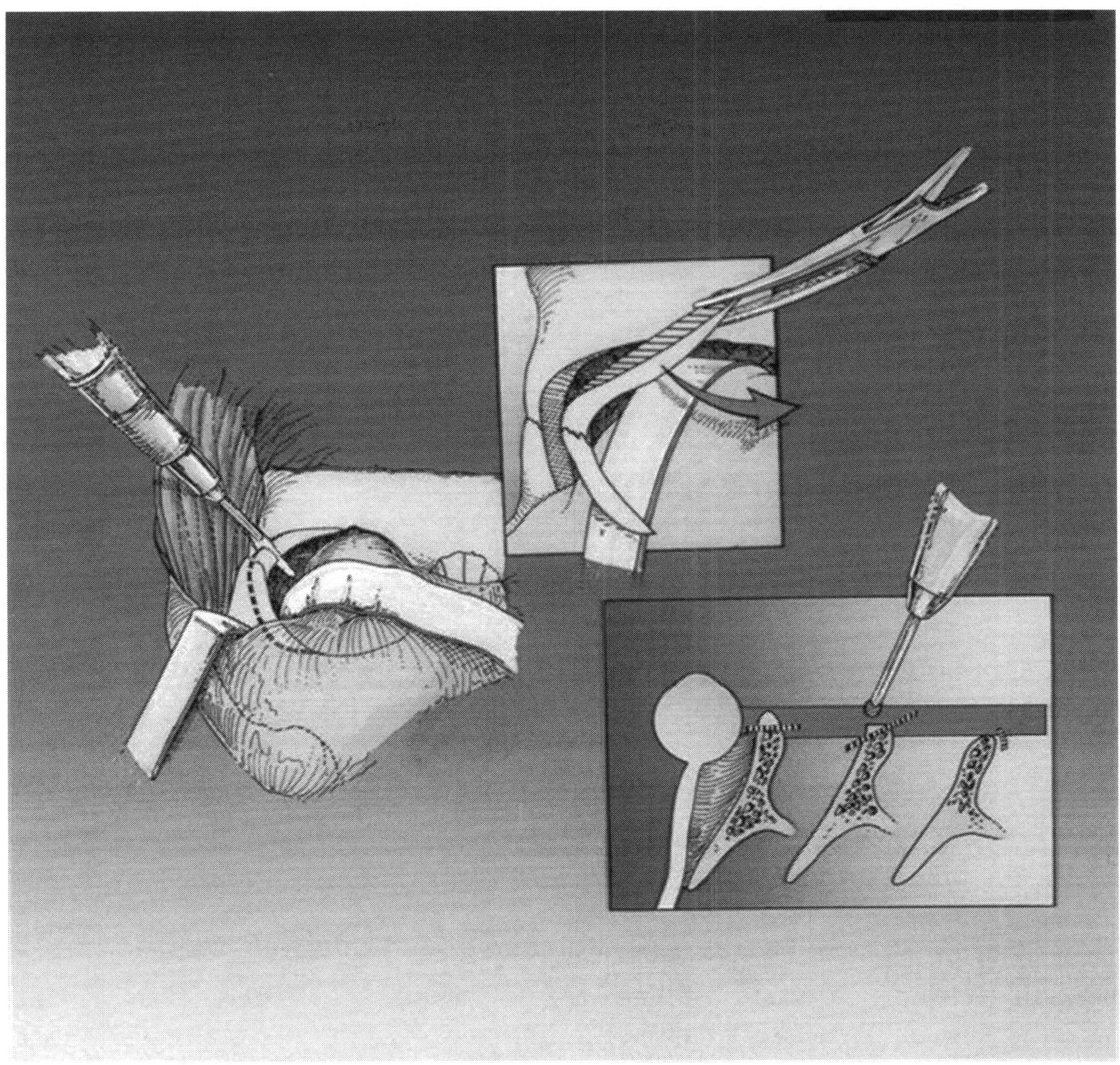

*Fig. 7.18 Tessier's drawings showing removal of a portion of the lateral orbital rim*

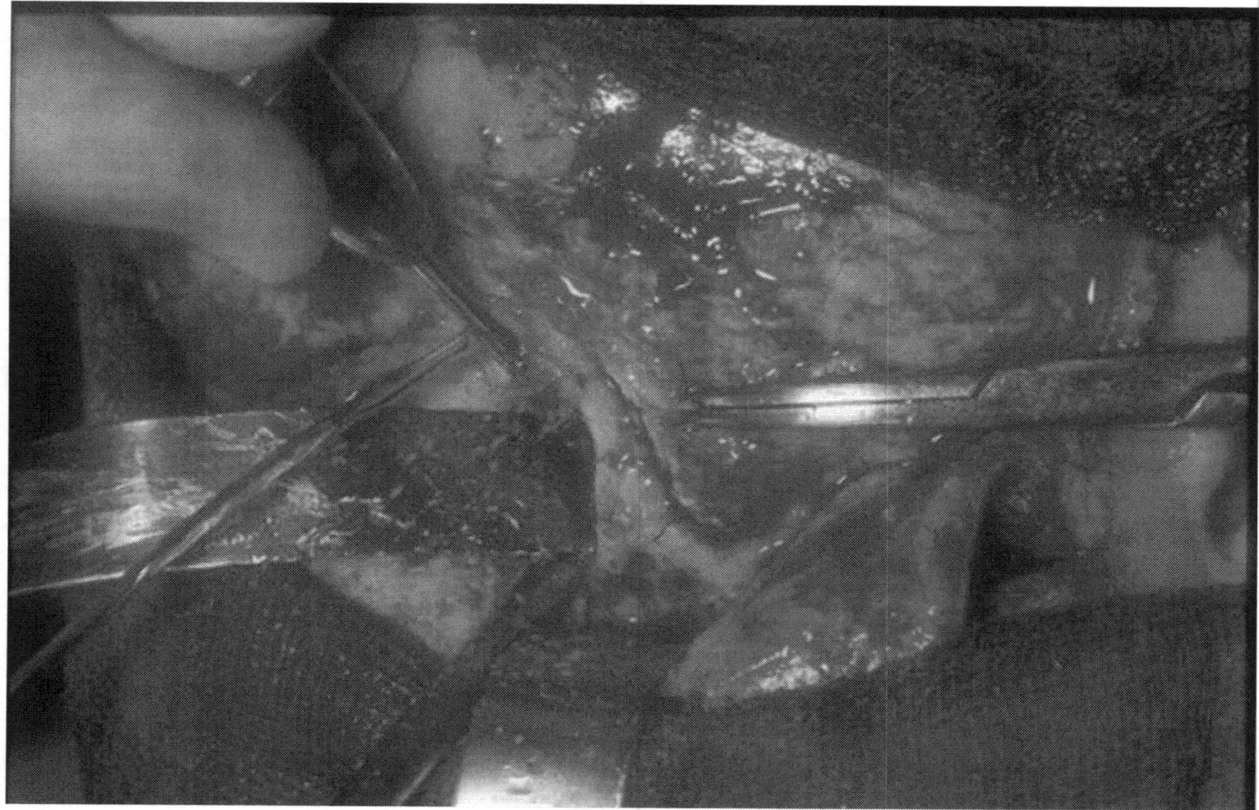

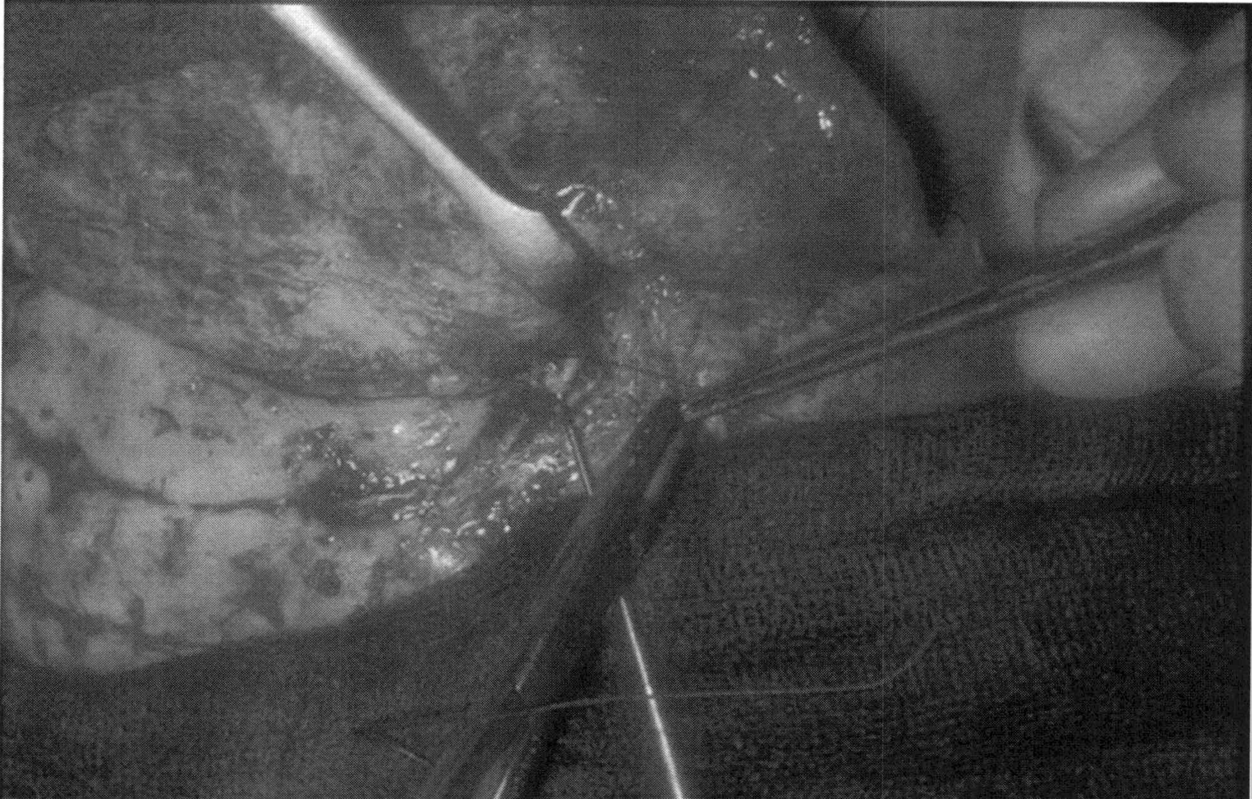

*Fig. 7.19 Operative pictures showing burring of the lateral orbital rim, and performing a lateral canthopexy to the temporal aponeurosis.*

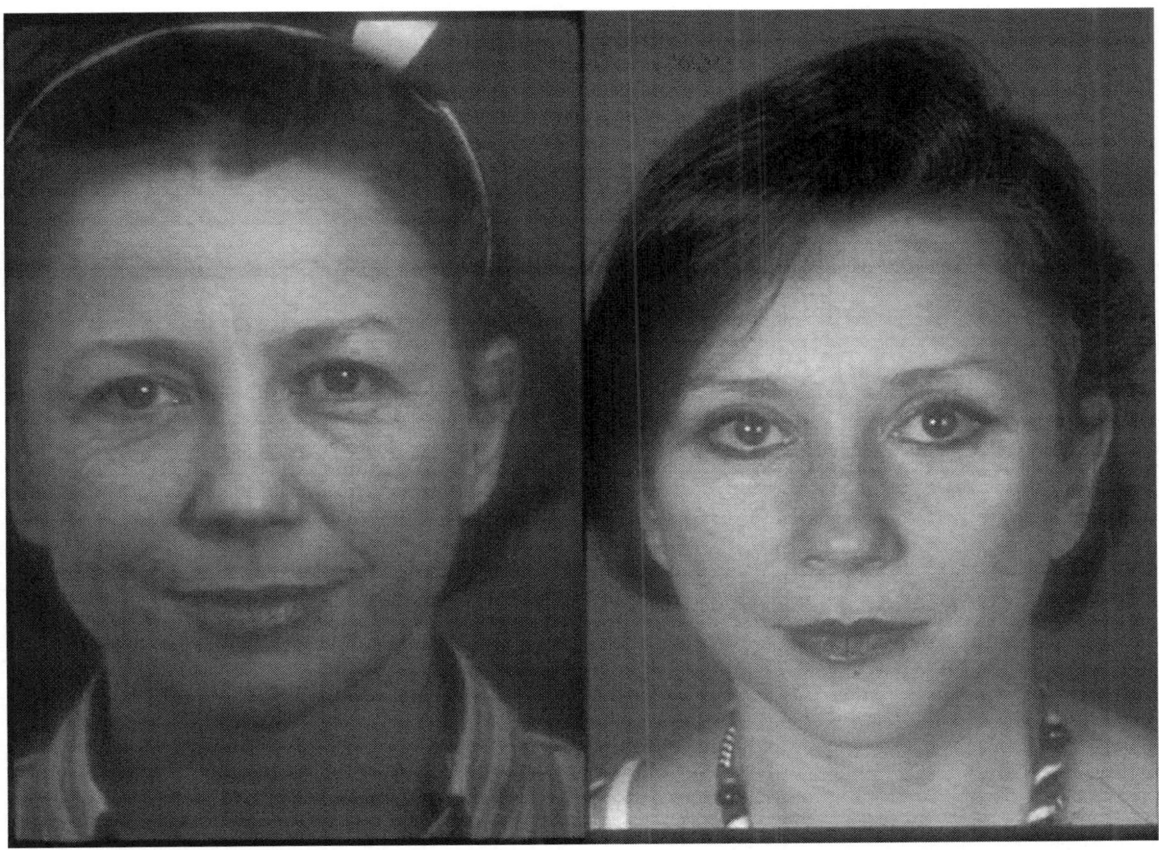

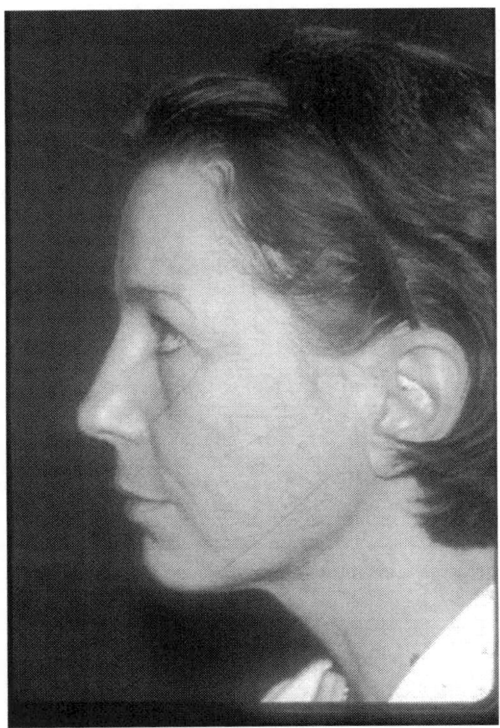

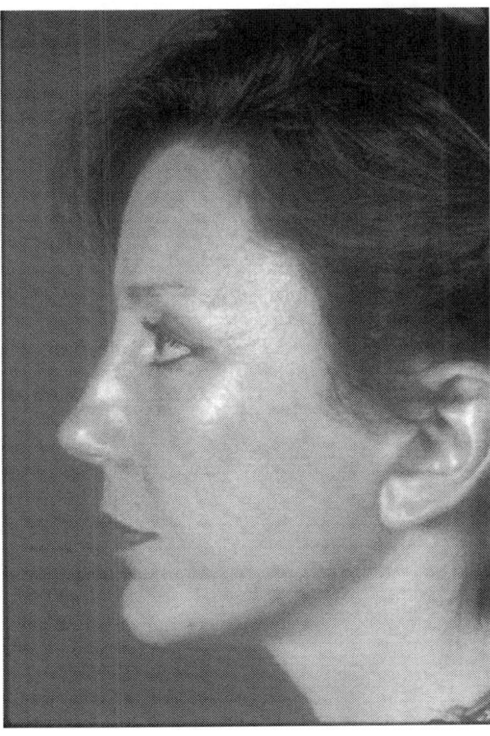

*Fig. 7.20 Darina Krastinova, Dr. Tessier's successor as chief of the plastic surgery service at Hôpital Foch, after a "mask lift," zygomatic bone grafts, a genioplasty, a face lift, and a minor nasal revision performed by Dr. Tessier. Darina has herself subsequently become one of the world's most expert practitioners of the mask lift. In later years, Dr. Tessier performed zygomatic osteotomies rather than onlay bone grafts since he felt they were smoother and more predictable.*

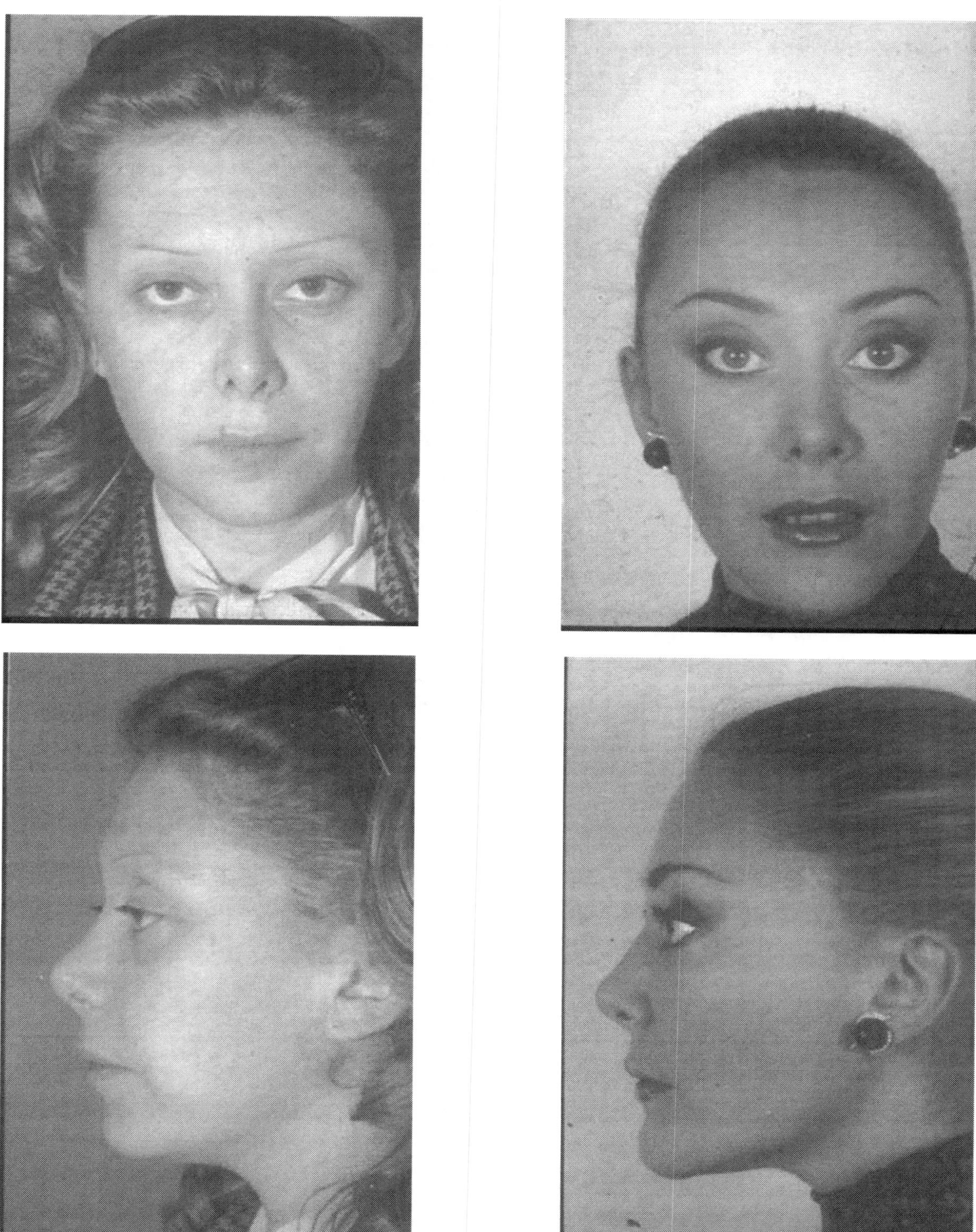

*Fig. 7.21 This patient was shown by Dr. Tessier in his lecture on craniofacial surgery at the International Society of Plastic and Reconstructive Surgery meeting in Rio in 1979. The striking result was obtained with a mask lift, an alteration of the lateral orbital rim and lateral canthus as described above, a genioplasty, and a lengthening of the nose with cartilage graft—and, obviously, some makeup and jewelry. This case had a profound influence on aesthetic surgery, and many surgeons went home and tried "subperiosteal facelifts." Unfortunately, without Dr. Tessier's skill—both with soft tissue and bone—and a deep understanding of the relationships between the orbit, globe and lateral canthus, few (if any) were able to obtain similar results.*

# Chapter 8

## The Societé Française d'Ophthalmologie Report

Paul Tessier also had close ties to ophthalmologists. Gabriele Sourdille of Nantes had been one of his teachers and he invited him regularly to Nantes to operate. Sourdille developed a procedure for correction of eyelid ptosis with another Nantes colleague, François Hervouët. Tessier also went regularly to Lille and worked with Michel Lekieffre and he also co-authored papers on orbital surgery with Marcel Woillez. Most of this work was orbital and eyelid repair—sequelae of orbital fractures, eyelid trauma, burns, and congenital malformations—but the ophthalmologists also knew what he was doing in craniofacial surgery and asked that he write a report for their society. "Chirurgie Plastique Orbito-Palpébrale" was published (several thousand copies were made) and sent to members of the French Society of Ophthalmology (1976). Approximately 90 percent of the book was written by Tessier—and almost all of the cases shown are his—but he insisted, with his usual modesty, on multiple authorship. The somewhat dog-eared copy of the book that I translated into English is shown below.

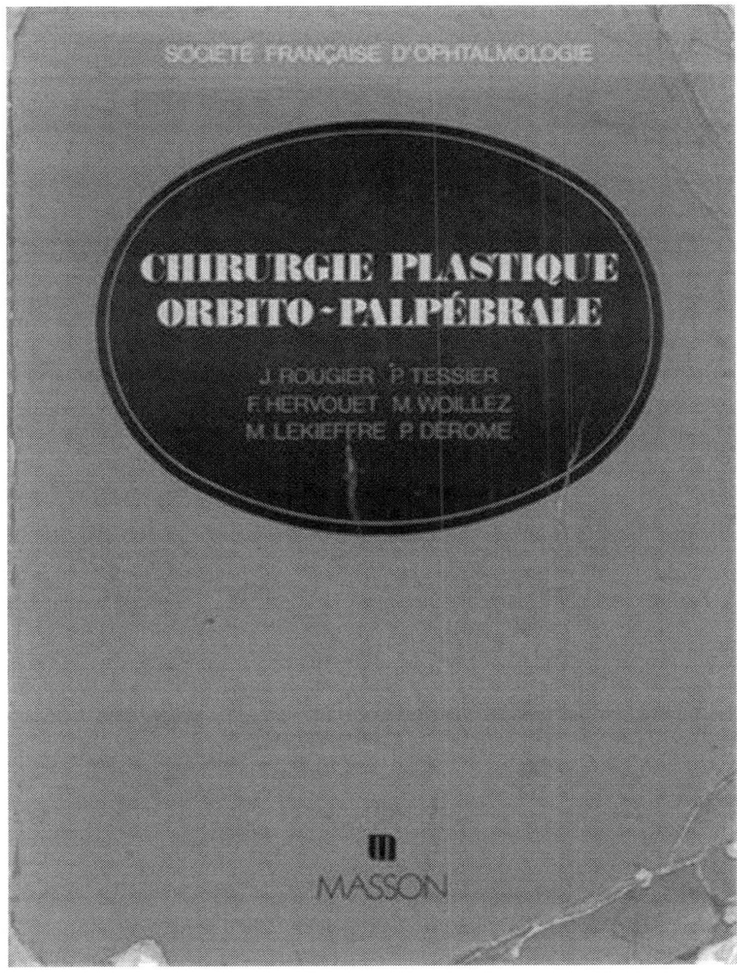


*Fig. 8.1 Paperback copy of the S.F.O. report.*

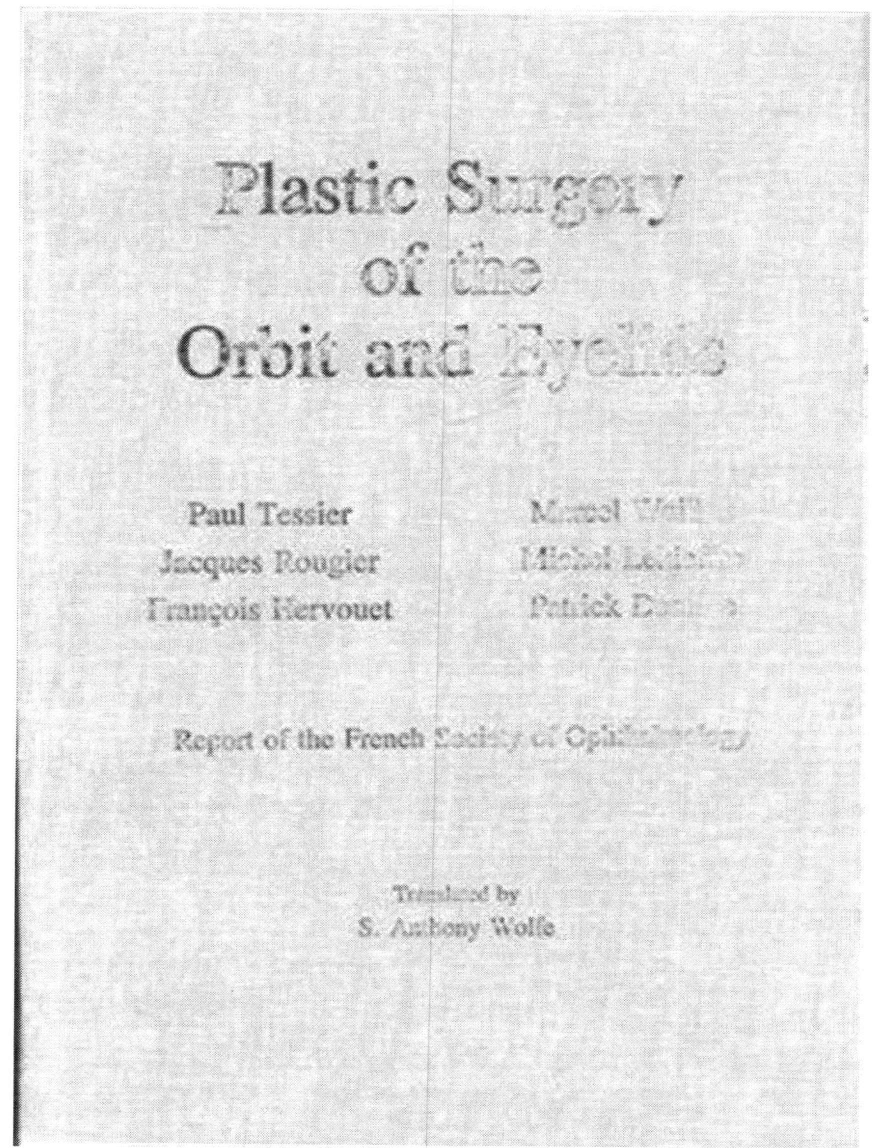


*Fig. 8.2 Hardcover copy of the translation.*

In my translation, which I hope would not offend Dr. Tessier, I moved his name to the front of the pack. A copy of this translation can be ordered on a DVD through my office.

In the original French, the writing style is quite spare. Dr. Tessier might say something is characterized by a, b, c, d, and e, which he would make into a bulleted list. I maintained that form since I felt it was better than standard English usage where things would be in one long sentence. I also used his anatomical terms, "supero-lateral angle of the orbit," for instance, which is not seen in English texts. I felt this was more clear. Some of my friends have criticized the translation for this reason, but I disagree with them: this is the way Dr. Tessier wrote, as will be evident in most of his notes and essays that have been translated and inserted into the Appendixes.

This is really the only book that Dr. Tessier wrote on craniofacial and orbital surgery. Certainly many developments occurred in the two decades following its publication, including using the transcranial approach more frequently, harvesting cranial bone grafts, employing plate and screw fixation, and implementing distraction osteogenesis. But what is in the book, with the excellent, anatomically correct drawings by Francine Gourdin, is still valid over thirty years later.

# Chapter 9

## Tessier Classification of Facial Clefts. Published in 1976

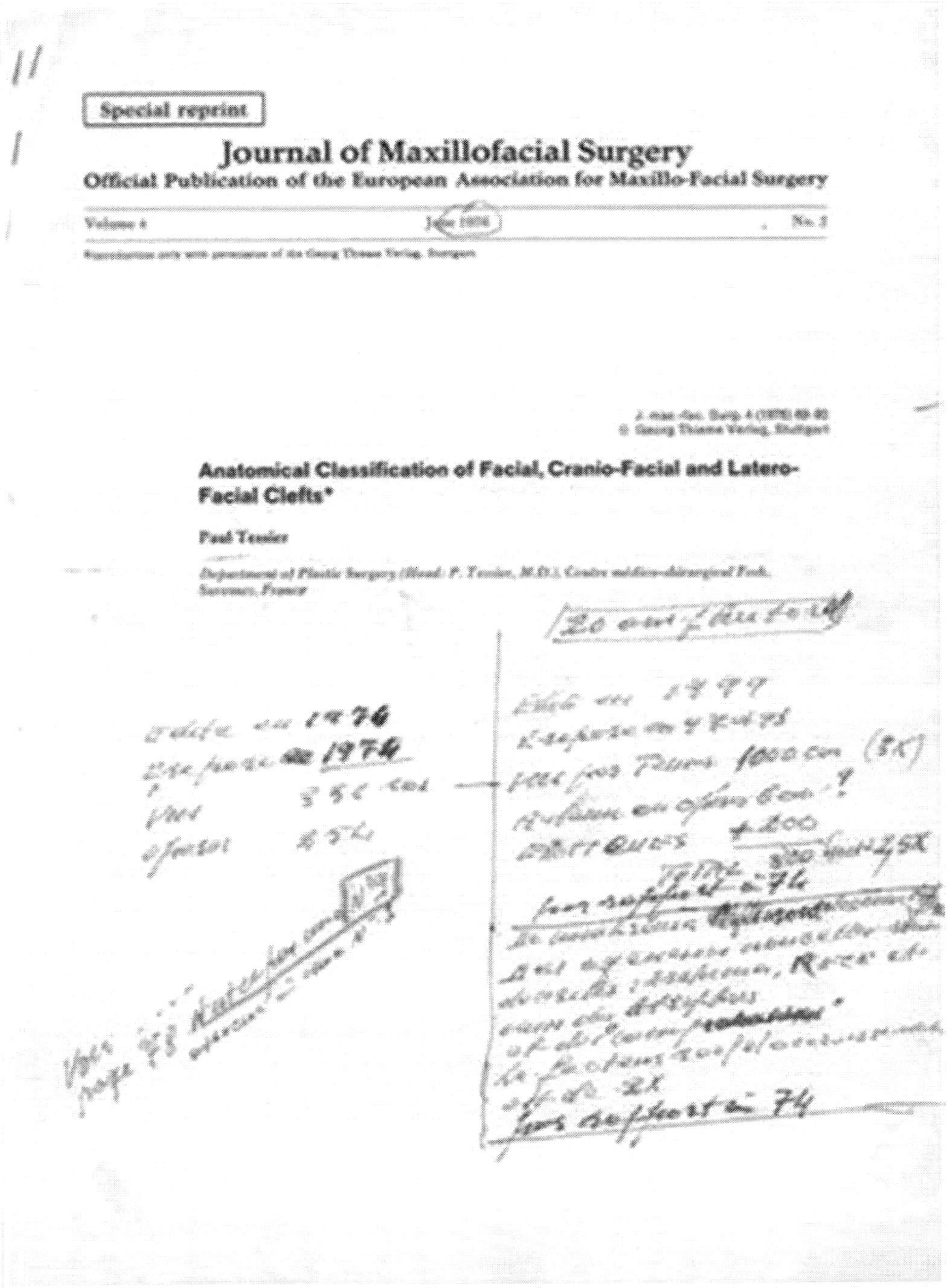

Special reprint

**Journal of Maxillofacial Surgery**

**Official Publication of the European Association for Maxillo-Facial Surgery**

**Anatomical Classification of Facial, Cranio-Facial and Latero-Facial Clefts***

Paul Tessier

*Fig. 9.1 Dr. Tessier's copy of his 1976 paper with his notes about bringing the classification up to date.*

Below: Dr. Tessier's cleft classification with several examples.

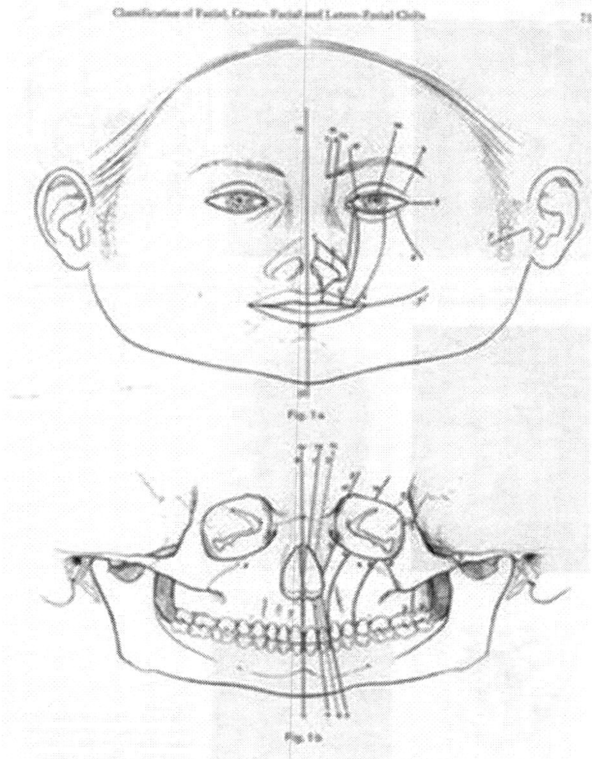

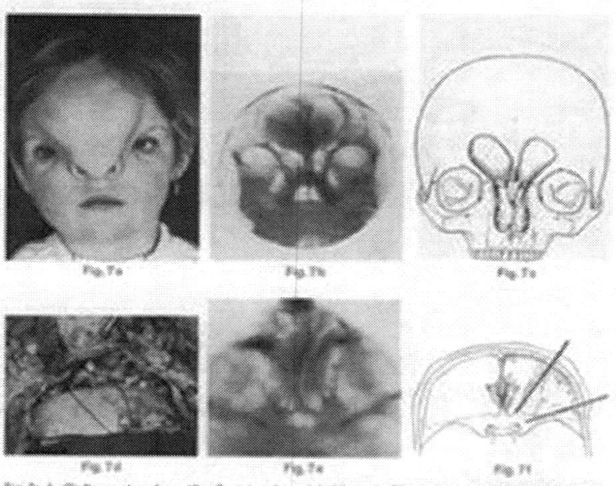

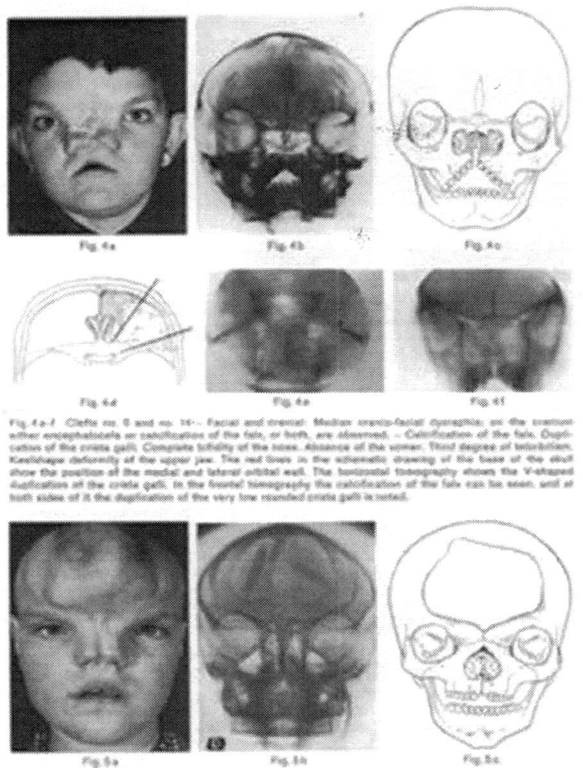

CLEFTS and AGENESIAS: an ANATOMICAL CLASSIFICATION: the "C.A.A.C."

*Fig. 9.2 The new classification, (and examples), the C.A.A.C.*

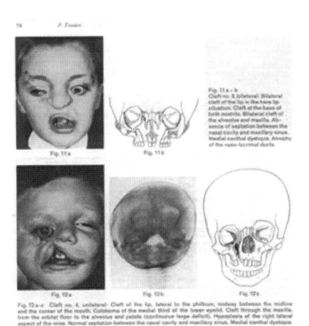

No. 4 Cleft below:

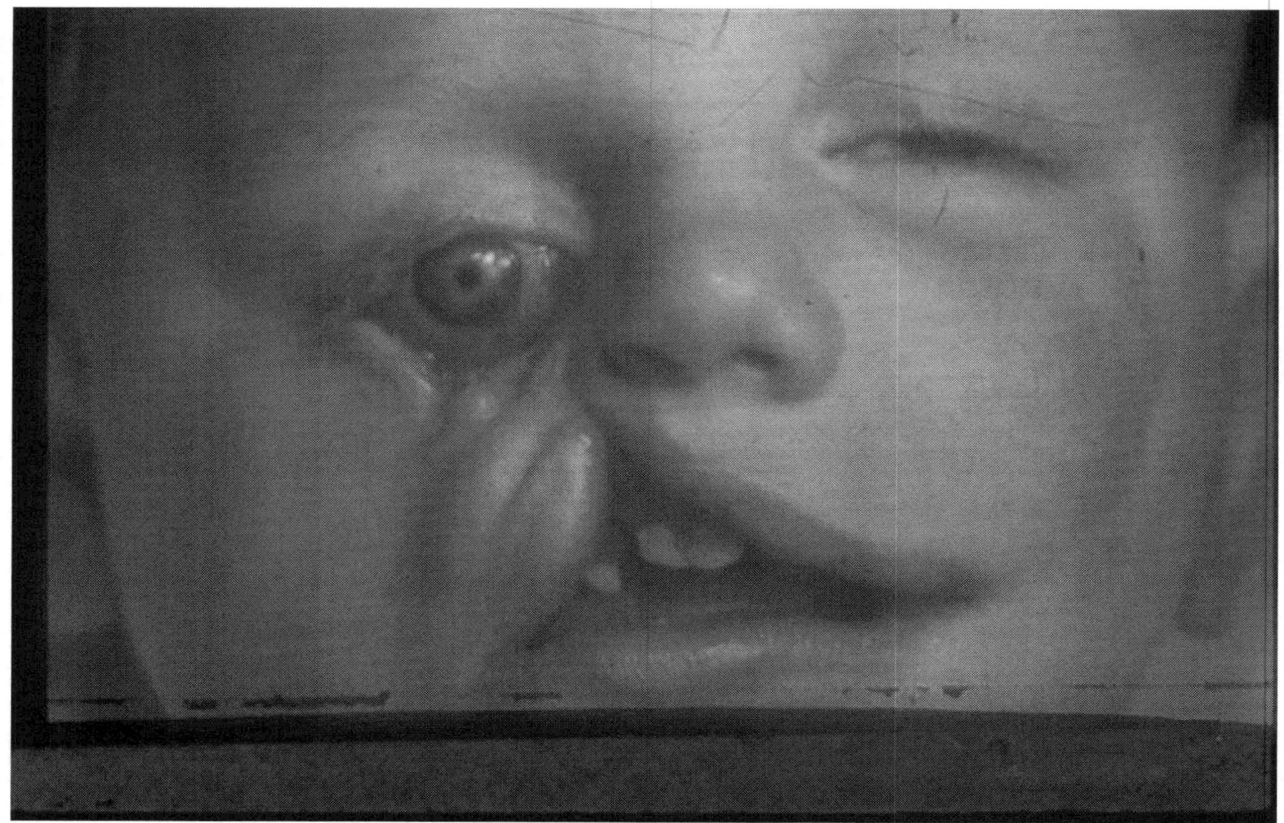

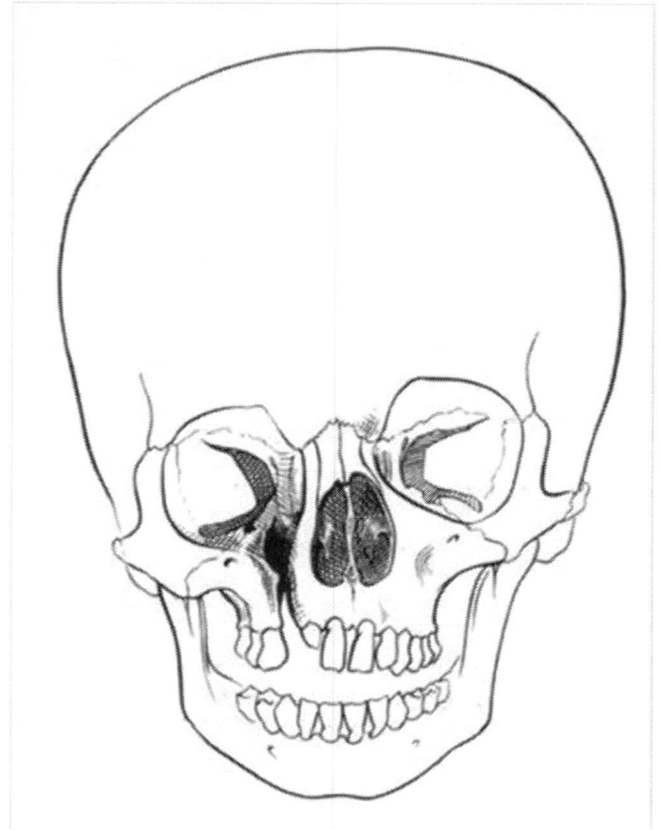

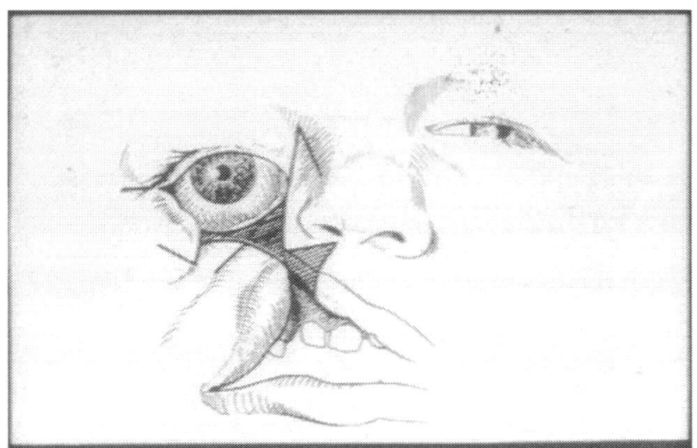

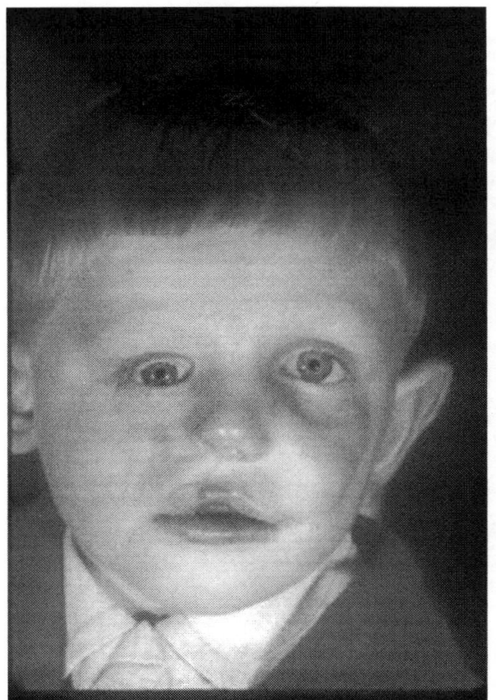

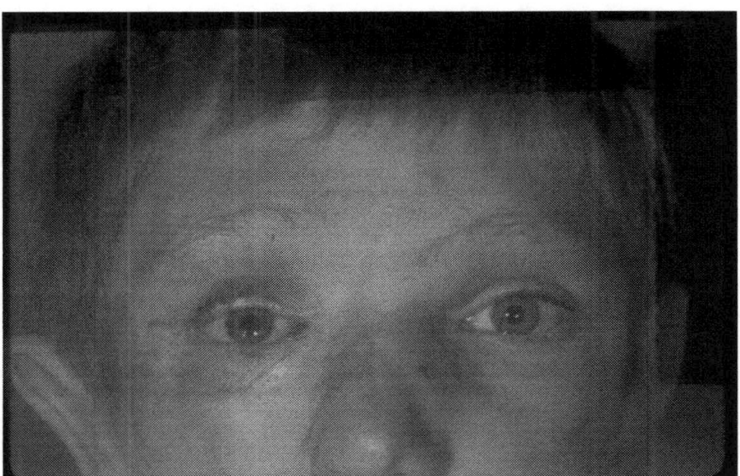

*Fig. 9.3 Patient with a Tessier Number 4 oro-ocular cleft, and drawings of his method of correcting the deformity. Since the right orbital floor was not bone grafted early, the globe prolapsed into the defect and a vertical orbital dystopia developed. The final photo shows the patient after correction of the orbital dystopia (achieved by elevating the orbit through a transcranial approach).*

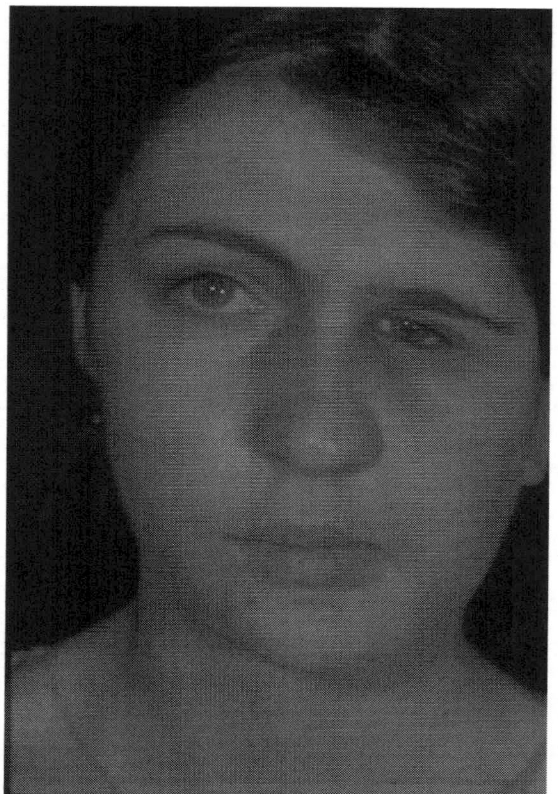

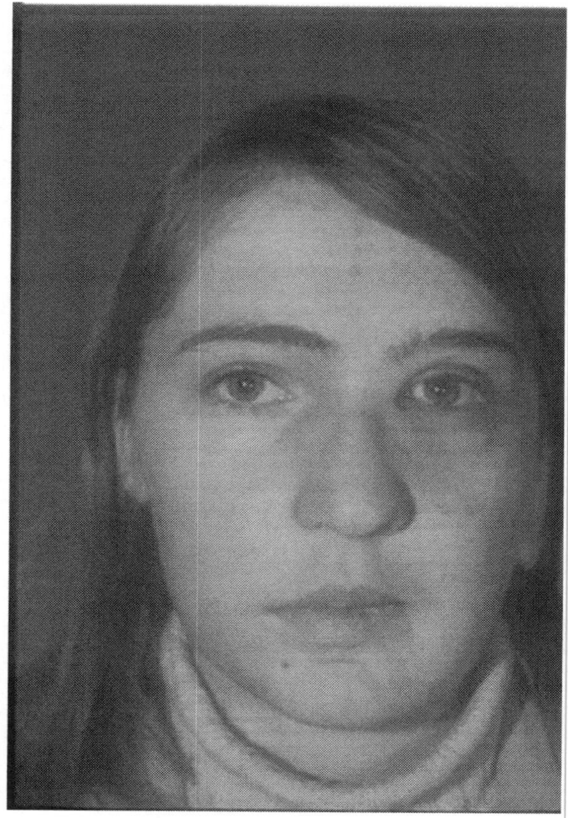

*Fig. 9.4 Another patient with a significant left orbital dystopia due to torticollis (note that the left ear is lower and the neck is shorter on the left), before and after correction through a transcranial approach.*

# Chapter 10

## The "Mise au Point" of Craniofacial Surgery

*Mise au point* is a wonderful term in French. "Bringing to the point where it is just right" might be the best English translation. When one goes down the list of conditions that are treated by craniofacial surgeons, in virtually all cases the method of correction was developed by Paul Tessier. He based his treatment on his understanding of how the anatomy—particularly the skeletal anatomy—was abnormal. Then he determined what would be needed to bring it to normal, either by moving existing skeletal structures or constructing them with autogenous bone grafts. Conditions for which he developed the surgical treatment include:

- Crouzon's disease—the Le Fort III-type osteotomy, later with simultaneous frontal advancement (BOFORT), then with the Monobloc Frontofacial Advancement (after the publication in 1978 by his friends Fernando Ortiz Monasterio and Antonio Fuente del Campo*ref.). The first monobloc in Mexico City was done October 1976 (personal communication, Antonio Fuente del Campo).

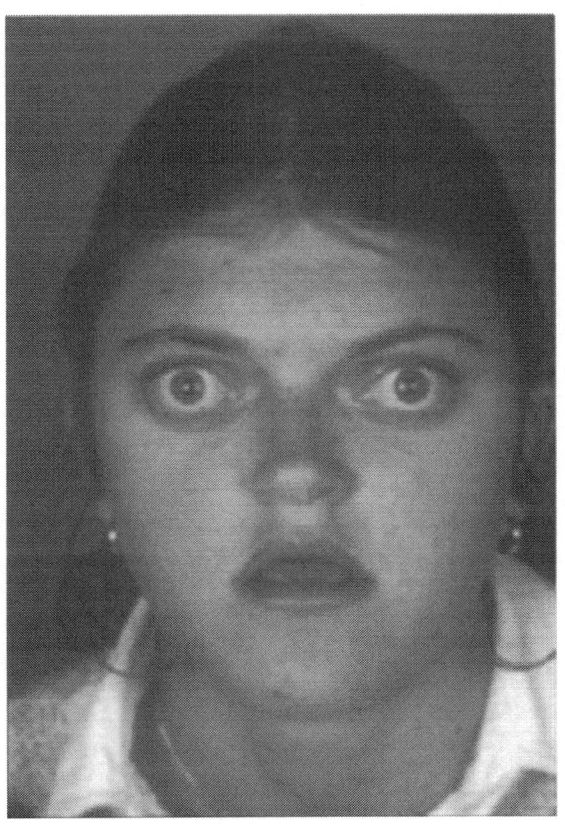

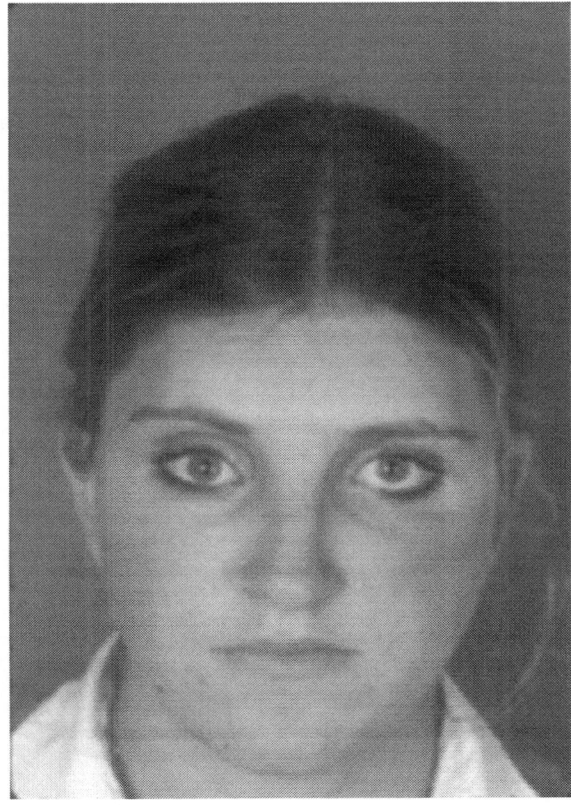

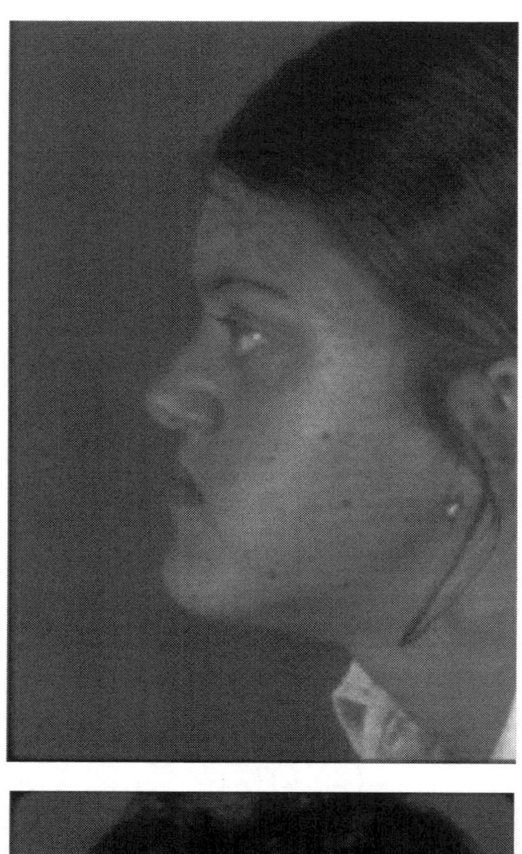

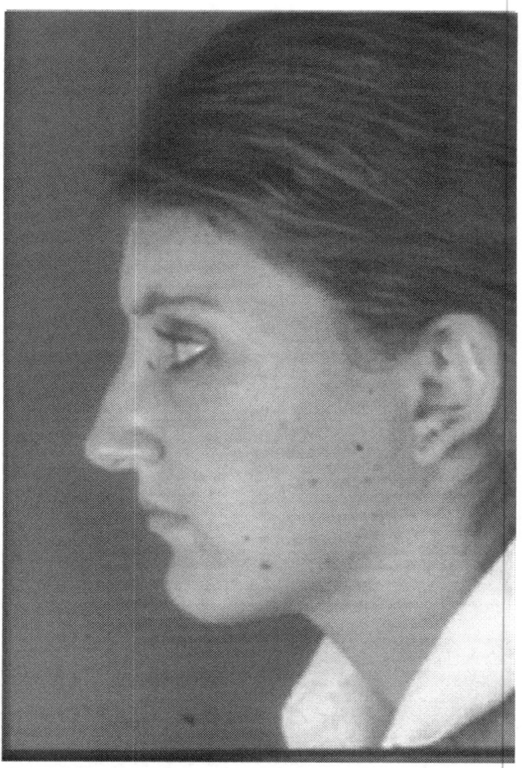

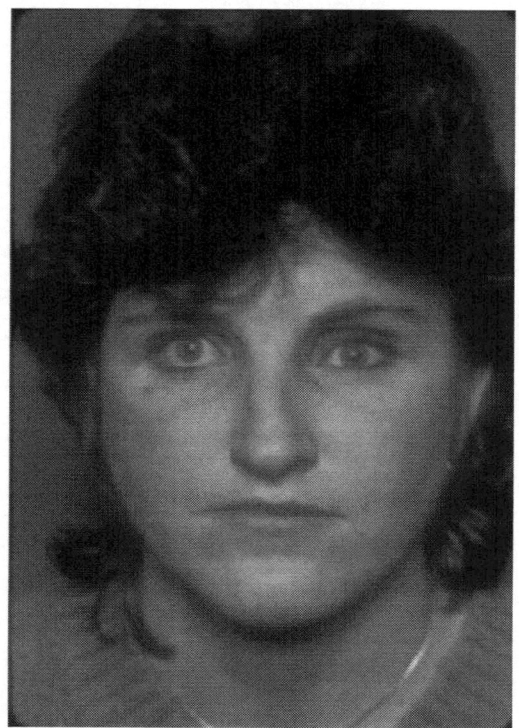

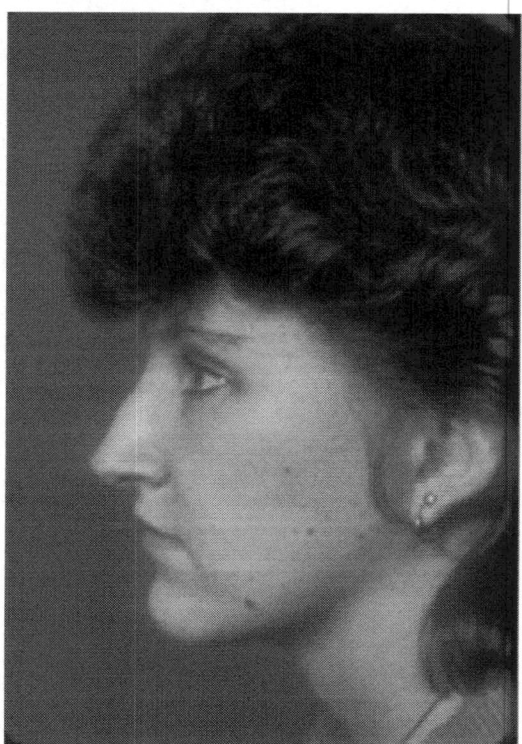

*Fig. 10.1 Young woman with Crouzon's disease, shown before and after a Le Fort III-type osteotomy. She is an ideal candidate for this procedure due to her prominent forehead, moderate proptosis, and short nose and midface. The early post-operative result is nearly perfect, but if one looks carefully, the upper eyelid crease on the left is a bit deeper than the right, and there is a suspicion that the left globe is a bit lower. On the twelve-year post-op pictures, she has definite enophthalmos on the left side, with a minor degree of hypoglobus. Long-term follow-up is important in craniofacial surgery.*

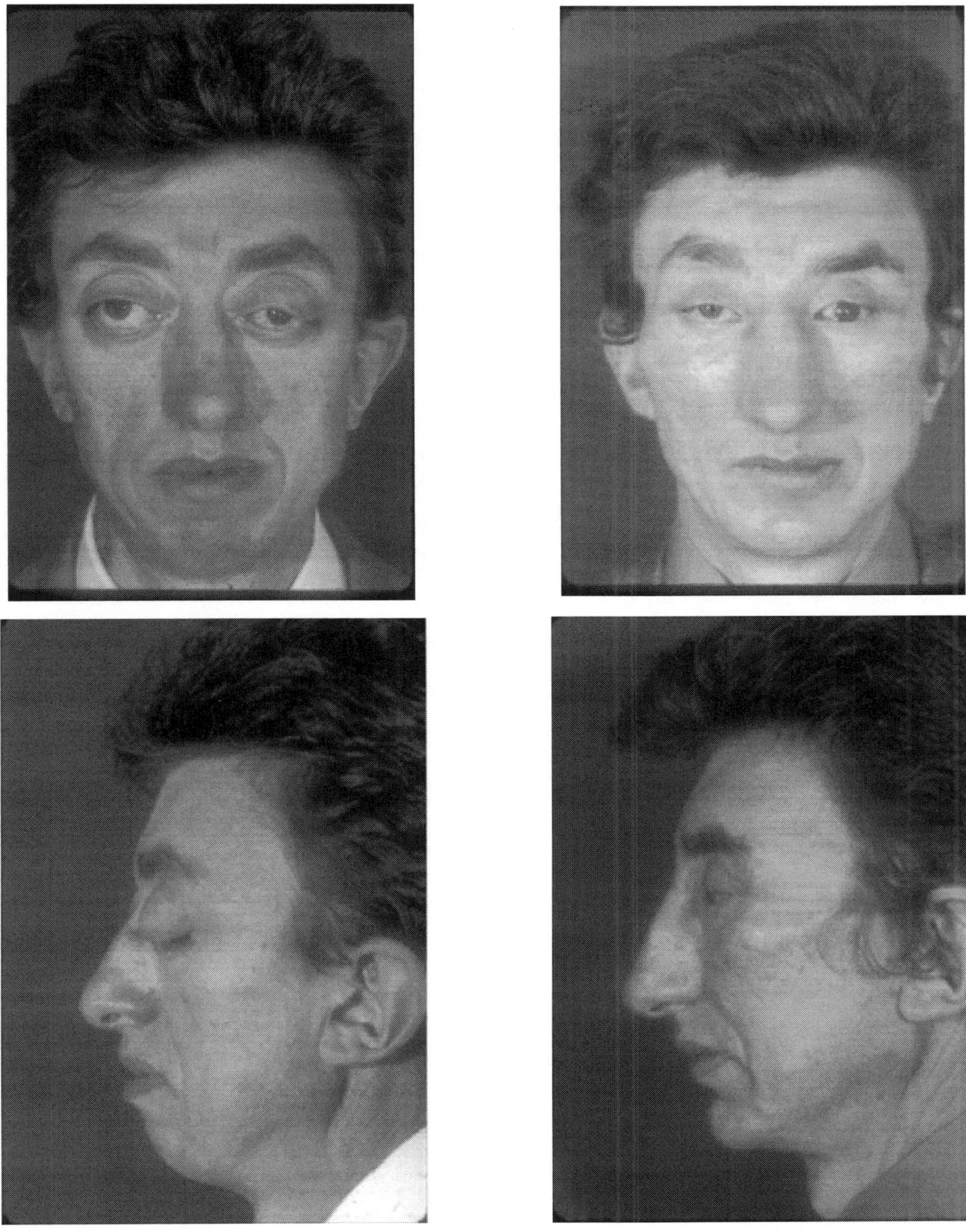

*Fig. 10.2 This patient is not such a good candidate for a Le Fort III. He does not have a prominent forehead preoperatively, and his nose and midface are already long. After the Le Fort III, his nose is even longer. The proptosis is well corrected. The genioplasty helped—as it almost always does—but the final result is not a normal face. This type of result led Dr. Tessier to shift to an increasing use of the intracranial approach with simultaneous advancement of the forehead and midface.*

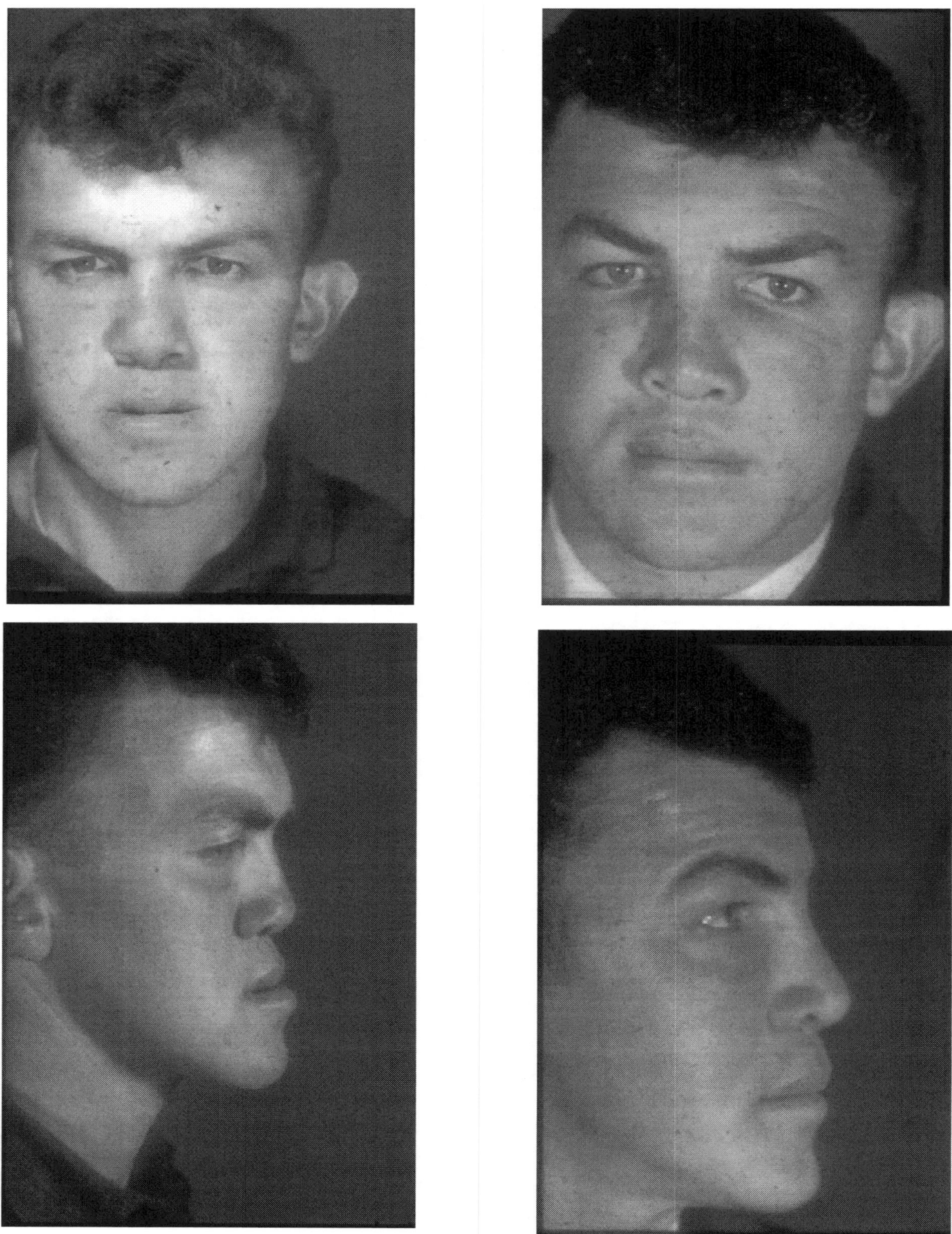

*Fig. 10.3 In this patient with Binder's syndrome (nasomaxillary hypoplasia), Dr. Tessier has advanced and lengthened the midface with a Le Fort III-type osteotomy. The result is good, and he has managed to avoid producing enophthalmos with the increase in orbital volume that occurs with the Le Fort III by extensive bone grafting of the orbital floors to bring the orbital volume back to normal.*

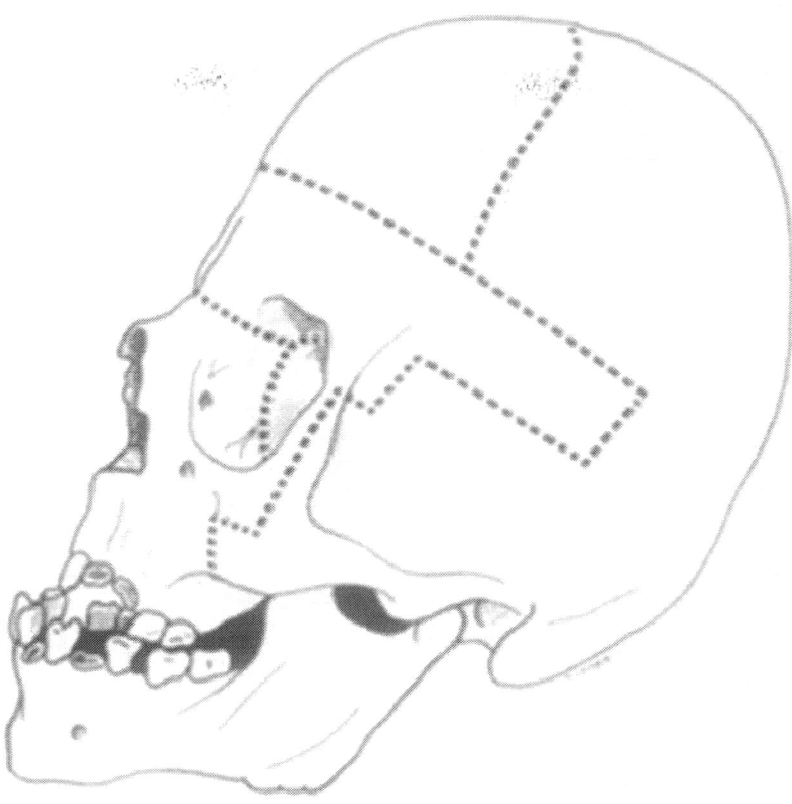

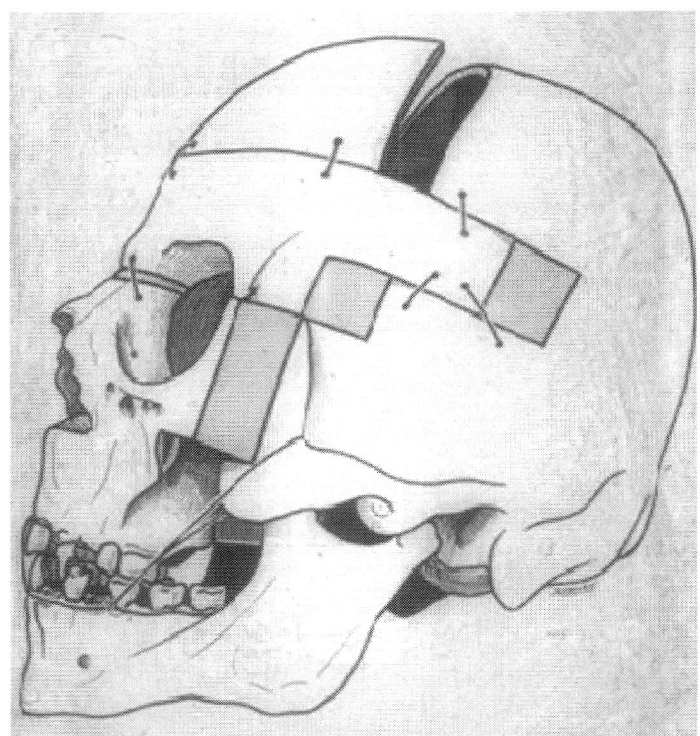

*Fig. 10.4 The "BO-FORT" (Le Fort III plus orbito-frontal bandeau and frontal bone) procedure was developed by Dr. Tessier in the late 1960s because of his dissatisfaction with the sub-cranial Le Fort III, as shown in Fig. 10.2. This was, in essence, a Le Fort III, with a fronto-orbital advancement at the same time.*

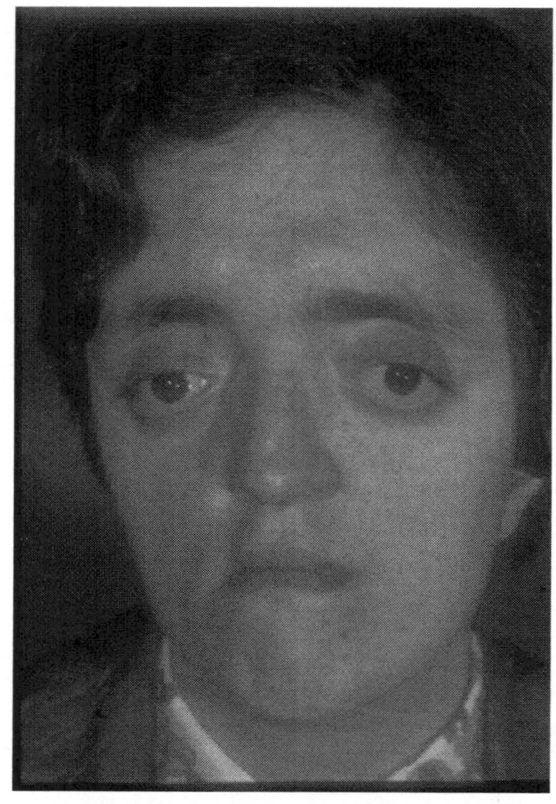

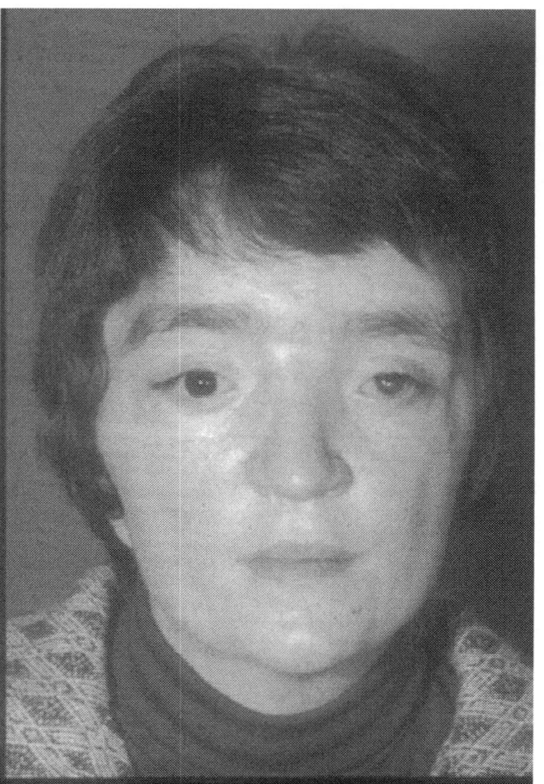

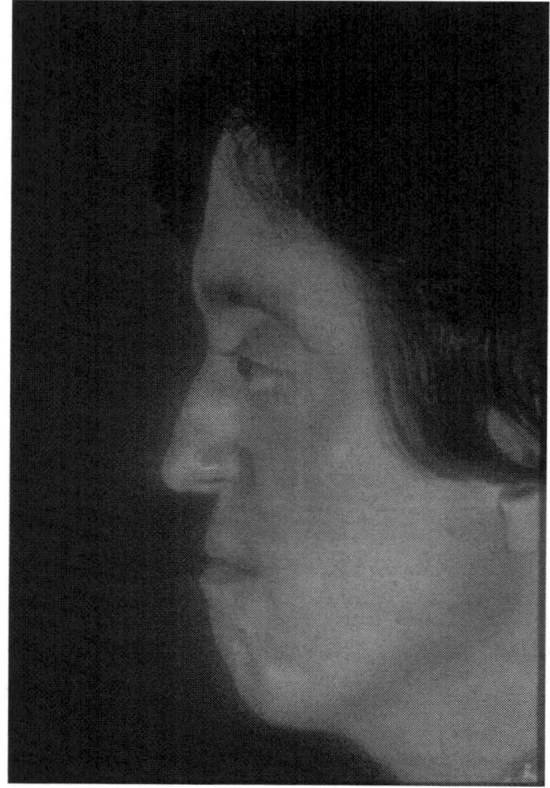

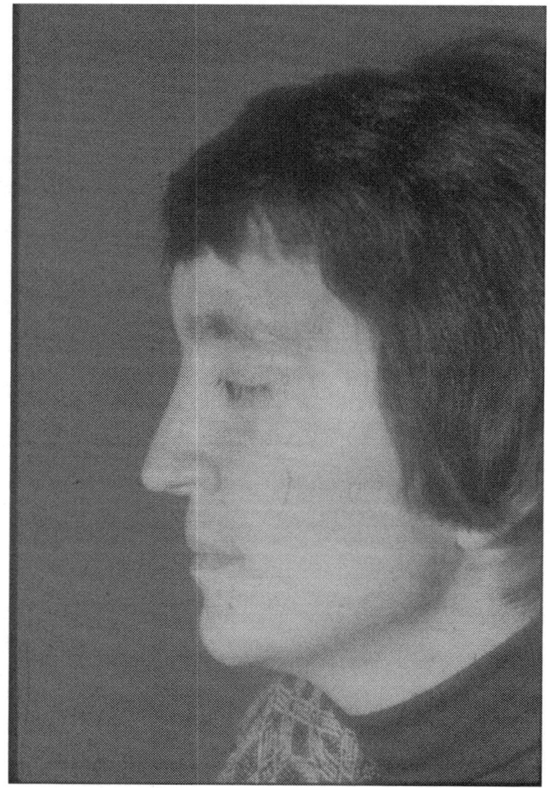

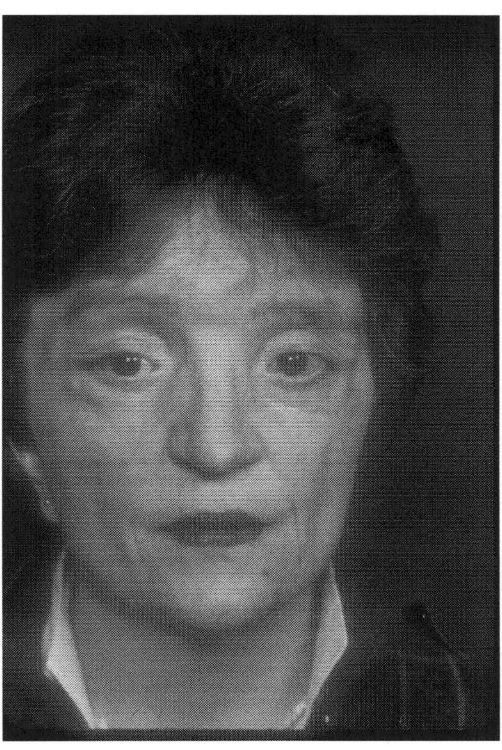

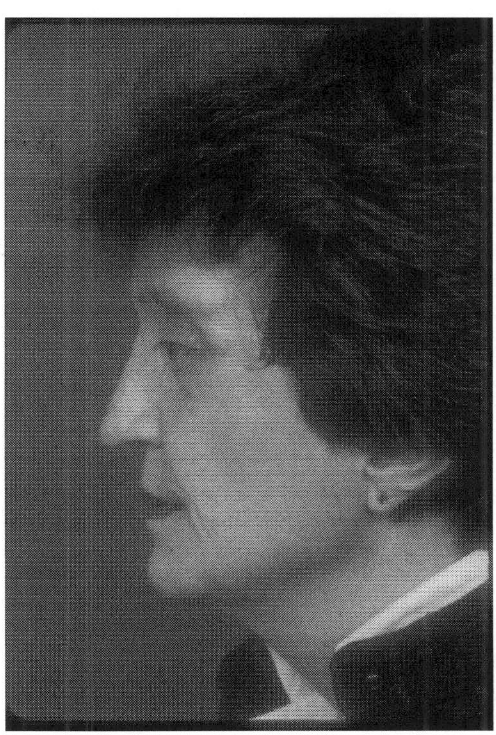

*Fig. 10.5 Patient with Crouzon's disease who was treated with the "BO-FORT" procedure in the mid- 1960s. The early result is shown, and the thirty-year post-operative result shows excellent stability. However, there were a few infections in the first six of these done, so Tessier placed the procedure on the "back burner."*

*Fig. 10.6 Paul Tessier and his good friend Fernando-Ortiz Monasterio enjoying each other in Mexico City, ca. 1985. Fernando's late wife, "Pollito," is to Tessier's left. Fernando, and his junior associate, Antonio Fuente del Campo, published the first report of a true "monobloc" advancement, where the outer orbit was advanced with the midface in one piece and not two, as Tessier had done with the "BO-FORT" procedure. Tessier had been concerned that moving the entire circumference of the orbit–since the orbit in the cases was congenitally small—might push on the globe during advancement. Antonio and Fernando showed that this was not the case, and Tessier took to the new procedure like a duck to water—and he was always careful to give Fernando credit for introducing the procedure. This is one of the few core procedures of craniofacial surgery not developed by Tessier, but once he recognized its value, he went on to do the procedure better than anyone.*

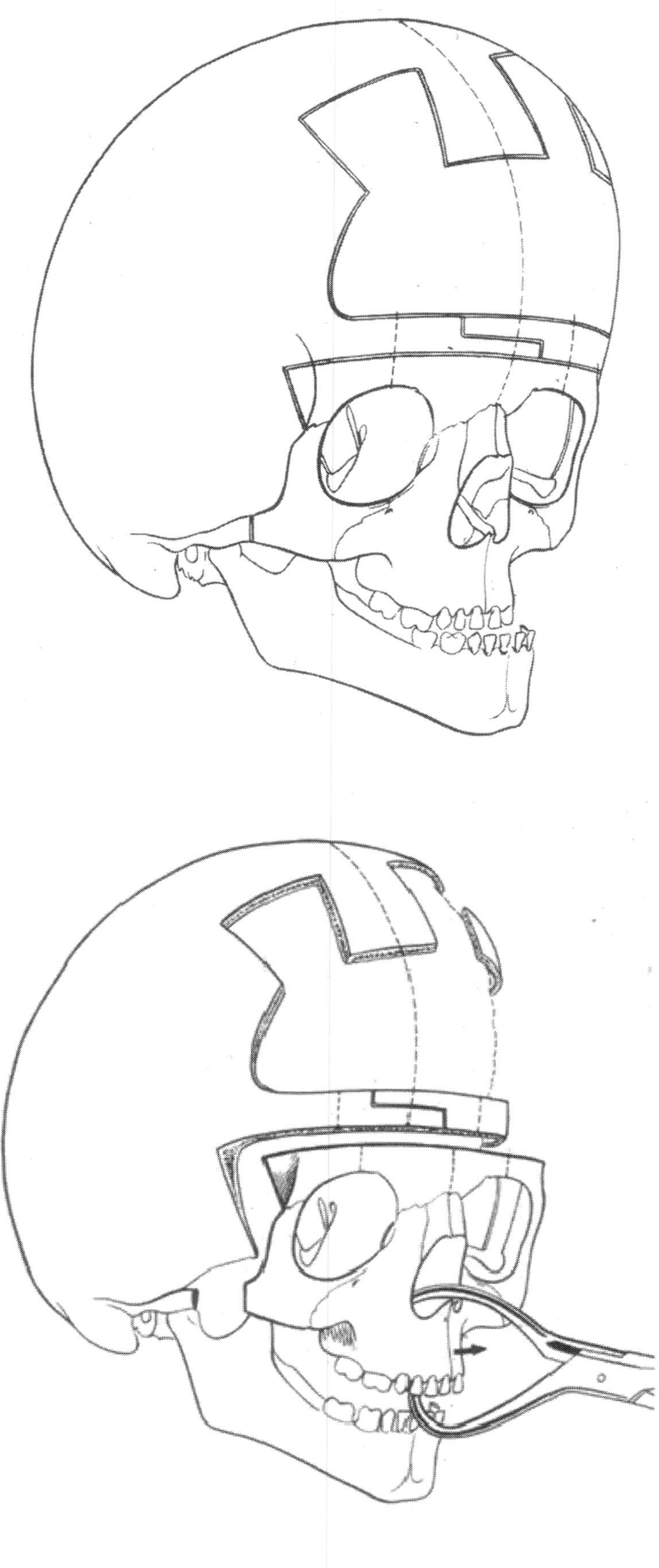

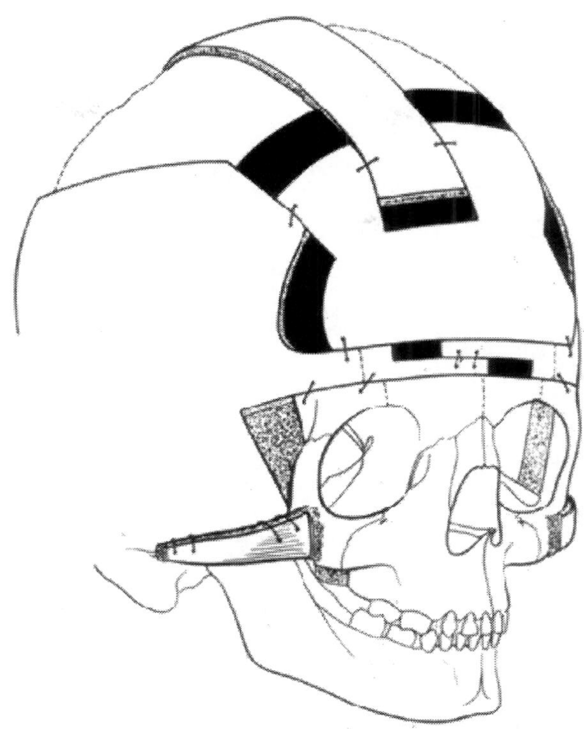

*Fig. 10.7 One of the methods of monobloc fronto-facial advancement developed by Paul Tessier. He is expanding the frontal bandeau to provide a fixed structure to which he could attach the advanced midface and frontal bones. This is bone carpentry at its best.*

Illustration of expansile bandeau technique in a two-year-old child with Apert's syndrome

CHIRURGIE ORTHOGNATIQUE

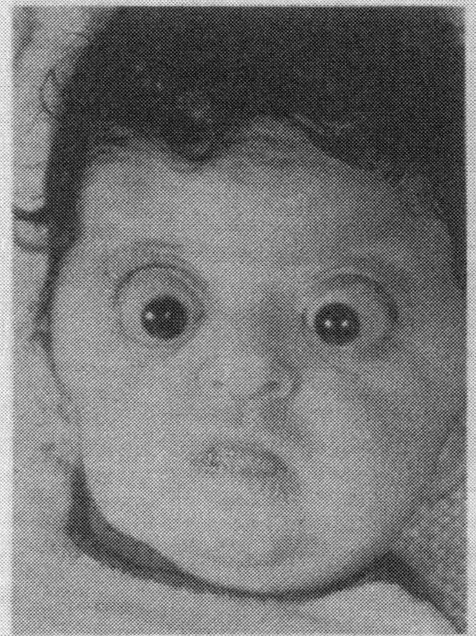

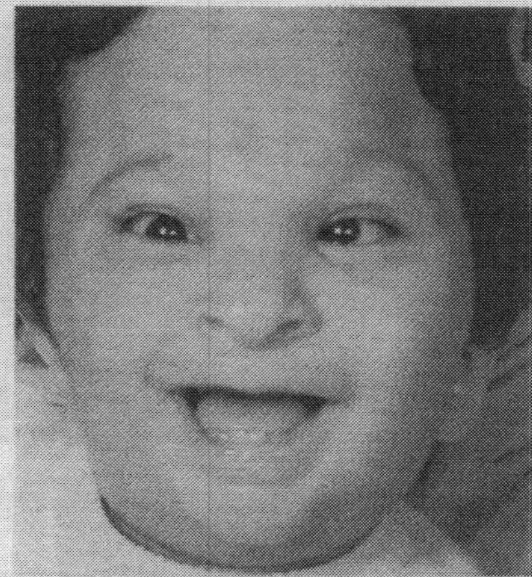

Fig. 6 a-b - Cranio-faciosténose type syndrome d'Apert ayant entrainé une hypoplasie considérable du massif facial avec sévère exophtalmie.

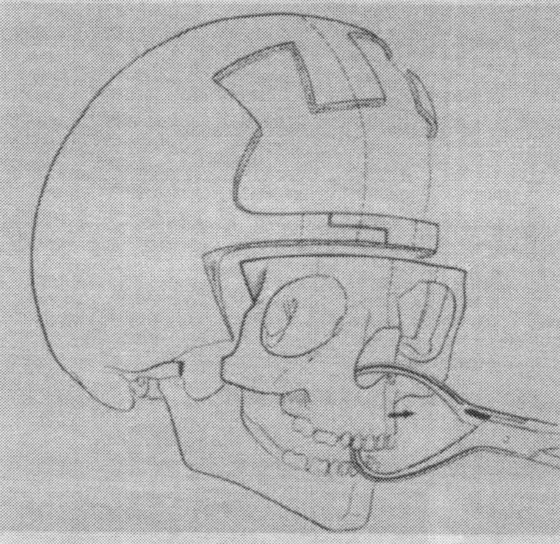

c-d - Schémas illustrant l'avancement fronto-facial et la stabilisation par des greffes osseuses.

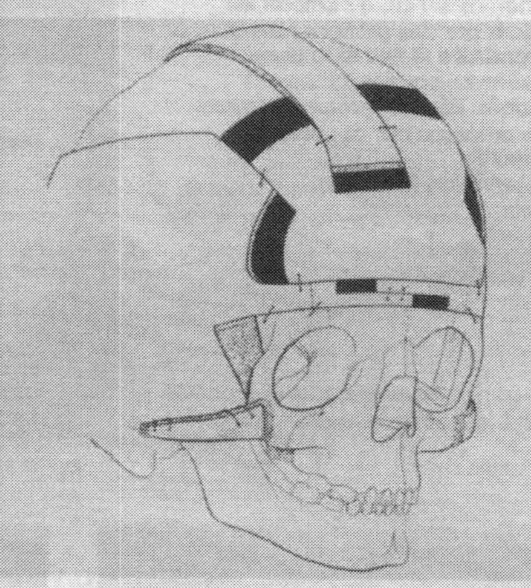

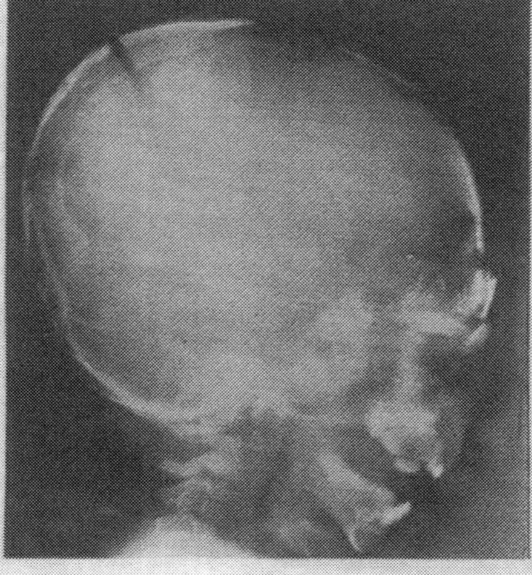

e - Après avancement du massif fronto-facial et greffes osseuses à l'âge de 2 ans. L'énophtalmie est intégralement corrigée. (observation P. Tessier).

*A PARAITRE EN MAI*
**3ème et dernière partie**

**LES OBJECTIFS ORTHOGNATIQUES**

**Esthétiques** : J.F. Tulasne

**Parodontaux :**
J.M. Dersot et J.L. Giovannoli

**Cranio-mandibulaires :**
C. Mannai et A. Sanial.

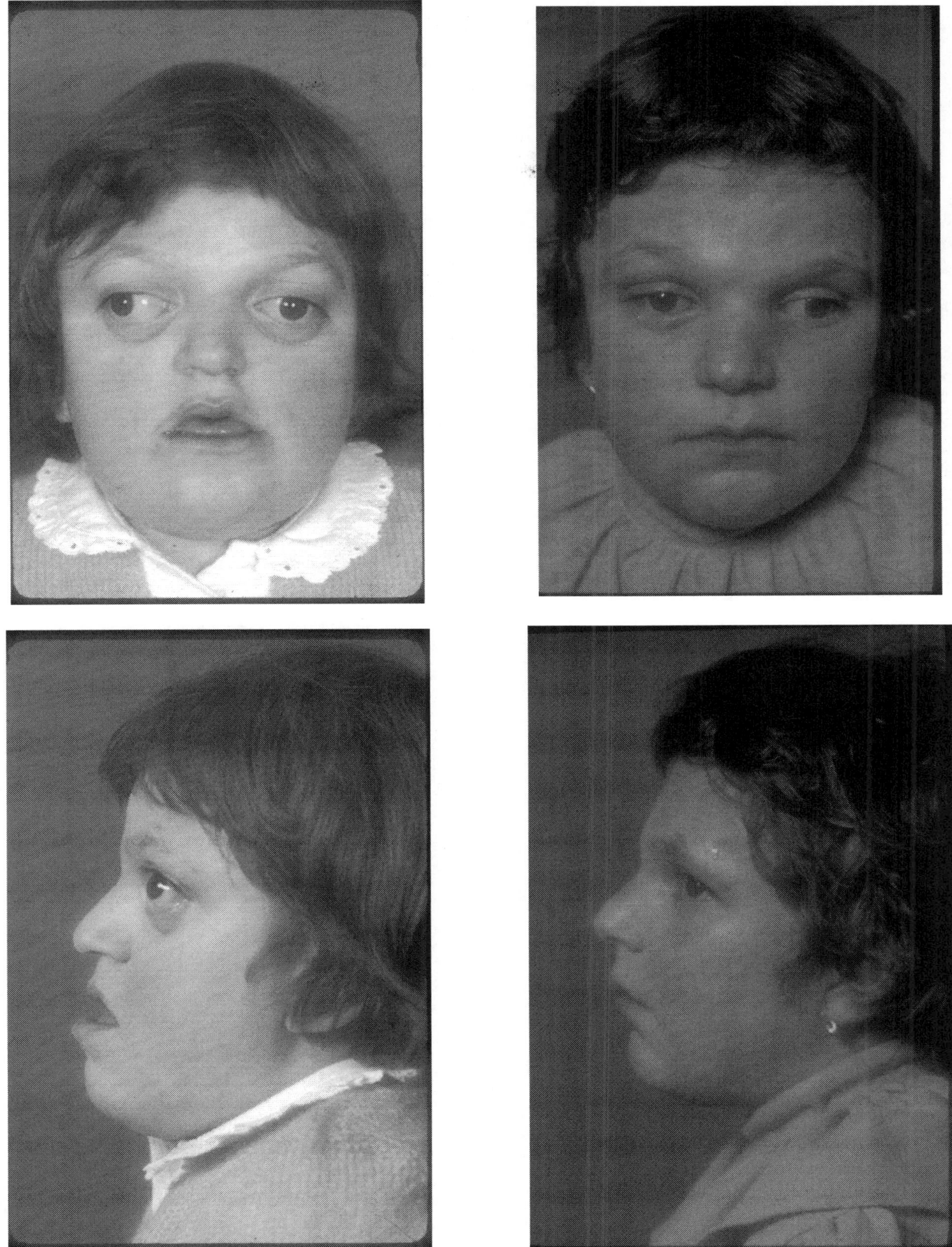

*Fig. 10.8 Patient with Crouzon's disease treated by Tessier with a transcranial monobloc frontofacial advancement (M.F.F.A.) in the early 1980s. The patient is normal post-operatively, which she would not have been with the Le Fort III-type osteotomy.*

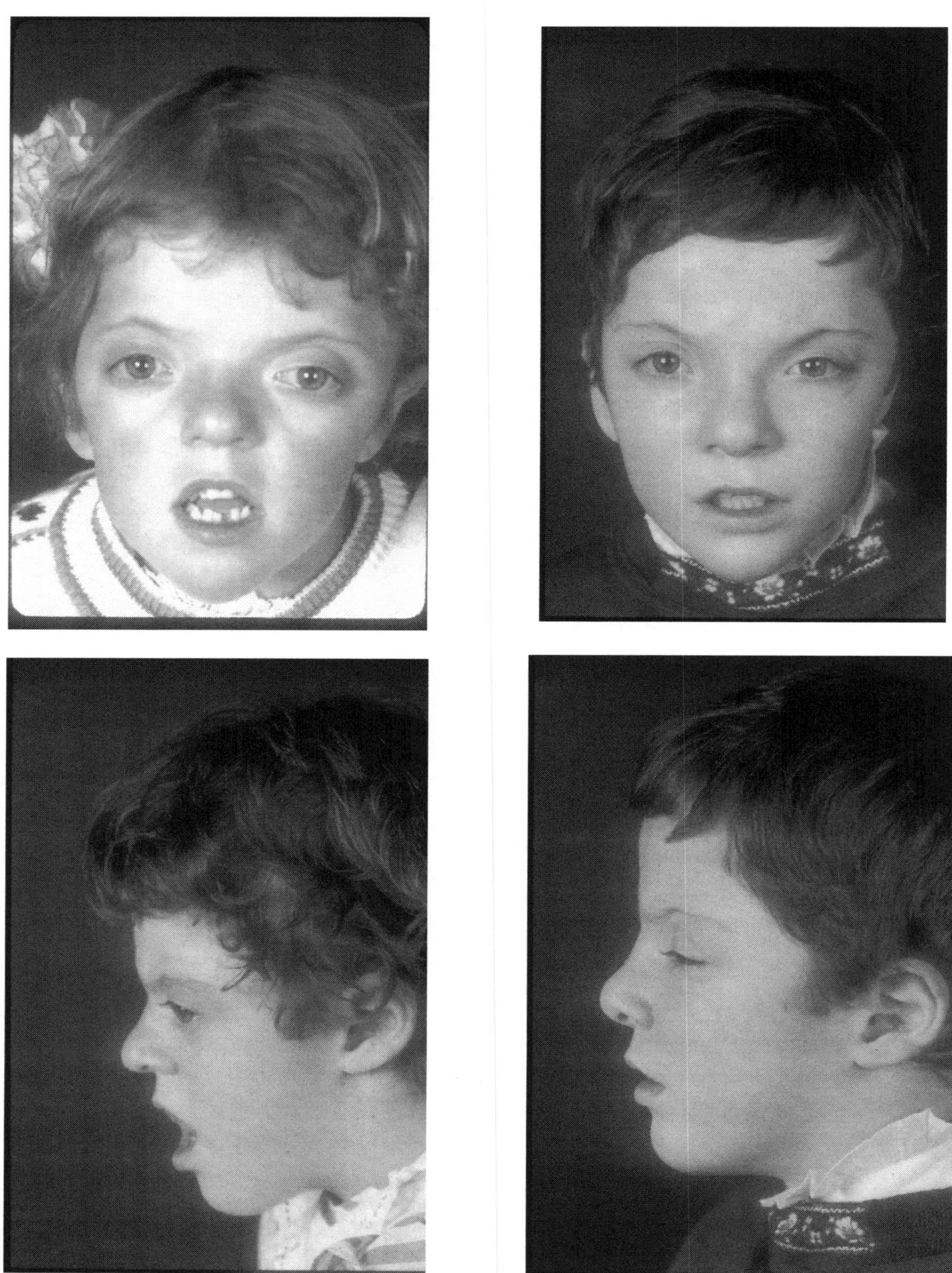

*Fig. 10.9 Another young patient with Crouzon's disease with a result close to normal except for mild orbital hypertelorism, mid-1980s.*

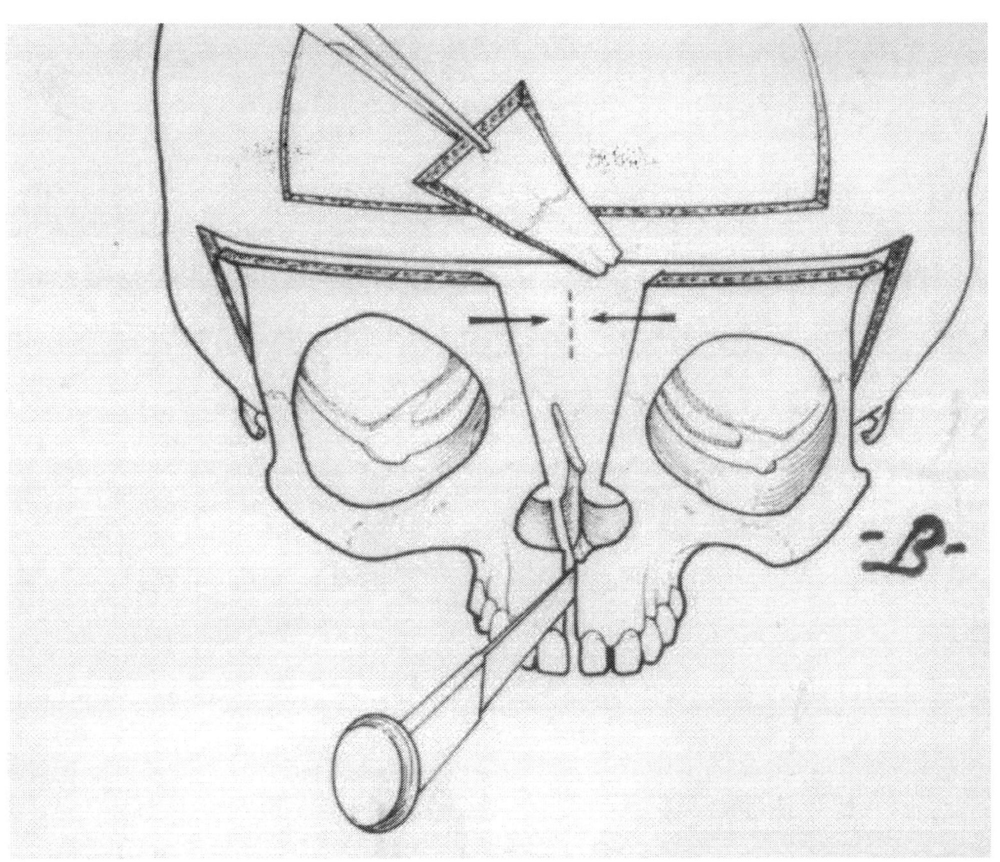
-B-

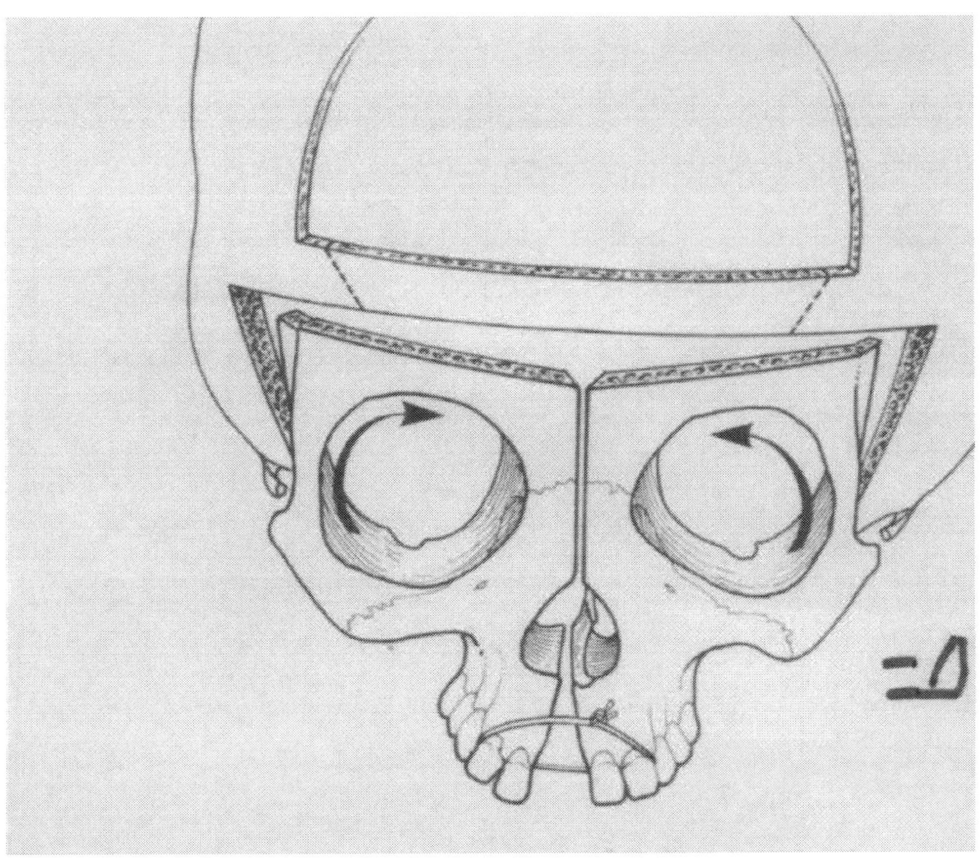
-D

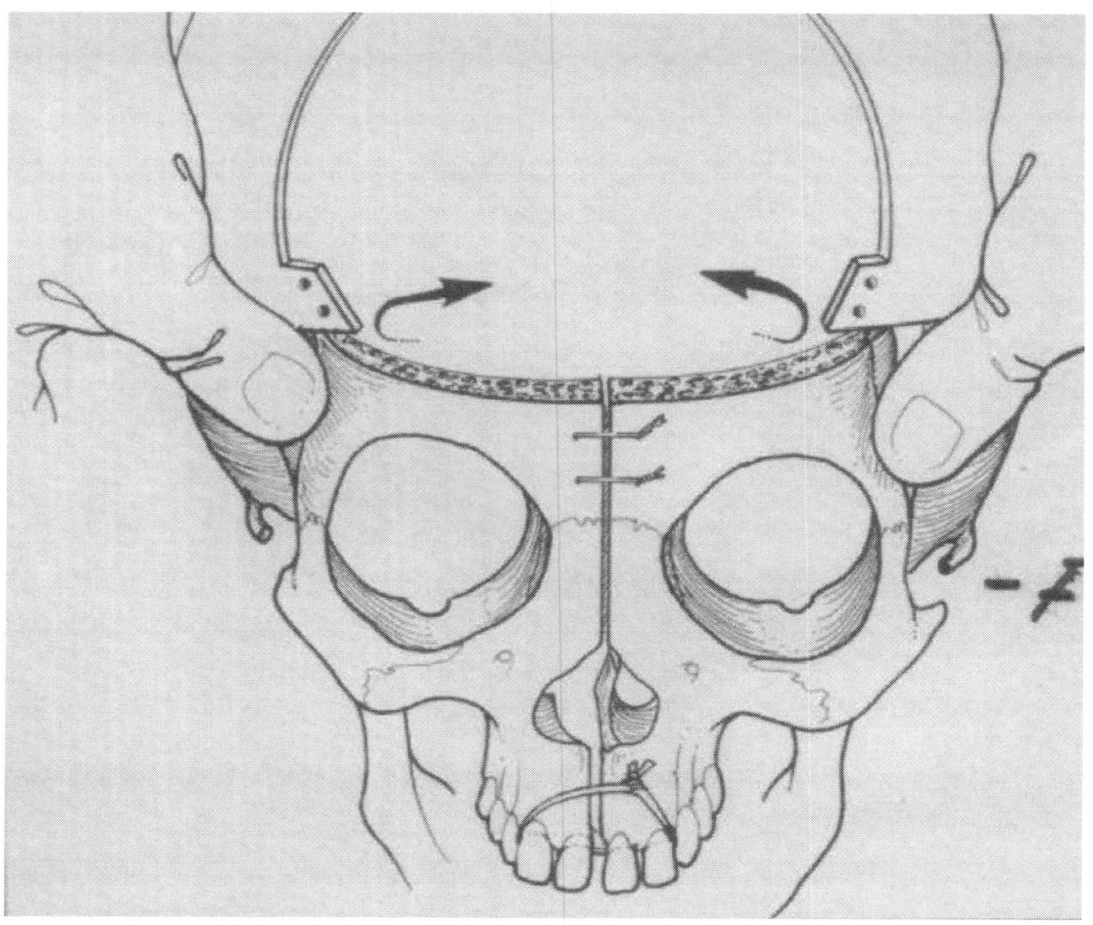

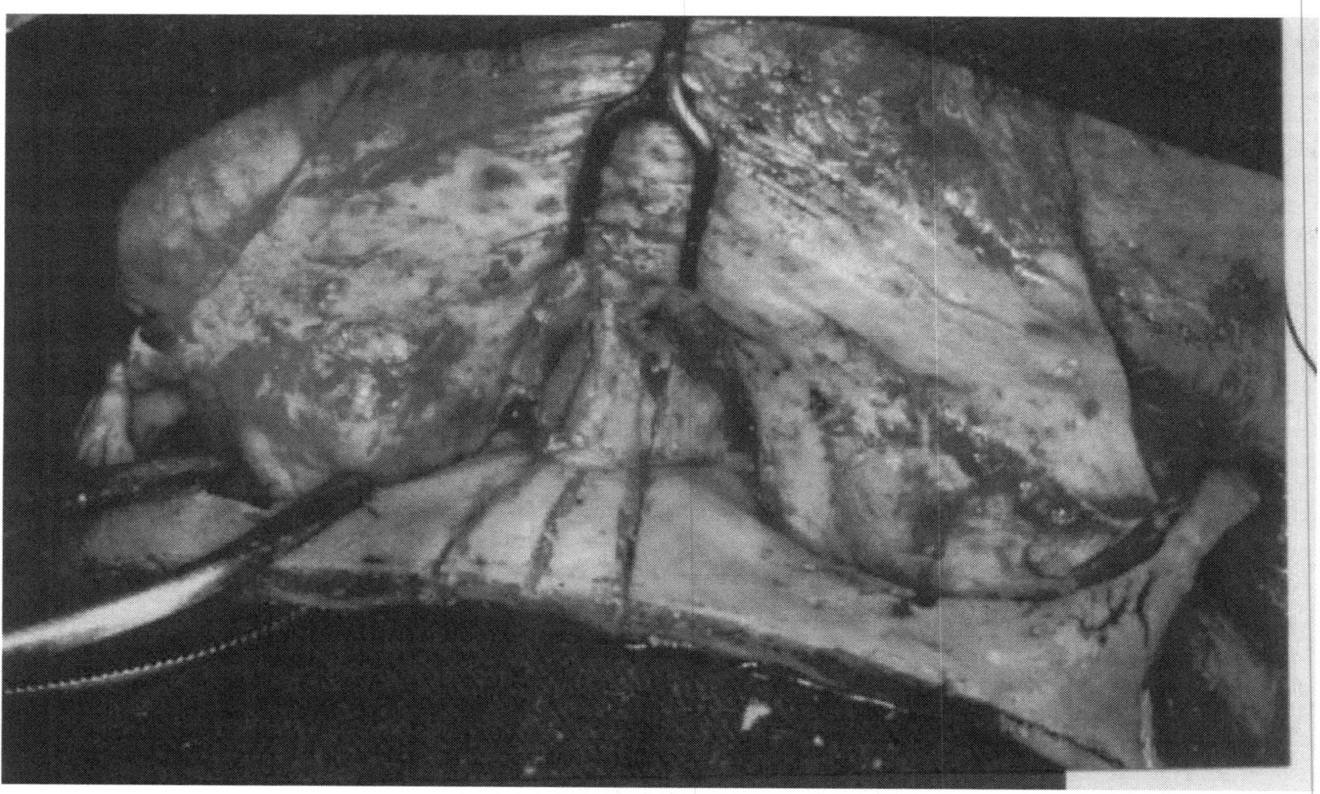

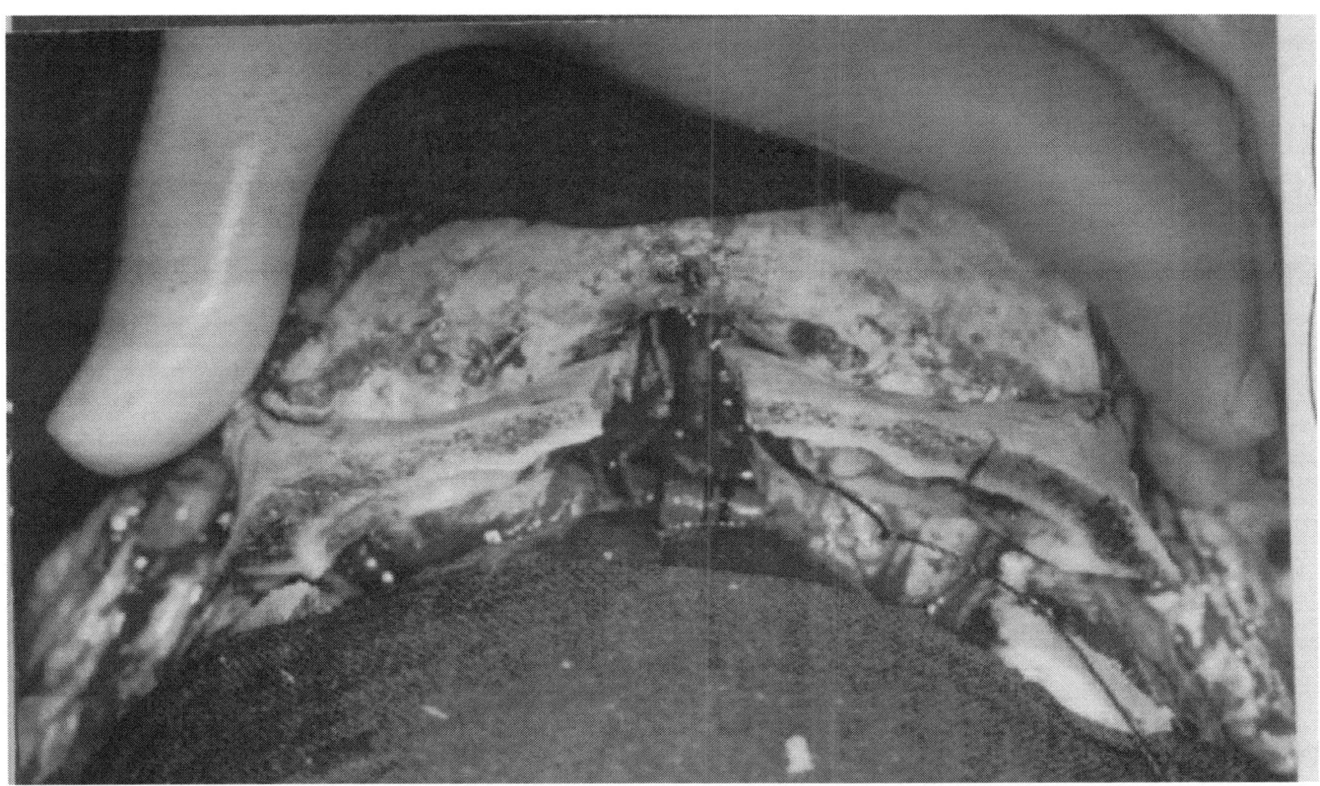

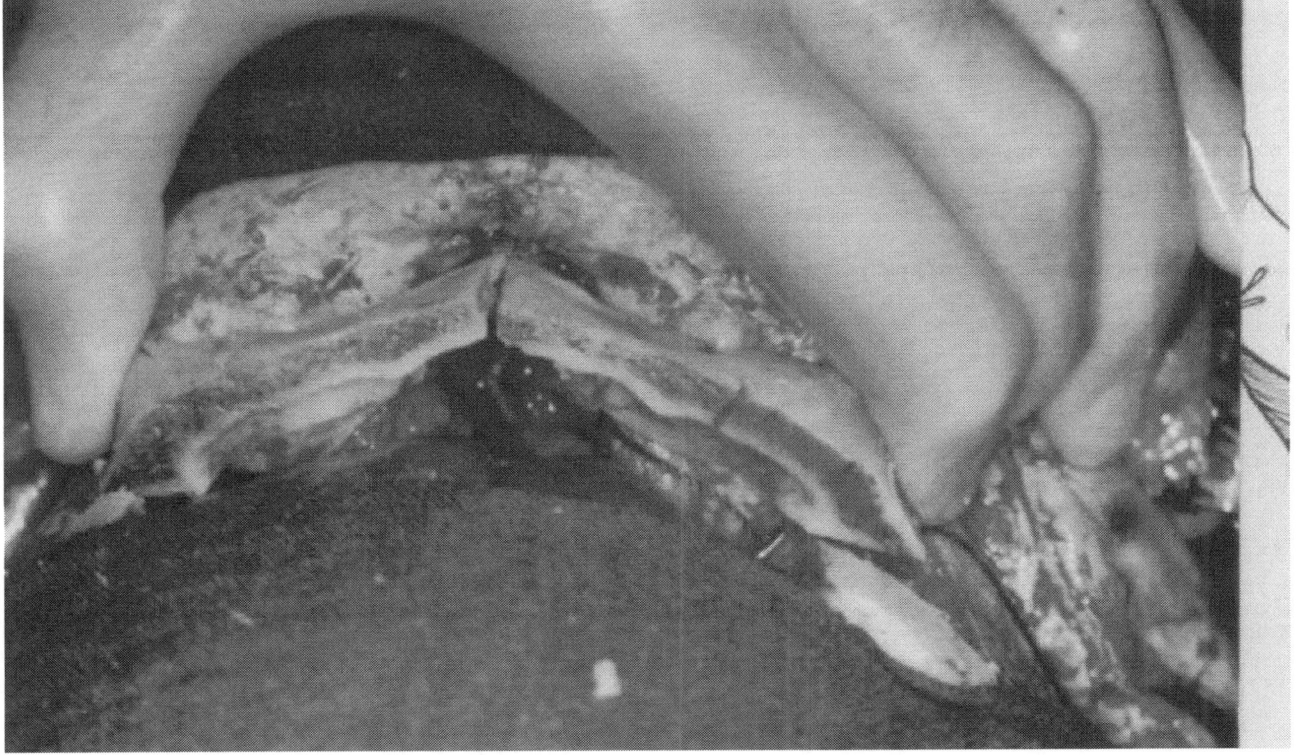

*Fig. 10.10 M.B.F.F.A with facial bipartition, which also corrected the hypertelorism. In patients with Apert's syndrome, the forehead and midface are flat, and if one makes a new frontal bandeau with proper curvature, the midface can be "bent," as illustrated, to correct this portion of the Apert deformity.*

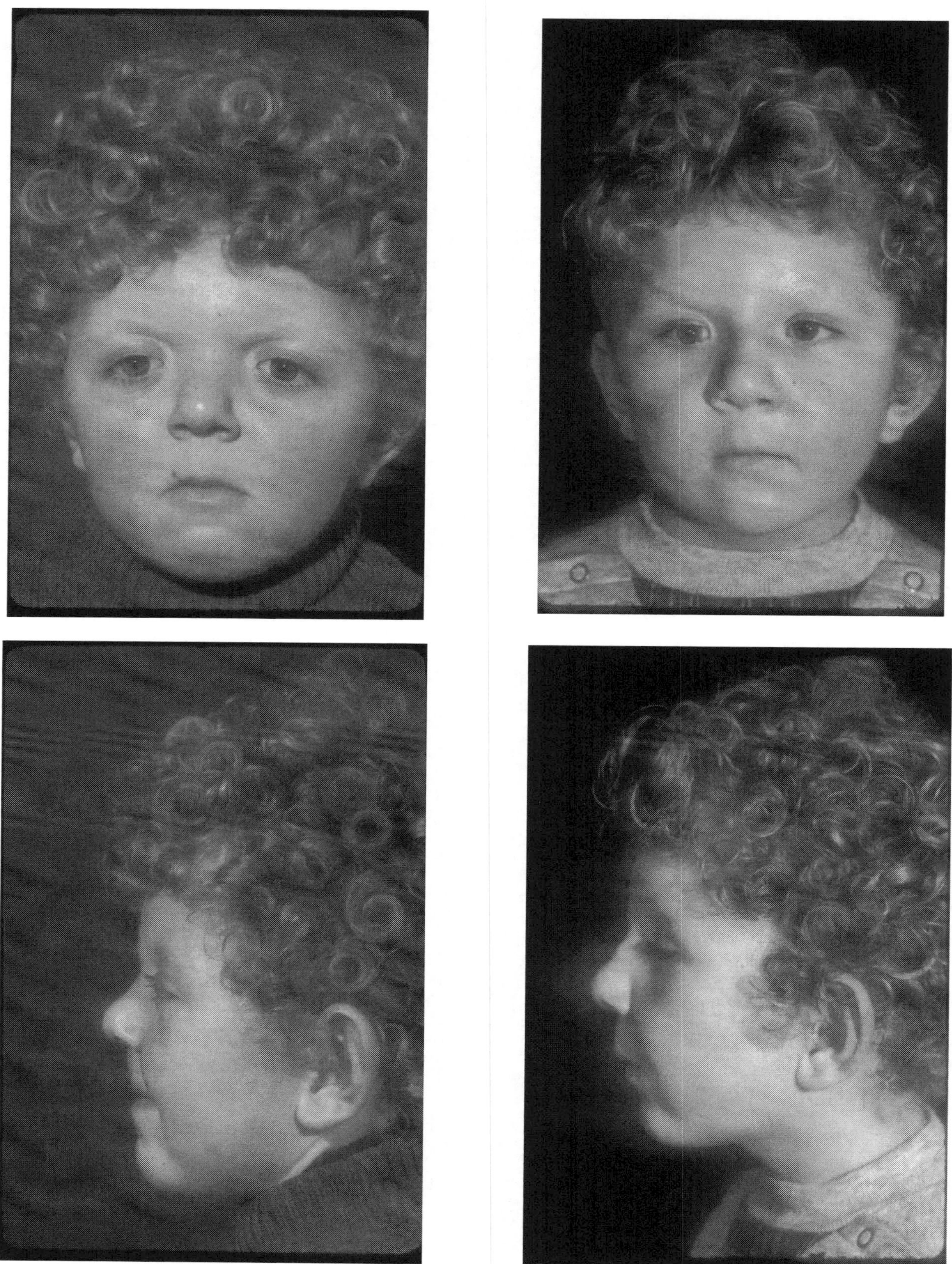

*Fig. 10.11 Young boy with Apert's syndrome, before and after M.B.F.F.A. (plus facial bipartition and correction of the hypertelorism and bending of the midface). Except for the minimal malposiiton of the right medial canthus, he has created a normal face for this child.*

- Sphenoethmoidofrontal encephalocoeles.
- Treacher Collins syndrome: initially ribs, then cranial bone, for construction of the missing cheekbones; later developed the integral procedure, which rotated the midface (lengthening the posterior portion of the upper jaw and the lower jaw, which, besides the missing cheekbones, is part of the malformation).
- Orbito-ocular clefts and other rare facial clefts.
- The arrhinias.

Other contributions:

- The Barron-Tessier flap for intraoral reconstruction.

  John Barron of Salisbury, England had described subcutaneous island flaps in facial reconstruction where a circular portion of tissue was cut free with only some underlying soft tissue connections, then moved to another area to fill a defect. Tessier's contribution was the use of a large paddle of skin from over the clavicle which could be provided circulation through the platysma, a thin muscle and fascia layer immediately below the cervical skin; this tissue could then be moved into the mouth. Tessier, with characteristic and insistent modesty, attached Barron's name to the flap as well, even though Barron never performed the procedure.
- Using the BT and other flaps, along with bone grafting methods that he had developed, he pioneered new methods of reconstruction for ballistic injuries. Much of this experience was gained operating in Iran and Iraq, after their war, and could be applied to civilian casualties as well.
- Methods of harvesting bone grafts:

  Tessier showed plastic surgeons how to harvest and work with bone from the hip, ribs, and, later, skull, and he developed a number of instruments specifically designed to make this easy

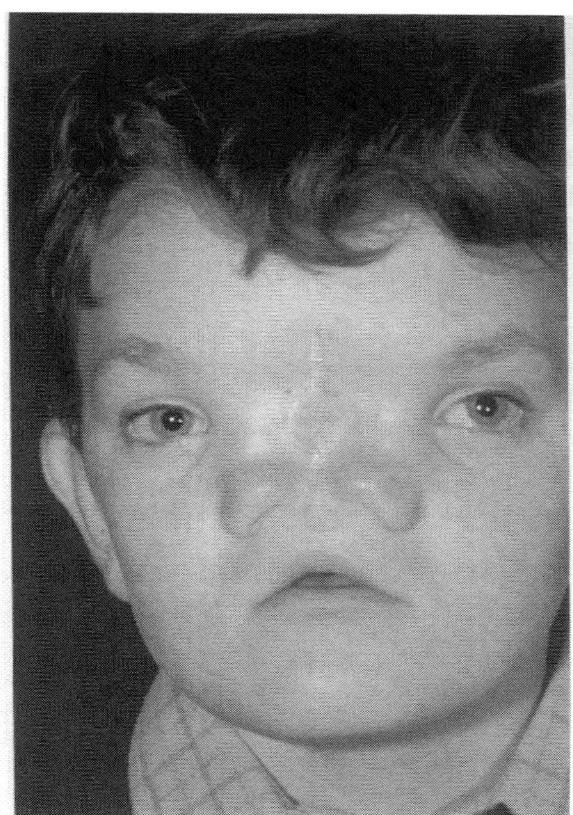

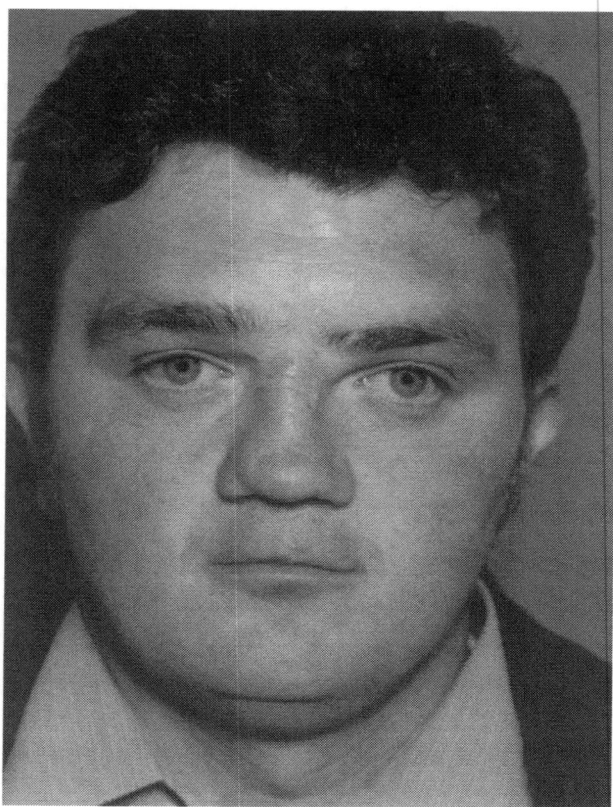

*Fig. 10.12 Burgaud as a boy with wide orbital hypertelorism (62 mm between the orbits, rather than a normal distance of around 20 mm due to No. 0-14 cleft), and as an adult after transcranial correction and nasal correction with iliac bone graft, conchal cartilage grafts, and a forehead flap.*

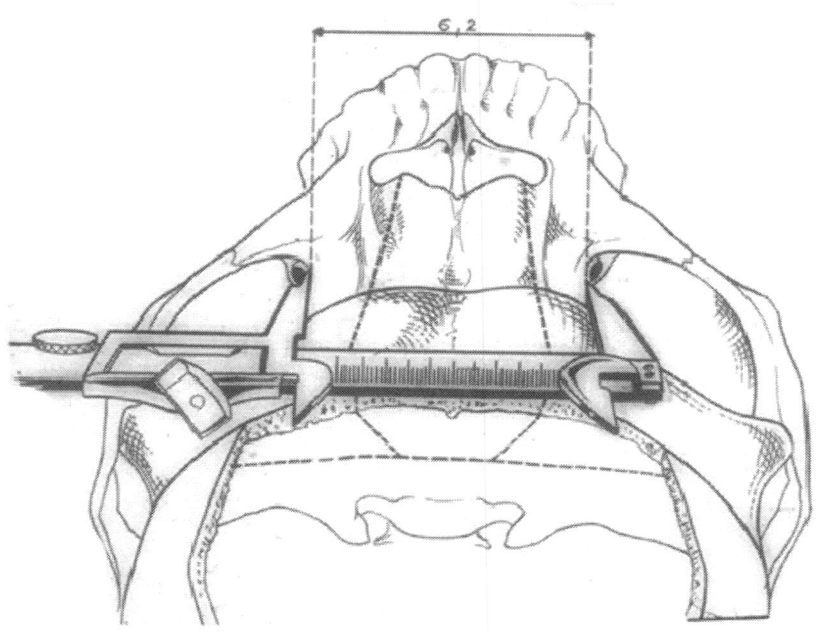


*Fig. 10-13 Francine Gourdin drawing showing calipers measuring interorbital distance at its narrowest point, just above the lacrimal fossa.*

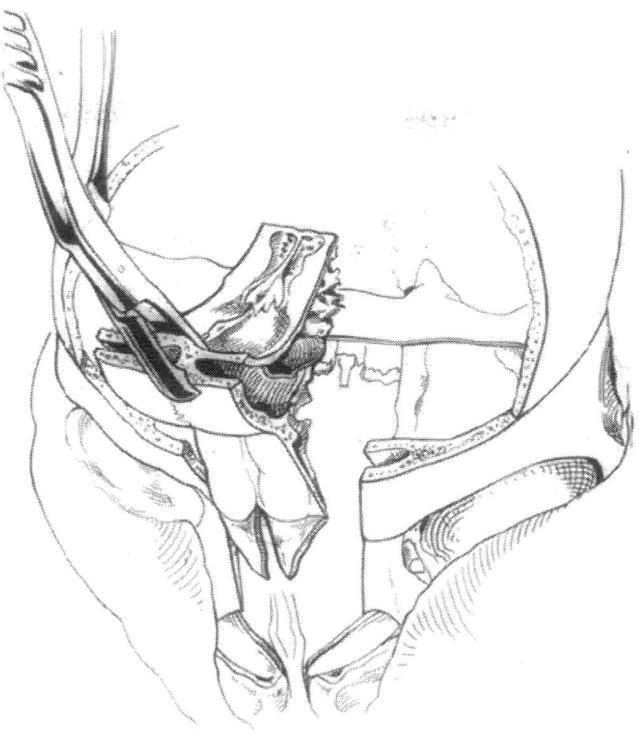

*Fig. 10.14 Bone clamp removing the bone segment-containing cranial base with entire cribriform plate, ethmoid, and nasal bones.*

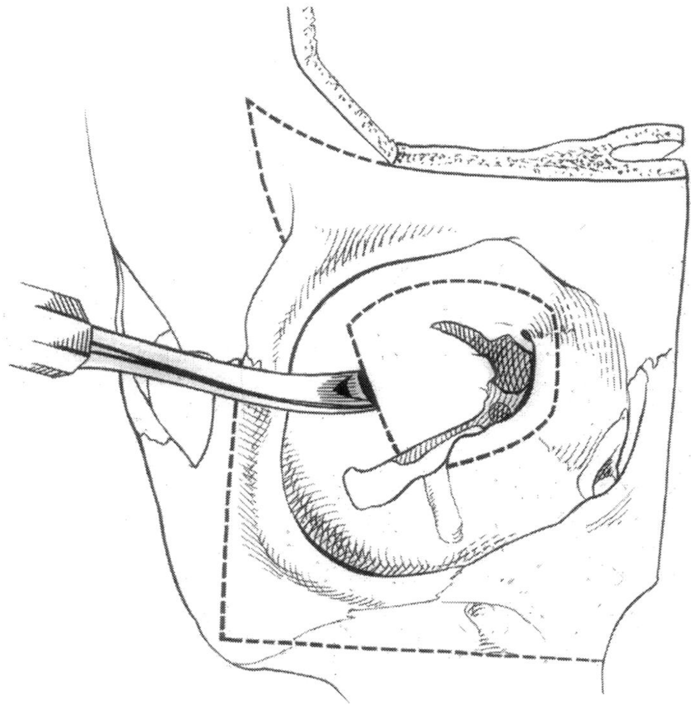

*Fig. 10.15 Internal orbital osteotomy extends into inferior orbital fissure inferiorly and is circumferential. When the external orbital osteotomies are complete, the bony box of the orbit can be moved, carrying the eyeball with it. The posterior portion of the optic pedicle, with the origins of the extraocular muscles and the optic nerve, does not move.*

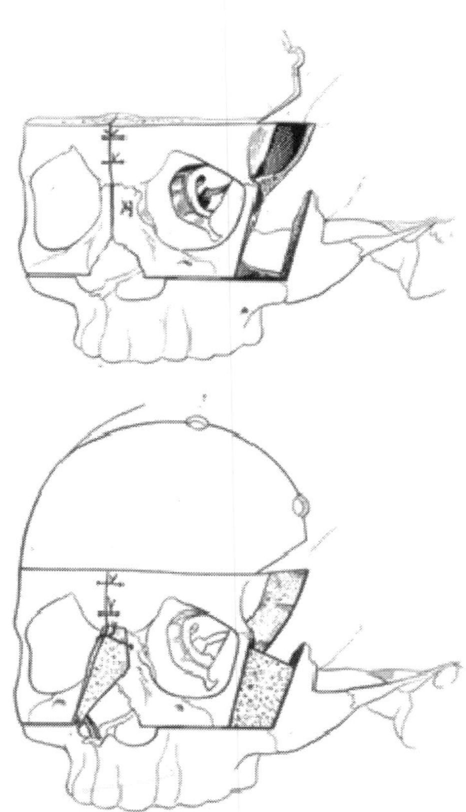

*Fig. 10.16 After medial translocation of the orbital segments and nasal and zygomatic bone grafts.*

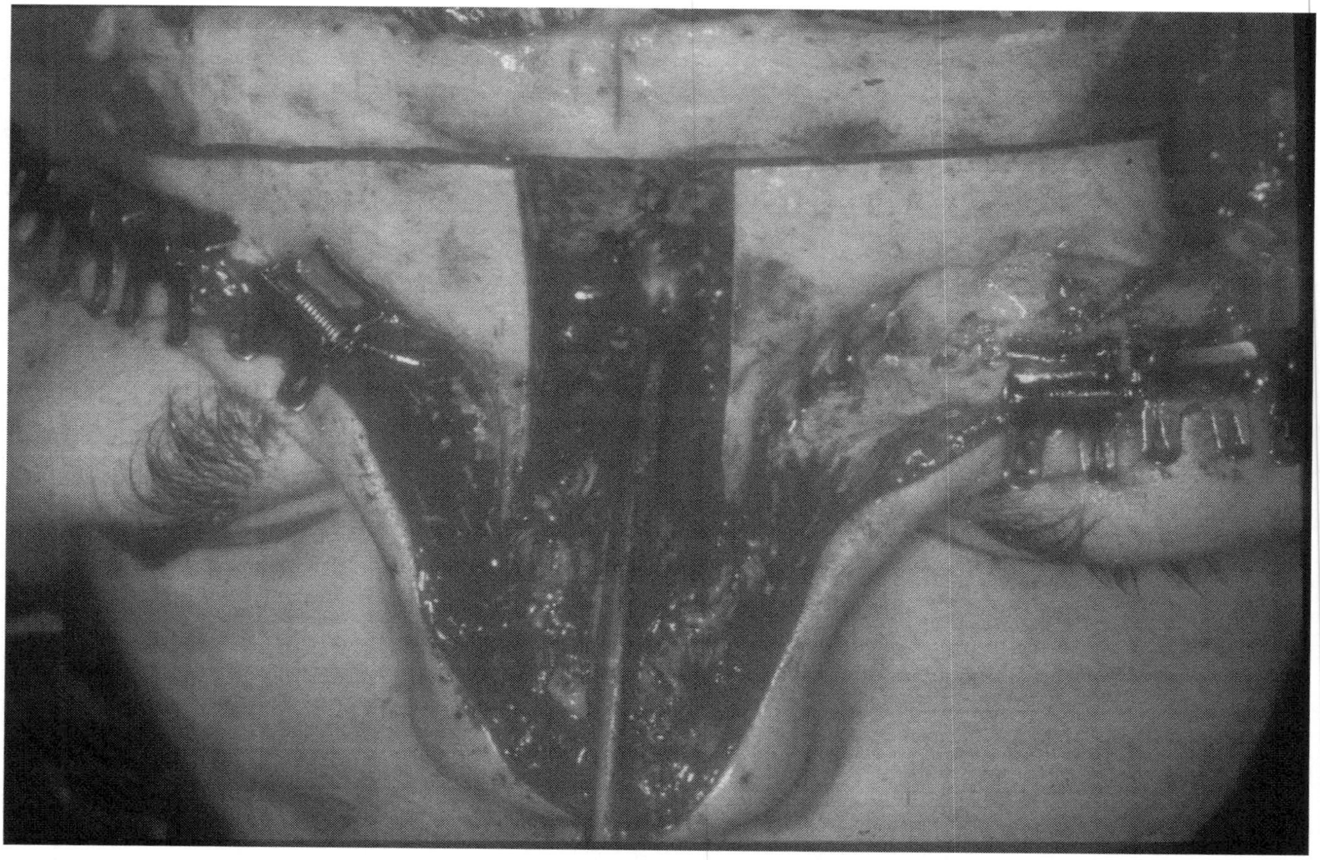

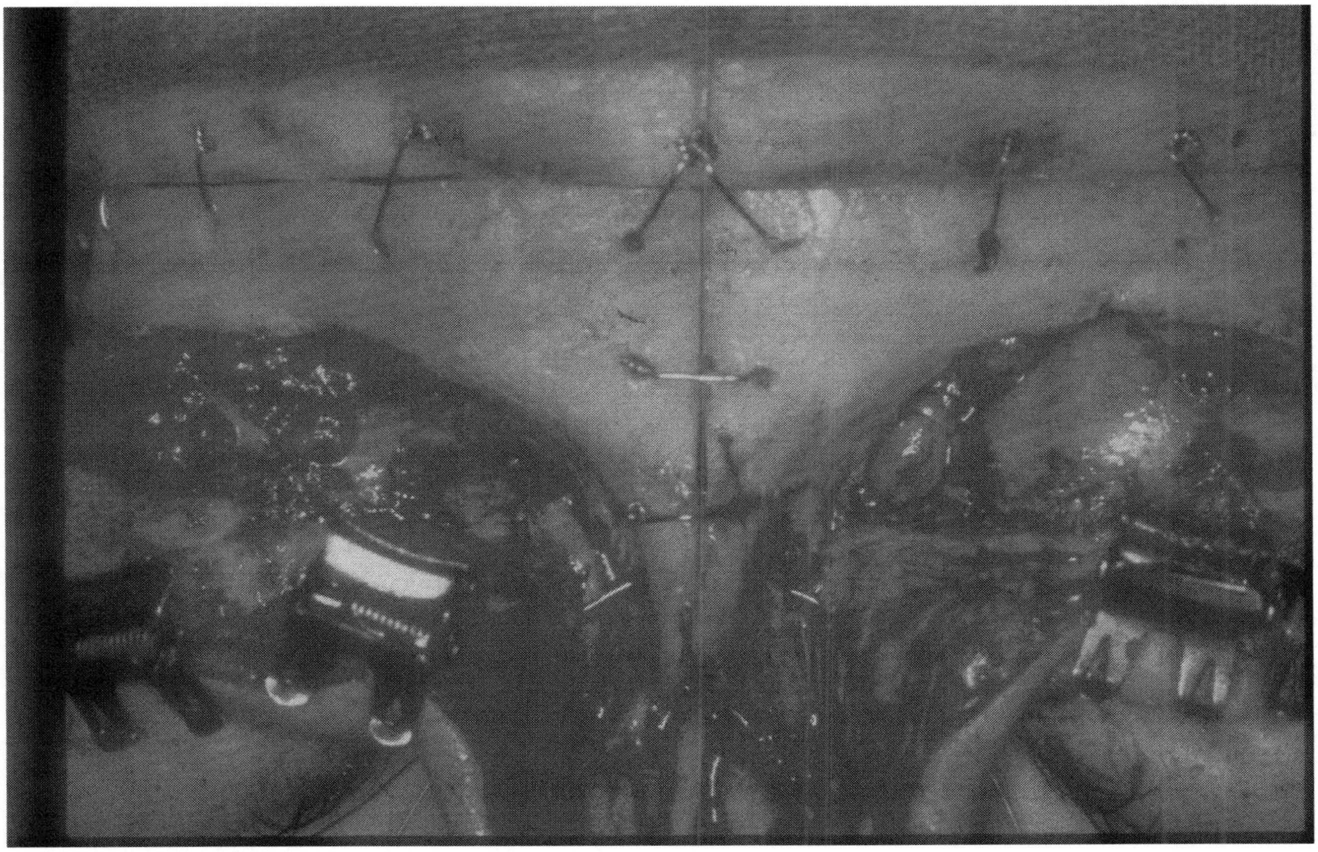

*Fig. 10.17 Operative photos of Burgaud showing the precision of Tessier's bone work. The frontal bandeau, a Tessier innovation, has been scored to register the midline. The interorbital distance has been overcorrected to something in the range of 12 mm, and transnasal medial canthopexy wires are evident.*

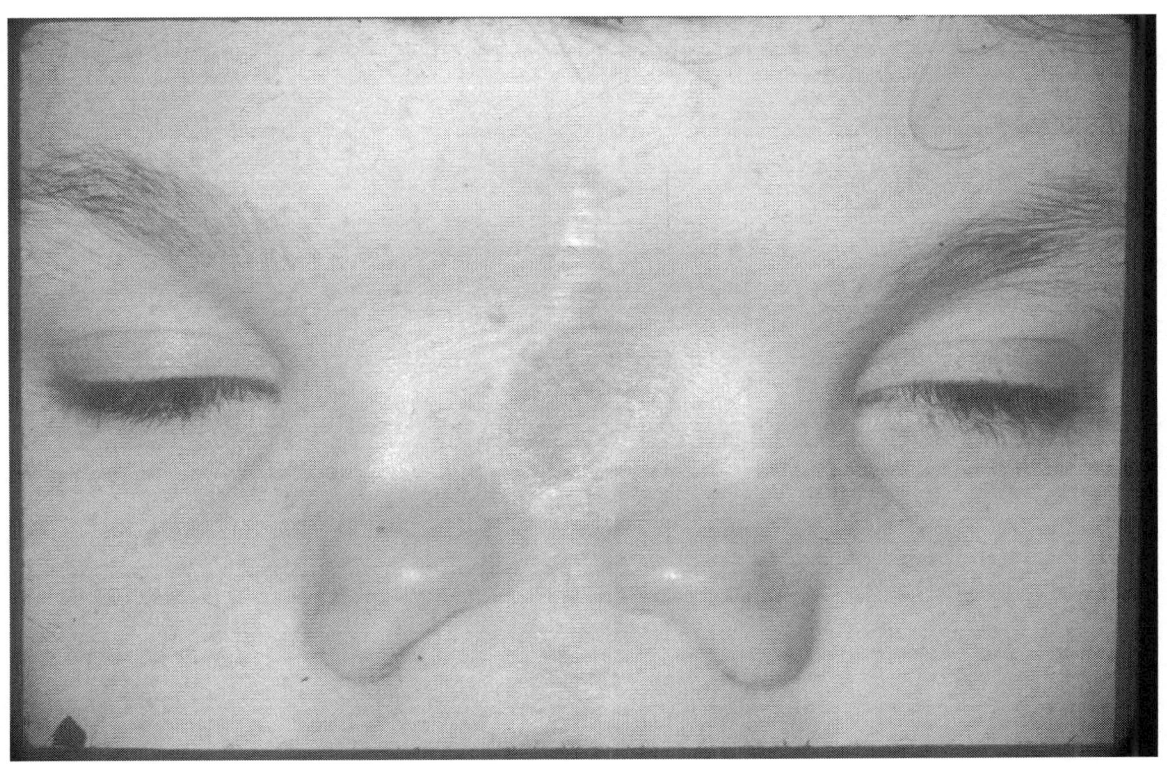

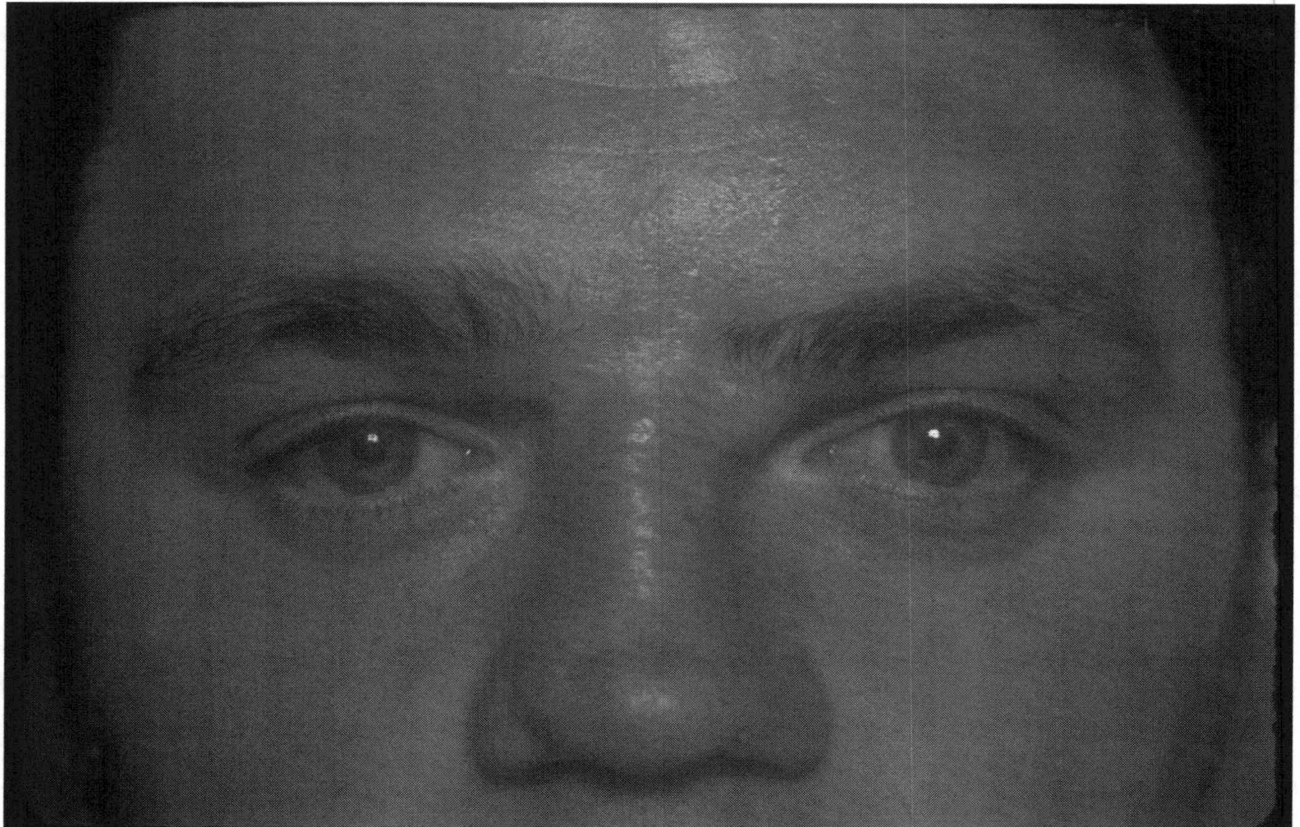

*Fig. 10.18 Pre- and post-op photos of Burgaud. This case, done in the early 1970s, is the best reported result of hypertelorism correction ever.*

Orbital hypertelorism means simply that the distance between the orbits is too great. Tessier often used the term "hypertelorbitism" (HTO) which he felt was semantically more correct, but which did not become widely accepted. He stressed that it was a *symptom*, and not a primary diagnosis. The HTO resulted from a facial cleft, such as in Burgaud, or other causes such as craniosynostosis (brachycephaly or bilateral coronal synostosis) or fronto-nasal dysplasia.

There were a number of technical innovations and concepts that he developed that made this radical type of procedure possible. First, there was "C.O.D." (DOC in French), circumferential orbital dissection. This had been something that he had often done in late trauma cases. Then, there was the introduction of the "effective orbit" concept, which meant that portion of the orbit, when moved, would carry the eyeball with it. Before Tessier's demonstration that this was possible, which began with Le Roy, no surgeon had tried this. After cutting the inner and outer perimeters of the orbit, a box was obtained, which, when moved, would move the globe in any direction—to the midline (HTO correction), apart (hypotelorism correction), and up or down (vertical orbital dystopia).

But what makes Burgaud such an extraordinary result, over thirty years later, is the quality of the individual parts of the operation: overcorrection of the orbits, the transnasal medial canthopexies, the bringing together of the eyebrows, and the nasal reconstruction.

Dr. Tessier once said—partly as a joke, but also with a certain truth to it—that HTO correction was nothing more than an extended rhinoplasty: the orbits were brought together so that the nasal reconstruction would look normal. Tessier conceptualized that, as in the Le Fort III-type osteotomy, the monobloc frontofacial advancement, with or without facial bipartition represented a radical surgical procedure that could make people with severe deformities look *normal*.

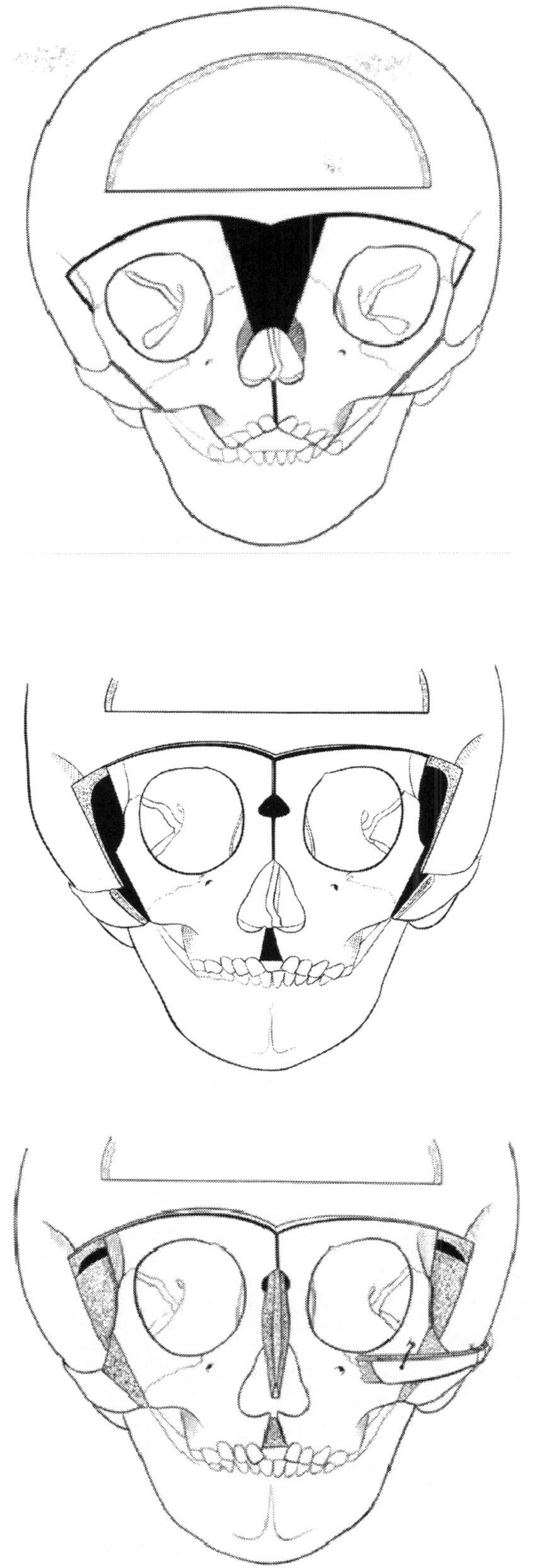

*Fig. 10.19 Another young patient with No. 0-14 cleft and orbital hypertelorism, corrected by a transcranial facial bipartition that also expanded the maxilla and became Tessier's preferred approach for HTO correction in children.*

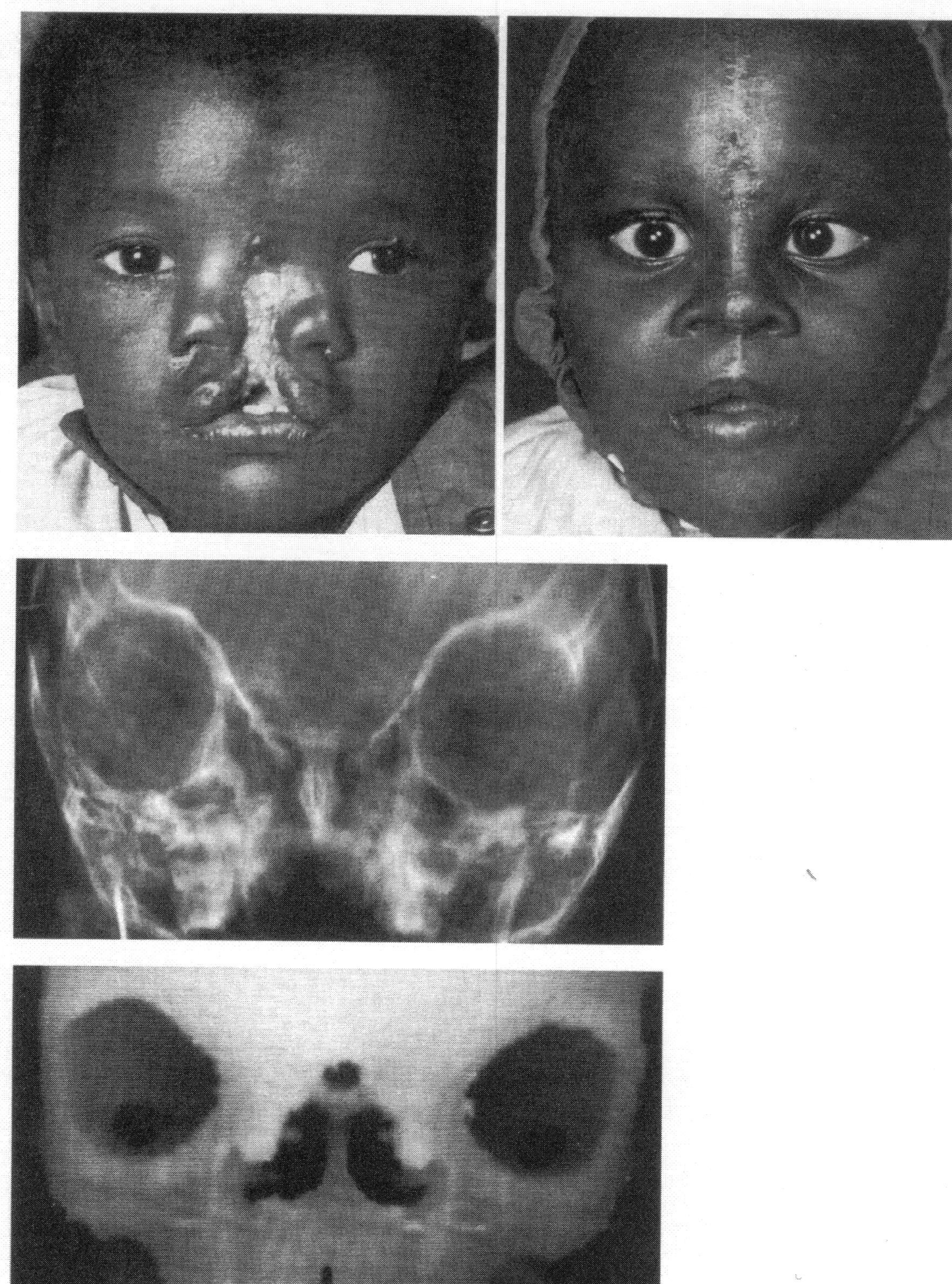



*Fig. 10.20 No. 0-14 cleft and HTO, corrected by transcranial facial bipartition. The mid-line forehead and nasal scar is unavoidable here.*

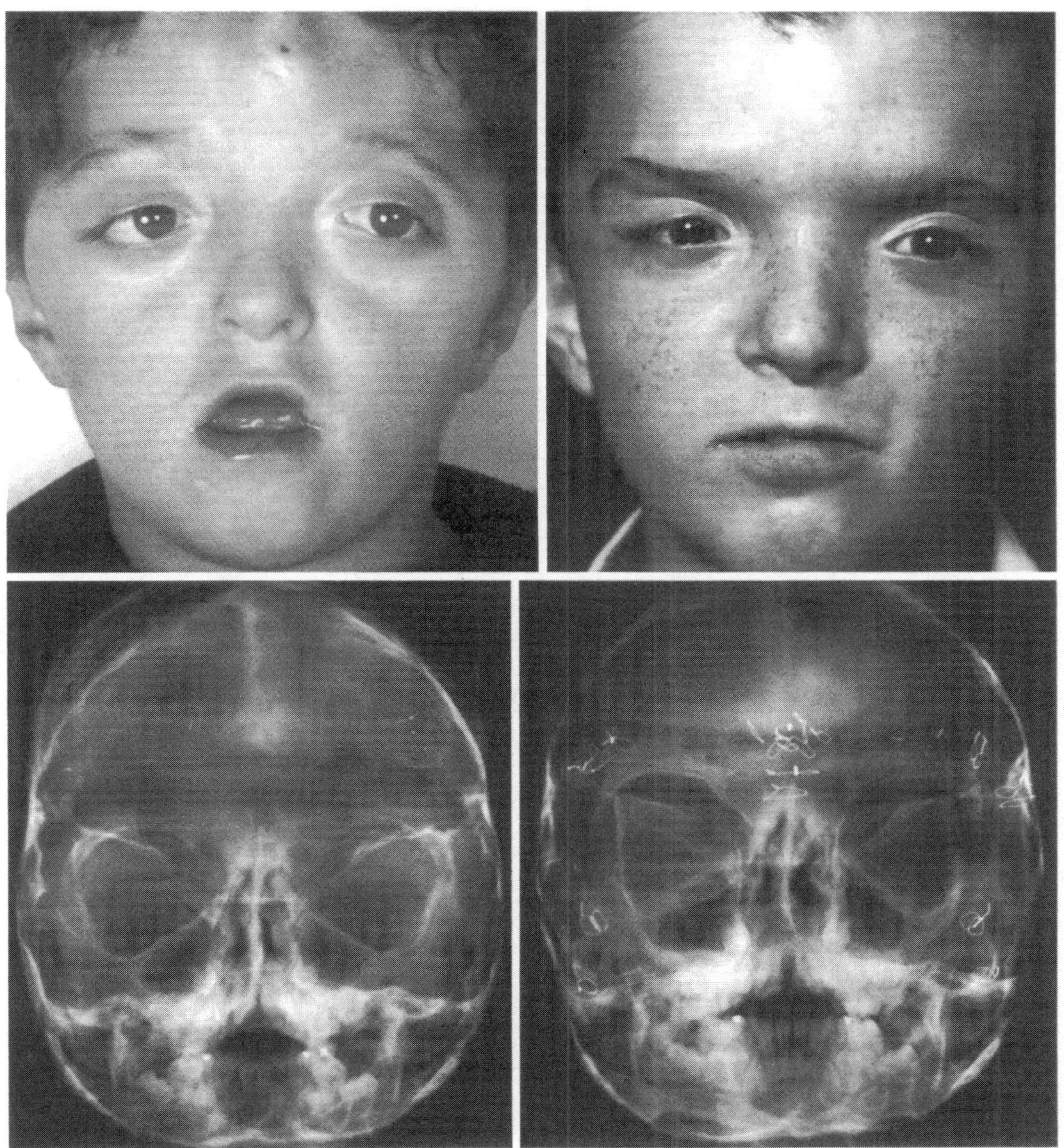

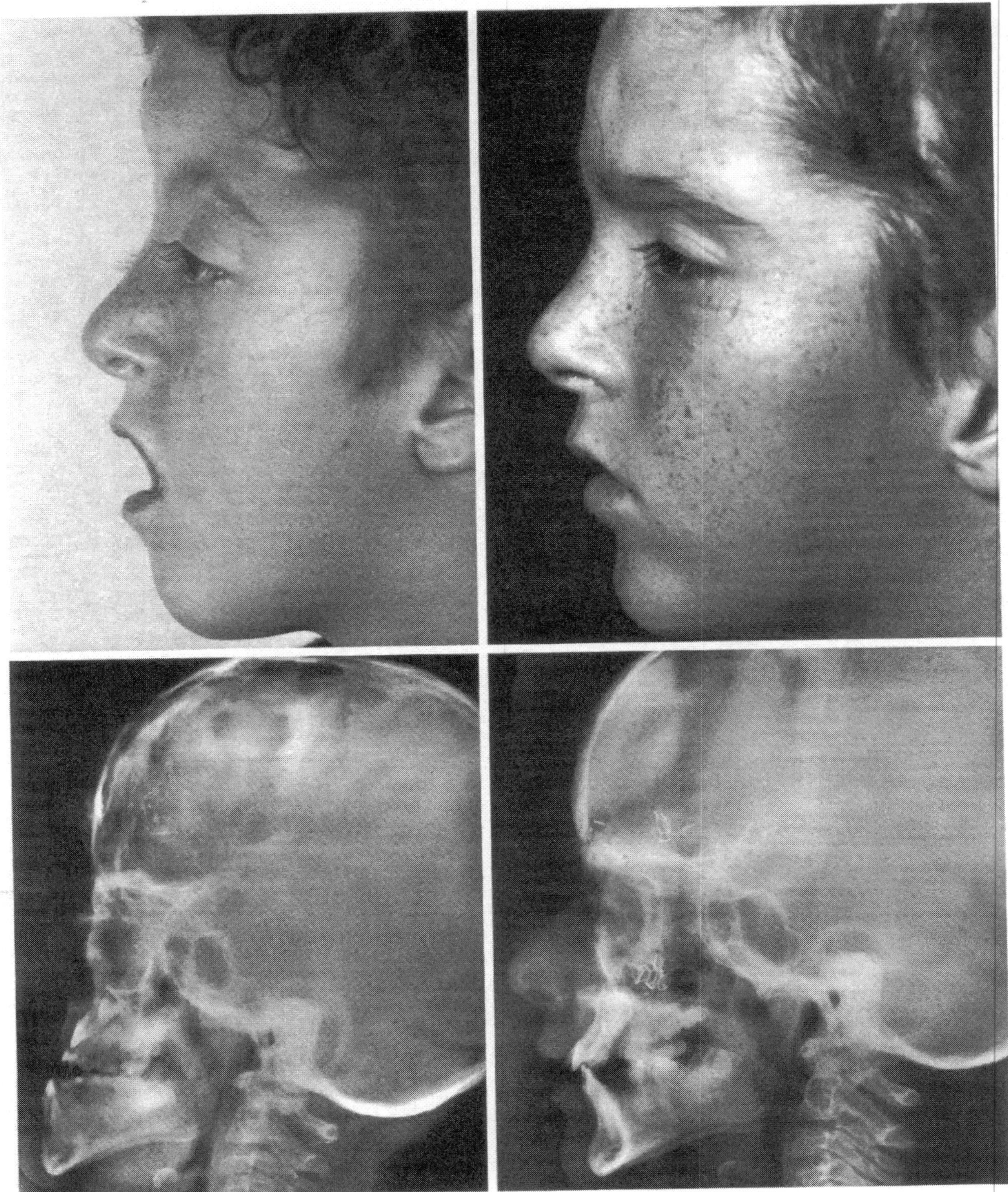

*Fig. 10.21 Child with Apert's syndrome and moderate orbital hypertelorism, treated by monobloc fronto-facial advancement and simultaneous facial bipartition. Note how the face is taken from flat to round, and it is narrowed by reversing the bulging temporal bones.*

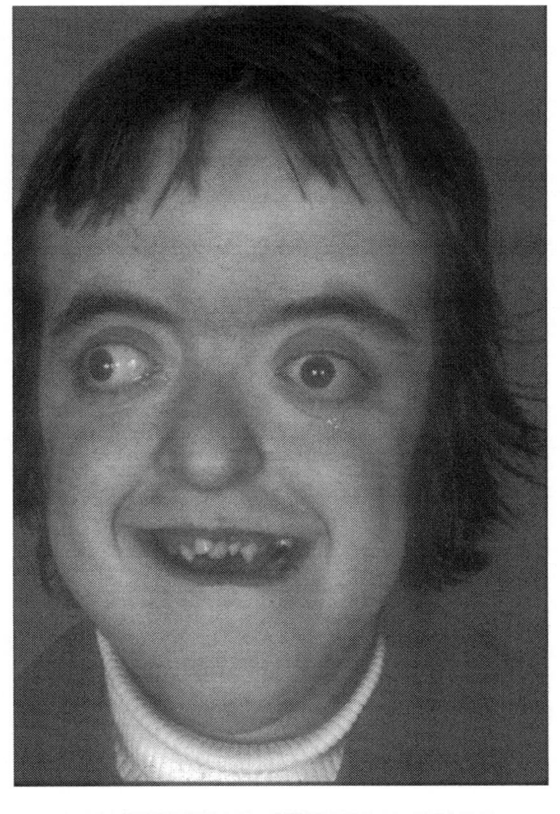

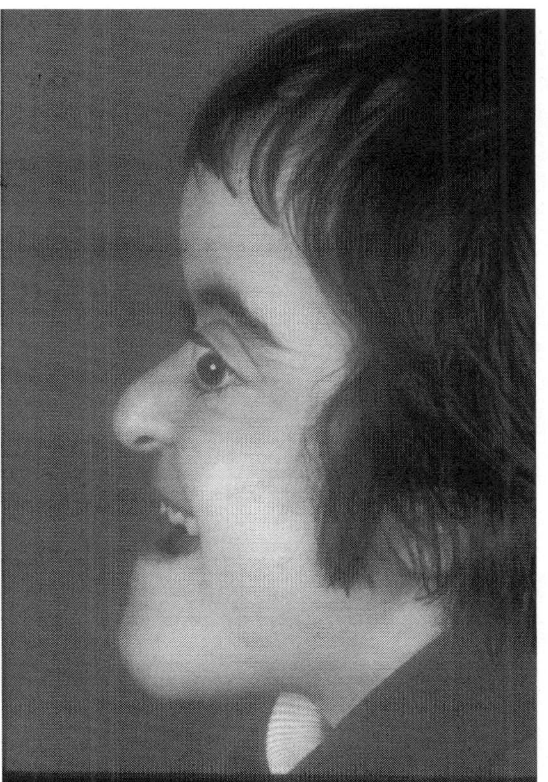

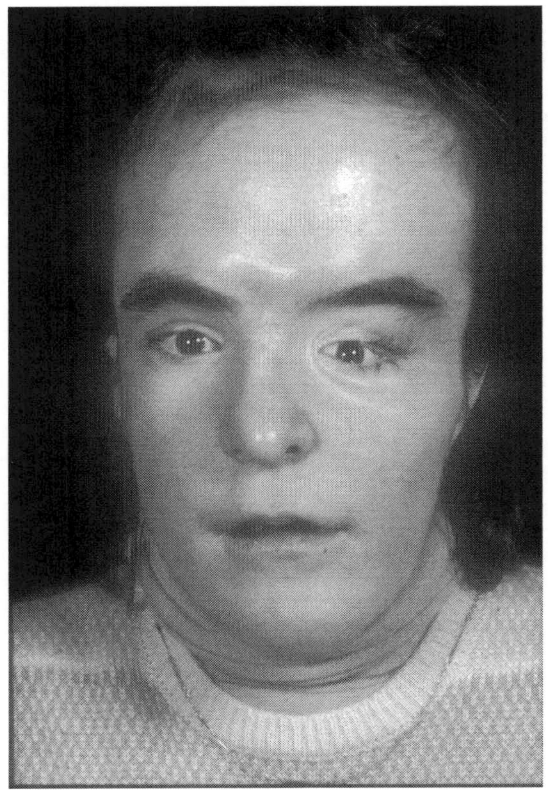

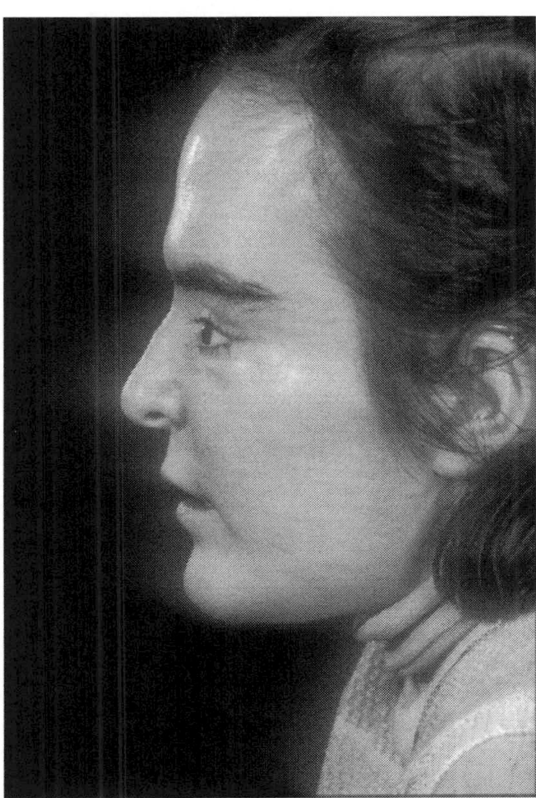

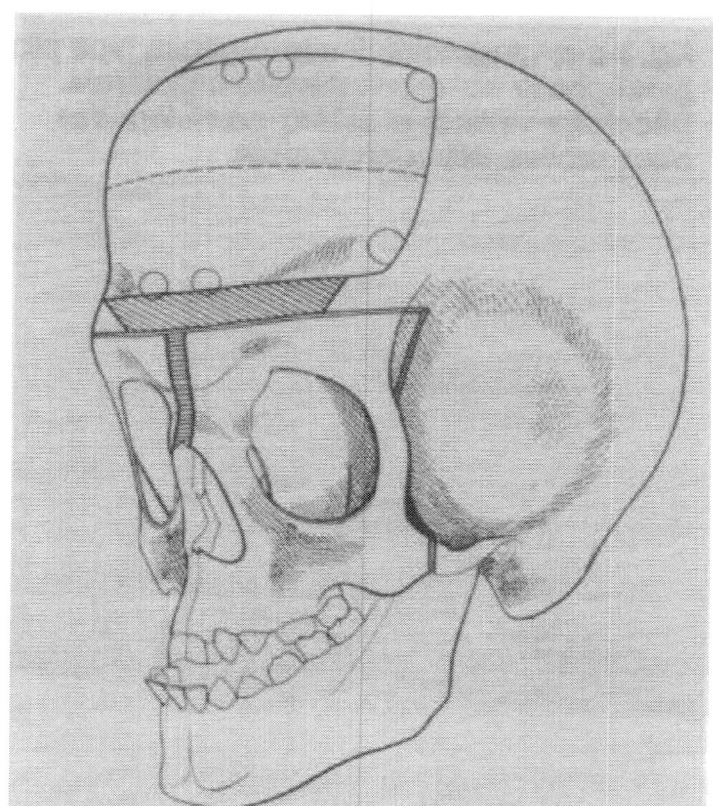

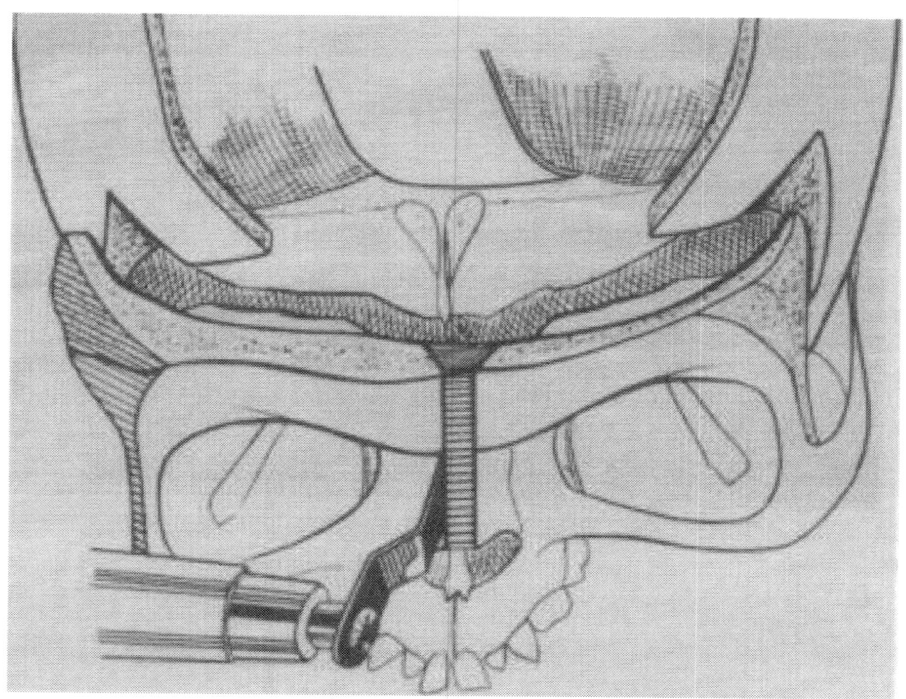

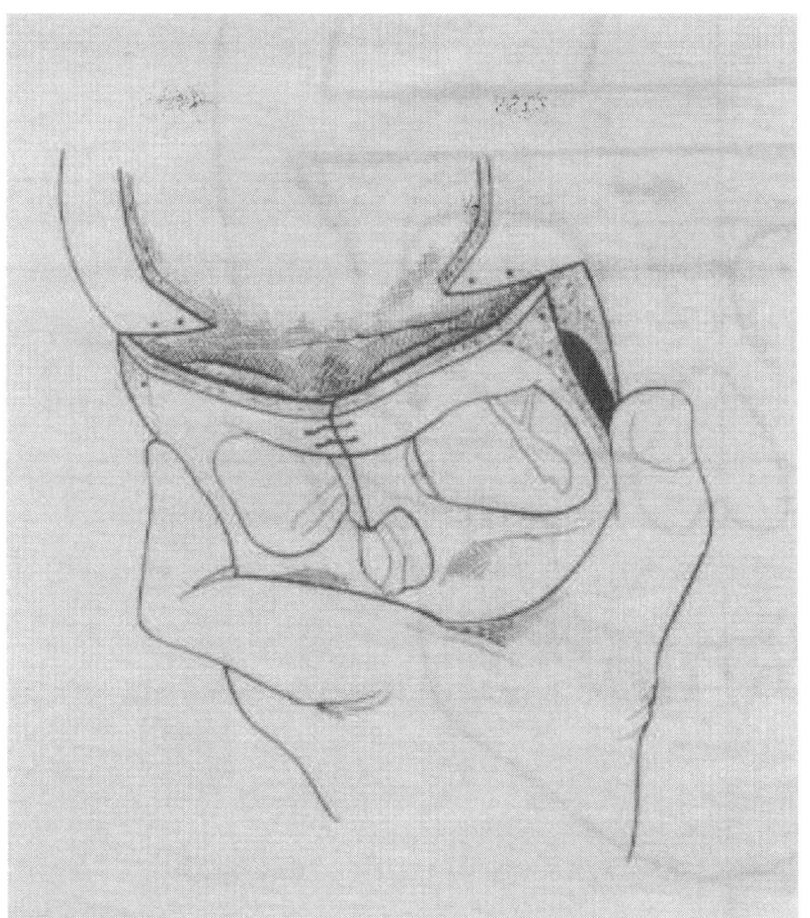

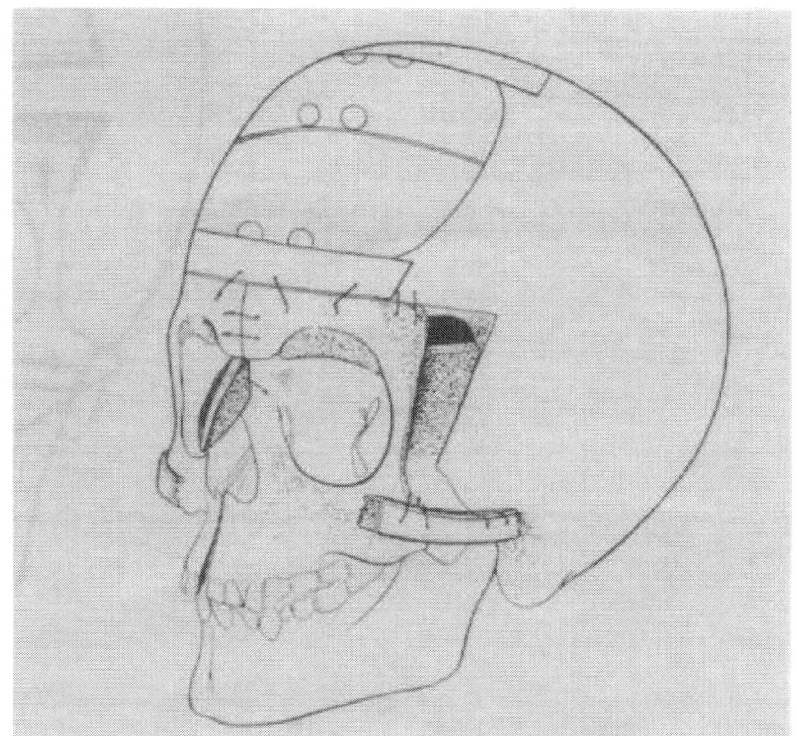

*Fig. 10.22 Sequelae of craniosynostosis: the plagiocephalies*

Daniel Marchac working in a pediatric department, did far more of these cases in France than Paul Tessier, and the few that Tessier did were generally on older patients. Nevertheless, his results were, again, the gold standard

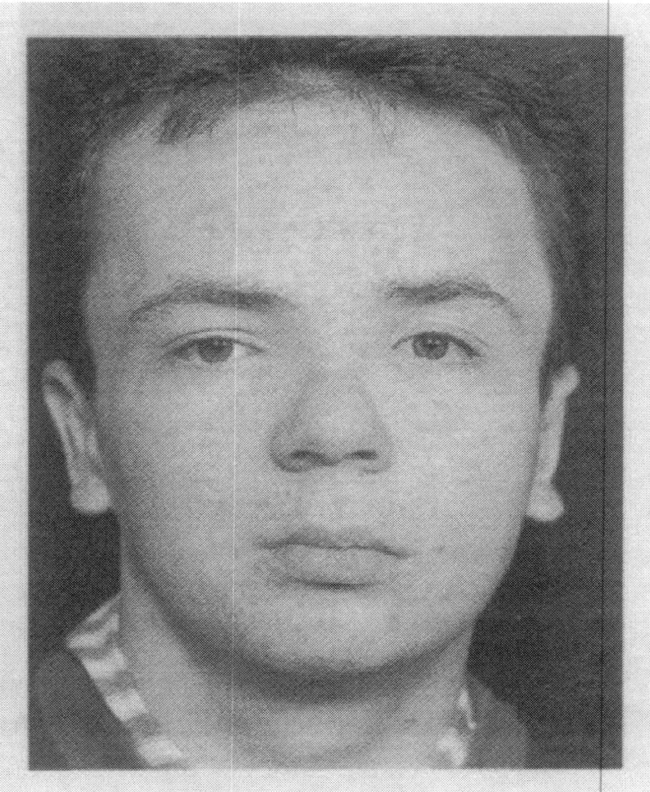

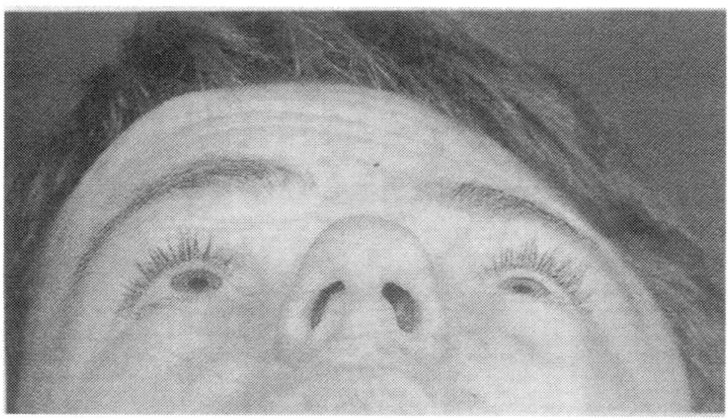

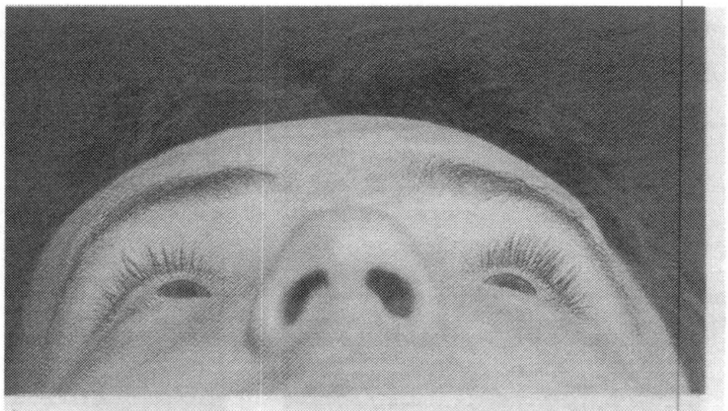

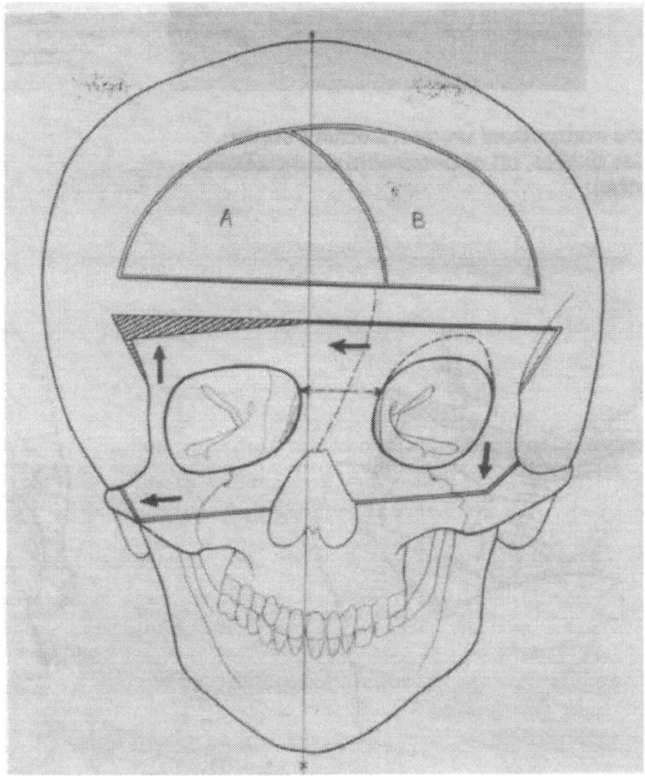


*Figs. 10.23c-e Correction complex plagiocephaly in an older patient.*

## The Arrhinias

Here was another condition for which Dr. Tessier developed a corrective procedure. The average pediatric plastic surgeon may see two or three patients with this condition in his or her entire career; Dr. Tessier had operated on over fifty. Dr. Tessier divided them into three groups: hemi-arrhinia (H.A.R.), hemi-arrhinia with proboscis lateralis, and total arrninia (T.A.R.). He had prepared a virtually complete manuscript on the subject; but, as was the case with other papers, he had a form of writer's cramp that prevented him from finishing the paper and getting it off to a journal. With only some minimal changes, and one case of my own, his paper has now been posthumously published in *The Scandinavian Journal of Plastic and Reconstructive Surgery and Hand Surgery (Paul Tessier, Frank S. Ciminello, S. Anthony Wolfe. M.D., 1009; 423: 177-196).*

Dr. Tessier had several bits of advice. First, he felt it was important to establish a *hole* for the new nostril. In unilateral cases, the hole could pass to the other side; in a total arrhinia, it should pass to the pharynx. And he advised waiting until at least 10-12 to perform the nasal reconstruction using a flap of skin from the forehead.

During the last year of his life, as related in Chapter 41, I had the occasion to visit him in the hospital with Mireille. Since I knew that arrhinias were one of his favorite subjects, I brought him the photographs and x-rays of an unoperated total arrhinia that I had been sent from Colombia. Although he was quite ill and uncomfortable, he held the x-ray up to the light, pointed to one area, and said, "*Faites-le bas,*" meaning make it (the hole for the nasal passage) low.

There have been a number of plastic surgeons who have shown cases of arrhinia where they did not make the hole. They have either said that the patient did not want it or that it was not necessary for the result. They should compare their results to his. Dr. Tessier felt that making the hole was important not for providing nasal air flow, but to make the nose look like a *nose*. Without the hole, it would be an artifice and not a nose.

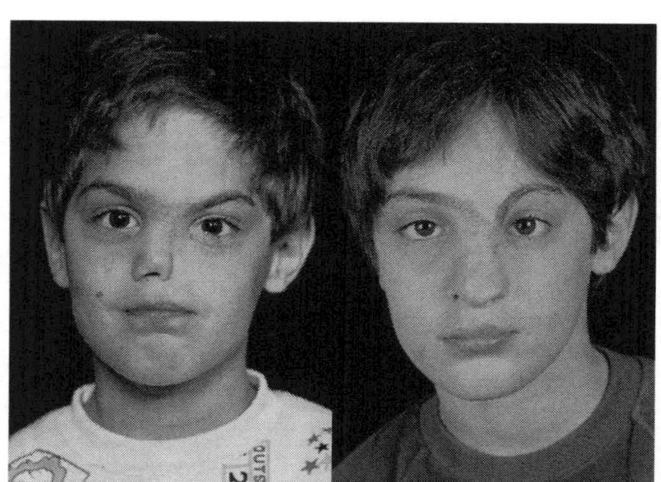

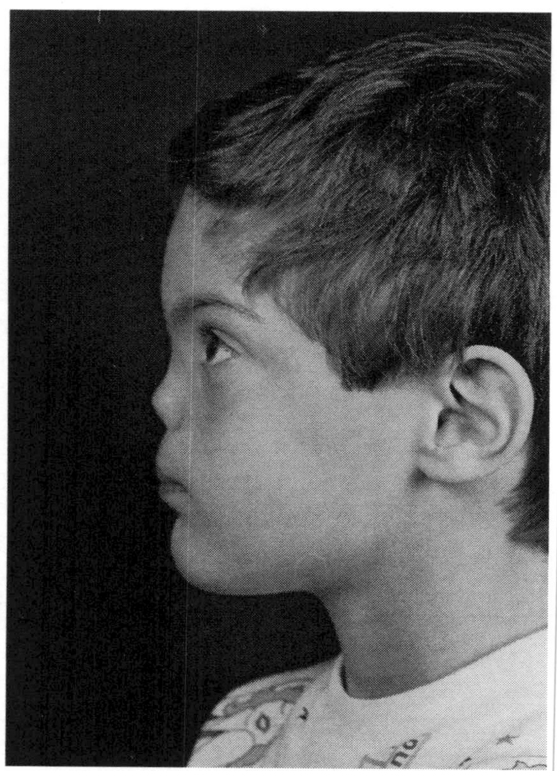

*Another older plagiocephaly correction.*

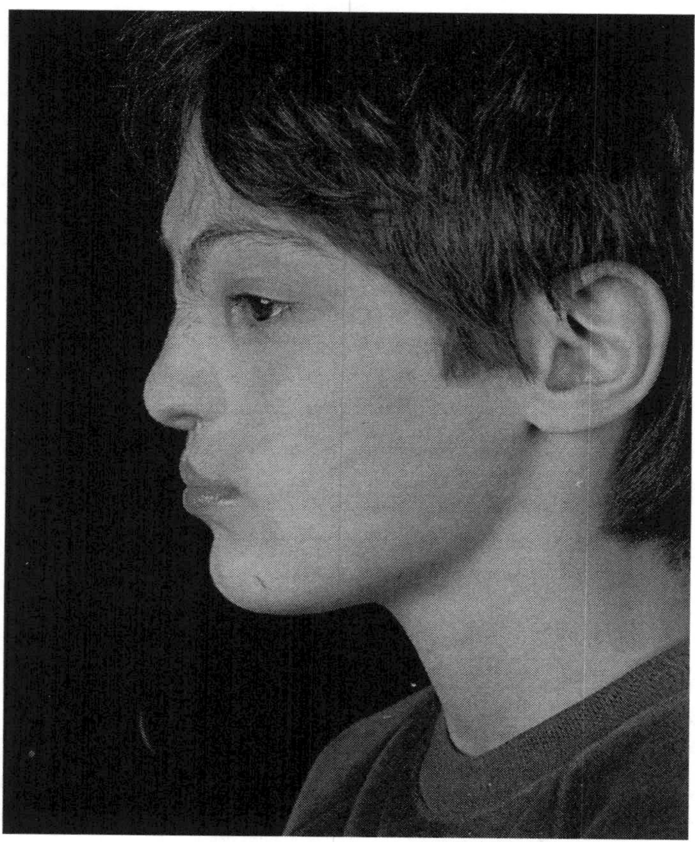

*Fig. 10.24 Patient with hemiarrhinia treated by Dr. Tessier with a forehead flap. Note that, in addition to creating the left half of the nose (with a nostril passage), the entire nose has been significantly lengthened.*

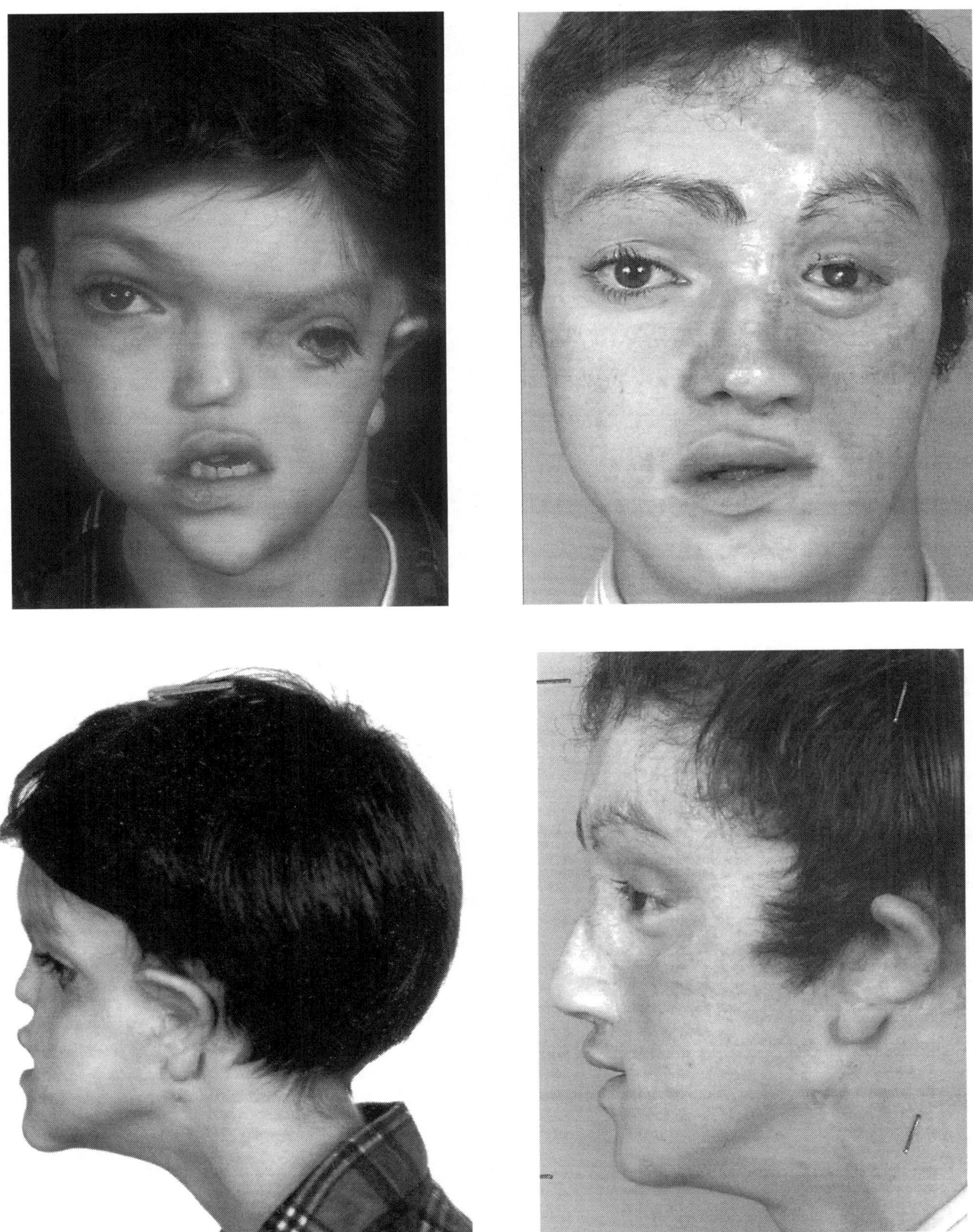

*Fig. 10.25 Another patient with hemiarrhinia treated by Dr. Tessier in Houston. Besides creating an excellent nose, with a nostril passage, he has straightened the face by two-jaw surgery and elevated the left orbit. A silicone ear prosthesis placed by Tom Cronin has also been raised.*

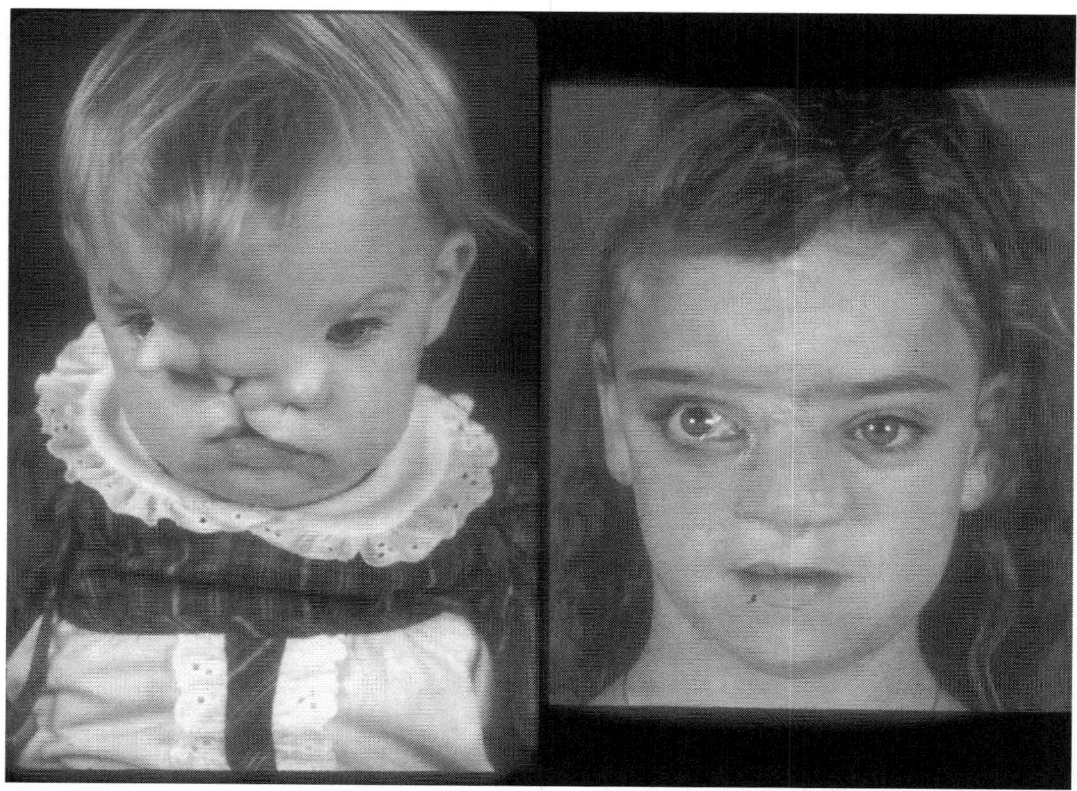

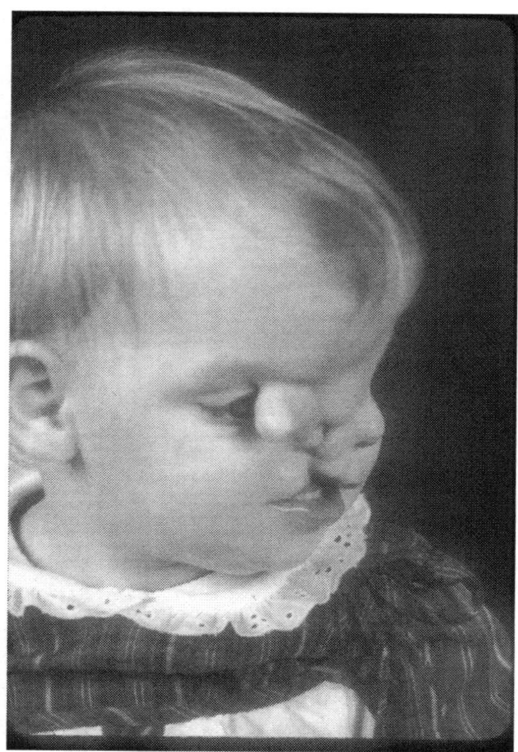

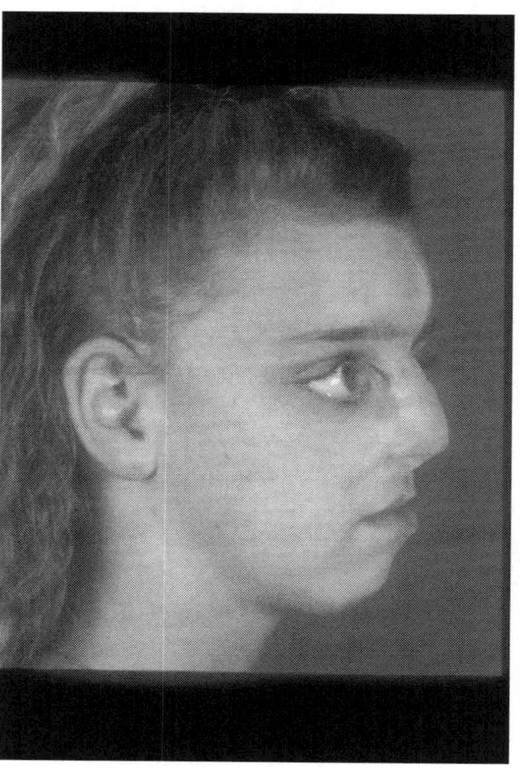

*Fig. 10.26 This patient, also treated in Houston, shows a complex malformation of cleft lip and palate, hemiarrhinia with a proboscis lateralis, coloboma of the right upper eyelid, and orbital hypertelorism. This, in Dr. Tessier's opinion, would have been an unfinished result. If he had the opportunity, he would have done more work on the nasal reconstruction and, without doubt, a genioplasty.*

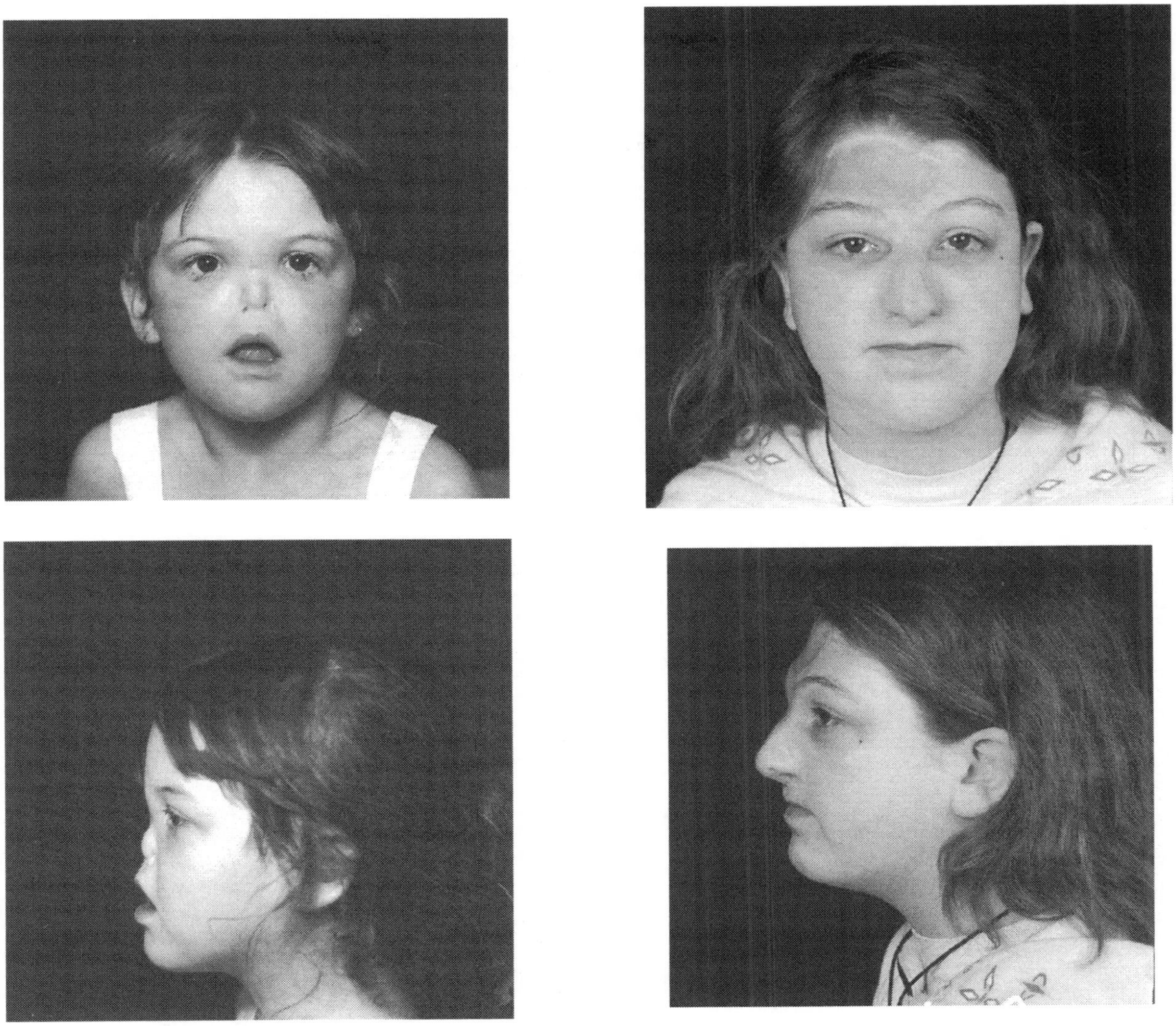

*Fig. 10.27 Patient with total arrhinia treated by Tessier first by creating a nasal passage and then by reconstructing a nose with two forehead flaps (one for lining, one for cover) and an iliac bone graft.*

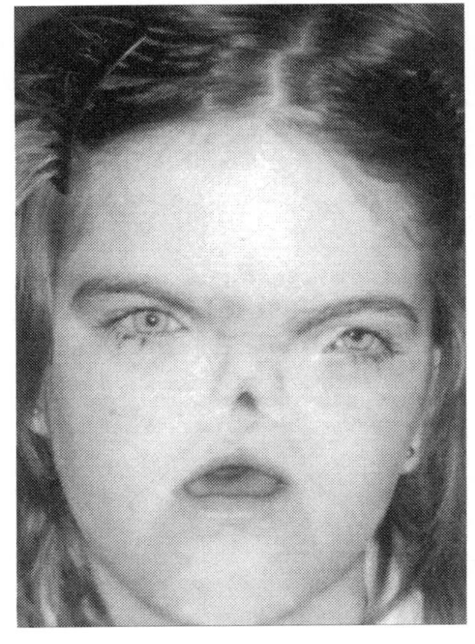

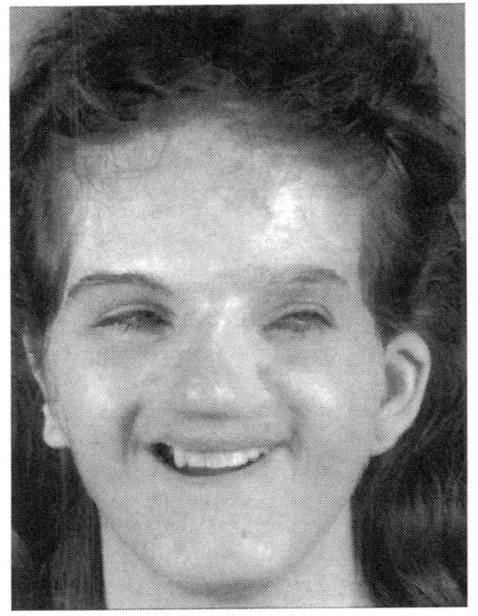

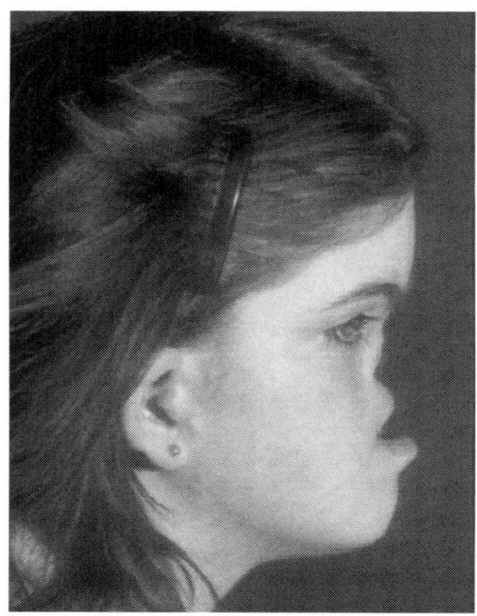

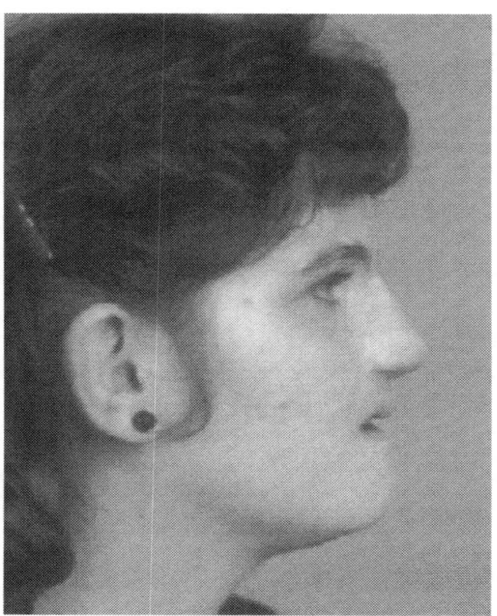

*Fig. 10.28 Another patient with total arrhinia, treated by transcranial facial bipartitition to correct the hypertelorism and expand the maxilla and nasal passage. This patient also exhibits an Abbé flap, followed by two forehead flaps and a nasal bone graft.*

## Trauma

Here Dr. Tessier returned to his roots—almost all his initial surgical experiences involved the treatment of burns and facial trauma. But now he had a whole panoply of new techniques, many of which he had developed in the treatment of congenital facial malformations, and began using them for the treatment of trauma with extraordinary results.

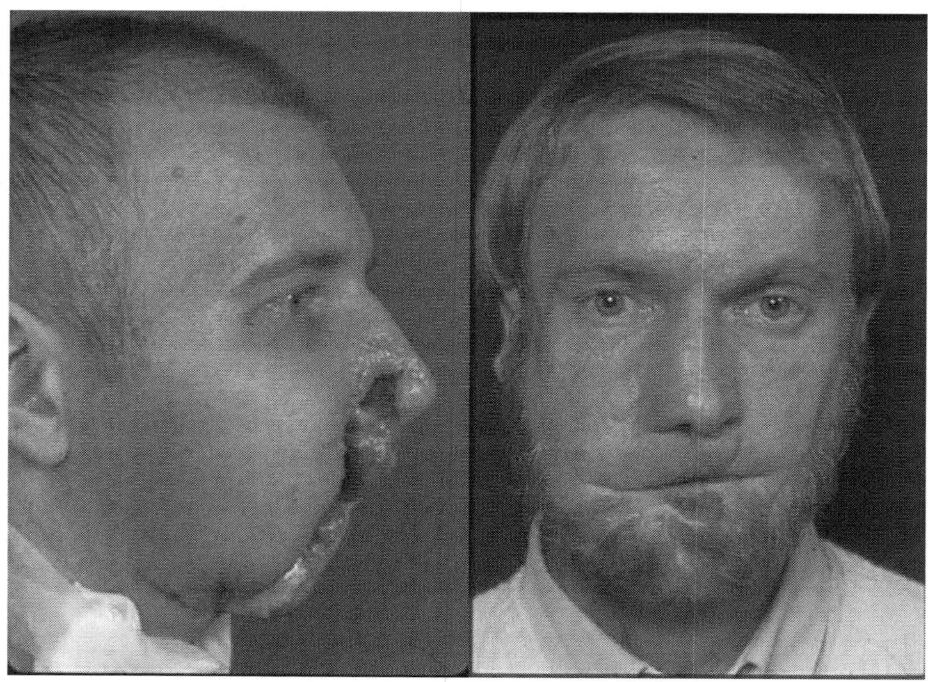

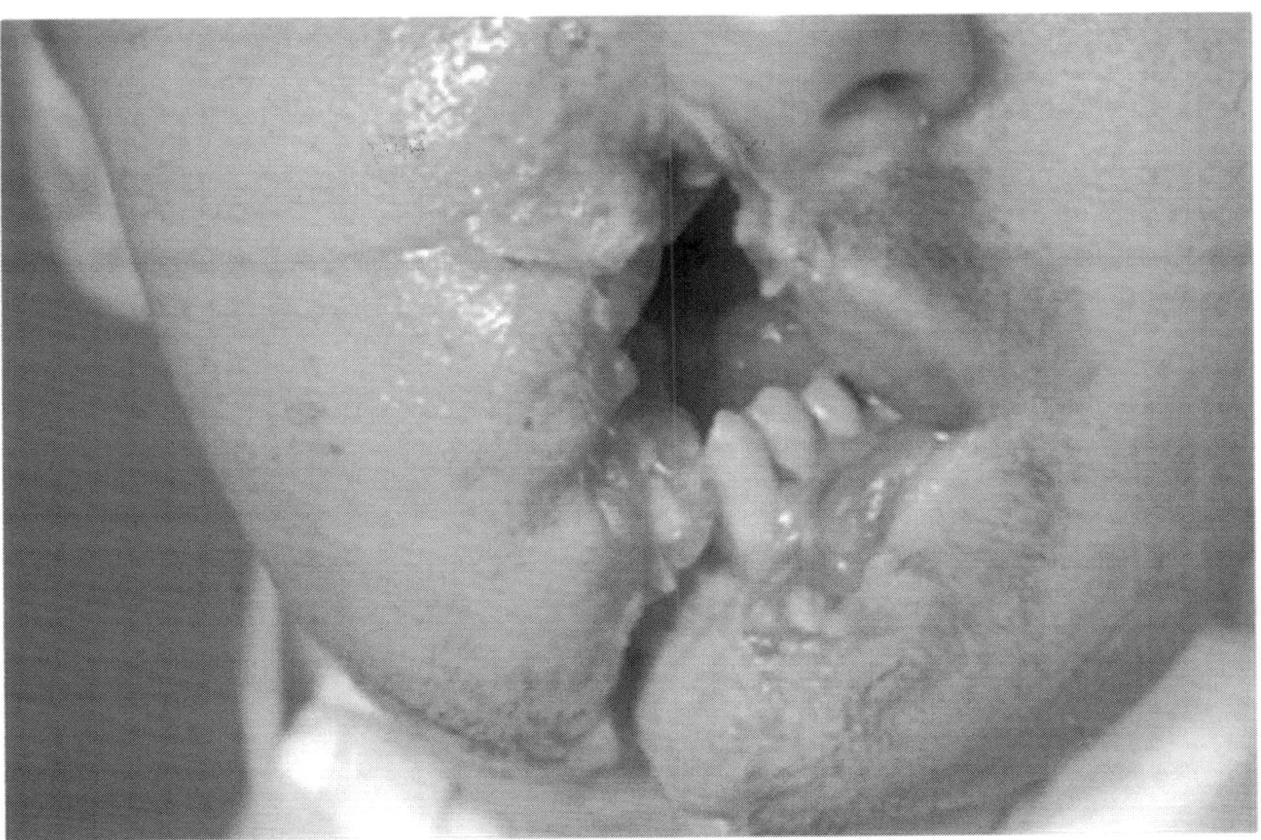

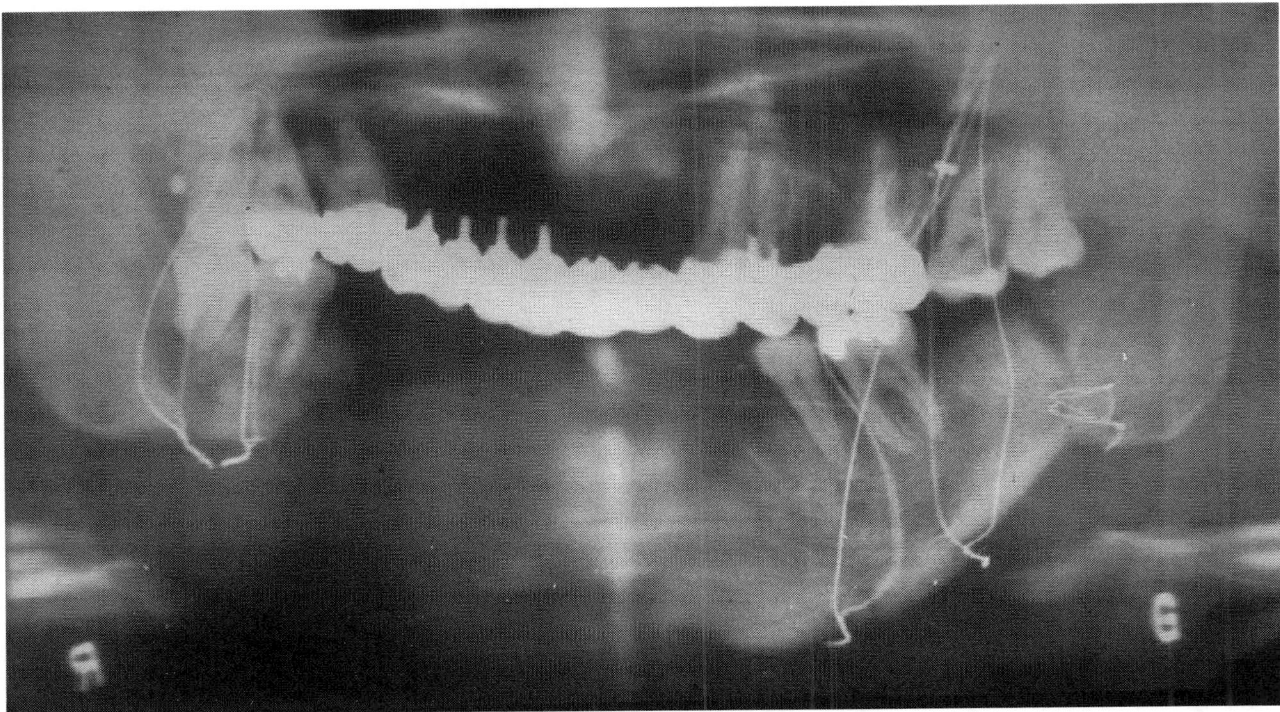

*Fig. 10.29 Patient shown after gunshot wound to the face (with initial treatment elsewhere). The panoramic x-ray shows that the attempt to stabilize the remaining mandibular segments to the remaining maxillary segments was only partially successful.*

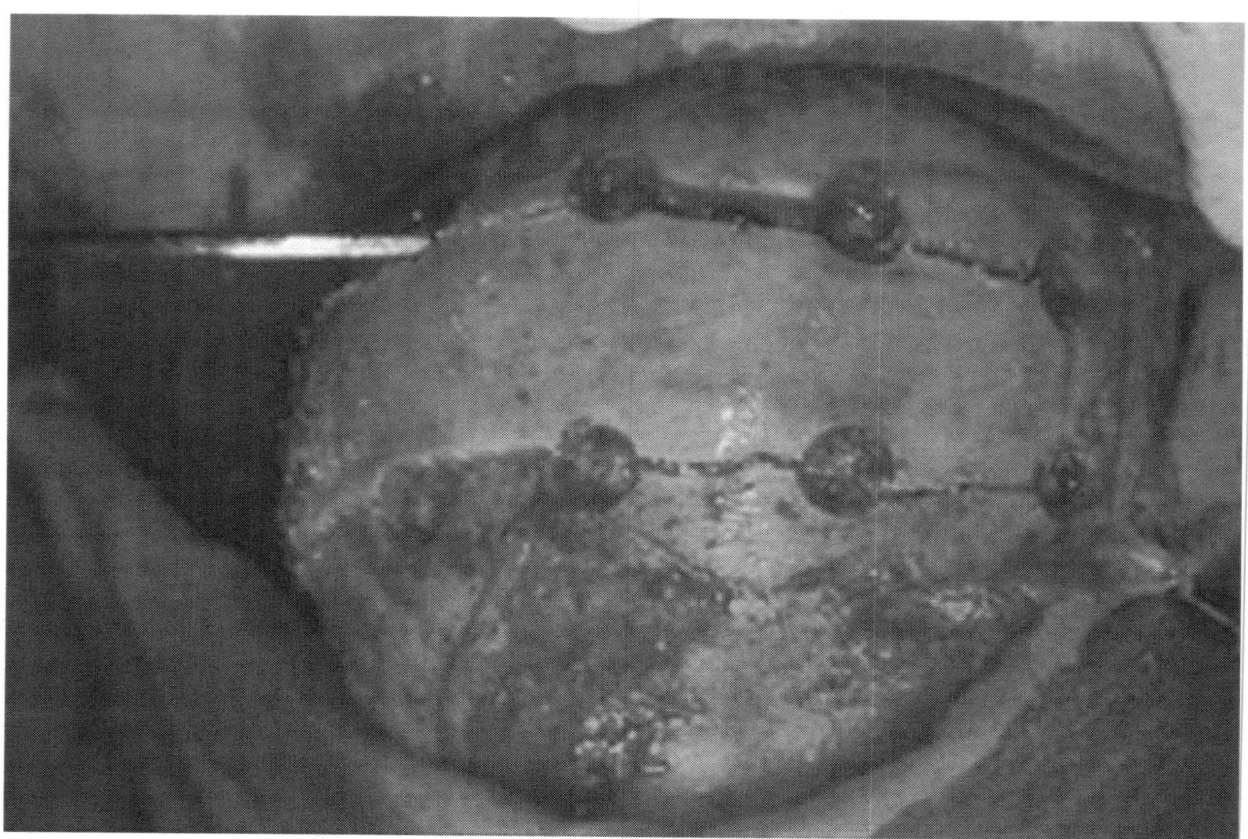

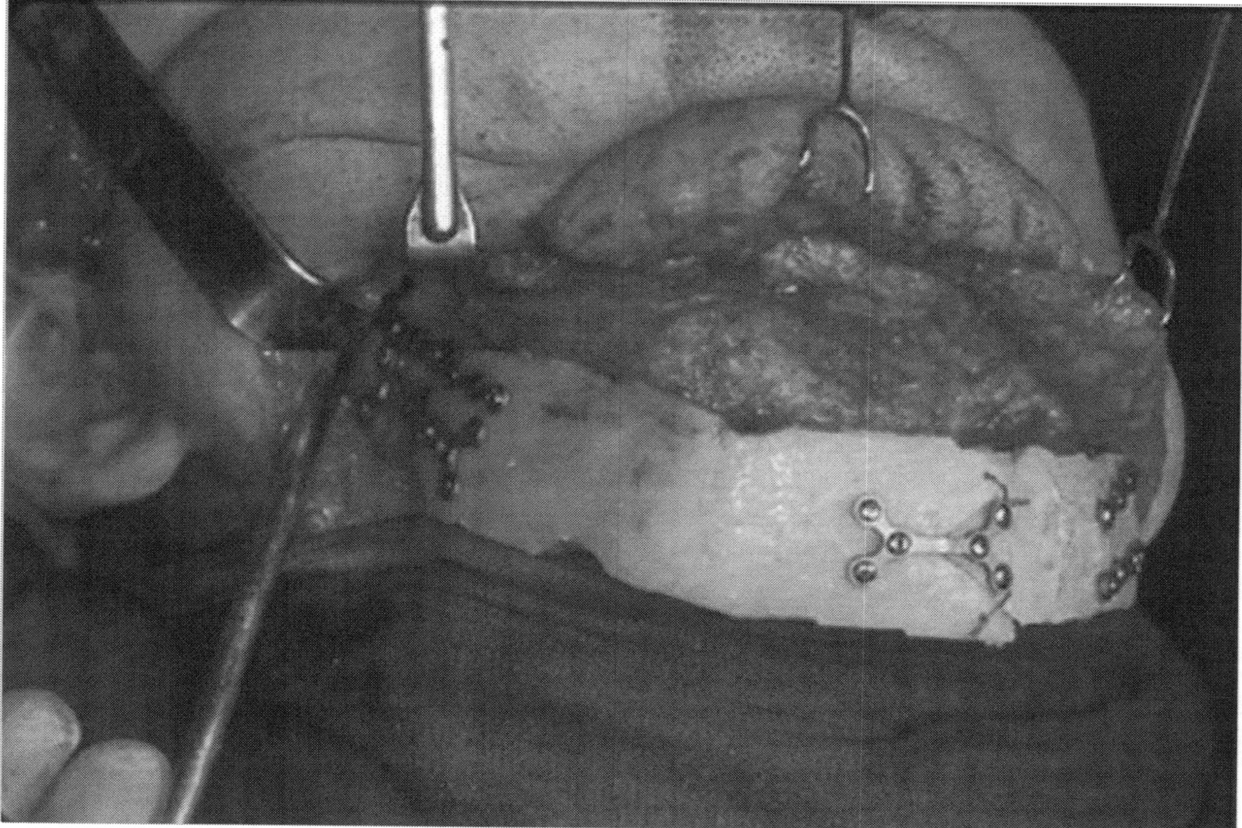

*Fig. 10.30 Craniotomy to harvest a full-thickness segment of cranial bone to reconstruct the mandible.*

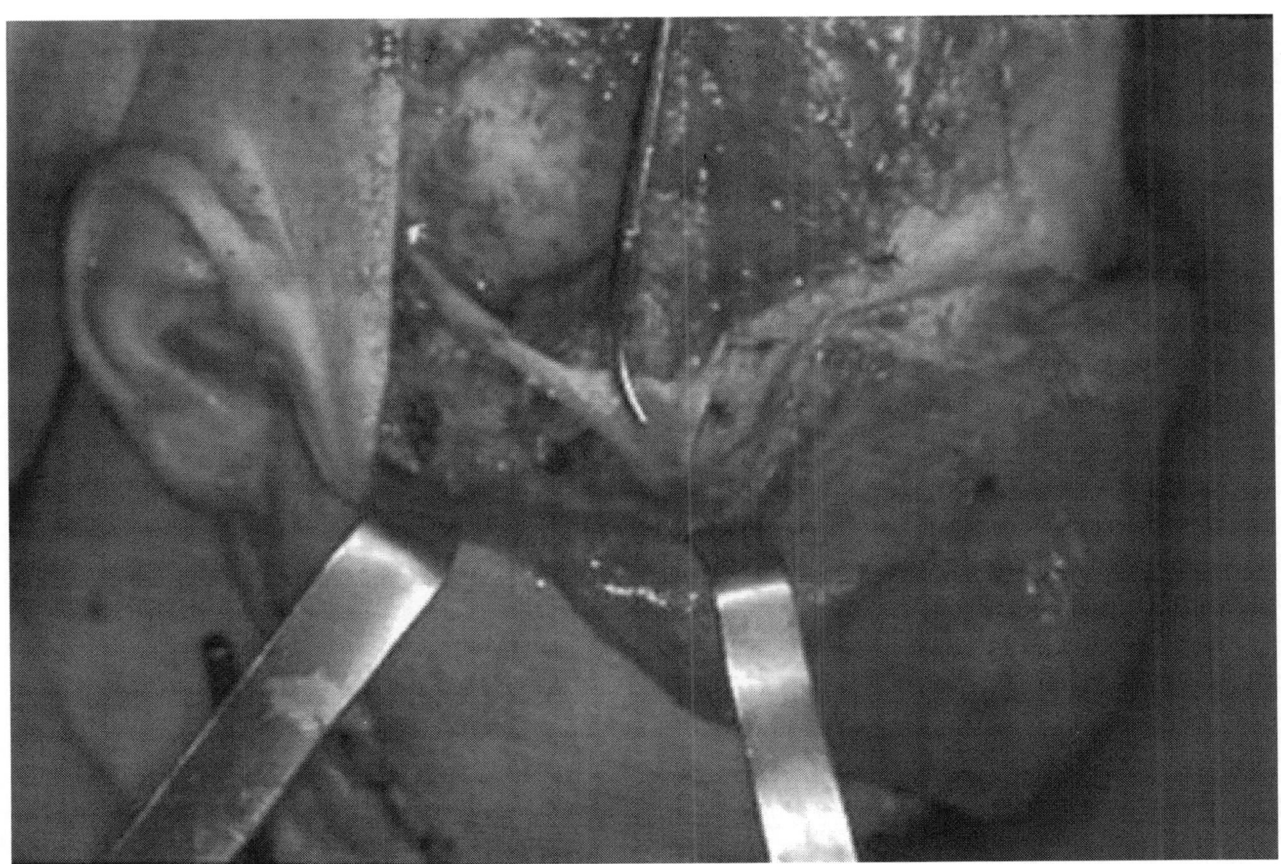

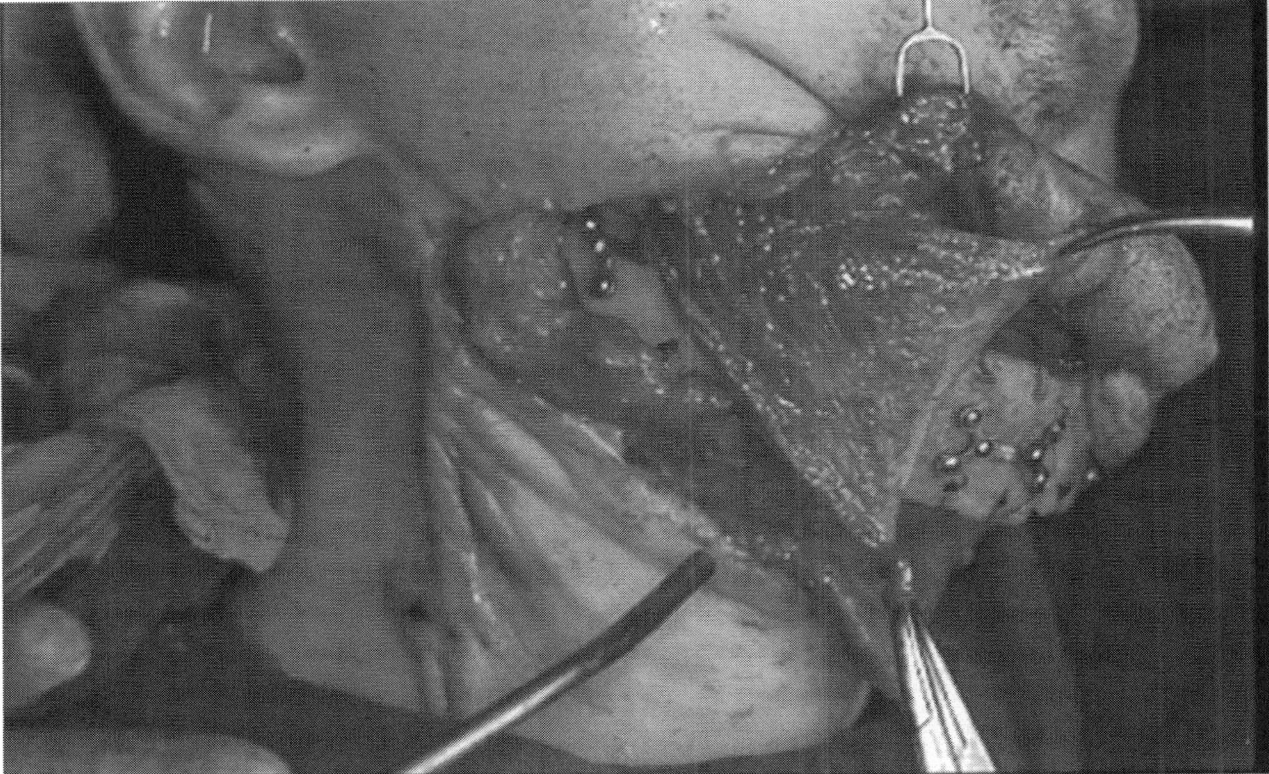

*Fig. 10.31 The zygomatic arch is removed to allow passage of a portion of the temporalis muscle to cover the mandibular bone graft.*

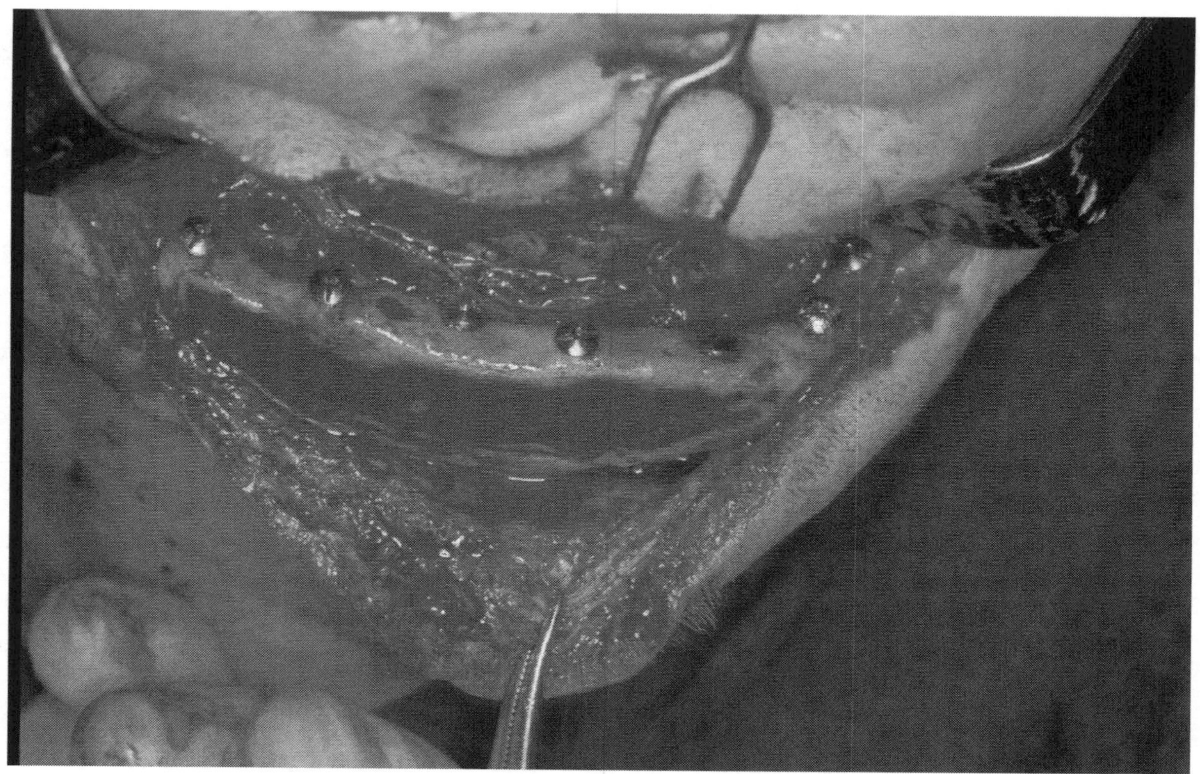

*Fig. 10.32 The mandibular reconstruction at a later date, with osseointegrated implants placed by Jean Francois Tulasne to allow ideal dental rehabilitation.*

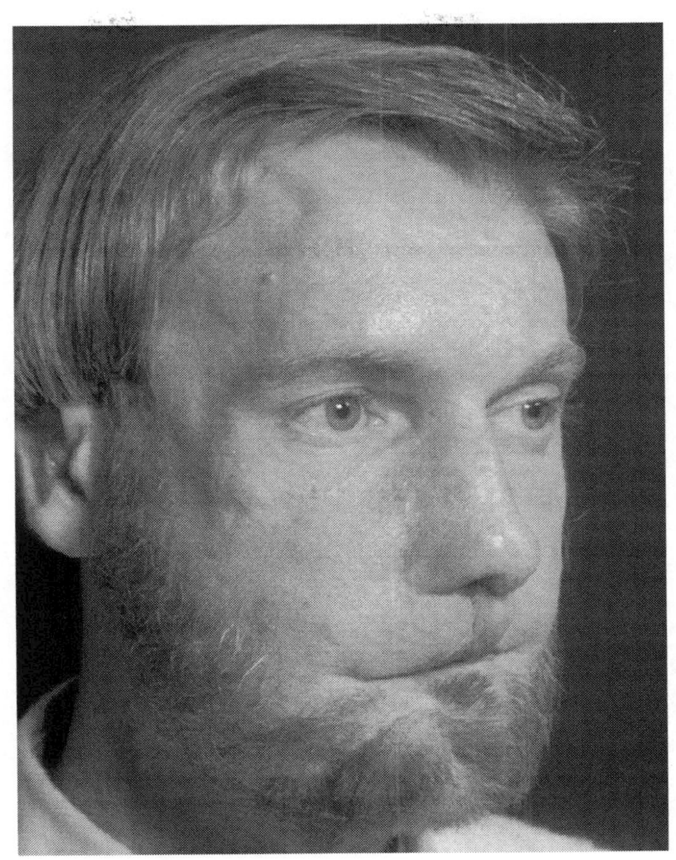

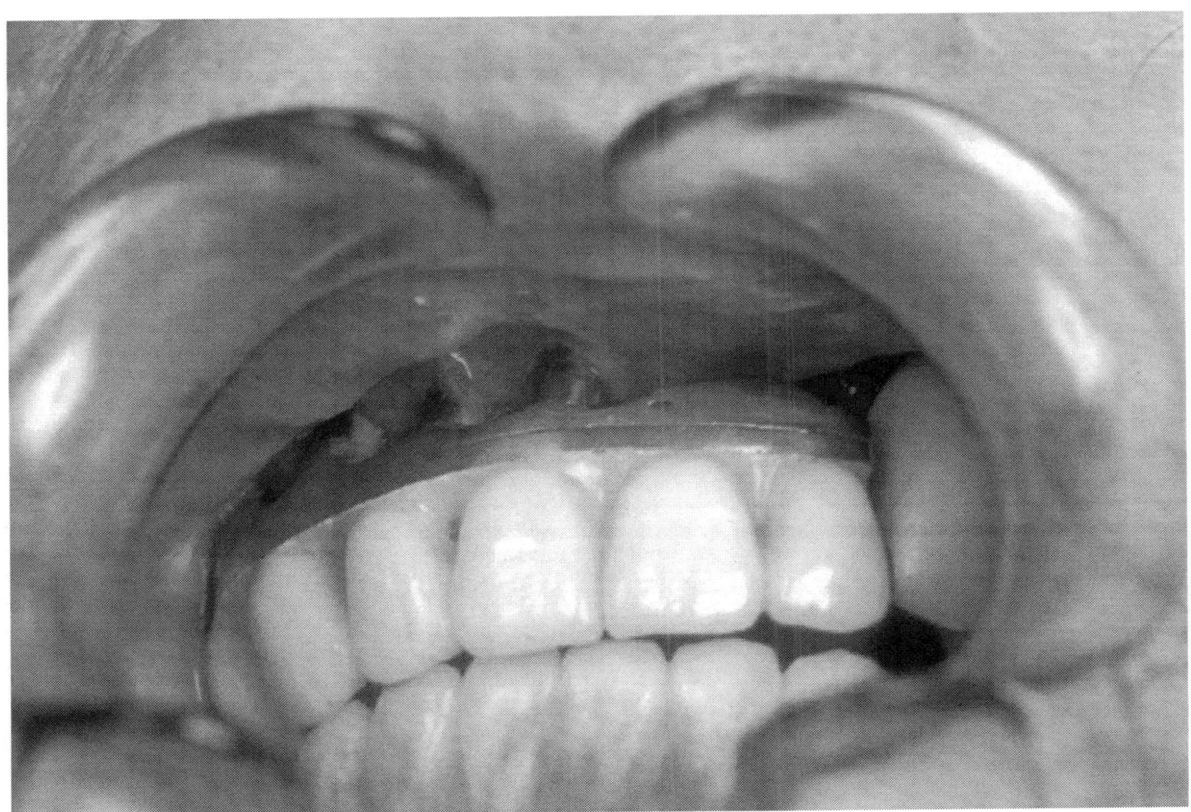

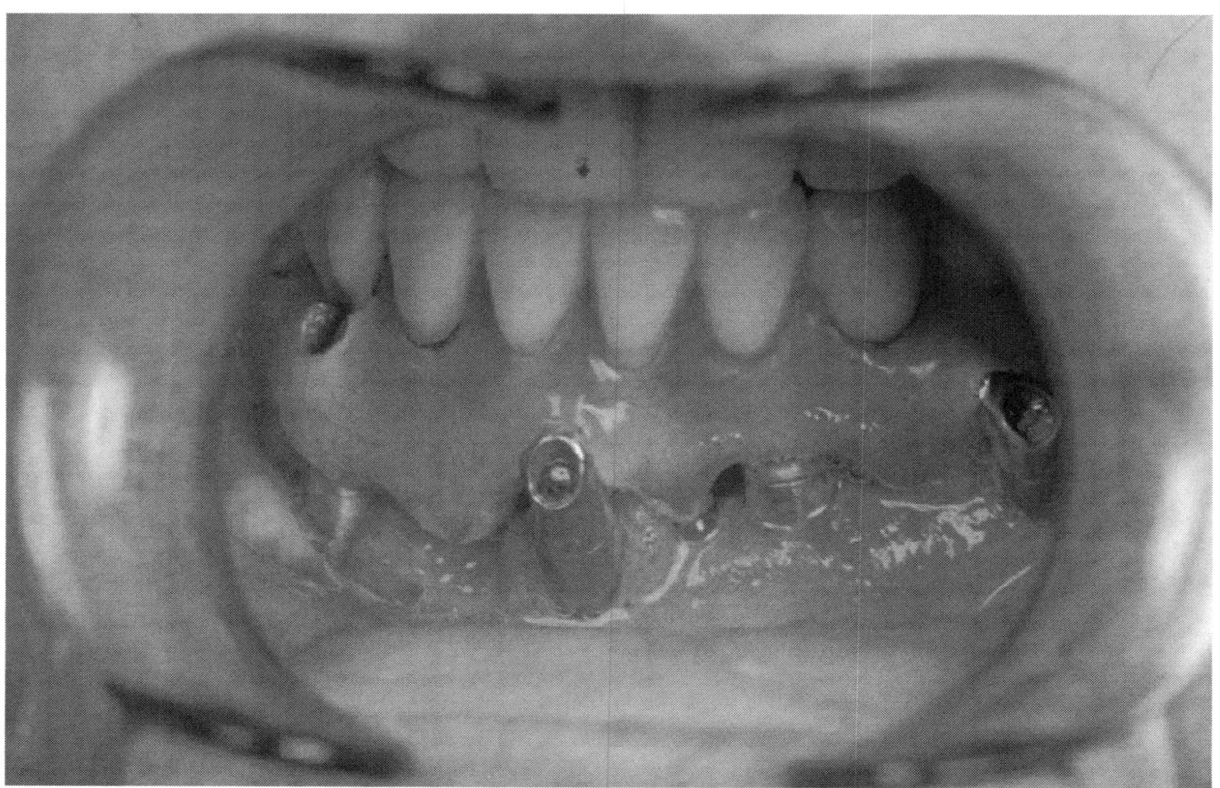

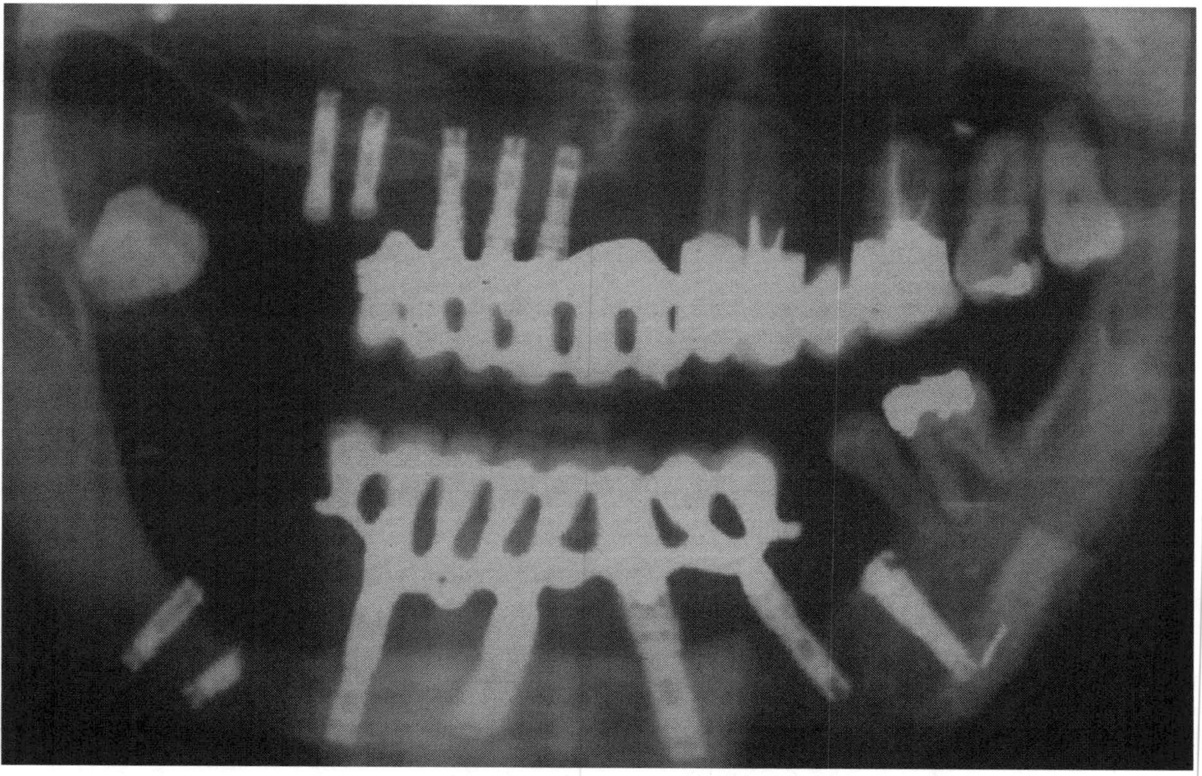

*Fig. 10.33 Final result, with mandibular and maxillary reconstruction, osseointegrated implants and attached dentures, and reconstruction of the nose and lips. This patient appeared in the "Techniques and Tools" Supplement to Plastic and Reconstructive Surgery that won Dr. Tessier his second James Barrett Brown Award.*

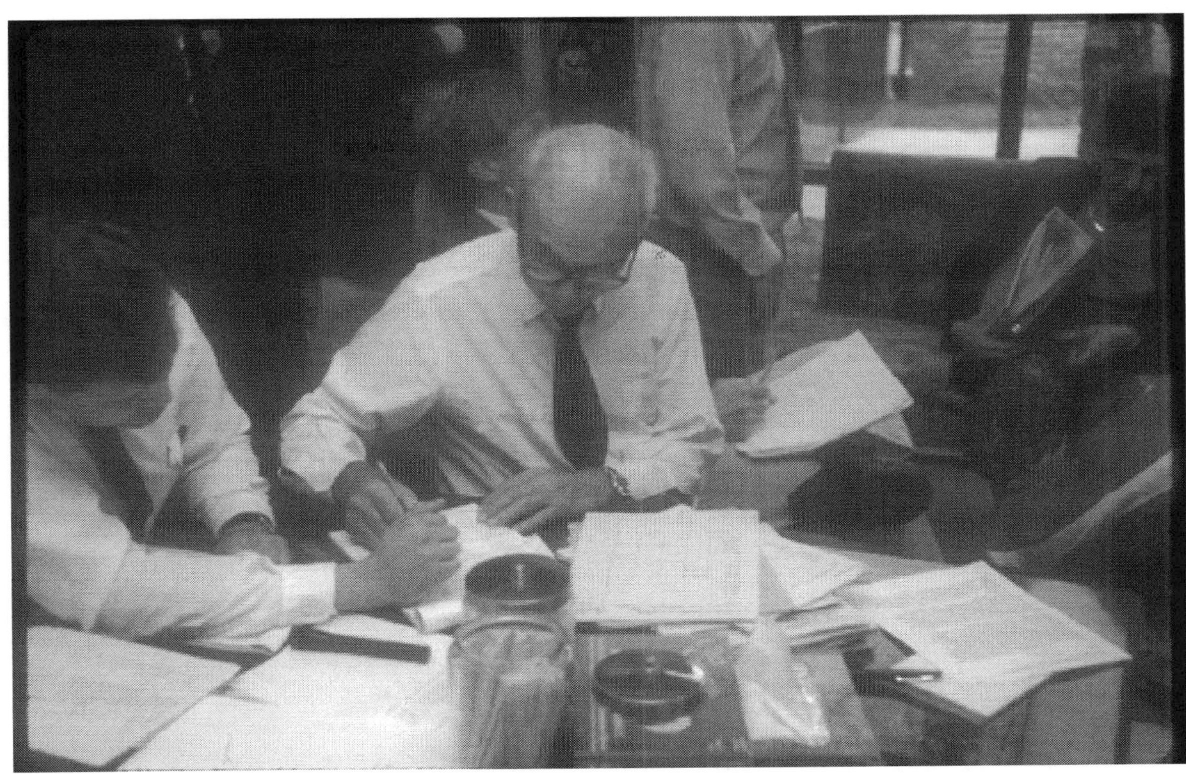

*Fig. 10.34 Dr. Tessier believed in his own medicine. Years of cigar smoking and poor dental care during the World War II resulted in the loss of many of his maxillary teeth. Two cranial and one iliac bone graft were taken by Jean Francois Tulasne from Paul Tessier (under local anesthesia!) to allow placement of the maxillary implants. The arrow points to the visible donor defect, as seen during a consultation in Charlotte.*

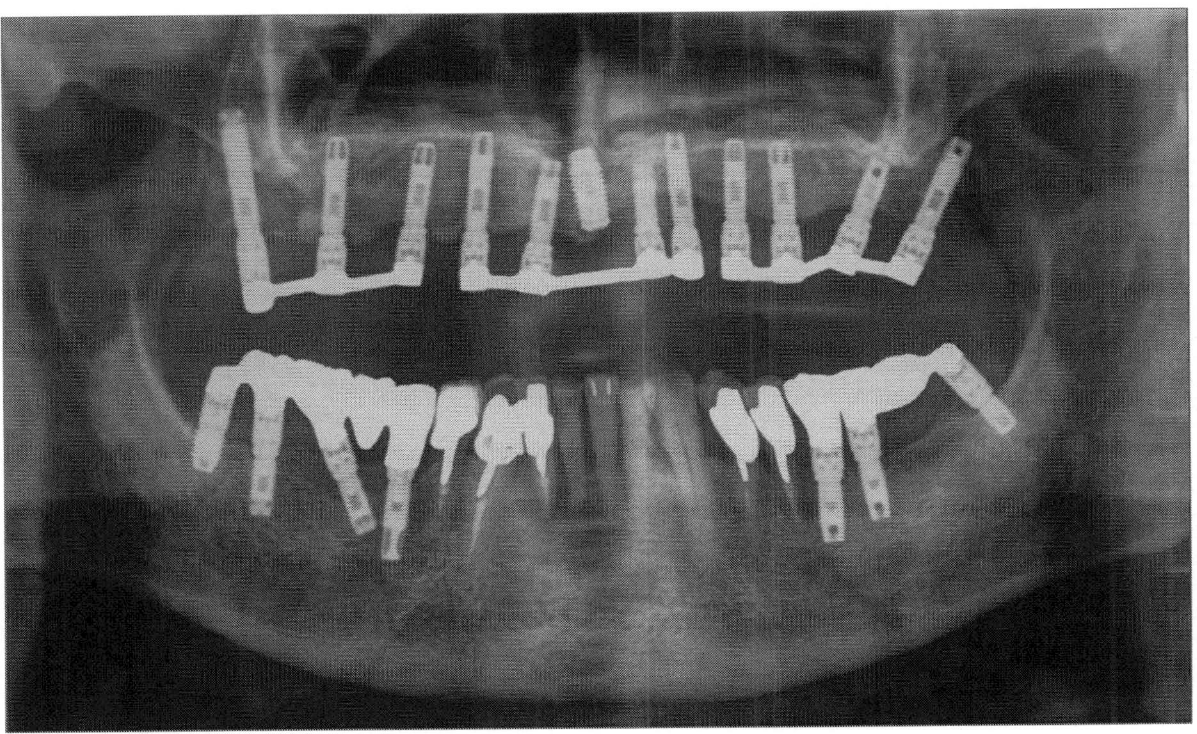

*Fig. 10.35 Paul Tessier's panorex, showing a record 19 osseointegrated implants. He was delighted with the result, and he would not hesitate to grab his upper front teeth and shown how solid they were.*

## The Barron-Tessier flap.

Dr. Tessier developed the plastysmal island flap for intraoral reconstruction in the early 1970s. And, with characteristic (and perhaps excessive generosity), called it a B-T flap, recognizing the contributions of John Barron, an English plastic surgeon who wrote about subcutaneous island flaps for facial reconstruction.

What Tessier had developed, however, was a true *myocutaneous* flap, since the cervical platysma muscle was used to nourish the cutaneous portion of the flap. This was another paper that he had almost completely finished, but never published due to "writer's cramp." David Matthews showed the procedure to one of his E.N.T. colleagues in Charlotte who went on to use it hundreds of times. This paper will also be published posthumously in a special edition of *Annals of Plastic Surgery* which will be devoted to Dr. Tessier.

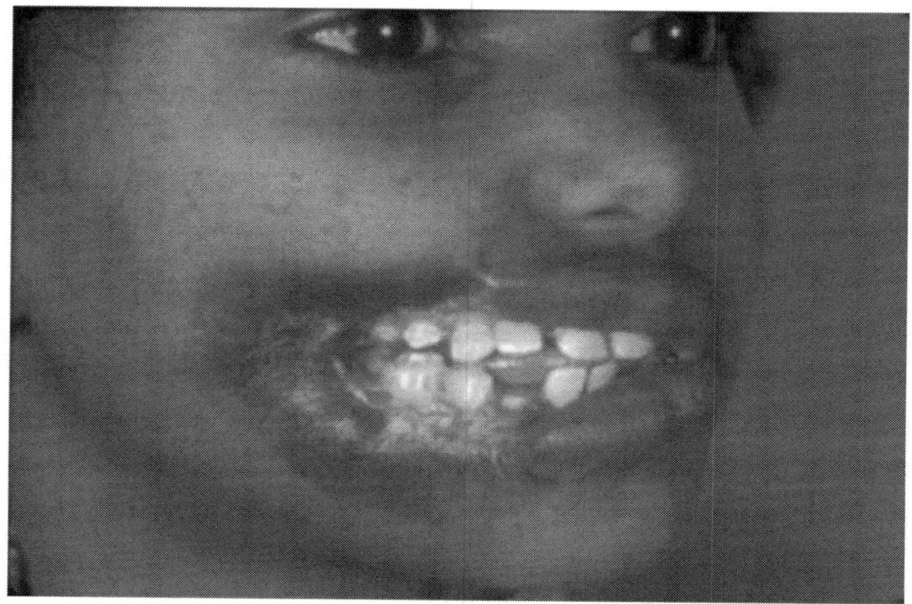

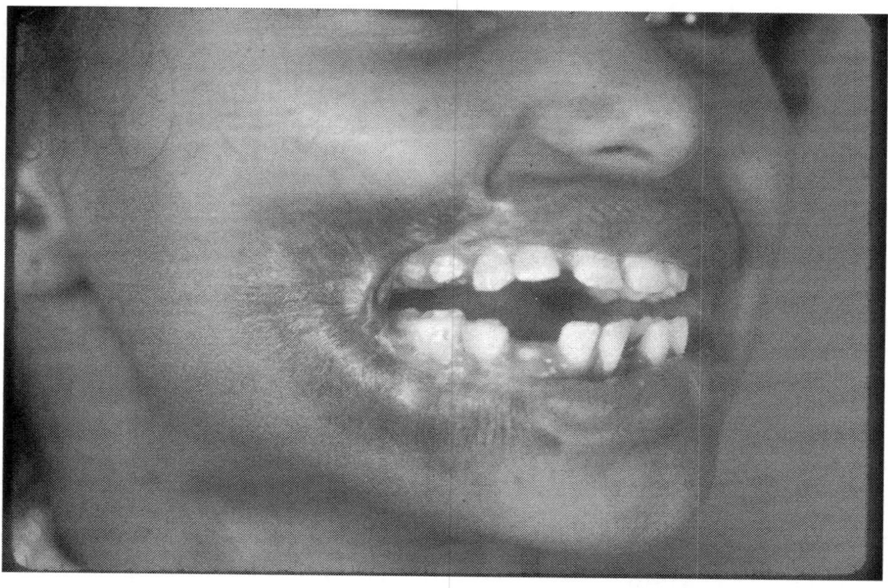

*Fig. 10.36 Patient originally from Africa who Dr. Tessier treated in Paris for sequelae of noma, a spirochetal infection seen in developing nations and associated with malnutrition, but rarely seen in the West (except in some patients undergoing chemotherapy). She has lost part of her lips and cheek, and has lost the ability to open her mouth due to a fibrous ankylosis.*

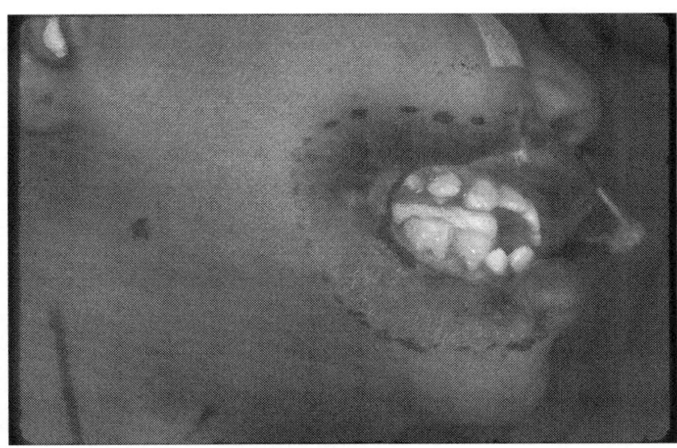
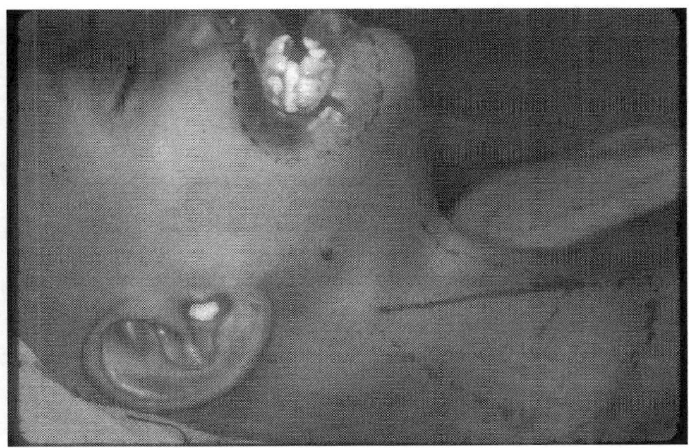

*Fig. 10.37. Dr. Tessier's markings for resection of scar tissue and the B-T flap.*

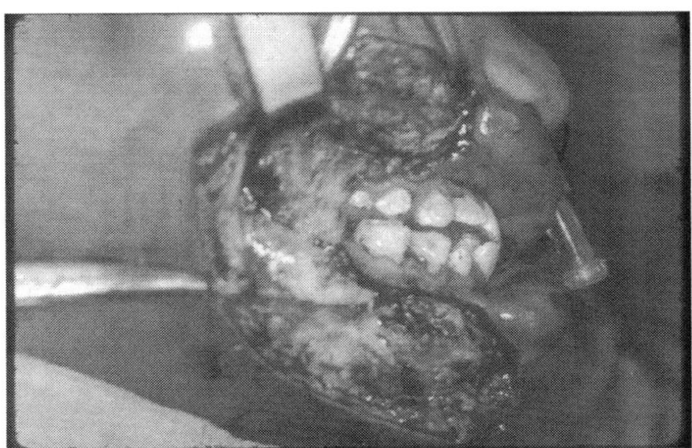
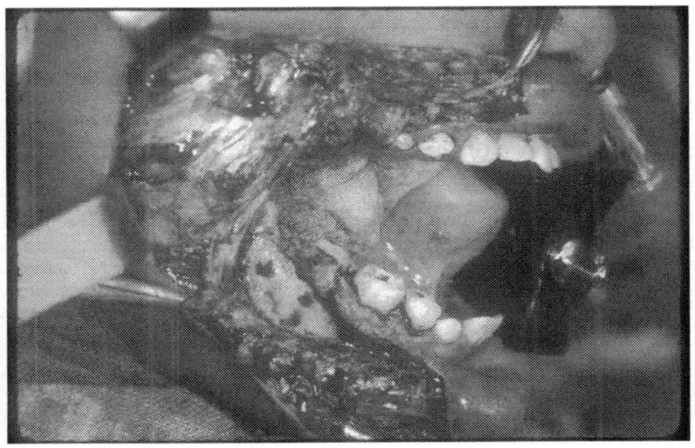

*Fig. 10.38 After resection of the fibrous ankylosis, the mouth is opened, exposing a portion of the mandible.*

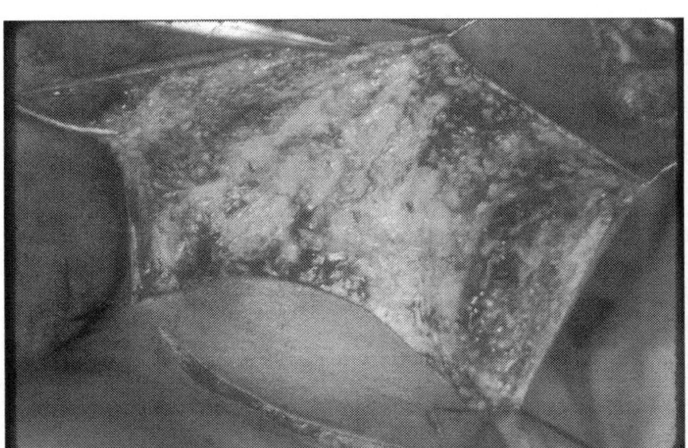
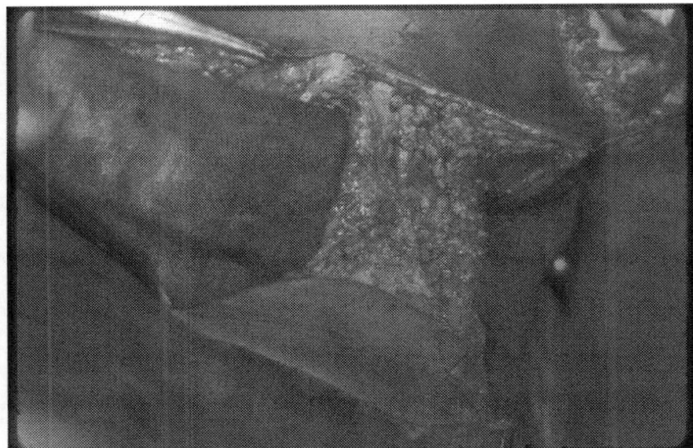

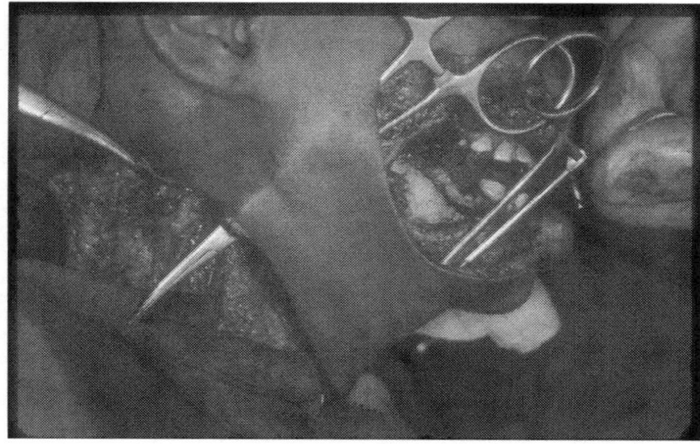

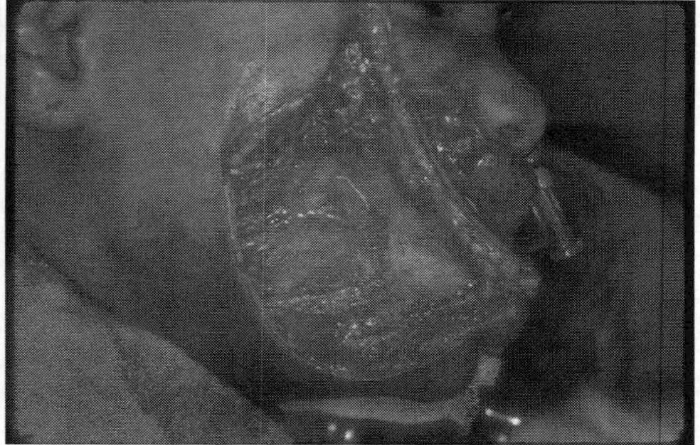

*Fig. 10.39 Steps in the dissection, mobilization, and transfer of the flap to provide oral lining, with the skin surface now facing inside the mouth.*

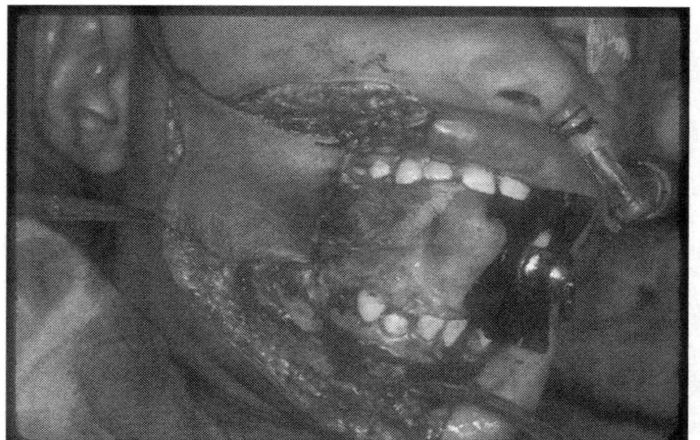

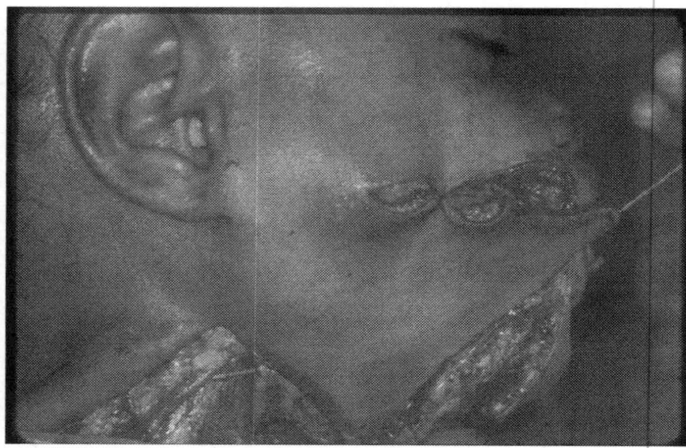

*Fig. 10.40 Silk sutures attach one end of the flap to the retromolar area. The other end, with two hemostats attached, will be swung forward and sewn to the inside of the oral commissure. A separate cervical flap is dissected to provide outer cover.*

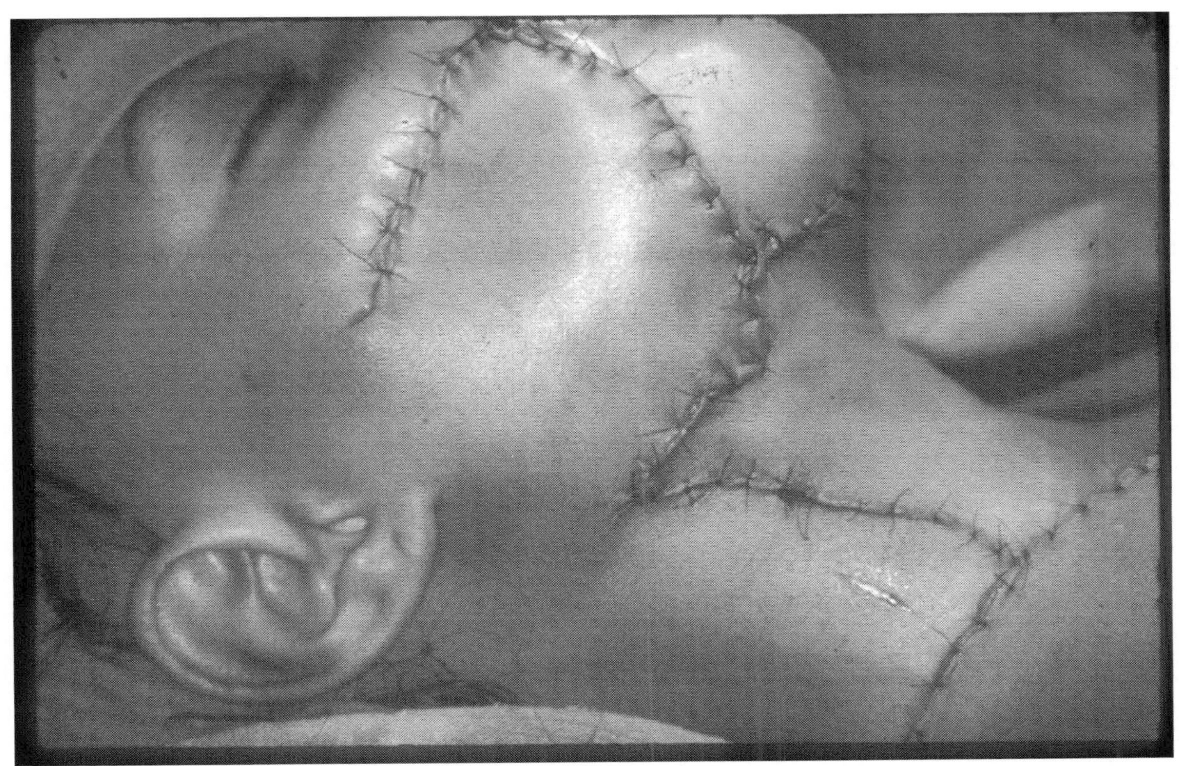

*Fig. 10.41 Flaps in place at the end of the procedure.*

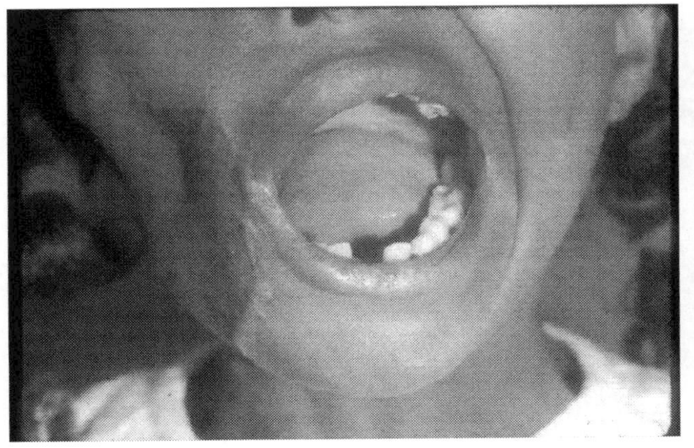

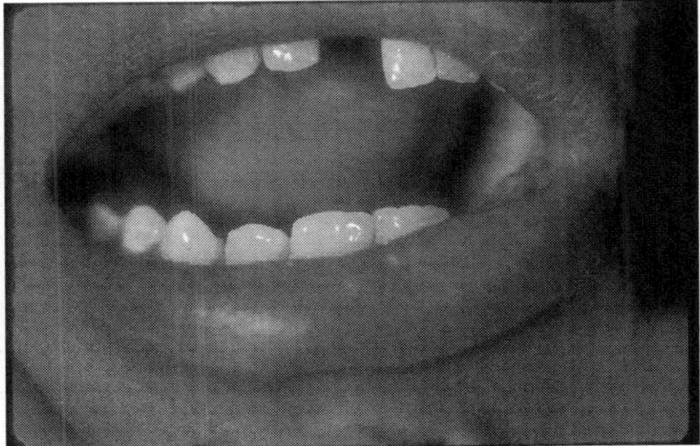

*Fig. 10.42 Early result showing good mouth opening and a portion of the flap next to the tongue.*

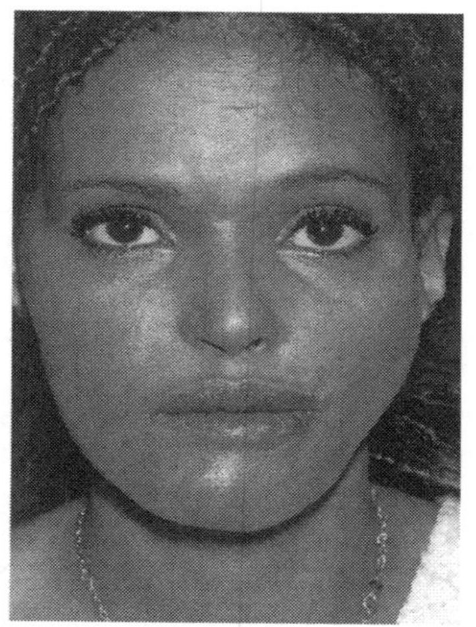

*Fig. 10.43 Twenty-five-year follow-up pictures of the patient, courtesy of Darinova Krastinova, who continues to follow her at Hôpital Foch.*

T.S. Eliot wrote that, "Only those who will risk going too far can possibly find out how far one can go." Tessier did push everything to the limit: the number of hours he could work per day and the number of patients he could operate on, for example. In surgery, he pushed everything to the limit: nasal bone grafts to lengthen the nose were inserted under great tension and occasionally protruded through the skin, requiring a trimming. One time, he divided a forehead flap at five days. All present and observing were against, but the flap survived.

On his hunting trips to Africa, he pushed himself, and all of those with him, to the limit. He rose before dawn and marched through the bush for 40 km some days.

He would take the Concorde to New York, have a brief meeting, and fly back to Paris on another Concorde the same night.

What made him this way? I can only conclude that it was his *will*, his enormous determination to have surgical procedures turn out as he wished—and they generally would, since the will was coupled with vast experience and tremendous technical ability. He sought perfection in his quest to make people, and children, *normal*. And, in cases such as Burgaud, he found it.

# Chapter 11

## *Secteur "T"*

In the late 1950s, Tessier went hunting for the first time in Africa. He traveled to Gabon with an old friend who introduced him to elephant hunting.

After consulting with other hunters and several big game guides, he began going to the Central African Republic, arriving in Bangui. From there, the expeditions would be staged, once or twice with a guide, and then, often, by himself. The logistical preparations for these trips were like a moon shot, and André Collesson, his nurse anesthetist, would record (during operations) the various objects that he would need. From Bangui, he would go by Land Rover or Dodge truck (which he bought and kept there) toward his preferred hunting area, on the banks of the Chinko River. He thought (erroneously, it turned out) that the large elephants (rogues or "solitaires") who had the biggest tusks would not be found around the villages eating mangos; they would be far from such villages. He arranged the lease of a large territory on the west side of the Chinko, which appears on some maps as "*Secteur T.*"

There is a story, confirmed by Tessier himself and others, about the arrival in Paris in 1970 of Hans Peter Freihofer, his first foreign fellow, sent to him by Hugo Obwegeser of Zurich, the renowned maxillofacial surgeon. Hans Peter arrived, and Tessier asked him, "Hans Peter, you have a dental degree, don't you?" "Why, yes, sir, I do," answered Freihofer. "Well, then, come to Avenue Kléber [where Tessier lived, behind his offices]; I have a job for you."

The job turned out to be taking "dental impressions" of two large "teeth", the very large tusks of an elephant that Tessier had shot. He also had a number of drawings created by Francine Gourdin—essentially architectural or engineering drawings—and on the basis of these and Hans Peter's impressions, brass tusk holders were made so that the tusks could be displayed as Tessier wanted: in front of a mirror.

*Fig. 11.1 Paul Tessier showing the tusks of his largest prey, Central African Republic, ca. 1960 (photo courtesy of Joël Cornet). These weighed 60 kg each and, according to Joël Cornet, were listed in Rowland Ward's "Records of Big Game."*

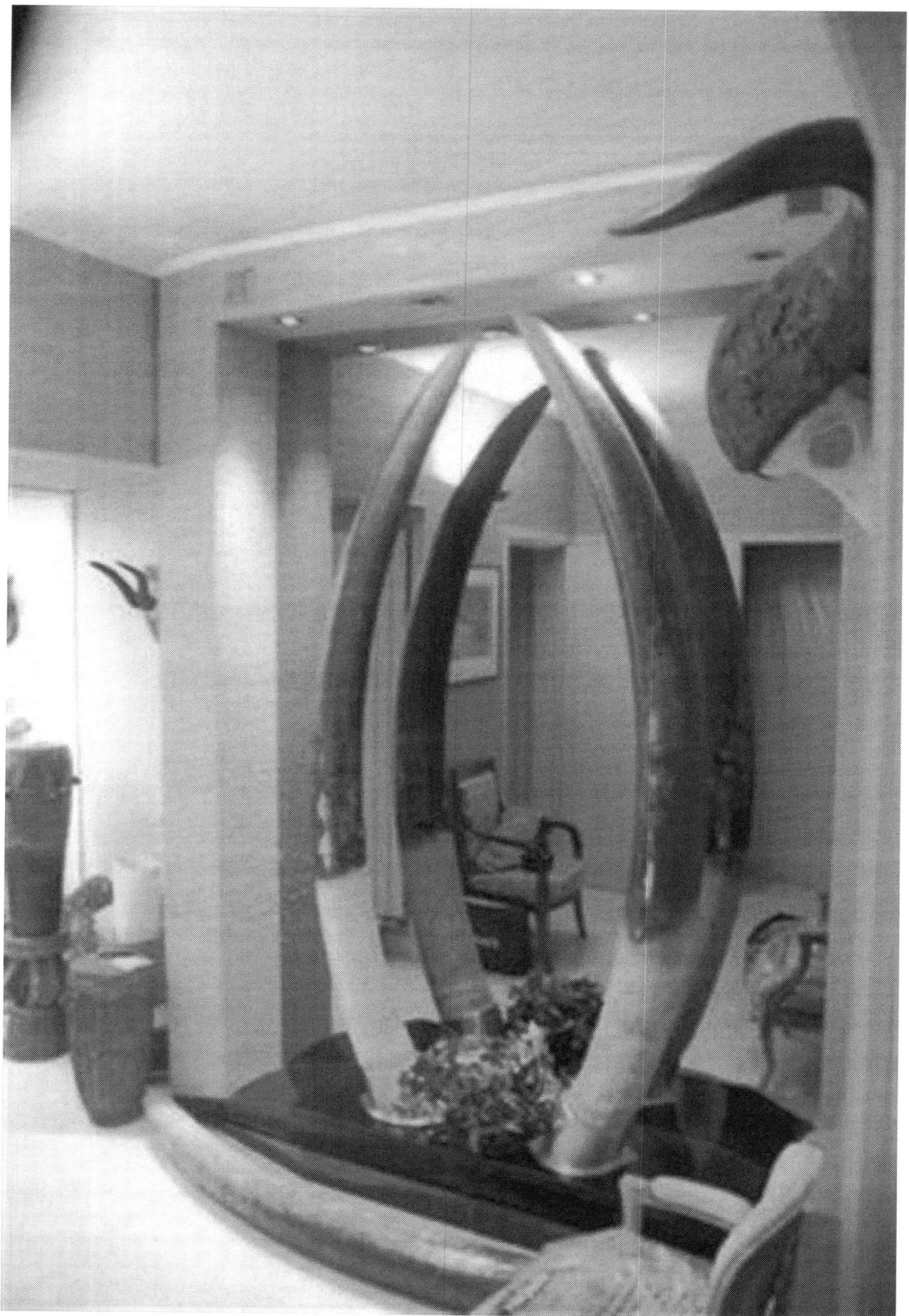

*Fig. 11.2 The same tusks, on display in the entry to his Boulogne apàrtment. They are mounted in brass receptacles of his design, in front of a mirror. Another can be seen on the floor in front of them.*

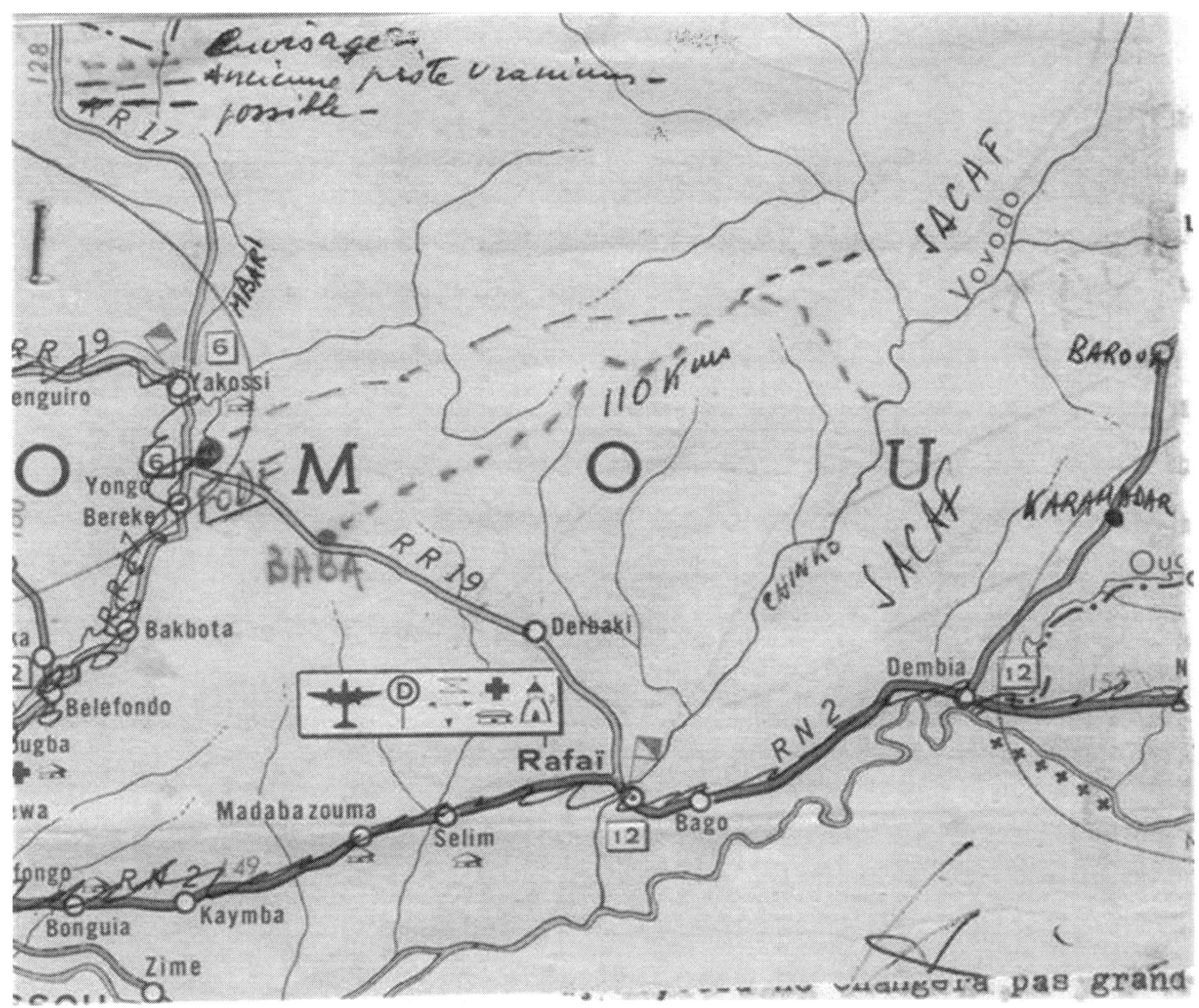


*Fig. 11.3 Dashes indicate one possible route; solid blue dashes represent an old trail of the uranium miners.*

To get to *"Secteur T,"* the expedition would leave Rafai and head east toward the little villages of Karamandar and Aliwaza, where about twenty porters would be recruited.

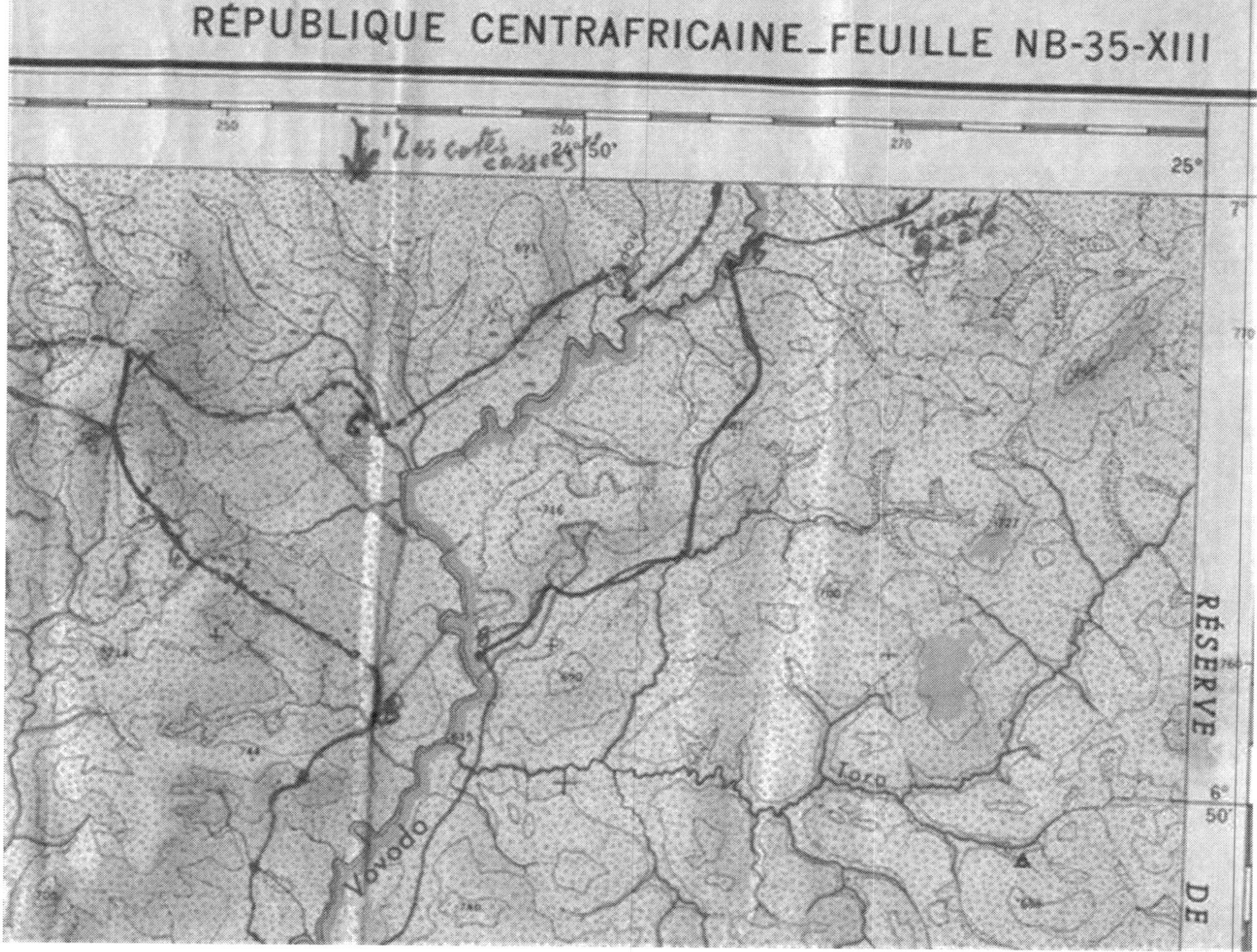


*Fig. 11.5 At the top of the map, Tessier has indicated where he broke several ribs. He was being pursued by an angry elephant and fell against a tree trunk.*

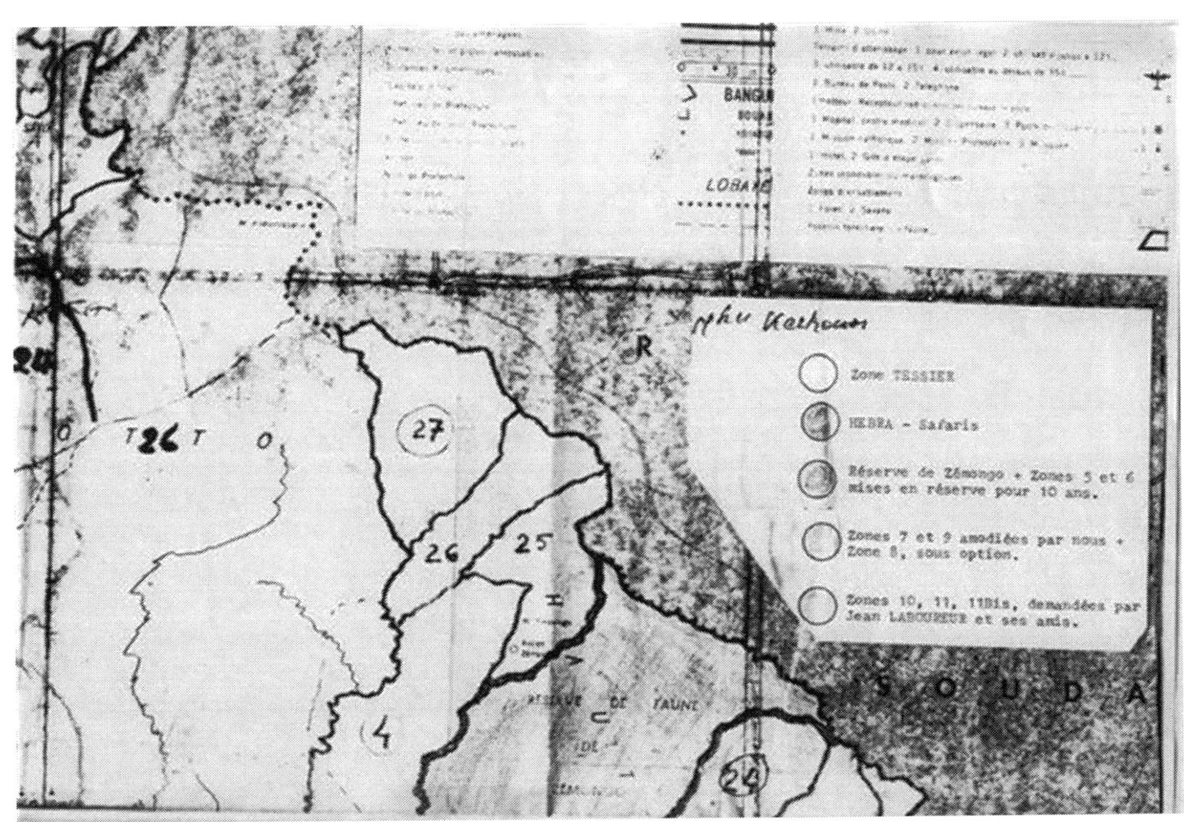


ROBERT J. MONTVOISIN

GUIDE DE CHASSE

TCHAD - BP SARH

E C A - BP BANGUI

BP. 795. Douala

RUC

*Fig. 11.7 Montvoisin's map of various hunting areas, including "Secteur T."*

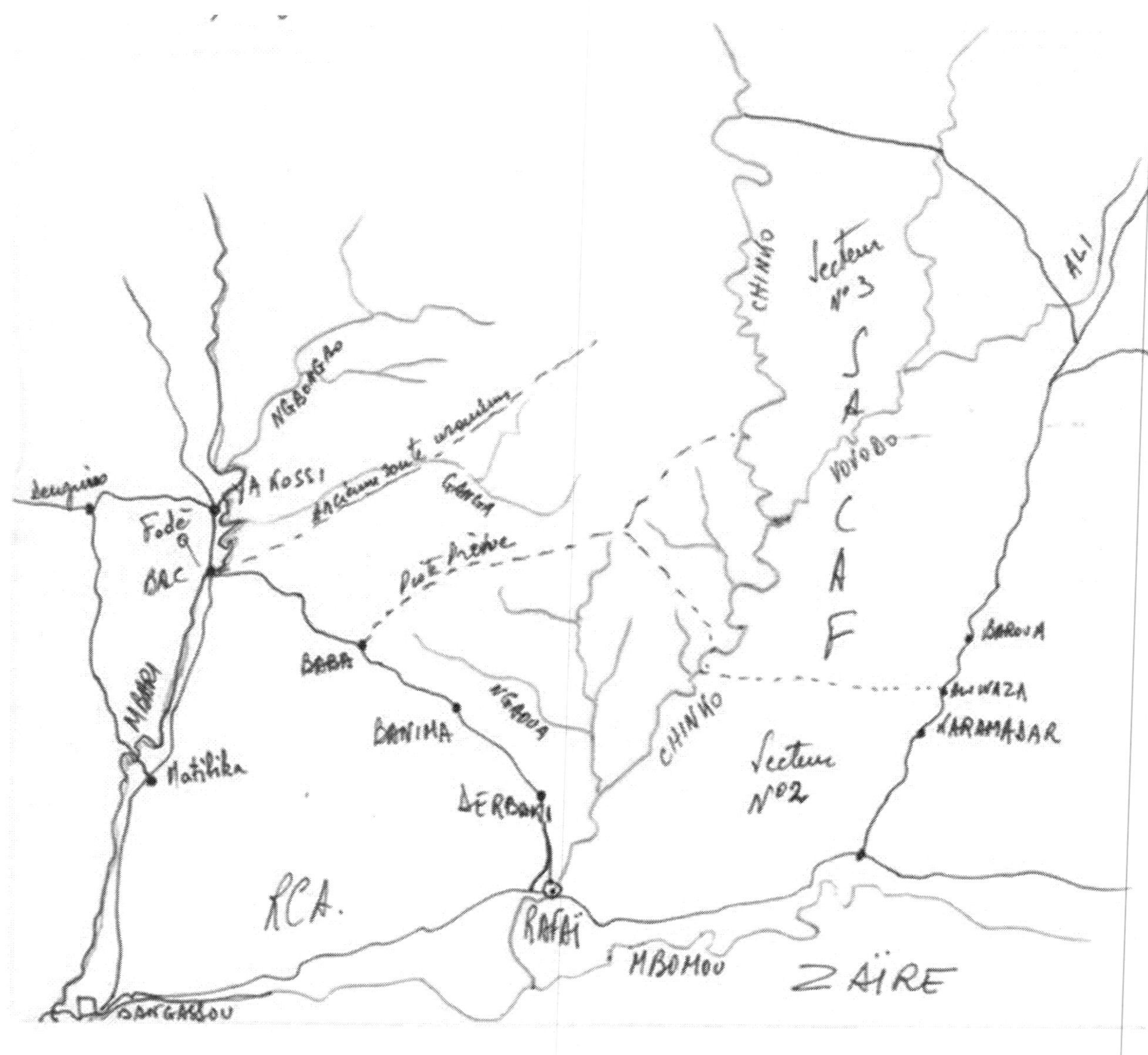


*Fig. 11.8 Drawing from a letter to Tessier by Robert Montvoisin, a hunting guide. What is shown as "Secteur No. 3" became "Secteur T" after Tessier arranged to lease the territory from the government of the Central Aftrican Republic as his exclusive hunting reserve.*

*Fig. 11.9 Paul arriving in Rafai by air, with Mireille and his friend Maurice Lamit, ca. 1976.*

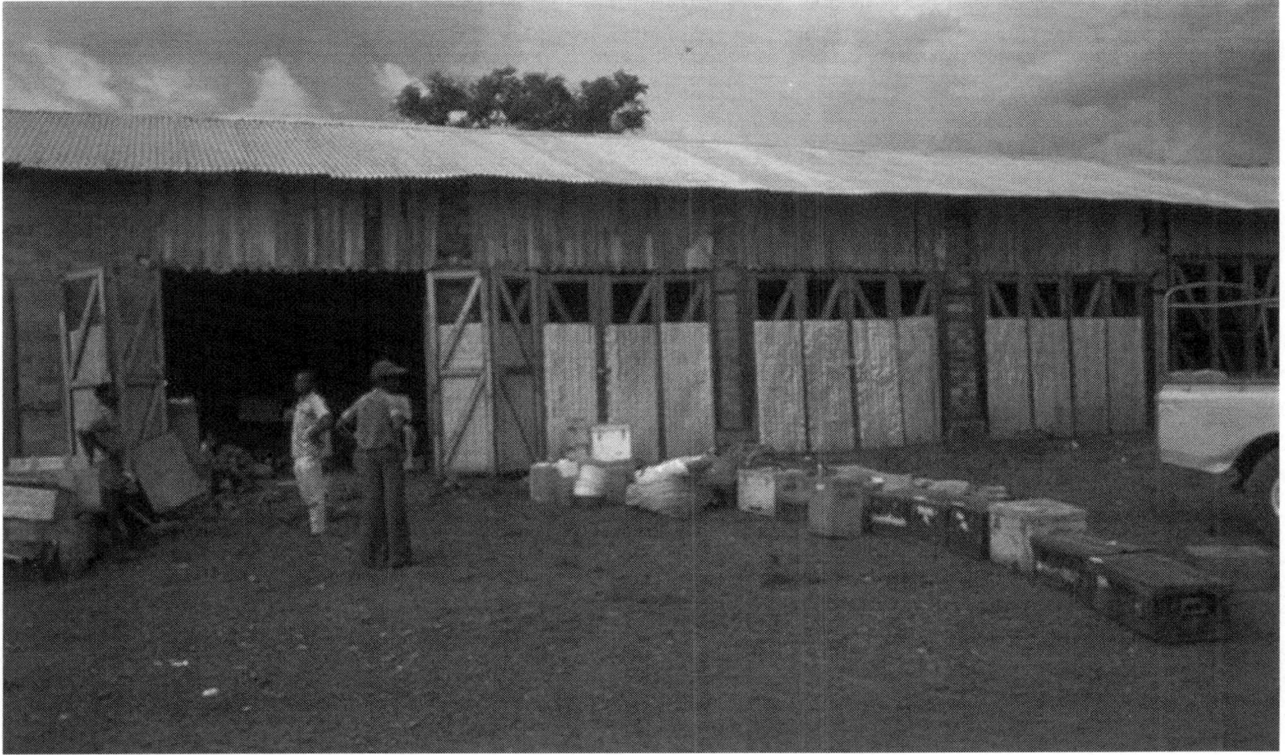

*Fig. 11.10 Gathering together provisions for the expedition at a warehouse in Rafai. The Land Rover is partly visible to the right.*

*Fig. 11.11 Leaving Rafai on foot, 1976.*

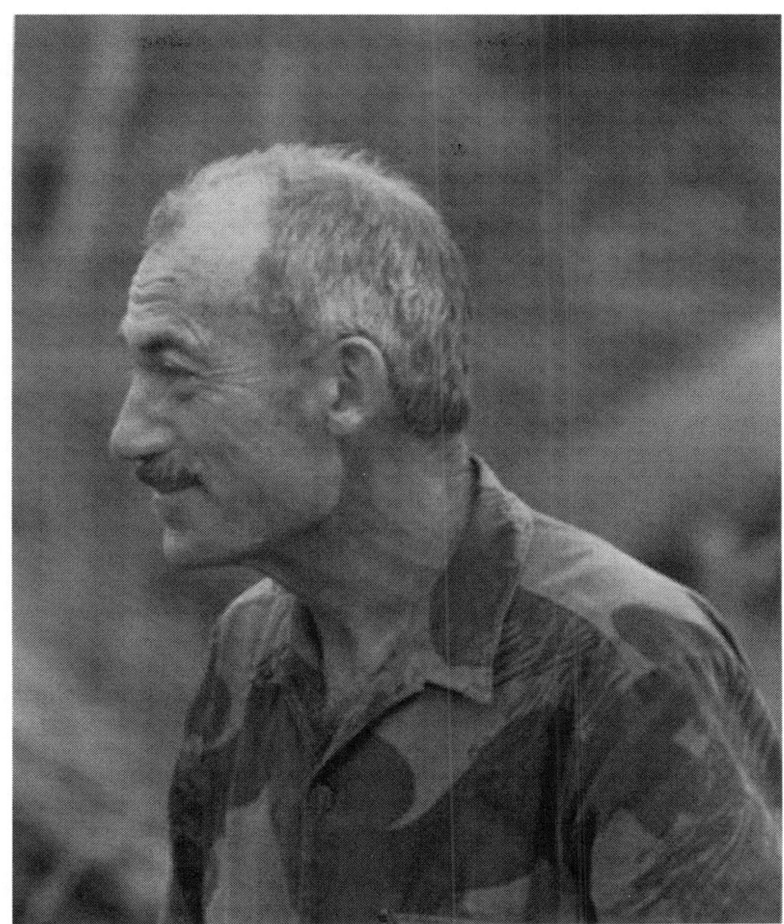

*Fig. 11.12 Paul Tessier on one of his African hunts, ca. 1980. Here he felt he was at his happiest.*

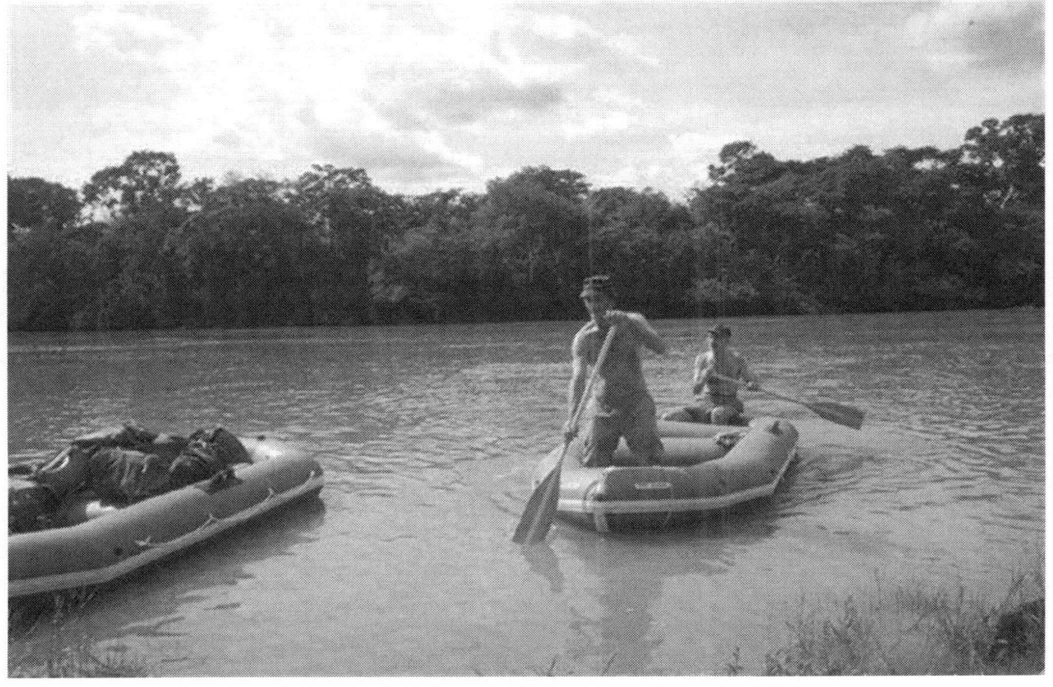

*Fig. 11.13 Tessier (paddling at the stern) on the Chinko.*

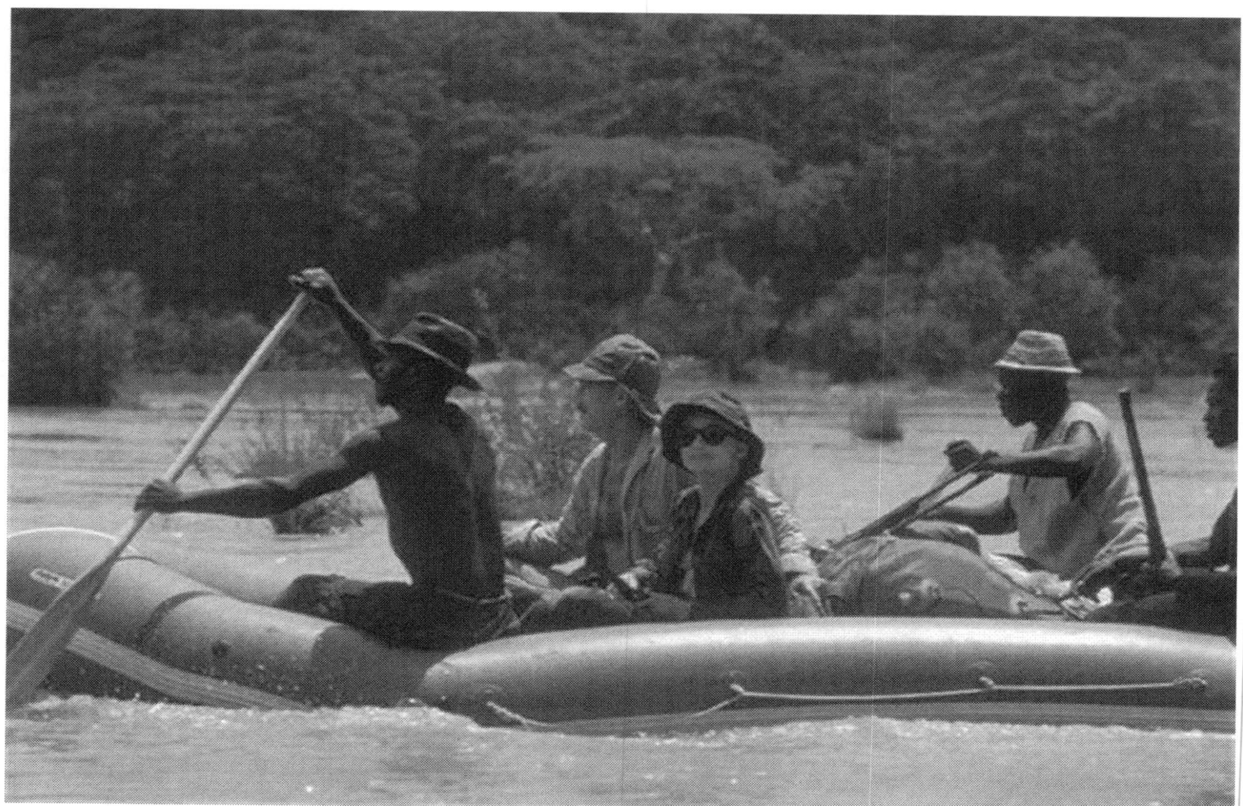

*Fig. 11.14 Paul and Mireille Tessier on the Chinko in a heavily laden Zodiak.*

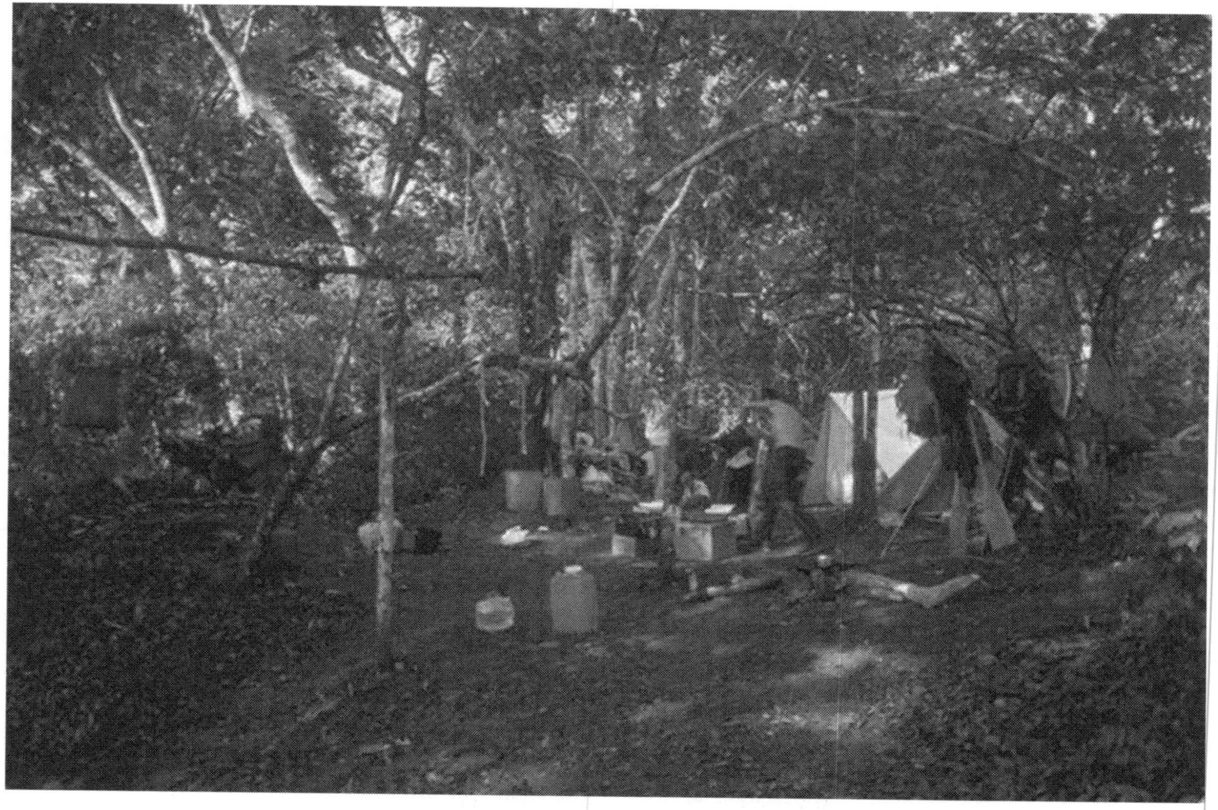

*Fig. 11.15 Setting up the "portable camp."*

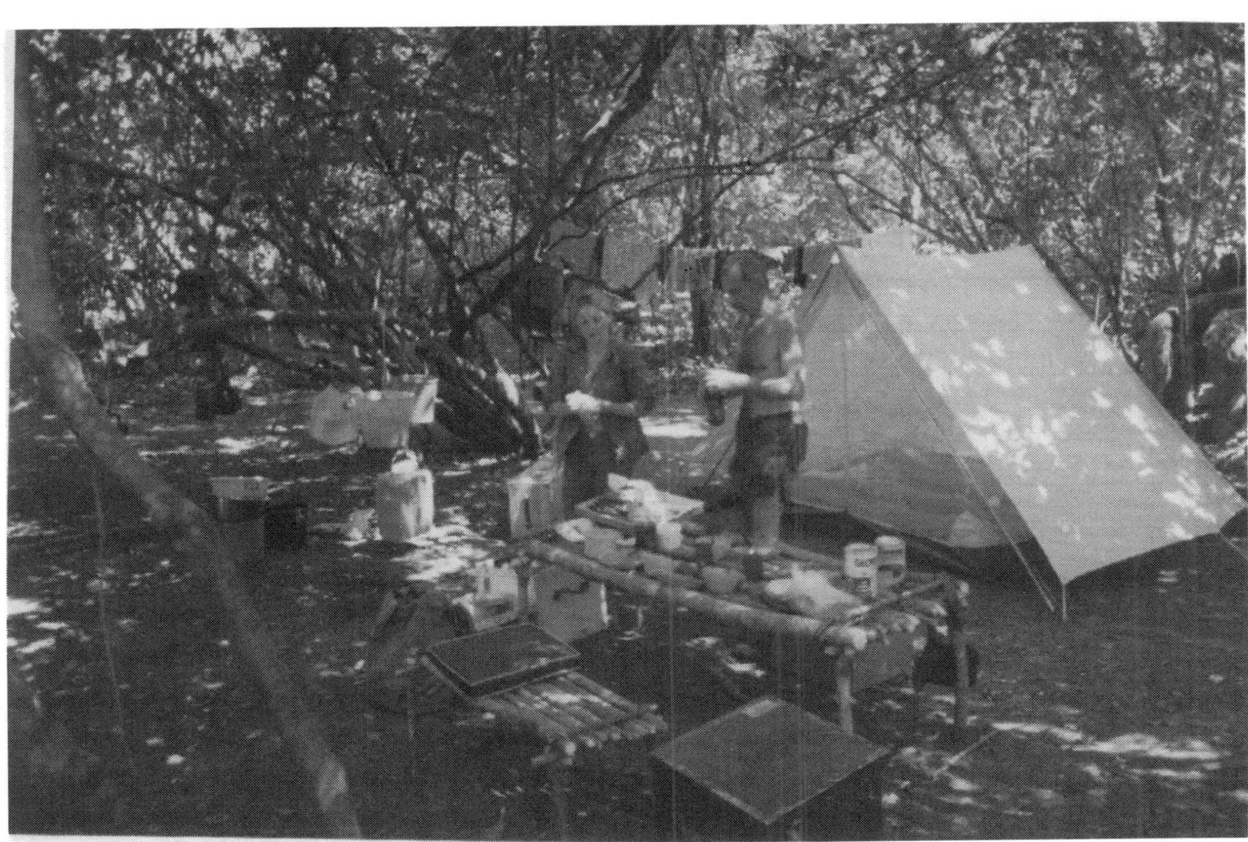

*Fig. 11.16 Paul and Mireille Tessier in camp.*

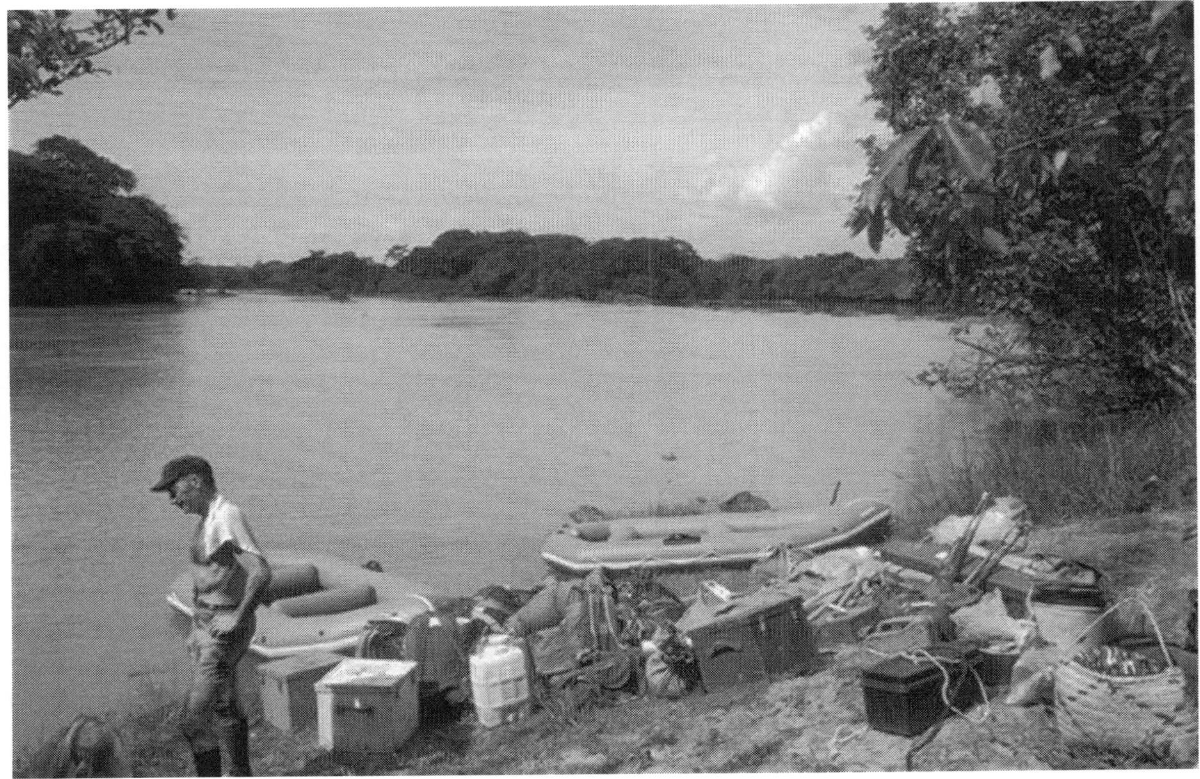

*Fig. 11.17 Paul Tessier and two Zodiaks and their contents, on the banks of the Chinko.*

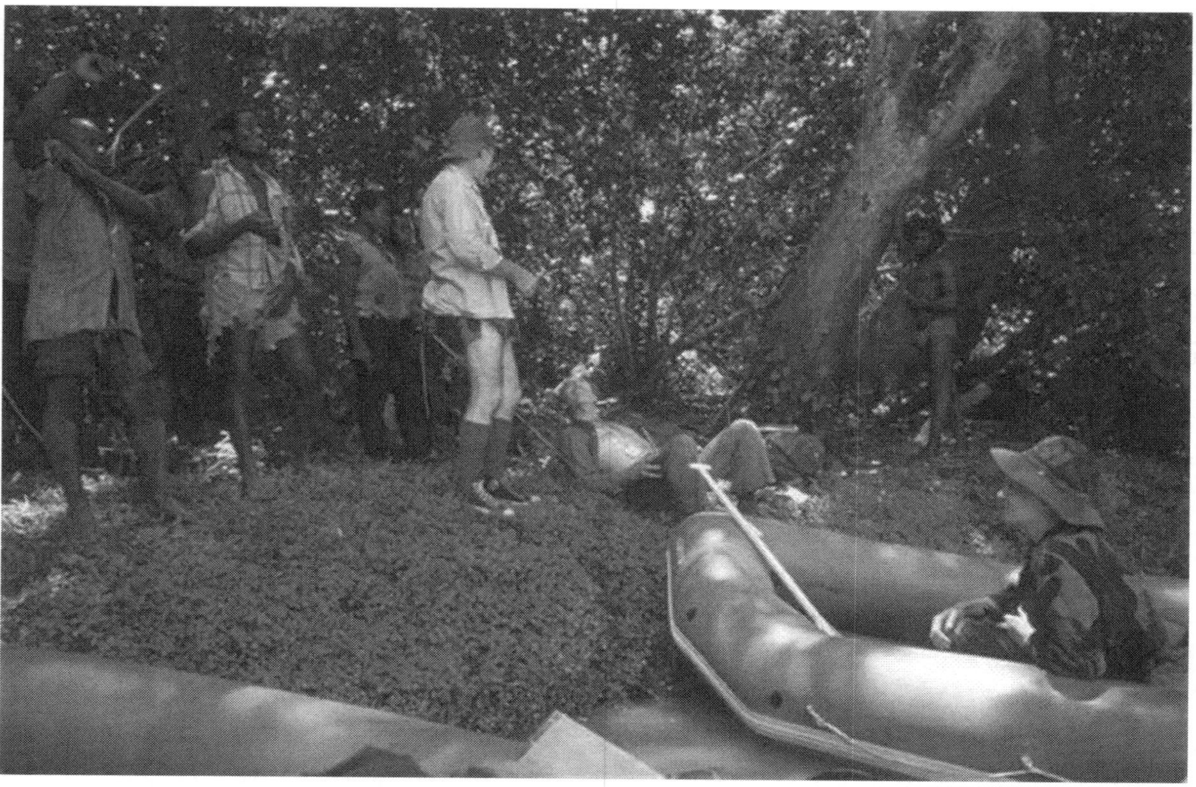

*Fig. 11.18 Tessier, in an outfit of his own design used for long marches on jungle trails: hightop canvas sneakers, knee socks, light shirt with multiple pockets, hat with front and rear brim.*

*Fig. 11.19 Tessier leading the expedition, with a large grin.*

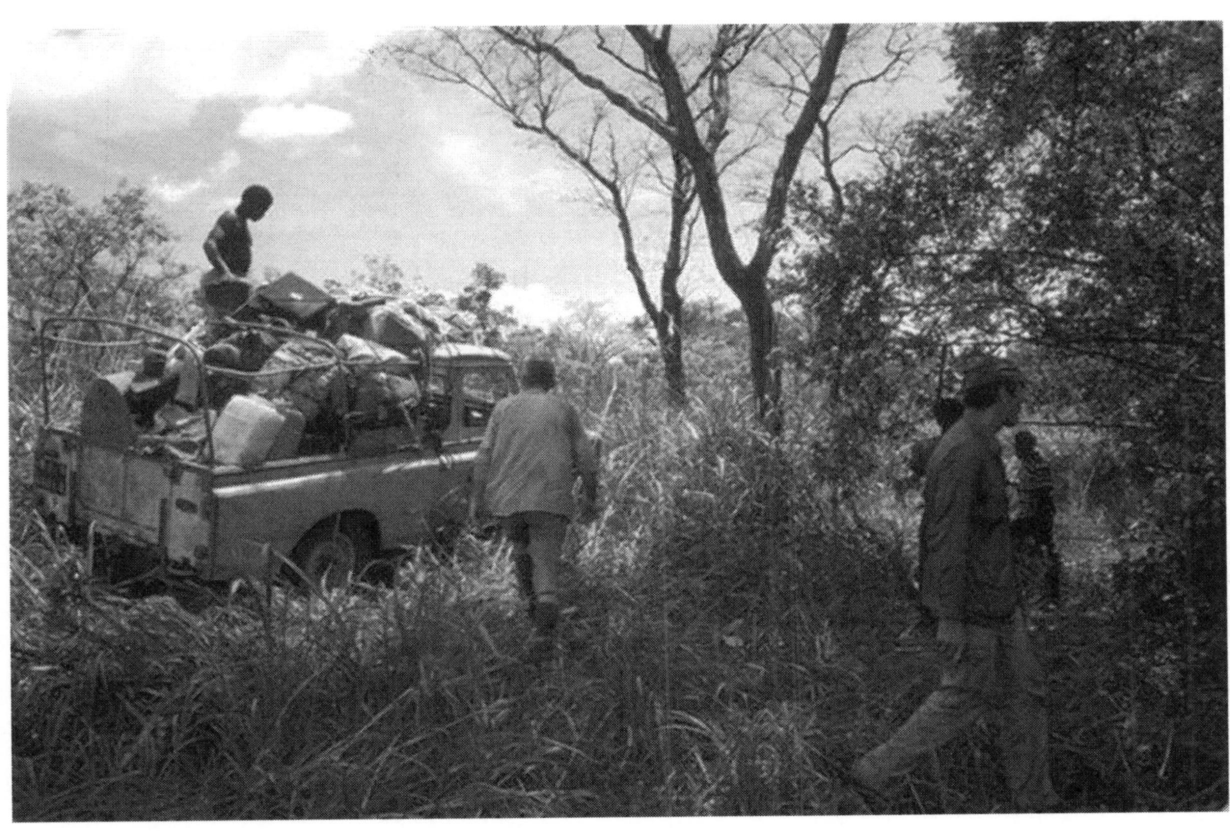

*Fig. 11.20 Tessier going to inspect the Land Rover since they had reached an impasse—or, rather, since the trail had run out altogether.*

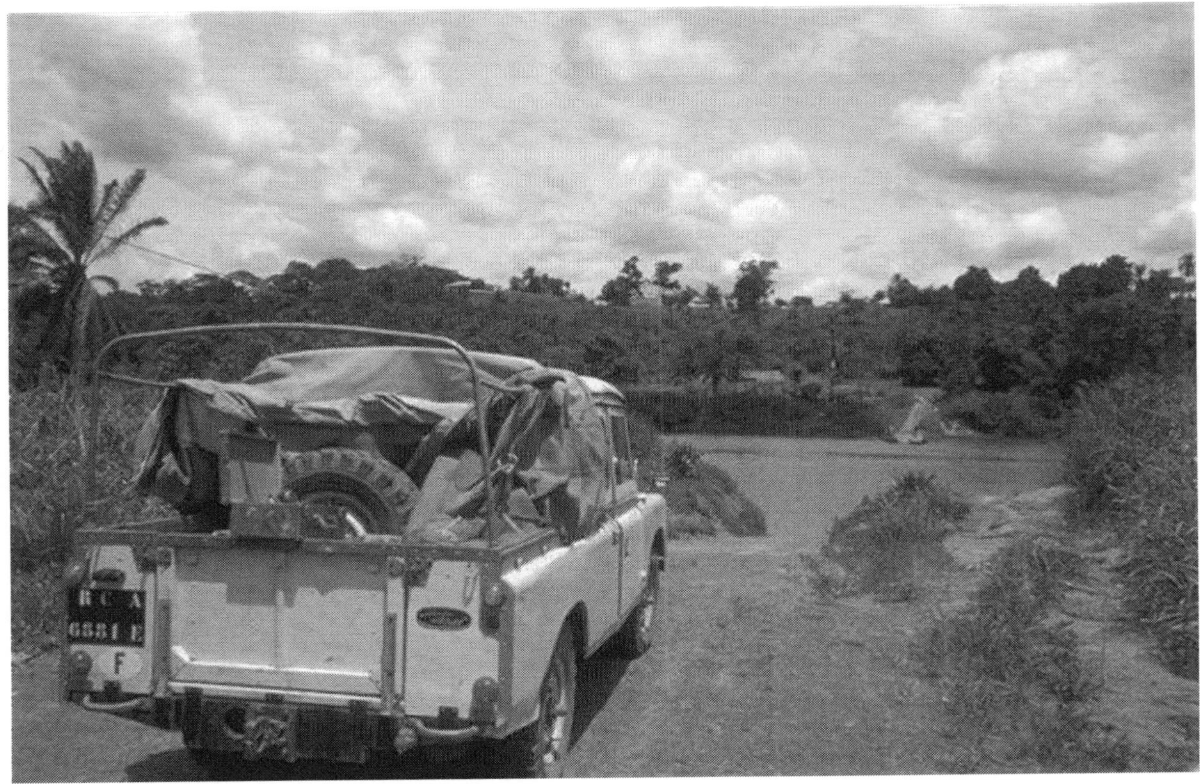


*Fig. 11.21 Waiting for the ferry to cross the Chinko.*

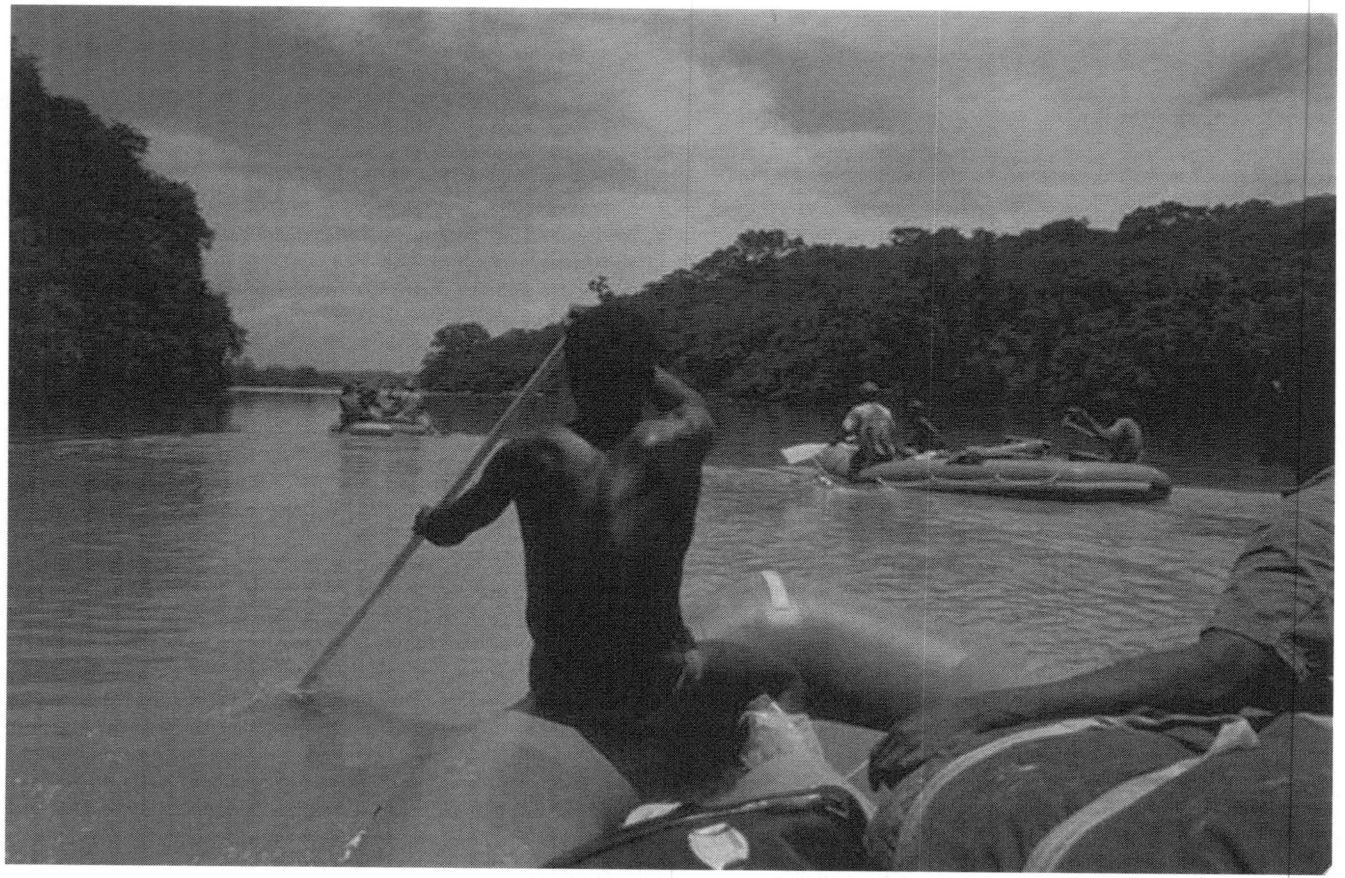

*Fig. 11.22 Tessier's armada heading downstream on the Chinko.*

*Fig. 11.23 Tessier with one of his porters.*

*Fig. 11.24 Family of elephants heading across the Chinko.*

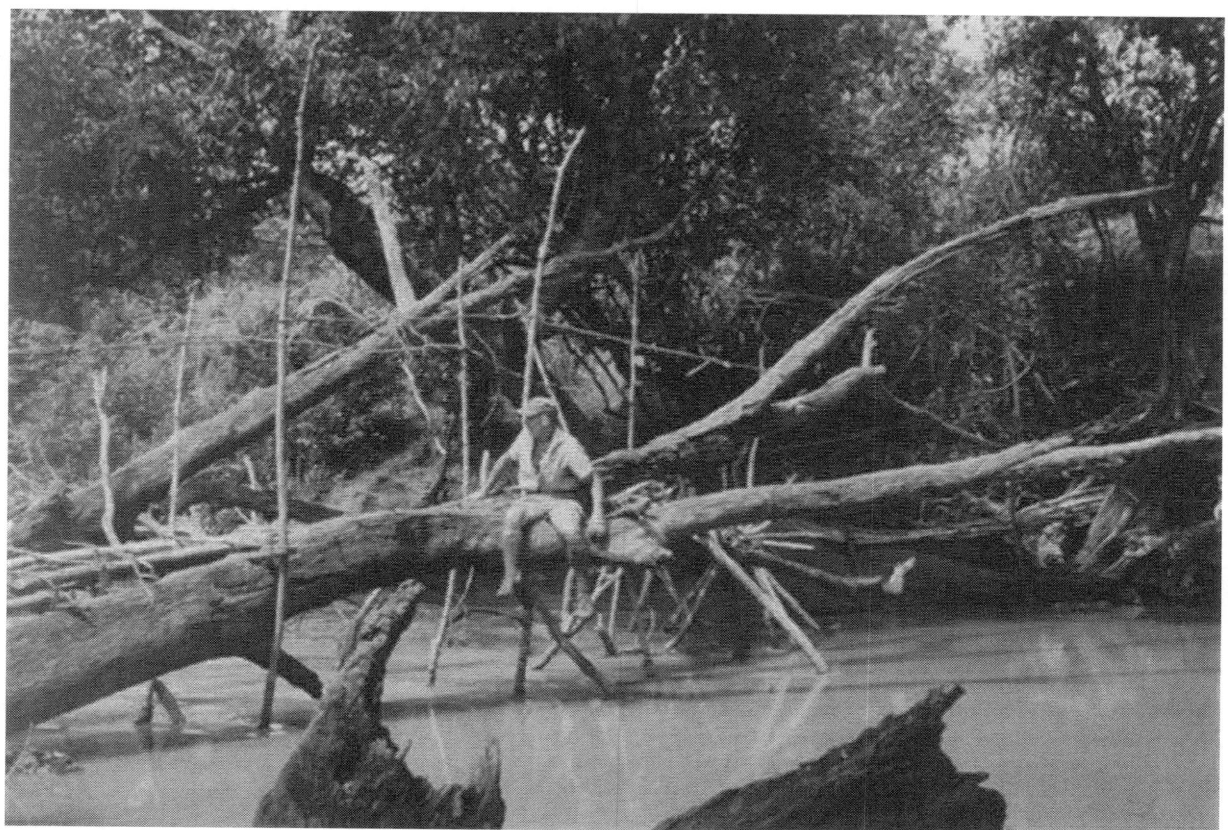

*Fig. 11. 25 Tessier on a "bridge," heading across one of the tributaries of the Chinko.*

*Fig. 11.26 Large elephant just ahead! More often than not, the elephants were just photographed. Only those with large tusks would be considered for hunting.*

*Fig. 11.27 Paul Tessier and an elephant regarding one another. This one was to be photographed, not shot.*

Tessier's trips to the Central African Republic to hunt elephants were his greatest passion and something that he started planning for months ahead of time. Just as in his preparation for major surgical procedures, every step was thought out and documented. And, when he returned to Paris, he wrote a long evaluation of the trip, with criticisms, just as he did with his operative notes.

See Appendixes/Africa for Tessier's planning, comments, criticism, and grades for his African trips.

# Chapter 12

## The early SCUBA diver

Paul met Jacques-Yves Cousteau in the early 1940s when Cousteau was developing his prototype, the Aqua-Lung. Tessier, in 1949, began to dive with a Cousteau-trained team in various sites in the Mediterranean. When David Hemmy went to pick up Tessier in Philadelphia, (from an Air France flight in the early 80s), he introduced him to Cousteau, with whom Tessier had just flown. Tessier introduced him to David as the "Godfather" of—David recalls his son, named Gillies or something similar. That, of course, sounds like his grandson, Gilles. Mireille, however, doubted this relationship. In any event, there is no question that Cousteau and Tessier were good friends, and the "Godfather's" comment may have been a joke on Tessier's part.

*Fig. 12.1 Paul Tessier wearing fins, ready for the sea, ca. 1956. Courtesy of Joël Cornet.*

In a paper published in *Annals of Plastic Surgery (*Vol. 20, No. 6, June 1988), Edward Lamont (1908-1988) wrote a memoir about plastic surgeons he had known, including Harold Gillies, Archibald McIndoe, John Stage Davis, A.A. Limberg, Vilray Blair, and J. Eastman Sheehan. Lamont had been a plastic surgeon in Hollywood, California. He wrote about Tessier: "Before formally entering plastic surgery, Tessier visited me in 1952, interested in learning about the specialty but primarily concerned with country and western music and scuba diving, a sport in which he held several European deep-diving records. I obtained the records for him through a studio and flew him to La Jolla in a small Navion, where he made several deep scuba-diving attempts. After leaving me, he spent several years with Jacques Cousteau, furthering his finesse in the art of scuba diving, before blossoming into a renowned plastic surgeon."

Tessier, in turn, discussed his trip to the United States in a conversation with Fernando Ortiz-Monasterio (Paul Tessier, *In Memorium*, privately printed by Fernando Ortiz-Monasterio). Tessier notes, "When I arrived in Los Angeles, when I saw this marvelous ocean, I said to myself that I cannot stay here for 6 weeks without going 'underwater hunting' (la chasse sous marine). Because I had done it since 1949, in France. It might have been Lamont who put me in contact with a Frenchman who had opened a business there, and who represented the spirotechnic material, and the Cousteau apparatuses. He sold 1000 of them to the US Navy, which proved that it was good material, for the US Navy to buy foreign material. Then, this Frenchman put me in touch with a man who I still remember, who was T. Ricor. He was an American who had trained the American commandos in the Pacific during the war against the Japanese. But Ricor was about 5 feet tall, and his coworker was a giant of German origin who was well over 6 feet. In me they saw a Frenchman who was enthralled with spear fishing. We went out a little north of Santa Barbara in an inflatable boat. All of the equipment had been strapped down inside the boat. And when I saw the enormous rollers, these huge waves of the Pacific coast, I said to myself that we would never be able to get into the water in all of that. There was nothing but huge waves of water. And then, after the fourth or fifth one, we passed the mark, and found ourselves in calm water, marvelous, very clear. And we fished. I haven't continued to do this. But I did in 1949. There were very few people doing it. There have been errors written about this: that I dived with Cousteau. It was not with Cousteau but with the first team that Cousteau had trained. I did some every summer. I went to the Midi. I did it for 3 years. There were fish then. Now there are none."

We see that Tessier did know Cousteau, and was involved in scuba diving early on in the development of the equipment. But he did not dive with Cousteau—rather, he went diving with one of Cousteau's teams. There is no evidence that he continued the sport beyond the late 1950s.

# Chapter 13

## The stock car racer

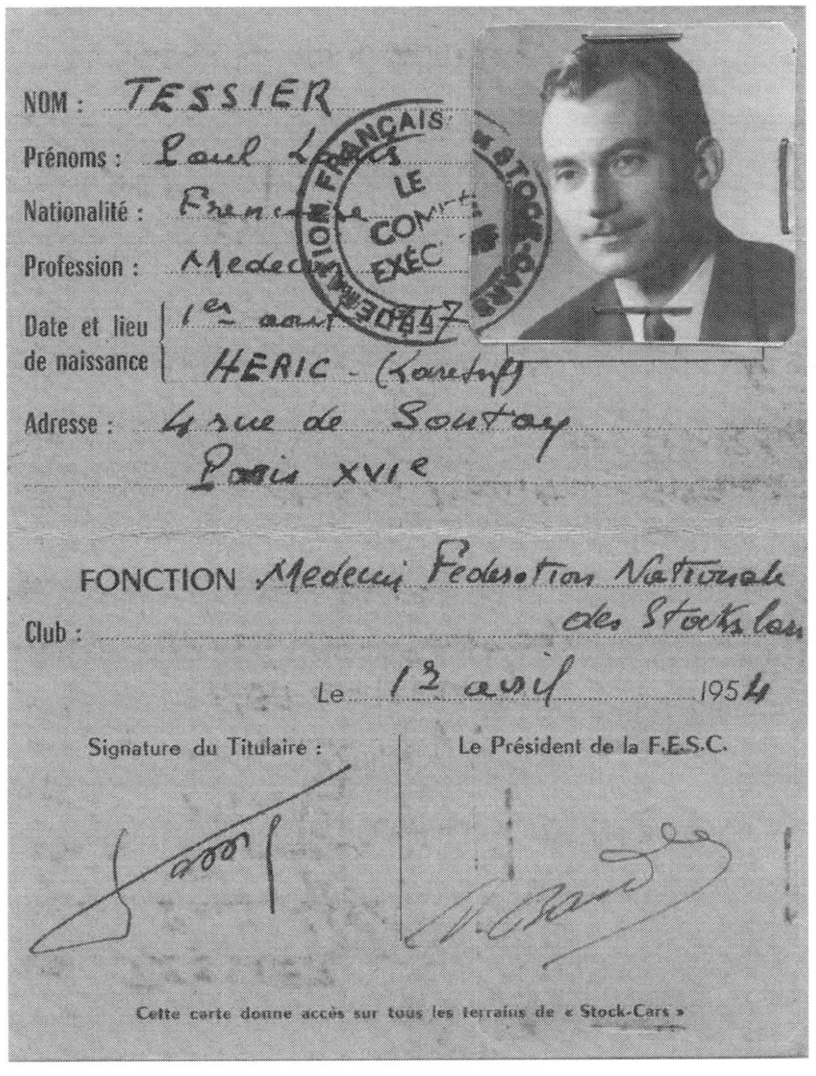

NOM : TESSIER

Prénoms : Paul L...

Nationalité : Fran...

Profession : Medec...

Date et lieu de naissance : 1er ...

HERIC - (Loire-Inf)

Adresse : 4 rue de Soutay

Paris XVIe

FONCTION Medecin Federation Nationale des Stocks Cars

Club :

Le 12 avril 1954

Signature du Titulaire :

Le Président de la F.E.S.C.

Cette carte donne accès sur tous les terrains de « Stock-Cars »

*Fig. 13.1 Tessier's identity card for the National Federation of Stockcars, 1954.*

Tessier's identity card identified him as a physician; but he was also a racer, racing under the names "Harry Covert" and "John Duff." (French: haricot vert=green bean, jaune d'oeuf= egg yolk)

Tessier first met his friend, Bob Maloubier, in 1949, and Bob was also a stock car driver. They went to the Buffalo Stadium in Vanves and raced without seat belts or helmets. Bob reports that Tessier was a fiercely competitive driver, but he did not have much time for the social aspects of the Stock Car group since he was so busy with his surgical work. His racing days ended when there was an accident that involved a fatality (which was responsible for new, restrictive security rules). They left with a few bumps and good memories.

This early experience as a racing driver was evident in Tessier's later life. In the 1960s he had a series of Alfa Romeos, and, in the mid-1970s, when I was there, it was an orange BMW, a 3-series, with a special–order, 6-cylinder engine. All of these cars were driven to their limit.

*Fig. 13.2 Paul Tessier and his special BMW, ca. 1983.*

I drove with him once in his car from Nantes to Paris, and I think he must have set the track record. Those who drove with him in Paris traffic remember him as a fast driver, but always under control. At age eighty, when he insisted on doing all of driving on the Tour de Bretagne (Chapter 37), he took me and Henry Kawamoto (and our wives Deirdre and Kathy). He had the rented Audi A4 "pedal to the metal" the whole time. Some might say that driving as he did was reckless, but it was completely consistent with his character and his will to push everything to the limit. He did it safely.

# Chapter 14

## International Society of Plastic and Reconstructive Surgery: Rome, 1967

The first meeting of the International Society of Plastic Surgery took place in Stockholm in 1955, and Paul Tessier, Sir Harold Gillies, Tord Skoog, Varaztad Kazanjian, and Ralph Millard (who presented his rotation-advancement for the first time here) were all present. It is unknown what interactions took place between these past, present, and future luminaries of plastic surgery, but Gillies and Millard were almost certainly in contact. None of the others mentioned above likely had any idea, at the time, who Paul Tessier was.

There were later meetings of the ISPRS (which is now known as IPRAS—International Plastic and Reconstructive and Aesthetic Society) that occurred in London and Washington, and the 4th meeting took place in Rome, in 1967. Before this meeting, hardly anyone in the English-speaking world knew who Paul Tessier was; after the meeting, however, virtually everyone knew. Tessier's presentations in Rome on the Le fort III osteotomy (there were also presentations about the correction of orbital hypertelorism and oro-ocular clefts) had an enormous impact on all who were present.

Partly, this was because all could see the enormous changes that had taken place in his patients, but they were impactful because they had been so carefully prepared. The clinical photographs were all of the highest caliber, and the illustrations, by Francine Gourdin, were of a quality never seen before in medical illustration. It is interesting to reread this paper more than forty-two years later. Tessier had waited nine years after he performed his first Le Fort III to present his results. It is hard to imagine any other plastic surgeon of that time (or this time, for that matter) sitting on something like this.

Tessier mentions at the outset the previous work of Sir Harold Gillies. In 1942, Gillies was on the Isle of Wight (most likely to play golf), and he ran across a nursing student who he described as having "oxycephaly." He arranged for her to come to London where he developed a procedure that would cut her midface free and hold it forward onto a plaster head cap. When the wires were removed after three weeks, her midface underwent an almost total relapse. In 1949, Gillies operated on her again, expanded her orbits, placed ox cartilage over her zygomas, and performed a rhinoplasty— all of which were attempts to c amouflage the underlying problem, which was still uncorrected.

This case is shown in Gillies and Millard (*Principles and Art of Plastic Surgery*[1]), and Hugo Obwegeser was the assistant during the 1949 operation. The case was published in *The British Journal of Plastic Surgery*[2] in 1950. Gillies, according to Obwegeser, told all of his trainees that this was an operation that should never be done again. However, years later, Obwegeser said that the father of a child with Apert's syndrome had come to see him in Zurich with a letter from Gillies, saying that the patient should go to London so an operation could be performed.

The second thing that is interesting about Tessier's paper is his focus on the ophthalmologic aspects of his procedure: the dissection of the inferior oblique, preservation of the superior oblique, and avoidance of the lacrimal system and canthal tendon. This came no doubt from his enormous experience with orbital surgery.

The key difference between the Tessier procedure and Gillies's—besides having the osteotomy line behind rather than in front of the lacrimal system—is the use of autogenous bone grafts. Here, Tessier goes into great detail describing the shape and positioning of each graft and how he saved unused bone and cartilage for later use either in the bone bank or subcutaneously in the chest.

Although Tessier had presented this same paper several months earlier to a French audience in Montpellier, this was the first presentation on the international scene, and it is considered by many to be the moment of birth for craniofacial surgery.

Following is the paper that Tessier submitted for the transactions of that meeting, with my English translation. He was fifty years old at the time.

**DYSOSTOSES CRANIO-FACIALES**
**(Syndromes de Crouzon et d'Apert)**
**Ostéotomies Totales de la Face**

PAUL TESSIER

Hôpital Foch, Paris, France

Les dysostoses cranio-faciales sont caractérisées par une synostose prématurée des sutures coronales (acrocéphalies), sagittales (scaphocéphalies) ou de toutes les sutures (oxycéphalies).

De cette atrésie de la base du crâne, on peut déduire que l'orbite osseuse, n'ayant pas atteint des dimensions normales propulse le globe et cette protrusion est appelée exophtalmie. Or, cette exophtalmie n'est que relative, par rapport à un massif facial en retrait. De plus, le crâne ayant pris un développement vertical anormal, aux dépends de son développement antéro-postérieur, ne permet pas de mesurer l'exophtalmie en fonction d'une arcade sourcillière et d'un malaire hypoplasié.

L'oeil semble luxé en avant d'un rebord orbitaire en retrait (exorbitisme) que l'intervention revèlera souvent comme très grêle. La rétrusion du massif facial participe donc à l'exorbitisme et constitue le rétrognathisme maxillaire (faux prognathisme mandibulaire).

*La pourquoi de l'intervention*

Une ostéotomie totale de la face se propose donc d'augmenter la profondeur de l'orbite et de rendre au massif facial et à l'arcade maxillaire supérieure, une protrusion normale.

Puisqu'une synostose prématurée de la base du crâne a bloqué la projection du massif facial, il faut désolidariser celui-ci du crâne et l'avancer en bloc. Pour cela, il suffit de reprendre les traits d'une disjonction cranio-faciale qui, puisqu'elle recule le massif facial, doit lui donner assez de liberté pour le propulser. L'ostéotomie totale ou ses variantes atténuées, s'étend aussi bien aux déformations traumatiques qu'aux malformations congénitales.

En 1950, Gillies avait proposé une ostéotomie sur la crête lacrymale antérieure et sur le bord inférieur de l'orbite. Ce tracé restait donc en avant du petit oblique, du sac lacrymal, du ligament palpébral et, avec lui, des paupières. On restait éloigné d'une véritable disjonction cranio-faciale. Or, il est possible de reporter l'ostéotomie sur la face interne de l'orbite, en arrière du système lacrymal, pour l'avancer en bloc avec les paupières. On ne craint alors plus ni l'obstruction du sac par un fragment osseux, ni la section du canal lacrymo-nasal, ni la coudure des canalicules lacrymaux. D'autre part, il est prouvé qu'on peut désinsérer le petit oblique même d'un seul côté sans provoquer de diplopie. Il suffit d'en laisser les insertions solidaires du cône fibreux de l'orbite qu'est son périoste pour que les relations des différents muscles ne soient pas modifiés.

*Les conséquences majeures* de l'avancement en bloc du massif facial sont:

— une correction complète du rétrognathisme supérieur,
— une réduction de l'infragnathie si elle existe,
— parfois, car on provoque une expansion de l'orbite, une enophtalmie sans dommage ni pour la vision binoculaire, ni pour la motilité du globe.

Comme *effets seconds*, mentionnons:

— une projection normale du nez qui révèle alors ses véritables dimensions (soit hypertrophie banale, soit véritable rhinomégalie);
— une rétrogénie (paradoxale si l'on tient compte du 'prognathisme') que fait apparaitre la projection du maxillaire supérieur et du nez.

774

*Fig. 14.1 Paul Tessier's paper on the Craniofacial Dysostoses*

Below is my English translation of same.

**The Craniofacial Dysostoses**
**(Crouzon and Apert Syndrome)**
**Total Osteotomies of the Face**

**PAUL TESSIER**
**Hôpital Foch, Paris, France**

The craniofacial dysostoses are characterized by a premature synostosis of the coronal (acrocephalies), sagittal (scaphocephalies) or of all of the sutures (oxycehalies).

From this atresia of the base of the skull, on can deduce that the bony orbit, not having attained normal dimensions, pushes the globe forward and this protrusion is called exophthalmia. But, the exophthalmia is only relative, in relationship to a midface which is retruded. In addition, the skull having taken an abnormal vertical development, at the expense of its anterior-posterior development, does not permit the measurement of the exophthalmia relative to a subraorbital ridge or malar bone which are hypoplastic.

The eye seems to be luxated in front of a retruded orbital rim (exorbitism) which, at operation, is often found to be very frail. The retrusion of the mid-face participates therefore in the exorbitism and also involves a maxillary retrognathism (false mandibular prognathism).

*The Why of the Operation*

A total osteotomy of the face is proposed therefore, to augment the depth of the orbit and to give to the midface and the arch of the upper jaw a normal protrusion.

Since a premature synostosis of the base of the skull has blocked the projection of the midface, it is necessary to separate this from the skull and advance it en bloc. To accomplish this, it is sufficient to reproduce by osteotomy the lines of a cranio-facial disjunction which, because it moves back the midface, should also give it enough freedom to move it forward. The total osteotomy or its lesser variations is quite applicable both to traumatic deformities and to congenital malformations.

In 1950, Gilles proposed an osteotomy along the anterior lacrimal crest and the inferior border of the orbit. The osteotomy line, therefore, remained in front of the inferior oblique, the lacrimal sac, the palpebral ligament, and with it, the eyelids. This was from a true cranio-facial disjunction. But, it is possible to carry the osteotomy along the inner surface of the orbit, behind the lacrimal system, to adnce en bloc with the eyelids. One does not have concern now about the obstruction of the sac by a bone fragment, or the section of the naso-lacrimal canal, nor the suturing of the lacrimal canaliculi. And, it has been shown that one can disinsert the inferior oblique been just on one side without causing a diplopia. It is sufficient to leave intact the insertions on the fibrous cone of the orbit, which is its periosteum, for the relations of the different muscles not to be altered.

*The major consequences* of the advancement of the midface are:

— a complete correction of the upper retrognathism.
— a correction of the infragnathia, if it exists.
— sometimes, because one is causing an expansion of the orbit, an enopthalmia, without interfering with either binocular vision, or the motility of the globe.

As *secondary effects,* we mention:

— a normal projection of the nose, which reveals its true dimensions (either banal hypertrophy, or a true rhinomegaly).
— a retrogenia (paradoxical, if one recalls the ‘prognathism’) which appears after the projection of the upper jaw and the nose.

Plate I. Case No. 1.

References:

1. Gilles, H.D., and Millard, D.R., Jr. The Principles and Art of Plastic Surgery. Little, Brown & Co. Boston 1957, pp. 551-553.
2. Gilles, H.D. and Harriso, S.H. Operative Correction by Osteotomy of Recessed Malar Maxillary Compound in a case of Oxycephaly. Brit. J. Plast. Surg., 2:123, 1950.

DYSOSTOSES CRANIO-FACIALES

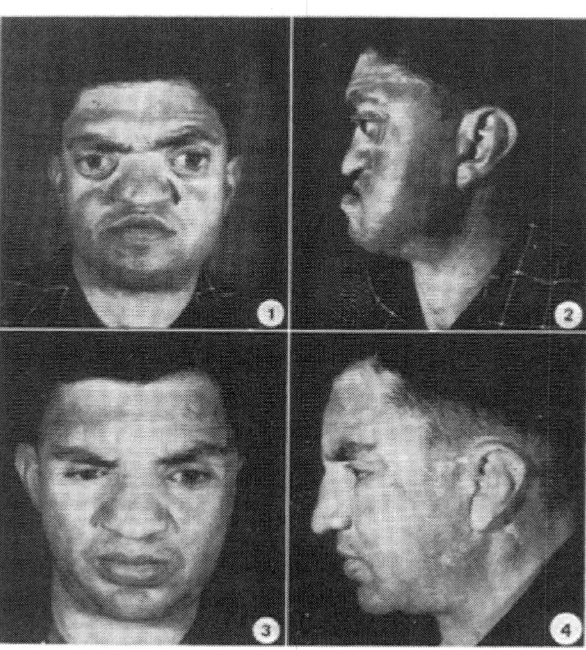

*Planche I, Cas n° 1.*
*Figs. 1, 2.* Avant. Maladie de Crouzon.
*Figs. 3, 4.* Après. Ostéotomie totale de la face — greffe osseuse du menton.

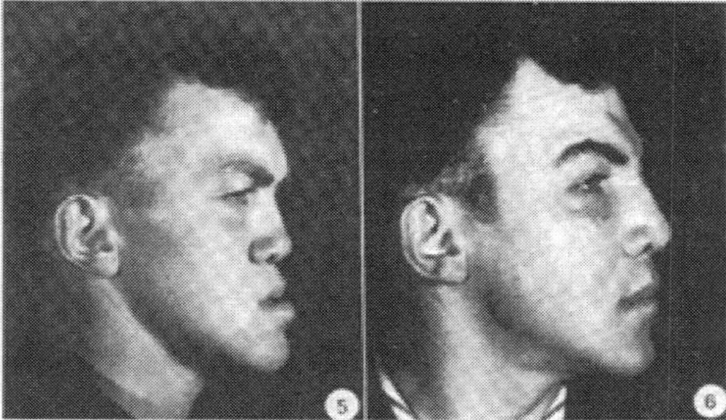

*Planche II, Cas n° 2.*
*Fig. 5.* Avant. Rétrusion du massif facial.
*Fig. 6.* Après. Ostéotomie totale de la face.

## QUELS SONT LES DANGERS ET LES ECUEILS?

*1. Le risque respiratoire*

Sujets fragiles, brièveté du cou, blocage inter-maxillaire parfois, mais surtout risque d'obstruction par un voile inerte, par des mèches inter-ptérygo-maxillaires, ou par des caillots, c'est plus qu'il n'en faut pour exiger une trachéotomie à titre de premier geste.

2. *L'ethmoïde*

Pour projeter harmonieusement le nez avec le massif facial, pour déplacer 'en bloc' le système lacrymal sans risque de sténose, l'ostéotomie doit passer au large du sac. Pour cette raison et pour d'autres, elle doit donc raser la base du crâne.

Le repérage radiologique ne devrait pas laisser place au risque.

Mais il faut tenir compte des données suivantes:

*a.* d'un écart inter-canthal exagéré pouvant résulter un prolapsus de la lame criblée;

*b.* l'obliquité de l'étage antérieur de la base du crâne est parfois très important dans le syndrome de Crouzon;

*c.* enfin, une dysostose cranio-faciale, même en l'absence de dystrophie ou d'hypertélorisme peut masquer une rarissime méningo-encéphalocèle de la base (un cas).

3. *Le système lacrymal*

Ici, point n'est besoin de la contourner au plus près (hypertélorisme et ostéotomies cranio-faciales). Il suffit de repérer le sac, d'abaisser son dôme pour accéder à la face interne de l'orbite, de désinsérer le petit oblique pour entailler, dans la profondeur, l'angle inféro-interne.

4. *Les muscles obliques*

La poulie du grand oblique n'est pas interessée par la rugine. Par contre, une désinsertion bien réglée du petit oblique est indispensable pour conserver à celui-ci, par l'intermédiaire du périoste, des rapports constants avec les autres muscles oculo-moteurs.

5. *La pseudarthrose possible*

Il s'en faut que l'ostéotomie totale de la face connaisse les larges surfaces de contact de l'ostéotomie cranio-faciale des hypertélorismes. Une fois la face libérée du crâne, des diastasis se creusent entre le frontal et le nez, mais davantage encore entre les deux fragments du malaire, et aussi entre le maxillaire et les ptérygoïdes. Certes, des greffons peuvent rétablir la continuité au deux premiers points critiques, mais dans l'espace inter-ptérygo-maxillaire, aucun contrôle à vue, aucune greffe n'est possible. Aussi, importe-t-il de pallier à ce déficit par un renforcement des contreforts antérieures (fronto-nasal) et latéraux (fronto-malaires). Aussi faut-il exiger de la contention, des qualités toutes particulières: traction continue en avant pour vaincre les sollicitations postérieures, stabilité exceptionnelle, indépendance vis à vis de la mandibule.

6. *Quels sont les autres écueils frôlés par une telle intervention?*

L'artère palatine postérieure qu'il paraît difficile d'épargner à coup sûr. Nous l'avons pu éviter jusqu'alors semble-t-il, mais il serait étonnant qu'il en soit toujours ainsi.

Le pédicule sous-orbitaire dont l'élongation semble impossible et qui cependant suit le mouvement, sans rupture.

L'artère maxillaire interne sur la face postérieure du sinus maxillaire qu'il faut ruginer de très près.

La veine angulaire qu'il suffit de recliner dehors avec le périoste.

L'artère ethmoïdale antérieure qui est chaque fois sectionnée (hémostase à la cire).

Les ailerons internes et externes qui subissent une forte tension et s'opposent temporairement à une ouverture normale des paupières.

7. *Les sollicitations musculaires*

Les sollicitations par les muscles masticateurs pourraient être considérables, aussi faut-il rester à distance de l'aponévrose temporale et de l'invincible masseter. Aussi, l'ostéotomie en gradins permet-elle de contourner en avant toutes ces insertions.

## PREPARATION

*Elle comporte:*

Mise en état de la bouche et des dents.
Pose d'arc dentaires.
Rassemblage de l'instrumentation spéciale et du 'diadème' à ancrages crâniens.
Trachéotomie.
Suture des paupières entre elles (pseudo-blépharorraphie) pour prévenir le risque oculaire per-opératoire.

## EXECUTION

Nous proposons donc un traitement radical qui reproduit une disjonction faciale, qui respecterait les ptérygoïdes et l'arcade zygomatique. Les voies d'abord sont au nombre de huit.

*a. La voie palatine double* — en dedans et en arrière de l'arcade dentaire, permet d'exécuter: au centre l'ostéotomie transversale du palais, un centimètre en avant du voile, et

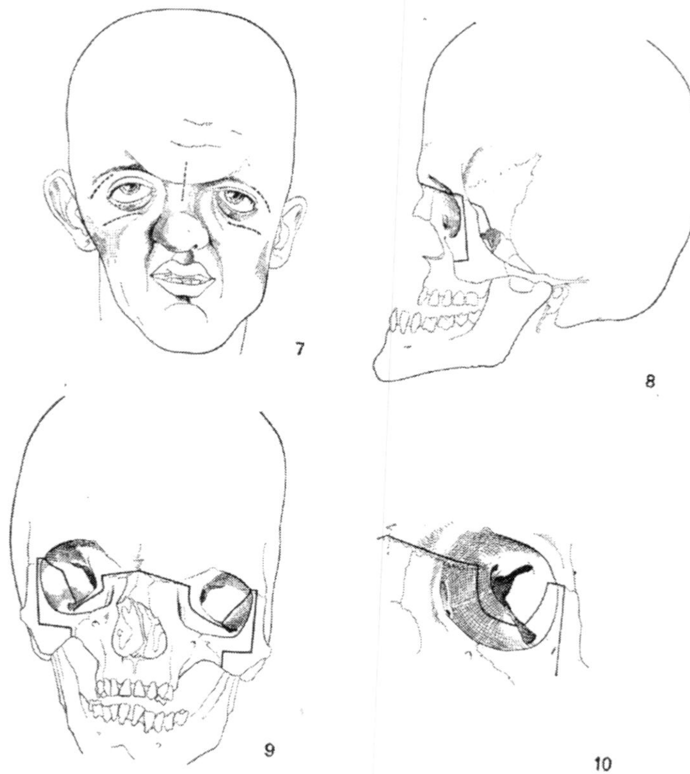


*Planche III — Planche technique.*
*Fig. 7.* Les voies d'abord.
*Fig. 8.* Tracé des ostéotomies.
*Fig. 9.* Tracé des ostéotomies.
*Fig. 10.* Tracé des ostéotomies orbitaires.

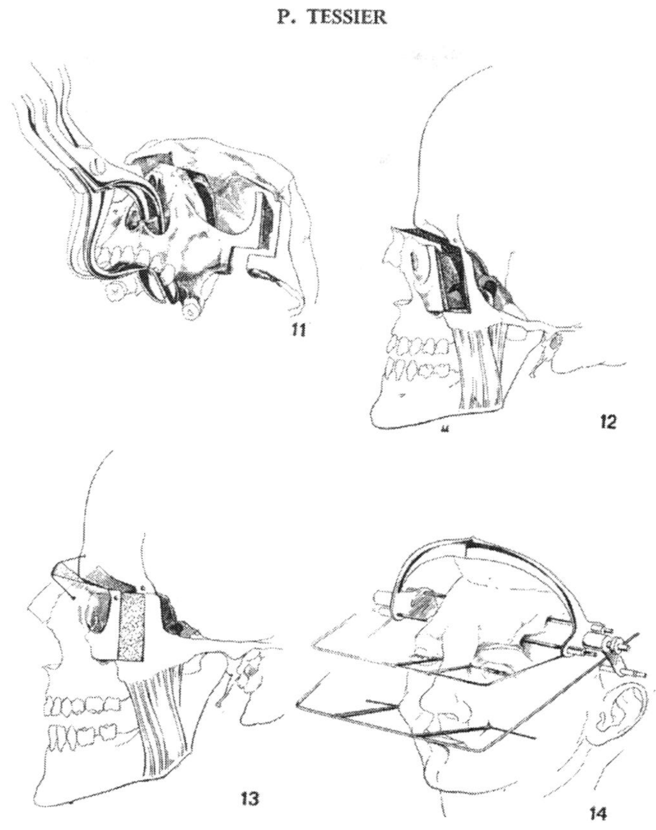

*Fig. 11.* Avancement de la face à la pince de Rowe.
*Fig. 12.* Les diastasis.
*Fig. 13.* Les greffes osseuses.
*Fig. 14.* Traction sur le maxillaire et le nez par l'intermédiaire du diadème Delbet-Tessier.

de chaque côté d'amorcer au ciseau courbe la disjonction inter-ptérygo-maxillaire. Au besoin, une incision palatine antérieure prévient toute tension excessive sur le voile.

*b. La voie vestibulaire bilatérale* — ouvre le chemin:

— à la suture maxillo-malaire (ostéotomie verticale ou plutôt en gradins);

— à la fosse ptérygo-maxillaire (section de la face postérieure du sinus maxillaire à la rugine coudée).

Là subsiste la seule incertitude du procédé car aucun écarteur, aucun miroir ne permet de contrôler 'à vue' ni l'ostéotomie, ni une hémorragie possible (maxillaire interne).

*c. La voie orbitaire externe bilatérale*, longue de 24 mm sous la queue du sourcil, permet 3 manoeuvres:

— l'ostéotomie sagittale à la scie oscillante de l'apophyse externe du malaire;

— l'ostéotomie horizontale à la fraise de la valve interne de cette apophyse dans l'orbite;

— l'ostéotomie verticale à la scie alternative de la paroi externe de l'orbite dans la fosse temporale, en avant de la suture sphéno-malaire, jusqu'à la fente sphéno-maxillaire.

*d. La voie sous-orbitaire bilatérale* donne accès à la face antérieure du malaire (section en gradins) et au plancher de l'orbite, dont la partie postérieure est sectionnée à la rugine coudée depuis l'unguis en dedans, jusqu'à la fente sphéno-maxillaire en dehors.

*e. La voie fronto-nasale unique*, verticale (scie oscillante ou alternative) pour l'ostéotomie oblique sous-ethmoïdienne de la paroi interne des orbites au dessus du ligament et du sac lacrymal. Par cette même voie après un début de mobilisation, on fait une section presque verticale de la cloison au ciseau courbe, dirigé vers l'épine nasale postérieure puis utilisé comme levier.

*Après ces ostéotomies, quels éléments s'opposent encore à la projection du massif facial?*

Des travées osseuses multiples mais fragiles, la plus puissante d'entre elles est la crête turbinale postérieure. Enfin, les muqueuses, toutes les parties molles, la peau et ses connexions profondes qu'il faut épuiser par distension.

*Amorcer la disjonction*

Cette face disjointe présente trois points faibles:
— les deux premiers sont les sutures maxillo-malaires, fragilisées par la gouttière sous-orbitaire.
— le troisième est la suture intermaxillaire, lorsqu'une division palatine (2 cas) en diminue la résistance.

Une traction trop puissante risque de rompre ces sutures et de transformer un monobloc idéal en un puzzle dont la contention s'avèrerait presque insoluble. Aussi, convient-il d'amorcer les diastasis et, au gré des résistances rencontrées, de compléter de ci, de là, au ciseau frappé, l'autonomie de la face.

Après toutes ces manoeuvres, la double pince de Rowe, emporte le massif facial (maxillaire, palais, nez, malaire, tout le système lacrymo-palpébral, la lèvre supérieure, et les joues). La projection doit être totale d'emblée. Il faut même rechercher une hypercorrection pour vaincre à coup sur toutes les résistances parasites.

Seul le pôle postérieur du sinus maxillaire et, avec lui, la partie la plus postérieure du plancher de l'orbite restent solidaires de la base du crâne.

*Que signifie une disjonction inter-maxillaire?*

Nous l'avons subie deux fois (un cas de division palatine, un cas de disjonction cranio-faciale) et chaque fois nous avons pu réduire une endognathie. D'un incident opératoire nous avons pu ainsi tirer un profit inattendu, et une déduction: si une endognathie est manifeste, ne pas hésiter à rompre la suture inter-maxillaire, mais seulement après accomplissement de la réduction en monobloc.

## GREFFES OSSEUSES

La consolidation ne peut s'imaginer que par l'intermédiaire de greffe osseuses fronto-nasales, orbitaires inférieures, orbitaires externes et malaires. Seuls les diastasis inter-ptérygo-maxillaires ne peuvent retenir une greffe osseuse. En l'absence de ces deux puissants points d'appui postéro-inférieurs, que constituent les ptérygoïdes, les autres doivent y suppléer par une solidité exceptionnelle.

Aux greffes osseuses revient donc un quadruple rôle:
— fermer les diastasis de trois parois de l'orbite,
— participer à la projection de la face ou du moins s'opposer à sa rétrusion,
— parfaire la correction de l'infragnathie,
— activer la consolidation osseuse.

*Greffon fronto-nasal (1)*

Greffon plat, ou cunéiforme, à base antérieure, il est la clé de l'édifice. C'est un greffon large, cortico-spongieux, affleurant la face interne des orbites. Il sert de point d'appui à l'ostéosynthèse fronto-nasale dont il amplifie l'efficacité mais en contre-partie, il comble l'angle fronto-nasal. Aussi faut-il le surmonter d'autres greffons restaurant la glabelle et l'arcade sourcillière toujours hypoplasiée (syndrome d'Apert).

Quand plus tard la consolidation est acquise, il n'est que d'encocher cet ancien greffon pour rétablir un 'stop' normal.

*Greffons malaires* (2)

Ce sont deux prismes rectangulaires insérés dans l'ostéotomie sagittale de l'apophyse orbitaire externe et du malaire.

*Greffons pré-maxillo-malaires* (2)

Si le bord inférieur de l'orbite est nettement aplasié.

*Greffons du plancher* (2) et de la *paroi externe* (2)

(Minces lamelles cortico-spongieuses).

## OSTEOSYNTHESES

L'ostéosynthèse fronto-nasale entre la crête lacrymale et la glabelle: avance la face, bloque le greffon, s'appuie sur celui-ci qui amplifie l'efficacité de sa traction antérieure.

L'ostéosynthèse fronto-malaire s'oppose à un déplacement latéral. Elle favorise l'impact de la région malaire et limite l'abaissement du bloc incisivo-canin. Elle participe faiblement à la protraction.

## LE DIADEME, FIXATEUR EXTERNE A ANCRAGES CRANIENS

Nous avons exprimé ailleurs les raisons du remplacement du casque traditionnel, inconfortable, imprécis et souvent inefficace par un fixateur externe à points d'appui crâniens.

Rappelons seulement que grâce à lui nous pouvons réaliser non seulement des tractions antérieures, mais encore une contention précise, rigoureuse, et jamais limitée dans le temps.

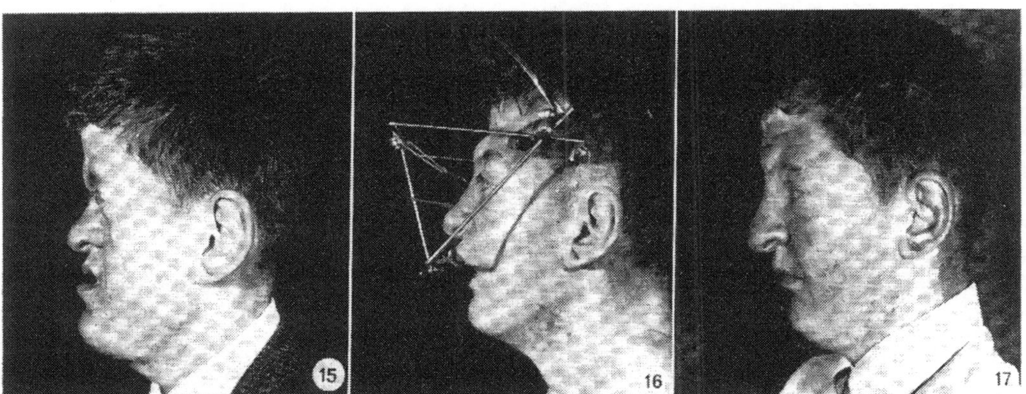


*Planche IV, Cas n° 3.*
*Fig. 15.* Avant. Syndrome d'Apert.
*Fig. 16.* Pendant. Ostéosynthèse extra-faciale sur le diadème Delbet-Tessier.
*Fig. 17.* Après. Ostéotomie totale de la face.

L'autonomie complète ainsi acquise vis à vis de la mandibule est inappréciable. Certes, il convient d'ajuster l'articulé par un blocage inter-maxillaire mais celui-ci peut n'être qu'intermittent ce qui évite toute sollicitation des foyers d'ostéotomies. De plus, de cette façon, les mouvements mandibulaires, employés à la mastication favorisent les impacts postérieurs.

A cet appareil peuvent en outre être reliés: une traction sur le malaire, une broche transfaciale ou, à la manière de Federspiel, une ostéosynthèse extra-focale branchée sur l'extrémité postérieure de l'arc maxillaire.

DYSOSTOSES CRANIO-FACIALES

## SOINS ET SUITES POST-OPERATOIRES

Mettre en réserve à la banque d'os, le surplus d'un prélèvement massif.

Si l'on constate une aplasie marquée du maxillaire ou une rétrogénie, faire en même temps que le prélèvement iliaque un prélèvement costal immédiatement mis en réserve sous-cutanée thoracique. Plus tard, après disparition des oedèmes, implanter ce cartilage ou les greffons de banque. On aura ainsi évité au patient un deuxième prélèvement, toujours pénible.

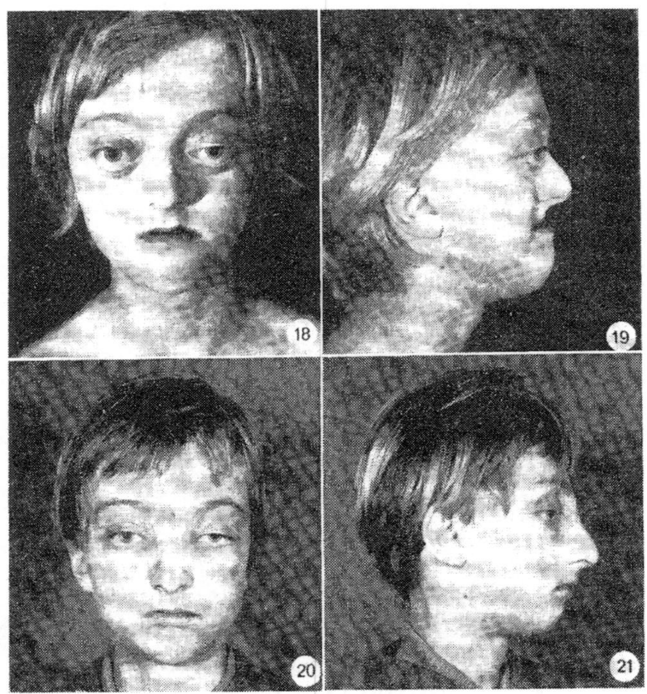

*Planche V, Cas n° 4.*
*Figs. 18, 19.* Avant. Maladie de Crouzon.
*Figs. 20, 21.* Après. Ostéotomie totale de la face.

Achever l'opération par des tractions élastiques inter-maxillaires, et une aspiration pharyngée. Calmer la dysphagie toujours intense.

Au 2e ou 3e jours, supprimer la pseudo-blépharorraphie.

Une diplopie peut se manifester pendant quelques jours. Peut-être est-elle provoquée par la désinsertion du P O ou par les bouleversements du plancher, ou par l'enophtalmie, ou par les tireillements sur les droits par l'intermédiaire des ailerons.

Au 3e jour, démécher le nez, et retirer progressivement le tamponnement inter-ptérygo-maxillaire. L'arrêt du saignement parfois important est toujours spontané.

Vers le 8e jour, abandonner le trachéotomie.

Vers la 4e semaine, enlever le fixateur externe.

## OPERATIONS COMPLEMENTAIRES

La correction est immédiatement spectaculaire, d'autant plus manifeste qu'étaient importants exorbitisme et rétrognathie. Une fois acquise, elle souligne des malformations passées inaperçues jusque là.

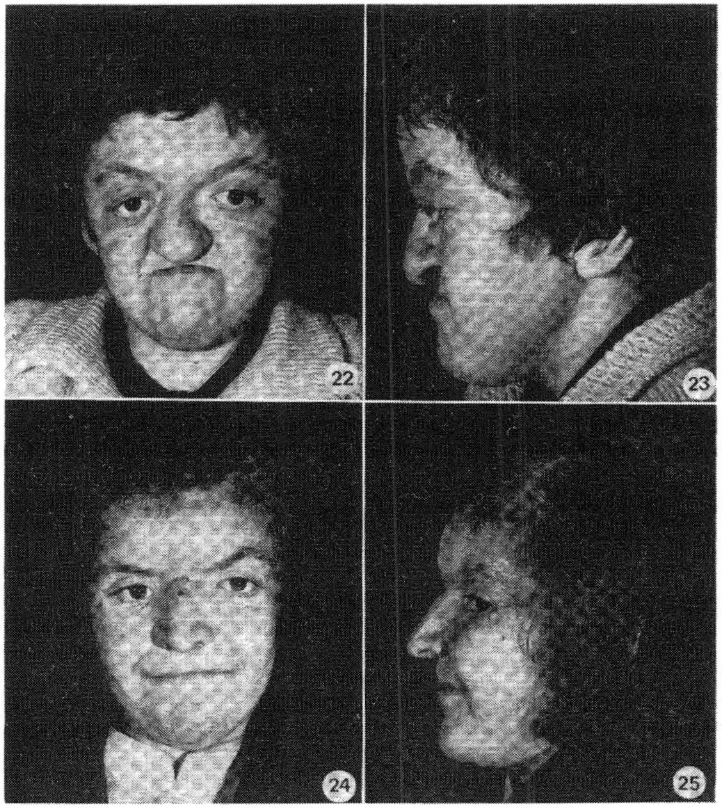

*Planche VI, Cas n° 5.*
*Figs. 22, 23.* Avant. Syndrome d'Apert.
*Figs. 24, 25.* Après. Ostéotomie totale de la face — rhinoplastie.

1. Hypoplasie du maxillaire (voire du malaire), prédominant sur le bord inférieur de l'orbite et sur la région sous-orbitaire:
greffe osseuse (réserve de banque) ou greffe de cartilage costal (réserve sous-cutanée).
2. Rhinomégalie fréquente dans le syndrome d'Apert:
réduction nasale, au besoin par voie externe.
3. Comblement de l'angle fronto-nasal par le greffon osseux:
restauration du 'stop' par évidement du greffon.
4. Obstruction nasale:
résection septale (au besoin utiliser le cartilage septal comme matériau de comblement sous-orbitaire).
5. Rétrogénie:
greffe de cartilage ou inclusion de silicone.
6. Aplasie glabellaire et frontale:
greffe d'os ou de cartilage.

Cette hypoplasie frontale, très inconstante dans la maladie de Crouzon, est parfois très accentuée dans le syndrome d'Apert.

Le projection de l'apophyse orbitaire externe même dédoublée est très importante; elle peut faire saillie dans la paupière supérieure et participe peut-être au ptosis provoqué par le retrait relatif du globe. On est donc parfois amené à disséquer le sommet de cette apophyse.

Toutes ces révisions peuvent s'effectuer en un ou deux temps, quatre à 6 mois après l'ostéotomie totale.

## DISCUSSION

Certains ont suggéré de limiter les ambitions à la réduction du rétrognathisme maxillaire.

C'est là une vue erronée et très incomplète du problème car rien n'intervient alors contre les malformations orbito-nasales.

Depuis 6 ans, l'ostéotomie totale de la face nous a confirmé le bien fondé des ostéotomies totales 'retro-lacrymales'. Elle a donné naissance:

— au cadre orthopédique à ancrages crâniens (diadème),

— aux osteotomies sous-ethmoïdiennes
(hypertélorismes modérès de cause faciale),

— aux ostéotomies d'expansion de l'orbite
(scaphocéphalies, atrésie des cavités anophtalmes et même exophtalmies basedowiennes),

— enfin aux ostéotomies sub-totales de la face,
(reliquats des disjonctions cranio-faciales).

Figs. 1,2 Before. Crouzon's disease.

Figs 3,4. After. Total osteotomy of the face—bone graft of the chin.

Fig. 5Before. Retrusion of the midface.

Fig. 6 After. Total osteotomy of the face.

WHAT ARE THE DANGERS AND THE PITFALLS?

1. *The respiratory risk*

Fragile patients, short necks, sometimes intermaxillary fixation, but particularly risk of obstruction by an inert soft palate, by inter-pterygomaxillay packing, or by clots, are more than are required to require a preliminary tracheostomy.

2. *The ethmoid*

To harmoniously project the nose with the midface, to displace 'en bloc' the lacrimal system without risk of stenosis, the osteotomy should pass around the sac. For this reason, and for others, it should be flush with the base of the skull.

Radiologic studies should remove the possibility of risk.

But one should take account of the following facts:

a. An exaggerated intercanthal separation can be associated with a prolapsed of the cribriform plate.
b. The obliquity of the anterior cranial base is sometimes quite important in the Crouzon syndrome.
c. Finally, a craniofacial dysostosis, even in the absence of dystrophy or hypertelorism, can mask on rare occasions a meningo-encephalocoele of the cranial base (one case)

3. *The lacrimal system*

Here, it is not necessary to go around it very closely (hypertelorism and craniofacial osteotomies). It is sufficient to locate the sac, and to reflect inferiorly its dome in order to give access to the medial wall of the orbit, to disinsert the inferior oblique in order to cut through the infero-medial angle of the orbit deeply.

4. *The oblique muscles*

The pulley of the superior oblique is not damaged by the periosteal elevator. To the contrary, a clean disinsertion of the inferior oblique is indispensible to preserve, through the periosteum, the constant relationships with the other oculo-motor muscles.

5. *The possibility of pseudoarthrosis*

It is necessary that the total osteotomy of the face has large surfaces of contact of the cranio-facial osteotomy of the hypertelorisms. Once the face is freed from the skull, gaps open up between the frontal bone and the nose, and even more so between the two segments of the malar bone, and also between the maxilla and the pterygoids. Certainly, bone grafts can reestablish the continuity of the two first critical points, but in the inter-pterygo-maxillary space, where one cannot see, no graft is possible. Thus, it is important to compensate for this deficit by a reinforcement of the anterior (fronto-nasal) and lateral (fronto-malar) buttresses. It is also necessary to insist that the contention has very particular qualities: a continuous anterior traction to overcome posterior pull, exceptional stability, and independence from the mandible.

6. *What are the other pitfalls to be avoided in such an operation?*

The posterior palatal artery, which it seems is difficult to completely spare. We have been able to avoid it so far, it seems, but it would be astonishing if that remained the case.

The infra-orbital pedicle, the elongation of which does not seem possible, and which nevertheless follows the movement, without rupture.

The internal maxillary artery on the posterior surface of the maxillary sinus, where dissection will need to be quite close.

The angular vein which is sufficient to dissect beneath, with the periosteum.

The anterior ethmoidal artery which is sectioned in every case (hemostasis with wax).

The medial and lateral canthal tendons which undergo considerable tension which temporarily interferes with normal opening of the eyelids.

7. *Restraint by the muscles*

The restriction by the masticatory muscles can be considerable, and one has to remain at a distance from the temporal aponeurosis and the invincible masseter. Thus, a step osteotomy makes it possible to stay in front of all of these insertions.

PREPARATION

*This involves:*

Getting the mouth and teeth in good shape.

Application of arch bars.

Getting the necessary instruments together, and a 'diadem' for cranial anchorage.

Tracheostomy

Suture of the eyelids (pseudo-blepharrophy) to prevent the risk of intra-operative ocular damage.

EXECUTION

We therefore propose a radical treatment which reproduces a facial disjunction, which respects the pterygoids and the zygomatic arch. The access incisions number eight.

*a.* *A double palatal incision*—inside and behind the dental arch, permitting the following to be carried out: in the center, a transverse osteotomy of the palate, one centimeter in front of the soft palate, and

Plate III. Technique.

Fig. 7. The access incisions

Fig. 8. Outline of osteotomies

Fig. 9. Outline of opsteotomies

Fig. 10. Outline of orbital osteotomie

Fig. 11. Advancement of the face with the Rowe forceps.

Fig. 12. The gaps

Fig. 13. The bone grafts.

Fig. 14. Traction on the maxilla and nose with a Delbet-Tessier diadem.

Retraction on each side in order to introduce a curved chisel to perform the inter-pterygo-maxillary disjunction. If necessary, an anterior palatal incision can prevent excessive tension on the soft palate.

*b.* *Bilateral vestibular incisions*—open the way to:

— the maxilla-malar suture (vertical or step osteotomy).

— the pterygo-maxillary fossa (posterior section of the maxillary sinus with a curved rugine).

Here lies the only uncertainty of the operation, since no mirror can help control the osteotomy, or possible bleeding (internal maxillary) under "direct vision."

*c.* *Bilateral lateral orbital incisions,* 24 mm in length, under the root of the eyebrow, permitting 3 manoeuvres:

— the sagittal osteotomy with the oscillating saw of the lateral apophysis of the malar bone;

— the horizontal osteotomy with the burr of the medial portion of this apophysis in the orbit;

— the vertical osteotomy with the alternative saw of the lateral wall of the orbit (step osteotomy) and of the floor of the orbit, of which the posterior portion of which is sectioned with a curved rugine until the palatal bone medially, and to the spheno-maxillary fissure laterally.

d. *The bilateral infraorbital* incisions provides access to the anterior surface of the maxilla (step osteotomy) and to the floor of the orbit, of which the posterior portion is sectioned with a curved rugine up to the lacrimal bone medially, and up to the spheno-maxillary fissure laterally.

e. The *single fronto-nasal incision,* vertical (oscillating or alternating saw) for the oblique sub-ethmoidal osteotomy of the medial walls of the orbits above the [canthal] ligament and the lacrimal sac. Through this same incision, after beginning the mobilization, one carries out an almost vertical section of the septum with a curved chisel, directed to the posterior nasal spine then used as a lever.

*After these osteotomies, which elements still oppose the projection of the midface?*

Multiple small, fragile bony bridges, the strongest of which is the posterior crest of the turbinate. Finally, the mucous membranes, all of the soft tissues, the skin and the deep connections which must be weakened by distension.

*Begin the disjunction*

This disjuncted face has three weak points:

— the first two are the maxilla-malar sutures, wakened by the infra-orbital groove.

— the third is the intermaxillary suture, which when there is a cleft palate (2 cases) weakens the resistance.

Traction which is too strong risks breaking these sutures and transforming an ideal monobloc into a puzzle, the contention of which turns out to be almost impossible. Also, it is good to begin with the diastases, and, depending on the resistances encountered, to finish here and there with chisel blows to lead to the autonomy of the face.

After all of these manoeuvres, the double Rowe forceps, holding the midface (maxilla, palate, nose, malar, all of the lacrymo-palpebral system, the upper lip, and the cheeks). The projection should be total from the beginning. One should even try for a hypercorrection to overcome all of the parasitic resistances.

Only the posterior portion of the maxillary sinus and, with it, the most posterior portion of the floor of the orbit remain attached to the base of the skull.

*What does an inter-maxillary disjunction signify?*

We have had this happen twice (one case of cleft palate, one case of cranio-facial disjunction) and each time we have been able to reduce an endognathia. From an operative incident, we have thus been able to obtain an unexpected profit, and a deduction: if the endognathia is manifest, do not hesitate to break the inter-maxillary suture, but only after having competed the reduction as a monobloc.

## BONE GRAFTS

Consolidation cannot be imagined without the use of bone grafts in the fronto-nasal, inferior orbital, lateral orbital and malar areas. Only inter-pterygo-maxillary diastases cannot accept a bone graft. And in the absence of these two powerful posterior–inferior points of support, which the pterygoids provide, the others should compensate with an exceptional solidity.

The bone grafts have therefore a quadruple role:

-- to close the diastases of the three walls of the orbit,

-- to participate in the projection of the face or at least to oppose its retrusion

-- to complete the correction of the infragnathia,

-- to activate the bony consolidation

*The fronto-nasal bone graft (1)*

A flat, or cuneiform graft, with an anterior base, it is the key of the edifice. It is a large, cortico-cancellous graft, estending to the medial walls of the orbits. It serves as a point of support of the fronto-nasal osteosynthesis, of which it amplifies the efficacy but it also fills in the fronto-nasal angle. One should also place on it other grafts restoring the glabella and the supraorbital ridge, which is always hypoplastic (Apert's syndrome).

When later the consolidation has been obtained, one has only to hollow out this old graft to reestablish a normal "stop" [fronto-nasal angle].

## THE DIADEM, EXTERNAL FIXATOR WITH CRANIAL ANCHORAGES

We have already stated the reasons for the replacement of a traditional [plaster] headcap, uncomfortable, imprecise, and often ineffective, by a fixator with support points on the skull.

We will recall only that thanks to it we can achieve not only anterior traction, but also a precise contention, rigorous, and never limited in time.

Plate IV. Case No. 3

Fig. 14.5. Before. Apert's syndrome.

Fig. 14.6. During. Extra-facial osteosynthesis onto the Delbet-Tessier diadem.

Fig. 14.7 After. Total osteotomy of the face.

The complete autonomy from the mandible is inappreciable. Yes, it is convenient to adjust the occlusion with intermaxillary fixation, but this can only be intermittent, and avoids any demands on the areas of the osteotomies. And, in this fashion, the mandibular movements, used in mastication, favor posterior impaction.

To this apparatus, one can also attach: a traction on the malar, and a trans-facial pin where, in the manner of Federspiel, an extra-focal osteosynthesis is attached to the posterior end of the maxillary arch.

## POST-OPERATIVE CARE AND EVOLUTION

Keep in reserve in the bone bank any leftovers from the massive harvesting.

If one notes a marked aplasia of the maxilla or a retrogenia, carry out at the same time as the iliac harvesting a costal harvesting immediately placed in reserve in the thoracic area subcutaneously. Later, after the edema has subsided, implant this cartilage or bone banked in the bone bank. One will thus have avoided a second harvesting, always painful.

Plate V. Case No. 4.

Figs. 14.8, 14.9. Before. Crouzon's disease.

Figs. 14.10. 14.11. After. Total osteotomy of the face.

Finish the operation by inter-maxillary elastic traction, and an aspiration of the pharynx. Treat the dysphagia, which is always intense.

On the second or third day, remover the pseudo-blepharrhaphy.

A diplopia can be present for several days. Possibly it is caused by the disinsertion of the inferior oblique or the disturbances in the floor, or by the enophthalmia, or by the effects on the recti through the canthi.

On the third day, take the packing out of the nose, and progressively remove the inter-pterygo-maxillary packing. The bleeding, which is often significant, always stops spontaneously.

Towards the 8th day, remove the tracheostomy.

Towards the fourth week, remove the external fixator.

'COMPLEMENTARY OPERATIONS

The correction is immediately spectacular, the moreso if the exorbitism and retrognathia were important. Once obtained, it points out malformations which were not appreciated until then.

Plate VI. Case No. 5.

Figs. 14.12, 14.13. Before. Apert's syndrome.

Figs. 14.14, 14.15. After. Total osteotomy of the face—rhinoplasty.

1. Hypoplasia of the maxilla (or the malar), predominant on the inferior border of the orbit and on the infra-orbital region: bone graft (stored in the bone bank) or costal cartilage graft (stored subcutaneously)

2. Rhinomegaly, frequent in Apert's syndrome: nasal reduction, through an external approach if needed

3. Filling in of the fronto-nasal angle with a bone graft: restoration of the "stop" by burring down the graft.

4. Nasal obstruction: septal resection (if need, use the material to fill in the infra-orbital area).

5. Retrogenia: cartilage graft or silicone implant

6. Glabellar and frontal aplasia: bone or cartilage graft

This frontal hypoplasia, very inconsistent in Crouzon's disease, is sometimes quite accentuated in the Apert syndrome.

The projection of the lateral orbital apophysis, even when overlapped, is quite significant; it can cause a projection under the upper eyelid and participate in the ptosis caused by the relative retrusion of the globe. On occasion one has to dissect and diminish the apex of this apophysis.

All of these revisions can be carried out in one or two sessions, four to six months after the total osteotomy.

DISCUSSION

Some have suggested limiting the ambitions of the reduction of the maxillary retrognathism.

This is an erroneous and very incomplete view of the problem because nothing is then done for the orbito-nasal malformations.

After 6 years, the total osteotomy of the face has confirmed for us the correctness of the total "retro-lacrymal" osteotomies. It has given birth to:

— in the area of orthopedics, to cranial anchorages (diadem),

— to sub-ethmoidal osteotomies (moderate hypertelorisms due to a facial cause)

— to osteotomies for expansion of the orbit (scaphocephalies, aresia of anophthalmic orbits or even basedowiennes exophthalmias),

— finally to sub-total osteotomies of the face, (sequelae of cranio-facial disjunctions.)

# Chapter 15

## Mireille and a Second Chance at a Family

In 1964, Paul Tessier met a young attorney named Mireille Bernard. Mireille was born in Millau, near Montpellier, where her father Louis was an attorney as well. She went to law school in Montpellier, and practiced family law. There was nothing between them for some time, but they became reacquainted in 1971, at which time a real courtship began. After decades of total immersion in his work following his divorce in 1963, Paul had finally met his other half in this beautiful, young blonde who could understand and appreciate the importance of his work—and, at the same time, be a companion, mother, and homemaker for him.

*Fig. 15.1 On one of their first dates—Mireille and Paul at the Lido, 1971.*

*Fig. 15.2 Tessier and Mireille on their wedding day, August 1974, in Millau.*

They had been in La Baule before, and, to save time, they chartered an airplane to take them, their witnesses, and Max (the cocker spaniel) to Millau. The plane made a stop at Nantes to pick up Solange, his sister, and after the marriage they all returned by plane to La Baule in time for dinner. Mireille said that her real honeymoon did not take place until they went to Venice in 2003!

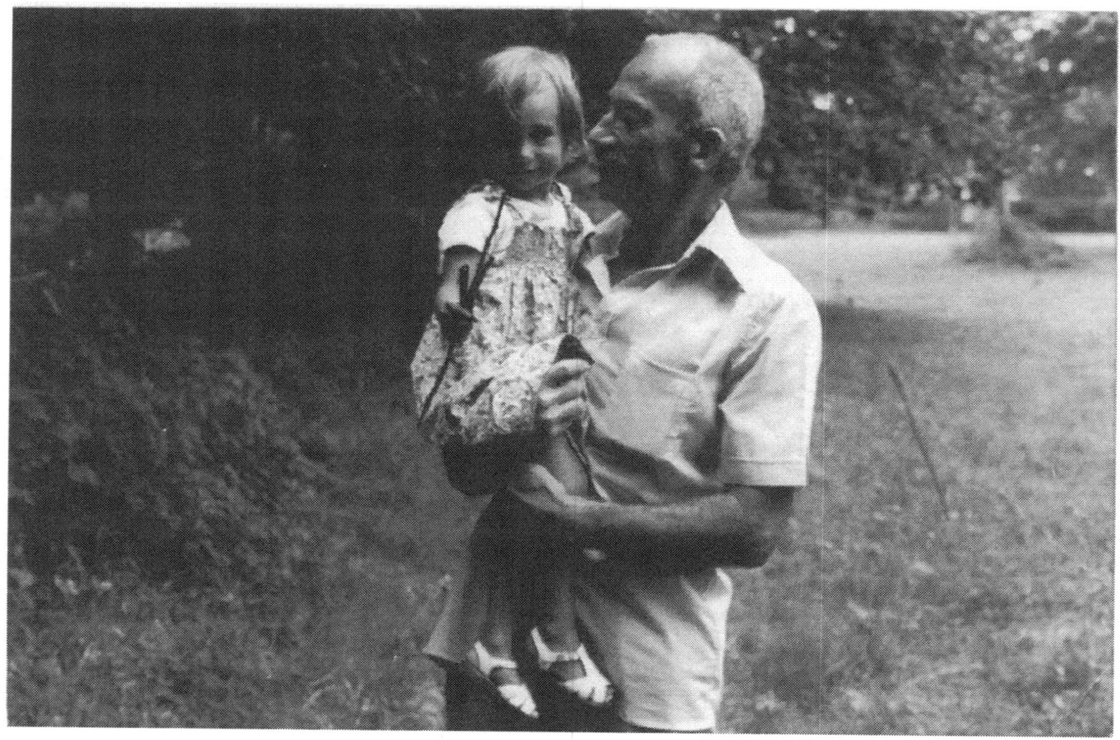

*Fig. 15.3 Paul and Laurence, ca. April 1977.*

Laurence was born in 1975 at Clinique Belvédère, and I can recall quite well that I was assisting him on an abdominoplasty when a nurse stuck her head inside the door and said, "Monsieur, your wife has just had a daughter!" He then mused on possible names: Apertine? Crouzonette? Fortunately, Mireille prevailed.

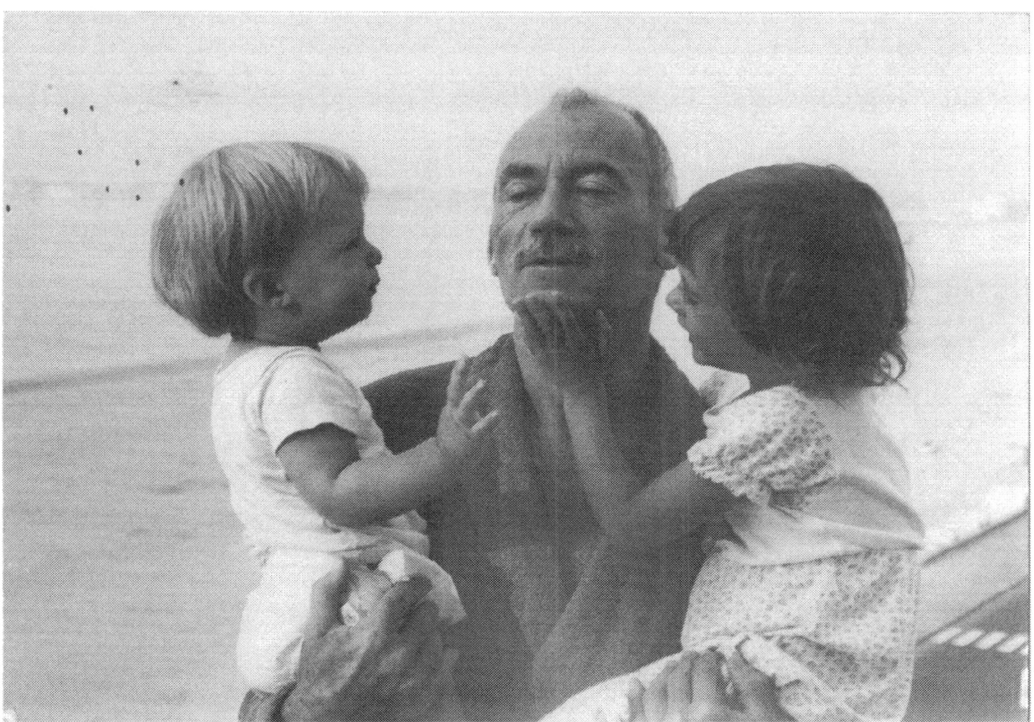

*Fig. 15.4 Tessier with Jean-Paul and Laurence, ca. 1978.*

*Fig. 15.5 Laurence, Jean-Paul, and Tessier, ca. 1983.*

*Fig. 15.6 Max, the beloved "Cocker," and his master, La Baule, ca 1983.*

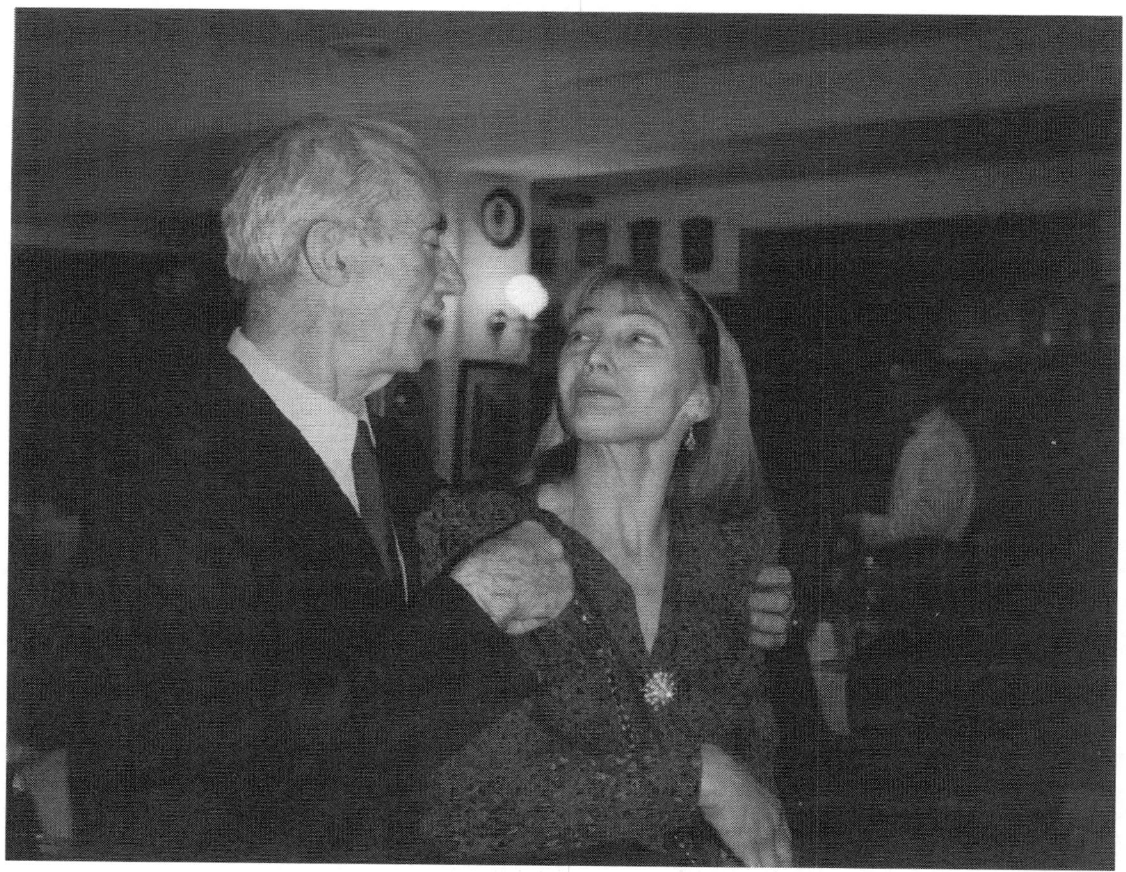

*Fig. 15.7 Paul and Mireille, ca. 1985.*

*Fig. 15.8 Mireille and Paul in a festive moment, ca. 1988.*

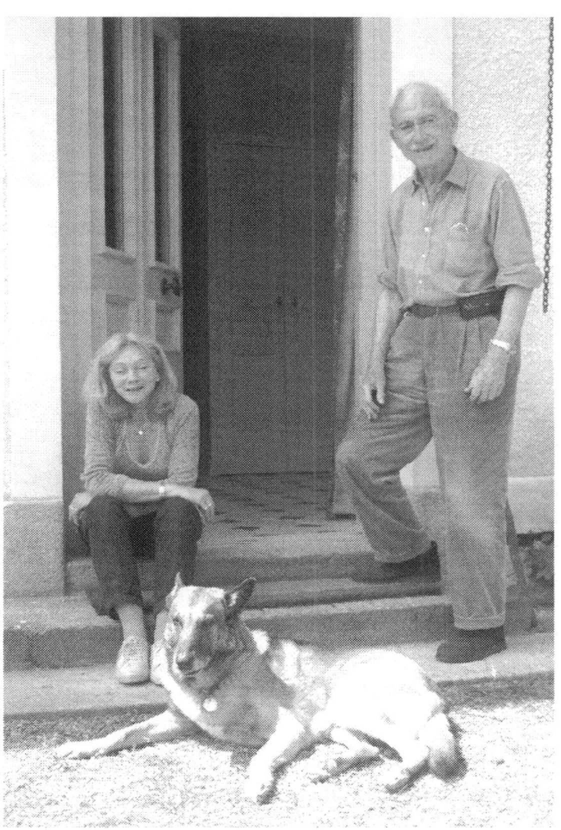

*Fig. 15.9 Mireille, Enzo (Max's replacement), and Paul on the front steps of Bonne Hygie, summer 2003.*

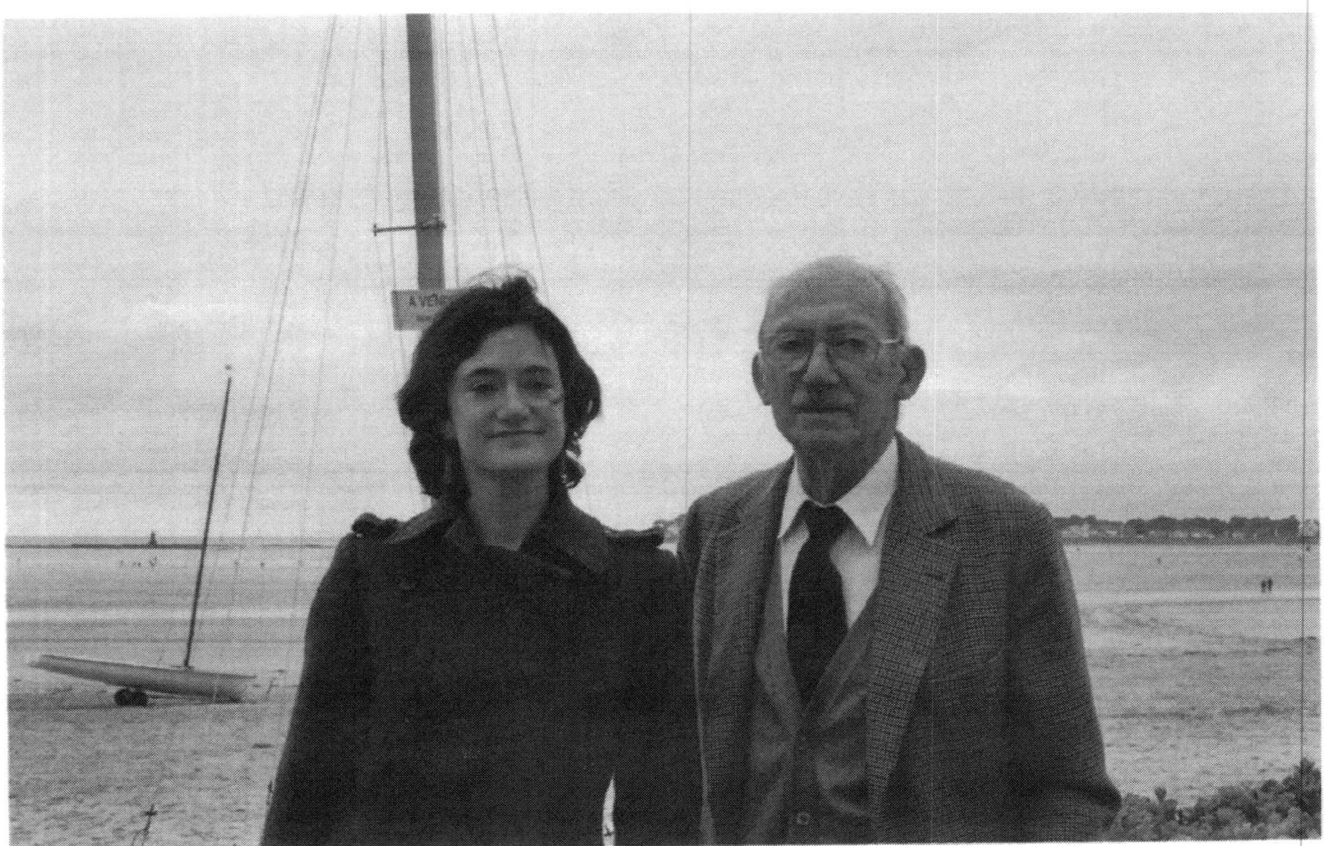

*Fig. 15.10 With Laurence, on his last trip to La Baule, Easter 2006.*

There was no question about Paul's love for his children and his happiness in the milieu that Mireille had created for them. But there were problems that were difficult, if not impossible, for him to resolve. First and foremost, there were the demands that were being put on him due to his growing reputation as the foremost reconstructive plastic surgeon in the world. This led him to his "suicidal" operative schedule—six or even seven days per week, until the late hours—which left him little time for his wife and children.

The family continued to live in the apartment space off of the office at 26 Avenue Kléber (several blocks from the Etoile in the center of Paris), which was far from ideal for a family with several young children. He had bought a piece of land in Saint-Germaine, outside of the urban area of Paris, and plans were drawn up to build a house. This never came to be, so several floors in an apartment building across the street from the Roland Garros tennis stadium in Boulogne were purchased, extensively refurbished, and henceforth referred to by Paul as "S.A.P.P." (*Stupide Apartement Parisien de Prestige*, or Stupid Pretentious Paris Apartment). See Chapter31.

Laurence attended dental school in Paris and is currently doing post-graduate work in anthropology in Berkeley, California. Jean-Paul attended law school and works in a Paris law firm, where he has a particular interest in intellectual property rights.

*Fig. 15.11 Jean-Paul and Laurence Tessier, June 2009.*

*Fig. 15.12 Paul and Mireille, London, 2006*

Mireille was able to bring levity, warmth, stability, and children into Tessier's life, which was filled to overflowing with work. Although life with him was not always easy, her love, admiration, and unflinching support were always evident.

In the last few years of his life, a constellation of medical problems beset him, and she was a true angel of compassion and constant support. When he was in the hospital, she would visit him every day with a small picnic to entice him to eat. When at home, she made his study into a place where he could be as self-sufficient as possible. Although he had great difficulty walking due to the problems that occurred after his hip surgery, his mind and curiosity stayed as sharp as ever.

It's also worth noting that, without Mireille's support and encouragement, this book would have never been written.

# Chapter 16

## Paris in 1974-75

I was present at Dr. Tessier's first presentation in North America, at the American Society of Plastic and Reconstructive Surgery meeting in Montreal, in 1971. Senior general surgery residents at the Peter Bent Brigham Hospital were given the opportunity to go to several scientific meetings of their choice and, because I had not completely decided what my long term plans were, I decided to go to the A.S.P.R.S. meeting. Plastic surgery was one of my interests, but I knew little about it since, at that time in Boston, there was little plastic surgery being done in the academic centers—aside from Donald McCollum and George Gifford's cleft lip work at Boston Children's Hospital. Joe Murray, at that point, was still heavily involved in renal transplantation.

I had never heard of Paul Tessier but, after hearing his presentation in Montreal, I was totally in awe of the results that he showed and my decision about further training was finalized. I wrote him a letter in French saying that I would like to come for further training with him after finishing my plastic surgery training, but I never heard back from him. I looked around for what I felt would be the best place to train in plastic surgery, and I decided to go to Miami with Ralph Millard who, at that time, was establishing himself as a major figure both in reconstructive and aesthetic surgery. Fortunately for me, Ralph knew Paul well (Paul had visited with him on one of his North American trips), and after he had written a letter on my behalf, a positive response came from Dr. Tessier.

There was no discussion of any salary or reimbursement, so I went about rounding up what funding I could from The International College of Surgeons and a generous gift from a colleague who was at that time doing only aesthetic surgery. I had various places in Paris that I could stay rent free for about four months, but beyond that the future was uncertain.

When I arrived at Clinique Bélvédere, I found that there were already several dozen potential assistants there; so, for the first month or so, I was part of the crowd looking over the sheet taped to two IV poles that kept people from getting too close to the operating team. I found that most of these visitors tended to drift off as evening and dinner time approached, but I always stayed to the end of the operating schedule, which was often around 11 p.m. or midnight. During the day, Dr. Tessier had little to say to the peanut gallery, but later in the evening, if I was the only one there, he seemed happy to have some companionship and politely asked me about Ralph and other American surgeons that we both knew.

As the year progressed, these late evening discussions continued on a wide range of topics. One subject that had doubtlessly been mulled over for centuries was whether, and for how long, consciousness might continue after one's head was severed by the guillotine. Various signals, such as blinking the right eye twice, were discussed.

There was also Dr. Tessier's idea about what would constitute the ideal way to die. He felt that having a black panther leap upon him at the same moment that he plunged a knife into the belly of the panther would be his exit of choice. Dr. Tessier was a fan of *contrepèteries*, which translates to Spoonerism in English. This is a word game where transposing two letters changes the meaning of a word completely. One I remember him mentioning was *les Anglaises qui aiment le tennis en pension,* which translates to *English girls who like tennis while staying in a pension house*. Change the T in *tennis* with the P in *pension,* however, and the French becomes *English girls who like the erect male organ*. One day, Dr. Tessier gave me a present, a book entitled *Les Contrepèteries*. This type of word game is much more popular in France that in the English-speaking world.

Watching Dr. Tessier operate was a completely new world for me. He was the master at working with bone—harvesting it, bending it to shape, cutting it, displacing it, fixing it into position. Exquisite carpentry of the human facial skeleton; everything fit so perfectly together. Ralph Millard, my teacher, was a master of soft tissue surgery but had little interest in bone. Tessier did both well.

After a month or so, I received a tap on the shoulder from Elizabeth, the instrumentiste, asking me to scrub in to assist on a case, probably a facelift. My task was to suture things up after Dr. Tessier had put in several key sutures and, most likely, Elizabeth was there to see if I could do a decent job of suturing. Apparently I passed the test, because I became one of the regular assistants, along with Martine Peyronie and Yvon Raulo. Unfortunately, when I was occupied suturing up an abdominoplasty or a facelift, I was missing the craniofacial case in the next room—but, eventually, I began assisting with them too.

After about the 3rd or 4th month in Paris, the relatively small amount of funds that I had on hand began to dwindle, and I no longer had free rent. So, for several months—even in November and December—I was staying in the cheapest lodgings I could find. I stayed at places in the five dollars per night range, which meant that there would be little if any heating (and the 1974-75 winter was cold!) and the only bathroom was down the hall. If one wanted to take a bath, one would have to ask the landlady to come draw the bath. And more than once per week was considered profligate.

At least, though, Dr. Tessier started to pass on to me (albeit irregularly) a check from one of his American patients. Thus, I was able to rent an apartment on Rue Boileau, on the 8th floor of an old building. There was a small gas heater that one could fire up by putting coins in it, a small kitchen, and a bathroom.

Within a month, I heard from the French government that I had been granted a *bourse,* meaning scholarship, of 2,000 Francs per month, which was about five-hundred dollars then. This, plus Dr. Tessier's occassional checks, left me rather flush, and I was able to use the surplus to buy a number of vital instruments to take back to the United States. I bought a number of Heljestrand osteotomes, which are superb, and which I continue to use to this day. Unfortunately, the company no longer exists.

*Fig. 16.1 Dr. Tessier in 1975 at Yvon Raulo's graduation ceremony. Dr. Tessier has in his hand a Heljestrand (Swedish) osteotome, made of what he felt was the very finest steel, which he was presenting to Yvon (who is to the far right; Elizabeth Hecht is on the left in the foreground; and Andreé Collesson, the nurse anesthetist, is to Raulo's right)*

Yvon Raulo had been Dr. Tessier's assistant between 1974 and 1975 and, following his graduation, went into practice with Dr. Tessier at 26 Avenue Kléber. He worked with Dr. Tessier for a number of years, and then went on to become the chief of plastic surgery at Creteil, a hospital on the outskirts of Paris.

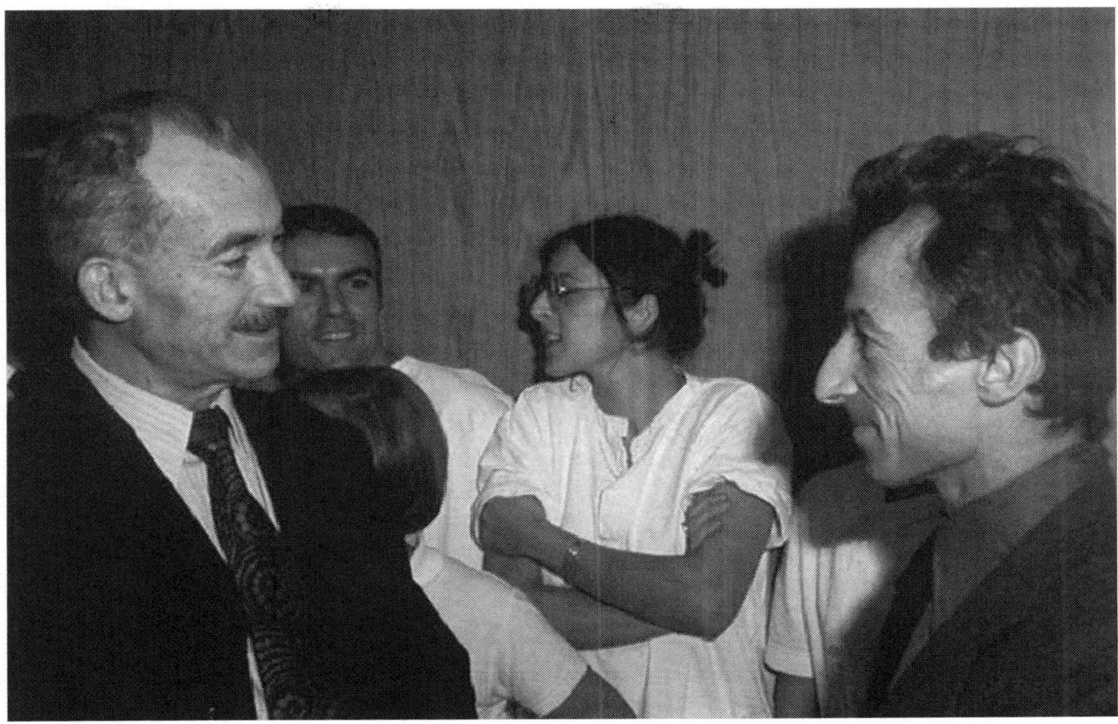

*Fig. 16.2 Immediately behind Dr. Tessier is Frank Trepsat, who is now a well-respected aesthetic surgeon in France. Yvon Raulo faces his ex-patron, now colleague.*

*Fig. 16.3 Andrée Collesson (on the left, above Raulo's shoulder) was Dr. Tessier's nurse anesthetist for thirty-seven years, and Elizabeth Motel Hecht, in front of Tessier, was his main scrub nurse for much of that time.*

*Fig. 16.4 Hans Peter Friehofer, to Tessier's left.*

Hans Peter Freihofer was Dr. Tessier's first foreign fellow. A Swiss-German, he was sent by his boss, Hugo Obwegeser, to learn craniofacial surgery. He went on to be the chief of maxillofacial surgery at Nijmigen, in the Netherlands, and editor of The European Journal of Maxillofacial Surgery.

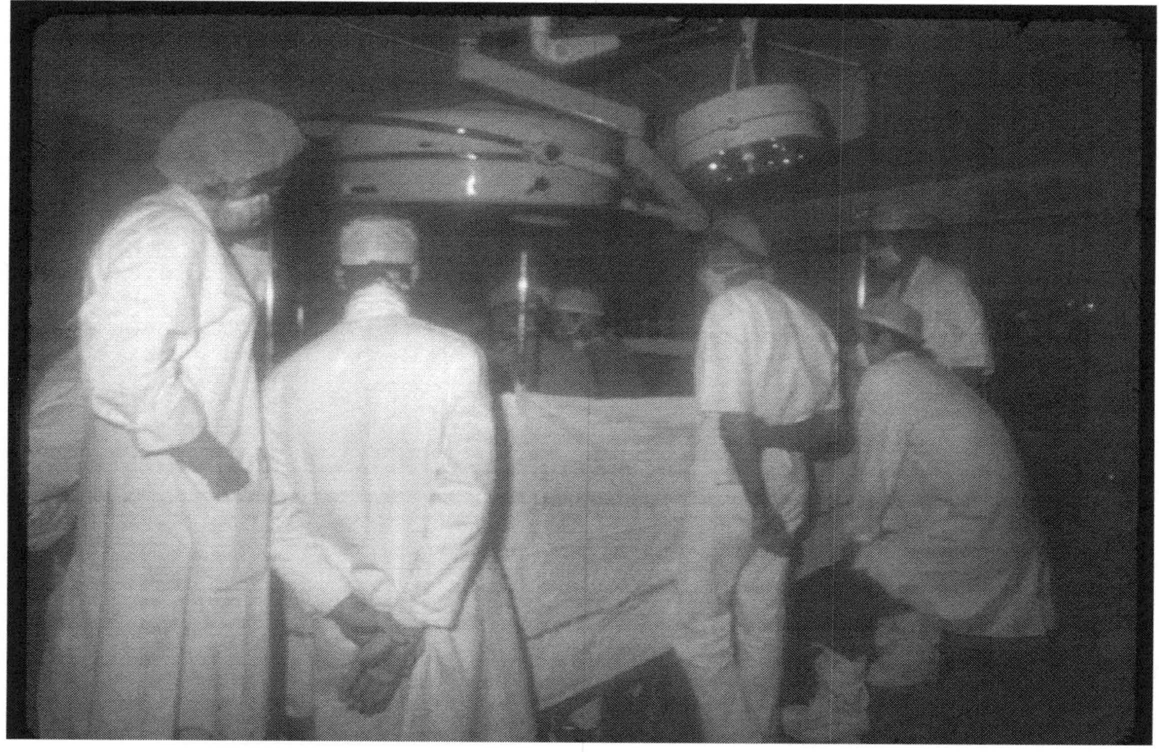

*Fig. 16.5 A sheet was taped between two IV poles to keep the visitors at bay. At times, there would be more than a dozen.*

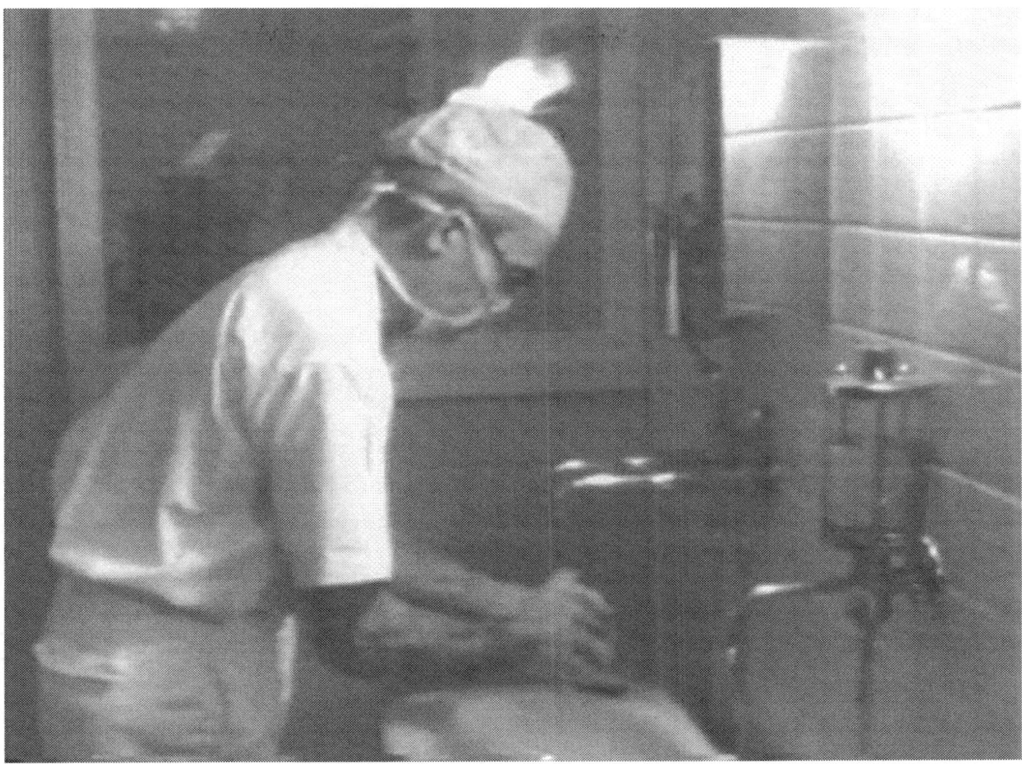

*Fig. 16.6 Dr. Tessier at his scrub sink. The day's schedule is taped to the wall on his left.*

The handwritten operating list for the day was usually drawn up the night before or that morning. Fridays and Saturdays were often the longest days. A typical list in the mid-80s might read like this:

Enf. A.B. Plagio/Derome (Child A.B.—correction plagiocephaly. Neurosurgeon Patrick Derome)

Mme. C.D. Lifting frontal, FL, paup. (Mrs. C.D. Forehead lift, facelift, eyelids)

P.R. HTO/ Derome. (hypertelorism correction, Derome)

Mlle. A.F. Nez esth. (Miss A.F. aesthetic rhinoplasty)

Mme. P.S. Seins/proth./abdo (Mrs. P.S. breast augmentation, abdominoplasty)

M. J.Q. Ptosis OG (Mr. J.G. correction ptosis left upper eyelid)

T.H. GO orb g. (bone graft to left orbit)

M. P.O. Seq. brul. (Mr. P.O. burn scars)

R.R. Le F I/G.O. Cr. (R.R. Le Fort I advancement and cranial bone graft)

G.H. Div. Abbé (G.H. Division Abbé flap)

D.D. Div. lamb. Fr. (D.D. Division of forehead flap)

F.V. Nez esth, genio (F.V. aesthetic rhinoplasty, genioplasty)

This comes to twelve cases, two of them intracranial. Some days it would get up to fifteen. This would be a full *weekly* schedule for a plastic surgeon in the United States, if not an entire plastic surgery service. How could he possibly do so much work in a day? First of all, he had absolutely no waiting between cases, something that can chew up hour after hour in a typical American teaching hospital. He would finish with one patient, take off his gloves, rescrub, and go on to the next. And with no lack of eager surgical assistants, he could have most of the closure of a case done by someone Elizabeth certified as capable for him. And then he would just keep operating until the schedule was finished—even if this was, on occasion, well after midnight.

And how could he be physically up to this grueling schedule, day after day? He performed most of his operations standing, pointing out that the more joints one had available to use, the more mobility one had. He felt that operating while standing erect was the most "ergonomic" method. To keep the veins in his legs from bothering him, he wore compressive stockings from the Jobst company that he purchased in the United States. His hands had enormous strength, with fairly short, but thick fingers. These fingers, particularly the index, would pass behind a mobilized maxilla and exert a very considerable force to have it move forward to where he wanted it to be. He was a thin man, a bit over six feet tall, but his forearms were thick and muscular, reminiscent of Popeye.

Fatigue? This was a word that was banned from his vocabulary. Between cases, he had an extraordinary ability to lie down on a stretcher and immediately fall into a deep sleep that lasted only five to ten minutes but allowed him to awaken completely refreshed.

Needless to say, the pace he set was hard on the staff, but this was a "volunteer army," and everyone stayed until the end. They had a sense of pride in being part of the best team in the world for this type of surgery. And everyone knew that, no matter how hard they were working, Tessier worked harder. Elizabeth directed the whole show and probably worked harder than anyone besides Tessier. The autoclaves at Bélvèdere were slow, so all of the instruments for all of the cases of the day were arranged the night before and kept on tables covered by a sterile drape. When the day's work was over, Elizabeth would often have to stay another hour, cleaning up and getting organized for the next day. In an e-mail from November 29, 2009, she said, "Yes, there were several times that I was upset with the Patron on the subject of work. Otherwise, I always respected him. There was a lot of work in sharpening the osteotomes and the rugines. I was often tired since I did not always have good help, either from the assistants or the nurses. To have a good assistant was primordial for the smooth functioning of the team. I was simply shocked by his last day of work, and not being warned about this ahead of time [He chose the last day to be 14 July, the French National Holiday, and ended surgery at 3:00 am., at which time he simply left without a word.] But that is life … and I knew we got along well together. He was happy to see me when I visited him during his convalescence. Outside of his work, he was a delicious man, but in his work he demanded perfection. He was an exceptional man."

If a patient came to see Dr. Tessier in consultation on Monday, and he or she was from Martinique and wanted the surgery done while in Paris, it was no problem—he would just add them to the list, no matter how long it already was. And if patients had a complaint about a result (for instance, some fat in the neck not dealt with during a face lift), they would find themselves back on the schedule later in the week.

I recall a patient from Miami—a doctor's wife—who came to see me about enlarging her cheek bones after I had started my practice. She brought a *National Geographic* magazine with her to the consultation that contained a feature on the Maori, a native group of New Zealand who had truly enormous cheekbones. This was what she wanted. I ventured that that might be a bit much, but that my approach would be to take bone grafts from the skull to add to the cheekbones. This was done without incident. Fairly soon, she politely told me that she felt it was not quite enough. Another operation was scheduled and more bone was added. Again, after time went by, she –again, politely—said she wanted more.

After an appropriate interval, a third bone grafting was done. By this time she was approaching Maori cheekiness, but she *still* felt it was not enough. I told her that I felt it would be in her best interest to put a moratorium on further bone grafting. She did not argue, but I began hearing from colleagues in New York, San Francisco, and Los Angeles that she had been in to see them. They all agreed with my moratorium idea.

She then flew to Paris and saw Dr. Tessier. Here was a patient operated on by one of his trainees, and she was not content. He operated on her and added even more bone (he sent me a picture of the state of the bone grafts that I had placed). True to form, she politely complained to him that it was not enough, and she was put back on the schedule the next week for more bone. I have not seen her since, but wonder at times how she looks, and how much bone remains in her skull!

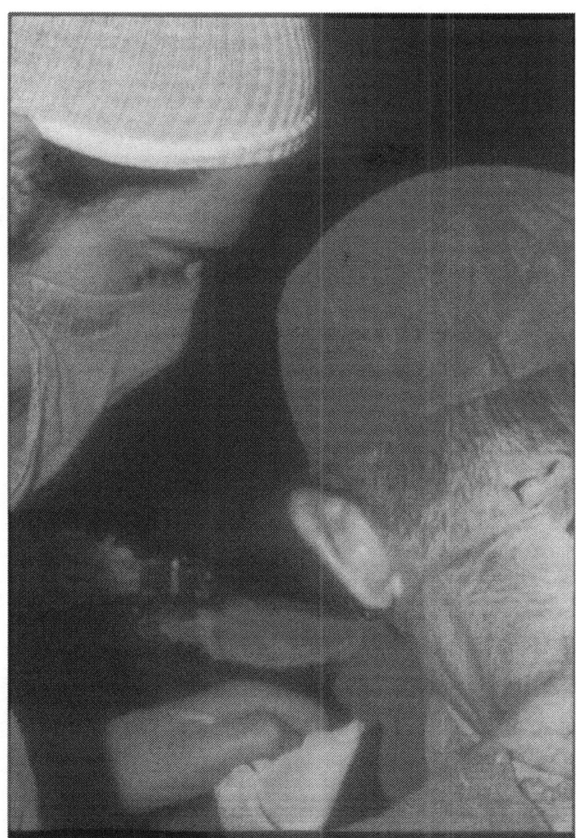

*Fig. 16.7 View over Dr. Tessier's shoulder. One can appreciate his Celtish ear.*

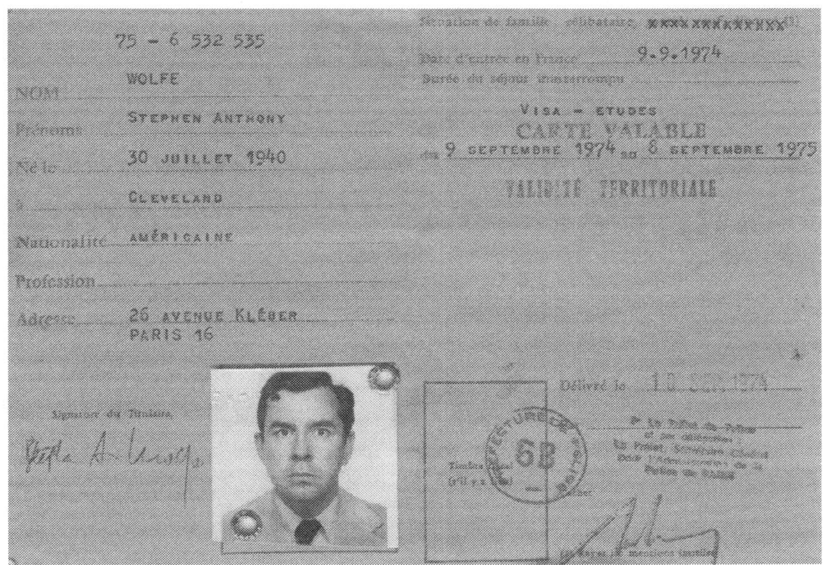

75 – 6 532 535

NOM WOLFE

Prénoms STEPHEN ANTHONY

Né le 30 JUILLET 1940

à CLEVELAND

Nationalité AMÉRICAINE

Profession

Adresse 26 AVENUE KLÉBER
PARIS 16

Date d'entrée en France 9.9.1974

VISA – ETUDES

CARTE VALABLE

du 9 SEPTEMBRE 1974 au 8 SEPTEMBRE 1975

VALIDITÉ TERRITORIALE

Délivré le

68

*Fig. 16.8 Visa to stay in France as a student for one year, issued in September, about the time my funds were beginning to run out. This shows in the picture.*

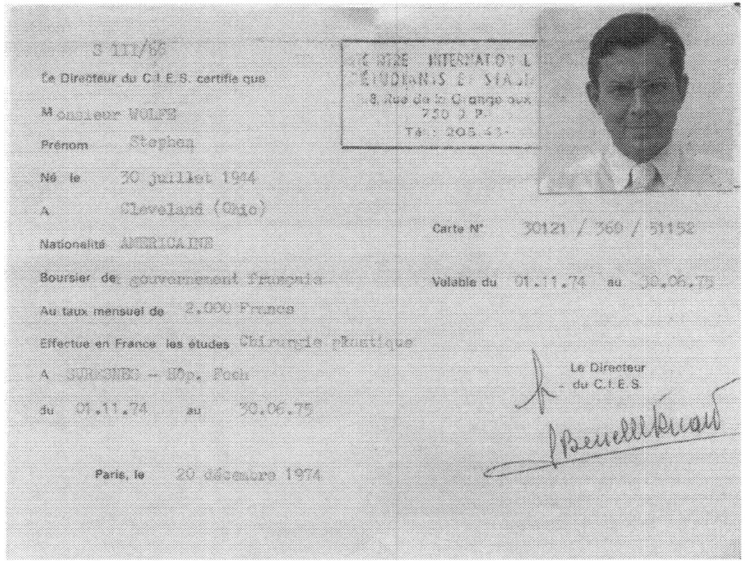

S 111/66

Le Directeur du C.I.E.S. certifie que

Monsieur WOLFE

Prénom Stephen

Né le 30 juillet 1944

A Cleveland (Ohio)

Nationalité AMERICAINE

Boursier de gouvernement français

Au taux mensuel de 2.000 Francs

Effectue en France les études Chirurgie plastique

A SURESNES - Hôp. Foch

du 01.11.74 au 30.06.75

Paris, le 20 décembre 1974

Carte N° 30121 / 360 / 51152

Valable du 01.11.74 au 30.06.75

Le Directeur du C.I.E.S.

*Fig. 16.9 My bourse, good for six months. This was related somehow to the Fulbright program that supported French scholars working in the United States. The photograph shows that things were looking up.*

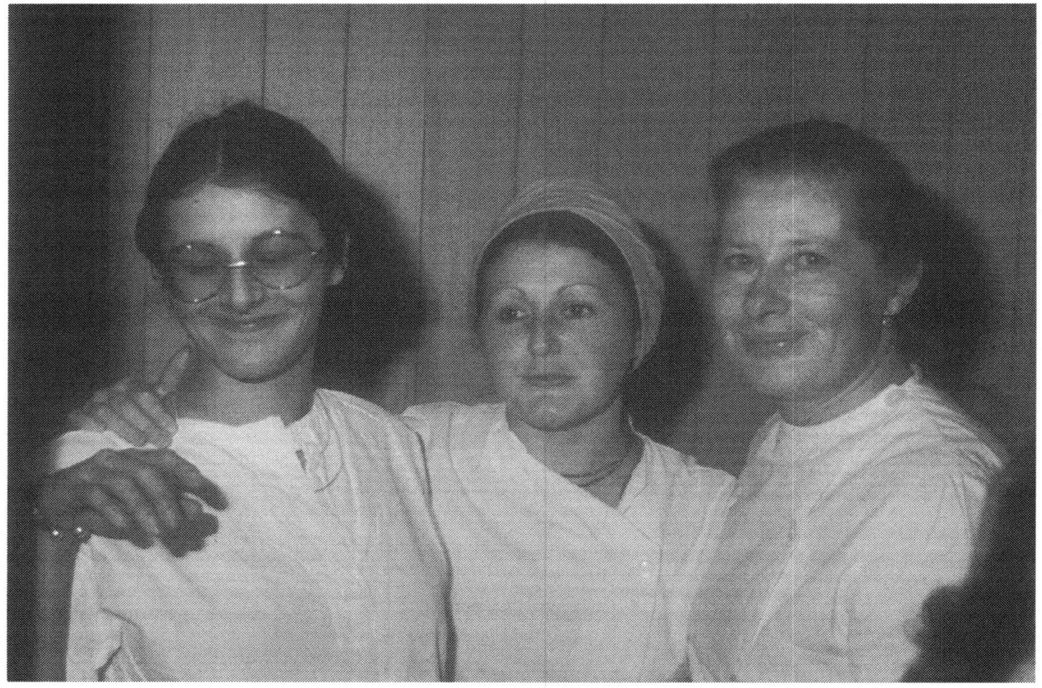

*Fig. 16.10 Cecile, an instrumentiste, (scrub nurse), on the left, and several panseuses (circulating nurses) at Bèlvédere. Everyone that worked for Dr. Tessier was paid by him, including the orderlies. The Clinique provided nothing other than operating rooms and hospital beds.*

shame that his name did not appear anywhere on the publication, but I think most people know by now that it was his idea. (See further discussion in Chapter 25.)

I opened my practice in Miami in 1976 and, from time to time, would see a patient for Dr. Tessier. One time in the early 80s, a young woman from Chicago came in with a forehead flap nasal reconstruction in place and the pedicle not yet divided. She said that Dr. Tessier had done it, and that she didn't like it and wanted it removed. I explained to her that this was not at all a finished result, and that she should return to Paris to let him divide the pedicle and do any further work that he felt was necessary. I said he was a superb surgeon and that she should be patient. I told her I was sure that the result would be outstanding.

She returned to Paris for her next procedure. I heard from Henry Kawamoto that, two days before her scheduled surgery, she flew from Paris to Los Angeles to ask Henry to remove the nose. He, of course, declined as well. She then returned on the next flight to Paris for her scheduled surgery.

I heard later from Dr. Tessier that, after dividing the forehead flap, the patient returned for a post-operative visit with a number of the sutures disrupted. He said he realized at that point that the original nasal deformity came from her self-mutilation. He also stated that she returned a year later with no nose, having cut it off herself … and she eventually went on to kill herself.

My learning experience with Dr. Tessier began in 1974, and it continued until his death in 2008.I learned from him how to examine a patient, record my observations, and make a long-term plan. I learned from him the importance of having proper instruments and having the ones that need to be sharp (rugines, osteotomes) undergo regular sharpening. I learned the proper way to hold the instruments—subperiosteal dissection is done with the suction cannula in the left hand, acting as a kind of retractor, and the rugine is in the right hand, raising an intact sheet of periosteum. I learned how to use an index finger to explore areas that I could not see (the pterygomaxillary space, the vomer behind the maxilla). And, although I will never be able to match it, I remember the great strength he had in his hands and forearms. I remember his determination and will. When I finish a long operating day (for me, at 8 or 9 in the evening), completely worn out, I remind myself that he was able to do twice as many cases, and operate for another four or five hours beyond what I had done.

Dr. Tessier was, without doubt, the greatest orbital surgeon of all time. His abilities working with bone were phenomenal. And I think, if it had not been for him, plastic surgery would have been a specialty that only dealt with the soft tissues. Dr. Tessier taught plastic surgeons (some, at least) how to work with bone, which is at the center of the specialty of craniofacial surgery.

If he had a weakness, it was the way he dealt with teeth and occlusion. In the early and mid-1970s orthodontics was still not a mature specialty in France. Instead of having a patient who had had prior orthodontic preparation with arches aligned, dental interferences removed, and brackets on the teeth with a rigid arch wire with surgical hooks (as was the cases with patients treated by Tessier in the United States), most of the French patients had to have arch bars applied at the beginning of the case. We tried to keep Tessier out of the room when we were doing that, because if he came in to "help" (always anxious to keep things moving along), he would soon become impatient and sometimes apply more force than the teeth were used to sustaining. He did recognize this as a lacuna in his own training, and in 1976 Jean Francois Tulasne (who had had dental training) joined him and dealt with the dental aspects of the cases.

When Tessier was out of town, he urged us to go and spend a few days with Jacques Dautrey. Dautrey had been at Foch on the service of Ginestet in the 1950s and 60s, before he moved to Nancy, a town midway between Paris and Zurich. The two were good friends and, at one point, had been considering going into practice together. Dautrey was strong in the areas where Tessier was weak. He was a superb mandibular surgeon. Walter Pepersack, a Belgian who was part of Hugo Obwegeser's team in Zurich, would sneak away from Zurich to spend a day or two with Dautrey whenever he could. He would use Dautrey's method—gentler, more precise, and more sparing of the alveolar nerve—rather than the classic Obwegeser method, but he had to keep his eye on the door to be sure that Hugo didn't come in and see such blasphemy. Dautrey had a special type of arch bars made, which bear his name and are still the best available. He would do the orthodontic treatment on his surgical patients himself, which was (and still is) a rarity. Several times per year, Dautrey would have a teaching session in Nancy, with four or five invitees. He would perform the limited number of operations that he had in his repertoire: the sagittal split of the mandible, posterior segmental maxillary molar osteotomies (Schuchardt) to close open bites, remodeling of the condyle to TMJ arthrosis, and the "Dautrey procedure," where he sectioned the zygomatic arch and bent the anterior portion down to prevent TMJ dislocation. Ultimately, we would see patients who had been operated on the week before, months before, or years before—all showing the results of his procedures.

Dautrey was the best mandibular surgeon that I have ever seen. His weakness, however, was Tessier's strength. Once we saw a patient with Crouzon's disease in which Dautrey had moved the mandible back to correct the malocclusion. He did not know how to do a Le Fort III, which would have moved the midface forward and properly corrected not only the occlusion, but also the entire facial deformity.

*Fig. 16.15 Jacques Dautrey*

Nevertheless, Jacques Dautrey was the best surgeon any of us had seen for procedures on the mandible. We had Dr. Tessier, the ultimate master of the orbit and midface, to thank for sending us to the ultimate master of the sagittal split of the mandible.

After returning to the United States, I started to put to use the techniques I had learned in Europe. This resulted in a number of publications in *Plastic and Reconstructive Surgery*, almost all of which were the result of my use of the procedures and techniques that I had seen used by Dr. Tessier: correction of lateral facial microsomia, cranial bone grafts for alveolar clefts, application of craniofacial surgical principles to orbital deformities, rationale for the treatment of exophthalmos and exorbitism, expansion of the orbit, genioplasty for correction of neck deformities, shortening and lengthening the chin, usage of the temporalis muscle for orbital and maxillary deformities, monobloc frontofacial advancement, lengthening the nose, treatment of post-traumatic, post-surgical deformities, and a few others. None of these were original, but all validated the techniques developed by Paul Tessier and showed that good results could be obtained, even in the hands of lesser surgeons.

The Textbook that I wrote with Sam Berkowitz, my orthodontist, was entitled *Plastic Surgery of the Facial Skeleton* (Little, Brown and Company, Boston, 1989) and had chapters covering each part of the face, from cranium to chin. On some level, I must have realized that Dr. Tessier would not be writing such a textbook and that someone would have to do it for him.

# Chapter 17

## Training with Tessier

As his renown increased over the 1970s and 1980s, surgeons from all over the world would come to Paris to see Dr. Tessier operate. It often got to the point that, during the day in Clinique Belvédère, there would be as many as twenty visitors. It became necessary to put up several IV poles and attach a sheet to them to create a barrier to keep this horde from interfering with the surgical team. As the day went on, the numbers would start to drop, and around dinnertime most of them drifted off. He often continued operating until 11 p.m. or midnight and, by that time, almost all of them had gone. If you stayed on until this hour, he would know that you were really interested and would willingly engage in conversation. Some of the questions asked by the daylight-hours visitors were so inane that they rarely got a response: "Dr. Tessier, when will you remove the sutures?" would generally not get an answer. But, toward midnight, he would open up. He was more than ready to share his remembrances of Harold Gillies or provide wicked comments about some of the idiotic things done by supposedly world famous surgeons.

D. Ralph Millard, Jr., M.D., F.A.C.S.
S. Anthony Wolfe, M.D., F.A.C.S.
Walter R. Mullin, M.D.
The Plastic Surgery Center
1444 N.W. 14th Avenue
Miami, Florida 33125

Plastic and Reconstructive Surgery — Phone 325-1441

November 4, 1985

Mary McGrath, M.D., Chairman
Ethics Committee, ASPRS
Geo. Washington Univ. Medical Center
2150 Pennsylvania Avenue, NW
Washington, D.C. 20037

Dear Dr. McGrath:

There have been a number of instances recently where members or prospective members of ASPRS have been having a bit of difficulty because they have put down that they were "trained by" Paul Tessier.

I had the opportunity at the Kansas City meeting to discuss this with Dr. Tessier, and he proposes the following classification for people who have spent time with him in Paris.

Greater than 1 year: Assistant
Six months-1 year: Fellow
2 months-6 months: Visitor
Less than 2 months: Tourist

When Dr. Tessier returns to Paris, he may wish to confirm this new "Tessier classification" to you in writing.

Yours truly,

S. Anthony Wolfe, M.D., F.A.C.S.
SAW:tm

CC: Paul Tessier, M.D.

*Fig. 17.1 1985 letter about another "Tessier classification."*

When the daylight visitors returned to their own countries, it was not unusual for them to advertise that they had been "trained by Tessier." On a number of occasions, when shown the brochures, he would have no remembrance of the individual. This became an ethical issue in the United States. The "Tessier classification" of those who had visited or spent time with him is shown above.

There were certainly some abuses of the process. One surgeon from Colorado put on the brochure for his craniofacial team that he had been "trained by Tessier." Tessier had no memory of the individual having been there, and when this became an issue for the ethics committee, the only thing the individual could produce on his own behalf were some notes that he had taken during the few days that he had been a *tourist*. In another situation, I was called by someone on the credentials committee of a north Florida hospital. An oral surgeon was demanding to be given privileges in cosmetic surgery and said that he had been "trained by Tessier." It turned out that he had been there several months, but this hardly constitutes a formal plastic surgery residency.

The important thing to understand was that there was *no* formal fellowship with Dr. Tessier. Surgeons could come and watch him operate, and some who were regulars could be tapped to assist him on operations. After a certain period of time, you might become *un de mes anciens* (one of my helpers, a confidant). But there was no French accrediting agency; most of his work was done in a private clinic. You watched, you learned, and, if you were motivated, you began to do some of this unusual reconstructive work in your own practice after you returned home.

In the United States, we have a well-developed bureaucracy for medical education. The ACGME (Accreditation Council for Graduate Medical Education) and the R.R.C.s (Residency Review Committees) have strict requirements for residency programs in plastic surgery, and there are now a few ACGME-accredited craniofacial fellowships.

The main problem with these bureaucracies, in my opinion, is that they do not look at the *quality* of the work being done. You could learn an enormous amount watching Dr. Tessier operate, since he was a superb surgeon with extraordinarily good results. Under the ACGME purview, you can be a very bad surgeon with extraordinarily poor results and still have an accredited program as long as all of the paper work was filled out properly.

*Fig. 17.2 Dr. Tessier's favorite picture of himself, taken by Jim Fletcher, ca. 1975.*

The closest that Dr. Tessier ever came to having any kind of certification of fellowship was to hand out a copy of the above picture. It was taken by Jim Fletcher, who was Ralph Millard's photographer in the early 1970s. Jim later went to Chicago where he worked for Sam Pruzansky, and then he returned to work for Millard and me before heading off to medical school and an eventual career as a psychiatrist. The picture has an inscription to Dr. Tessier's right. The ballpoint writing has faded almost to illegibility and I can barely read it, but the inscription reads, "To one of my favorite sons, Tony Wolfe … Tessier." One can detect the slight ptosis of the left upper eyelid, which, three decades later, would be corrected by Serge Morax.

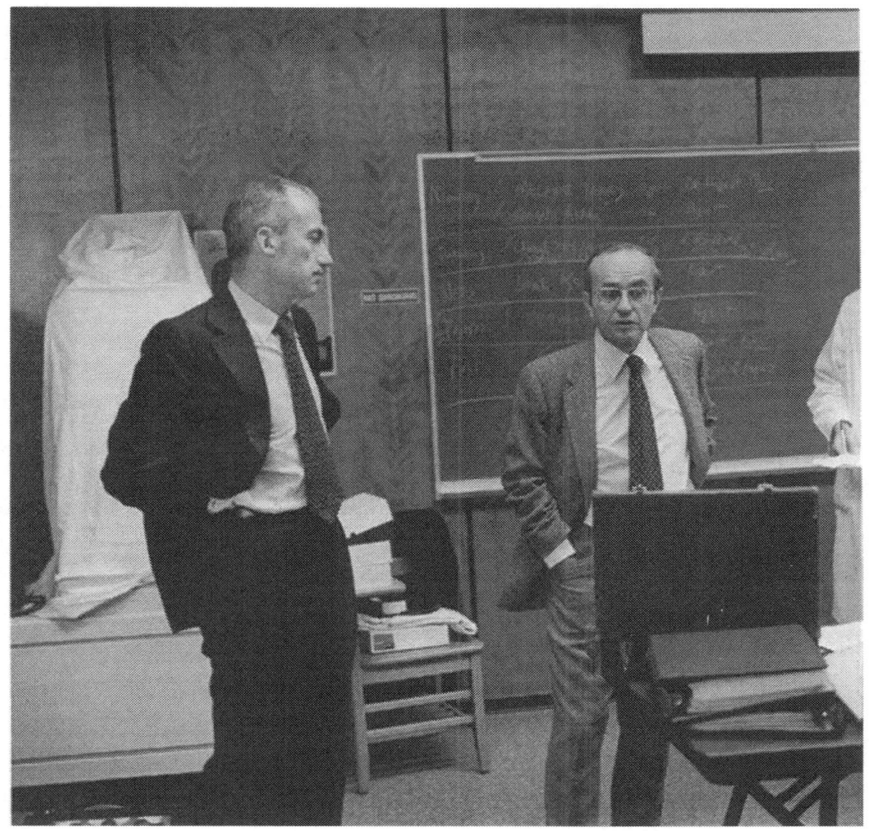

*Fig. 18.3 Sam Pruzansky had been following a large number of patients with various craniofacial anomalies at his Center for Craniofacial Anomalies (CCFA) at The University of Illinois, and he first invited Tessier to operate there in 1972.*

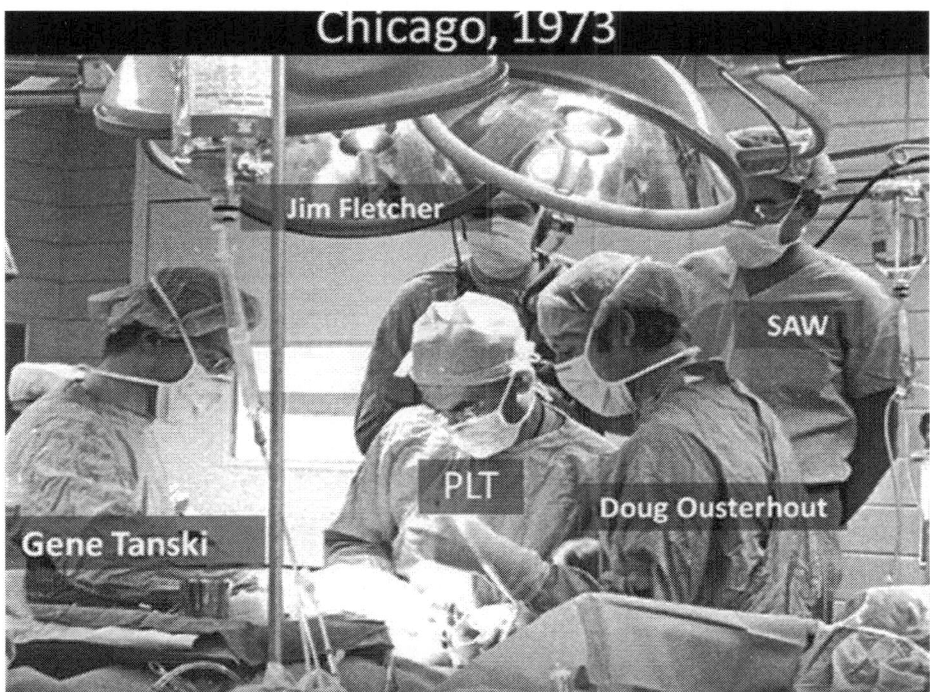


*Fig. 18.4 Paul Tessier, operating in Chicago at Rush-Presbyterian Hospital, 1971. Gene Tansky is to Tessier's right, and Doug Ousterhout is to his left. Jim Fletcher (who later worked as a photographer for Ralph Millard and me in Miami) and I stand behind them.*

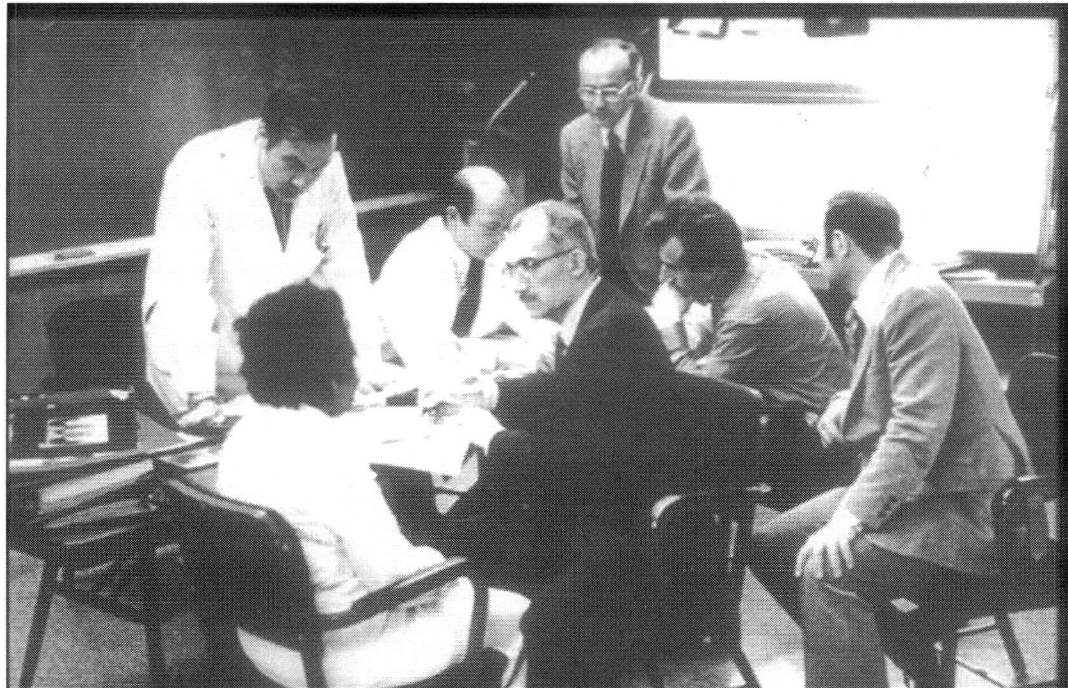

*Fig. 18.5. Patient consultations, Chicago, 1974. On the right of Sam Pruzansky is Howard Aduss, another orthodontist on the CFFA team.*

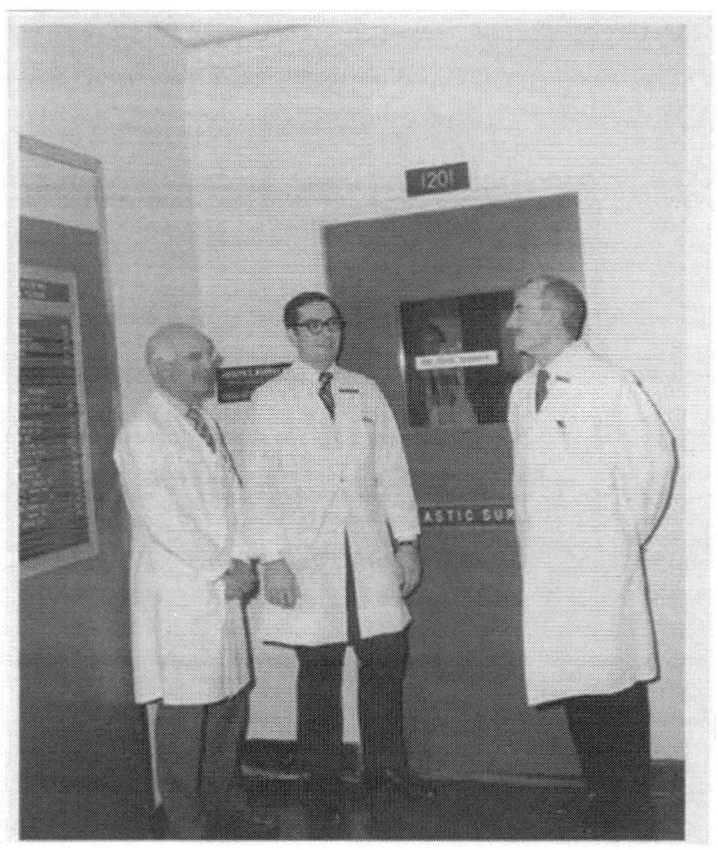


*Fig. 18.6 Joe Murray, Leonard Kaban and Paul Tessier, Boston Children's Hospital, 1980. Tessier's name is now officially on the door, and he had obtained a Massachusetts Medical License with the help of Murray.*

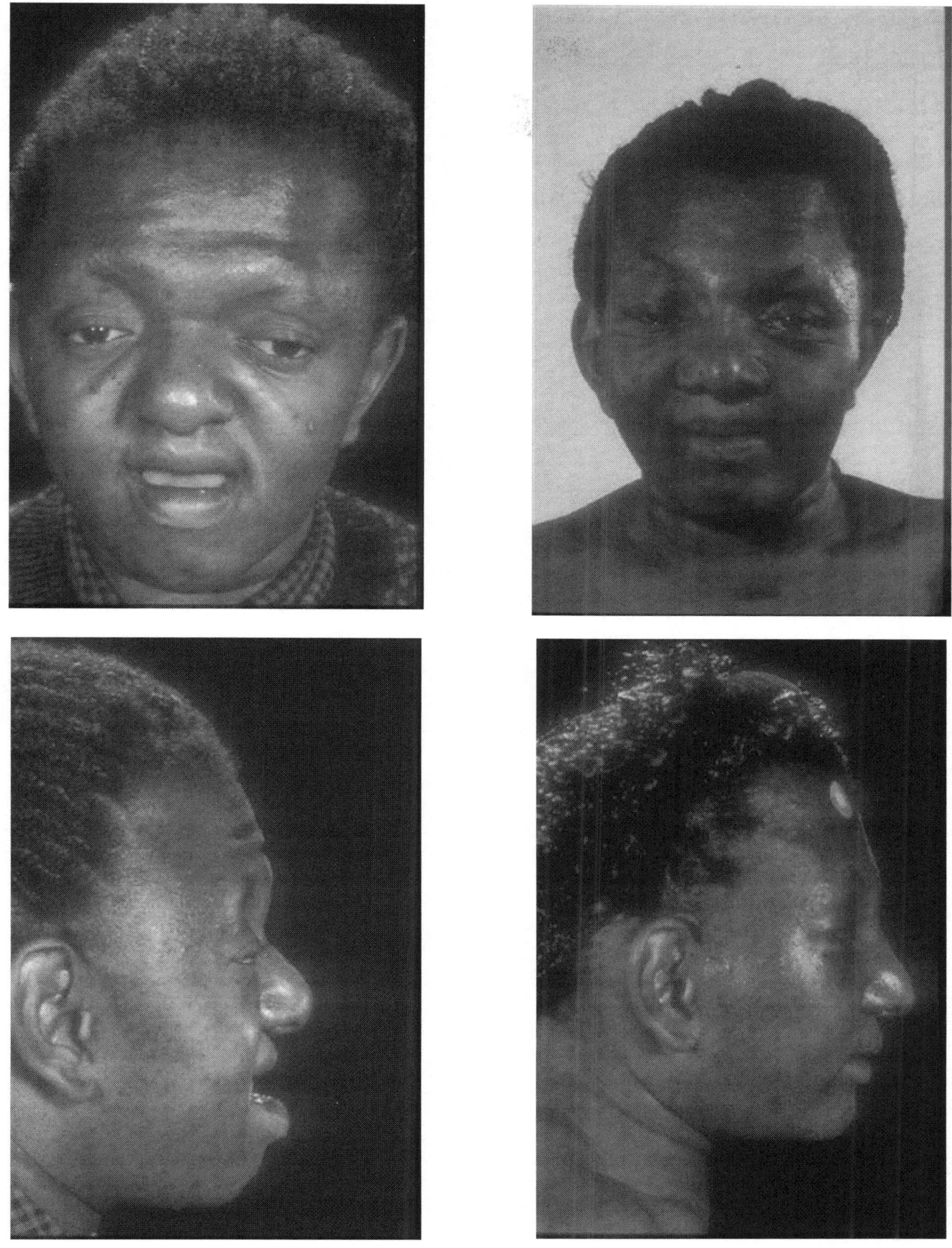

*Fig. 18.3-d Apert patient operated on at Great Ormond Street Hospital in London with Harry Jones when Dr. Tessier was in his late 70's.*

Of the various centers, there were a few that Tessier enjoyed and returned to regularly. Usually his decision would be made on the basis of his relationship with the local division chief, and the number and type of patients available to be operated upon.

Kansas City was a regular stop, since Fred McCoy (another big game hunter) and Tessier got along famously. Houston was a regular stop, and Ray Brauer and Tom Cronin were congenial hosts there.

For a number of years, Boston was a favorite destination, and Joe Murray, chief of plastic surgery at Boston Children's and The Peter Bent Brigham Hospital, wanted him there.

# Chapter 19

## The Tessier Consultation

When Dr. Tessier came to operate on a plastic surgery unit in the United States, it was usually for one or two weeks, and with several major intracranial cases a day, when he left the intensive care unit would be full to overflowing with recently operated patients.

The day usually started early on a Sunday morning, when the consultation began. During the course of the day he might see seventy to eighty patients, ending late in the evening.

Each patient was examined in the same careful, methodical manner. He felt the top of the head and worked his way down the structures of the face, and he ended with a look at the hands. Then he would make his notes, which for many of us were almost more instructive than seeing him operate. After noting all of the salient points of the physical exam, he would write "TT" which meant treatment. Here, some understanding of the many abbreviations he used became vital to deciphering his notes. For example, "R.I.O." meant *rebord inférieure orbitaire*, or infra orbital rim; "G.O." meant *greffe osseuse*, or bone graft. (A partial list of abbreviations is found in Appendixes).

And, for him, having examined the patient was almost as important as having operated. Whenever he discussed his experience with a condition, it would be: X number seen; Y number operated.

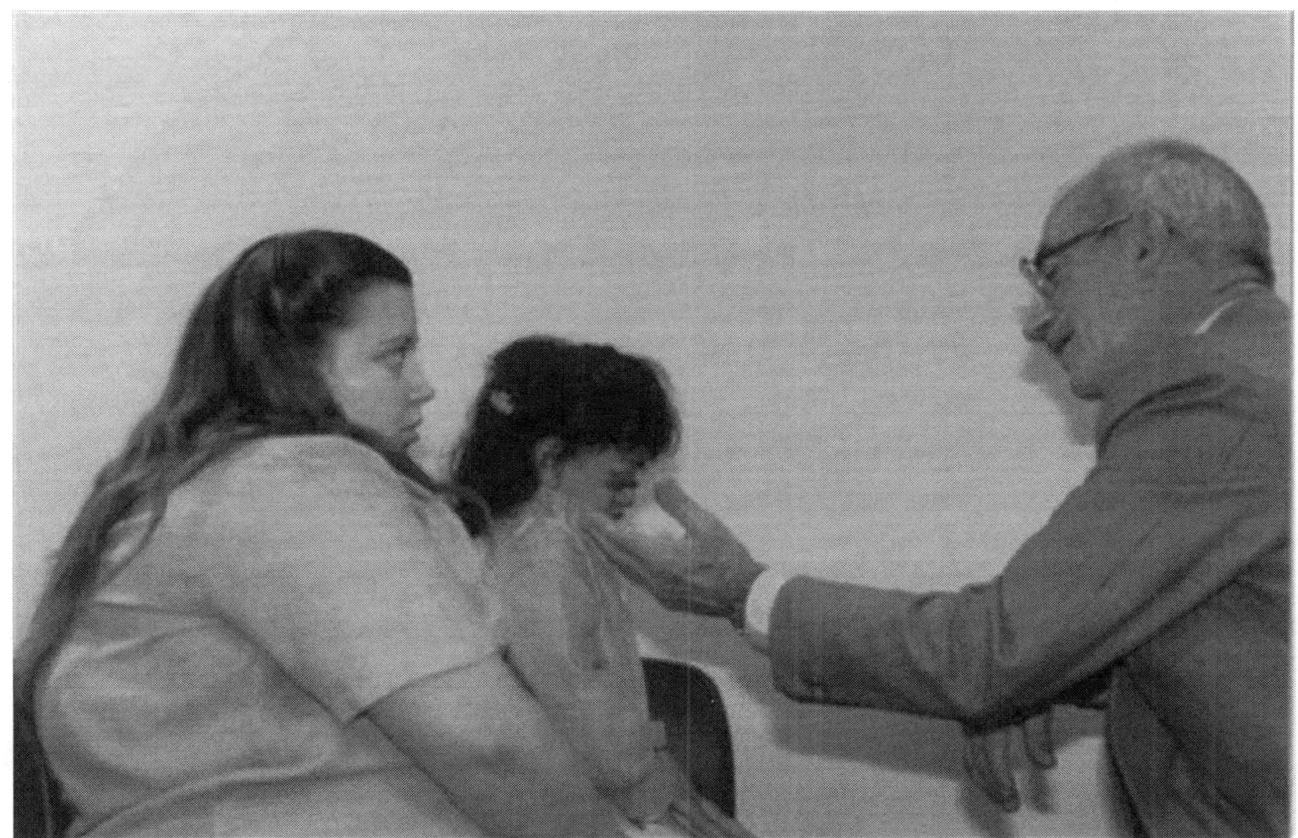

*Fig. 19.1 Kansas City, late 1980s. Reassuring a Crouzon patient.*

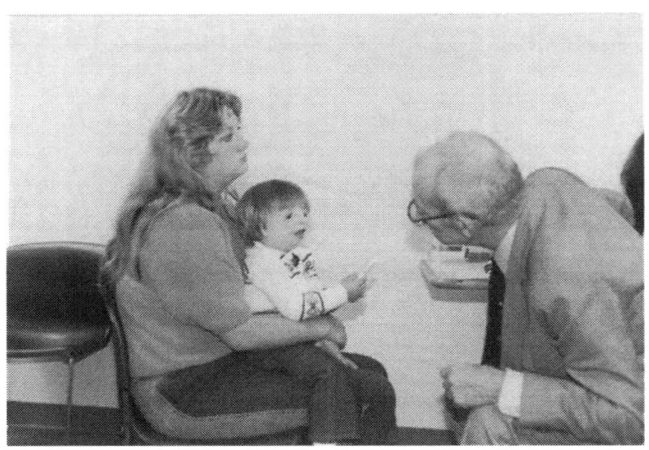

*Fig. 19.2 Tessier is saying hello to a Treacher Collins Franceschetti patient*

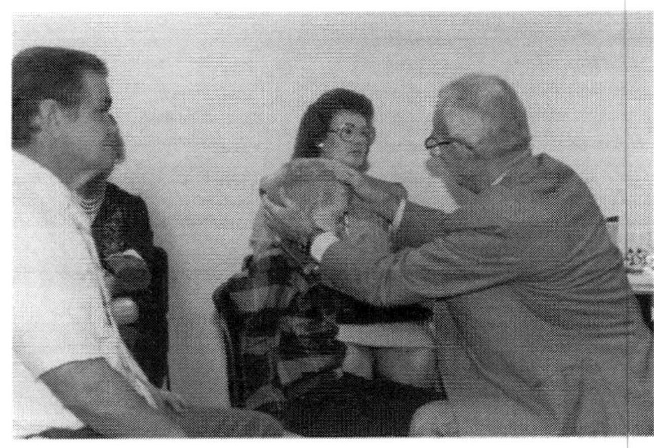

*Fig. 19.3 Palpation of a Crouzon's skull.*

*Fig. 19.4 Explanation to the plastic surgeons present; Elizabeth Hecht is in the background.*

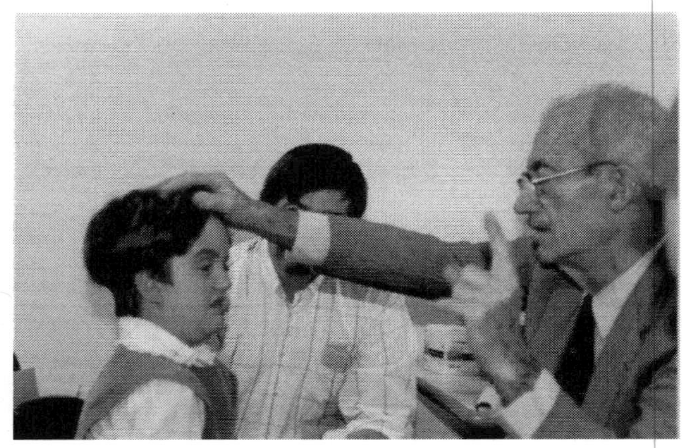

*Fig. 19.5 Check of extraocular muscle function.*

*Fig. 19.6 Let's see the occlusion.*

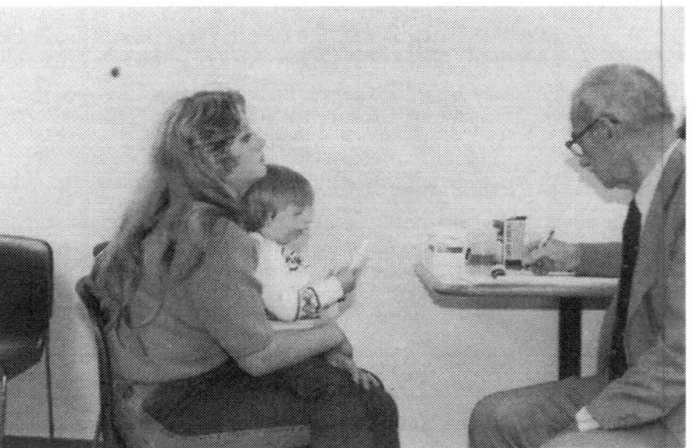

*Fig. 19.7 And always taking notes.*

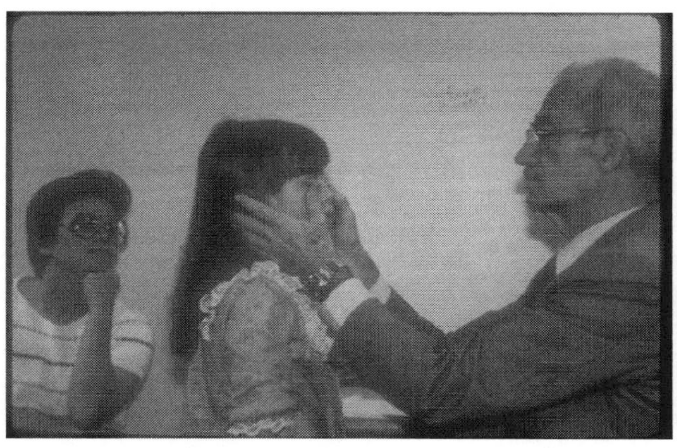

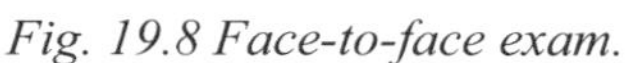

*Fig. 19.8 Face-to-face exam.*

*Fig. 19.9 In Charlotte, North Carolina, ca. 1993. David Matthews, Henry Kawamoto, SAW, SAW's Fellow Lou Bucky, Tessier.*

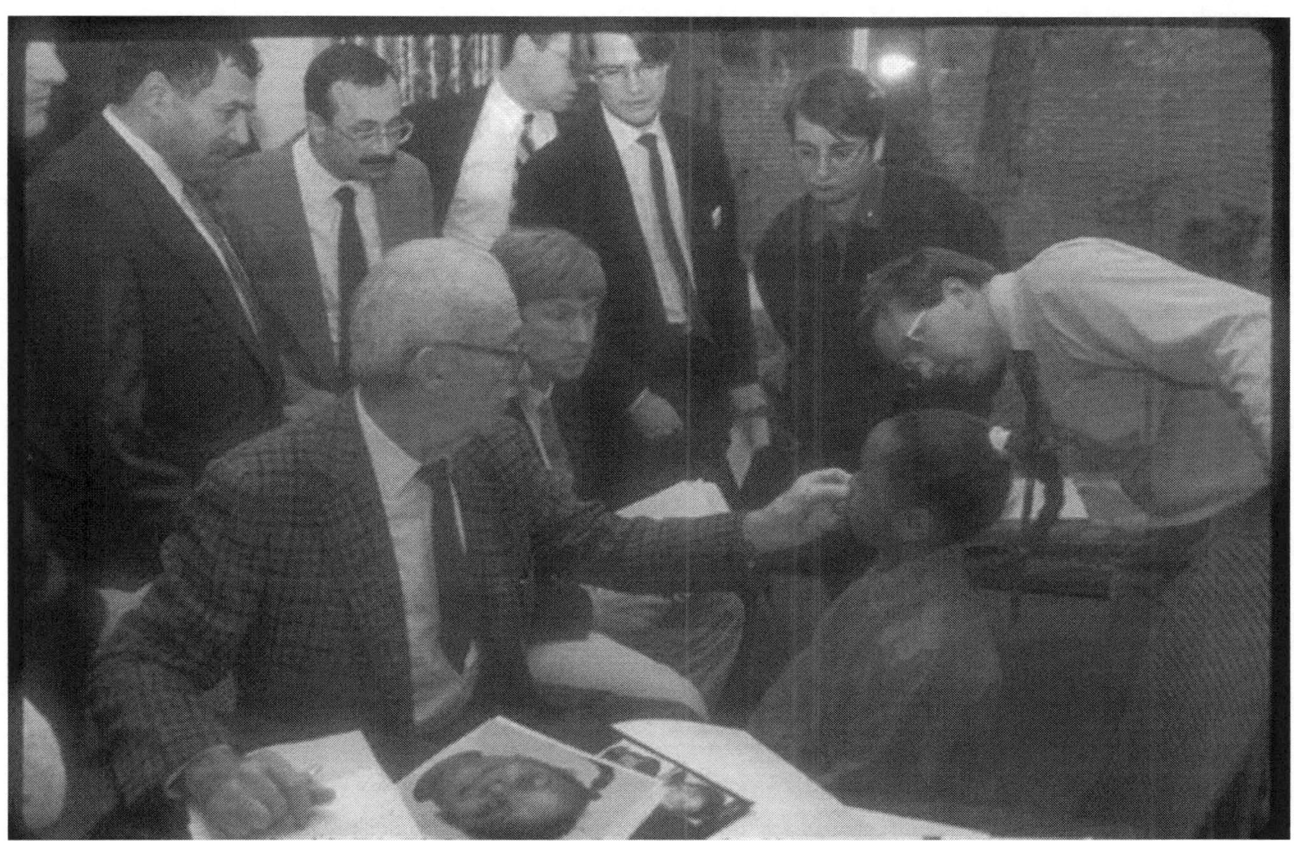

*Fig. 19.10 Explaining a fine point to David Matthews et alia.*

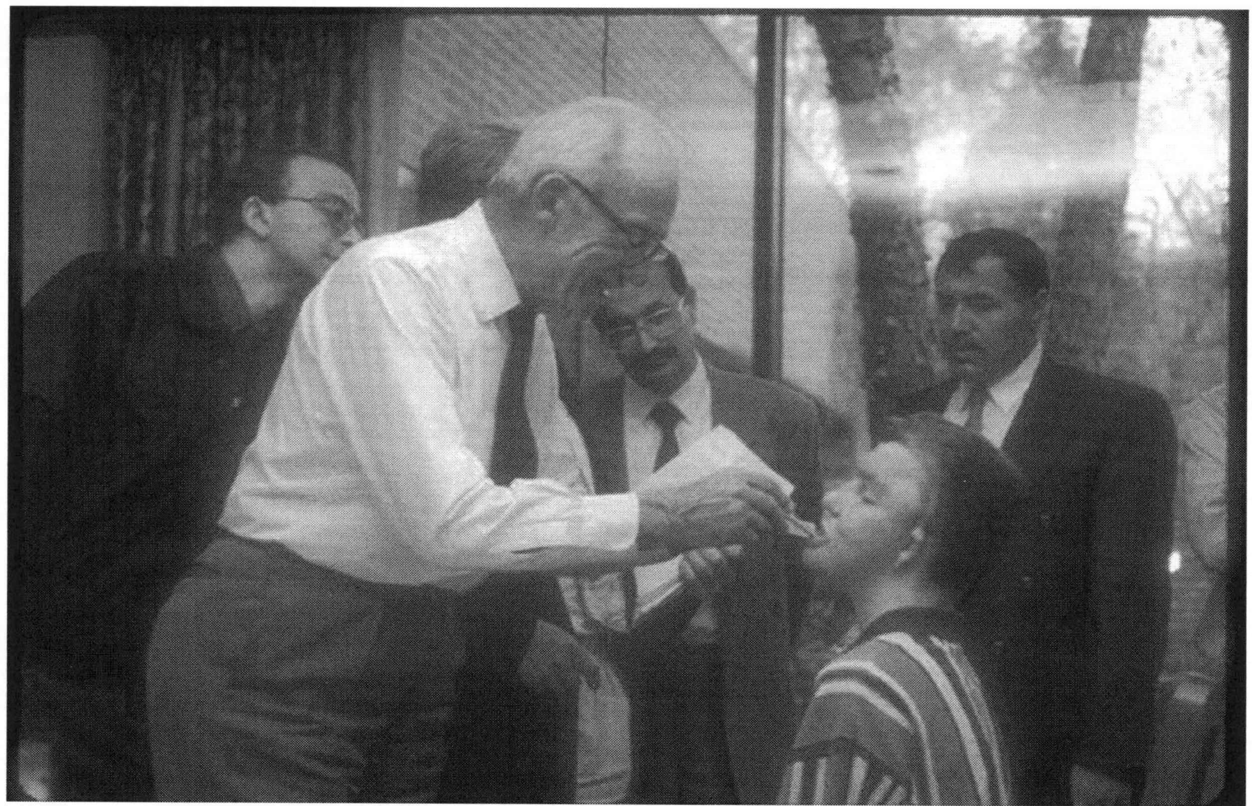

*Fig. 19.11 Yes, I see the occlusion.*

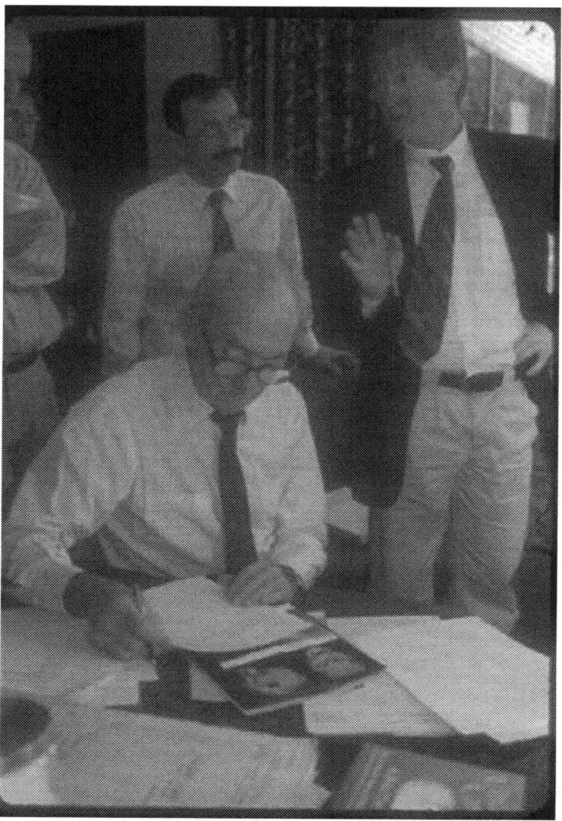

*Fig. 19.12 Tessier checking his previous notes.*

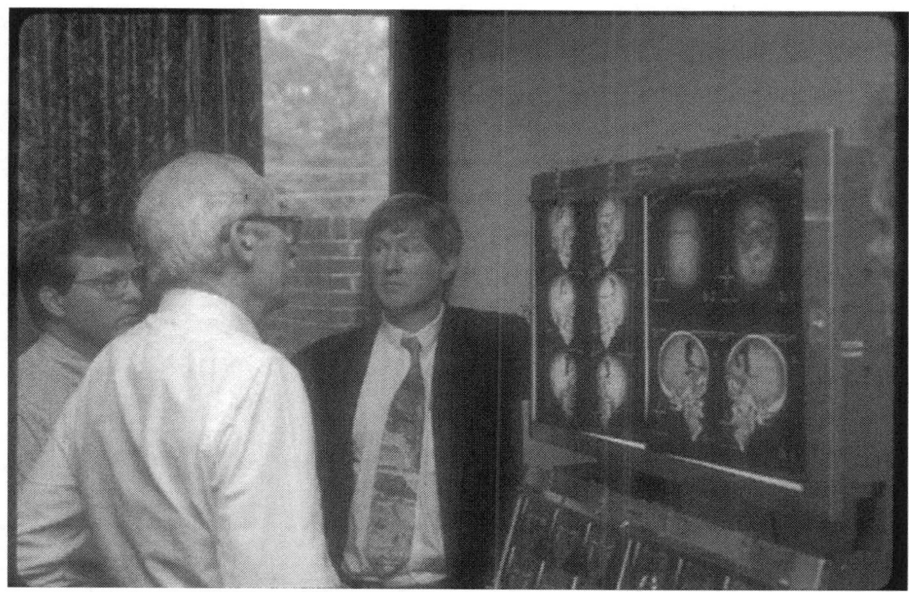

*Fig. 19.13 David Matthews, Tessier's neurosurgeon, Tessier, and 3-D CT scans.*

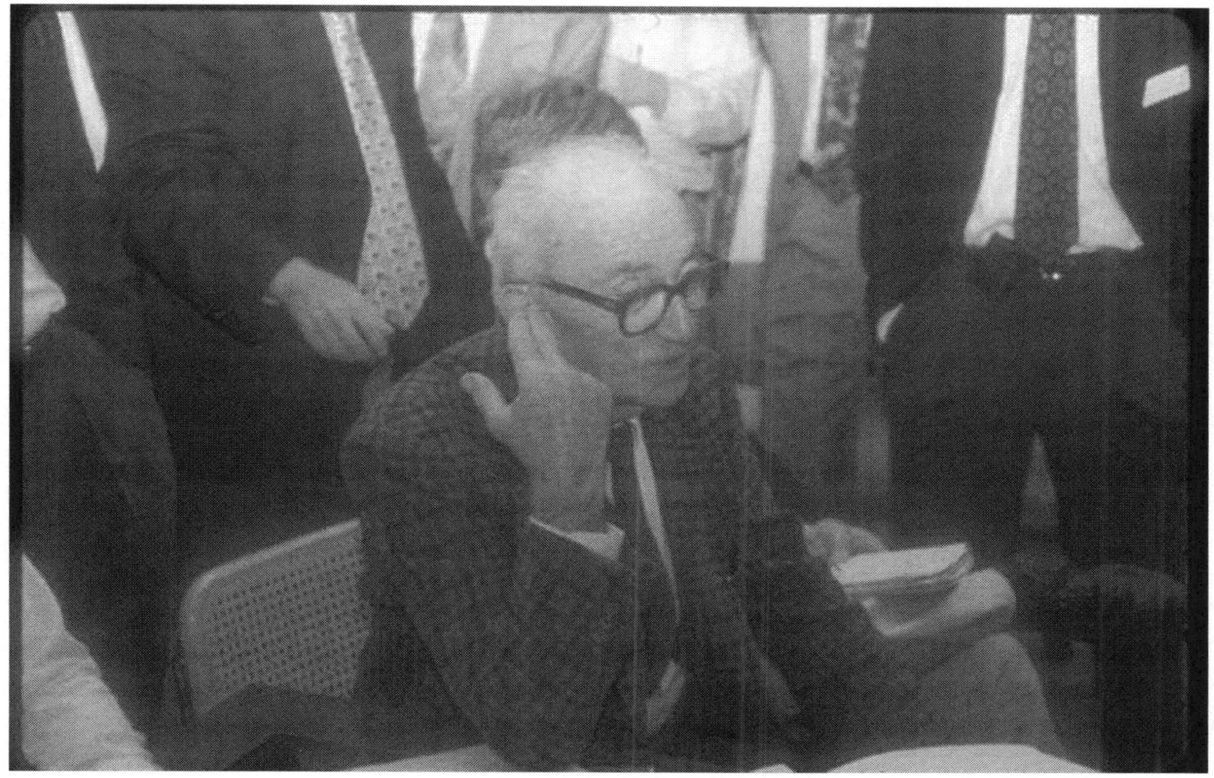

*Fig. 19.14 Tessier teaching and making a point. One was much more likely to hear him expound in the United States than in Paris (where he was so overwrought with work).*

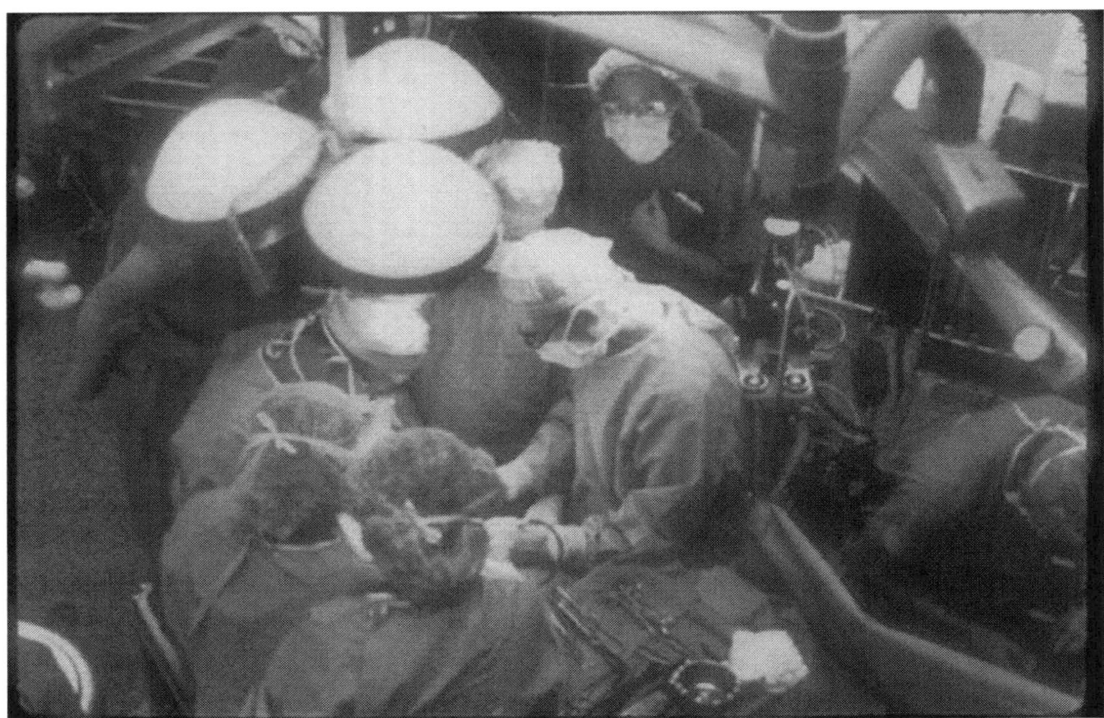

*Fig. 19.15 Tessier operating with Gerald Verdi, Louisville, late 1980s.*

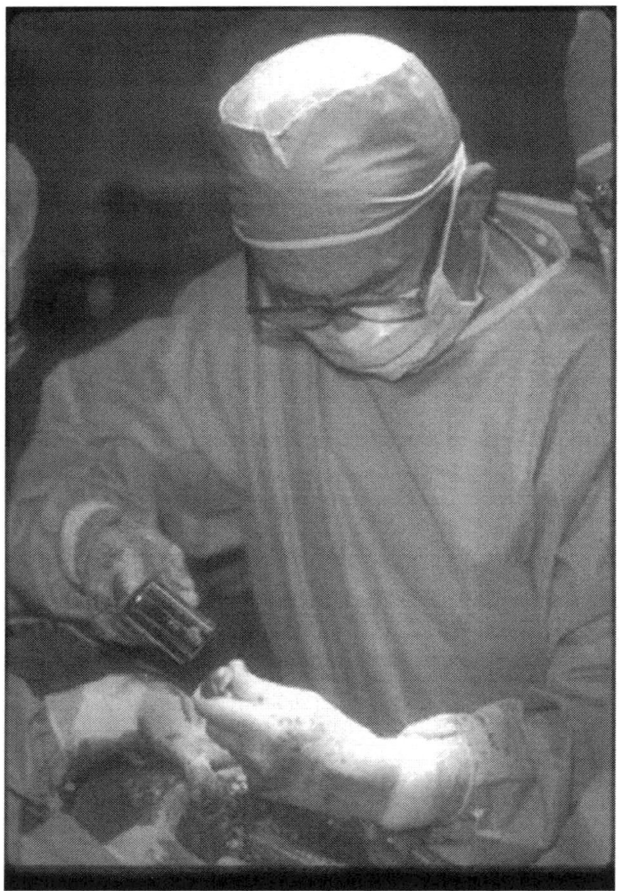

*Fig. 19.16 PLT harvesting a cranial bone graft, Charlotte, 1995.*

# Chapter 20

## Trips to Miami

Dr. Tessier passed through Miami on numerous occasions, but we never arranged for him to operate there. In the late 1970s, he would usually stop off when we were on our way to Brazil to operate with Cassio Raposo do Amaral. In later years, Tessier would stop off for a day or so en route to Mexico—or, if he had a day or two to spare, he would stop off between engagements in the United States.

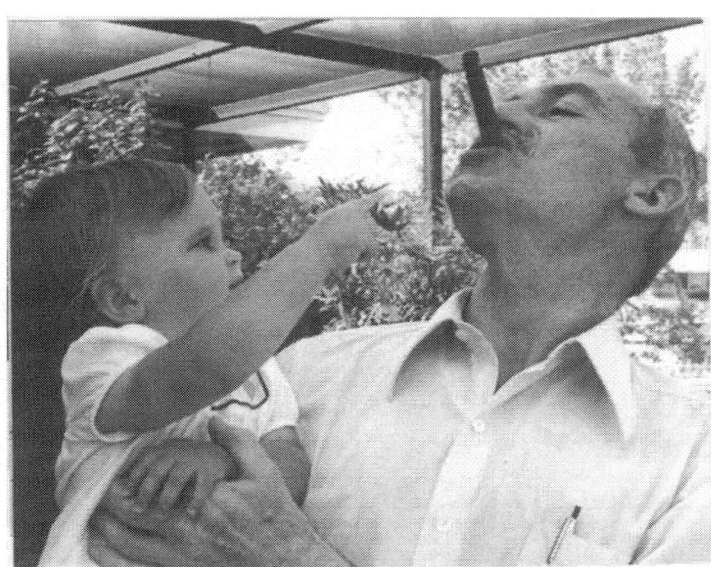

*Fig. 20.1, 20.2 Johanna Wolfe in 1978, admiring the Tessier cigar.*

*Fig. 20.3 An older Johanna and Tessier with cigar around 1991.*

On another trip to Miami, we arranged for there to be a small ad hoc symposium on orbital surgery at the Bascom Palmer Eye Institute of the University of Miami. Participants were ophthalmologists on the staff, and an invitation was extended to American plastic surgeons who had spent time with Dr. Tessier in Paris.

*Fig. 20.4 From the left, going around the table: Mireille, Phil Hendel, Tessier, Barbara Millard, and Ralph Millard. Michael and Candy Schaefer are in the background.*

*Fig. 20.5 Tessier, author/Wolfe, and D. Ralph Millard, Jr.*

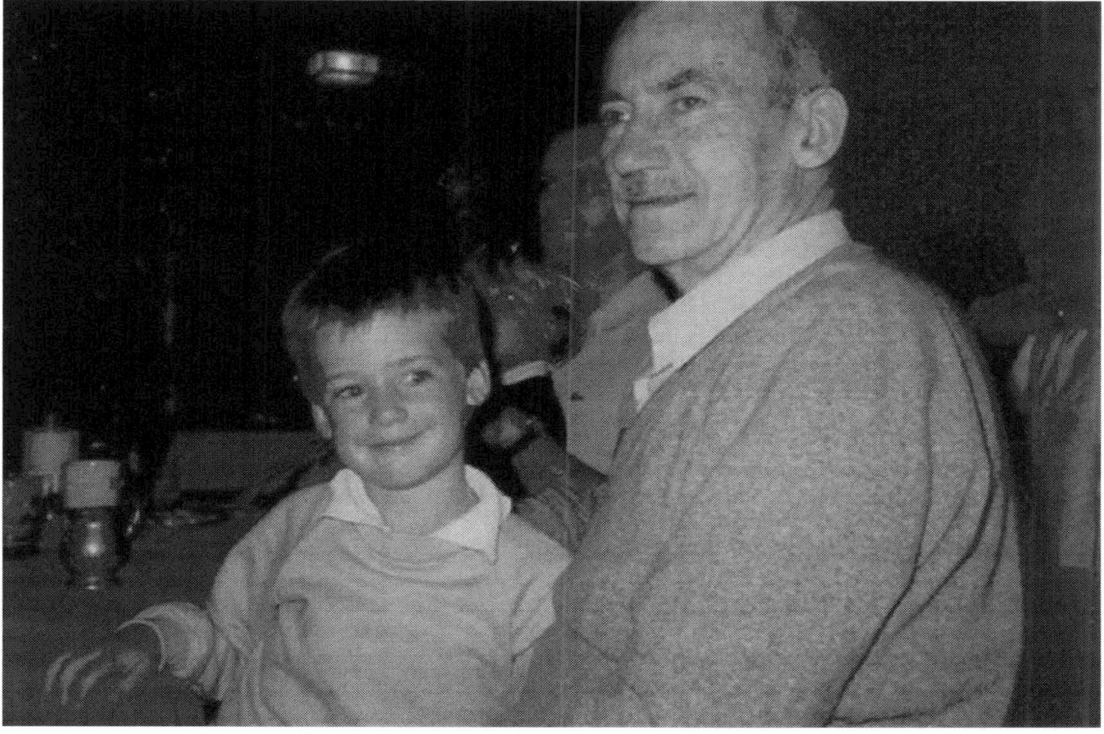

*Fig. 20.6 After the Bascom Palmer symposium, before leaving for Brazil, we squeezed in a trip to Disneyworld at the request of the wives. Jean-Paul Tessier on his father's lap, with Serge Morax and his child in the background.*

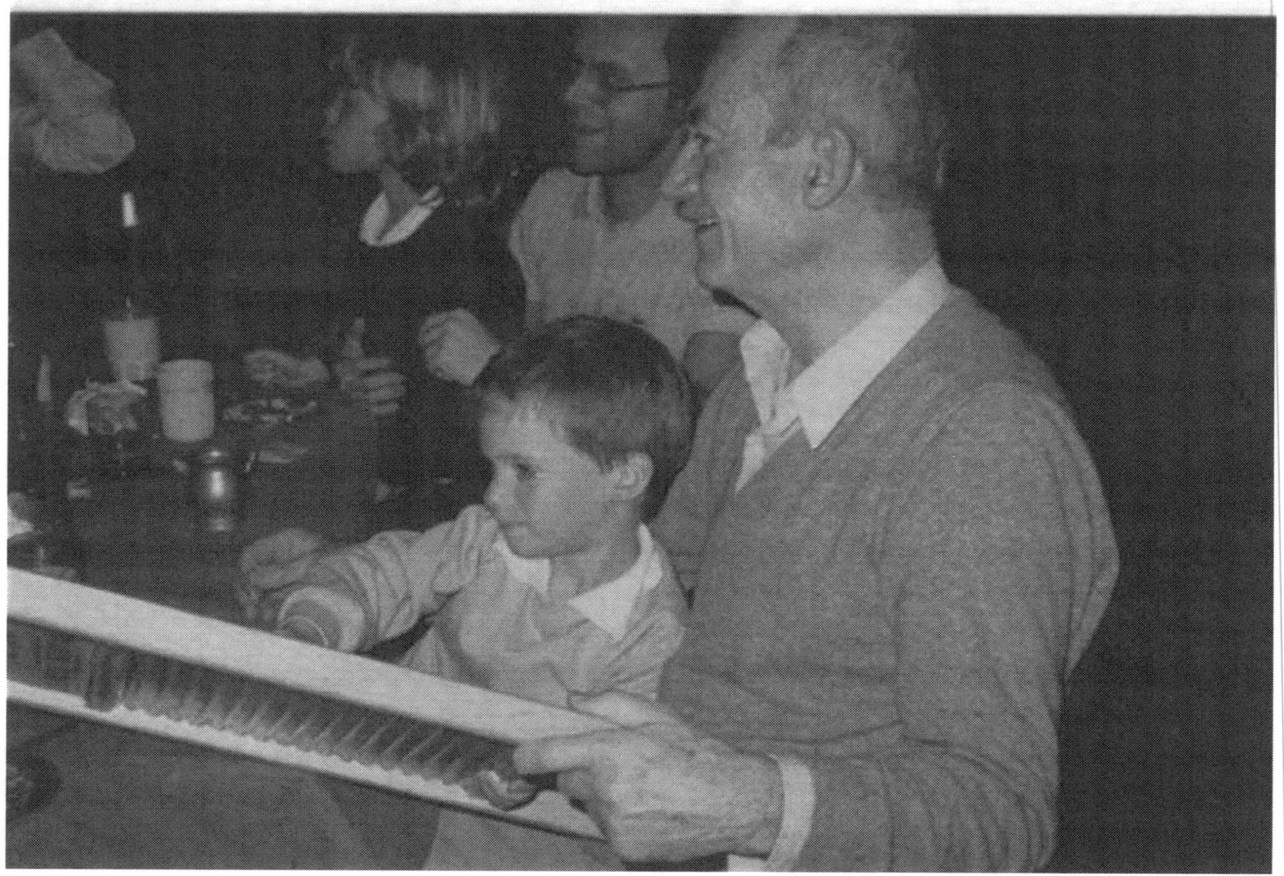

*Fig. 20.7 Playing the washboard came easily to Jean-Paul. Papa enjoyed himself, and the next day the wives and children and Serge returned to Paris. We decamped to Campinas, Brazil, to meet Henry Kawamoto and Cassio.*

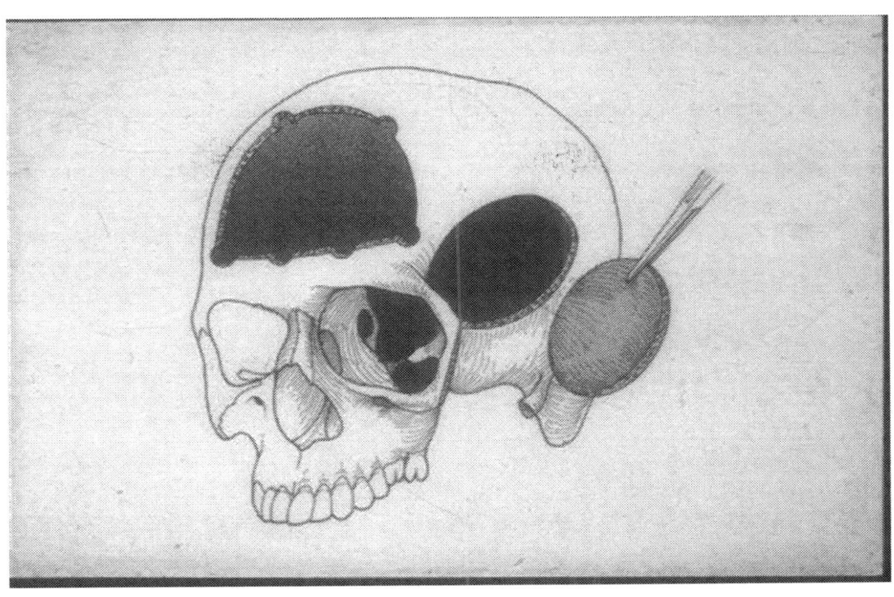

*Fig. 21.8 Fenestrating the temporal bone to allow passage of the temporalis muscle.*

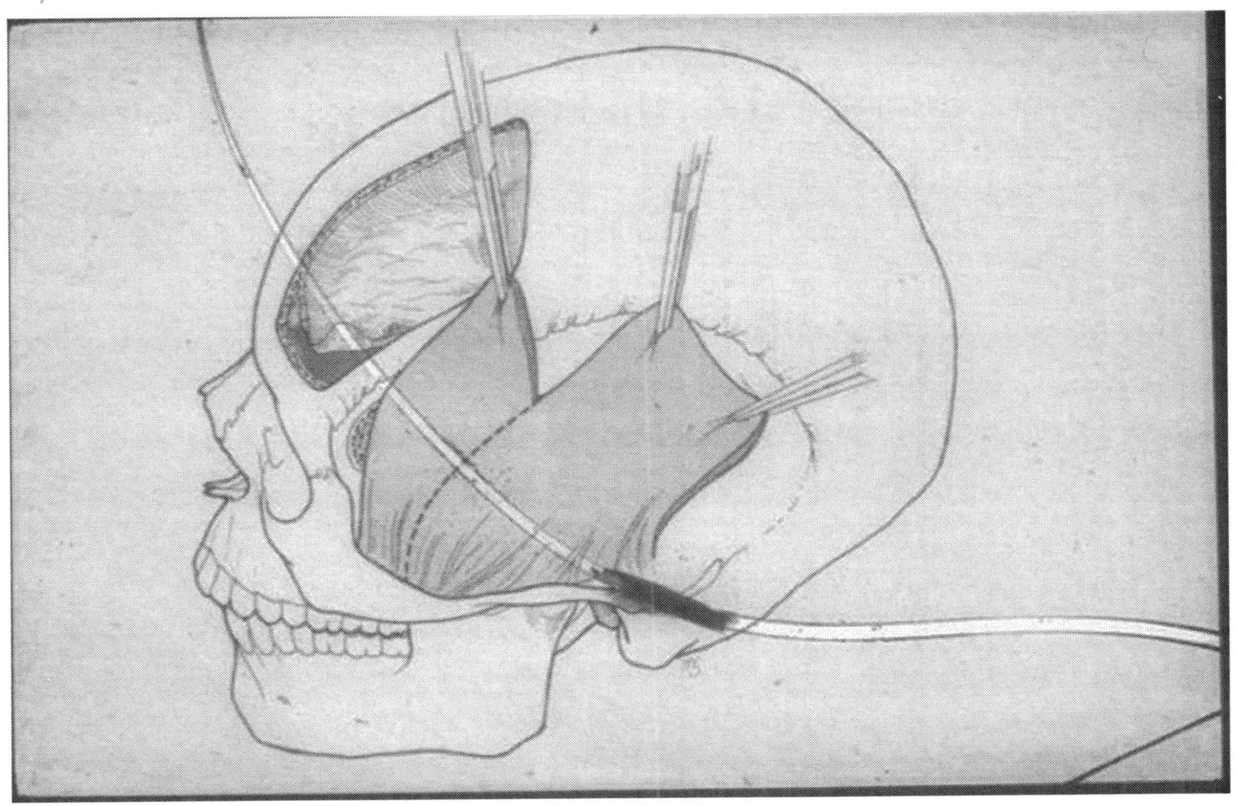

*Fig. 21.9 Mobilization of the temporalis muscle. The muscle is split, and the anterior portion will cover the cranial base defect. The posterior segment will be brought forward to avoid a temporal fossa depression.*

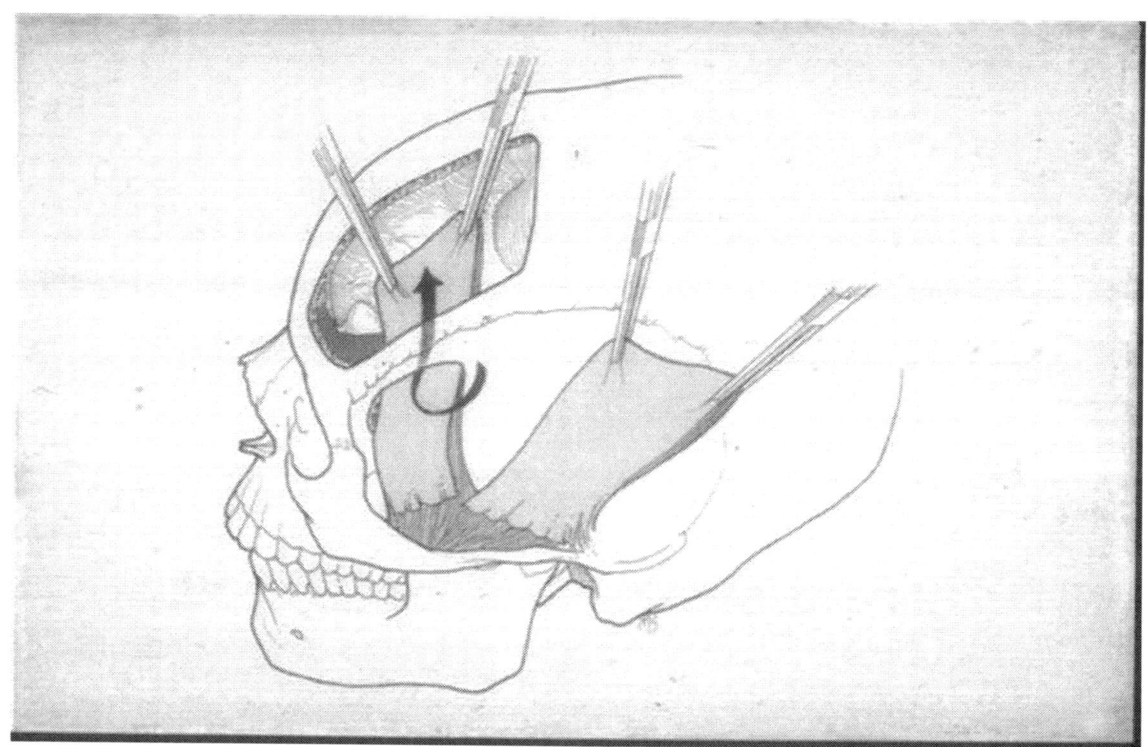

*Fig. 21.10 Passage of the muscle flap.*

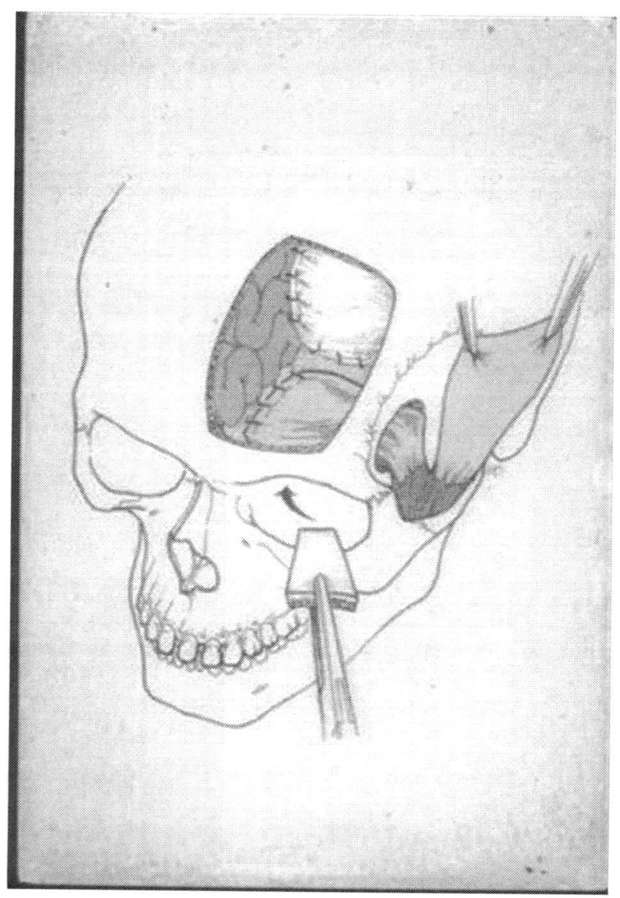

*Fig. 21.11 Bone graft to reconstruct the orbital floor.*

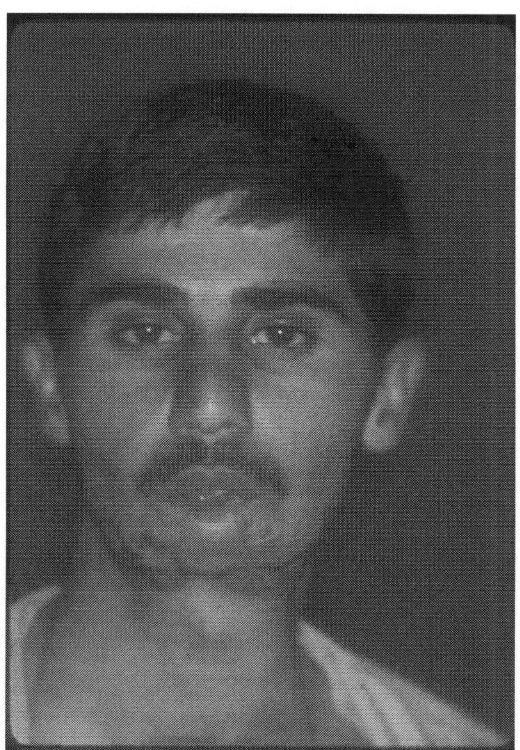

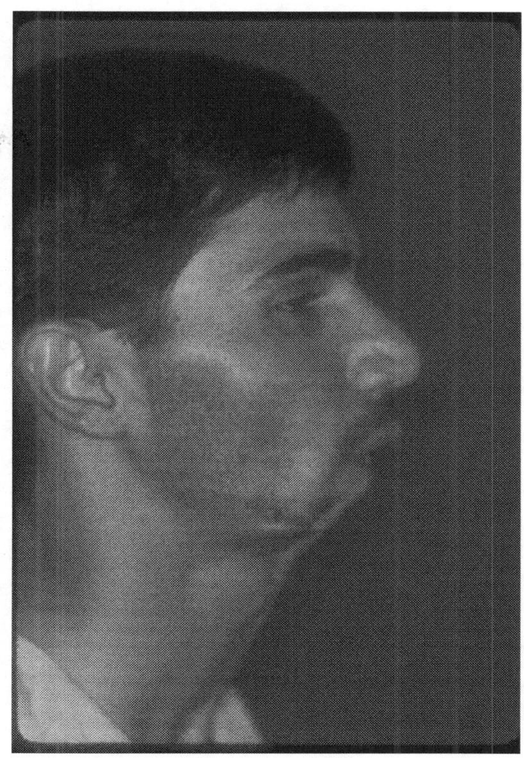

*Fig. 22.17, 22. 18 Similar patient, after an attempt at reconstruction with what appears to be a free flap. Inadequate result.*

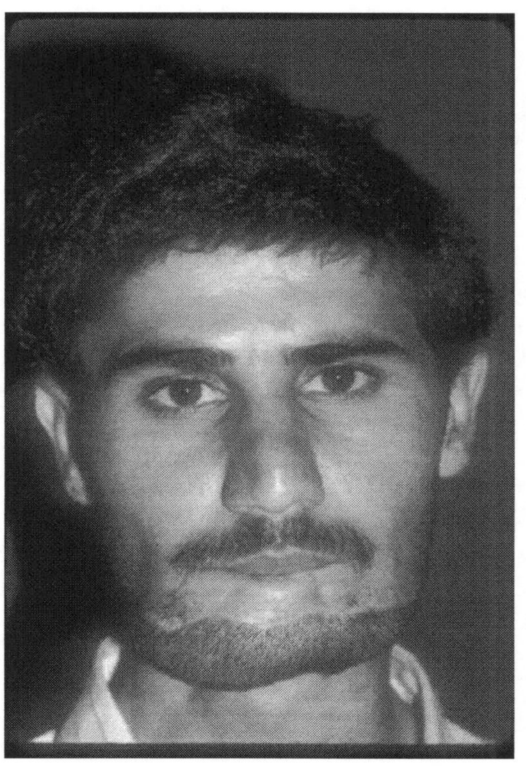

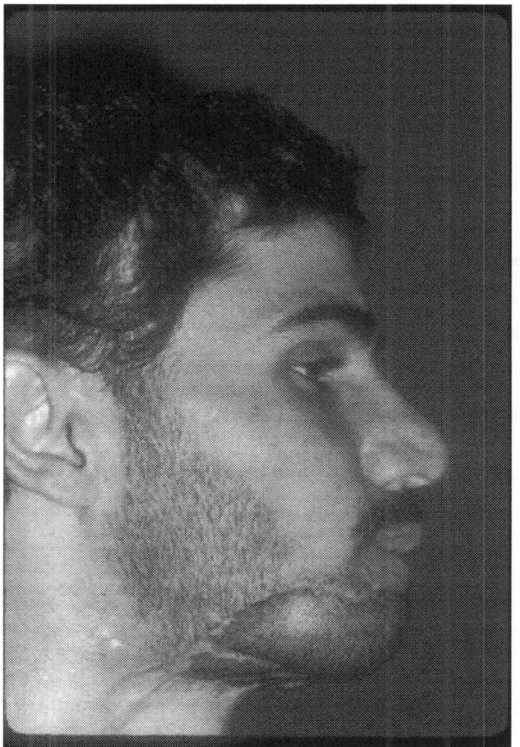

*Figs. 22.21, 22.22 Final result.*

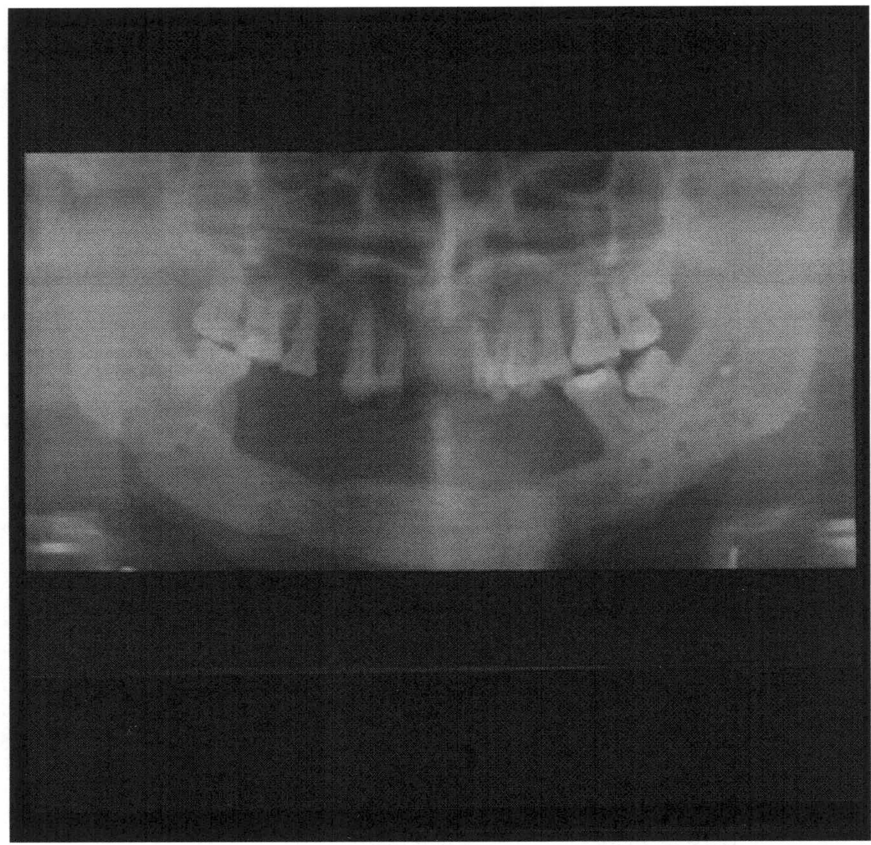

*Fig. 22.23 Post-op panoramic x-ray shows ample bone stock after Tessier's procedure.*

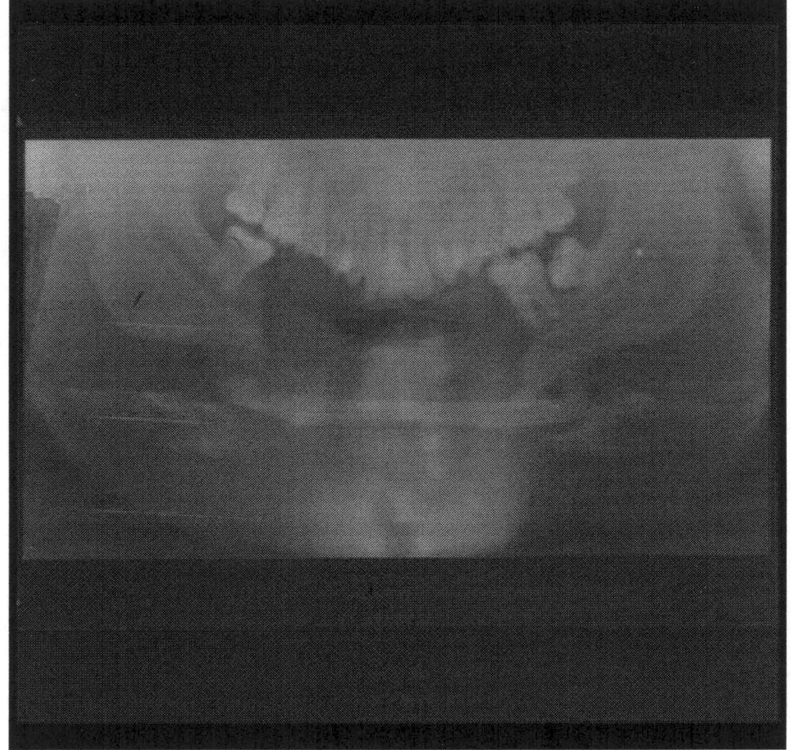

*Fig. 22.19 X-ray shows inadequate mandibular bone stock.*

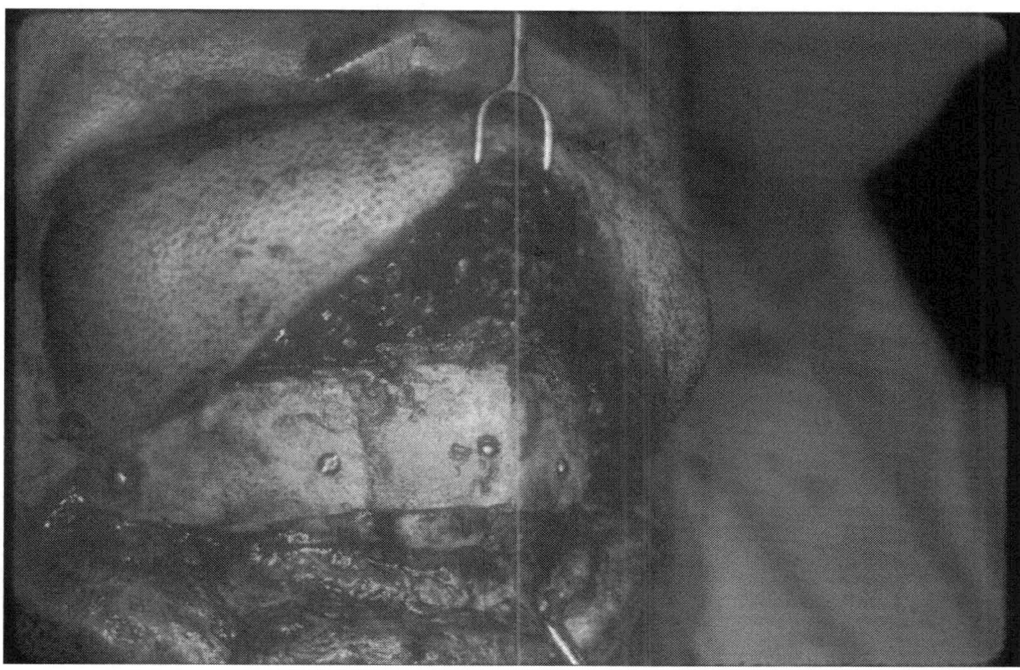

*Fig. 22.20 Massive mandibular bone graft made of cranial bone by Tessier.*

The two patients shown above received gunshot wounds to the central jaw in the Iran/Iraq conflict, and were operated on by Dr. Tessier in Teheran. The first patient was missing oral lining, and the BT flap is shown. Both patients had forehead flaps used for cover, and mandibles constructed with cranial bone grafts. There is ample bone stock in both for osseo-integrated implants, and Dr. Tessier's agreement with the Iranian authorities was that these would be done by Jean-Francois Tulasne. Unfortunately, due to various logistical problems, this was not done as often as it might have been.

These cases also reflect Dr. Tessier's reconstructive approach. He believed that most craniofacial reconstruction could be done with material available locally—this is known as "craniofacial autarchy." In most American teaching institutions, a microvascular procedure—usually of the fibula—would have been used. It is a tribute to Tessier's skill and confidence that he was able to obtain these results without microsurgical free flaps.

Dr. Tessier's experience with microsurgery had not been a good one. Many of the patients that he cared for in Teheran had already been operated on by German team s of microsurgeons, and the results were often blobs of tissue that filled holes but did not reconstruct a face. Dr. Tessier usually scrapped these flaps and began from scratch. I had discussions with him about microsurgery, and I am sure that if he had had someone he could have worked closely with, he would have incorporated it into his surgical planning.

# Chapter 23

## The 60th Birthday Party

This was meant to be a surprise party for Dr. Tessier, but whether it succeeded we will never know. The pretext given to get him to the Bateaux Mouches (large tour boats that go up and down the Seine) was that Andreé Colleson, Tessier's nurse anesthetist, and Jean-Claude de Wolf, a well-known photographer who had been her partner for many years, had finally decided to get married. When he went down the quay to the boat, though, the secret was certainly out of the bag since a large sign with an arrow announced "Dr. Tessier, Anniversaire." There were fifty or sixty celebrants on board—friends, colleagues and previous trainees—and we presented Dr. Tessier with his birthday present. Organized by Françoise Firmin, the previous assistants had all chipped in and bought him a rifle, specifically made for hunting elephants. It had a bore about the size of one's thumb. This particular one, an "Express," had been made in London in the 1920s, and it remained the gold standard for big game hunters.

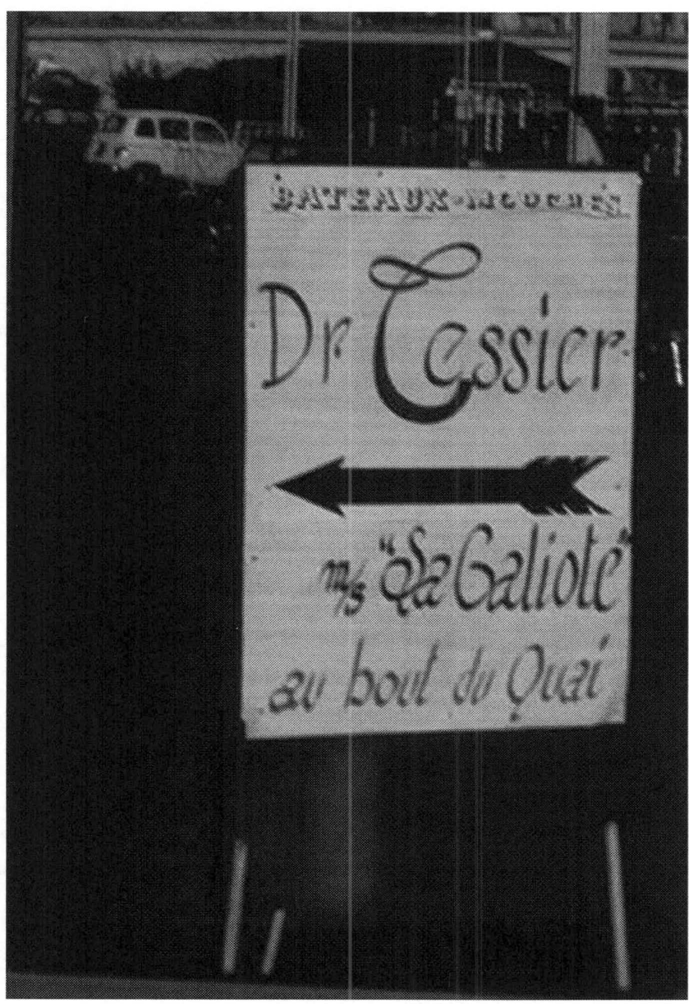


*Fig. 23.1 Sign pointing the way.*

*Fig. 23.2 André Collesson, party to the ruse.*

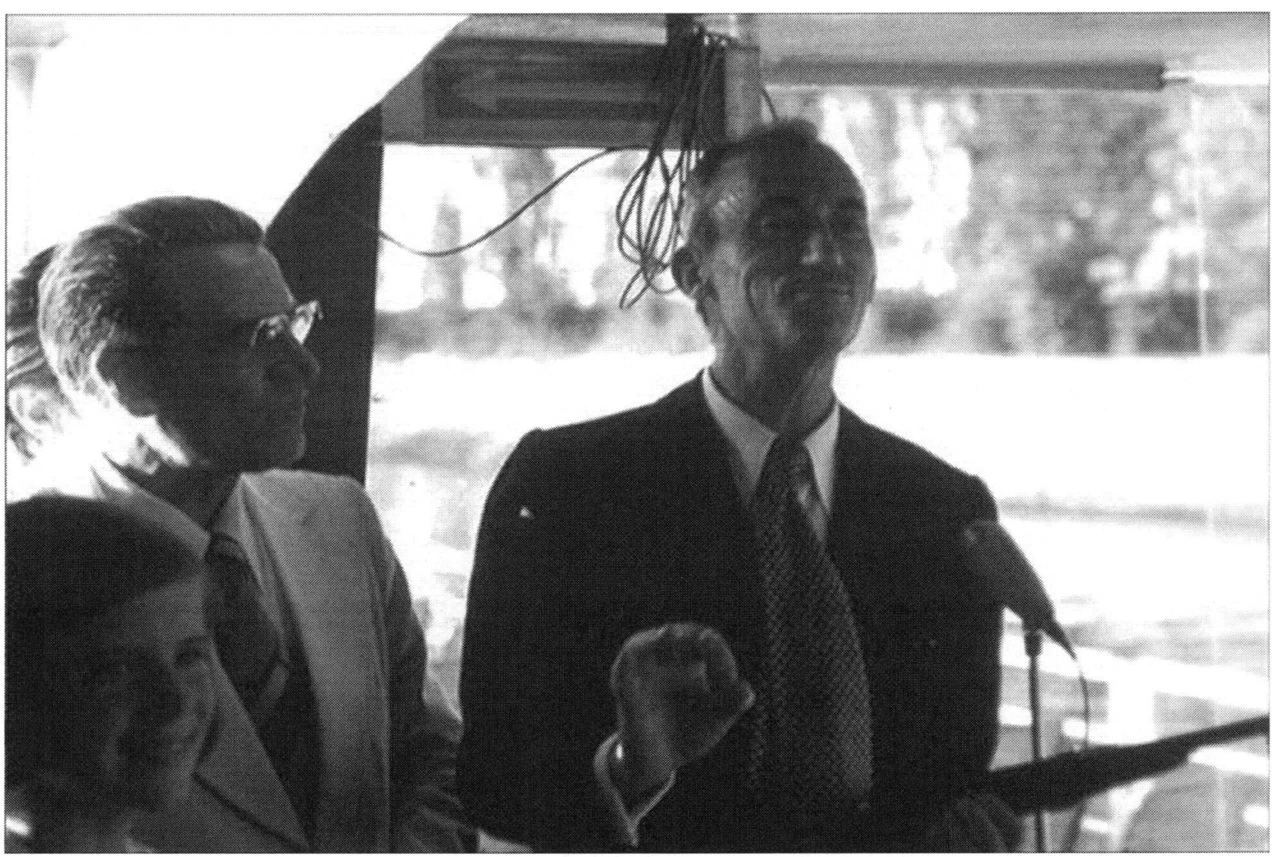

*Fig. 23.3 Tessier and his friend Karl Hogeman of Sweden.*

*Figs. 23.4, 23.5 Tessier explaining why the 475 Express made by Holland and Holland was the preferred elephant hunter's weapon.*

Here is what Paul Tessier said on that day:

"One fine day, by chance, I arrived at sixty years of age. Since I had never stopped in the past sixty years, it was a *pleasant surprise* to arrive there.

On a boat full to overflowing, this was also a *complete surprise* to see so many friends reunited from the sixty years that I had spent giving them a hard time. For me, this was very moving, in that so many of you have come on the invitation of my loyal assistants who, nevertheless, have betrayed me *by surprise.* But this was also a *magnificent surprise,* gathered from all points of the world by your generosity and your friendship. In the lower deck, enthroned in its leather case, is the most beautiful 475 "Express," Number 2 to come out of the famous shops of Holland and Holland and the hands of their artists.

I thank you for the force and the beauty of the work, for the memory that you have attached to it, and for the discrete suggestion which it gives me to go and surprise some beautiful elephants for several years yet to come."

## HISTORY

1851 - VIRCHOW coined the term "plagiocephaly" to describe the "twisted head" which results from a unilateral synostosis between the frontal and parietal bones.

1890 - LANNELONGUE performed the first linear craniectomy.

1952 - McLAURIN and MATSON advocated hemicoronal craniectomy, at a very early age, to prevent more extensive deformities.

1961 - NATHAN carried out a complete analysis of the radiological symptoms of three personal cases and of the roentgenograms of other cases reproduced in the literature. In case n° 1, x-rays exhibited a narrowing of the sphenofrontal, sphenoparietal and spheno-squamosal sutures.

1965 - ANDERSON and GEIGER recommended additional osteotomies of the frontal bone to restore the normal contours of the forehead.

1967 - FAURE performed a remarkable x-rays analysis and pointed out the lowering of the glenoid fossa.

1971 - SEEGER and GABRIELSEN pointed out on x-rays a frequent extension of the synostotic process to the sutures of the cranial base.

1972 - ROUGERIE reported on 14 cases treated by standard craniectomy associated with remodeling of the homolateral frontal bone. He subsequently changed his procedure to a unilateral advancement of the supraorbital margin and orbital roof as used to be done bilaterally in patients presenting with brachycephaly or craniofacial dysostosis.

1976 - HOFFMAN and MOHR reported on 10 patients treated by a similar technique which they called "lateral canthal advancement".

1981 - KREIBORG and BJORK described a dry young adult skull with a premature synostosis of the coronal suture on the right side accompanied by premature fusion of the right sphenofrontal suture.

*PERSONAL WORK ON U.C.S.* (Bde C. Romain gras)

*1968 - Local remodeling and displacement with ROUGERIE.*

*1976 - Lateral displacement of the naso-ethmoid bone with remodeling of the orbital cavities.*

*1978 - Lateral and vertical displacement of a fronto-orbito-naso-ethmoidal monobloc.*

*1980 - The anatomical description of a dry skull with a left-sided coronal synostosis (TESSIER's collection) was presented by TULASNE at the Volvo Craniofacial Seminar in Göteborg.*

## NOMENCLATURE

In English literature, the terms "unilateral coronostenosis", "unilateral coronal synostosis" and "plagiocephaly" have been used interchangeably. Since the initial definition by VIRCHOW, (1851), the word "plagiocephaly" is synonymous with unilateral coronal synostosis (U.C.S.). In fact, "plagiocephaly" literally means "oblique skull" and there are many causes of asymmetry other than U.C.S. Among them are cerebral hemiatrophy, subdural hematoma, brain tumor, congenital torticollis, n° 1-13 unilateral paramedian craniofacial cleft, n° 10 orbitocranial cleft, microphthalmos and even some cases of otomandibular dysostosis. It, therefore, seems more appropriate to use the word "plagiocephaly" exclusively as a descriptive term for skull asymmetries arising from U.C.S.

*Suggested name: UNILATERAL CORONAL SYNOSTOSIS (U.C.S.).* (Bde C. Romain)

In this name, "coronal" (crown) does not preclude a possible extension of the frontoparietal synostosis to the frontosphenoidal and/or sphenoparietal sutures.

PLACE IN CLASSIFICATIONS (Bde C)

Since the publication of LAITINEN and SULAMA (1956), U.C.S. is usually classified under "simple craniosynostoses".

GLOSSARY OF ABREVIATIONS (Bde romain.)

C.S.: Craniosynostoses.
U.C.S.: Unilateral coronal synostosis.
C.F.S.: Craniofaciostenosis.
I.C.H.: Intracranial hypertension.
S.O.M.: Superior oblique muscle.
I.O.M.: Inferior oblique muscle.
Stenotic: region or side directly affected by synostosis.
Telorbitism: orbital hypertelorism.
Recurvatum: curved contrary to normal, a backward bending.
Pachycephaly: means an abnormal thickness of the skull, but the word is often used to describe a unilateral flattening of the parieto-occipital area.
Homolateral: the side affected by the synostosis.
Contralateral: the side opposite to the unilateral synostosis.

## INCIDENCE

U.C.S. is rare among craniosynostoses in general:
66 out of 525 patients (12,6 %) SHILLITO and MATSON (1956).
44 out of 382 patients (11,5 %) ROUGERIE (1981).
4 out of 219 patients (1,8 %) BERTELSEN (1958).
18 out of 204 patients (8,8 %) ANDERSON and GEIGER (1965).
4 out of 185 patients (2,8 %) FAURE et al. (1967).
13 out of 161 patients (,7,7 %) MONTAUT and STRICKER (1977).
In our series it affects the right side more frequently than the left, and female patients more frequently than males.

## MATERIALS

### PATIENTS

operated: 32
not operated: 31

| SIDE | MALES | FEMALES | TOTAL |
|---|---|---|---|
| Right | 15 | 23 | 38 |
| Left | 7 | 18 | 25 |
| TOTAL | 22 | 41 | 63 |

### DRY SKULLS

| Diagnosis | N° | CITY | MUSEUM | CURATOR |
|---|---|---|---|---|
| Left U.C.S. | 100 | Paris | Private Collection | Dr. TESSIER |
| Right U.C.S. | 110 | Paris | Musée de l'Homme | Prof. COPPENS |
| Left U.C.S. | 113 | Paris | Musée de l'Homme | Prof. COPPENS |
| Right U.C.S. and Telorbitism | 120 | Paris | Musée Orfila | Prof. HUREAU |
| Right U.C.S. | 184 | Copenhaguen | Private Collection | Prof. BJORK |
| Right U.C.S. | 209 | Edimburgh | Royal College of Surgeons | Prof. SHIVAS |
| Left U.C.S. | 302 | Vienna | Pathologisch-Anatomisches BundesMuseum | Prof. von PORTELLE |
| Right U.C.S. | 310 | Vienna | | Prof. von PORTELLE |
| Right U.C.S. | 318 | Vienna | | Prof. von PORTELLE |
| Left U.C.S. | 328 | Vienna | | Prof. von PORTELLE |
| Left U.C.S. | 333 | Vienna | | Prof. von PORTELLE |
| Left U.C.S. and Telorbitism | 351 | Graz | Institut für Pathologische Anatomie | Prof. RATZENHOFER |
| Left U.C.S. | 368 | Vienna | Pathologisch-Anatomisch BundesMuseum | Prof. von PORTELLE |
| Postural Plagiocephaly (torticollis) | 105 | Paris | Musée de l'Homme | Prof. COPPENS |
| Postural Plagiocephaly | 112 | Paris | Musée de l'Homme | Prof. COPPENS |
| Postural Plagiocephaly | 114 | Paris | Musée de l'Homme | Prof. COPPENS |
| Postural Plagiocephaly (from | 151 | Amsterdam | Anatomisch-Embryologisch Laboratorium | Prof. van LIMBORGH |

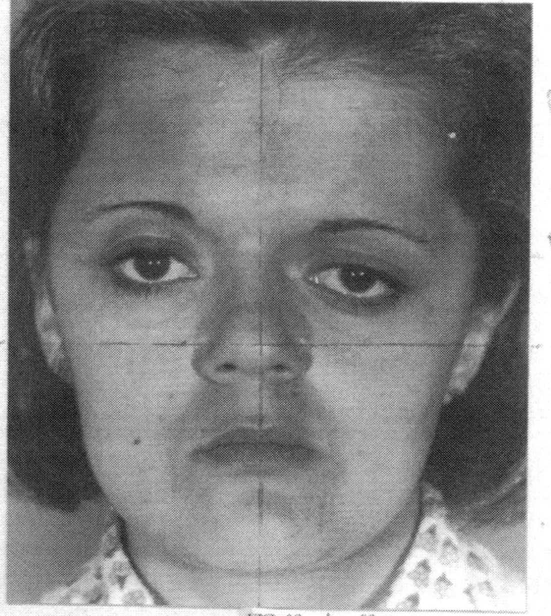

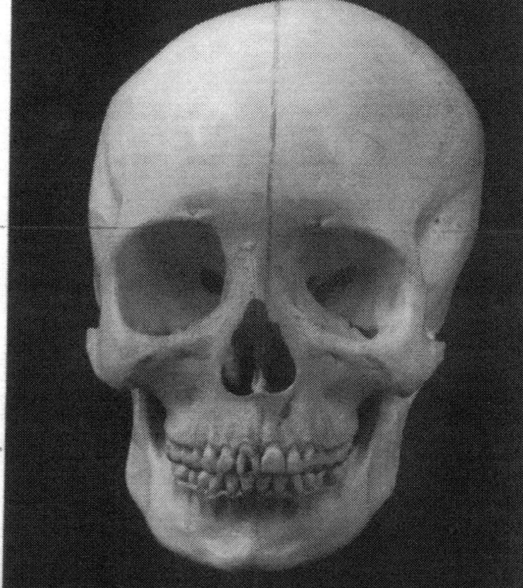

*FIG. 00 - chap. 00*
*Facial asymmetry in case of right U.C.S.*
*Absence of coronal suture on the right side. Homolateral deviation of the naso-ethmoid. The position of the eyebrows and upper eyelids reflects the differences in shape of the orbital cavities. Dental occlusion is close to the norm.*

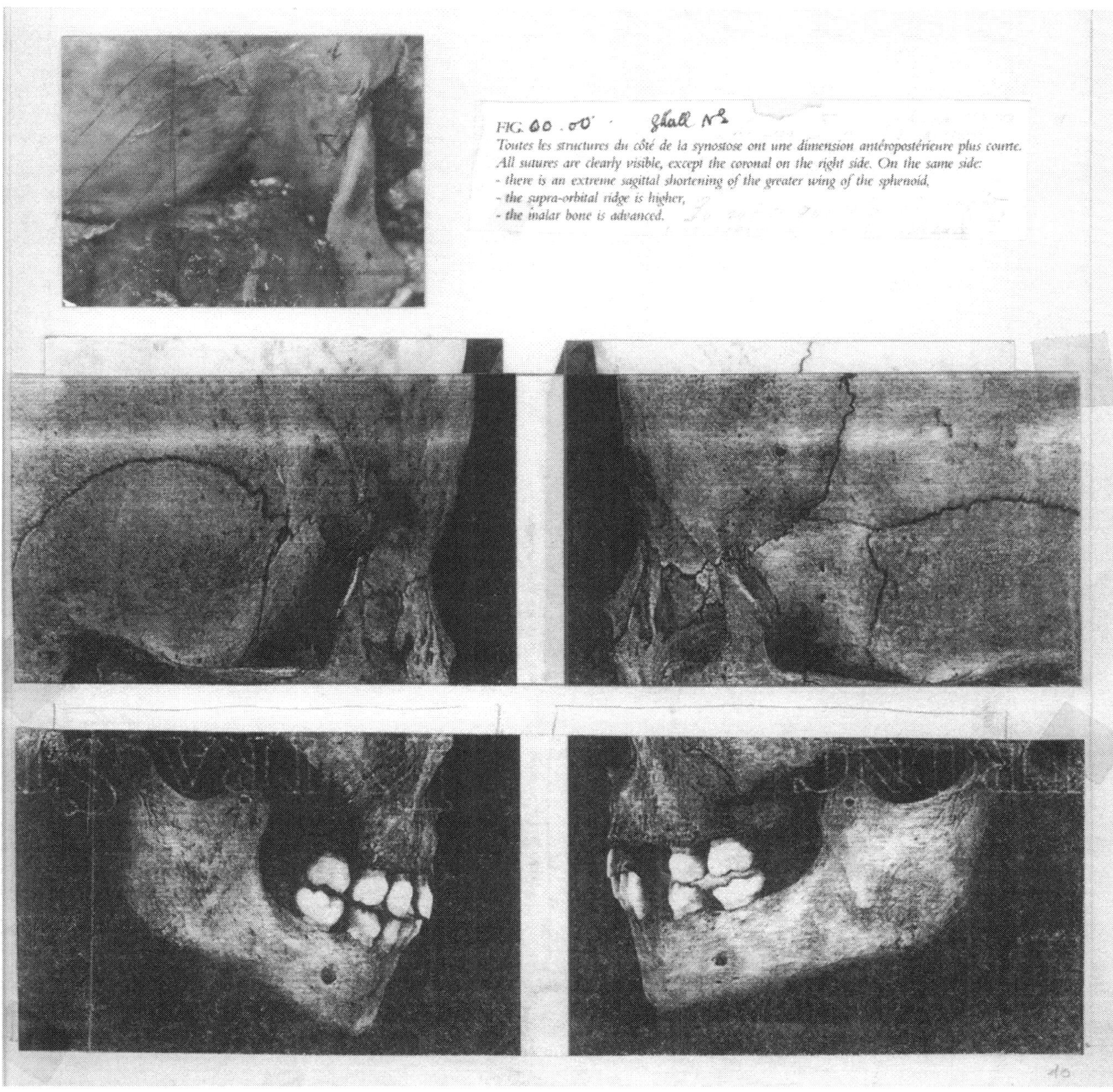
FIG. 00 . 00 · Skull N°2
Toutes les structures du côté de la synostose ont une dimension antéropostérieure plus courte.
All sutures are clearly visible, except the coronal on the right side. On the same side:
- there is an extreme sagittal shortening of the greater wing of the sphenoid,
- the supra-orbital ridge is higher,
- the malar bone is advanced.
10

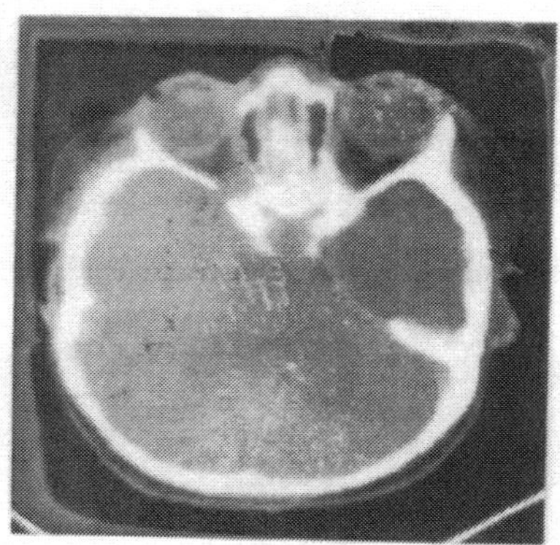

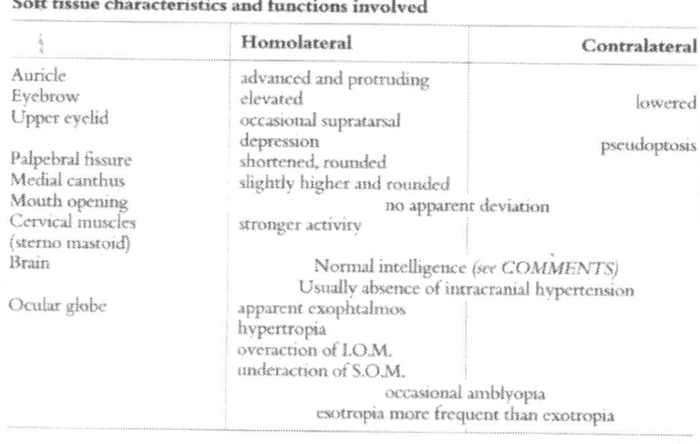

**Soft tissue characteristics and functions involved**

| | Homolateral | Contralateral |
|---|---|---|
| Auricle | advanced and protruding | |
| Eyebrow | elevated | lowered |
| Upper eyelid | occasional supratarsal depression | pseudoptosis |
| Palpebral fissure | shortened, rounded | |
| Medial canthus | slightly higher and rounded | |
| Mouth opening | no apparent deviation | |
| Cervical muscles (sterno mastoid) | stronger activity | |
| Brain | Normal intelligence *(see COMMENTS)*<br>Usually absence of intracranial hypertension | |
| Ocular globe | apparent exophtalmos<br>hypertropia<br>overaction of I.O.M.<br>underaction of S.O.M.<br>occasional amblyopia<br>esotropia more frequent than exotropia | |

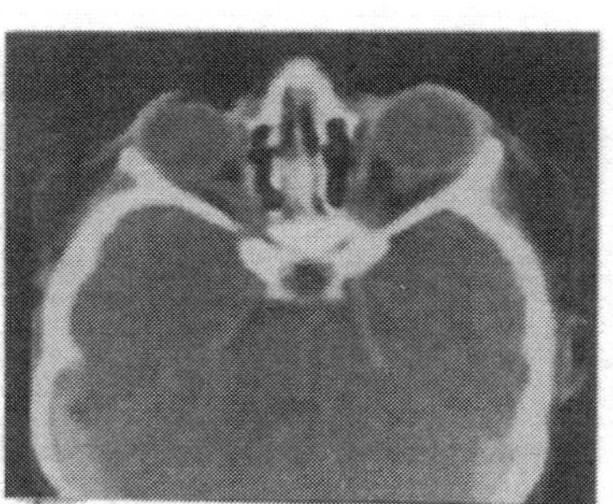

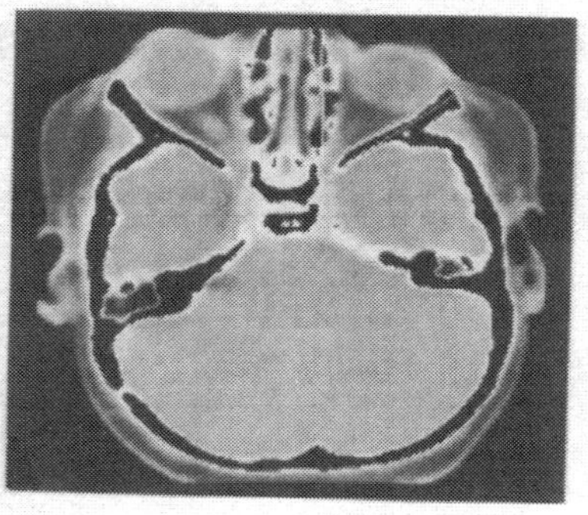

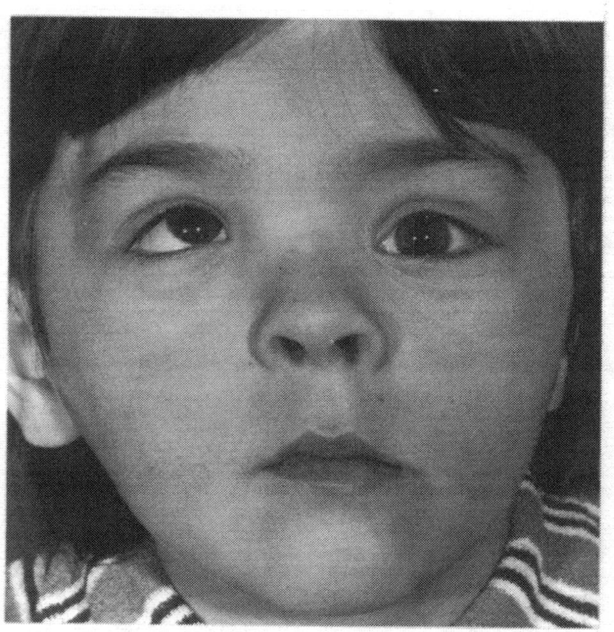

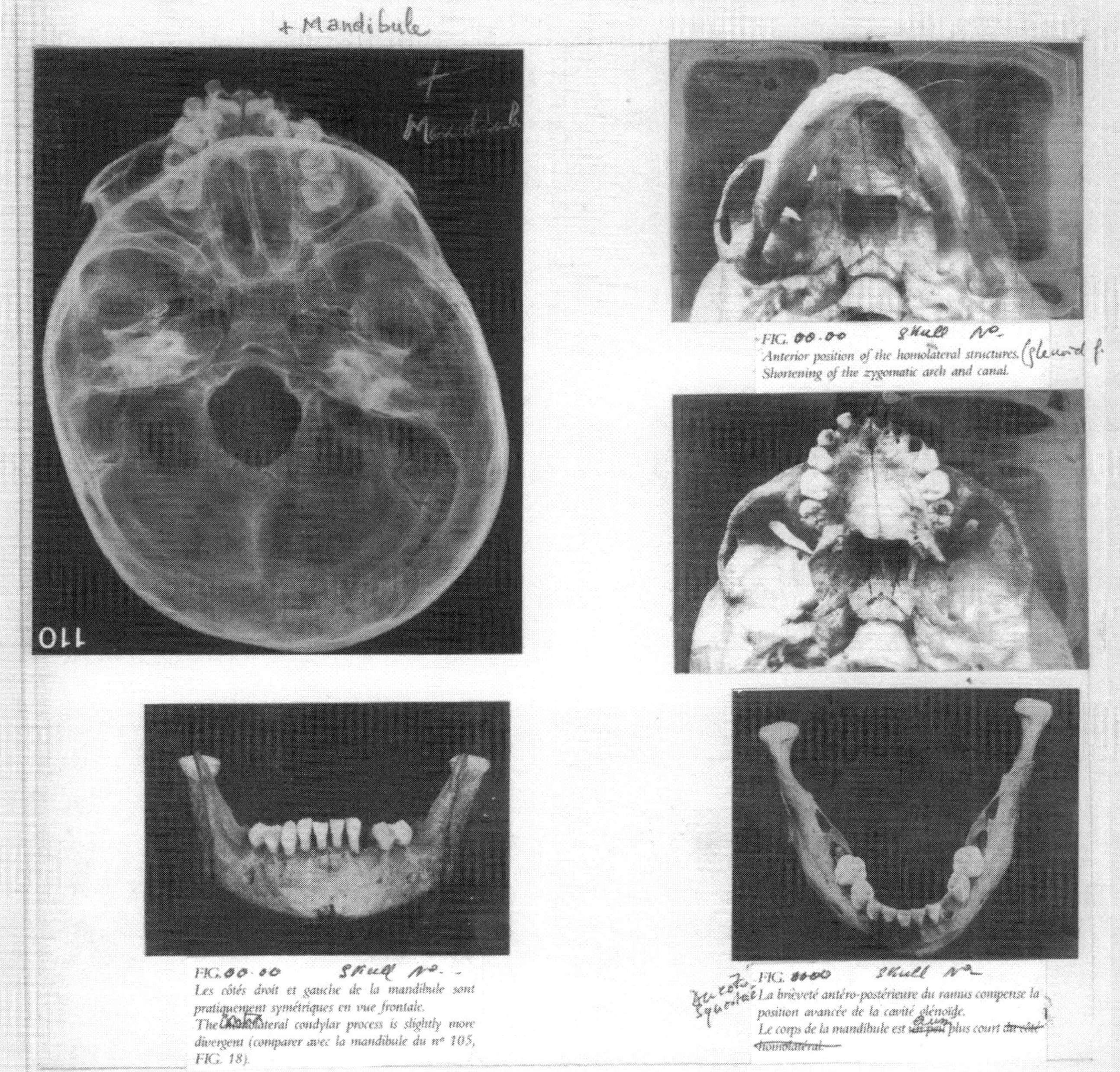


FIG. Skull No.
*Anterior position of the homolateral structures.*
*Shortening of the zygomatic arch and canal.*

FIG. Skull No.
*Les côtés droit et gauche de la mandibule sont pratiquement symétriques en vue frontale.*
*The homolateral condylar process is slightly more divergent (comparer avec la mandibule du n° 105, FIG. 18).*

FIG. Skull No.
*La brièveté antéro-postérieure du ramus compense la position avancée de la cavité glénoïde.*
*Le corps de la mandibule est un peu plus court du côté homolatéral.*

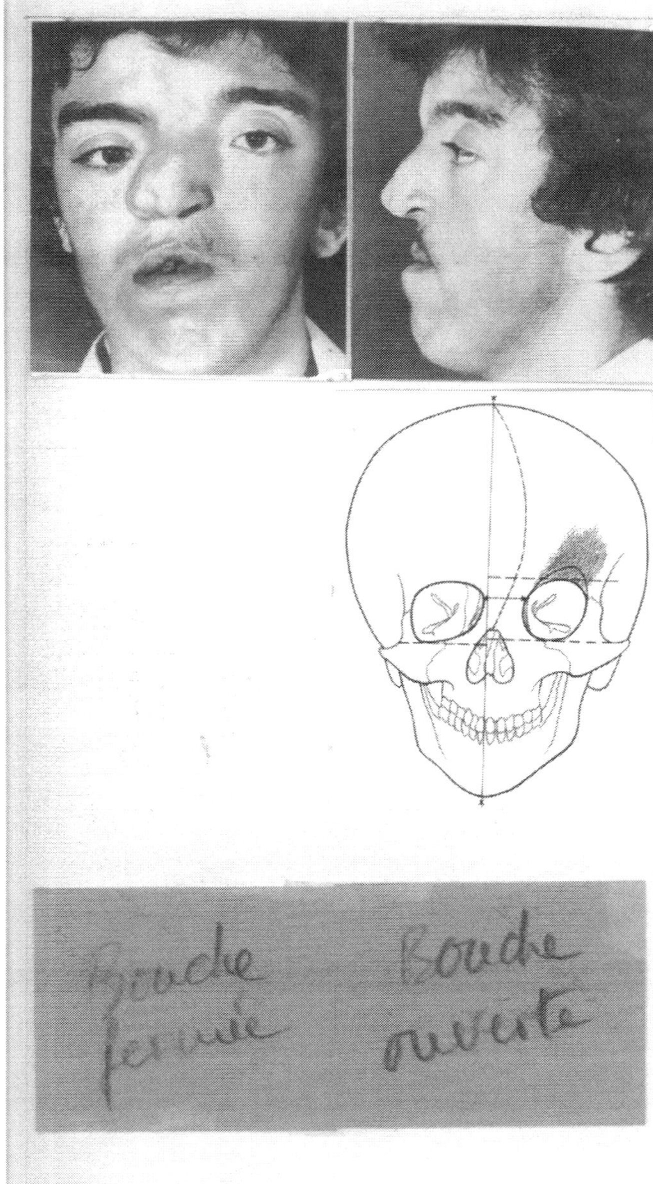


## ASSOCIATED MALFORMATIONS

- Cleft lip and palate is not mentioned in the literature, but there were three cases out of 63 in our series (5%).
- Cases of limb and trunk malformations associated with pure U.C.S. are not mentioned either, as far as we know, though we have personally encountered one case of syndactylism of the fingers and toes.

## SUMMARY

- The anterior position of the homolateral glenoid fossa is balanced by the correspondingly short sagittal dimension of the homolateral ramus. The body of the mandible is the least deformed facial structure. The occlusal plane is horizontal and the asymmetrical mandible functions symmetrically. It therefore seems logical to take the mandible as a reference for the orientation of the structures of the head.
- The ideal vertical axis, raised from the lower inter-incisie point, is projected to the contralateral anterior lacrimal crest. The root of the nose is deviated towards the side affected by the hemicoronal synostosis.
- Points, normally located on the vertical midline, are on a curved line; the concavity opens on to the contralateral side.
- One a frontal view, the most significant deformities are the distorsion of the naso-ethmoid towards the lateral synostosis and the ascending sphenoid ridge.

On a vertical view, the most obvious asymmetry is in the frontal region: recurvation of the homolateral superior orbital ridge and frontal bossing on the opposite side.

## GENETICS

Wether or not craniosynostosis is a hereditary malformation is an open question. The existence of several cases in the same family is not uncommon. Other types of craniosynostosis can also be seen in the same family (ANDERSON, 1965; FAURE, 1967).

## ETIOPATHOGENESIS

As in all types of craniosynostosis, the etiopathogenesis is unknown (See Comments on APERT's Syndrome). There are two main theories concerning the causes of premature obliteration of cranial sutures:

- injury to the blastemal suture anlage (PARK and POWERS, 1920),
- changes in the shape and position of the bones of the cranial base which alter the tensile forces of the dural tracts between theses bones and the neurocranial cranial capsule (MOSS, 1975).

spontaneous correction of the cranial asymmetry occu when the child's head reverts to its normal posture, except in perhaps 10% of the affected infants, especially those with congenital torticollis (CLARREN, 1981).

- Congenital torticollis is not infrequent: it was noted 120 out of 2.600 children observed in an orthopaedic surgical unit (MAJCZINO, 1972). It may result in severe craniofacial deformities: "scoliosis capitis" (NATHAN, 1961).

The main characteristics of the craniofacial asymmetry are not very different from those of U.C.S.:

- deviation of the naso-ethmoid,
- deformation of the orbital cavities,
- ascending sphenoid ridge,
- asymmetry of the cranial base.

However, the diagnosis is usually easy because of:

- the clearly abnormal posture of the head,
- the normal shape of frontal region,
- the deviation of the naso-ethmoid towards the side opposite the shortened cranial base,
- the normal frontal sinus,
- the absence of obliquity in the sagittal suture,
- the marked enlargement of the mastoid process on the affected side,
- the mandibular asymmetry, which is as much vertical as saggital,

- Hemicerebral atrophy.
- Space-occupying brain lesions including subdural hematomas and brain tumors.
- Craniofacial asymmetry following x-rays therapy during infancy.
- Hemihypertrophy.

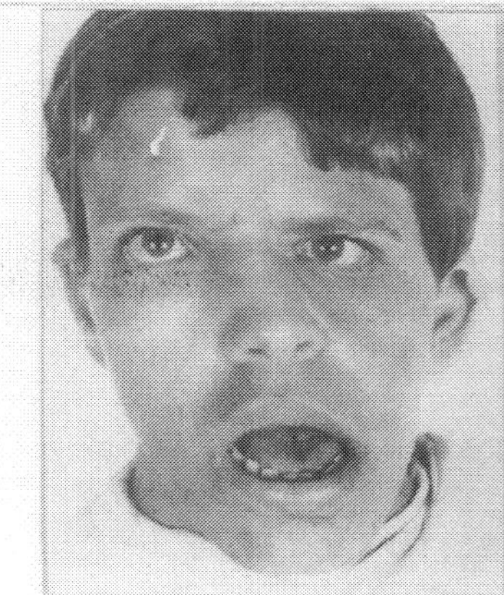

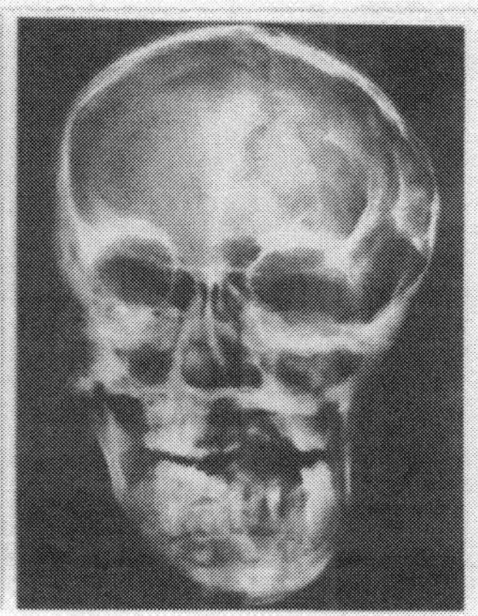

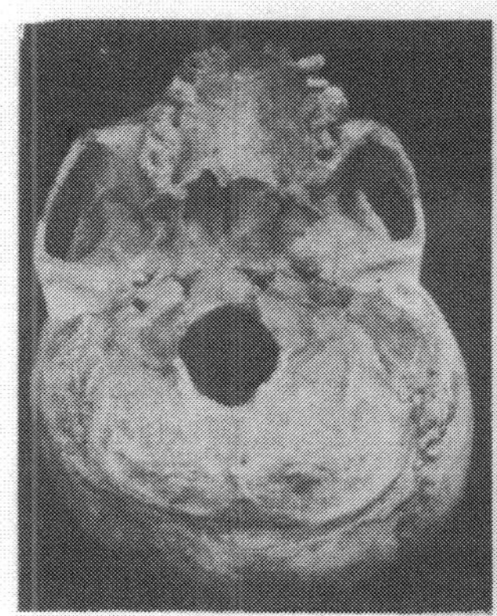

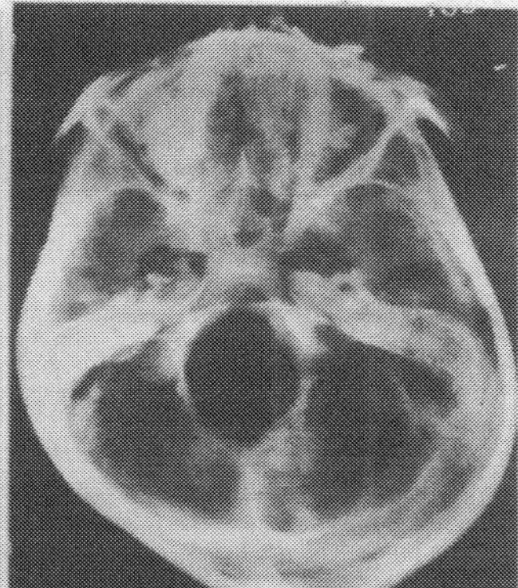

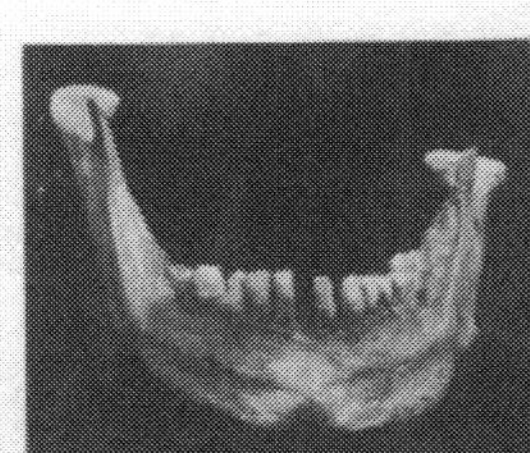

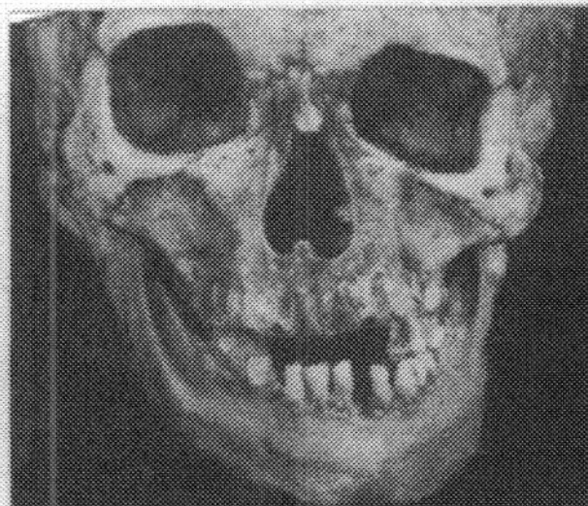

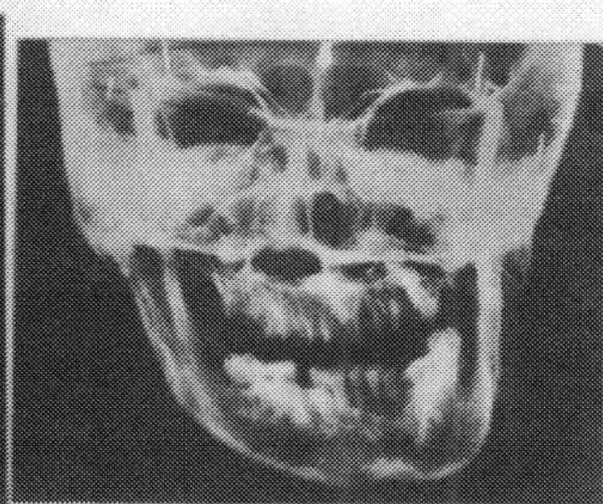

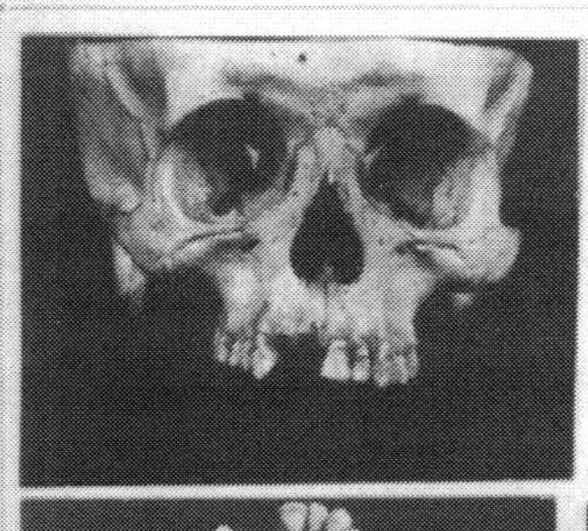

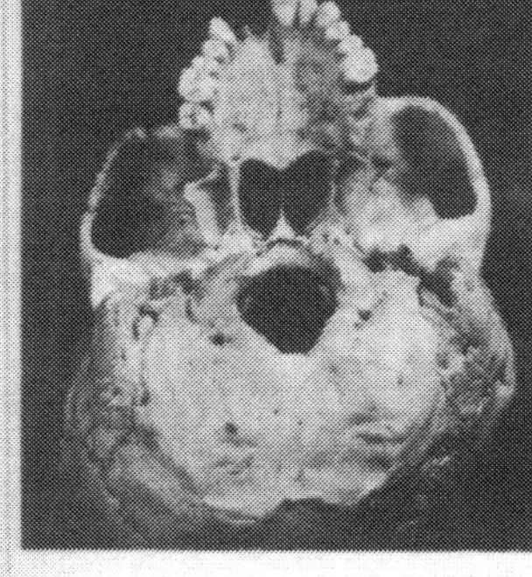

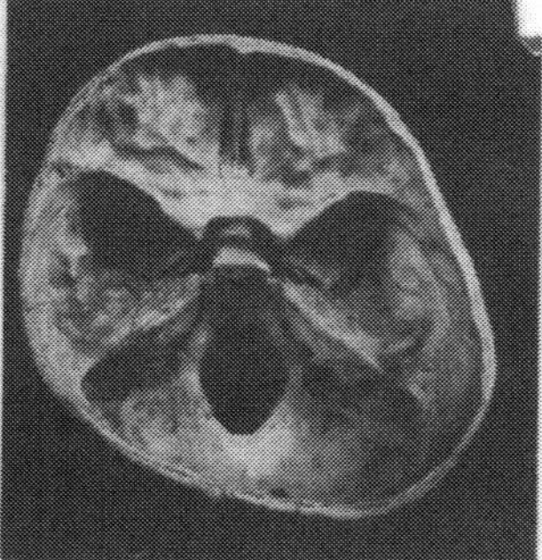

| **Differential diagnosis** | | | (Homolateral Signs) | | |
|---|---|---|---|---|---|
| Cause of Plagiocephaly | Thickness of vault | Digital markings | Suture involved | Lesser wing | Face |
| U.C.S. | – | + | – (hemi-coronal) | ↑ | Scoliosis |
| U.L.S. | – | + | – (one lamdoid) | N | N |
| Torticollis | N | N | N | ↑ | Scoliosis |
| Hemicerebral atrophy | + | – | N or – | ↑ | N |
| Space occuping brain lesions | – | + or – | N or + | | N |

## PROGNOSIS

Symptoms are usually present at birth:

- The deformity is progressive until full development of the brain (7 years of age).
- Intra-cranial hypertension (I.C.H.) does not develop when the coronal synostosis remains unilateral.
- There is a possibility of subsequent development of synostosis in other sutures.

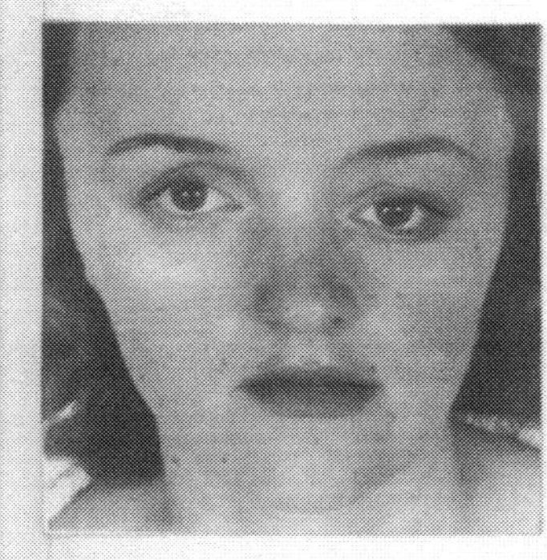

COMMENTS → Cap gras ?

1. The coronal suture and the "coronal system" *(See Skull no 000)*
*The coronal suture is the fronto-parietal suture. It is in fact a component of the "coronal system" which extends inferiorly to the cranial base and laterally to the medial cranial fossa. It is more visible in the external temporal fossa. Inferiorly the sutures involved are the fronto-ethmoidal and the sphenofrontal (lesser wing); laterally all the sutures lie between the greater wing and the three adjacent bones: they are the sphenosquamous, the sphenoparietal and the sphenofrontal sutures.*
*The coronal system thus forms a continuous ring, lying between the anterior and middle cranial fossae. Therefore there is a logical possibility of the sutures of the cranial base being affected by coronal synostosis. This has been borne out by the radiological studies of* SEEGER *and* GABRIELSEN (1971) *in affected new-borns and was responsible for early craniotomies extending to the anterior cranial base.*
*However, the typical orbito-cranial and naso-ethmoidal asymmetries described above may involve only a partial synostosis of the frontoparietal suture (See Skull nº 318). Conversely, a symmetrical face or cranial base may appear despite unilateral absence of the coronal suture (See Skulls nº 113, nº 209, and nº 302). Of the 13 skulls with U.C.S. which have been examined, the sutures of the cranial base were not fused in at least 9 of the skulls, even though the orbital and naso-ethmoidal deformities were typical. The absence of synostosis in a given suture does not necessarily mean that the suture functions frelly. What, then, are the indisputable criteria to distinguish between a free functional suture, or a free non-functional suture?*

2. McCARTHY *et al.* (1978) *suggested that the* sphenozygomatic suture *also formed part of the coronal system; topographically it does. He suggested that synostosis between the greater wing and zygomatic bone would occur as a primary phenomenon and that the coronal and other basal sutures probably closed in a secondary phenomenon. We have not personally observed sphenozygomatic fusion; we have, on the contrary, more frequently noted a widening of this suture between a facial bone and a cranial bone.*

3. *At first sight, it might be thought that study of UCS would provide a reliable* pathological model *for a better understanding of more extensive cranial synostoses and craniofacial dysostoses. There are several reasons for this:*
- *U.C.S. is a common and fairly well-known deformity,*
- *it is confined to a single suture on sutural system,*
- *the primary deformities are confined to a relatively small area,*
- *there is no damage to the brain.*

*However, the study of a significant number of patients has been disappointing. Our studies of dry skulls with U.C.S. show that it is not possible to extrapolate to* CROUZON's *or* APERT's *because apparently identical sutural fusions do not produce identical deformities on the homolateral or contralateral sides.*
*Moreover, a very minor synostosis can give rise to considerable primary malformations. Finally, we at present know very little about the density and extent of synostoses of the cranial base which may be the primary phenomenon.*

X Coronal System Normal
Photo crâne 3/4 endocrânienne

X Coronal System Abnormal
Dessin

X Dessin SCOTT

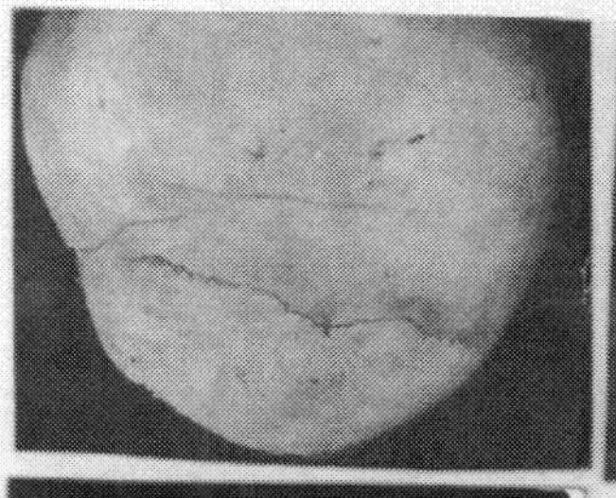

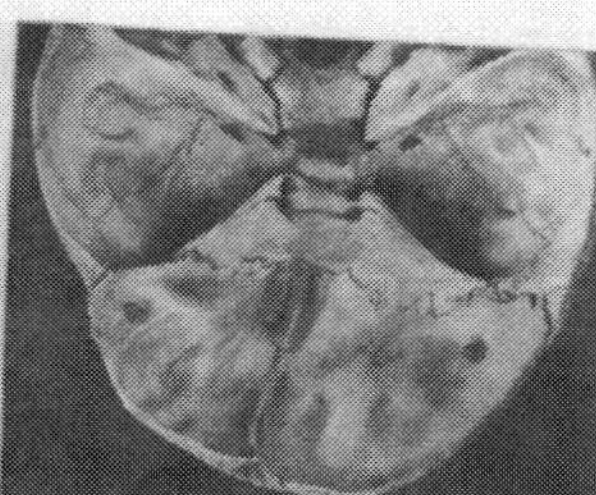

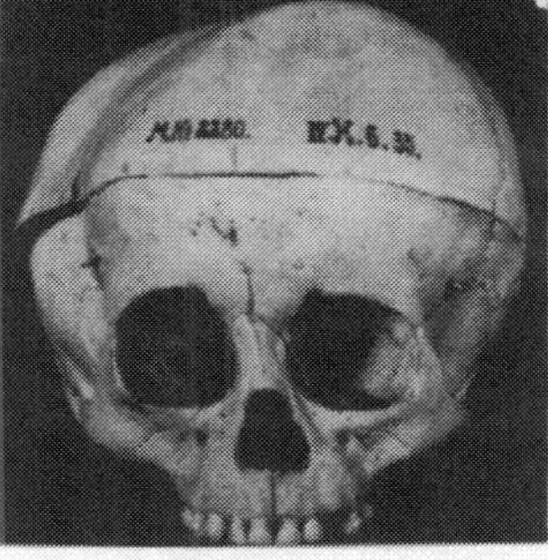

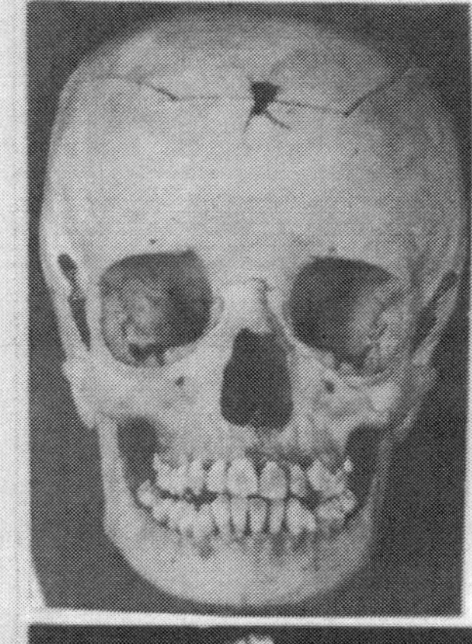

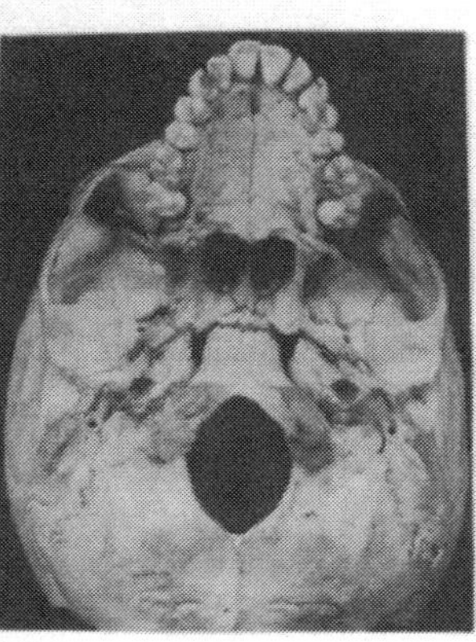

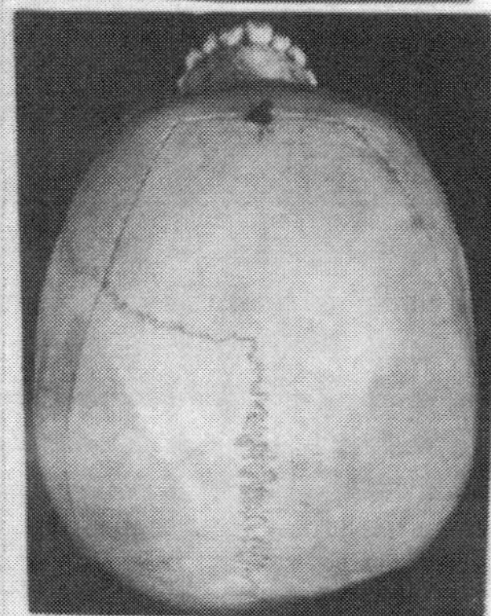

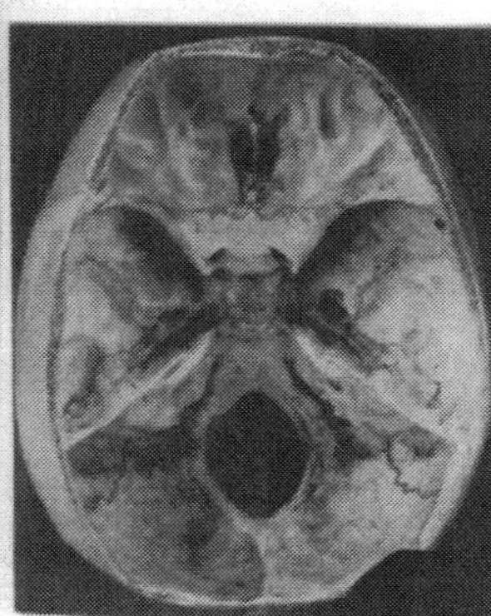

4. Primary and secondary deformities

*The primary malformation is cranial, unilateral and either complete or incomplete; it involves the fronto-parietal suture in which it is clearly visualized on x-rays, and, very likely, other sutures in the coronal system in which it is more difficult to diagnose. The primary malformations already described in... will be found in the vicinity of the fused cranial sutures.*

- *The secondary deformities consist of all anomalies noted at some distance from the affected sutures. The contralateral deformities are called "compensatory". They result from the displacement of cranial pressure from the side affected by craniosynostosis to the opposite side (which cannot be called "unaffected"). The frontal bossing and the prolapse of the orbital roof and supra-orbital ridge are in line with what has come to be generally accepted since the work of* VIRCHOW *(1851). The contralateral deformities may, however, also result from tensile forces in the malformed bones which are transmitted to the opposite side. But what is the cause of the hypoplasia or flatness of the malar bone on the opposite side?*

5. The elevation of the lesser wing *of the sphenoid bone is not pathognomonic of U.C.S. It may also occur in congenital torticollis, hemicerebral atrophy and space -occupying brain lesions (see Table II, p. )*

6. The deviation of the nasal bridge or septum *has been mentioned* (NATHAN, 1961). *As far as we know, the lateral deviation of the ethmoid has not been described. This naso-ethmoidal deviation from the vertical and sagittal median axis is substantial. At 6 years of age, it is 6 to 8 mm at the Nasion point and 12 to 14 mm at the glabella along the oblique line extended from the deviated nasal bridge.*

7. *The bony structures of the face are less displaced vertically than transversely or sagittally. For example, the homolateral orbit is not as high as might be expected clinically from the position of the eyebrow. The hypertropia of the homolateral globe combined with bossing of the forehead and ptosis of the eyelid on the contralateral side also lead to errors of appreciation with regard to the discrepancy in orbital level. These anomalies depend more on variations in the shape than on the position of the orbital cavities.*

8. The ocular **deviations** ***seem to be the direct consequence*** *of the malformations of the orbital cavities.* ***This statement calls for greater*** *reference to embryology, but this is not the place for this.*

*A study of 23 patients done by Serge* MORAX *(1982) showed that:*

- *60% of the patients presented with esotropia and 40% with exotropia. Sensorial perception or anatomical factors may be responsible for* horizontal ocular deviation.
- *90% suffered from hypertropia on the stenotic side with hyperaction of the inferior oblique muscle and a hypoaction of the superior oblique muscle. In 10% the hypertropia was contralateral.*

*Anatomical factors seem to outweigh sensorial factors in* vertical ocular deviation.

*Amblyopia was found on one side or the other regardless of the localization of the craniosynostosis.*

RX Hirtz PALLY (Asymétrie basale)

Pathogenesis

- *First, there is the* "ocular extorsion syndrome" *with a pseudo-ectopia of the macula, resulting from a deviated insertion of the rectus muscles on the sclera. It is caused by ovalisation of the orbital cavity whose major axis is directed obliquely downwards and medially.*
- *Then, in plagiocephaly, there is always a more porterior attachment of the trochlea; it is associated with shortness of the orbital roof and retrusion of the supra-orbital ridge in relation to the maxilla to which the I.O.M. is attached. This results in the S.O.M. being more oblique frontally than the I.O.M. The two muscles are not parallel. The I.O.M. - which is more sagittal-acts more rapidly and leads to hypertropia.*

*This anomaly persists after correction of the orbital deformities and their asymmetrical position* (ORTIZ-MONASTERIO, 19..). *The trochlea retains its insertion in the periorbitum whose relationship is changed with the frontal bone, but not with the eyeball.*

*9. The eye deviation induces malposition of the head and ocular torticollis. The acquired head malposition should not be confused with congenital torticollis (See differential diagnosis). Nevertheless, a persistent ocular torticollis may bring about a secondary deformity of the cervical spine. Hence the need to correct the eye deviation after the orbitocranial deformities have been balanced.*

10. The mandibular asymmetry, *is very interesting.* ~~*KREIBORG has pointed out that*~~ *it does not seem to be present at birth. But the glenoid fossa is more anterior and lower on the affected side in almost all our patients and in the dry skulls.* ~~*This implies a mandibular asymmetry even when the glenoid fossae are on the same level vertically.*~~

11. These is no lateral deviation of the mandible *when the patient opens his mouth, eventhough the mandible is asymmetrical. Is the mandibular deformity a consequence of a normal jaw function despite asymmetrically located glenoid fossa?* DELAIRE (1965), *has pointed out the possibility of compensatory growth of the mandible to adapt to an asymmetrical cranial base.*

*12. Many neurosurgeons consider that U.C.S. is not responsible for I.C.H. They do not advocate early surgery although* McLAURIN *and* MASTON (1952) *admitted that there is probably constriction of brain growth. This has been confirmed by the studies of* CARMEL *et al.* (1981) *who demonstrated on CAT scans anomalies of the middle cranial fossa consisting of distorsion of the brain structures with compression of the cerebrospinal fluid pathway resulting in a local increase in pressure in the brain at the closed suture. Moreover, a prominent cerebrospinal fluid space was found in postoperative seans at the site of the coronal craniectomy.*

*From a neurological viewpoint, it seems that the indication for U.C.S. is the same as for brachycephaly or plurisynostoses i.e. surgical management at the age of 3 to 6 months.*

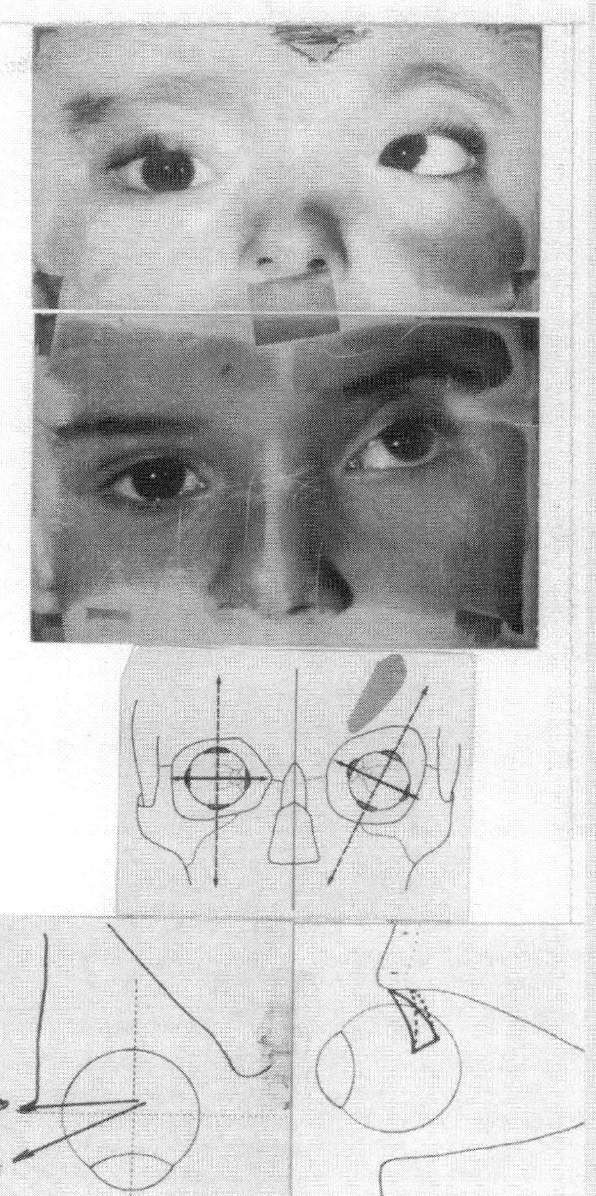

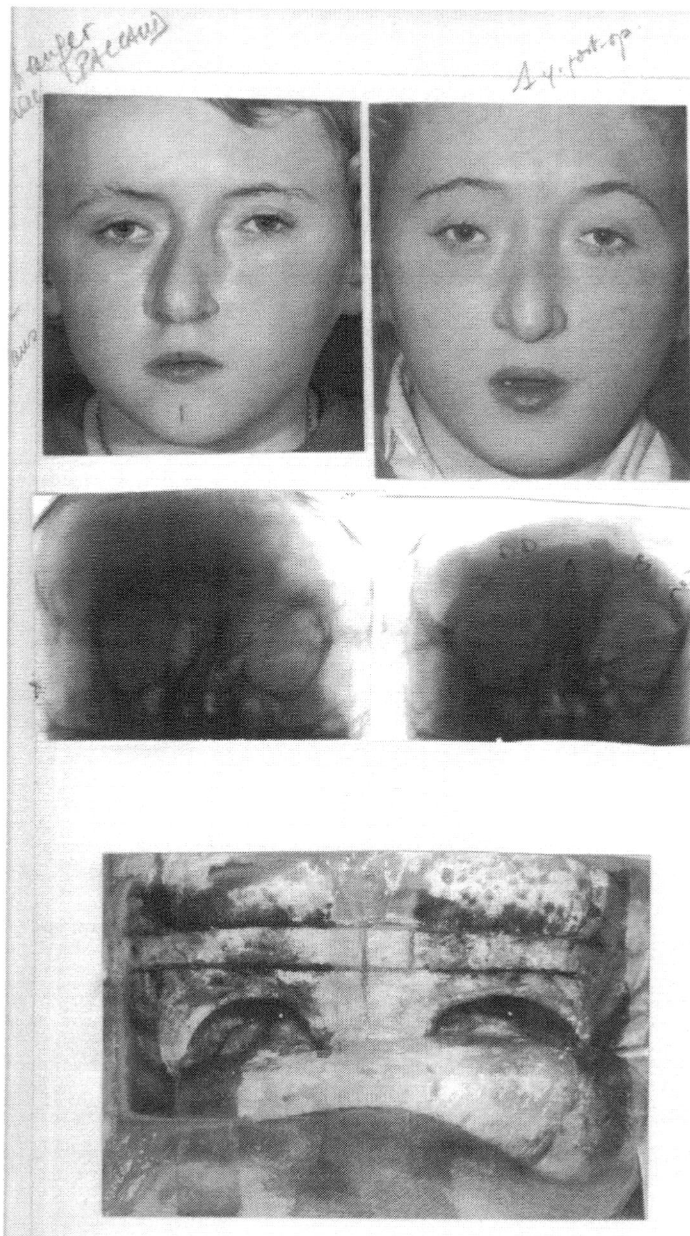

## SURGICAL MANAGEMENT

The objectives are to prevent local I.C.H., if necessary, and to prevent or correct:
- the orbito-cranial asymmetries and the orbital deformities,
- the naso-ethmoidal deviation, which is the most significant facial anomaly,
- the eye deviations.

The theoretical grounds for the choice of procedure and the age at which the operation is performed are the following:

● In pure U.C.S. there is no I.C.H., or, if there is, it is never severe, and does not in itself require early surgery. However, this view has been questioned by CARMEL (1981) (See Comment - 3) who recommended surgery in the first weeks of life.

● The orbito-frontal region cannot develop normally on the stenotic side because the brain cannot expand. Craniotomy should therefore be performed while the brain still has its full expansion potential, i.e. before the age of about 3 months. (See table 0 page 0).
Craniectomies have very little effect on orbito-frontal deformities in infants over one year old, so that they must be performed before the age of 6 months. When performed in due time, however, the craniectomy can be repeated one year later.

● The synostoses are assumed not only to involve the fronto-parietal suture, but also to extend from the hemicoronal system to the cranial base (where they may originate). Craniotomies must, therefore, extend to the anterior base of the skull.

● Craniotomies on the stenotic side do not correct contralateral deformities, so that primary surgery should also take in the contralateral side.

● Craniotomy is a neurological procedure intended to provide room for the expansion of the brain and to displace parts of the calvaria. It does not correct deformities in the segments which it encompasses. Additional contouring procedures should therefore be performed to correct the homolateral recurvation of the supra-orbital ridge and the contralateral frontal boss.

● Extension of the craniectomy, either laterally or to the base of the skull, is supposed to correct facial deformities which had come under pressure from the liberated brain, but, in our view, this is very debatable.

● Primary craniotomies are totally ineffective in infants of over 18 months. More radical surgery can then be delayed until the age of 3 to 4 years.

## PROCEDURES AND TIMING

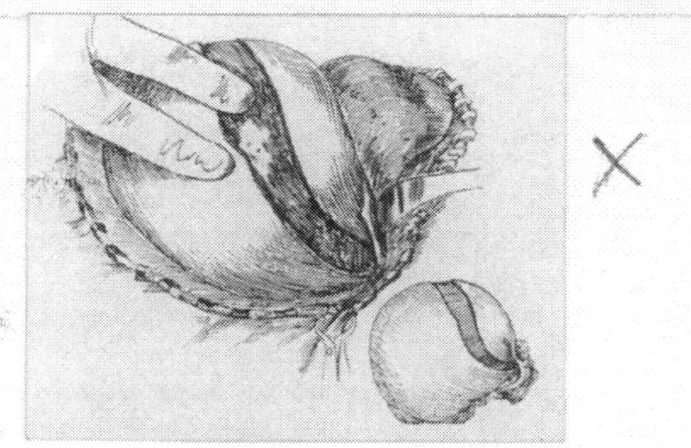

1. Unilateral linear craniectomy

The procedure consists of a linear craniectomy throughout the length of the hemicoronal synostosis. The craniectomy is then extended to the thickened pteryon and the orbital roof, as far as the vicinity of the olfactory groove. Spectacular results have been described by McLAURIN and MATSON (1952), BLUNDELL (1979) when "early" craniectomies had been performed in the first six months after birth. Postoperative correction of the homolateral "devil's eye" configuration has been shown on frontal x-rays by PRUZANSKY (1976). The most severe malformations should be operated on the first three months of life.

2. Advancement of the orbital roof with the supra-orbital ridge (ROUGERIE's procedure)

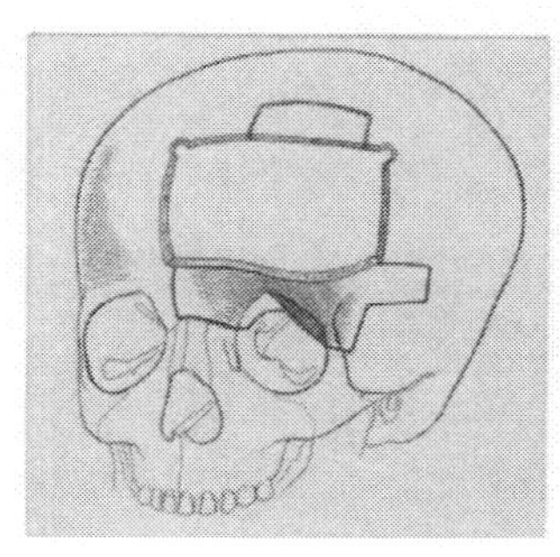

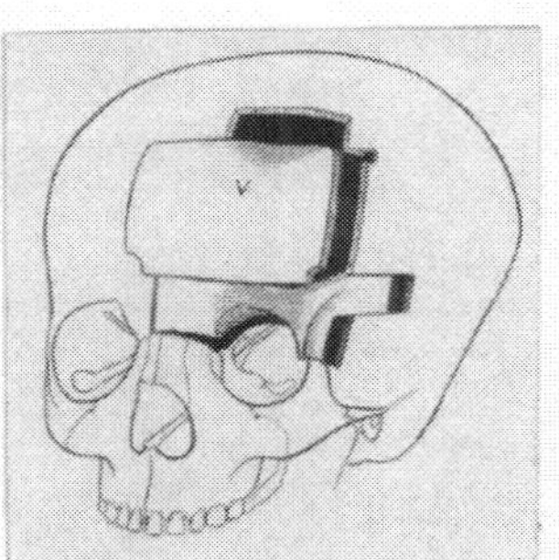

The results of a linear craniectomy are not consistently good even when extended to the anterior cranial base. For this reason, ROUGERIE (1972) followed by HOFFMAN (1976) and McCARTHY (1979) removed a segment of frontal bone and advanced the lower part of the frontal bone, the supra-orbital ridge and the orbital roof. Laterally, the fragment is maintained in an advanced position by a bone graft taken from the calvarium and wired to the temporal region. Although the procedure gives an immediate correction of the retrusive supra-orbital ridge, it does not correct the contralateral deformities or the transverse asymmetry.

3. MARCHAC's procedure is more radical and consists of:
- the removal of two portions of the frontal bone (separated by the sagittal suture),
- the removal of the orbito-frontal "bandeau" in its entire length,
- the bending of the homolateral supra-orbital ridge,
- the replacement of the orbito-frontal "bandeau" and its fixation to the fronto-nasal angle and to the homolateral fronto-zygomatic process in a more advanced position, with or without a bone graft,
- the interchanging of the two protions of the frontal bone.

The procedure derives from the "floating forehead" procedure. In fact, the orbito-frontal "bandeau" is not completely "floating", but can turn on the three hinge points around a horizontal axis (MARCHAC, 1982).

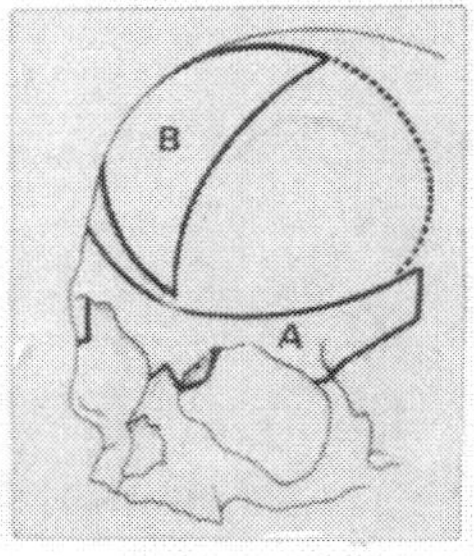


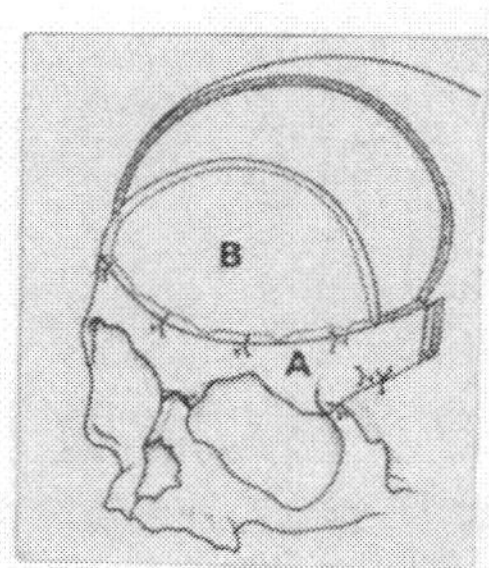

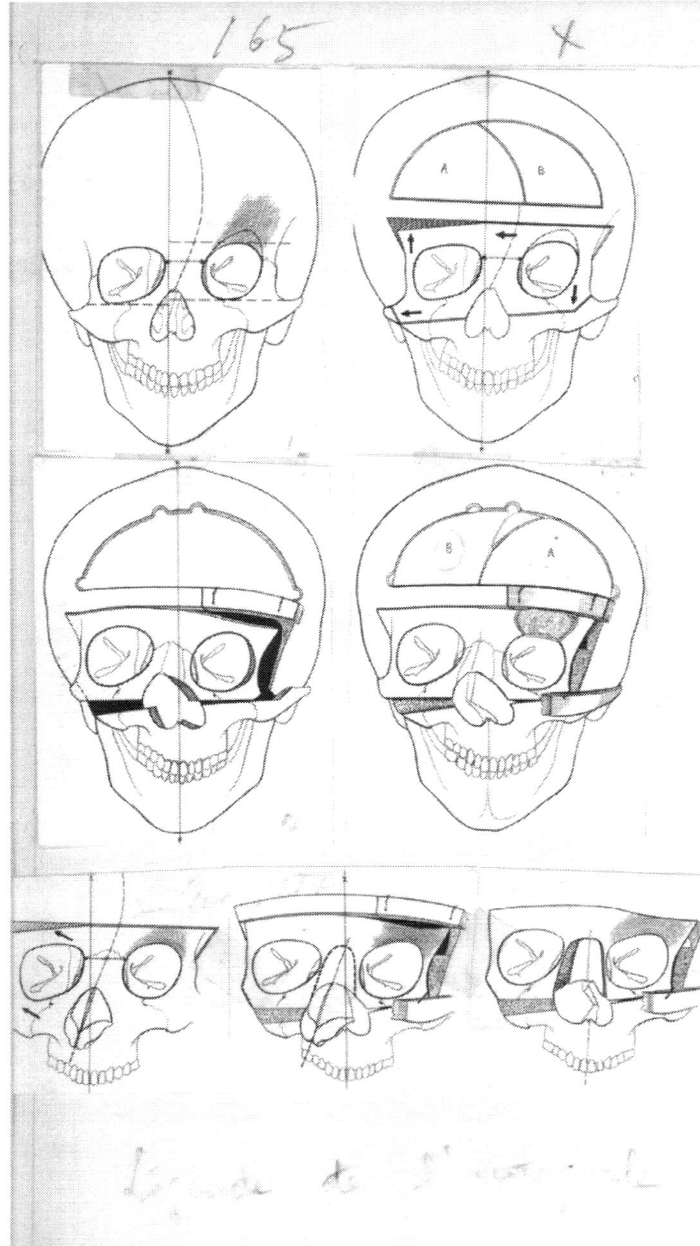

In considering these three procedures performed in early childhood, the following questions come to mind:

Are satisfactory results a consequence of the extensive surgery or was the synostosis less extensive or less severe than initially supposed?

Does early surgery prevent all secondary deformities whether homolateral or contralateral?

These three procedures are more efficient if they are performed early in life. Their efficiency results from the driving effect of the growing brain, which is considerable at 3 months, appreciable at 6 months, but almost exhausted at 12. There is nonetheless the possibility of a repeat procedure in infants of about 12 months old.

After 2 years of age, local craniotomies or local skeletal displacements cannot overcome acquired deformities of the orbital cavities, frontal regions or naso-ethmoidal structures. A more radical procedure must be planned for the proper time, which seems to be after the child has attained 3 years of age and when its cranium is no longer influenced by brain development.

4. TESSIER's procedure. A radical procedure for acquired deformities was developed in 1978. It basically consists of the displacement of a fronto-orbito--naso-ethmoidal monobloc fragment from the stenotic side towards the other. The main purpose is to re-center the oblique interorbital midline on its ideal vertical axis. The nose is displaced in the opposite direction within the limits of the monobloc. In addition to the linear displacement and rotation, the procedure includes a local remodeling by deep trimming and onlay bone grafts. This procedure has been performed on fifteen patients over a period of four years. Results have been almost invariably satisfactory.

Although this operation can be considered a major procedure mainly for cosmetic reasons, it constitutes a logical approach to the various malformations of U.C.S.

In a few cases of U.C.S. (See clinical form - 1) there is no lateral deviation of the orbito-naso- ethmoidal complex. The main deformity does not affect the facial axis, but consists of a vertical discrepancy in the orbital cavities. The traitment here consists of raising the lower orbital cavity (or, of course, of descending the upper cavity).

échanger avec DAL COL

## SECONDARY SURGERY AND RELATIONSHIP WITH OTHER CEPHALIC SPECIALITIES

● Whatever the timing of the primary surgery and whatever the procedure used, morphological deformities may subsequently appear.
They may consist of:
• atrophy of the homolateral ridge, requiring an additional onlay bone graft
• nasal or septal deviation,
• ptosis of the upper eyelid, frequently associated with U.C.S.
● Eye deviation. The surgical indications to treat the anomalies discussed above p. 00 are:
- Before the cranio-facial surgery, to prevent amblyopia or impairment of binocular vision, when it is present by...
- More generally to repair eye deviations six months after orbitocranial corrections.
- To correct strabismus when there is a risk of the strabismus leading to amblyopia. If a successful primary result is altered by the orbito-cranial procedure, it can be corrected by eye muscle surgery.
The usuol surgical procedure is used for horizontal deviation and a specific procedure on the oblique muscles is used to "disagittalize" the I.O.M.
● Dental malpositions
Gross deviations of the maxilla or mandible are rare in cases of U.C.S. but minor dental malocclusion is frequent and requires orthodontic treatment.
● Lateral deviation of the maxilla and mandible
It has already been pointed out that even though the mandible is asymmetrical, it functions symmetrically (See page 00 and COMMENTS 00 and 8); the axis of the mandible is therefore taken as a reference point for facial and cranial correction. However, in 4 cases out of 63, severe jaw malformations have been observed.
They consisted in deviation and rotation of the maxilla; consequently there is no dental malocclusion from a purely dental point of view. So, nevertheless, this jaw deviation in relation to the "ideal facial axis" becomes more obvious after the orbito-cranial deformities have been corrected. In these cases, the ideal axis was not taken from the mid incisive point but was assessed in relation to the overall facial morphology.
Surgery consists of a simultaneous derotation of the maxilla by a Le Fort I maxillotomy and a mandibular derotation by sagittal splitting on the contralateral side and vertical osteotomy on the homolateral side.

325

325

OJ à 5½ 3 y post-op

Légende
de l'Intégrale
(Suite)

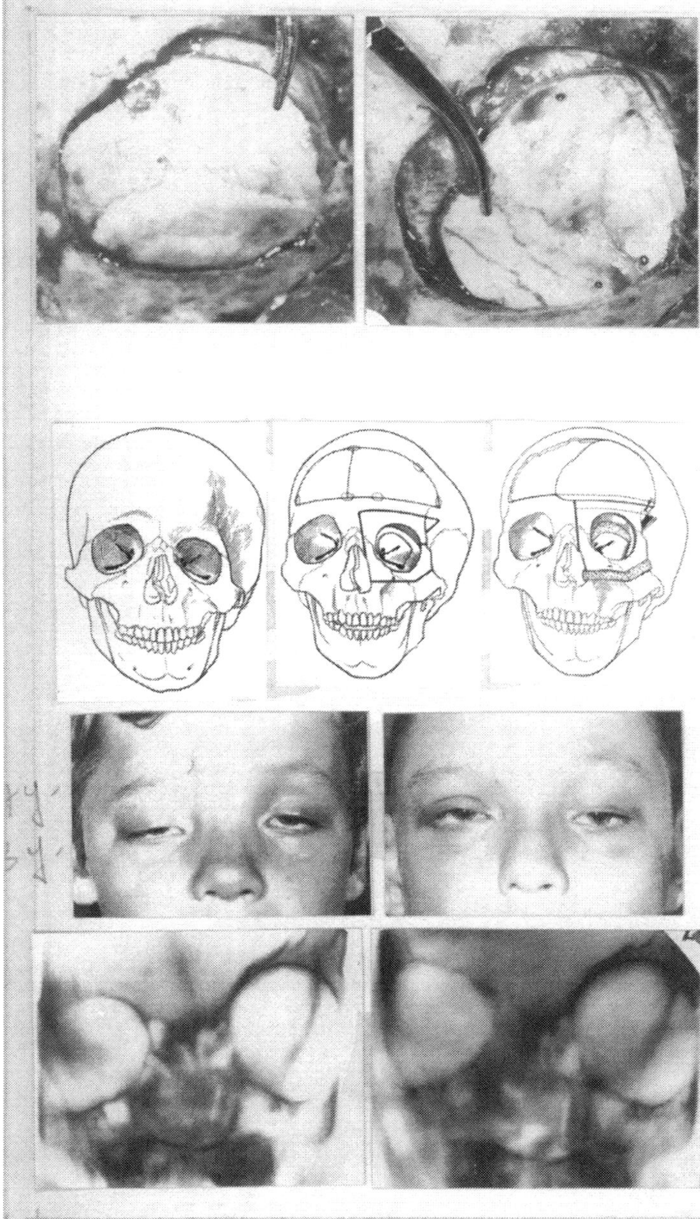

## CONCLUSIONS

Some interesting information can be gleaned from this study based on:

- observation of 17 dry skulls,
- the surgical treatment of 32 patients,
- observation of 31 other patients.

● The subject of "plagiocephaly" has been restricted to U.C.S. with possible extensions laterally or inferiorly to the cranial base.

● Considerable information has been provided by dry skulls, which display and demonstrate in three dimensions what has already been mentioned by different authors in different places over the past 20 years, especially NATHAN (1961) and FAURE (1967).

● The examination of dry skulls did not provide as many demonstrations of complete synostosis at the anterior cranial base as we had expected. X-rays of these dry skulls were all really significant.

● A description has been given for homolateral and contralateral deformities.

● The lateral deviation of the naso-ethmoidal complex is an important new feature, which, as far as we know, is here described for the first time.

● The lower and more anterior position of the glenoid fossa was mentioned by FAURE. We have pointed out herein that the abnormal position of the glenoid fossa is responsible for the asymmetry of the mandible and although asymmetrical, the mandible functions symmetrically with a normal or rotated maxilla.

● A vertical clinical form of U.C.S. without deviation from the axis has been described. It could represent a pure U.C.S. without extension either laterally or inferiorly.

● Several other clinical forms have been shown involving other synostoses associated with U.C.S.

● Among the primary procedures, preference is given either to the ROUGERIE procedure or the MARCHAC procedure. Both these procedures stem from the advancement and bending of the "orbito-frontal bandeau" that we started to perform in 1968 in the correction of brachycephaly and CROUZON's disease.

● A radical procedure has been described for patients over 3 years of age. It consists of centering an obliquely displaced upper mid face, on an ideal vertical axis elevated from the midincis or point, the jaws usually being unaffected.

● There were no serious complications, except for one case of seizure. There was also two partial sequestrations of bone grafts in the frontal region.

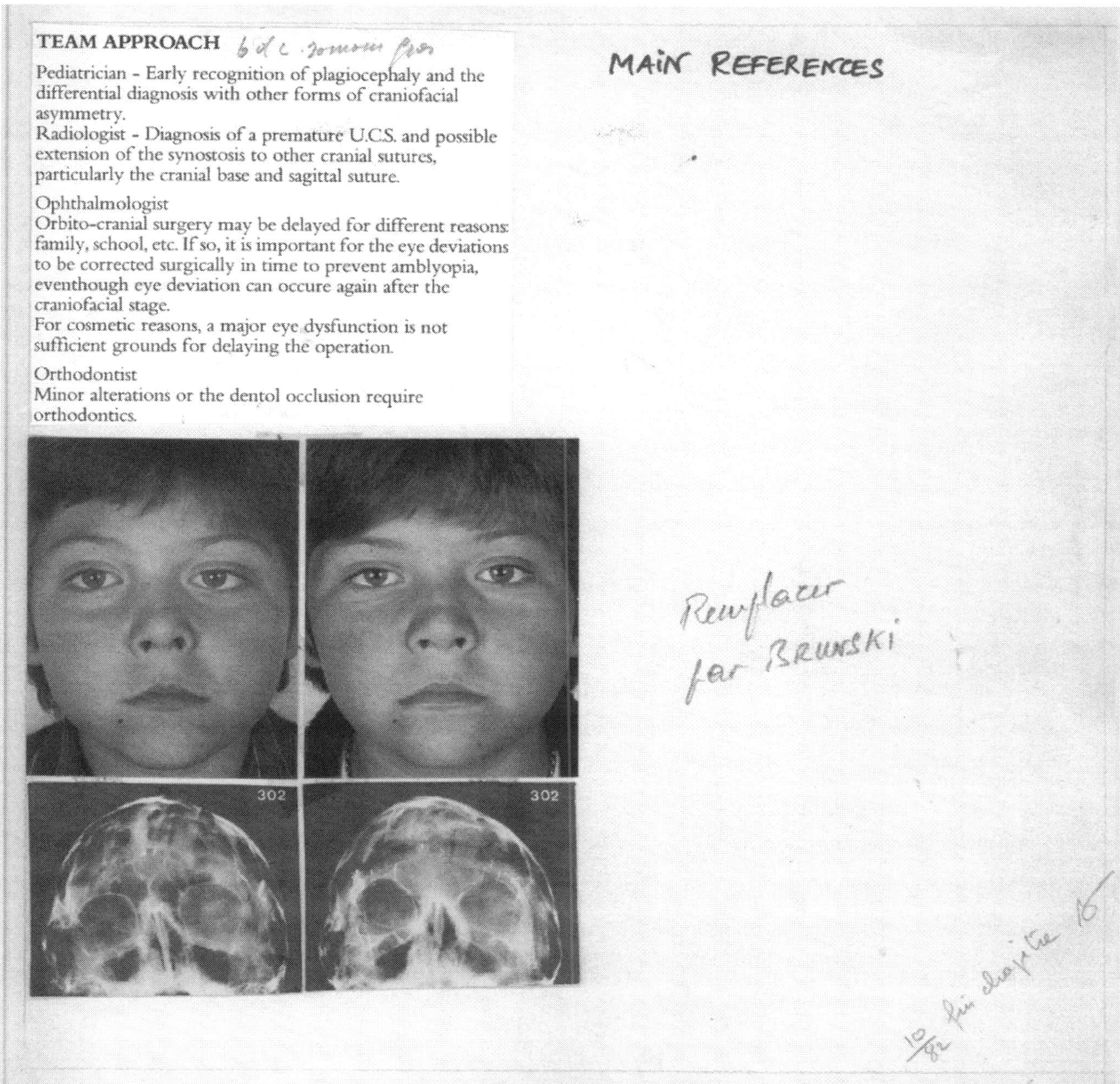
TEAM APPROACH

Pediatrician - Early recognition of plagiocephaly and the differential diagnosis with other forms of craniofacial asymmetry.
Radiologist - Diagnosis of a premature U.C.S. and possible extension of the synostosis to other cranial sutures, particularly the cranial base and sagittal suture.

Ophthalmologist
Orbito-cranial surgery may be delayed for different reasons: family, school, etc. If so, it is important for the eye deviations to be corrected surgically in time to prevent amblyopia, eventhough eye deviation can occure again after the craniofacial stage.
For cosmetic reasons, a major eye dysfunction is not sufficient grounds for delaying the operation.

Orthodontist
Minor alterations or the dentol occlusion require orthodontics.



*Fig. 24.6 Next to the last patient is written "Remplacer par Brunski" (Replace by Brunski)---- who was a particularly severe and distorted plagiocephaly patient that Dr. Tessier operated on in Los Angeles, and who had his subsequent jaw surgery performed by Henry Kawamoto. He is patient number 405-408 of the "London 2006" DVD.*

*Fig. 24.7 Guibor Herman, David Hemmy, and Paul Tessier, Philadelphia, 1984, in Dr. Herman's lab.*

*Fig. 24.8 Chad Perlyn presenting Tessier a set of the skull models he worked on with Jeff Marsh, Paris, ca. 2001.*

## Drawings by Merri Scheitlin

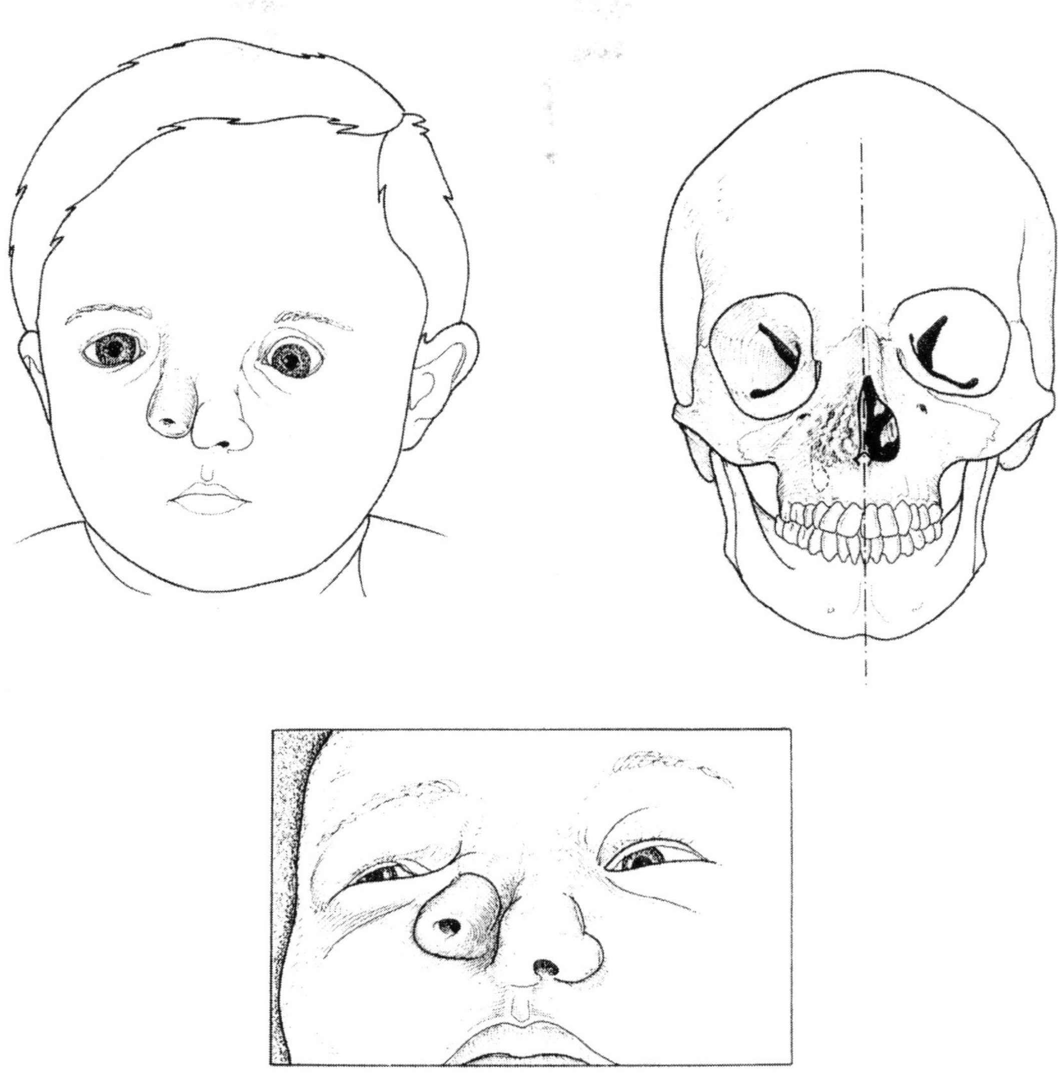

*Fig. 24.9 Drawings created by Merri Scheitlin for an eventual atlas of craniofacial malformations. This drawing depicts hemiarrhinia with a proboscis lateralis.*

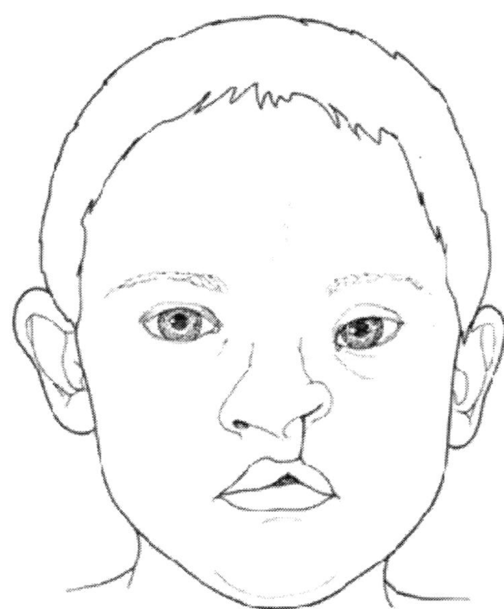

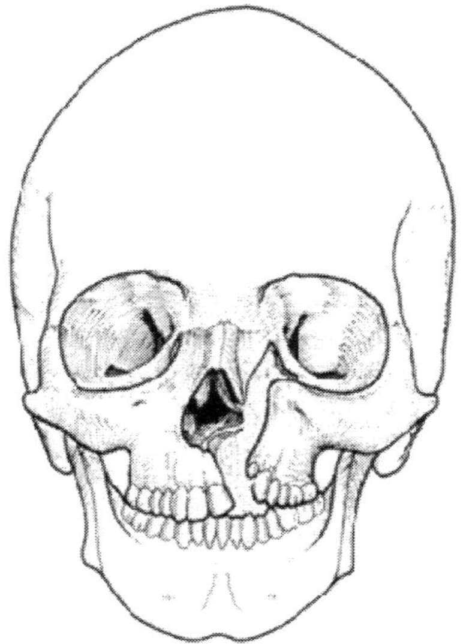

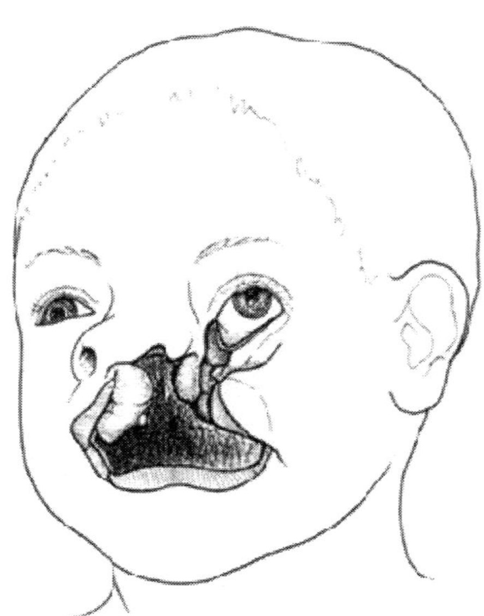

*Fig. 24.10 Tessier No. 3 cleft.*

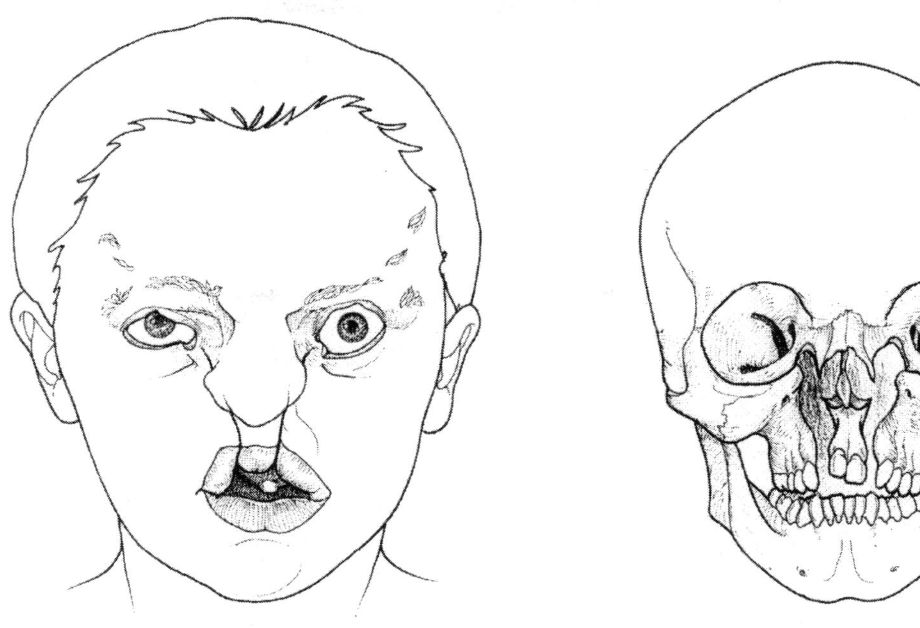

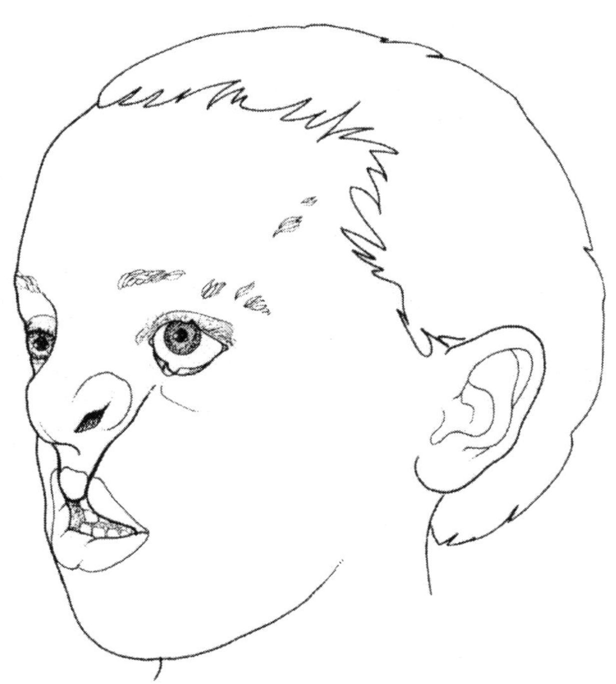

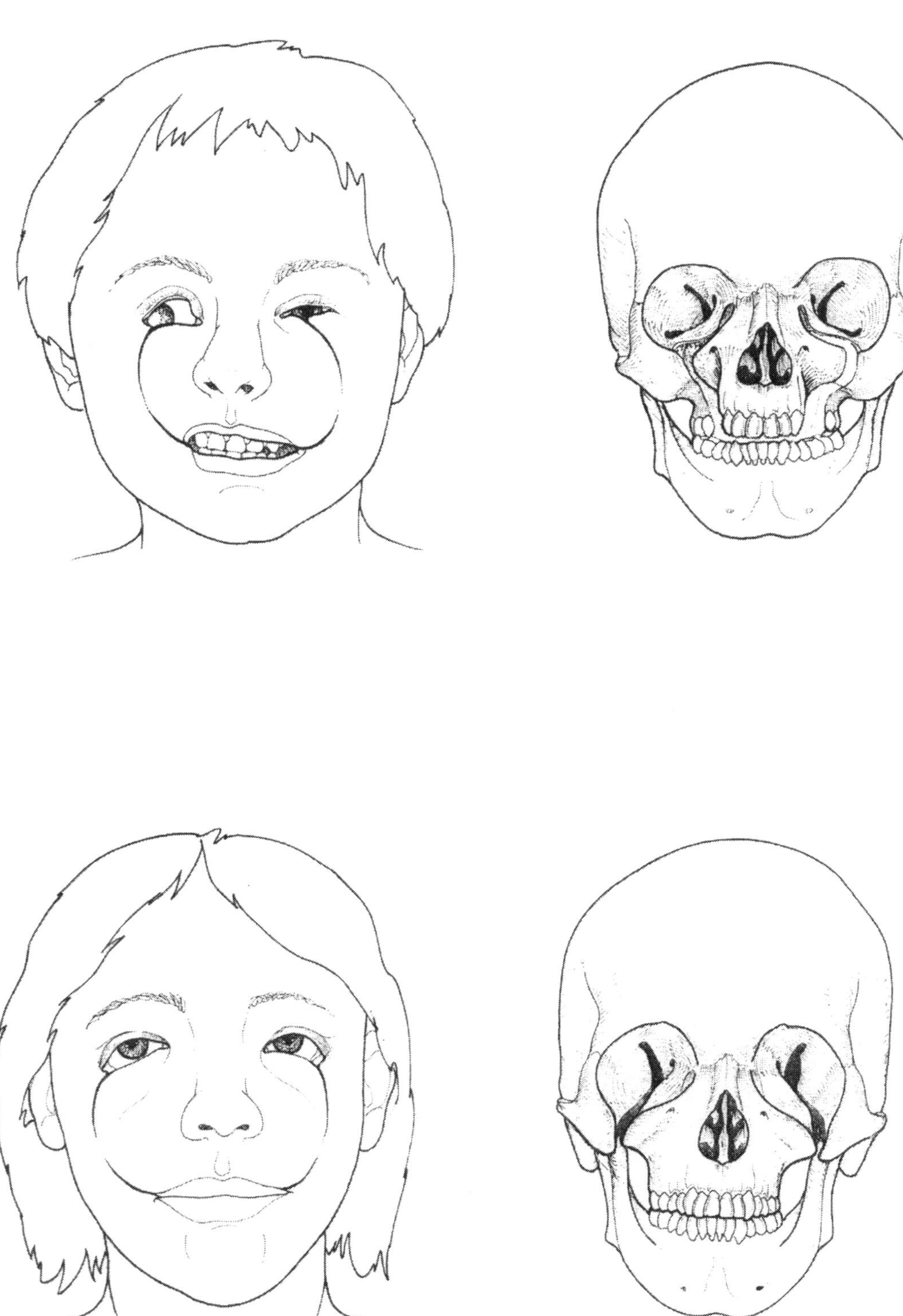

*Fig. 24.11 Bilateral No. 3 clefts.*

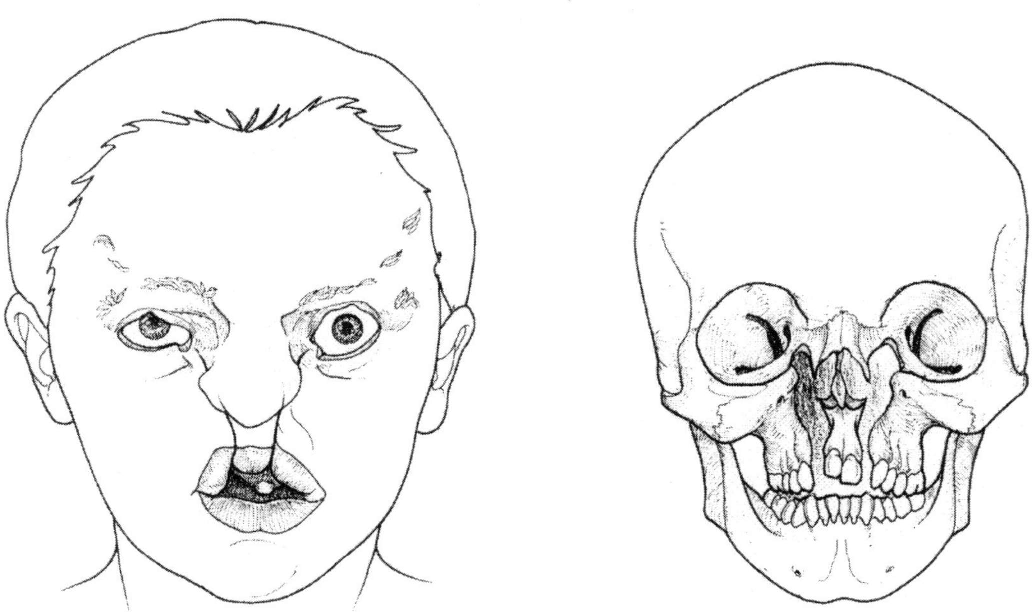

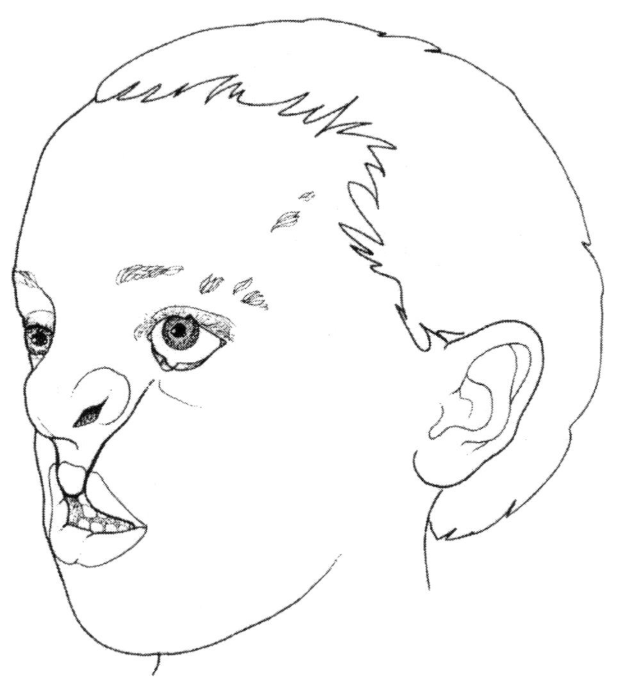

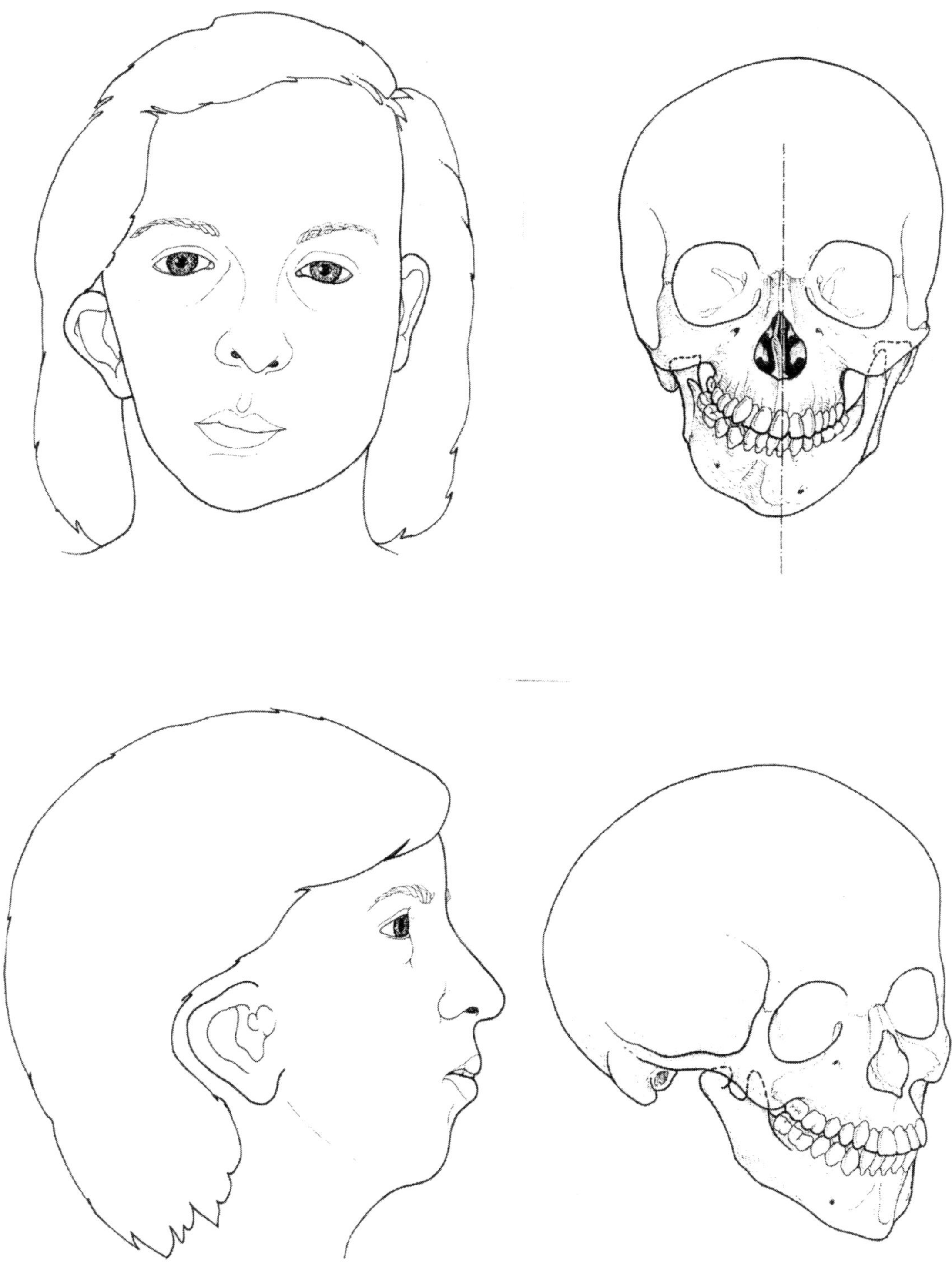

*Fig. 24.12, 24.13 No. 5 (top) and No. 6 (bottom) clefts, both very rare.*

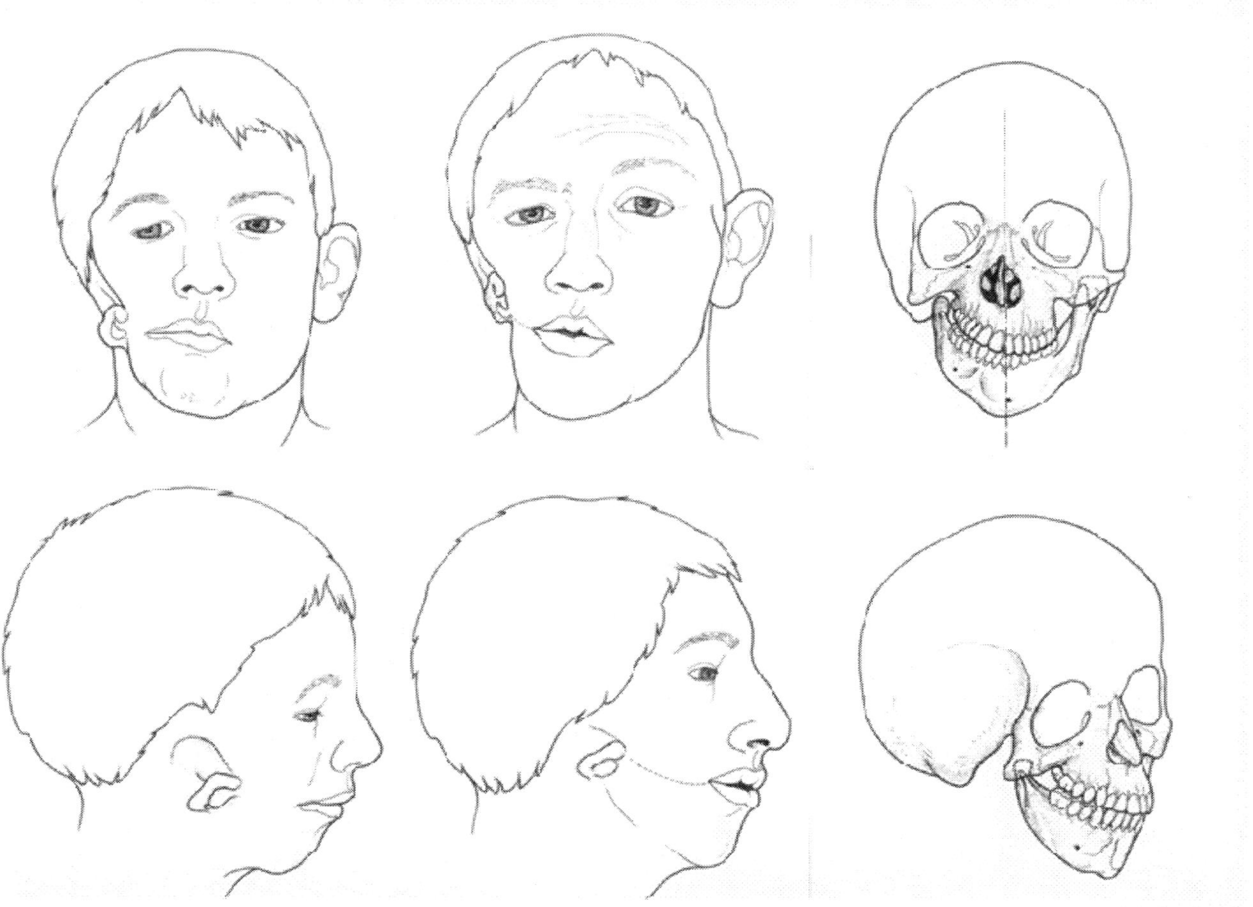

*Fig. 24.14 Hemifacial microsomia.*

*Fig. 24.15 Hemifacial microsomia.*

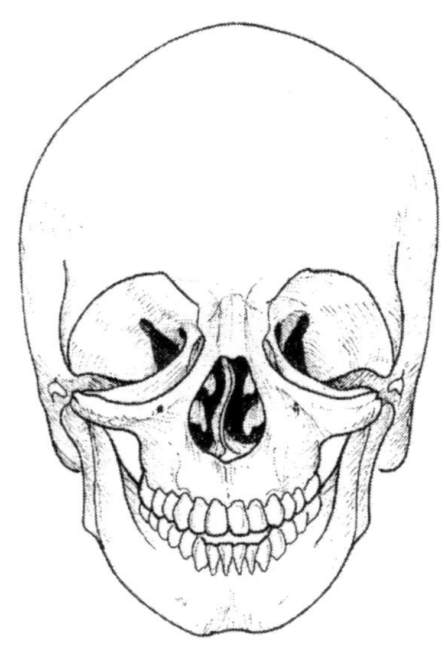

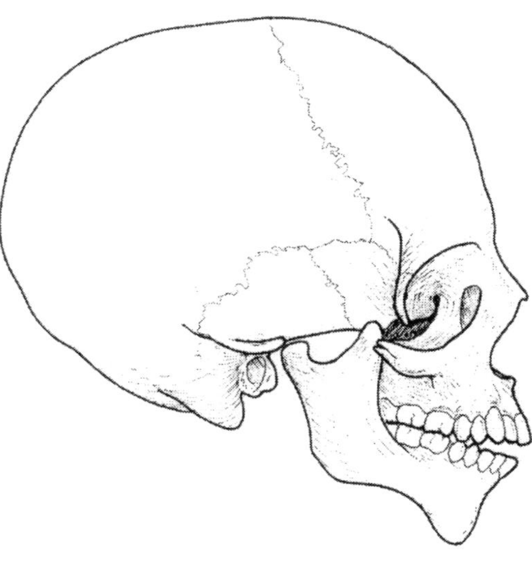

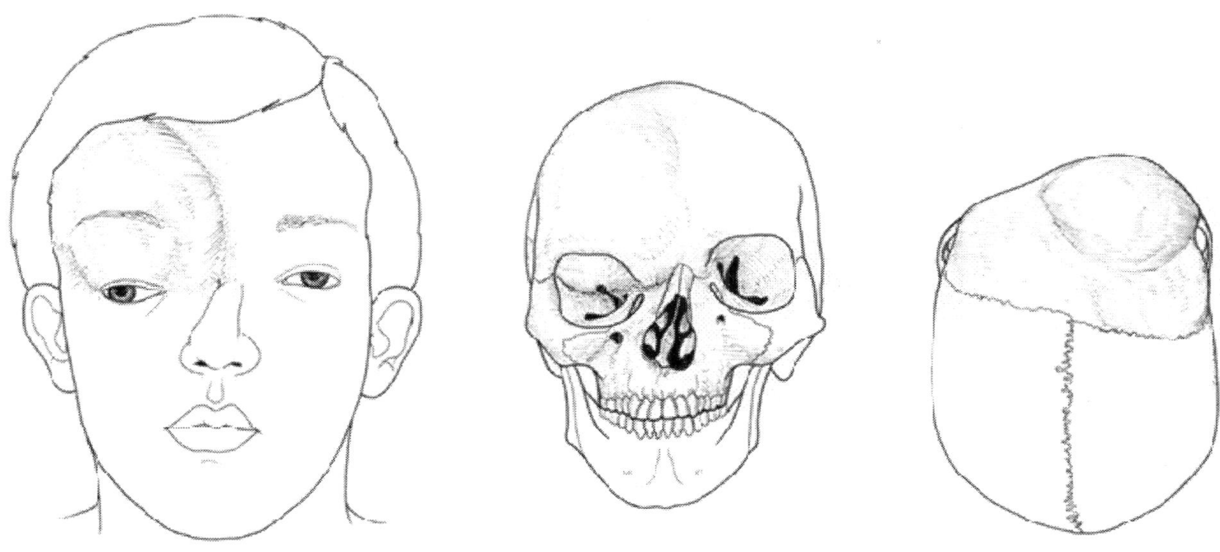

*Fig. 24.16 Treacher Collins Franceschetti syndrome.*

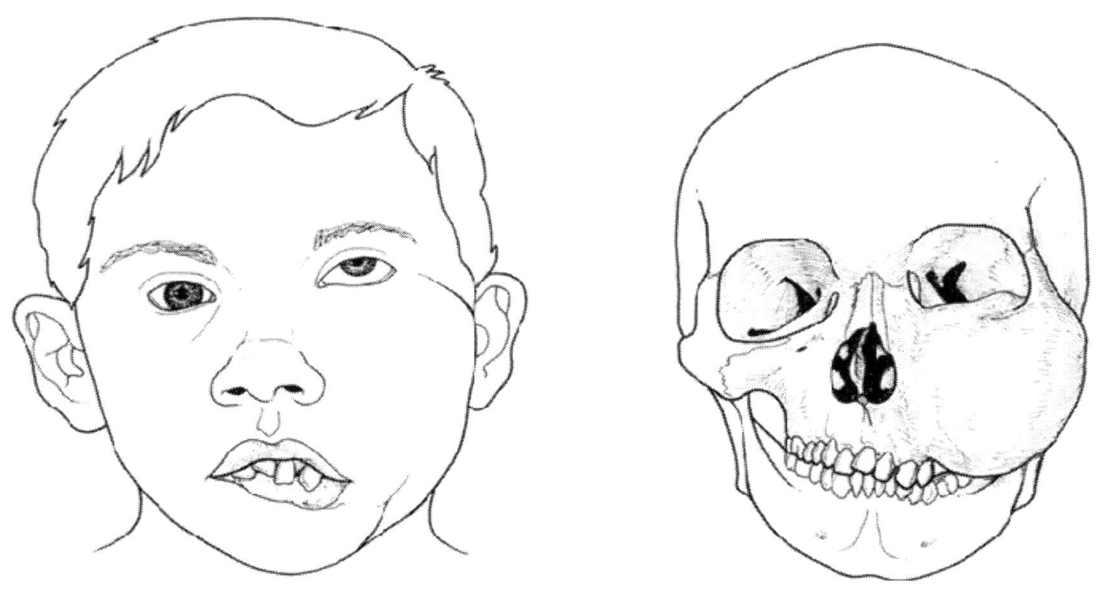

*Fig. 24.17 No. 10 cleft.*

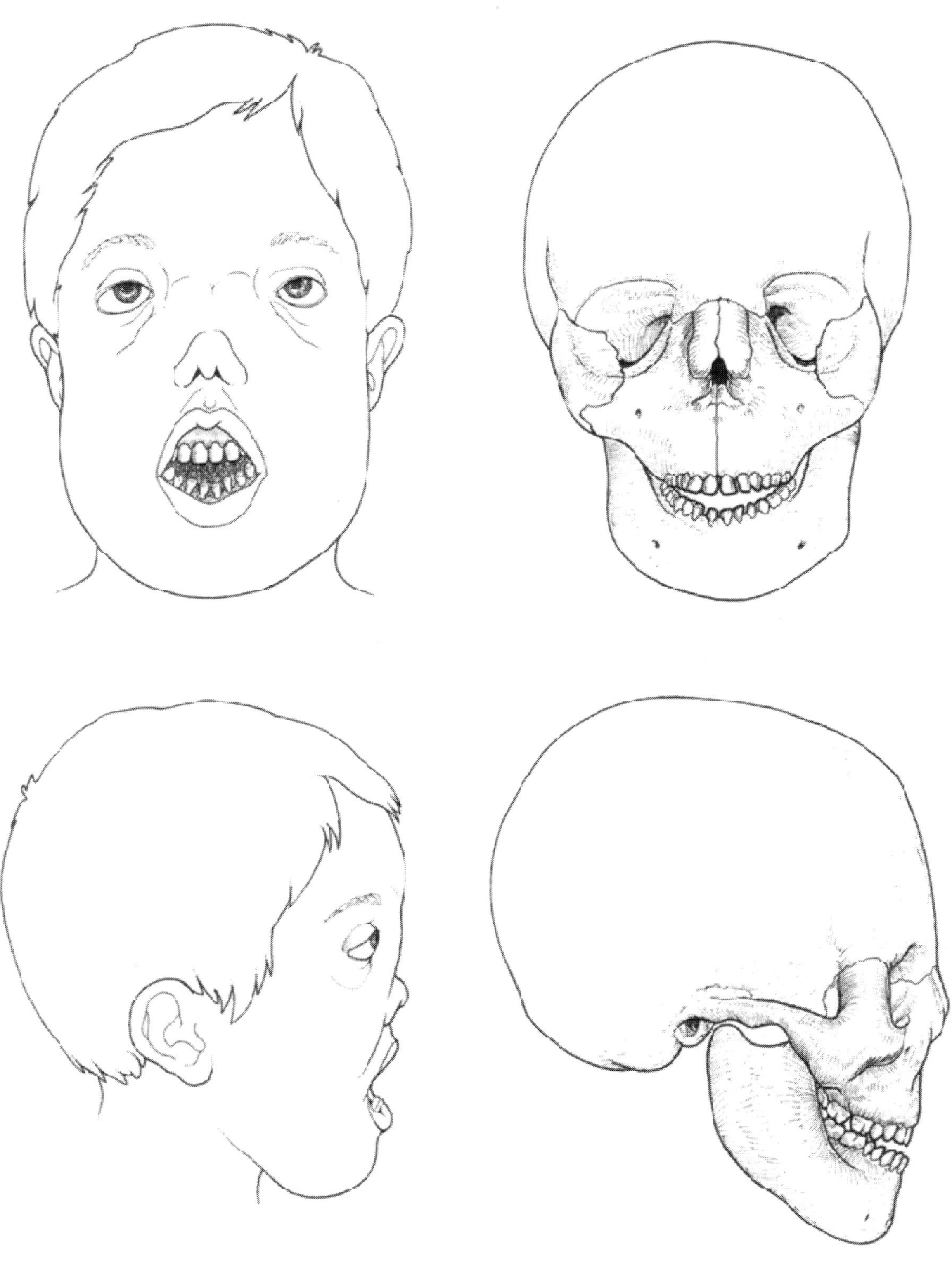

*Fig. 24.18 Fibrous dysplasia left maxilla and orbit.*

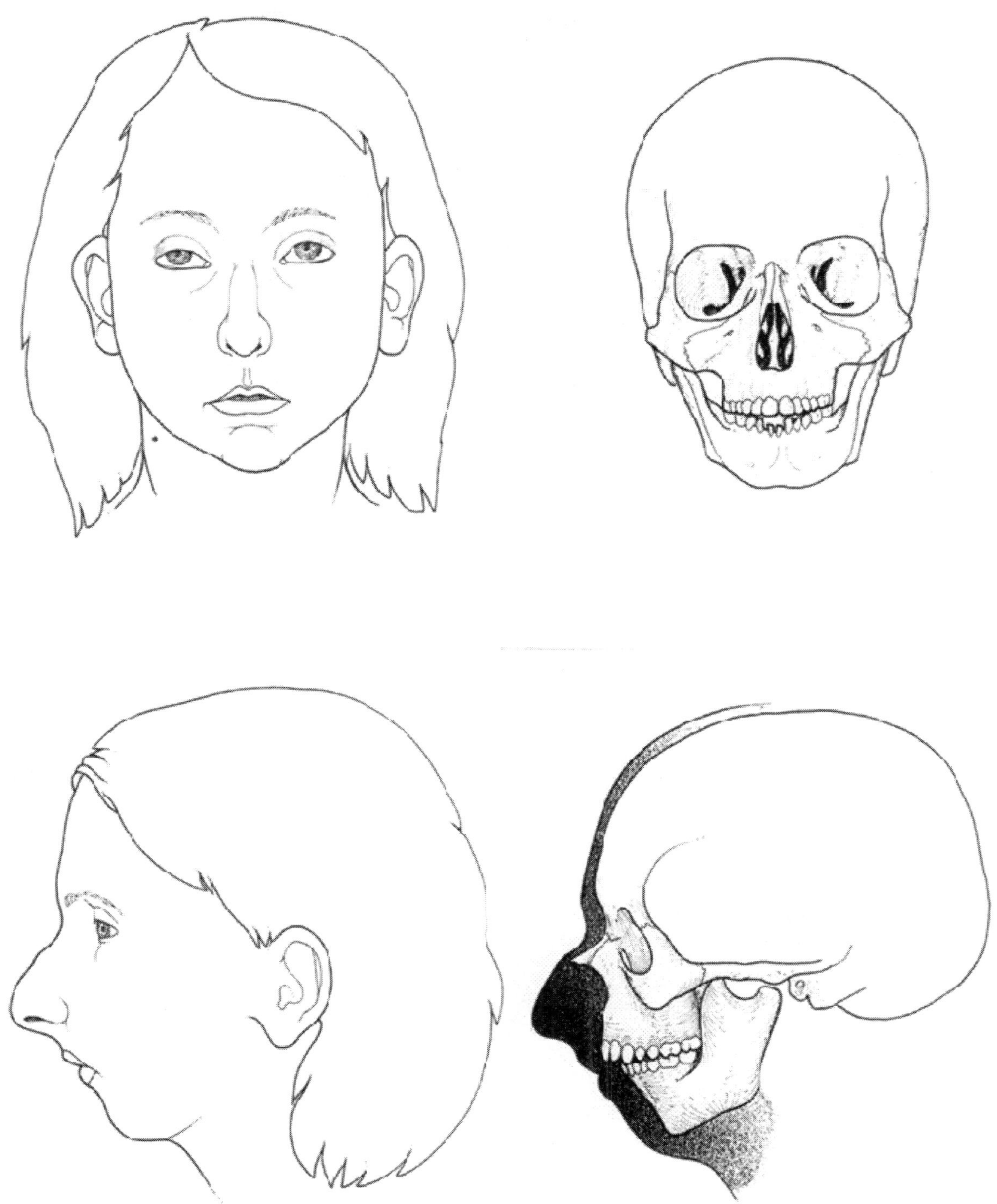

*Fig. 24.19 Cherubism*

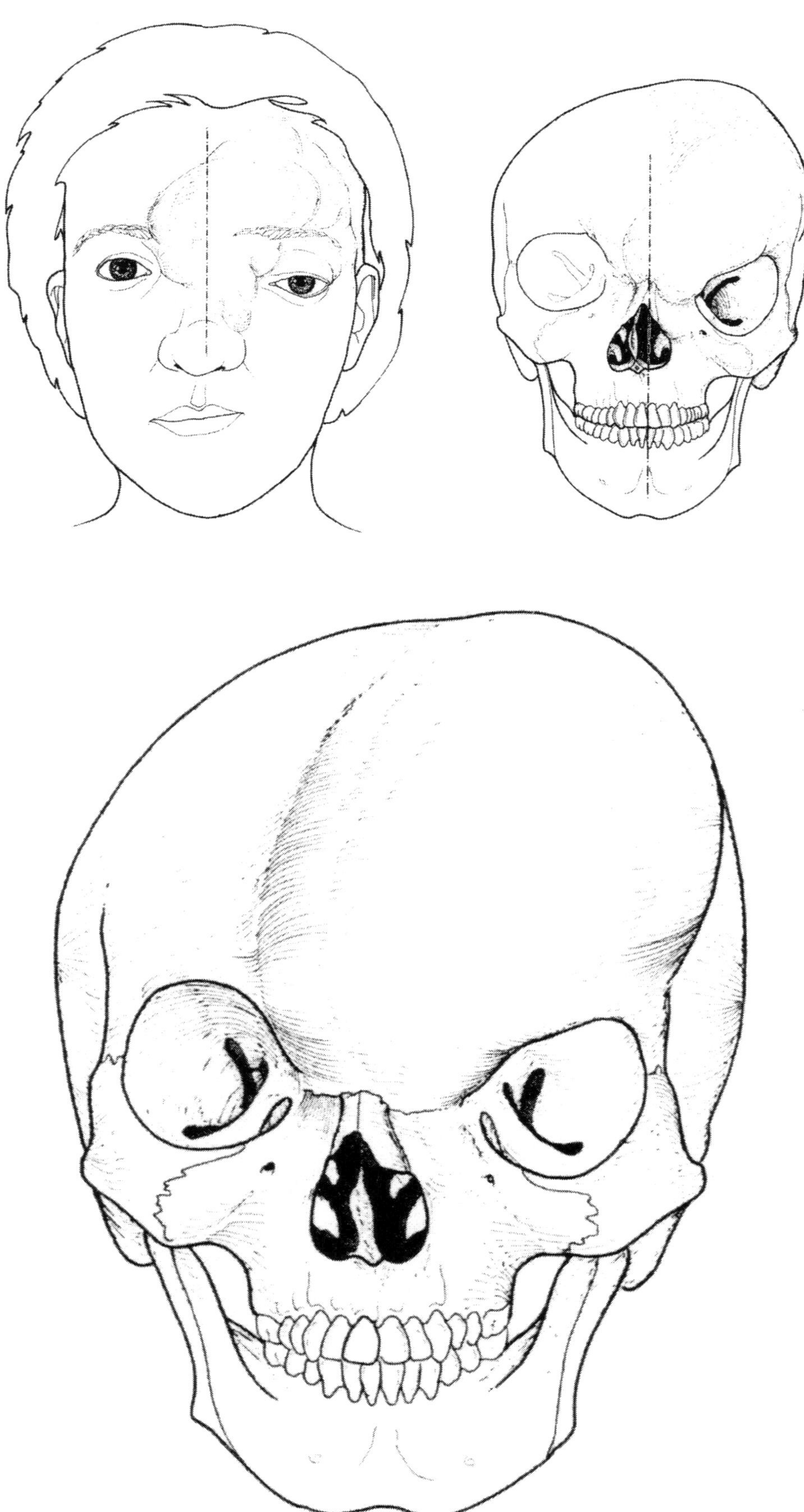

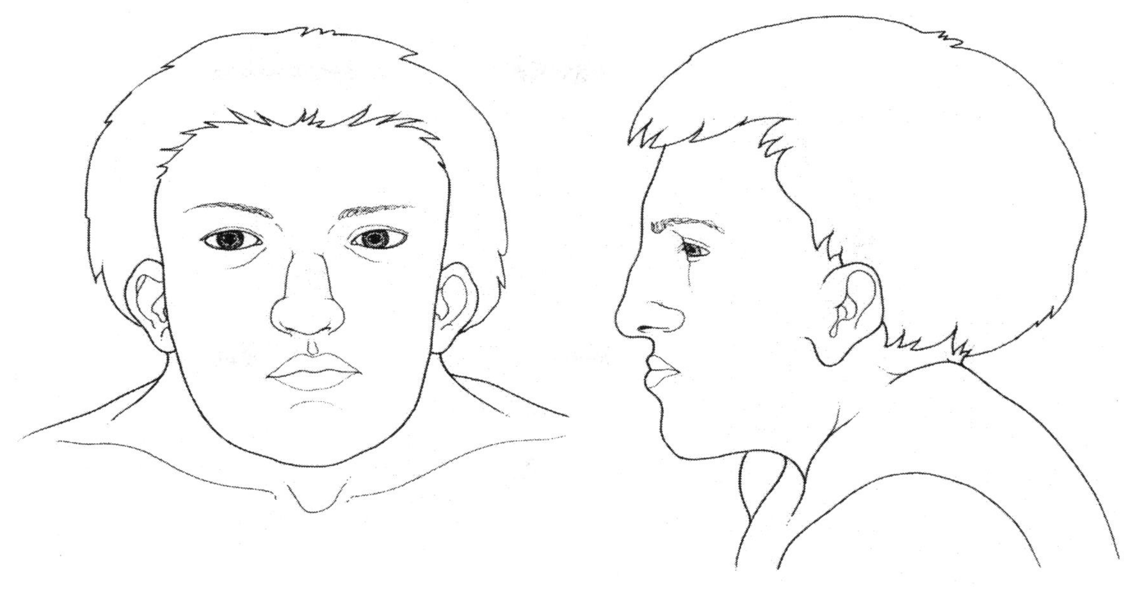

*Fig. 24.20 Hallerman Streiff syndrome*

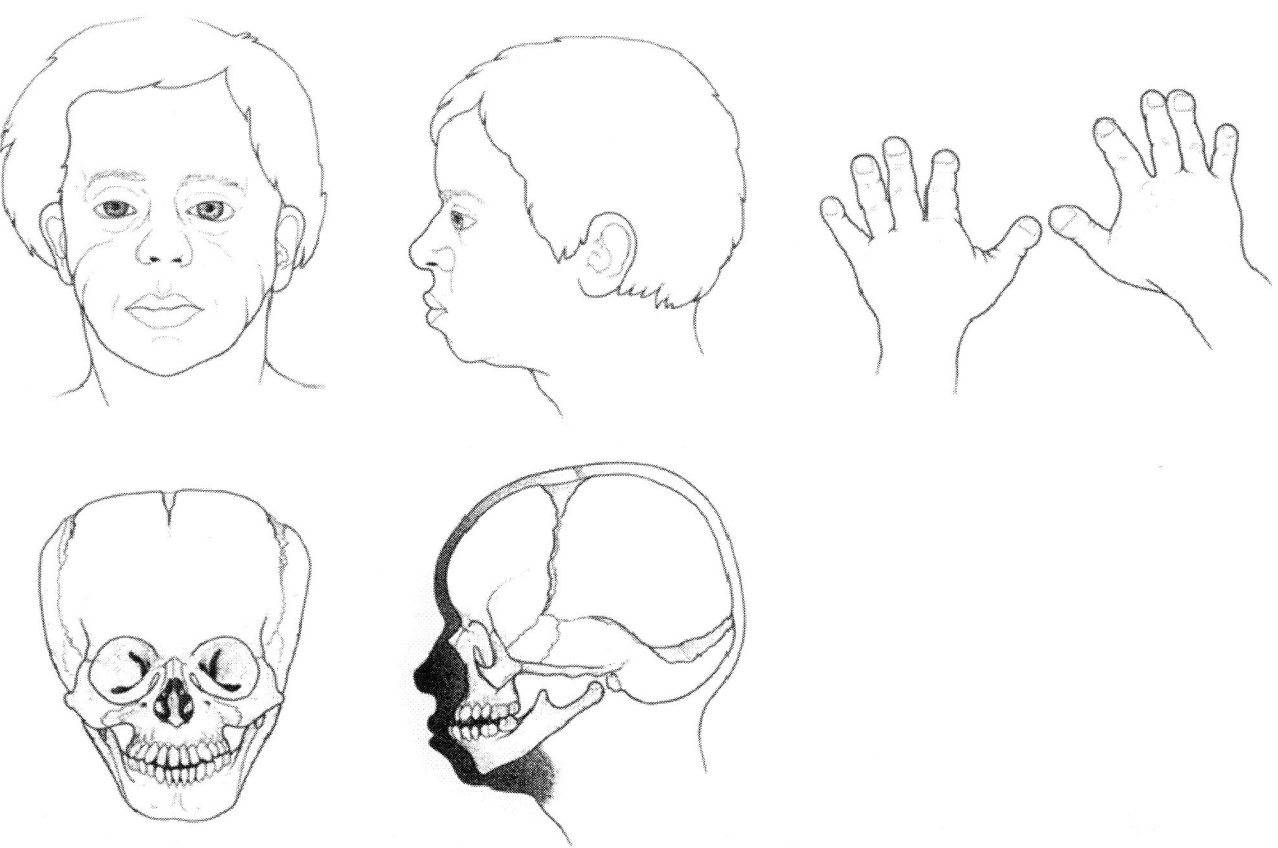

*Fig. 24.21 Klippel Feil syndrome*

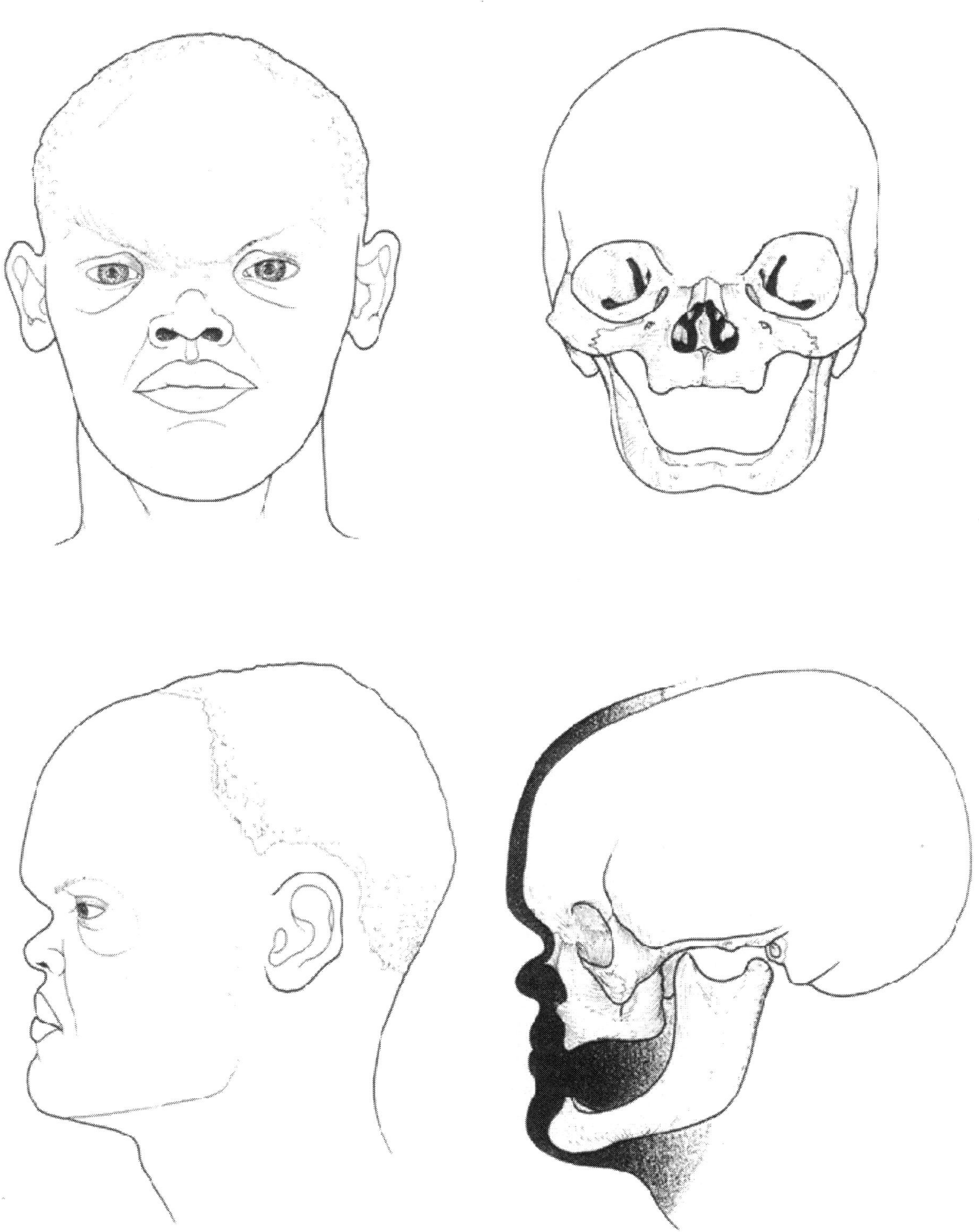

*Fig. 24.22 Achondroplasia*

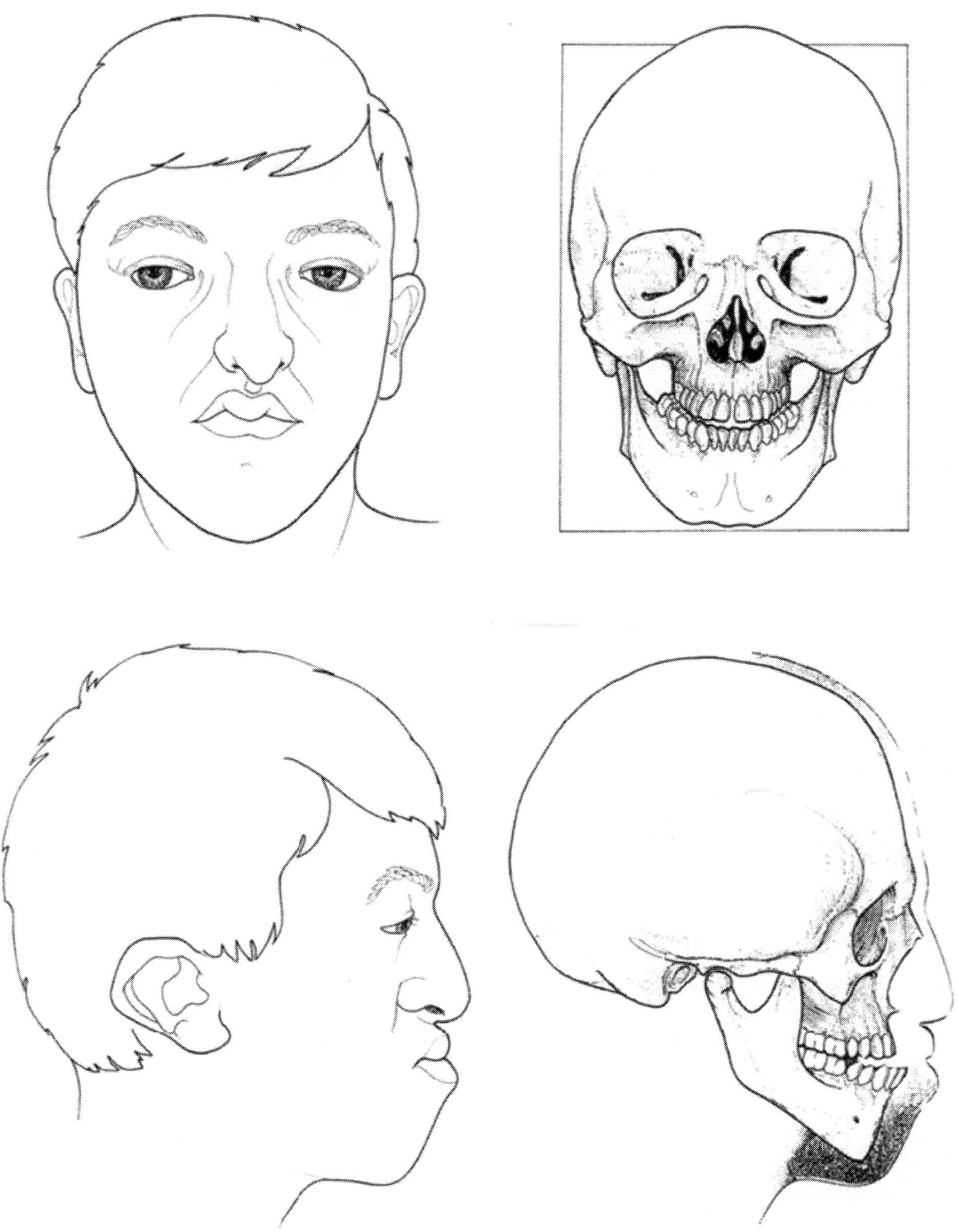

*Fig. 24.26 Blepharophimosis*

*Fig. 24.27 Mandibular prognathism*

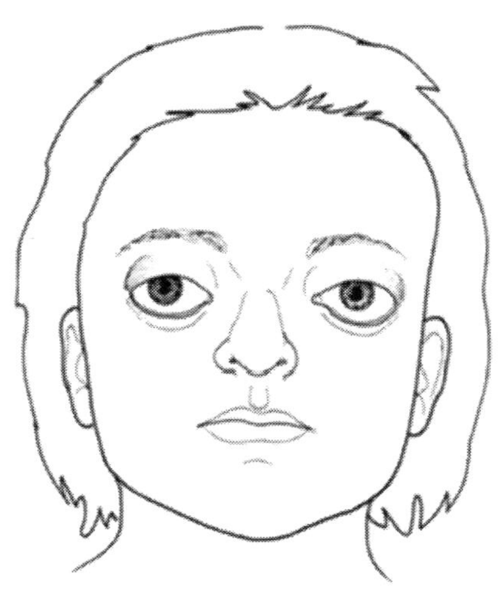

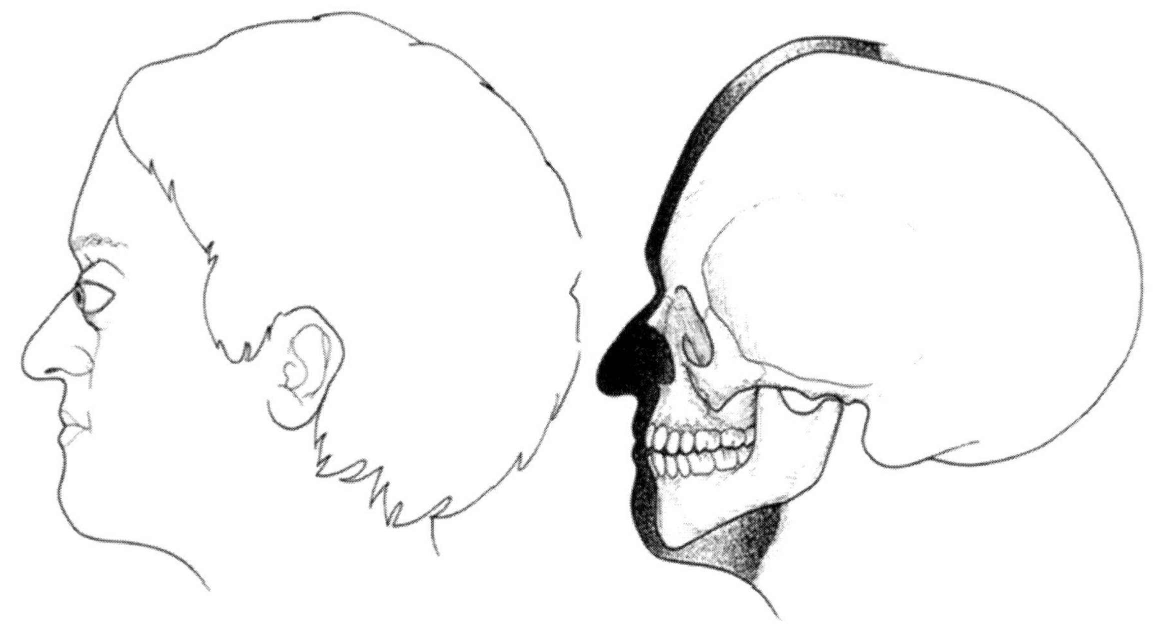

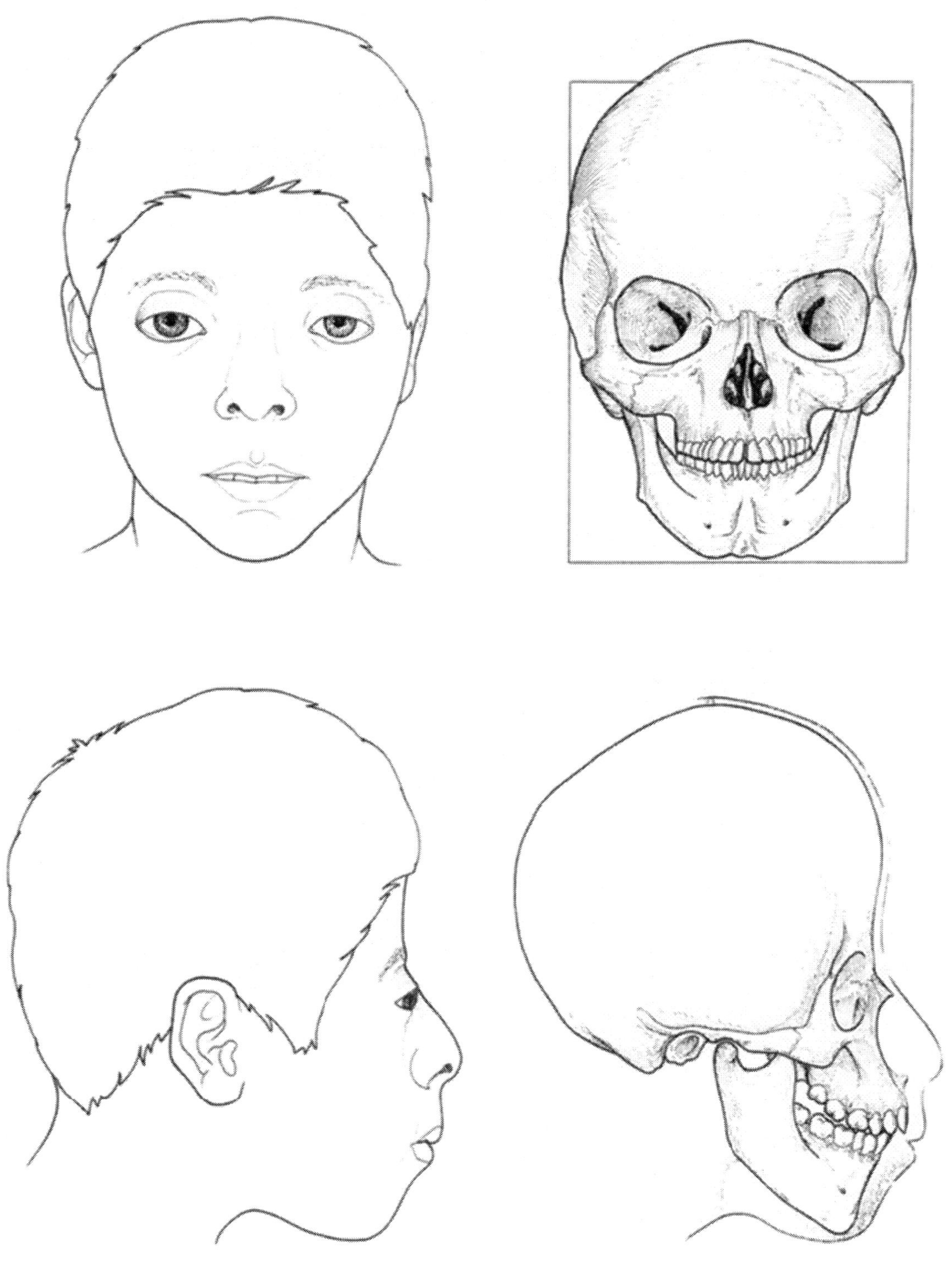

*Fig. 24.28 Crouzon's disease*

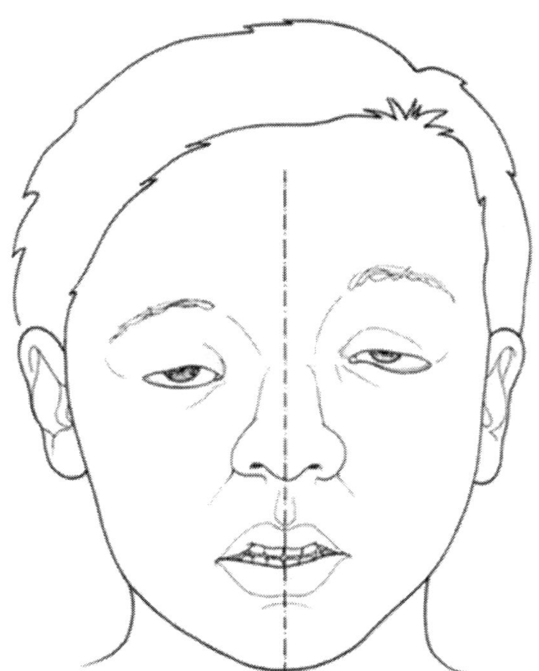

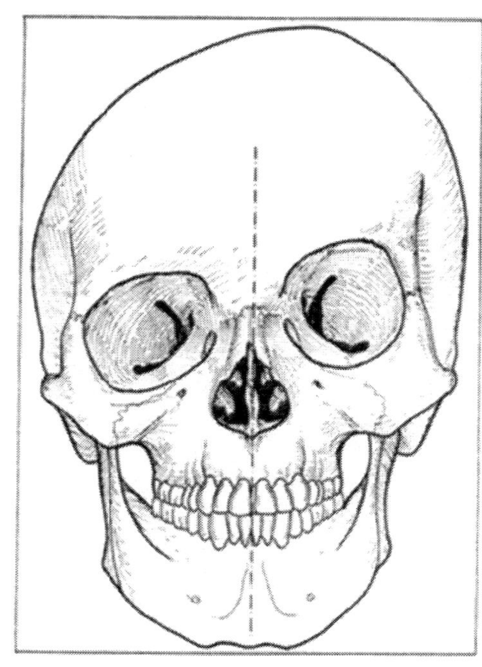

*Fig. 24.29 Saethre Chotzon syndrome*

*Fig. 24.30 Orbital dystopia*

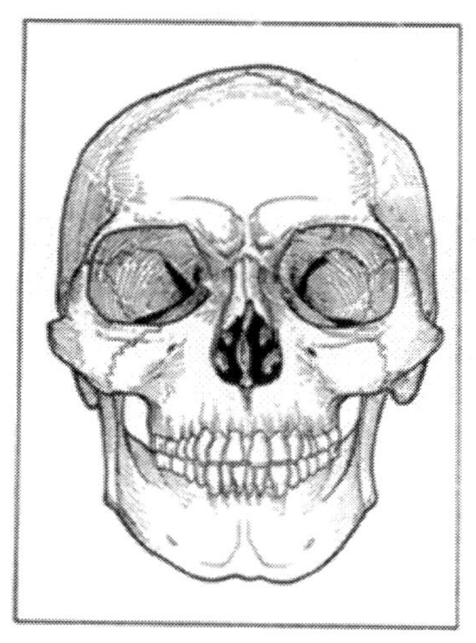

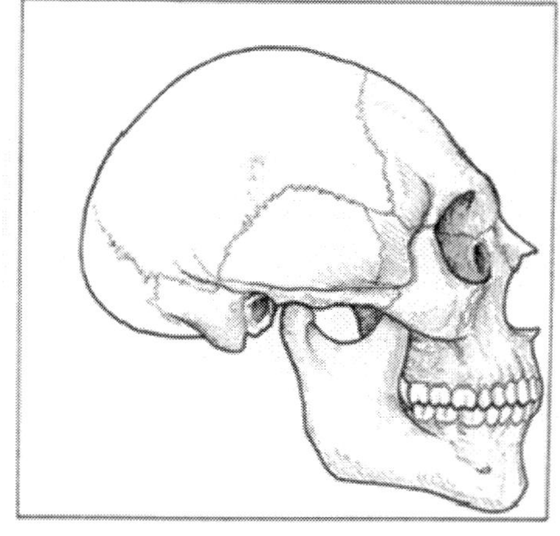

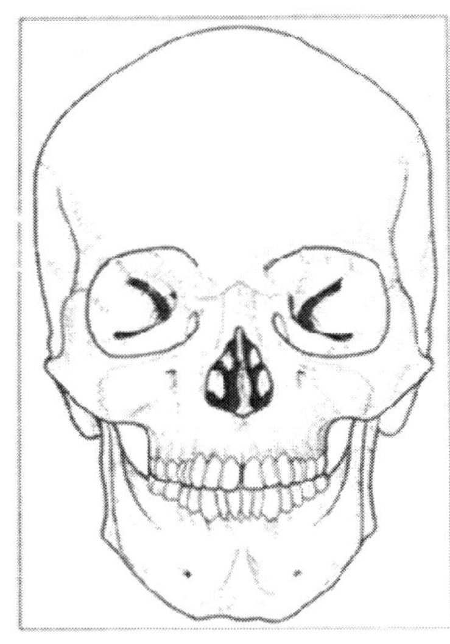

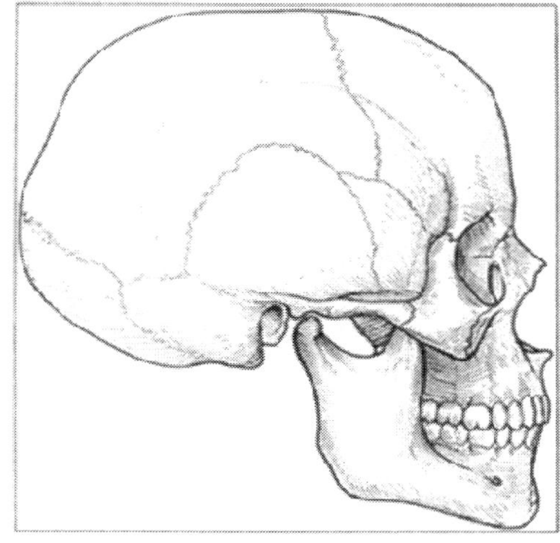

*Fig. 24.31 Microcephaly*

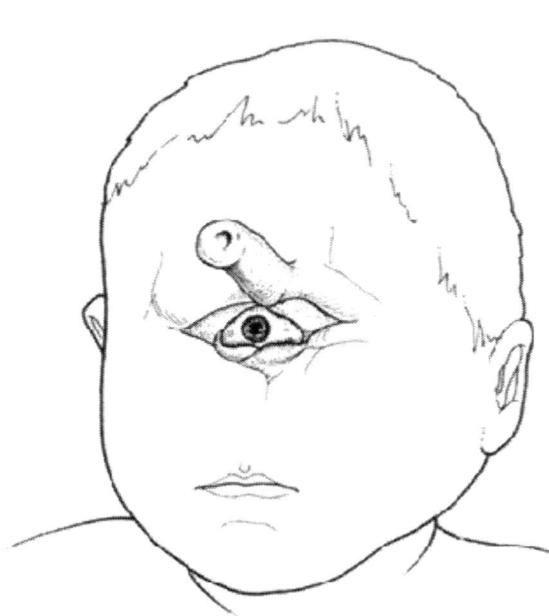

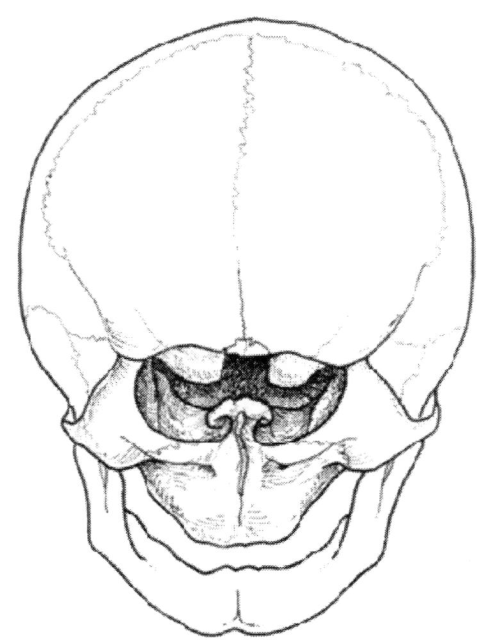

*Fig. 24.32 Cyclopia*

*Fig. 24.33 Normal skull*

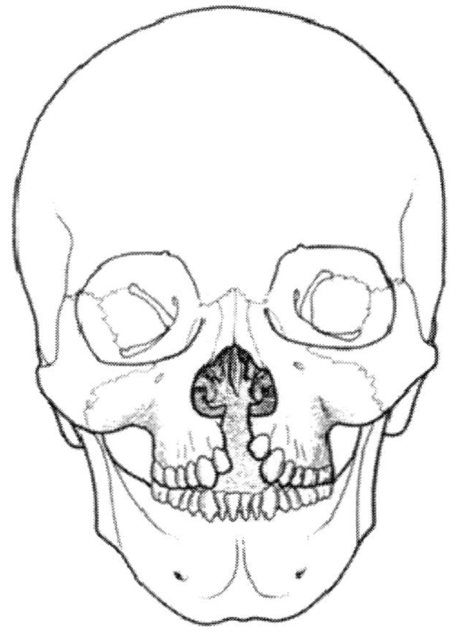

*Fig. 24.34 Midline cleft and hypotelorism*

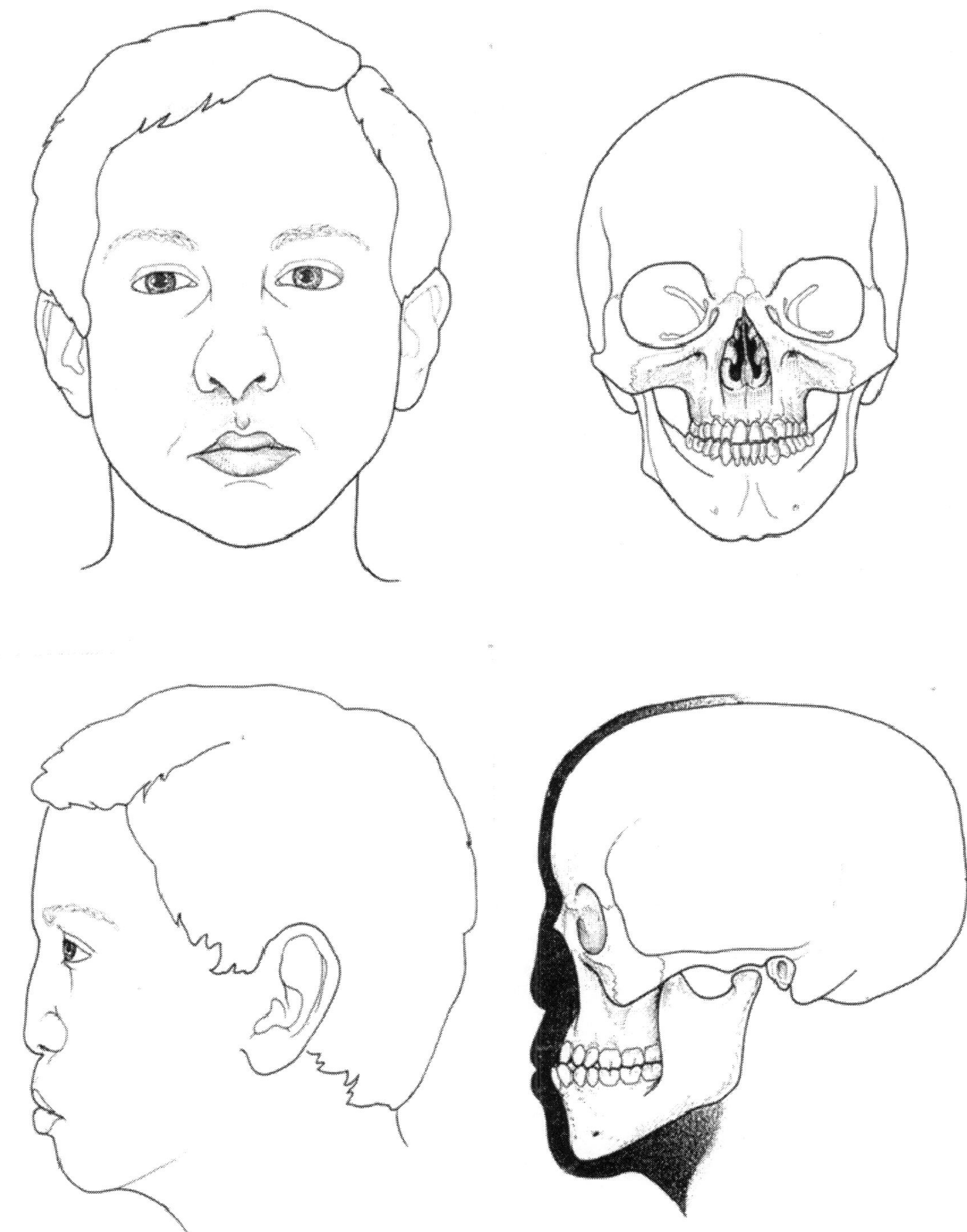

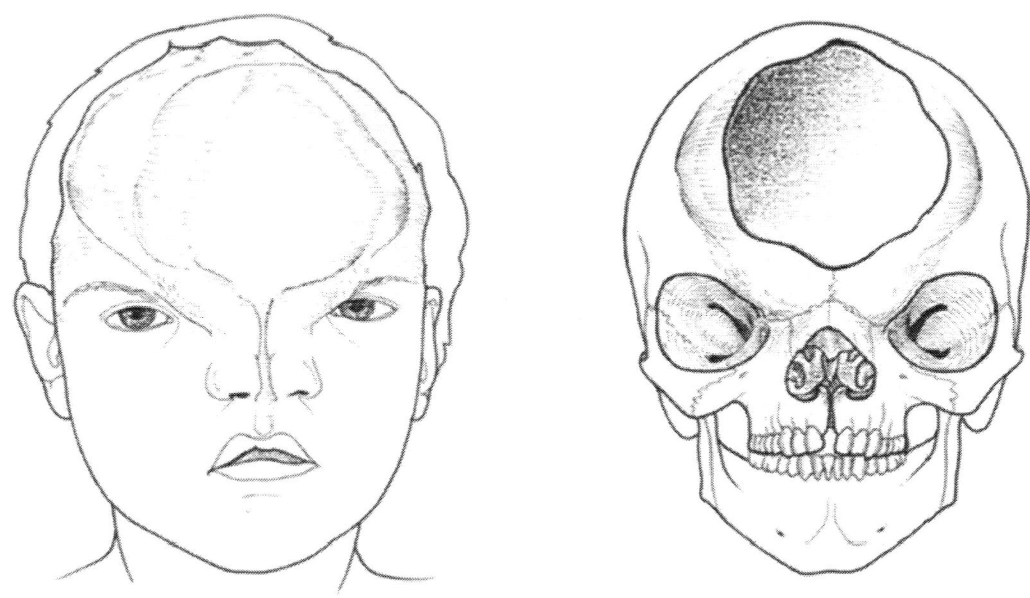

*Fig. 24.35 Frontoethmoida encephalocoele and pachydermatocoele*

*Fig. 24.36 Frontoethmoidal encephalocoele*

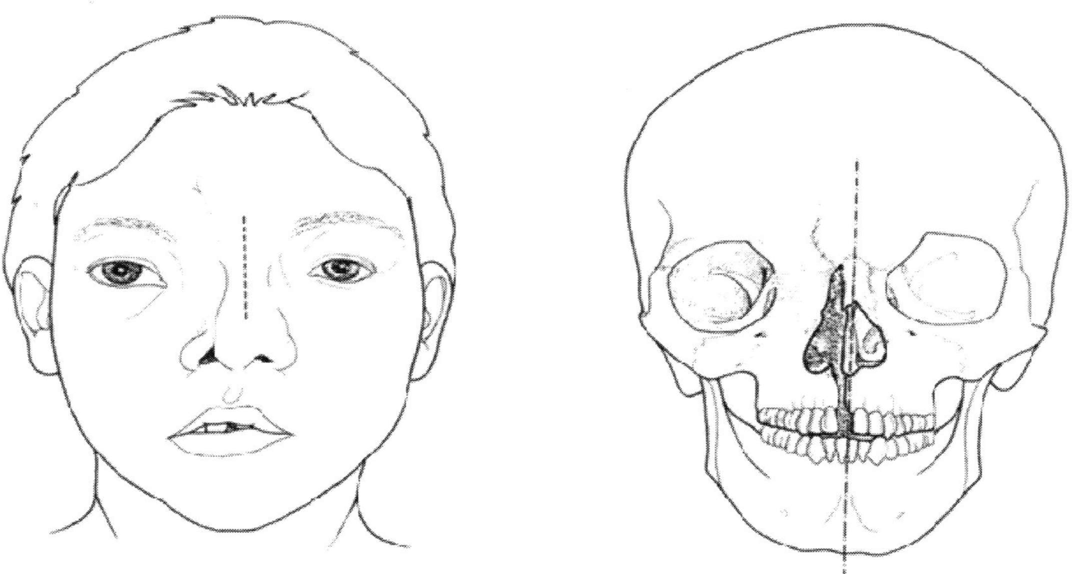

*Fig. 24.37 Hyperpneumatization of the frontal sinuses*

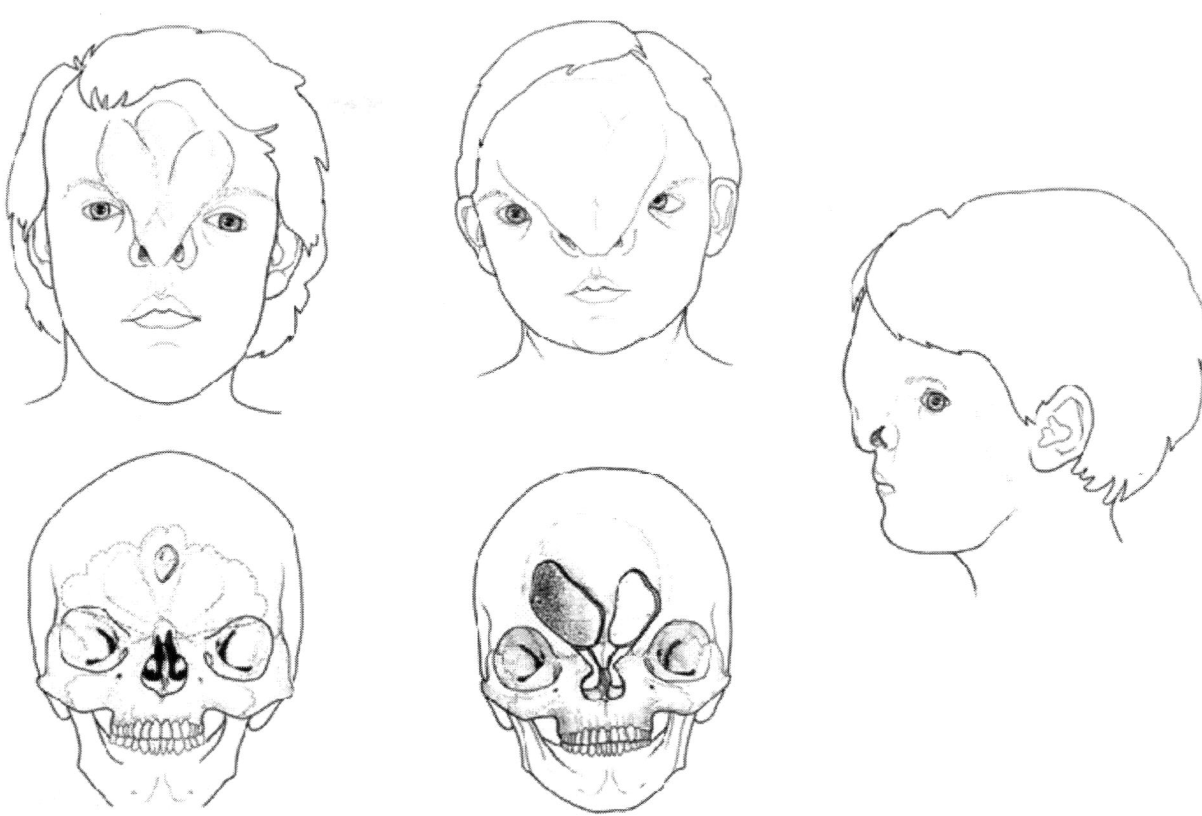

*Fig. 24.38 Orbital hypertelorism*

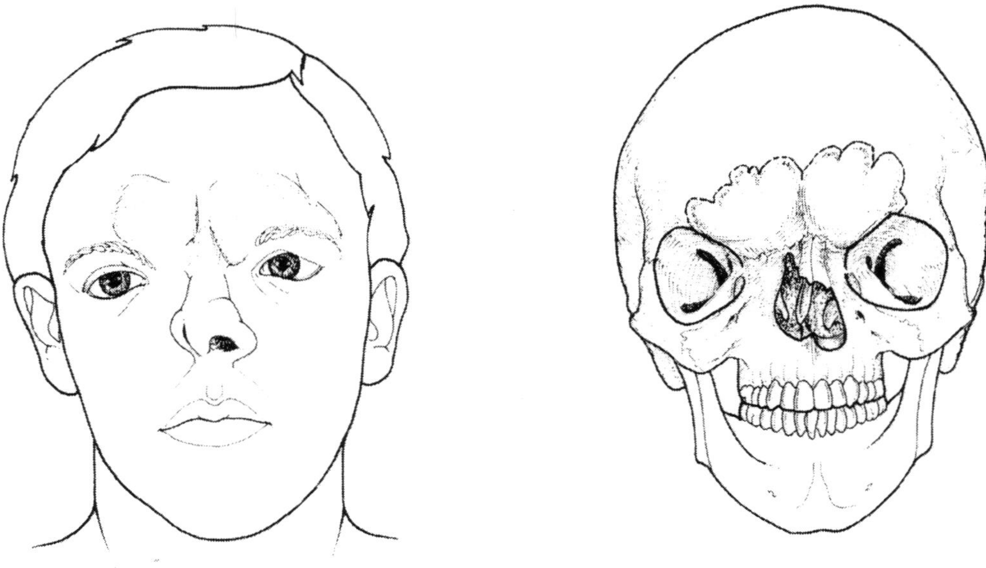

*Fig. 24.39 Frontonasal dysplasia*

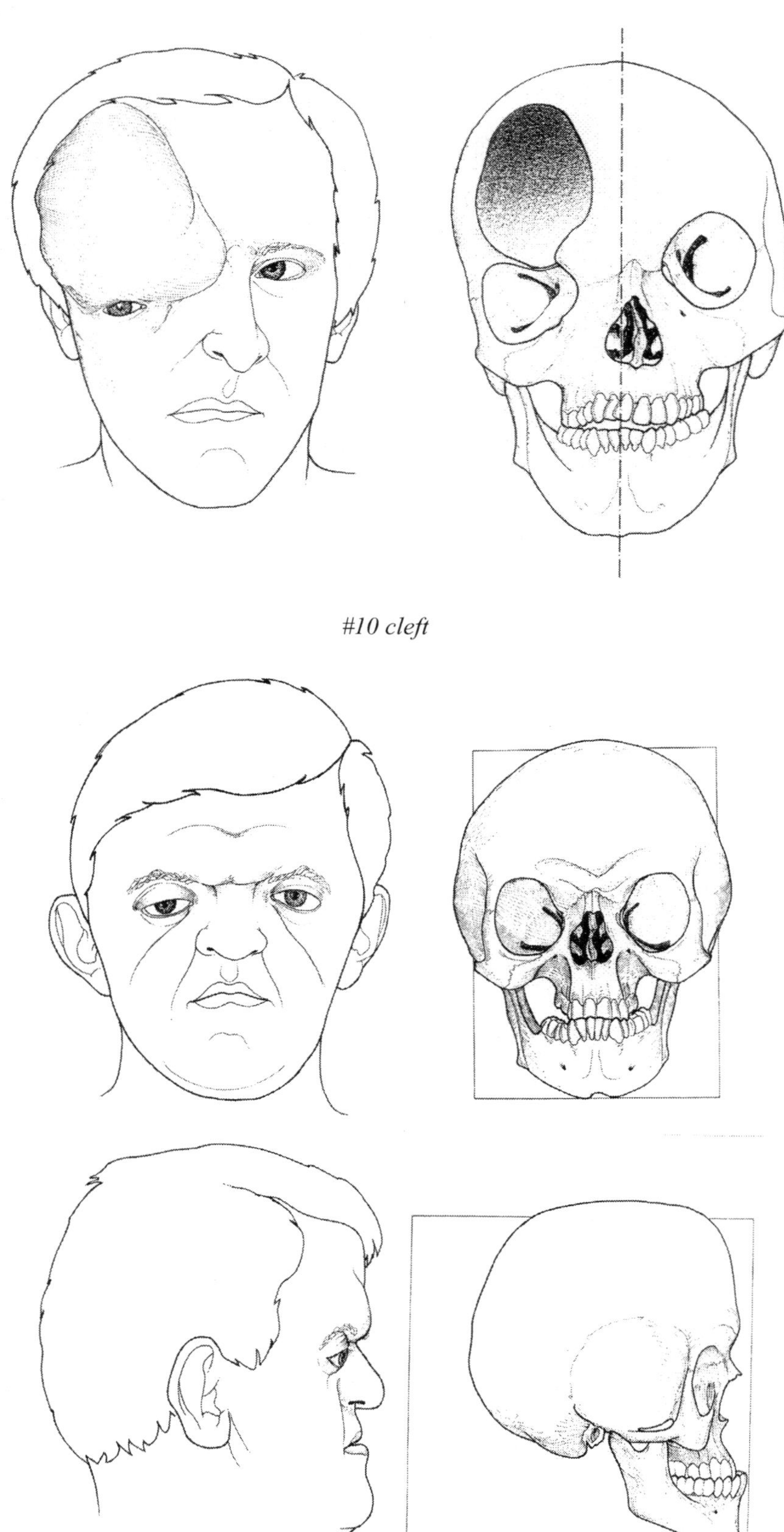

*#10 cleft*

*Apert's Syndrome*

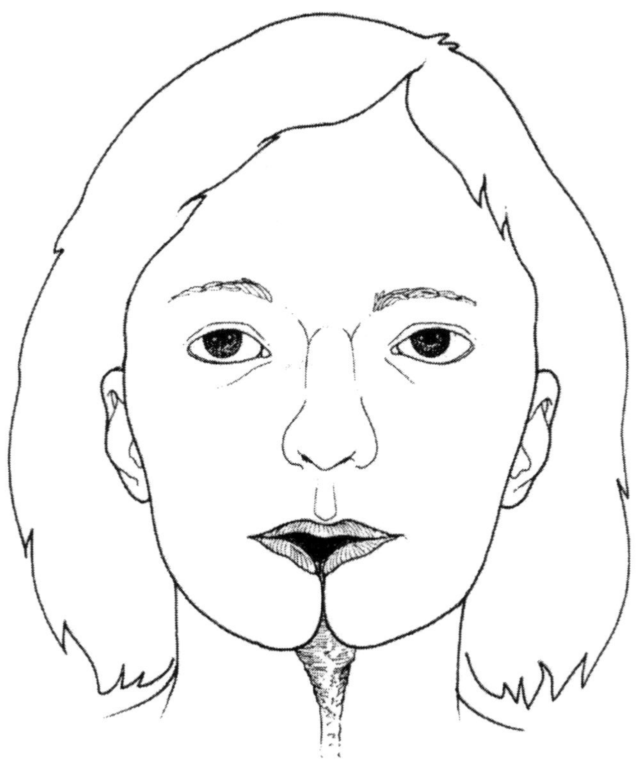

*Fig. 24.40 #30 cleft*

Dr. Tessier's skull collection is now housed at Amiens and will be part of the future Centre De La Face, at project of Dr. Bernard Devauchelle.

# Chapter 25

## Maltreatment in the United States and elsewhere, and final years of work in the United States in Charlotte

Paul Tessier's experiences in the United States had been mixed. Overwhelmingly, his relationship with the United States had been positive. Besides providing validation in the "big time," he was regarded with awe and admiration by most of the medical community. And parents of patients who sought him out were extremely grateful to be able to receive treatment from the acknowledged world authority.

And, in return, Dr. Tessier made many close friends in America. Fred McCoy of Kansas City and Reed Dingman of Michigan, both hunters, are two of the best examples.

However, there are several exceptions to this overall warm relationship that merit mention—not to "settle the score"; but, rather, to acknowledge that all was not roses.

1. As mentioned, Dr. Tessier did not return to Chicago after having operated there for several years when he learned that his cases had been turned over by Jack Curtin (a cosmetic surgeon who ran the teaching program at the University of Illinois), to his residents, who had little if any idea what they were doing. In many instances, Tessier's carefully thought out reconstructive plans were rendered impossible to complete.

2. In a Southeastern city where he went to speak at a meeting on orbital surgery in the mid-70s, he took several movies that he had made (depicting temporo-mandibular joint ankylosis and lacrimal reconstruction) to be shown. When he got back to Paris, he found that he had been copies of his own movies. Without being asked, they were copied—and he wasn't even given back the originals. The surgeon who seemed to be responsible for this breach made an effort at atonement by sending Dr. Tessier a present. This was a skull specimen of a patient with plagiocephaly (a deformity caused by premature closure of the coronal suture). Dr. Tessier felt the specimen was superb, and this was certainly the best gift that could have been offered him. Unfortunately, he took the skull to Foch the next day, and it was stolen from his locker.

3. He went to a northeastern city several times to operate in the early 1970s. He told me that one day he did two Le Fort 3 osteotomies on patients who had had posterior pharyngeal flaps (where a part of the pharynx is sewn to the back of the soft palate to improve hypernasal speech). He detached the flaps then reattached them after the maxillary advancement, something that he had done before.

   Around 1976, Millard, my senior associate, showed me a paper that had been sent to him to review for *Plastic and Reconstructive Surgery.* It was from the northeastern city and described two patients who had Le Fort 3 advancements who had pharyngeal flaps. Nowhere on the paper was Tessier's name mentioned. This seemed strange to me. I sent a copy of the paper to him, and he responded that these were indeed his cases. Nevertheless, he asked me not to say a thing, to let the paper be published. This happened, and he then demanded a written apology from Frank McDowell, the Editor of *Plastic and Reconstructive Surgery* at the time. The apology was finally published in very fine print at the back of the journal. Relations were cool between Paul Tessier and the senior author of the paper for quite some time.

4. In a southern city, a surgeon finishing his residency once called me and asked if I could put in a word for him with Dr. Tessier since he wanted to spend time with him in Paris. I did so, and he

spent six months there before returning to his teaching institution to join the staff. For five or six years , Dr. Tessier was invited to operate at this center, and he did so for two to three weeks at a time. Operating every day, with two or three major craniofacial cases per day, amounted to a lot of work. Typically, Dr. Tessier never asked about reimbursement—he was a gentleman and expected that he would be treated like one. The finances were left up to the institution that invited him. The staff of the plastic surgery service in the southern city was having an internecine battle that involved two factions. The chief, who was head of one faction, went to Tessier and told him that he should take a look at the monies collected for the cases he had done, and how much of it went to him. This distribution was being handled by his former fellow, who was in the other camp. It turned out that, for one period of time, close to a million dollars was collected, of which he was given about 100,000.

I got a call from Dr. Tessier in the early 80s on a Friday afternoon, asking me whether I had any plans for the following Monday. "No sir, what would you like me to do?" I replied. He asked that I meet him in the southern city, for he was mad enough about this situation to consider filing a lawsuit and was meeting with a lawyer. He felt it would be helpful to have me there.

It turned out that the former fellow was refusing to turn over the charts on the patients that Tessier had operated on, saying that this was "proprietary information (i.e., his), even though the patients had come from all parts of the United States to be operated on by Tessier.

I understand a final settlement was reached without going to court.

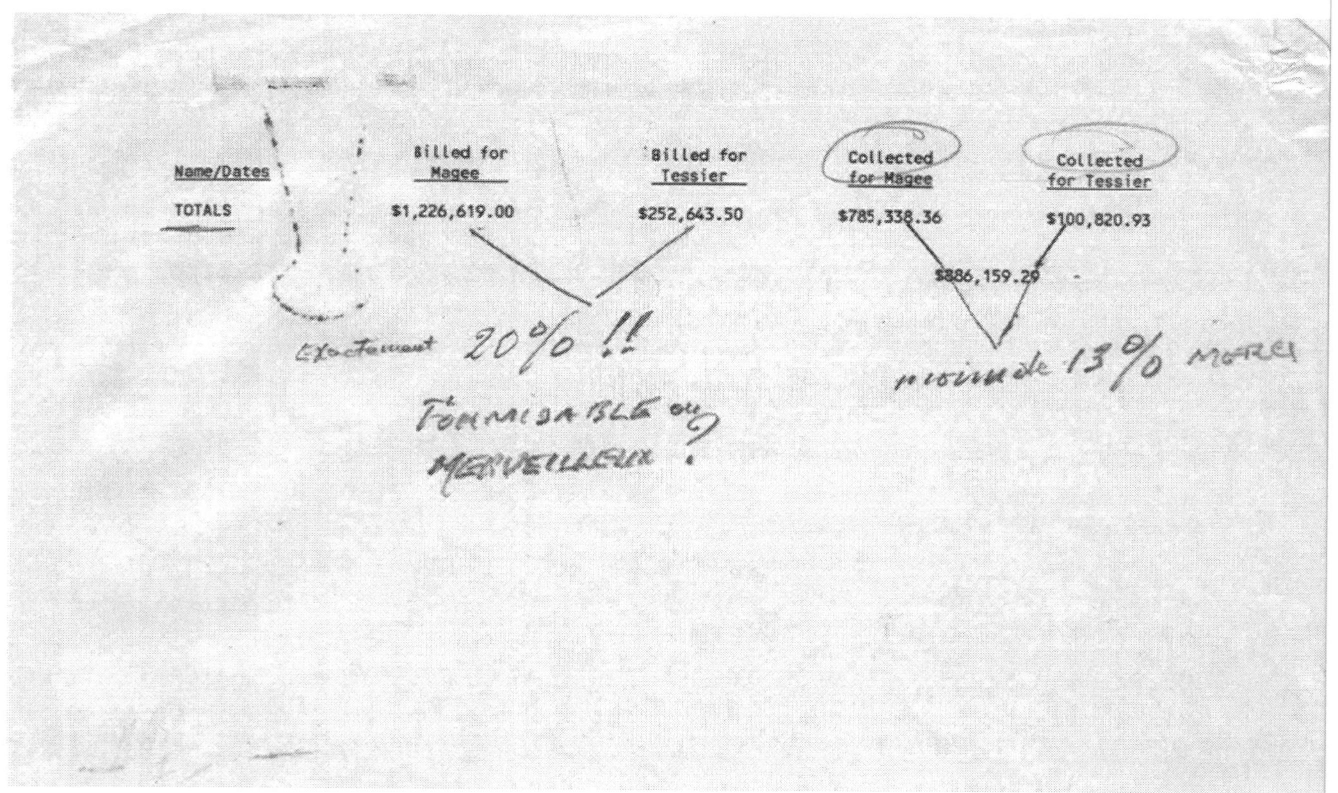

| Name/Dates | Billed for Magee | Billed for Tessier | Collected for Magee | Collected for Tessier |
|---|---|---|---|---|
| TOTALS | $1,226,619.00 | $252,643.50 | $785,338.36 | $100,820.93 |

$886,159.29

Exactement 20% !!

Formidable ou Merveilleux ?

moins de 13% Merci

*Fig. 25.1 Tessier's comments on the documents he received for the surgery he performed. He received 13 percent of the surgical fees that had been collected, and his local host received the rest. His note says "Exactly 20%!! Formidable or marvelous?" and "Less than 13%. Merci."*

The good that came out of the trips to the southern city was that David Matthews came to watch, and he got to know Tessier this way. David went to Paris for many short visits and became one of his favorites. Dr. Tessier developed so much confidence in David's surgical abilities that he made him part of one of the teams that were staffing the reconstructive enterprise in Iran—he was the only American to be included. For the last few operative years in the United States, David hosted Dr. Tessier in Charlotte, NC, and Henry Kawamoto and I went a number of times to see him operate in Charlotte.

**The Superficial Fascia of the Face.**

During my year in Paris, I attended the meeting of the French Society of Plastic and Reconstructive Surgery; Dr. Tessier was the president that year. I recall specifically asking Roger Mouly, the secretary, whether I could register at the resident rate since I was with Dr. Tessier. My request was denied, so I went ahead and paid full tariff and enjoyed the meeting. I kept the program, the front page, and an abstract of the topics presented.

The abstract reads:

"3. The Superficial Musculo-Aponeurotic System of the Face and Its Surgical Applications

F. Firmin, J. Le Pesteur, V. Mitz, W. Pepersack, M. Peyronie, H. Quilichini, Ch. Raybaud, P. Tessier, and A. Thion

[Note that with typical modesty, Tessier, whose idea the whole was, and who thought of the term S.M.A.S., placed himself as the next to last author]

The authors studied the particularities of the superficial facial fibro-aponeurotic structures using dissections, macro and micro sections, vascular studies and ultra fine radiographs.

This superficial musculo-aponeurotic system was studied on:

- The nose, where it extends above the periosteum and the perichondrium,
- The labial commissure,
- The forehead and the eyelids, the temporo-zygomatic area where it is the prolongation of the galea,
- The cheek, up to the ear, where it constitutes a fascia independent of the parotid fascia,
- The neck, and the submandibular area

And finally, over the frontier areas, in particular, the zygomatic arch.

The fascia receives the expansions of the muscles called "skin muscles" [platysma], between which it is an intermediate, and which it shares the action in an integrated fashion towards the deep surface of the dermis. There is therefore no completely isolated function of a mimetic muscle, but a nuanced result of the tension of the skin muscles.

The surgical importance of this superficial musculo-aponeurotic system is emphasized, as well as new uses which can be anticipated, in particular in rhinoplasty, face lifts, and major cranio-facial malformations."

The following exchange of letters occurred in *Annales de Chirurgie Plastique,* Vol. 26, No. 2, 1981, pp. 191-92:

The SMAS, Its "Little History"

By P. TESSIER Chief of the Service of Plastic Surgery and Burns

Centre Medico-Chirurgical Foch

40, rue Worth, 92151 Suresnes

The first publication concerning the SMA and using this appellation "SMAS" was done, under the names of V. Mitz and M. Peyronie, in PRS, July 1976, Vol. 58, No.1, pp. 80 to 88. But the study of the SMAS, was it done by them alone, and by their independent investigation? One could believe this according to other articles published on the same subject, using the same term; SMAS, and referring to this first publication and to its authors.

Let us go over therefore the "history" of this musculoaponeurotic system and of its name: SMAS.

During the preparation for, and during sessions of craniofacial surgery performed at Hôpital Foch in 1969 to 1972, we encountered a sub-cutaneous structure along the entire length of the incisions: coronal, temporal, infra-orbital, medio-nasal, mandibular angle. It seemed to me that this anatomic structure had until then been described in a fashion which was too fragmentary: both for the neck, in the parotid area, and the forehead. That is why, in 1973, I proposed a group study, in which the connections, which seemed to me to be evident, would be looked for between the different parts of what seemed to me to be a "system."

In February, 1974, I therefore assigned to several of my previous interns, familiar with the aspects of this surgery, the study of the different parts of the "system." This study was done by dissections, histologic slides and on horizontal macrosections. The tasks were divided up in the following fashion:

- Françoise Firmin and Jacques Le Pesteur: the nose and the perinasal areas
- Vladimir Mitz: the genioparotid zone
- Martine Peyronnie: the tempero-zygomatic zone
- Walter Pepersack: the lips and the commissures
- Hervé Quilichini: the orbits and the forehead
- André Thion: the neck
- Charles Raybaud, radiologist from Marseille, was in charge of the radiography of the sections.

I personally chose the term "SMAS," so that it could be used:

- either in French: Système Musculo-Aponeurotique Superficiel: SMAS
- or in English: Superficial Musculo-Aponevrotic System: SMAS

On 18 October 1974, at the Congress of the French Society of Plastic and Reconstructive Surgery, all of the authors of this work gave their presentations under the rubric "Return to the Sources." I kept for myself the showing of the methods of work developed in common, then, as a conclusion, gave certain surgical applications which I had already made of the SMAS.

The common work of my group should have been followed by a common publication accompanied with drawings in color, which was not done.

It is regrettable that, without asking for an agreement on separate publication and without having made a preliminary reference to all of their colleagues, that two of the authors of this common study took it upon themselves to appropriate the ticket, and in this fashion, the entire work.

I would have never thought of a exposition of this sort, four years after the publication in cause, if an initiative of Ralph Millard [3] had not reminded me that the case is not unique, and risks repeating itself. Four years after the inadmissible forgeries of L. Whitaker [8] (Philadelphia) in 1976, on the pharyngeal flap at the time of maxillary advancement, and his crude "excuses," I have still never tried to put the facts in a publication when called for. Colleagues such as Ralph Millard, rather revolted by the procedure, took it with humor. Thanks for having refreshed my memory.

References

1. Balch, Cl. Superficial musculo aponeurotic system suspension and buccinators placation for facial nerve paralysis. PRS, 1980, 6. No. 5, 680-683.
2. Mitz, V. Peyronnie, M. The superficial musculoaponeurotic system (SMAS) in the parotid and cheek area. PRS, 1976, 58, No. 1
3. Millard, R. Cleft Craft, vol. iii, p. 702
4. Owlsley, J. Q. Platysma fascial rhytidectomy. PRS, 60, No. 6 843-850
5. Reese, Th, Aston, S. A clinical evaluation of the results of sub-musculo-aponeurotic dissection and fixation in face lifts. PRS, 1977, 60, No. 6, 853-859

6. Reese, Th. Aesthetic Plastic Surgery. Chap. 23, pp. 634-683

7. Ruberg, R., Randall, P. Whitaker, L. Preservation of a posterior pharyngeal flap during maxillary advancement. PRS. 1976, 57, No. 3, 335-337.

8. Whitaker, L. An apology to doctor Tessier. PRS, 1976, 58, No. 3, 366.

---

## The True History of the SMAS

Response to Dr. Tessier

By V. Mitz

Service of Orthopedic and Repairative Surgery

Hôpital Boucicaut

78, rue de la Convention, 75730 Paris, Cedex 15

Paul Tessier is a giant in plastic surgery who sometimes goes ahead a little too fast.

I would like to recall that the title of the publication under discussion is "the SMAS in the genioparotid area," the objective of a work that Tessier assigned to me, as he confirms in his letter to the editor.

While Tessier had his intuitions, I published, as far back as 1972, with Lassau and Delecourt, work on the vascular anatomy of the genioparotid area. This article is cited in the bibliography of my article in PRS as number 10. I published with Ricbourg and Lassau, in 1973, articles on facial vascularization in the *Annales de Chirurgie Plastique;* these works were publicly shown at the Society of Plastic Surgery. These works, involving innumerable hemifacial dissections, led me to find what I called the fibrous skeleton of the face (SFIF= squelette fibreux de la face) ; I proposed, having become a young intern, much in admiration of Tessier, this work to my Chief. He magnificently extended it to an entire team for the year of "Return to the Sources," over which he presided. This monumental work was supervised by him, but I was the coordinator and the responsible one.

It was thus that the SFIF became the SMAS on the proposal of Tessier. The entire team was cited at the end of the article that we wrote with M. Peyronie: I solemnly affirm that I wrote Dr. Tessier before publishing this article to ask him, who would have been natural, to be a coauthor. He responded that a partial work did not interest him; he was planning on a group article. But Skoog and Couly worked on the same observations. I is important to take a date. I therefore published with my own documents. Tessier is designated at the end of the article as the Mentor of the work.

Three precise questions pose themselves as it happened:

1) To whom belongs the SMAS?

If Tessier had read the article, he would have seen that it was an Anglo-Saxon, Gray, who was the first to have described vaguely this formation. And I cited Gray at the beginning of the article.

2) Is the term SMAS what matters?

It is his, Tessier claims. I hold to the anatomical facts that I have discovered. The Americans are not fooled. The product is more important that the name one gives it. I am happy that the term SMAS has pleased them. But four years later, it is the work that I did which, finally, changed a bit our conceptions of the superficial facial anatomy—notably in making an entire system of the platysma—preparotid fascia and the frontal muscle.

3) To whom does a scientific work belong? To he who thought of it, or he who did the work?

I believe deeply that the time is over when the Chief, the authority, is the first author. A work should be accorded to he who did the work, in all honesty, responsibility and truth. I have always associated my chiefs with the work that they helped me carry out.

**The American Response**

By Linton A. Whitaker

Hospital of the University of Pennsylvania

4th floor, Silverstein Pavillion

3400 Spruce Street, Philadelphia, Pa. 19104

Thank you so much for sending me the letter to the editor as written by Dr. Tessier.

Dr. Tessier's contributions are monumental and none of involved in the article he cited in *Plastic and Reconstructive Surgery,* 57: 335, March 1976 wished consciously to detract from him in any way. The authors do, however, believe the facts are as recorded in the "apology" in *Plastic and Reconstructive Surgery,* 58,366, September, 1976. I am enclosing a copy of the article that explains the situation. In addition to the suggestion having originally been Dr. Randall's, he was actively participating in both operations, the patients were mine and Dr. Randall's and the surgery was done in Philadelphia.

The surgical procedure in question is one that has extremely rare application. It is unfortunate that a surgical event and misunderstanding which occurred seven years ago has resurfaced in this fashion.

---

These instances are both good case studies of medical ethics.Mitz and Peyronie I know well. He lived in my house in Miami when I was in France, and I stayed in his apartment in Paris. Martine was the other assistant to Dr. Tessier when I was there, and she was at his funeral. In 1974-75, I was present several times when the "Group d'Etudes" of which Tessier was the Mentor met. The whole thing was without doubt his idea, and under his direction.

Clearly Mitz should have just waited until everyone else had finished their part of the study, and sent his part in with the others. Ambition led him to jump the gun. And when I was reading *Paris Match* one time on a trans-Atlantic flight, there was an interview with Mitz, and he described himself as "The Inventor of the SMAS." I shook my head. Not so.

I had some involvement with what Henry Kawamoto once referred to as "The Philadelphia Flap."

In 1975, after I had returned to Miami and went into practice with Ralph Millard, he asked me to look at a paper he had been sent by PRS to review, saying that it was more up my alley. The paper described two patients in Philadelphia who--- the same day--- had undergone Le Fort 3 osteotomies, and had their pharyngeal flaps detached and reattached. Dr. Tessier had told me once that he had done two Le Fort 3's in Philadelphia on the same day, and that he took down and reattached the pharyngeal flaps. I didn't see any mention of him in the paper, so, after discussing this with Millard, sent the paper to Tessier for his comments. He sent it back with instructions to do absolutely nothing, and the rest of the story is given above. I recently ran across a comment in a book on memory (Martha Weinman Lear, *Where Did I Leave My Glasses*?) the following: "If you make use of somebody else's mental property and claim it as your own because you truly fail to remember that it is *not* your own, that is cryptomnesia."

Tessier did these two operations, and did something that he had done before: detached and reattached a pharyngeal flap. Certainly he discussed this with Peter Randall, since after all they were his patients.

Was this a case of group cryptomnesia? Perhaps. But one gets the feeling from Dr. Whitaker's letter that he felt that their actions--- clearly lacking in ethics--- were justifiable. Witness his putting quotation marks around the "apology," which makes it sound as if it were really not one. Relations between Paul Tessier and Linton Whitaker remained icy for quite some time after this episode.

"Paul"

---

Maher Anous, a naturalized American citizen of Egyptian background who speaks good French, spent a number of months with Dr. Tessier in the mid-80's. He then wrote an account of his time in Paris that he was considering publishing, which he entitled "Paul." He sent a copy of the manuscript to Dr. Tessier for his inspection. Since the account focused on Dr. Tessier's "anger" in the operating room, and engaged in some amateur psychoanalytic exploration of the reasons behind this, Dr. Tessier was not amused. He was a private person, and felt that this was presumptious on the part of someone who had spent relatively limited time with him. Dr. Tessier wrote Anous back, saying that perhaps he should send a copy to me and Henry Kawamoto for our comments. Anous did, and my letter to him, with Tessier's comment on my letter, are shown below.

Recently Anous went ahead and published his book, sending a copy to Mireille, Henry and myself. Mireille was not at all happy with it the book either, particularly since it had been dedicated to her children, another invasion of privacy.

My dear Tony,

I thank you for your letter of 17 May and for your response to Dr. ANOUS. It is perfectly pertinent; one could not do better. You know how to write, as you knew how to present in Beiriut: This is exactly what I expected from you.

I would very much like to see the response of Henry, if there was one, and if---as is habitual for him--- he did not let it go beyond the "deadline." But in this case, there is no deadline, except for this manuscript completely off target.

We will have dinner Sunday with Morax at Françoise's.

All the best,
Tessier

Dear Dr. Anous,

Thank you for the copy of your book, which you have obviously put time and your own money into.

It was considerate of you not to publish this while PLT was alive. As you properly documented, he dissociated himself from it.

But by the same token, it was inconsiderate to publish it as far as Mireille is concerned, and inappropriate to dedicate it to Laurence and Jean-Paul.

There is a lot in the book that is correct. There is a good bit that is correct, but incomplete. And there is quite a bit which is simply incorrect.

Start with the last.

Dr. Tessier died on June 5th, not June 6th. This is an understandable error, since many of the obituaries had it wrong.

He really didn't die from the Parkinson's, which was under very good medical control.

His great-grandfather, not his grandfather, was a blacksmith. His grandfather was a wine merchant.

He was never in a hospital in German territory; he was in a German military hospital in Nantes.

André Collesson is spelled with two "l's".

Tessier came up with the acronym "S.M.A.S," not Vladimir Mitz.

Marchac got sent to North Africa by Dufourmentel after his first case in Paris died.

The statement that he said he didn't know what to do when a pharyngeal flap tethered a maxilla does not ring true; as you know, he divided pharyngeal flaps twice in Philadelphia during the course of Le Fort III's, and found to his surprise that Linton Whitaker wrote up the operations without mentioning him-----in the early 1970's.

He certainly was not jealous of Ralph Millard. They had a cordial friendship, and when Tessier did a cleft lip, which sometimes occurred in No. 3 or 4 clefts, he called it a "Millard repair," not a Veau.

Consultations were at Avenue Kléber, not Avenue Foch.

The three cases of "mordures passionelles" involved French women, with Italian lovers.

I don't find you in the membership roster of ISFCS.

There are other errata, but nothing I would consider serious.

In the second category, for example, Idir was indeed married to a German woman. You didn't mention that they had met when she came to Paris for Dr. Tessier to operate on her Apert daughter.

Bill McGee was *persona non grata,* but you didn't mention why.

In the first category, it was good of you to report on your nightly conversations with Dr. Tessier when he was kind enough to drive you partway home. Certainly speaking French made it possible to have a conversation *un peu plus nuancé.* However, I must say that when you were there, his English was pretty good, and he was certainly able to get along well with Fernando, Henry K., and David Matthews, none of whom had much French.

Here's my problem with your book, and I believe I said essentially the same in my letter to you which you have in the book.

A lot of your statements were downright hostile.

I think this focus on moments of foul temper (have you ever been in the kitchen of a master chef) simply detracts from your book, and in my opinion, diminishes you. Sure, Dr. Tessier did get frustrated at times. I do too. Bending a defective instrument is done simply so that it will not appear in your instrument tray again.

You did capture certain other aspects of his personality nicely, but anyone who knew Dr. Tessier well is going to be annoyed by your critical remarks. You were essentially a guest in his house, and you behaved badly. It reminds me a bit of the jihadist Major in the Army who started shooting his fellow soldiers. Definitely in bad taste.

I would say I got to know Dr. Tessier a good bit better than you did, from 1971 and visiting him at least every year until the year of his death, and I would say my French is probably about as good as yours. Yes, I am an American, but the only Americans he didn't like were the ones who screwed him. The speech I gave at his reception of the Legion d'Honneur, I talked about Rochambeau, Lafayette and the French fleet, and 300 dead French soldiers at Yorktown, and said that we Americans owe our very existence to the French. And we returned the favor in the course of two World Wars.

I remember him as a kind man, a generous man, and as a wonderful teacher. He became my role model in life, and I took great pleasure in simply being with him. He was much more of a father to me than my own biological one.

He really did want to pass on to us what he had learned about craniofacial surgery. Yes, he had a strong personality, but he was not nearly as hard on the others around him as he was on himself. Let us excuse and understand the occasional tirade.

I think you were right in stating that his roots in Bretagne influenced his character. He loved his part of France, and one of the most enjoyable events in my life was when he drove Henry and I and our wives to the places that he liked best.

Simply put, I think your book would have been a better memoir if you had pressed the delete button for much of your criticism of your teacher.

You missed the point----which was that he gave us the opportunity to become craniofacial surgeons. Some of us did, some didn't.

I will mention your book in mine.

Yours truly,

S. Anthony Wolfe, M.D.

Chief, Division of Plastric Surgery

Miami Children's Hospital

# Chapter 26

## The Artists. Francine Gourdin and Merri Sheifflin.

In the mid 1960s, Tessier was on the search for a good medical illustrator. He had already mastered medical photography, and for his weekly clinics at Hôpital Foch he would arrive with a Nikon F (for 35 mm slides) and a Hasselblad (for 120 mm format prints) and a number of flash units (to provide back lighting).

He placed an ad for a medical artist in the help wanted section of a Paris paper. Francine Gourdin at the time was in her early twenties, and she was working as a jewelry designer for Cartier. She had had no experience with medical illustration whatsoever. Tessier told her to come to the operating room the next day so that he could give her a try for a few weeks. He said that he immediately recognized that she had a unique talent: she could support her artists pad with her left hand and forearm, look at the operative field, and do her sketch without once taking her eyes off of the field. Over the years she did thousands of drawings for him. Explaining to her how the drawing should be done and what it should show forced him to better understand what he had done—better than the words of an operative note.

For his presentation in Rome in 1967, he wanted the drawings of his new operations to be perfect in terms of their anatomic details and depiction of what he had done surgically. He went with Francine to the south of France (Nice, I believe), along with his patient photographs and x-rays, and they holed up in a hotel for a week. He felt that if he had stayed in Paris, the distractions of his practice would not allow dawn to dusk work.

Francine's husband is a nuclear physicist, working at CERN, the European Supercollider Facility, which is located in both France and Switzerland, straddling the border.

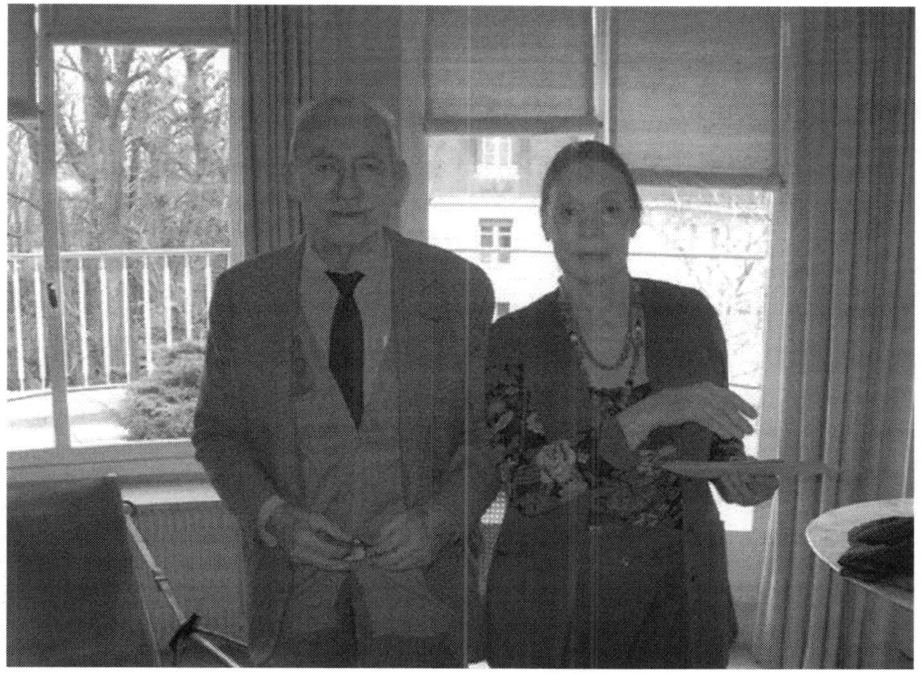

*Fig. 26.1 Paul Tessier and Francine Gourdin, on a visit to her apartment in Saint Germain, 2006.*

In the 1970s Francine left Tessier's employ, feeling that she wanted to do other things with her artistic abilities. He then met Merri Sheifflin on one of his trips to Chicago. He invited Merri to Paris for a trial and, after she passed, Merri started working for him and moved to Paris to do so full time. She married a Frenchman and has been there ever since. Notably, she recently hosted a reception for those who had been at the memorial Mass at Val de Grace on June 6, 2009 in her home/studio on Ave St Jacques, down the street from the Val de Grace Hospital and Chapel.

At a meeting in San Francisco in the early 1980s, I had breakfast with Dr. Tessier in a coffee shop across the street from our hotel (the cost of the breakfast being about one tenth that of the hotel). I knew that he had been placing onlay cranial bone grafts over the malar area as part of his "mask lift," but recently had changed to a malar osteotomy, which he said he preferred. He drew the procedure for me on a paper napkin, and when he got back to Paris, sent me these pictures by Merri Sheifflin. They have never been published, like much of his work.

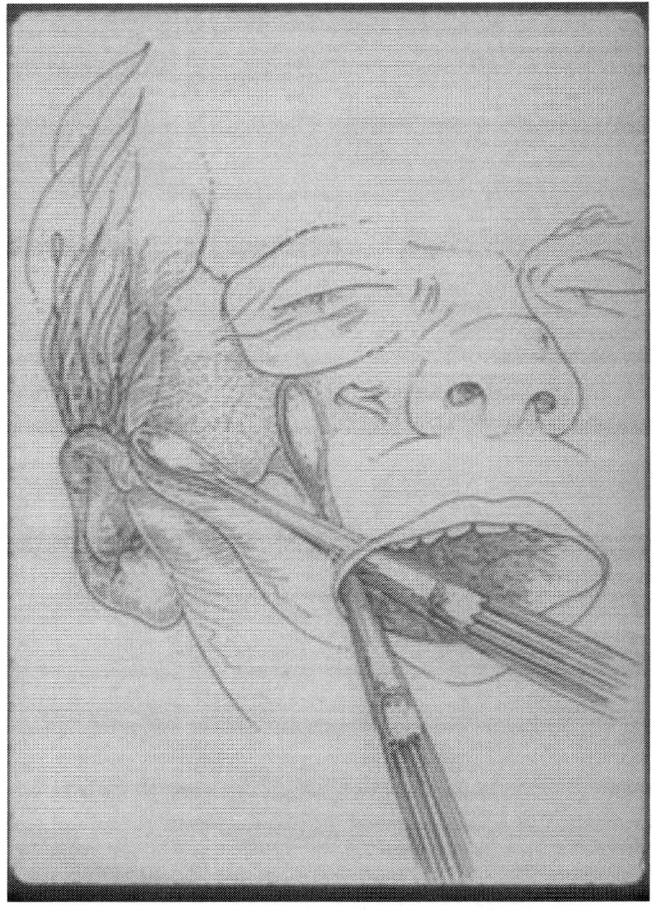

*Fig. 26.2 Dissection of the malar bone through an oral approach.*

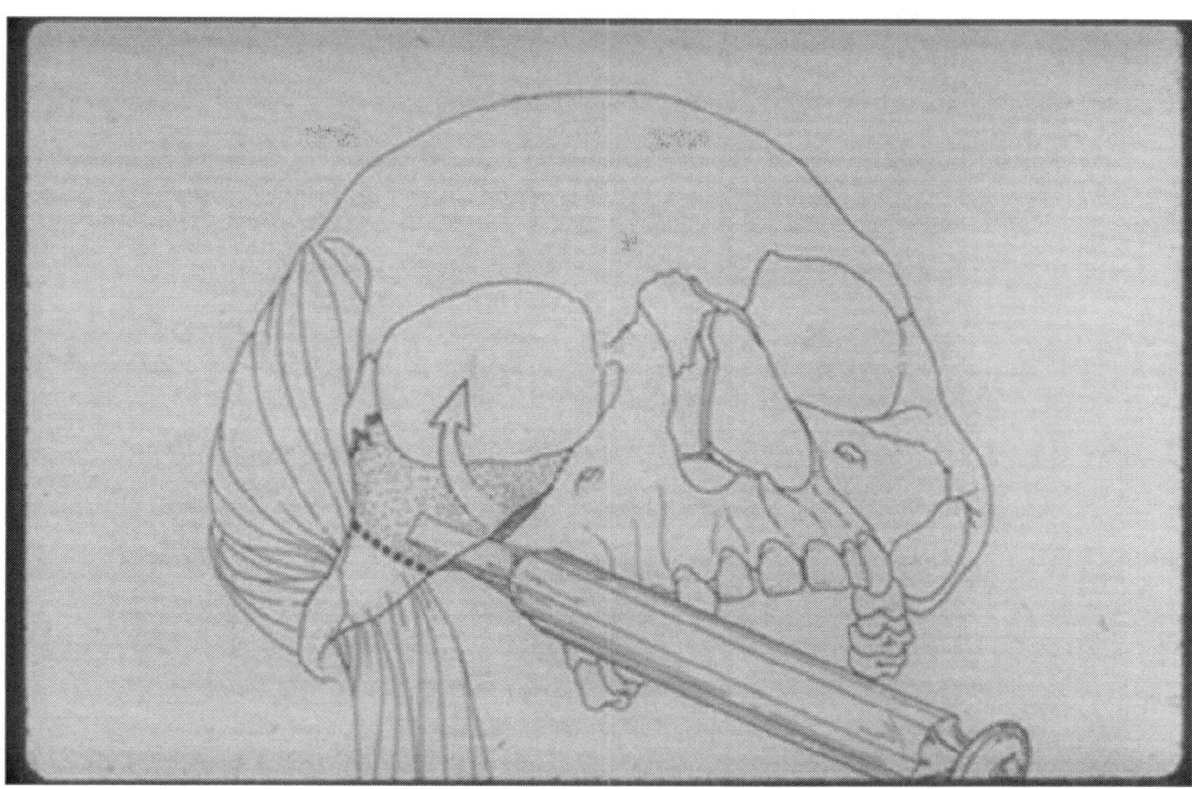

*Fig. 26.4 Tessier osteotome luxing the malar bone forward, after an oblique osteotomy near its attachment to the arch.*

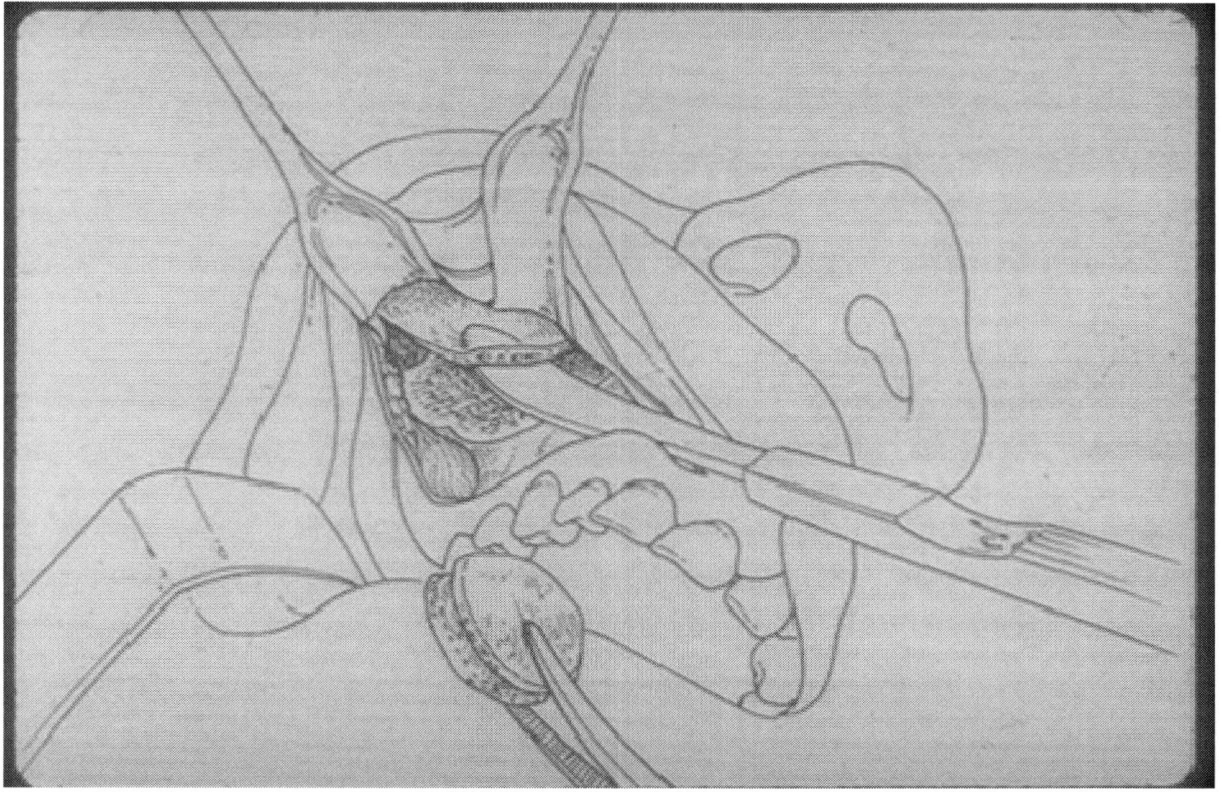

*Fig. 26.5 Elevation of the anterior portion of the malar bone and placement of an interpositional bone graft.*

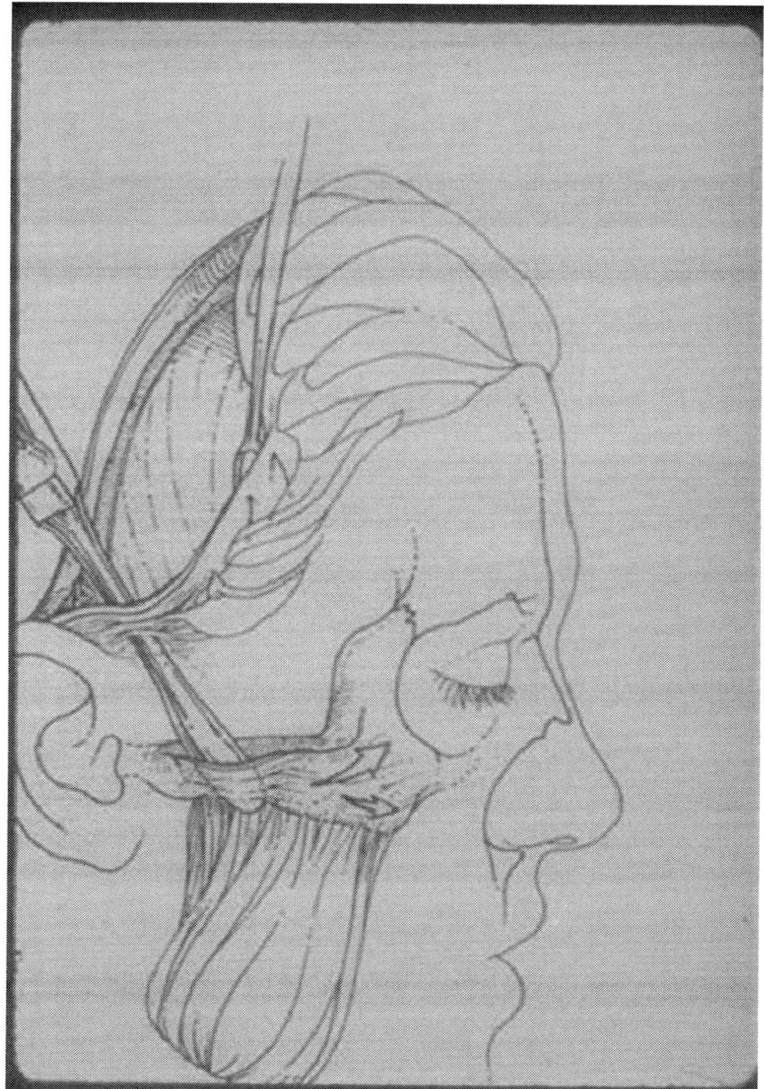

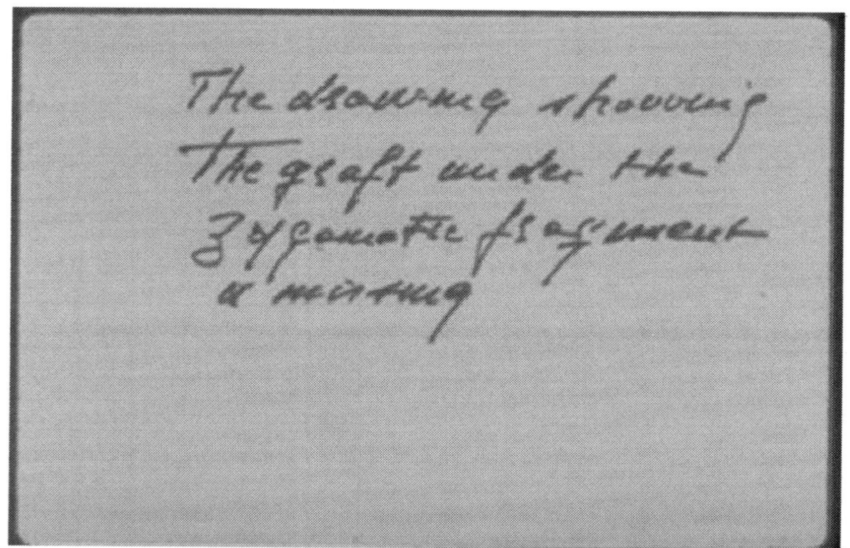


*Fig. 26.6 Midface elevation and suture, with Tessier's comments.*

*Fig. 26.7 Merri Scheitlin (Nordman), Paris, 2009.*

*Fig. 26.8 Laurence Tessier with Mme. Foste and Mme. Pelegrin, Dr. Tessier's secretaries (in Merri Sheifflin's studio, Paris, 2009). Cesar Raposo do Amaral is in the background.*

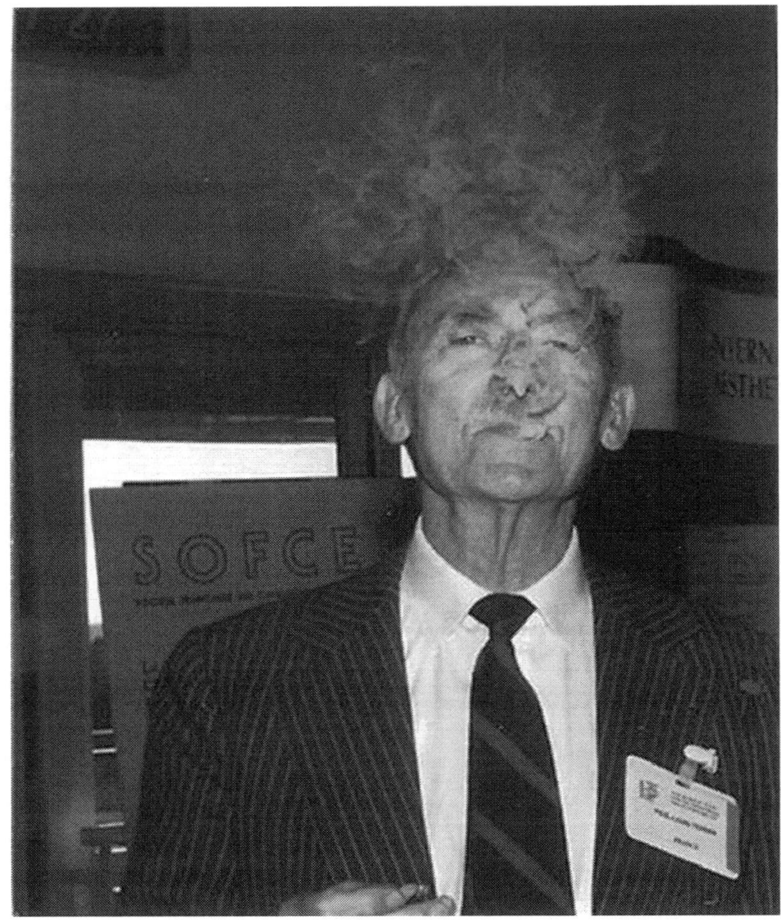


*Fig. 26.9 Photo by Merri Scheitlin of Paul Tessier in a cloud of cigar smoke, ca. 1998.*

*Fig. 26.10 Fernando Ortiz-Monasterio, SAW, Yvon Raulo, Jean-Francois Tulasne, and Tessier, Paris, ca. 1998.*

*Fig. 26.11 Drawing of Tessier by Merri Sheifflin.*

*Fig. 26.12 Merri Scheitlin with Jean-Paul Tessier and Laurence Tessier, La Baule, ca. 1979.*

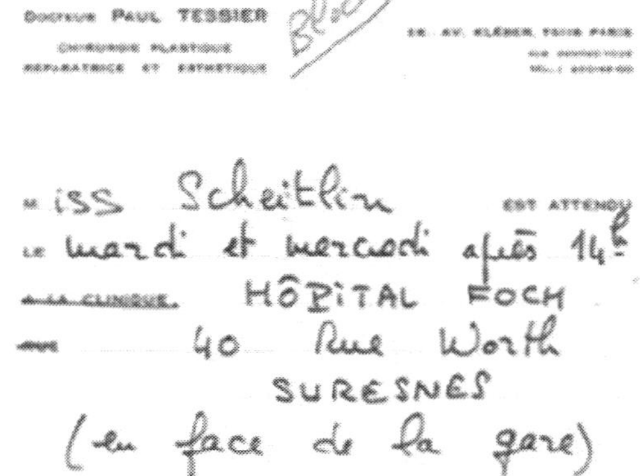
Docteur Paul Tessier
Chirurgie plastique
réparatrice et esthétique
Blanc
26, av. Kléber, 75116 Paris

Miss Scheitlin est attendu
le mardi et mercredi après 14h
à la clinique. HÔPITAL FOCH
40 Rue Worth
SURESNES
(en face de la gare)

*Fig. 26.13 Card given to Merri after her first conversation with Tessier, inviting her to come to the operating room at Foch to do some "test drawings."*

Below is a letter from Merri, discussing her years with Dr. Tessier:

Dear Tony,

I'm sure I'm way too late in getting back to you. I wanted to compile a visual narrative rather than just words but no one would believe that my computer died of a virus and by the time I repositioned and organized my slides my time had run out.

If nothing else, these are for you.

See you June 6. Le reception a suivre sera chez moi. Merri Sheifflin -Nordman

Following is a short sequence of events leading up to my working with Dr. Tessier.

U.of Illinois Medical School (Chicago) prosthetics class where I was introduced to the craniofacial work of PLT through Dr. Sam Pruzansky.

Became familiar with the surgery of Dr. Paul Tessier when employed at Presbyterian St. Luke's Hospital/ Rush University Illustration Department in Chicago 1972/73.

As Assistant Professor of Medical Biocommunication Arts, I took a 6 month sabbatical from the University of Illinois School of Basic Medical Sciences—Urbana/Champaign from October 1980-March 1981 to observe and work with Dr. Paul Tessier.

First meeting:

Arrived in Paris October 27, 1980

My first meeting with Dr. Tessier was arranged by a brief and last minute letter after several months of unanswered correspondence outlining my six-month sabbatical from the University of Illinois Medical Center. Standing in front of 26 Avenue Kléber at two-o'clock, Monday afternoon, the 29 of October, 1980 only 24 hours after arriving in France for the very first time with no french language skills, my nervousness was not diminished as I confronted with the monumental Hausmanien entrance and staircase. Cautiously mounting each step, I was standing before the oversized double doors with the famous brass name plate Docteur Paul TESSIER before me. After ringing, the secretary opened the door, (Mme. Foste) escorting me into a large empty waiting room with the drapes drawn. I was left on my own. Thirty minutes passed, one hour, a second hour went by and still no sign of being called in. Approaching the 3 hour mark and in spite of my resolve to resist the imminant flight or flight reaction, I was told that Dr. Tessier would see me now.

Stepping into his consultation office, I was at last face to face with Dr. Tessier, the afternoon sun highlighting him from behind his desk with two impressive elephant tusks dwarfing a floor to ceiling mirror.

"Ahhh, Miss Sheifflin. Tell me why you are here?"

What! Absolutely *no* recollection or recognition what-so-ever of the several letters exchanged during the past year outlining my reasons and purpose for sitting in front of him?

I was taken a back, but somehow managed to find a calm and sure voice explaining my six month sabbatical proposal to observe and illustrate his craniofacial surgery.

A short pause from the maître and his response:

"Come to Hospital Foch tomorrow at 14:00. My secretary will give you the details. Au revoir, Mlle Sheifflin."

Well, that was not exactly what I expected!

Suddenly, I was leaving 26 Ave Kléber after waiting 3 hours with a mere 5 minute Dr. Tessier interrogation and no clear idea of whether I was going to be able to fullfill my sabbatical proposal. This was going to be an unprecedented challenge!

Arriving at Foch the following day and locating the OR, I was announced.

Entering the OR, Dr. Tessier announced; "Clear the circus ring and let the artist perform!"

A stepladder was placed behind him and the command was,

"Okay, draw!"

Seven hours later and just as he was leaving the OR, he suddenly came over to me almost as an afterthought, asked to see my sketches and announced,

"Well, we'll see if you are an artist." and left the OR.

Voila, my welcome to the world of Dr. Tessier!

Determined to find a way out of this impasse, I questioned several of the doctors assisting Dr. Tessier at Foch and obtained the operating schedule at the Clinique Belvédère and Foch. They advised me to show up each morning at 7:00 a.m. and enter with a "Bonjour, Dr. Tessier."

After 2 weeks presence drawing in the OR from early morning until late at night there was no acknowledgement on the part of Dr. Tessier.

Another strategy was in order.

By talking to the assistants and learning of his skull collection and consultation hours, I finally mustered the courage to ask Dr. Tessier permission to draw from his skull collection of cranialfacial malformations during consultation hours at Avenue Kléber.

The day I arrived, I selected an Apert skull from the cabinet, set it on his bureau in the library, took out a piece paper, a No. 2B pencil and started to draw the "nature mort". Dr. Tessier came in between patients taking a cursory look at the progressing drawing without uttering a word.

Finished with the Apert sketch, I chose another skull, a Crouzon and kept on drawing. Just when my confidence was hitting dangerously low levels, Dr.Tessier entered the room came up to me and declared;

"Maybe, we can work together." and proceeded to invite me to dinner the next week.

The evening I arrived, I met Mme Tessier and their two young children, Jean-Paul and Laurence. An excellent diner of foie gras accompanied by a bottle of Chateau d'Yquem, a first for me! une pintade with wild mushrooms, cheese and dessert followed by cognac and a cuban cigar. Just when I thought it was time to take my leave and nearing midnight, Dr. Tessier announced,

"Now, we are going to go to work."

We returned to his bureau where he had prepared 20 hand-written surgical procedures on TM.

"You will start working tomorrow, here."

It had taken me just 2 months of concentrated effort at last to have my first illustration assignment!

July 1982

Asked to spend 5 days with Dr. Tessier and his family on vacation in La Baule to work on drawings for his publishing project on craniofacial surgery.

Dr. Tessier met me at the train station and brought me to their Corbusier inspired apartment building on the bay. I was installed in a room off the hallway to their apartment. After dinner, Dr. Tessier gave me instructions for several drawings to be completed and presented at lunch the following day. Working the morning in my room we met for lunch with the family and afterwards worked correcting the sketches and outlining new drawings, the afternoon was spent drawing in my room while Dr. Tessier took a short siesta on the beach. Again, in the evening after a family dinner, we continued working with new assignments for the next day. During the next 5 consecutive days, the schedule was established and strictly adhered to: breakfast-work, lunch-work, dinner-work. On my last day, Dr. Tessier said I must explore the beauty of the region, asked if I could drive and proceeded to hand me the keys to his red-orange BMW. I was given instructions to follow the scenic route and I left for my one and only "sortie"—a spectacular sunset drive along the coast in my sunset colored car. The next day, I boarded the train returning to Paris.

# Chapter 27

## Instruments, the Instrument Makers, and the "T and T."

Not only did Paul Tessier create the field of craniofacial surgery, he modified existing instruments or designed entirely new ones.

Since craniofacial surgery largely deals with the bones of the face, one might call it "orthopedic surgery of the face," and special instruments are required.

Developing his procedures for the various conditions treated by craniofacial surgery, the only power saw available was the Stryker electric system, with a curved semi-circular blade that rotated through a short arc, side-to-side. It was largely used as a cast cutter by orthopedic surgeons, and as a means of removing the skullcap at autopsies by pathologists. This had been developed by Homer Stryker, an orthopedic surgeon in Kalamazoo, Michigan.

> In the late 1960s, the Stryker Corporation came up with improved power equipment, run by compressed air. This system had three interchangeable handpieces: a drill, an oscillating saw (which rotated side-to-side) and a reciprocating saw (where the blade movement is straight ahead, back and forth). This is the system that Dr. Tessier was using in 1975 when I arrived; he had three or four of them. Claudette Foste, who was one of his secretaries at the time, tells that once in 1967, when the one Stryker that he had at the time was malfunctioning, he put her on a flight to New York to pick up a new one and bring it back with her. (See Appendixes/Memorials.)
>
> In the early 1980s, I visited Dr. Tessier and saw a strange new device in the operating room. There was a stand on wheels with a basket attached to it and arms that went out laterally, to which a sterile drape was attached. This was the Aesculap system, made in Germany. Instead of being air driven, it had an electric motor, which provided greater torque than the air-driven system.
>
> The Stryker system has subsequently come out with an electric system, which is also excellent. I have no favorites.
>
> There was a need for new types of surgical instruments for facial bone surgery, including instruments for the harvesting and shaping of bone grafts. Dr. Tessier modified an existing orthopedic instrument to develop special bone-contouring forceps, a heavy instrument with convex and concave surfaces that could bend rib or iliac bone to almost any shape he desired.
>
> The osteotomes he preferred came from the Heljestrand Company in Sweden. They were thin, but made of excellent steel. He said that all osteotomes needed to have either a mushroom cap of "T" extension at the end of the handle in case they became wedged in bone and needed a blow in the other direction to safely remove them.
>
> Special instruments were found in orthopedic catalogues for cutting bone—gigantic versions of fingernail clippers.
>
> A whole set of retractors was developed for harvesting bone from the hip and the rib, and special osteotomes with short handles were developed for harvesting cranial bone.

Special awls were developed for putting the hip back together after removing bone, and others were made, like an icepick, for precisely making a hole through the nasal bones for a transnasal canthopexy. Special soft, malleable retractors were developed for use in the orbit.

But the most important instrument to Dr. Tessier was what he called a "rugine" (*ruginer* in French means to scrape), with which he performed subperiosteal dissection, elevating the tough membrane that covers bone. He called this a bone scalpel, and insisted that it be sharpened regularly. Without sharp rugines, a proper dissection could not be done. When we went to Cuba (Chapter. 35), he gently chided me for the fact that my rugines were not properly sharpened.

## The Instrument Makers

In his trip to New York in 1971, Tessier needed a particular instrument for the demonstration operation he was going to perform for John Marquis Converse at NYU. Converse took him to a German he knew in New York who sharpened instruments. This was Walter Lorenz, and Walter was able to make the instrument Tessier needed on short order. Walter then formed his own company, importing surgical instruments from the small town in southern Germany where almost all surgical instruments are still made: Tuttlingen. Walter became a wealthy man when the titanium plate and screw sets were developed for facial bone surgery, and he marketed one of the early versions (the Würzburg system). The Walter Lorenz Company was sold, and is now called Biomet.

Karl Leibinger lived in Tuttlingen, and he and his brother owned a company (bearing his name), which made some of the first Tessier instruments. Karl made frequent trips to Paris to consult with Tessier about their design. One of the instruments that took multiple trips before it finally met with Tessier's satisfaction was what he called the "T.O.M."—the Tessier Osteo-Microtome. This was a bone mill that had the capacity to chew up hard cortical cranial bone segments to a hash of smaller particle size, which would be packed into defects. Eventually, the Stryker Corporation purchased Karl's company, which is now Stryker/Leibinger.

All of the behind the scenes details are not clear, but another company—originally Martin—was founded by another individual unrelated to the Karl Leibinger mentioned above, but with the same name. This company has metamorphosed into KLS-Martin.

Another major player is Synthes, which descended from the AO group in Switzerland (which was involved with the development of compression plating for orthopedic uses).

All of these companies produce similar equipment. The plating systems are similar—all titanium—and many of them sell instruments of Tessier's design. The interaction between a very demanding and particular Paul Tessier and the instrument makers resulted in the production of high quality instruments that make craniofacial surgery much easier. One can tout the wonderful qualities of cranial bone grafts, but without the proper equipment to harvest them, this practice becomes meaningless.

## Techniques and Tools

Dr. Tessier was more aware than anyone that at the core of craniofacial surgery lay a proficiency in harvesting and using autogenous bone grafts. The medical literature is replete with reports of "bone substitutes," ranging from cadaver bone to silicone to Teflon to various types of coral to titanium mesh to ivory, even. None of these substances can hold a candle to a bone graft taken from one's body—an autogenous graft. It heals, takes as a bone graft, has circulation, and is recognized by the body as self.

The debate has been raging for years between two camps in plastic surgery: one group uses strictly autogenous material (and Dr. Tessier was the best spokesperson for this group), and the other camp says that it prefers foreign materials, since autogenous grafts are hard to harvest and undergo absorption.

Dr. Tessier had been hearing this argument for years, and felt it was time to have his position heard. Autogenous grafts are not at all hard to harvest if you know how and have the proper equipment. At the meeting of the International Society of Craniofacial Surgery in Visby, Sweden, in 2001, he asked Henry Kawamoto, David Matthews, and me to have a little meeting. We found a small conference room in the quaint castle where the meeting was being held, and he told us his plan. He had had drawings made to illustrate the proper technique of harvesting iliac, costal, tibial and calvarial grafts, along with many cases illustrating their proper use. Would we be willing to collaborate in this enterprise, and who else might we suggest? Of course, there were Jean Francois Tulasne and Yvon Raulo, both collaborators and associates of Dr. Tessier. And then there was Jeff Posnick, who learned from Dr.Tessier when he came to Norfolk. So there was the group: Tessier, Tulasne, Raulo, Kawamoto, Matthews, Posnick, and Wolfe.

I was to survey the group and ask for numbers: how many of the various bone grafts had they done, and what had the complications been? I then requested that they send an illustrative case or two.

Eventually, after a number of snags, this paper was published as a *Supplement to Plastic and Reconstructive Surgery,* with the support of KLS-Martin. Dr. Tessier was at times pessimistic about ever seeing the presentation in print but, happily, it was published during his lifetime, and the members of The American Association of Plastic Surgeons awarded it the James Barrett Brown Award for the best paper published in *Plastic and Reconstructive Surgery* during the preceding year. He was able to receive this award in London in 2006. (See Chapter 39, Honoris Causa.)

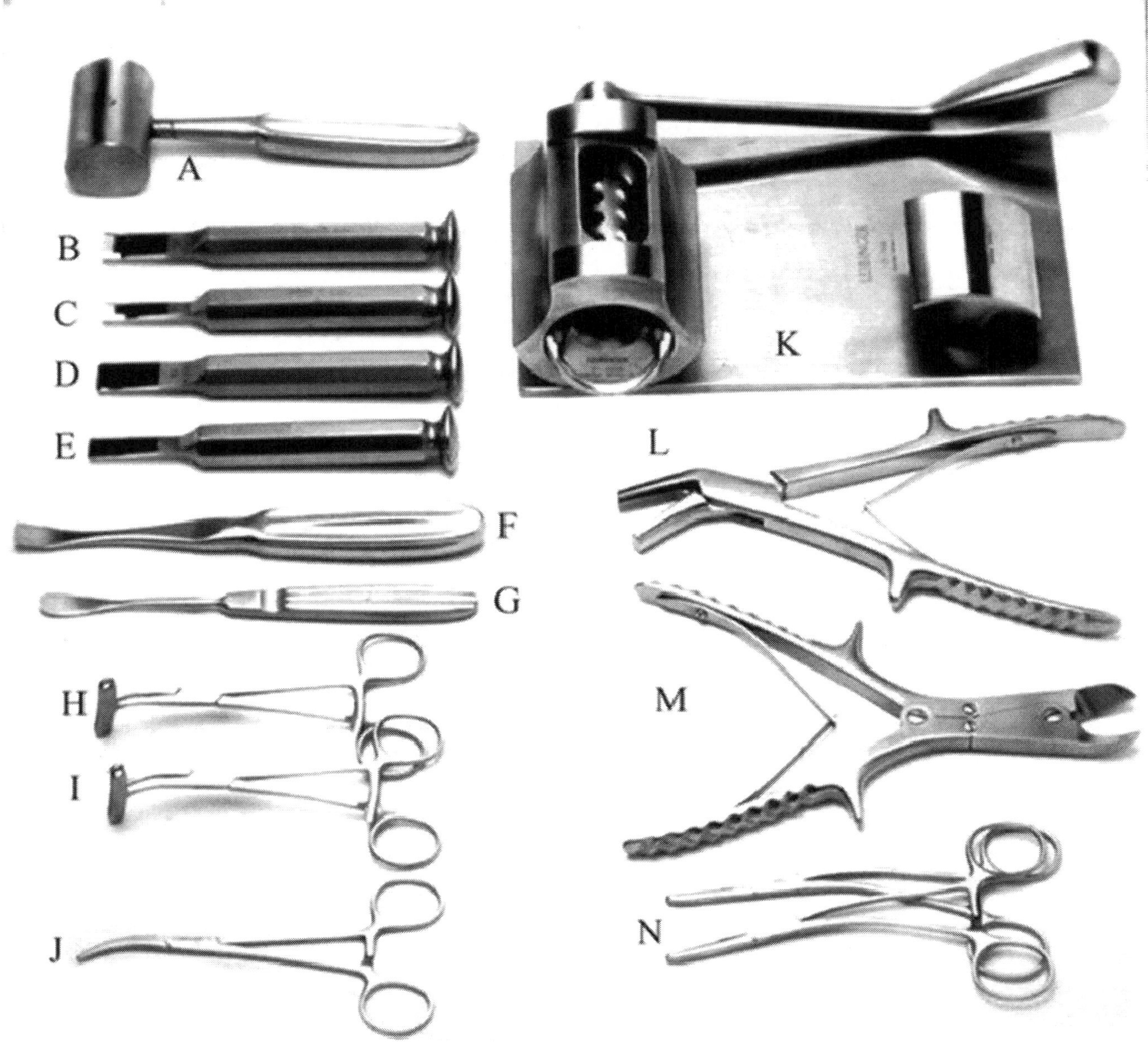


*Fig. 27.1 Tools of Tessier design: heavy mallet and special osteotomes for harvesting cranial bone, periosteal elevators, scalp clamp, and scalp hemostat (left); T.O.M. (Tessier osteo-microtome), bone bending forceps bone cutter, and bone clamps (right).*

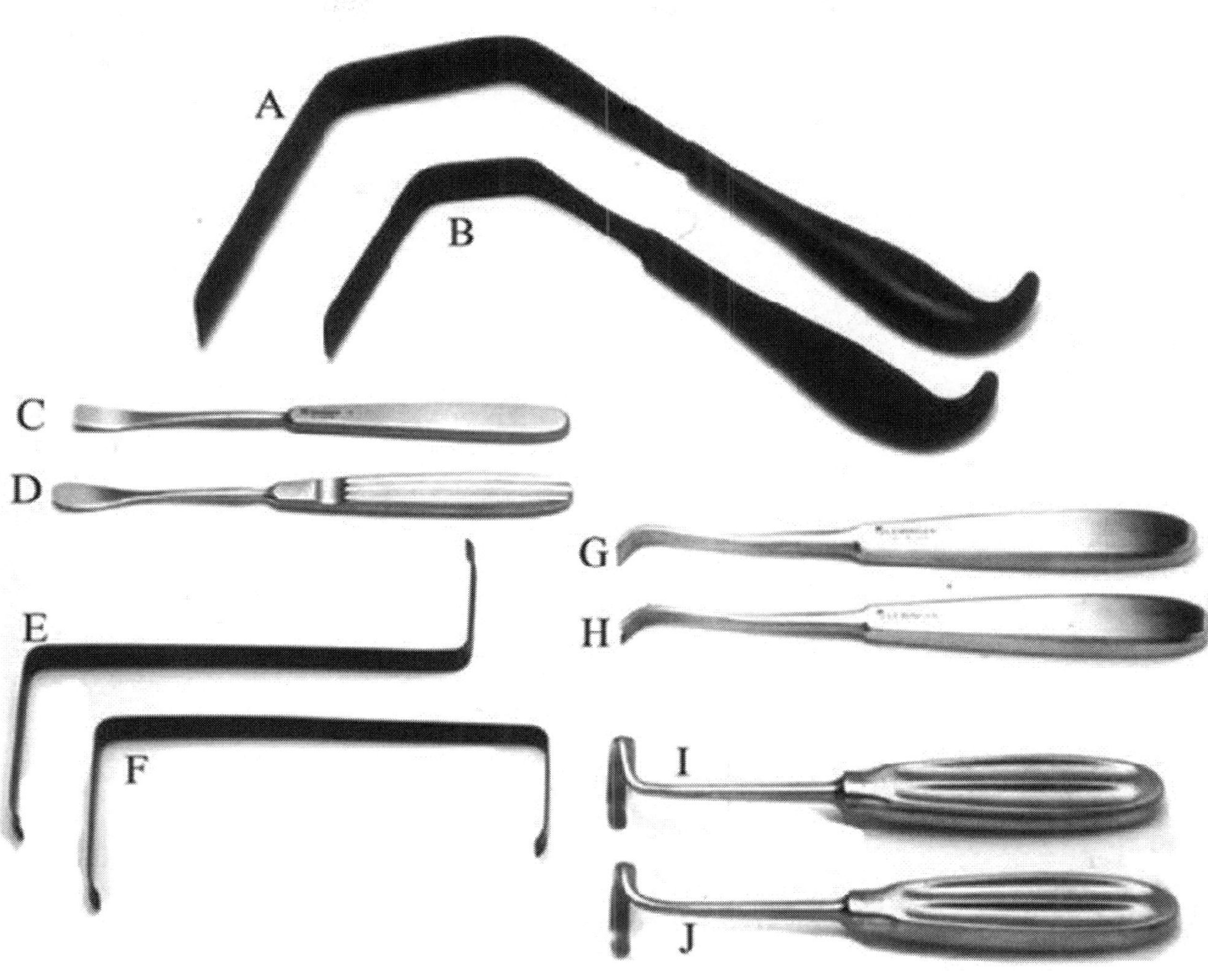


*Fig. 27.2 Tessier instruments for harvesting rib grafts.*

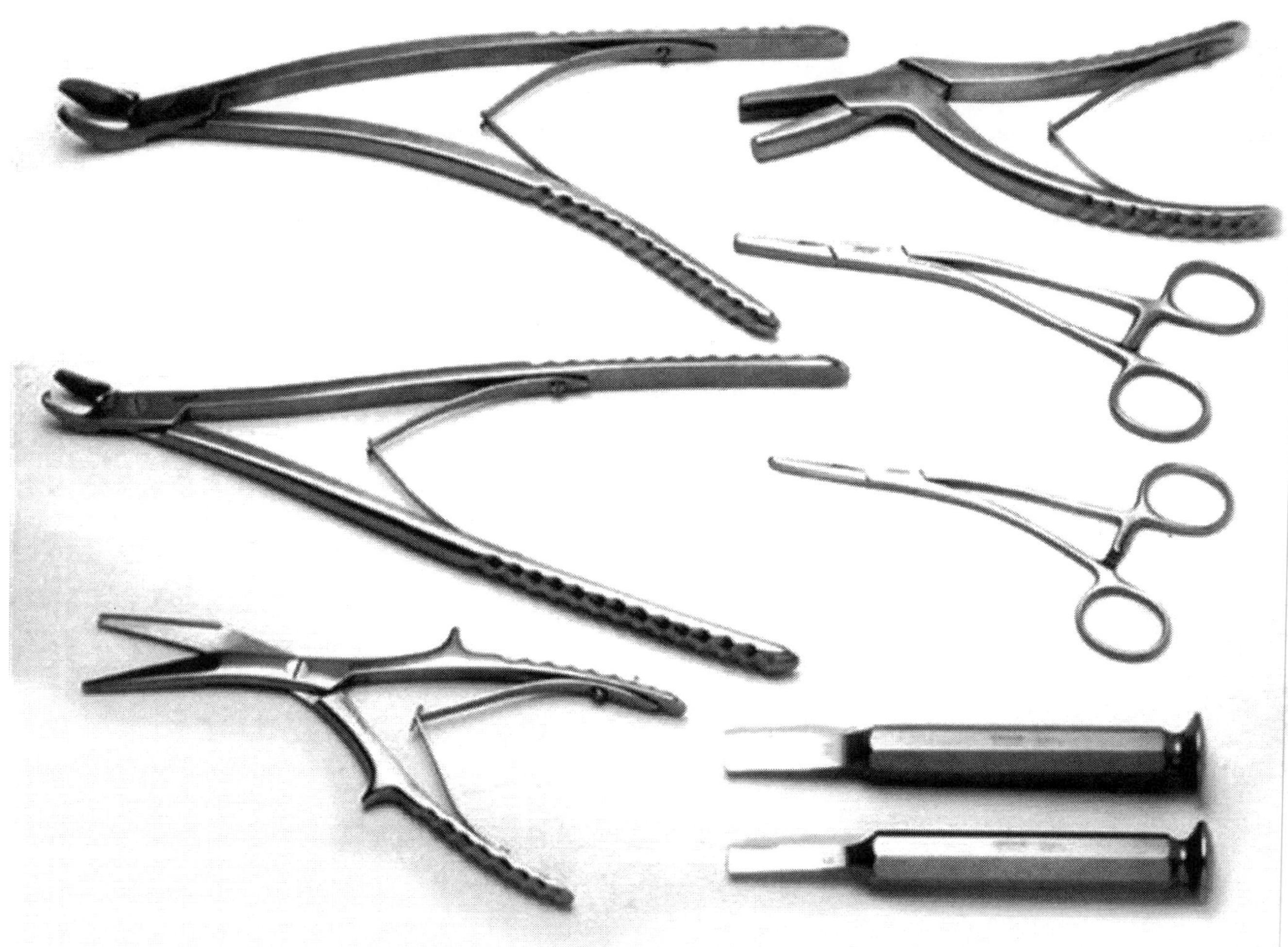

*Fig. 27.3 Rib cutters, bone cutter (left); bone bender, bone clamps, osteotomes (right) All of these tools were designed by Tessier.*

# Chapter 28

## The 70th Birthday Party

There was no effort to keep this celebration a surprise as there had been for the 60th birthday. The *Club de Chasse* (Hunt Club) was chosen as the venue, and there was a very good turnout of friends, colleagues, and previous trainees. Hugo Obwegeser was there from Zurich, as well as many of the previous American fellows. Dr. Tessier had said that he was not happy with the term *craniofacial surgery* (and even less so with the term *craniomaxillofacial*). *Orbito-cranial* would be a better term, he felt, and he often used it. An even better term, he felt, would be *orthomorphic surgery*, which would fit right in with orthodontic, orthopedic, and orthognathic.

One day at The New York Academy of Medicine, I came across a book dating from 1828 that used this term, so I had a copy made and framed. This was presented to him and, several decades later, turned up in Héric.

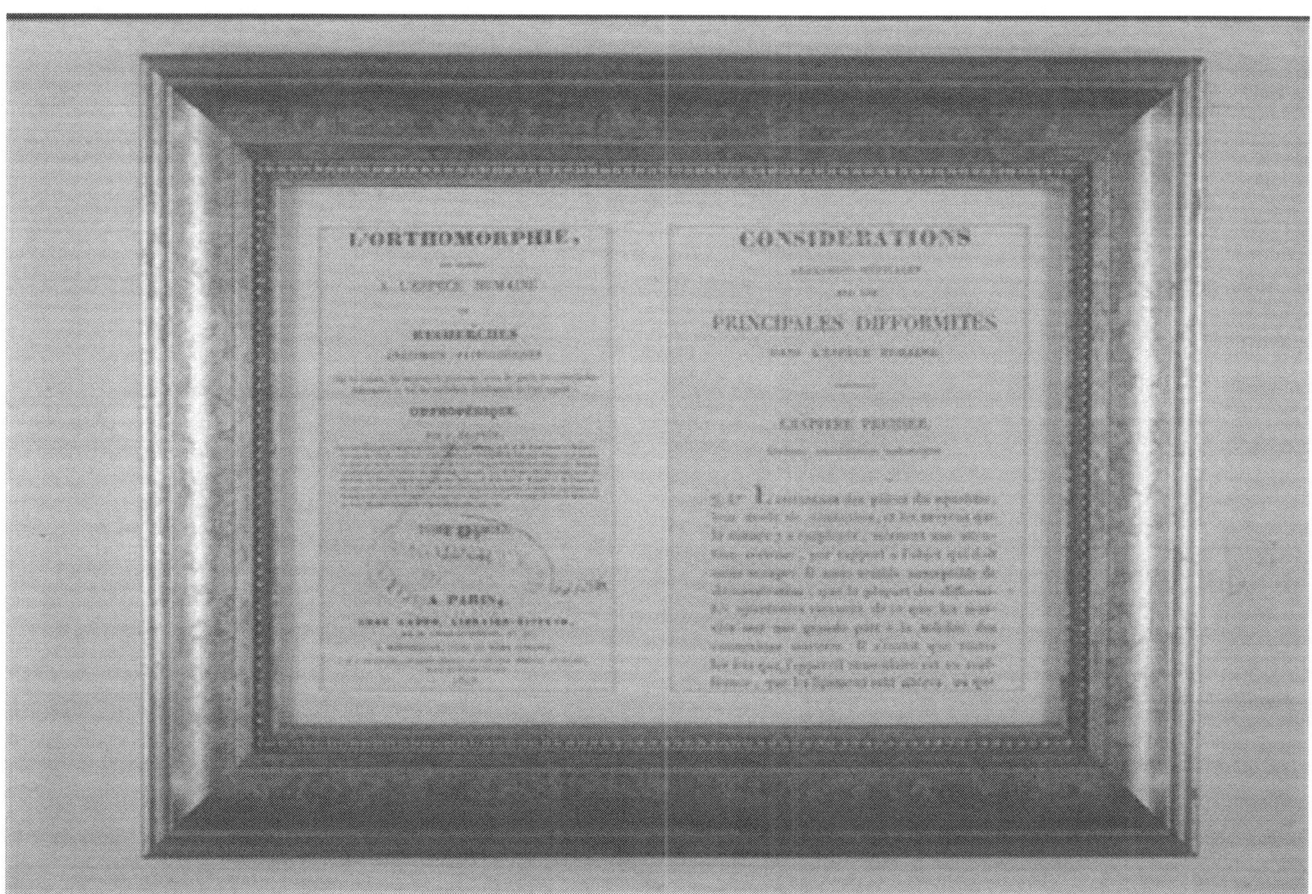
L'ORTHOMORPHIE,

A PARIS,

CONSIDERATIONS

PRINCIPALES DIFFORMITES

*Fig. 28.1 Frontispiece and first page of Delpech book, 1828, in which the term orthomorphic was used.*

*Fig. 28.2 Paul Tessier thanking the celebrants. Madame Deleague, an anesthesiologist who often came to Bélvèdere to give anesthesia to young children is to his left.*

# Chapter 29

## Lebanon, May 1994

Nabil Hokayem had been one of Dr. Tessier's favorite assistants. He worked with Tessier for several years in Paris and went with Jean-Francois Tulasne on the extensive tour to search for abnormal skulls in the museums of Europe, Great Britain, Mexico, and Asia (the "Jivaros" project). He was also one of the most productive team members on the trips to Tehran.

Nabil was a Christian, Lebanese man, and he returned to Beirut in the late 1980s. He had wanted to organize a meeting in Beirut for years and finally did so in 1994. For several years before this, downtown Beirut had been a battle ground between various Islamic factions. The active fighting, fortunately, had ceased with the entrance of the Syrian Army.

An invitation was sent by Nabil to all the members of Tessier's "Imperial Guard," and this was something that had to be accepted. For Americans, however, getting to Beirut was not an easy matter. It was not possible to purchase an airline ticket to Beirut, so we found that one could purchase a ticket to Damascus, Syria, with a stop in Beirut that allowed us to deplane there. The Lebanese authorities would be alerted to the fact that several Americans (Kawamoto, Matthews, and Wolfe) would be arriving, without visas. We had no problems whatsoever, and Nabil's meeting at the Hôpital Hôtel Dieu was a great success.

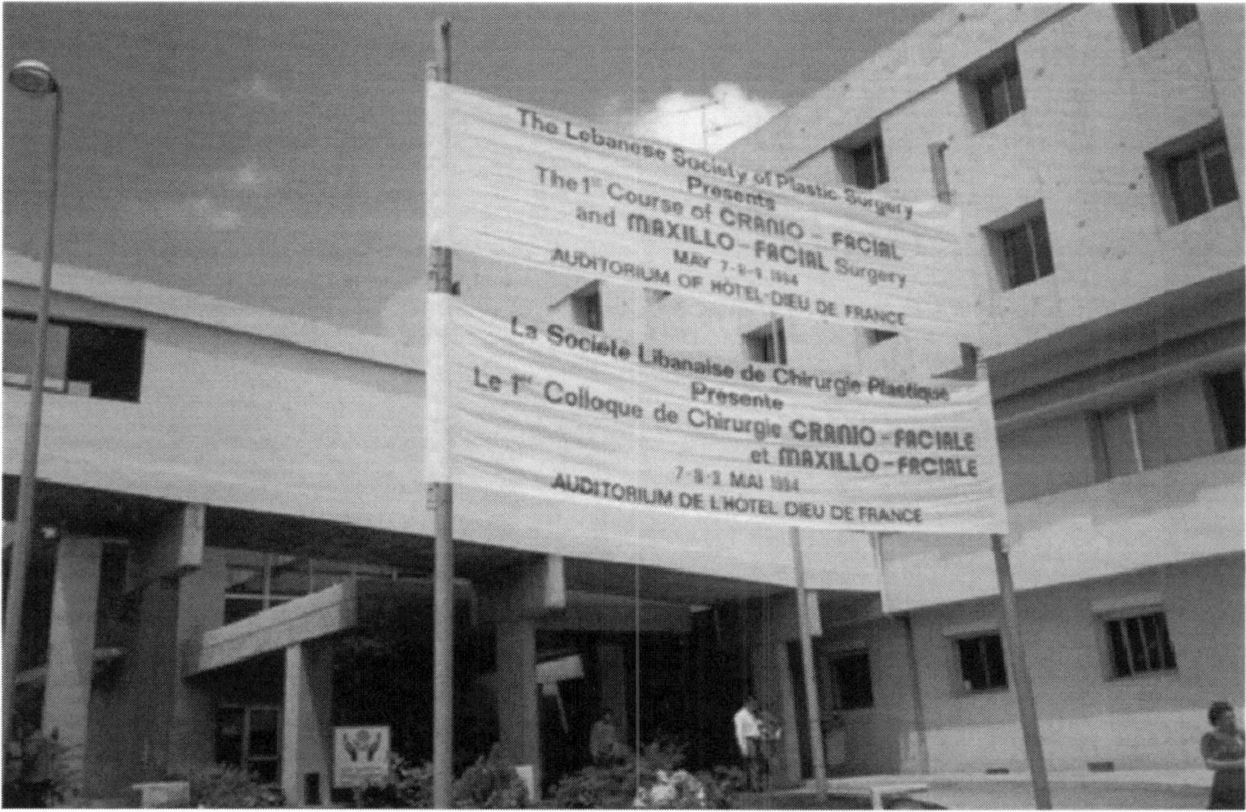


*Fig. 29.1 Signage in front of the Hôtel Dieu.*

*Fig. 29.2 Participants. From the left: Nabil Hokayem, SAW, Henry Kawamoto, Françoise Firmin, Tessier, David Matthews, and Jean Francois Tulasne.*

Unfortunately, Dr. Tessier came down with a fairly severe upper respiratory infection, and he was unable to give his lecture. He asked me to give his lecture for him—and it was on what he called his "impossible cases." Many of these patients had multiple facial clefts associated with wide orbital hypertelorism and severe nasal deformities; they were among the very most complex malformations that he had dealt with. Dr. Tessier passed off his carousel of slides to me and then went back to bed. In most of the cases—where he had done a dozen or more operations—I had little idea of what he had done. All I could say as I presented the cases was something like: "Here, Dr. Tessier was faced with a monstrous deformity. And here is his post-operative result, which, as you can see, is truly incredible."

What follows is a number of Dr. Tessier's "impossible cases." There is not a plastic surgeon alive (certainly including myself) who could obtain these results. These are children with truly monstrous malformations, made "normal," and thereby given the gift of a normal life.

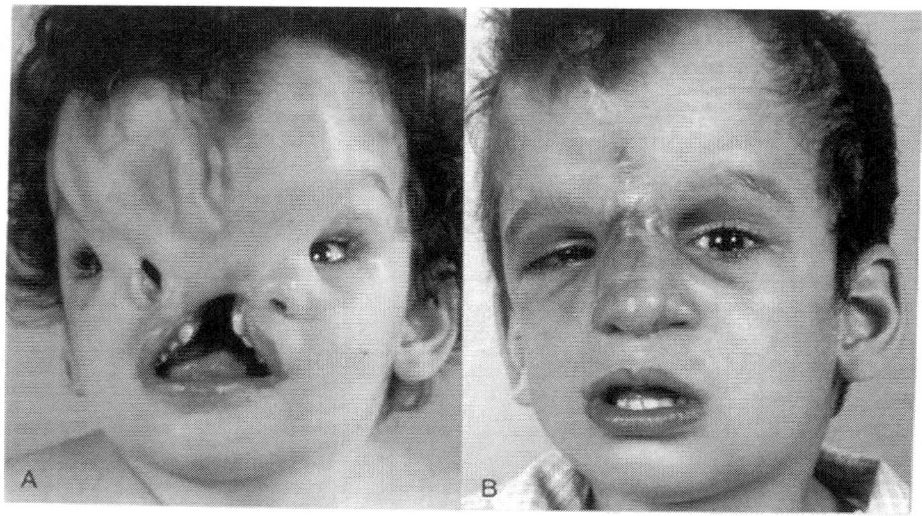


*Fig. 29.3 One of Tessier's "impossible cases": muliple facial clefts (0-14, 2-13), wide orbital hypertelorism, spehofrontoethmoidal encephalocoele.*

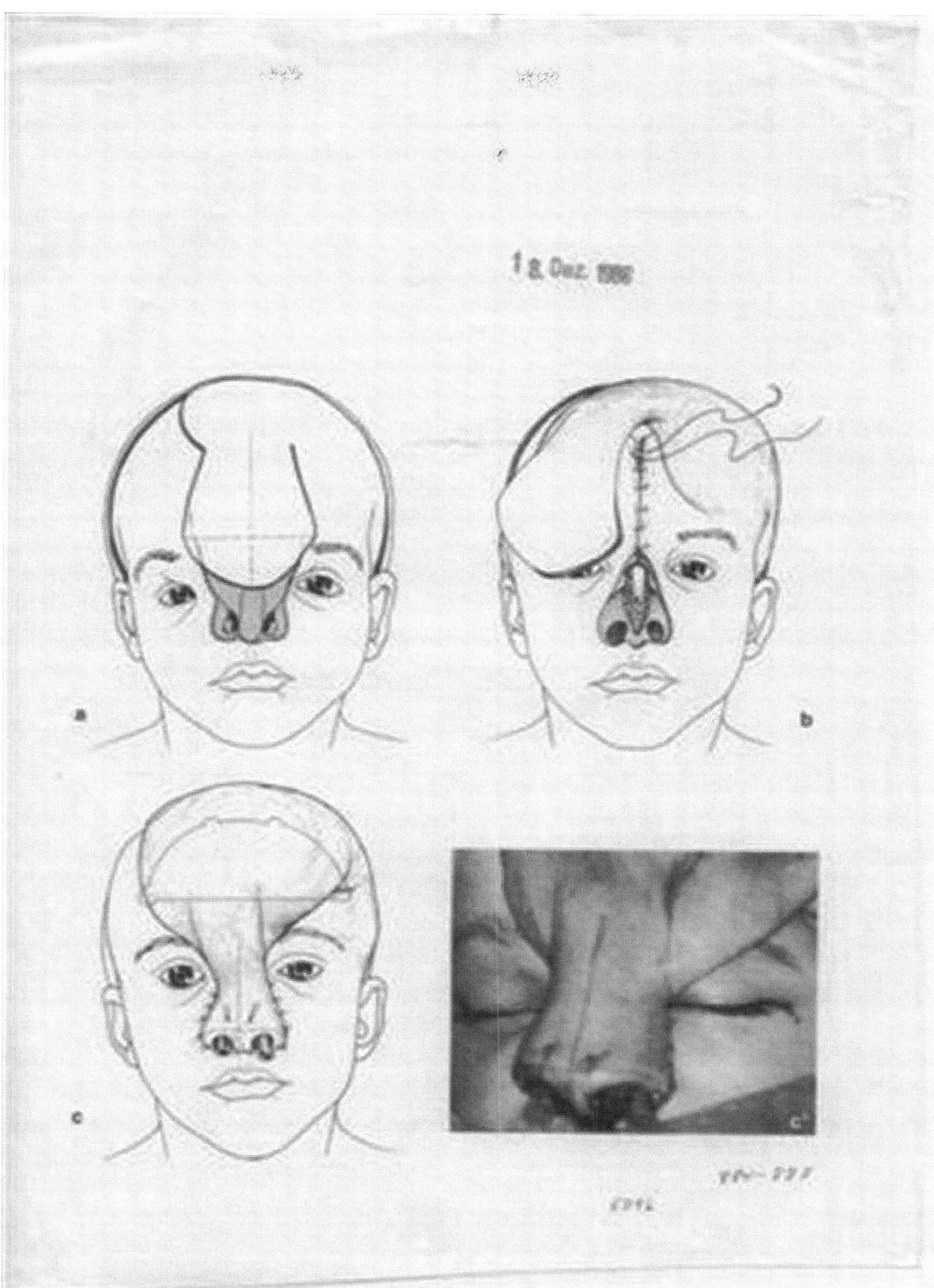

a
b
c
c'

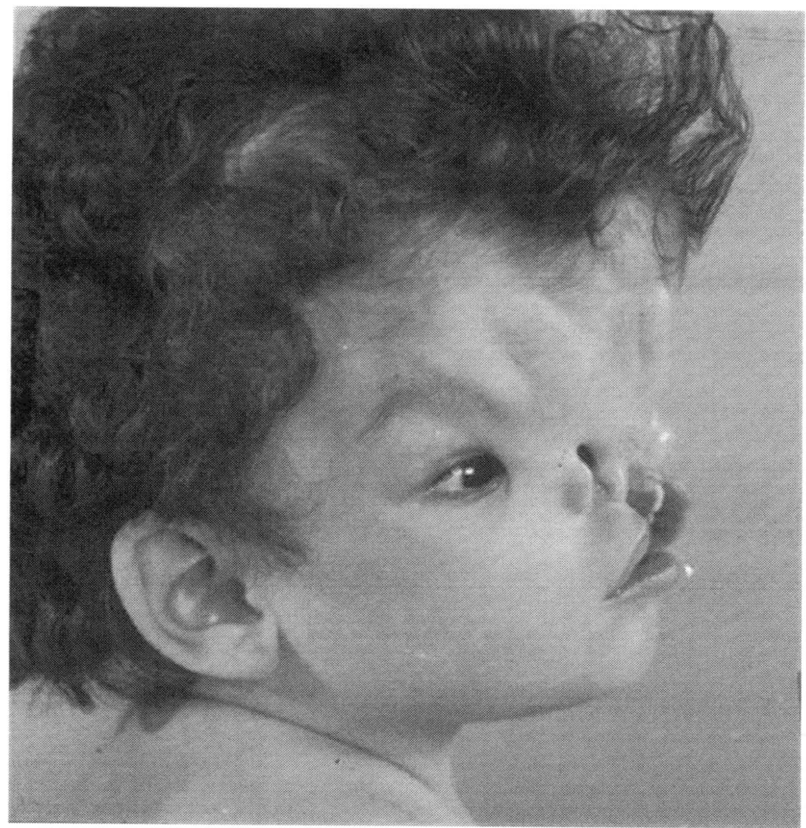

*Fig. 29.4 Lateral pre-op view.*

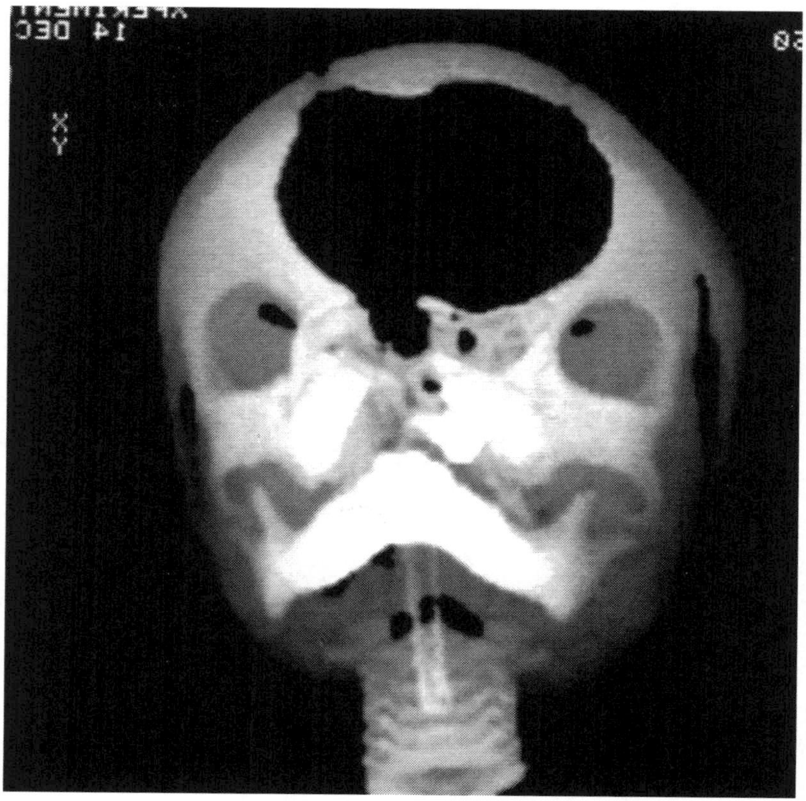

*Fig. 29.5 3-Dimensional CT scan showing large encephalocoele.*

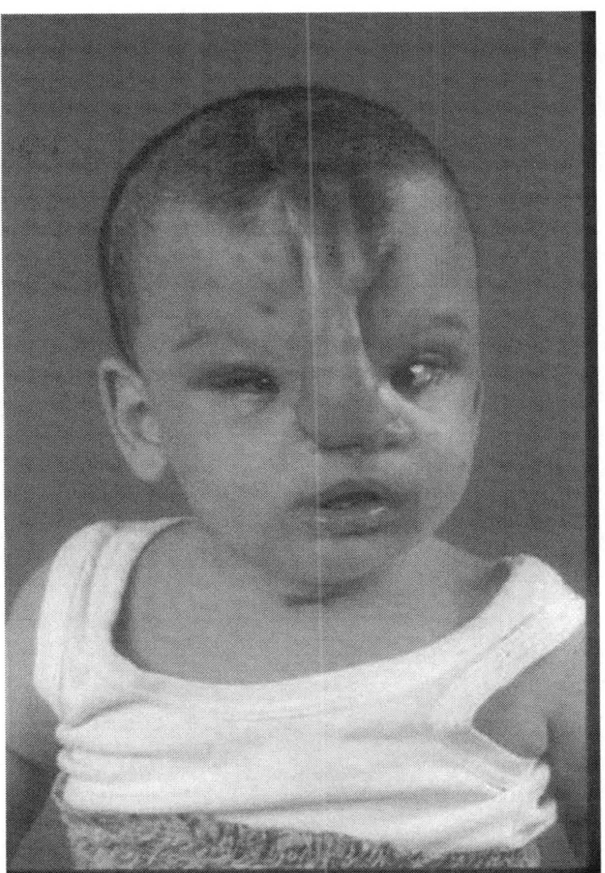

*Fig. 29.6 After transcranial correction of the encephalocoele and orbital hypertelorism, and before division of the forehead flap nasal reconstruction.*

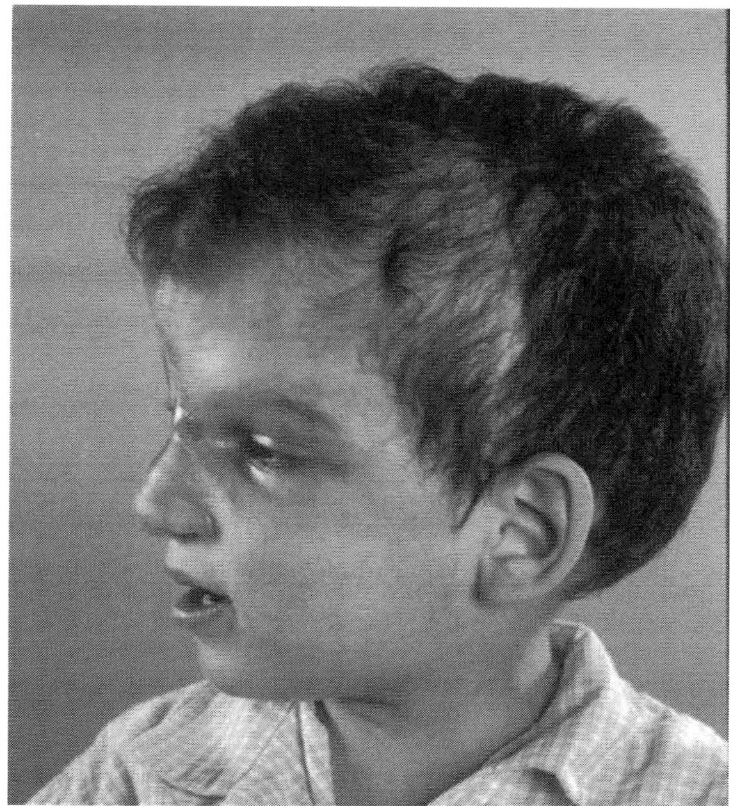

*Fig. 29.8 Post-op lateral. This case was done in Basel, Switzerland with Beat Hammer.*

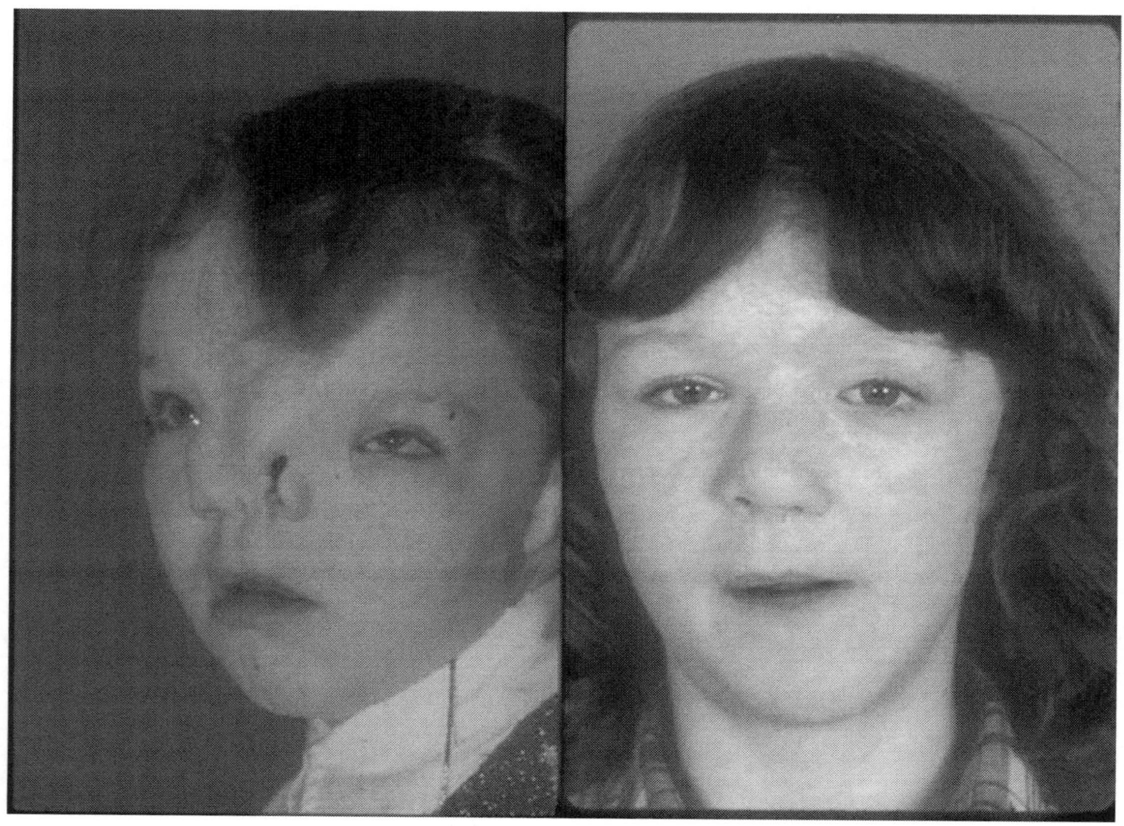

*Fig. 29.9 Hypertelorism, 2-13 cleft, encephalocoele. A superb result is depicted.*

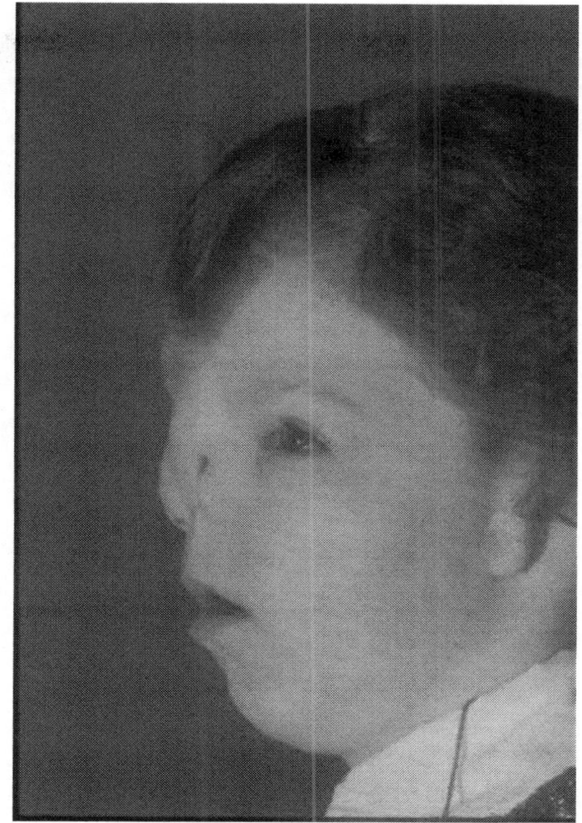

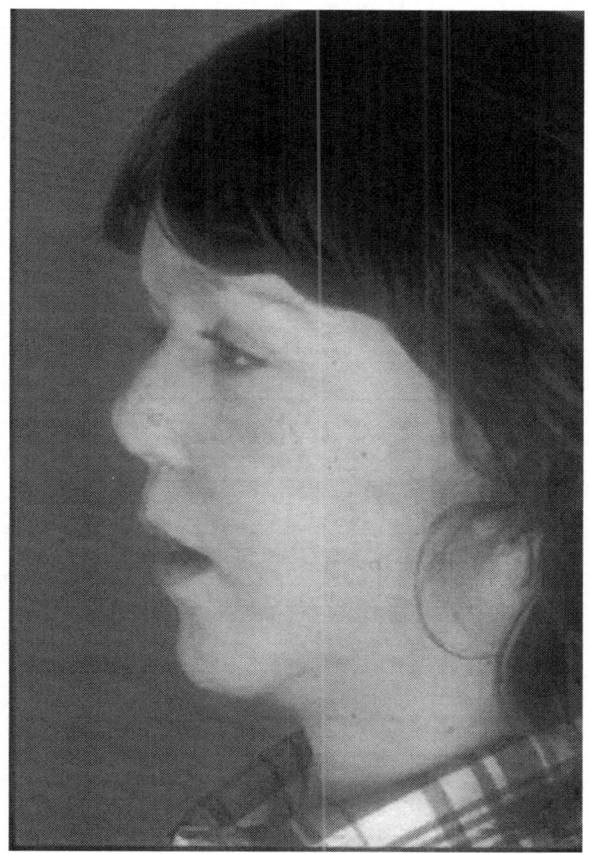

*Fig. 29.10 No. 2-13 cleft and hypertelorism. Lateral views.*

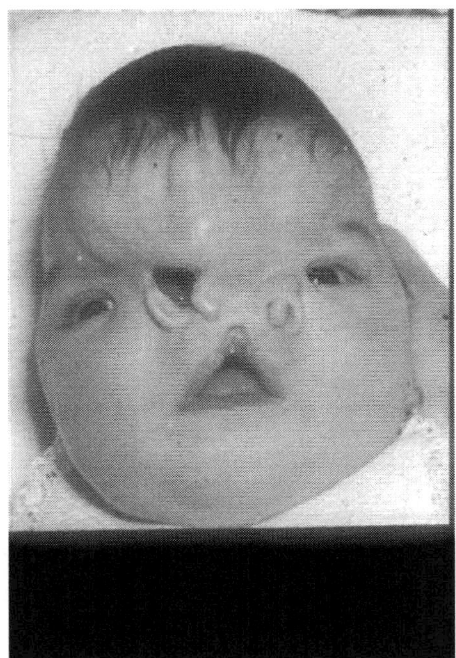

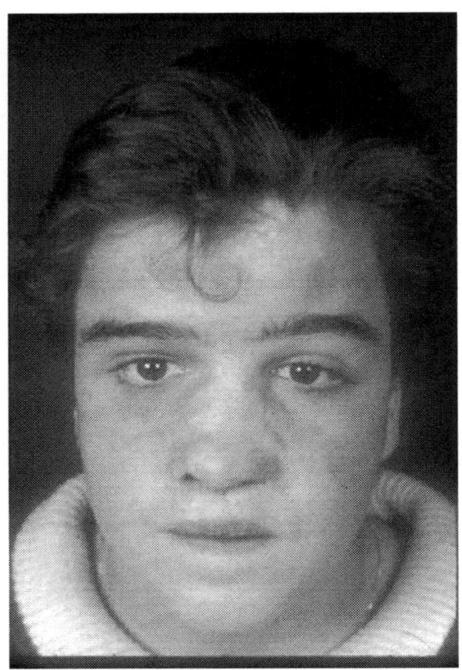

*Fig. 29.11a-b Sphenoidal encephalocoele and multiple facial clefts.*

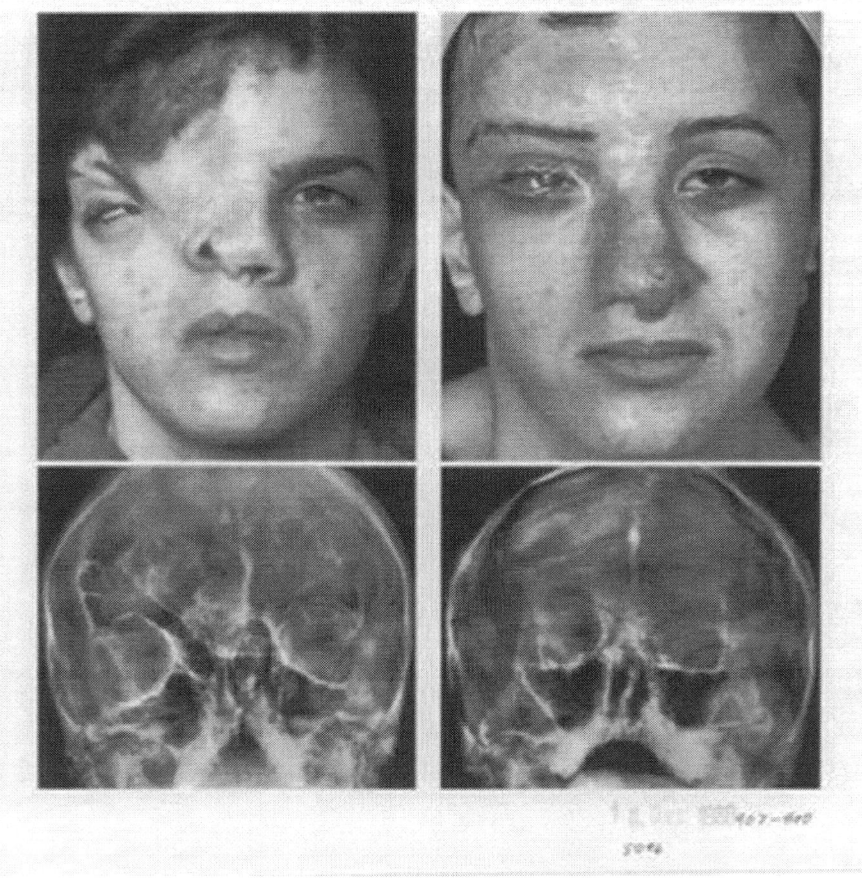

*Fig. 29.11c #10 Facial Cleft*

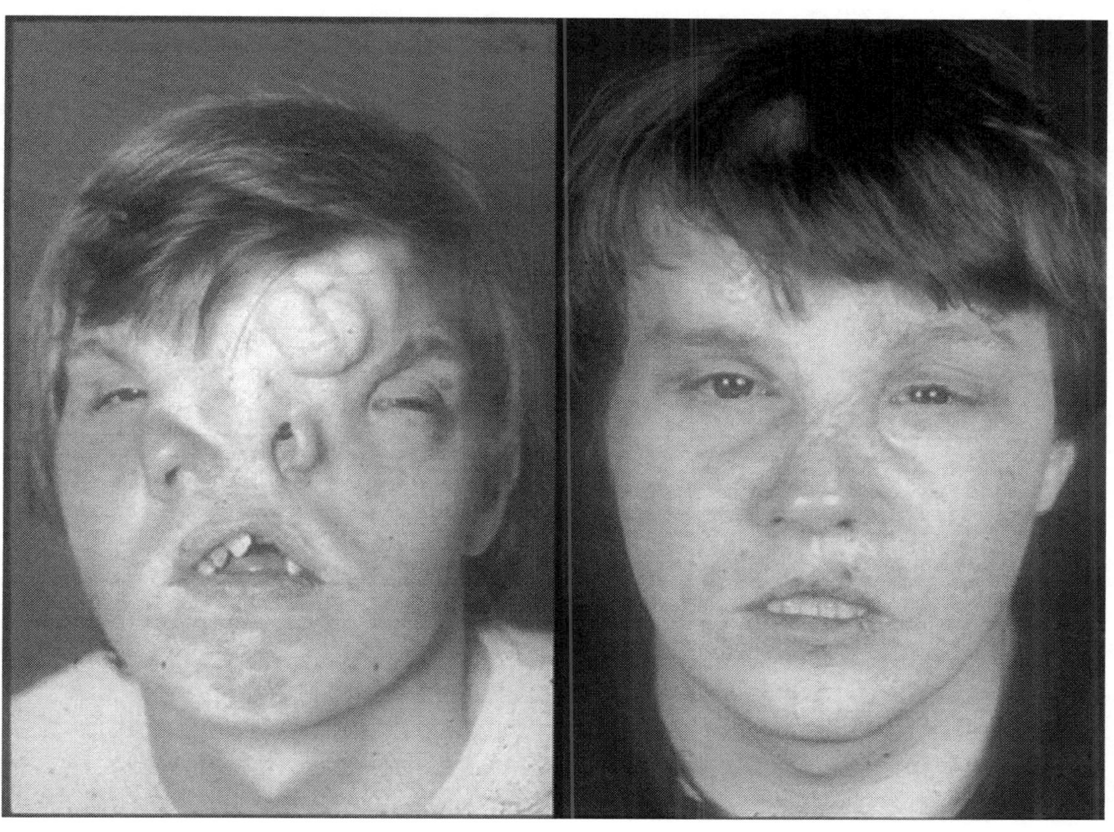

*Fig. 29.11 Wide orbital hypertelorism, 2-13 cleft, encephalocoele, pachydermatoclele. This shows an astounding result.*

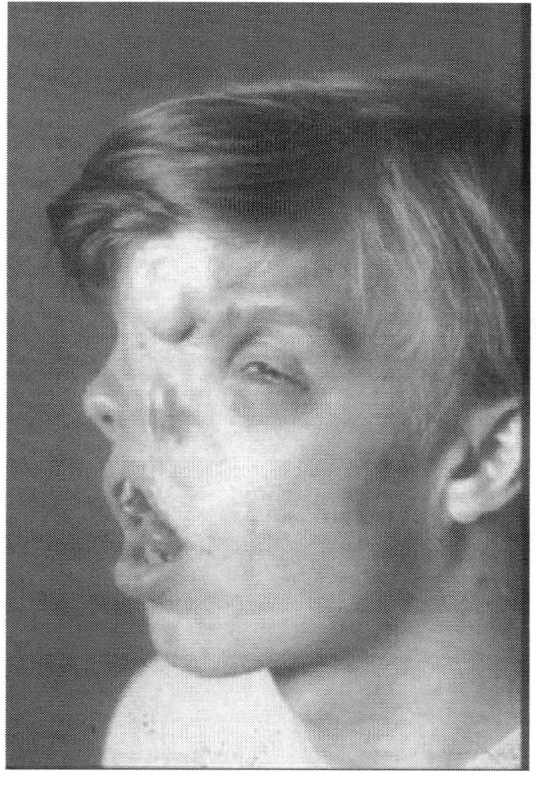

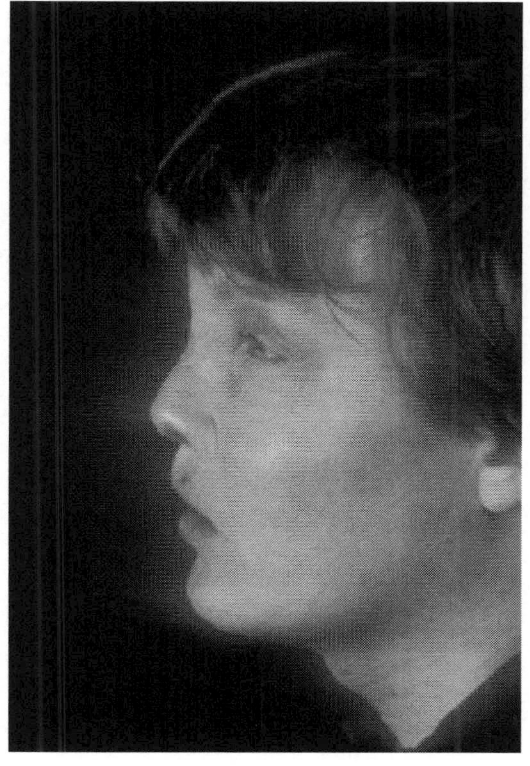

*Fig. 29.12 Lateral views.*

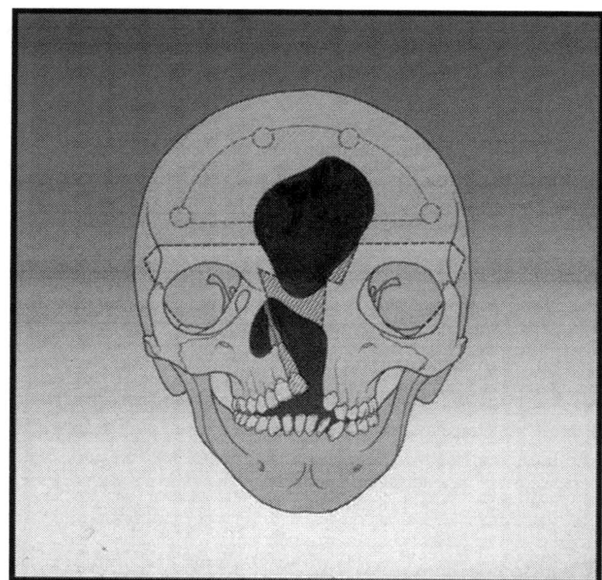

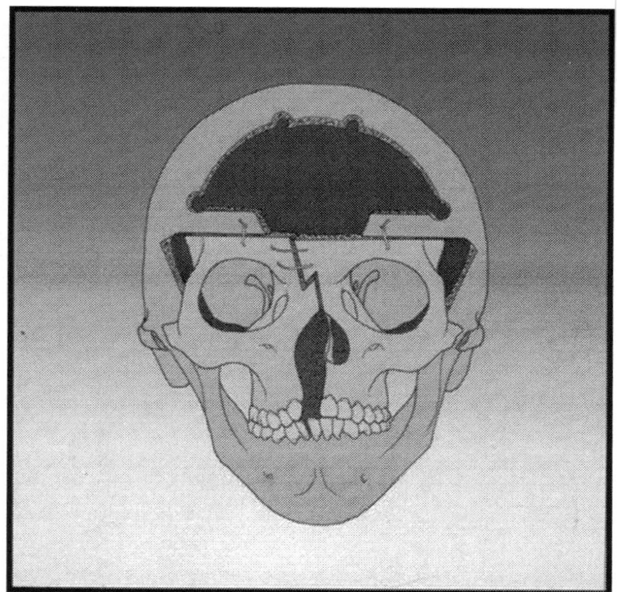

*Fig. 29.13 No. 2-13 cleft with orbital hypertelorism. The drawings show assymetric osteotomies for facial bipartition.*

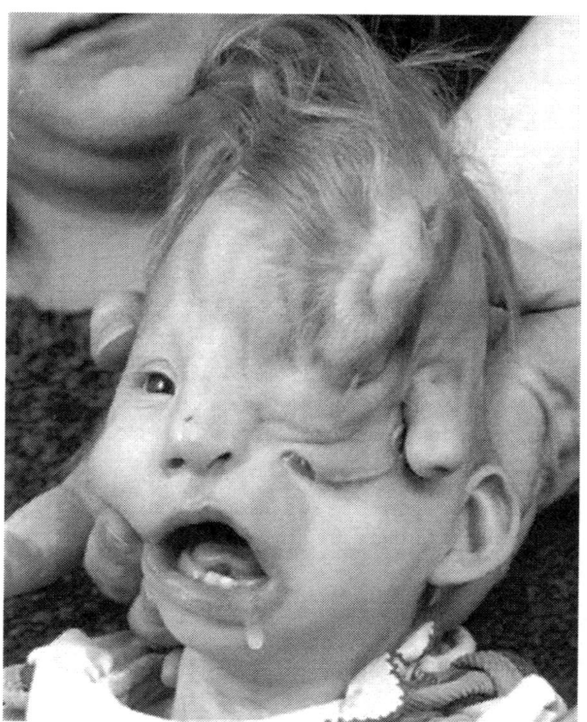

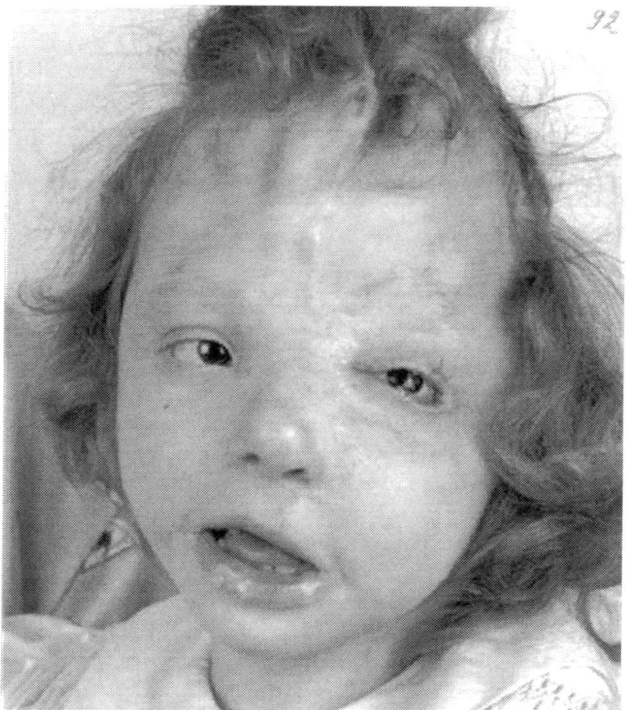

*Fig. 29.14 Encephalocoele, hypertelorism, and atypical proboscis lateralis, case done in Charlotte, North Carolina, with David Matthews.*

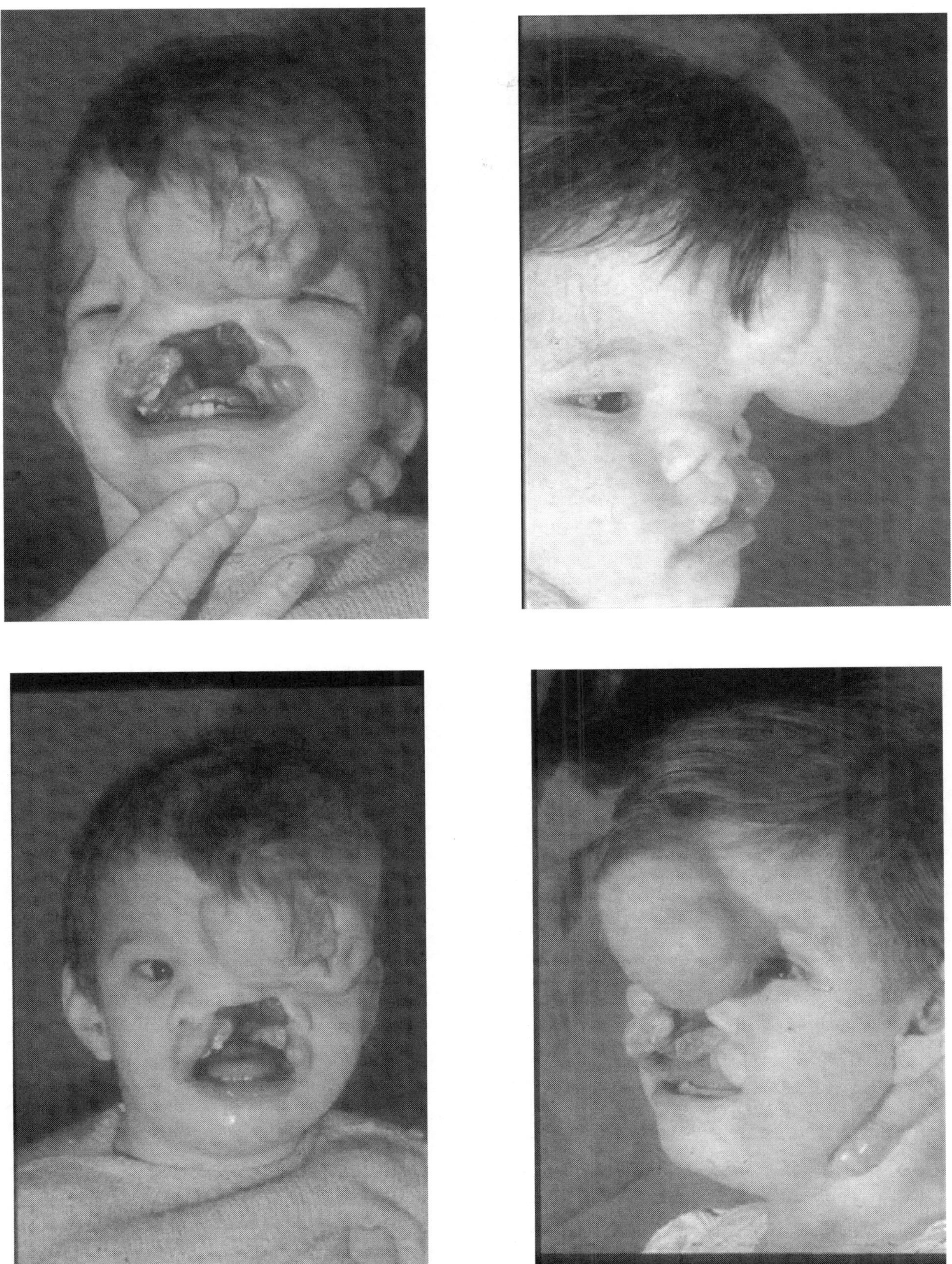

*Fig. 29.15 Frontal encephalocoele, wide hypertelorism, 2-13 cleft, pachydermatocoele.*

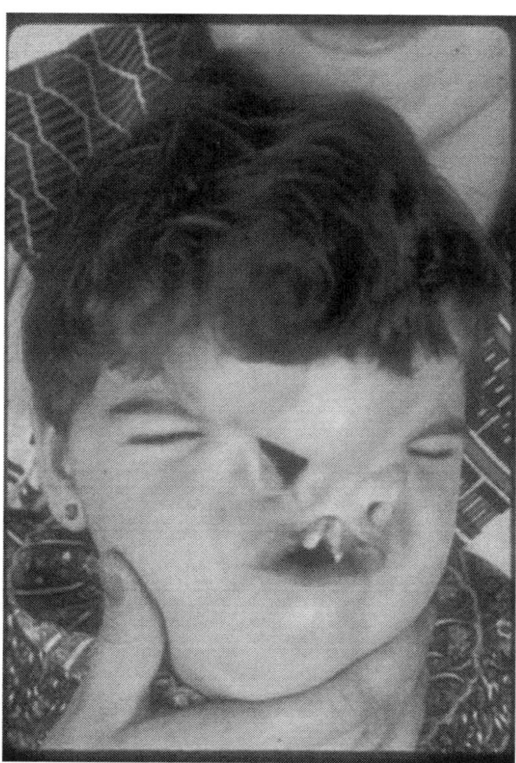

*Fig. 29.17 Encephalocoele, wide hypertelorism, multiple facial clefts.*

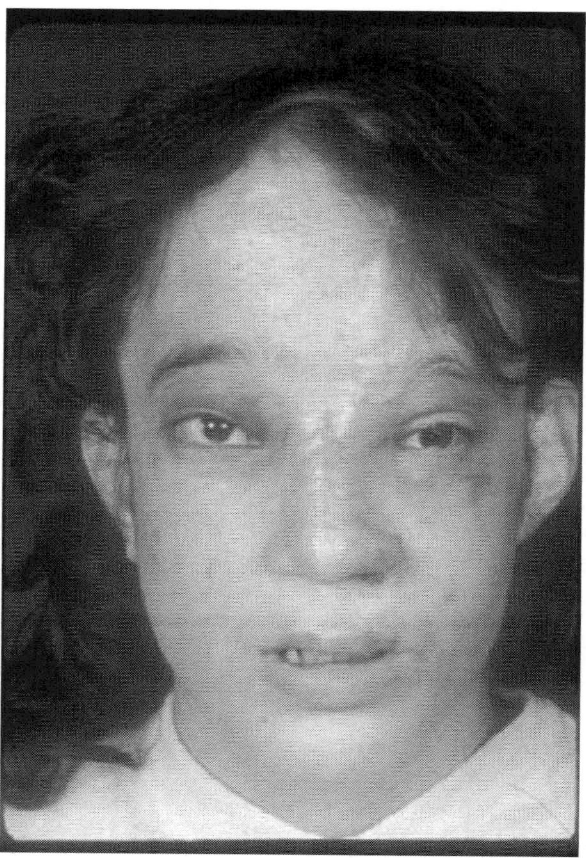

*Fig. 29.18 The post-operative result is unparallelled masterwork by the master.*

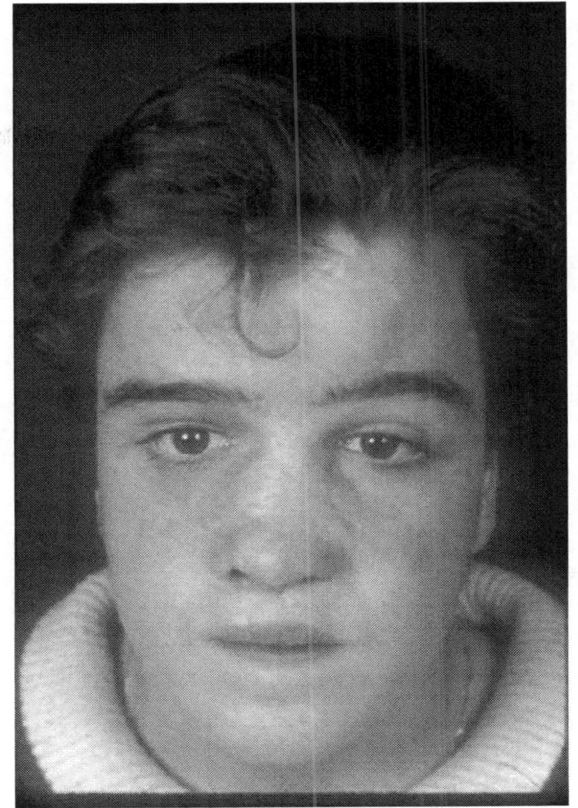

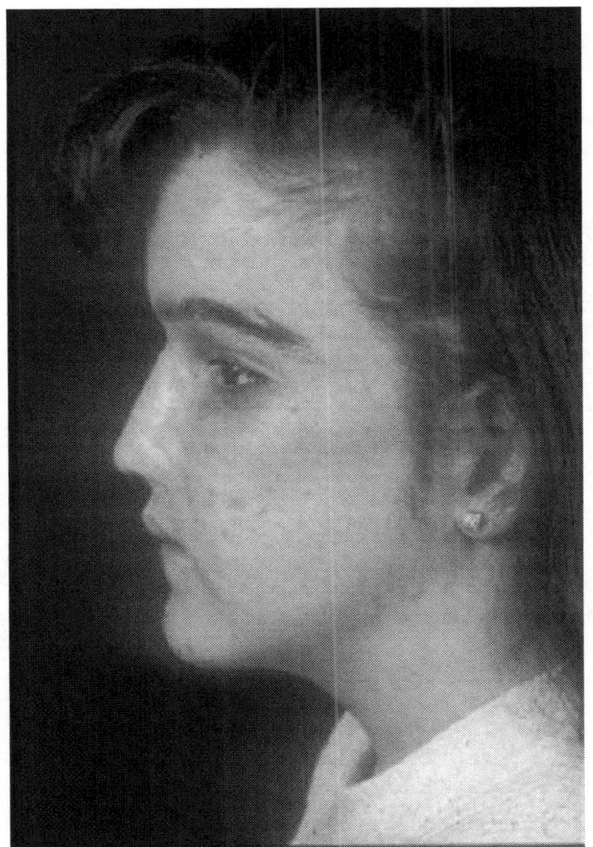

*Fig. 29.20 Early and later post-operative results. (Scolarité normale means doing well in school).*

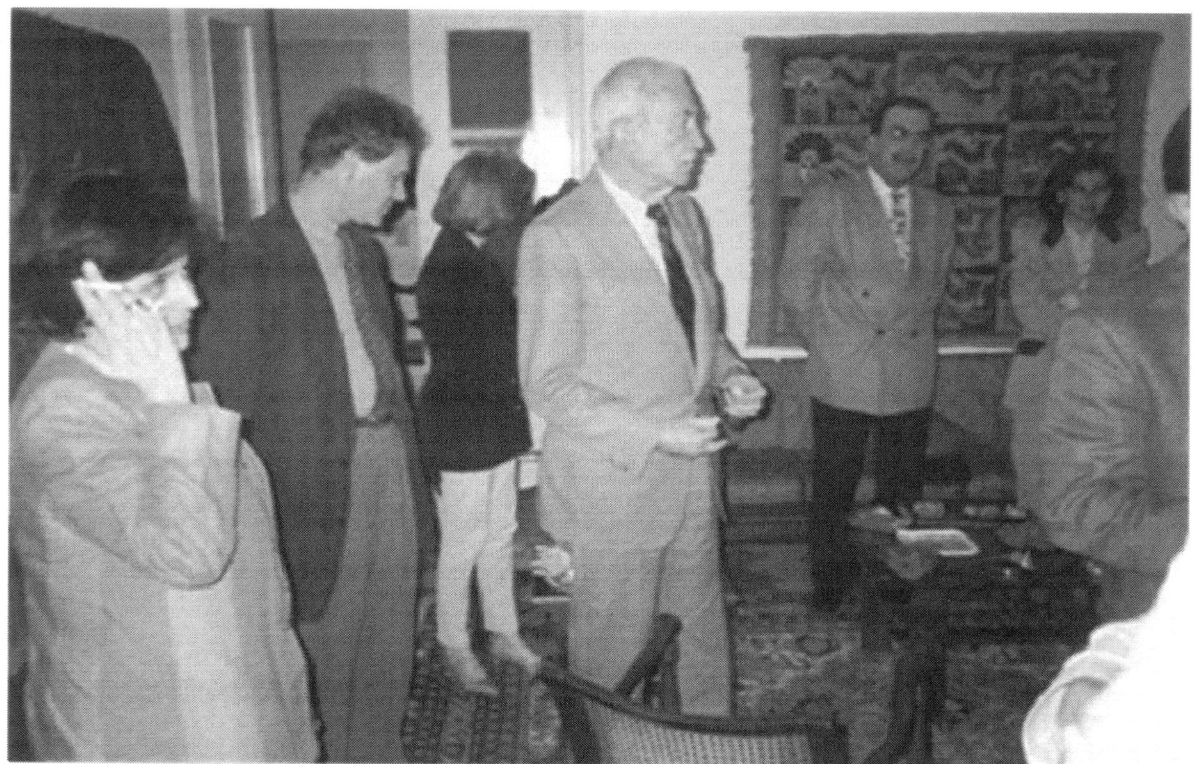

*Fig. 29.21 Serge Morax to the right of Paul Tessier.*

*Fig. 29.22 This had not been long after the civil war destroyed portions of Beirut. We took a tour of the downtown area, the "Green Zone," where most of the fighting and destruction was confined.*

*Fig. 29.23. Bullet pockmarks in downtown Beirut.*

*Fig. 29. 24 We left Beirut several times on expeditions, once to see the Cedars of Lebanon and the old Christian Maronite churches, and another time to go to a private club in the mountains high above Beirut. The road up the mountain was winding and steep, and there was no guard rail at all. Roger Khouri's father drove us in his Land Rover, and it seemed that his eyes were anywhere but on the road ahead. Looking across a steep ravine to the road on the other side, one can see a landslide with small dark objects here and there—those are cars that had slid off of the road.*

*Fig. 29.25 Club Faqwa, high above Beirut. It was an arduous drive to get there. Jean Francois Tulasne is on the right.*

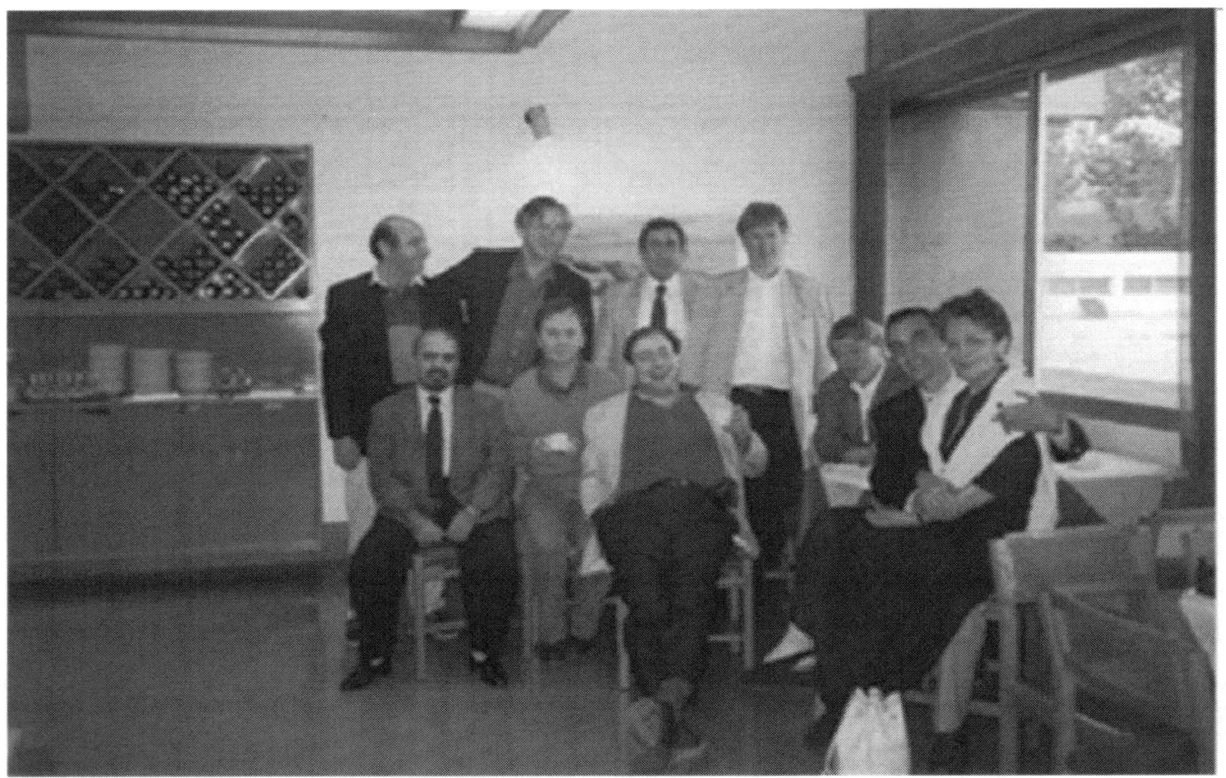

*Fig. 29.26 Club Faqwa: Back row from the left (unidentified), SAW, Nabil Hokayem, and David Matthews. Front row from the left (unidentified), Serge Morax, Roger Khouri, Henry Kawamoto, Jean Francois Tulasne, and Françoise Firmin.*

# Chapter 30

## Le Grand 26, Selling the practice.

"Le Grand 26"

In 1968, Paul Tessier accepted a lease on a second floor suite at 26, Avenue Kléber, a building dating from the mid-19th century and located several blocks from the Etoile (the Charles de Gaulle monument). The renovations he carried out took about a year, and, in 1969, he moved in. One entered from the street into a *Porte Cochère* and, on the right, there was a door to a large stairway with a very high ceiling that had red carpeting held in place by brass rods. On the second floor (first floor, to the French; for them the ground floor is the *rez-de-chaussée)* at the top of the stairs was an oak door with a brass plaque that read, "Dr. Paul Tessier." In later years, when his trainees Yvon Raulo and Jean-François Tulasne went on to become his associates, plaques with their names went up beneath his. Yvon Raulo finished as an assistant to Dr. Tessier in 1974, and then went to Tehran for six months. Following this, he returned to be Dr. Tessier's associate and was in the office with him at 26, Avenue Kléber until 1984. At this point, Raulo left to become chief of plastic surgery at a hospital in Creteil, on the outskirts of Paris.

Jean-Francois Tulasne first became acquainted with Dr. Tessier when he came to Nantes. Tulasne was in training with Dr. Jacques Delaire, a well-respected maxillofacial surgeon, and, after watching Tessier operate in Nantes, he started going to Paris on Saturdays to watch him there as well. Tessier asked Tulasne at one point if he would like to be a full-time assistant, and Delaire gave his blessing. After finishing his training, Dr. Tessier asked him to stay on as well, with the hope that he would take over his practice. Tulasne and another colleague did purchase Dr. Tessier's practice, and Tulasne continues to base his practice at Le Grand 26 with a few dental colleagues. For various reasons, Tulasne preferred to restrict his practice to orthognathic surgery, dental implants, and some aesthetic surgery. Thus, no one in France really picked up the mantle as Tessier's successor in the realm of orbito-cranial surgery.

Both Raulo and Tulasne accompanied Tessier on his grueling hunting trips in Africa.

When one rang the bell, the door would be opened by one of the secretaries, Madame Foste or Madame Pelegrin. If you were a patient, you would go to a large, high-ceiling waiting room on the right. If you were an assistant or visitor, you would go left and head down to a library/study at the end of the hall on the right. There was a good collection of plastic surgical texts, and Dr. Tessier's skull collection stretched across the mantle of the fireplace. On the left were the secretaries' offices and Dr. Tessier's consultation room. At the very end of the hall, if one turned left, a corridor headed to the private quarters where Dr. Tessier lived, avoiding any need to commute to the office.

Tessier had brought two of his trainees , Yvon Raulo and Jean-Francois Tulasne, into the office with him at 26 Avenue Kléber. Yvon, after ten years, left to become the chief of plastic surgery at a large hospital in Creteil, on the outskirts of Paris. Tessier had discussed selling his practice and the space at Avenue Kléber to Tulasne, but since he felt that the cost would be prohibitive for him (Tulasne) to bear alone, he suggested bringing in another surgeon. No one immediately came to mind but, finally, a young maxillofacial surgeon who neither Tessier nor Tulasne knew very well was mentioned. They should have recognized the warning bells going off when this individual went around town crowing that he was the new Tessier, but they did not. The transaction took place and, for a year or so, Tulasne and the new individual were in 26 Avenue Kléber together. Tessier was still there on occasion for consultations and to help the two younger surgeons with any of their cases if there were problems. Tessier did in fact help the new man in the office with a number of his complications but, for various reasons, the relationship soured and the new man, referred to now only as *le voyou* (the bum), left the office and, being a rather litigious person, brought a suit against Tessier.

This, however, did not turn out to be his last operation. He had helped his two younger associates with some of their cases and continued to go to Basel to operate with Beat Hammer. And, at age eighty, he went to Italy and operated with Ernesto Carroni, who was almost the same age as he. Tessier said that this operation almost killed him: he didn't have his scrub nurse, he didn't have his usual instruments, and everything was in a strange language. Plus it was a very difficult case: a facial bipartition and simultaneous nasal reconstruction that took over twelve hours. It was a bit strange to hear the man who routinely showed superhuman stamina—and would not allow the word *fatigue* to enter his vocabulary—to say that he had been tired.

# Chapter 31

## "S.A.P.P"—This is a typical Tessier acronym, meaning "Stupide Apartement Parisien de Prestige"—"stupid pretentious Paris Apartment."

Tessier had bought a good chunk of land in Saint-Germain well outside of Paris—several hectares—and had plans drawn up to build a house there. This would have involved a long commute into town, and Mireille was not enthusiastic about living out there in relative isolation. Therefore, he bought an apartment in a building in Boulogne, across the street from the Roland Garros tennis stadium, the previous owner of which had been the actor Omar Sharif.

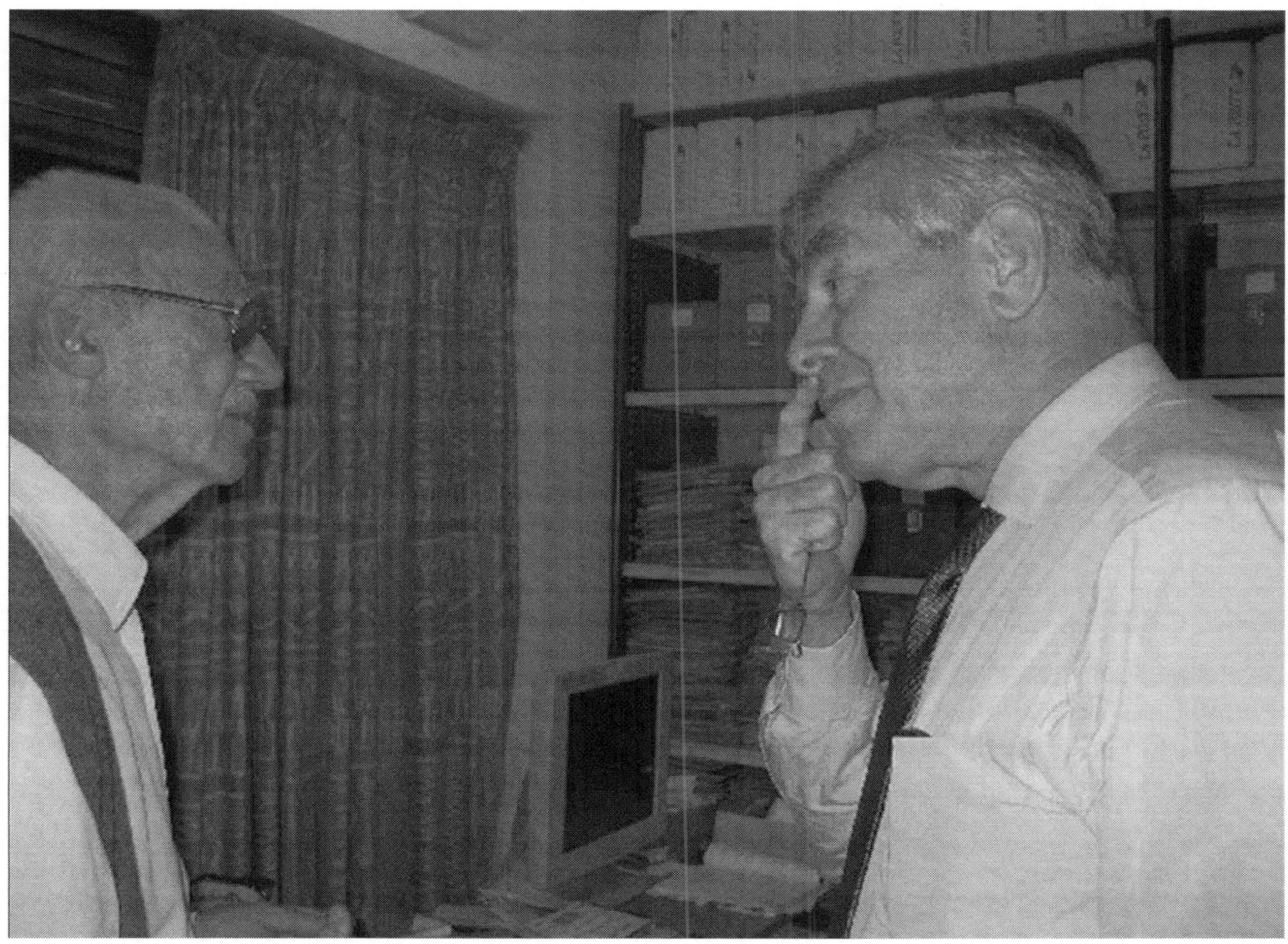

*Fig. 31.1 Tessier and SAW in the Tessier "archive room," SAPP. This was during one of the numerous three to four day visits that I made to go through all of his records, resulting in the long PowerPoint presentation that was shown at the London Honoris Causa meeting in 2006, and which is appended to this book in the DVD.*

The top two rows of the shelves have white French postal boxes, filled with almost a thousand drawings by Francine Gourdin. Beneath those are a number of skulls in their cases, and beneath those are patient charts.

*Fig. 31.2 The "work station" in the Tessier Archive room.*
*The Roland Garros tennis stadium is visible through the window.*

*Fig. 31.3 Patient dossiers (charts) and boxes housing the skull collection.*

*Fig. 31.4 More of the skull collection.*

*Fig. 31. 5 Slide trays, archive room, which no longer exists.*

The final resting place for all of Dr. Tessier's documents was up in the air for some time. *Las Gueles Cassée* is a French charity founded after World War I to care for soldiers with facial injuries. (Literally it means, "Smashed Mugs"). After the war, all of the proceeds from the National Lottery went to this charity, but with time and a lessening need for their services, only a percentage of those receipts went to the *Gueles Cassée*. The *Gueles Cassé* expressed an interest in finding a place to store the Tessier archives. Dr. Louie Argenta of Bowman Gray, University School of Medicine in North Carolina, put in an offer for the skull collection, but the French Society of Maxillofacial Surgery, under the urging of Bernard Devaunchelle, (who helped orchestrate the first face transplant done in the world which was performed in Amiens), put in a matching offer, wishing to keep the collection intact and in France. So, the final disposition of the Tessier archives will be that they will be part of the *Museè ?* which is being built in Amiens. The important thing is that all of this material will be available to interested scholars.

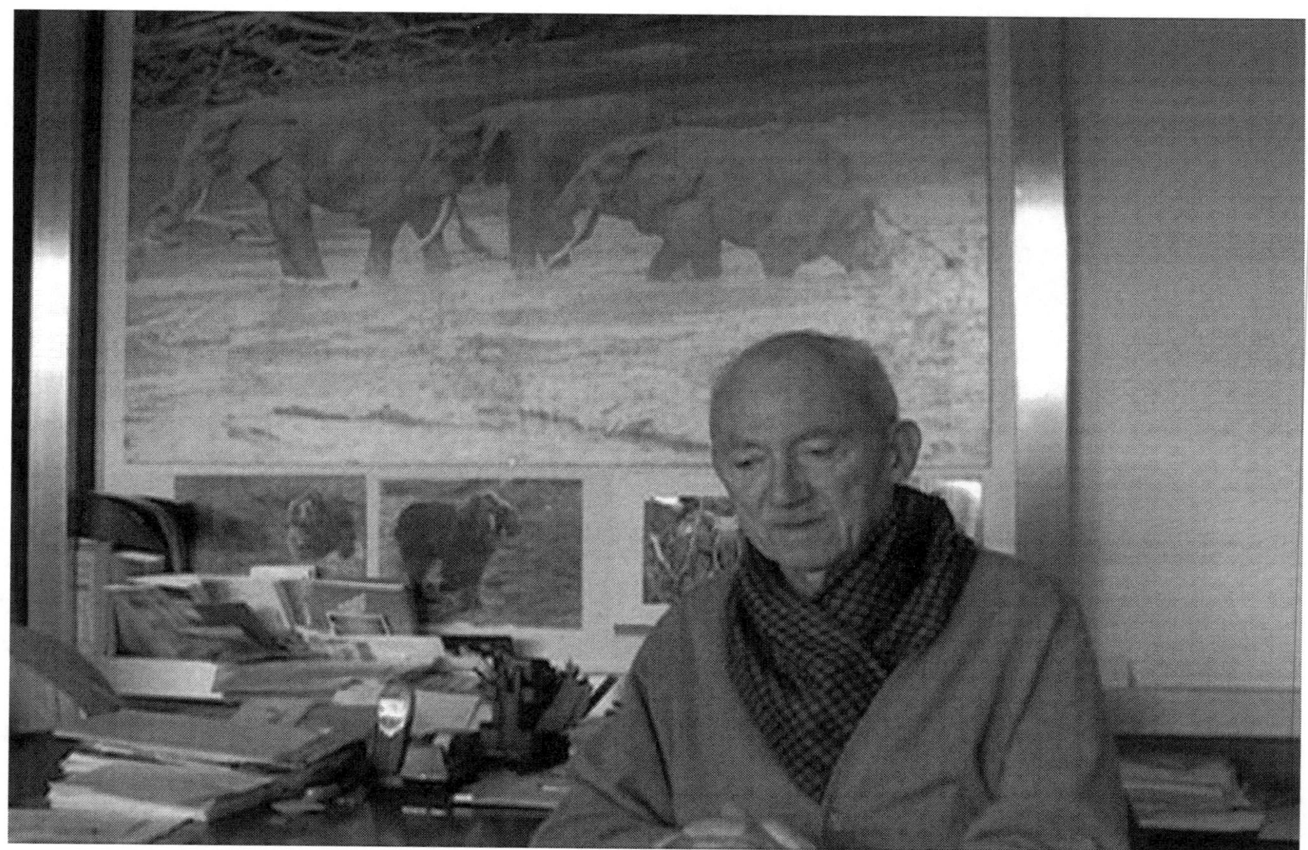

*Fig. 31..6 Paul Tessier at his desk in his office, in front of a picture of his beloved elephants. 2005.*

# Chapter 33

## Kudos

After the 1967 presentation in Rome, Paul Tesssier became a sought-after commodity. The invitations to speak came from all quarters, and were more than he could handle. At the International Society of Plastic Surgery meeting in Montreal in 1983, he was one of the keynote speakers. It was at this meeting that a number of craniofacial surgeons, largely at the urging of Ian Munro (who was still at the Hospital for Sick Children in Toronto—before his move to Dallas), got together to consider forming a new society dedicated to the new specialty that Dr. Tessier had formed.

Tessier was against establishing a formal society and suggested that there just be a travel club. However, the feeling of all of the others present was that there needed to be a formal society, so he said he would not oppose this idea but did not want to be heavily involved. He graciously agreed to be the first president, with the proviso that he would not have to do anything. Daniel Marchac of Paris said that he would arrange the first meeting, which was held in La Napoule, in the south of France, in 1985.

The original name for the society was the International Society of Craniomaxillofacial Surgery, which, in retrospect, was a mistake. Maxillofacial surgery is a separate specialty, involving largely the jaws, whereas craniofacial surgery involves the orbits and the skull. Of course, many craniofacial surgical patients will end up needing maxillofacial procedures, and it can be stated that one of the goals of craniofacial surgery is to convert a craniofacial deformity into a maxillofacial one. This unfortunate choice of terminology antagonized some who largely worked in the oral and maxillofacial surgery realm; they felt that the plastic surgeons were trying to make a "land grab" of their specialty. In response, the European Society of Maxillofacial Surgery changed its name to "Craniomaxillofacial" as well.

Another mistake was not inviting Hugo Obwegeser to be a founding member of the Society. Hugo was an outstanding jaw surgeon, and he had done more than anyone to develop the field of orthognathic surgery to correct jaw deformities. He had trained with Harold Gillies, and he had been part of the "jury" that Tessier convened several times in Paris to decide on the future of craniofacial surgery. Certain voices felt that he was no more than an oral surgeon, and that this new society was to be one of plastic surgeons. Mistakes can be corrected and, years later, our society formally changed its name to "Craniofacial," and Hugo Obwegeser was made an honorary member.

Tessier himself managed to stay above the fray, and Hugo Obwegeser was one of his longtime friends. Hugo's dental background and closeness with the dentists helped him become the leader in jaw surgery. Tessier's lack of a dental background, he felt, was always a limitation for him. And, in terms of orthognathic surgery, particularly on the mandible, he was not an Obwegeser. On the other hand, Tessier's background in ophthalmology and closeness to the ophthalmologists made him the leader in the area of orbital surgery, where, it might be said, Obwegeser was no Tessier.

*Fig. 33.1 Paul Tessier receiving an honorary doctorate from the University of Lund, 1974. Karl Hogeman is on the right, and his wife, Karen Wilmar (who received her PhD), is in the center.*

*Fig. 33.2 Keynote speakers at The International Society of Plastic and Reconstructive Surgery, Montreal, 1983: Ralph Millard, Paul Tessier, Bob Chase, and Bernie O'Brien.*

*Fig. 35.4 Paul Tessier giving his address at the Val de Grace Meeting in his honor. (See Appendixes/Addresses).*

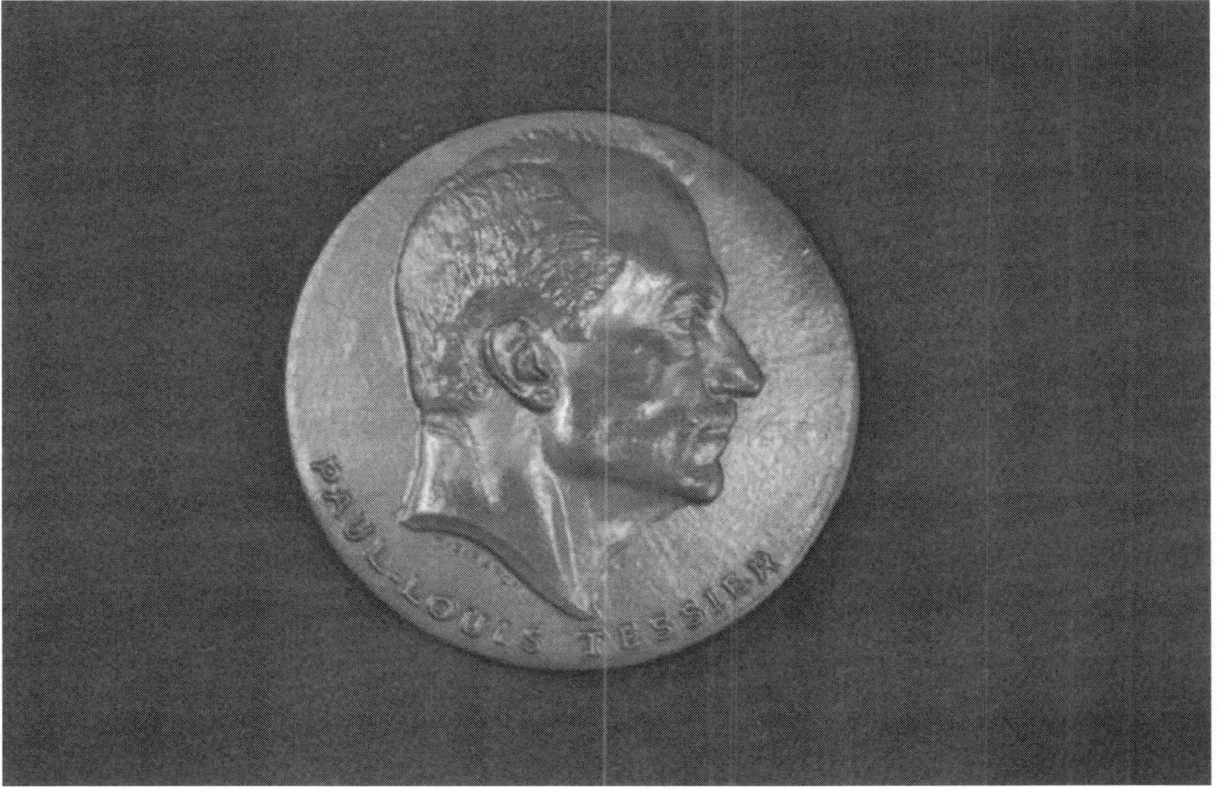


*Fig. 35.5 Another medal struck for Paul Tessier: "From his Students to the Founder of Cranio-Facial Surgery."*

The photograph on the left is of a sculpture that Jacques Levignac made out of wire and offered to Dr. Tessier at the Val de Grace meeting. It captures him remarkably with a fine economy of line.

The text on the right reads:

I am going to personally undertake something: to draw a portrait, with several lines in space, a Character Portrait. I see this as being "The Conquerer."

By these lines, I first establish a "noble posture" with the high forehead.

Then comes, on the forehead, a "vertical line of authority"

The eyebrows rise up high laterally, and bend, with a note of "arrogance."

The expression .... it is an expression which fixes you with a certain transparency, but I cannot render it here "interior quality"... it is looking inwardly, it is looking far away!

The nose. For the nose, it is easier. The nose is a nose with strong nostrils.

It is made to smell: the bitter aroma of a good Havana, the smell of the Atlantic Ocean, the warm odors of the Bush and the Hunt, several musky smells!

The upper lip is adorned with a moustache of stiff hair

Answering it, on the top of the skull, a crest of hair which advances in a point.

The lower lip advances easily, as in saying "Je" (I)

The chin is strong, voluntary, and the angle of the jaw matches it with a masseteric outline.

The cheek bones project.

The ears I have made large .... "ready to hear"

The material for this construction is not just any: rusty iron wire! But it is a noble rust, because this wire has had over the course of time the generous attachments of a vine growing in a difficult sun (in the Causse du Lot) where there is nothing but stones.

"Generous and Difficult".... such is the Man!

"Generous" because he has given us so much, and we know the interest that has in his students.

"Difficult"... I didn't mean that! He is difficult with himself.

If these lines in space have spoken to you like I wanted them to speak, and if you recognize here the essentials of a face and a character?

—Is it him?

Yes it's him! .... Paul Tessier.

Then all is well.

ANN CHIR PLAST ESTHÉT 1994 - VOL. 39 - N° 1 — *HOMMAGE À PAUL TESSIER* — 133

Je vais faire une tentative personnelle : celle de dessiner, avec quelques lignes dans l'espace, un Portrait-Caractère. Ce sera, vu par moi, « Le Conquérant » :

Par ces lignes, je le situe d'abord dans une « posture noble », avec le front haut.

Puis vient, sur le front, une « ligne verticale d'autorité ».

Les sourcils montent loin latéralement et se coudent, avec une note d'« arrogance ».

Le regard... C'est un regard qui vous fixe avec une certaine transparence, mais je ne peux rendre ici sa « qualité intérieure »... Il regarde en dedans. Il regarde loin !

Le nez. Pour le nez, c'est plus facile. Le nez est un nez avec de fortes narines.

Il est fait pour sentir : l'odeur âcre d'un bon Havane, les senteurs marines de l'Atlantique, les odeurs chaudes de la Brousse et de la Chasse, quelques odeurs musquées !...

La lèvre supérieure s'orne d'une moustache à poils durs.

Ici lui répond, sur le sommet du crâne, une crête de cheveux qui avance en pointe.

La lèvre inférieure avance facilement, comme pour dire « JE ».

Le menton est accusé, volontaire, et l'angle de la mâchoire lui correspond avec un relief massétérin.

Les pommettes saillent.

Les oreilles, je les fais grandes... « à l'écoute ».

La Matière même de cette construction n'est pas quelconque : un fil de fer rouillé ! Mais il s'agit d'une rouille noble, car ce fil a porté au cours du temps des grappes généreuses d'une vigne venue dans un sol difficile (dans le Causse du Lot) où il n'y a que des pierres.

« Généreux et Difficile »... tel est l'Homme !

« Généreux » car il nous a tant donné, et nous savons l'intérêt qu'il porte à ses élèves.

« Difficile »... Je n'insiste pas !... Il est difficile avec lui-même.

Si ces lignes dans l'espace vous ont parlé comme j'ai voulu qu'elles parlent, et si vous reconnaissez ici dans l'essentiel un visage et un caractère ?

– C'est lui ?

– C'est bien lui !... Paul Tessier

Alors c'est bien !

**Jacques LEVIGNAC**
*Secrétaire Général*
*de l'Association Française*
*des Chirurgiens Maxillo-faciaux*

*Fig. 35.7 Sculpture made by Jacques Levignac for Tessier of Tessier*

Jacques Levignac, Secretary General of the French Association of Maxillofacial Surgeons

*Fig. 35.8 Tessier complimenting Jacque Levignac on his work.*

There is some irony in the fact that Paul Tessier, for whom this special ceremony was held by The French Society of Maxillofacial Surgery (of which he was the first president), once received stern letters from "Médecin General," Gustave Ginestet, Chief of the Maxillofacial and Stomatology Service at Hôpital Foch. Ginestet, after all, forbade him to do any maxillofacial surgery in that institution.

# Chapter 35

## A Trip to Cuba

In the early 1980s, I received a reprint request from a surgeon in Cuba. And, though it was only a fifteen-minute flight from Miami, was worlds away. I sent him a number of papers and a note saying that I thought it was too bad that we couldn't get together since we were not far away. A number of months later, I received a call from the Cuban Interest Section, which I believe was in the Czech Embassy in Washington, asking whether I would like to go to Cuba. The first time I went, I was told that the only way to get there would be through Montreal or Mexico City, which seemed ridiculous for a destination that was only a hundred miles away. A friend who worked at the Miami airport told me that he thought there was a flight on Sunday nights, although it was not listed. Indeed there was, and my nurse and I found ourselves on a very old DC-3 leaving Miami International Airport, destination Havana. The first time I went, the Cubans were not prepared for our visit, so I gave a number of lectures and performed only a few operations. I got to know Harley Borges, who was the "Dean" of Cuban plastic surgery, having been a chief resident at the time Fidel Castro took over, and about the only plastic surgeon who did not emigrate.

Harley is a jovial man, and he arranged for me to come back several more times—at which times there was a good bit of surgery to do. I was also asked to care for the wife of a rather senior individual in the Cuban Protocol Department. She had a fairly extensive vascular malformation of one side of her face, and had had one prior operation in France. She and her husband came to Miami twice for surgery, staying about a month each time, and I recollect that all of the surgical fees and hospital costs were paid without any difficulty. They were very nice people, and we became good friends. During the trips to Cuba, they arranged excursions to various parts of the country and were quite hospitable. My trips to Cuba were entirely apolitical, but it certainly seemed like, under Communism, everyone was equal, but some were a little more equal.

In any event, in 1996, when I received another invitation, I thought of Dr. Tessier and his lifelong love affair with Cuban cigars. I asked the Cubans whether they would like me to see whether he would like to come, and they were delighted. We invited Henry Kawamoto, which was reminiscent of our trip to Brazil in the past, my wife, Deirdre (who was about six months pregnant), and his nurse, Rose DiBiase. This time we were fortunate that there was a scheduled flight from Miami to Havana on a United Airlines charter, and we met Dr. Tessier in Havana.

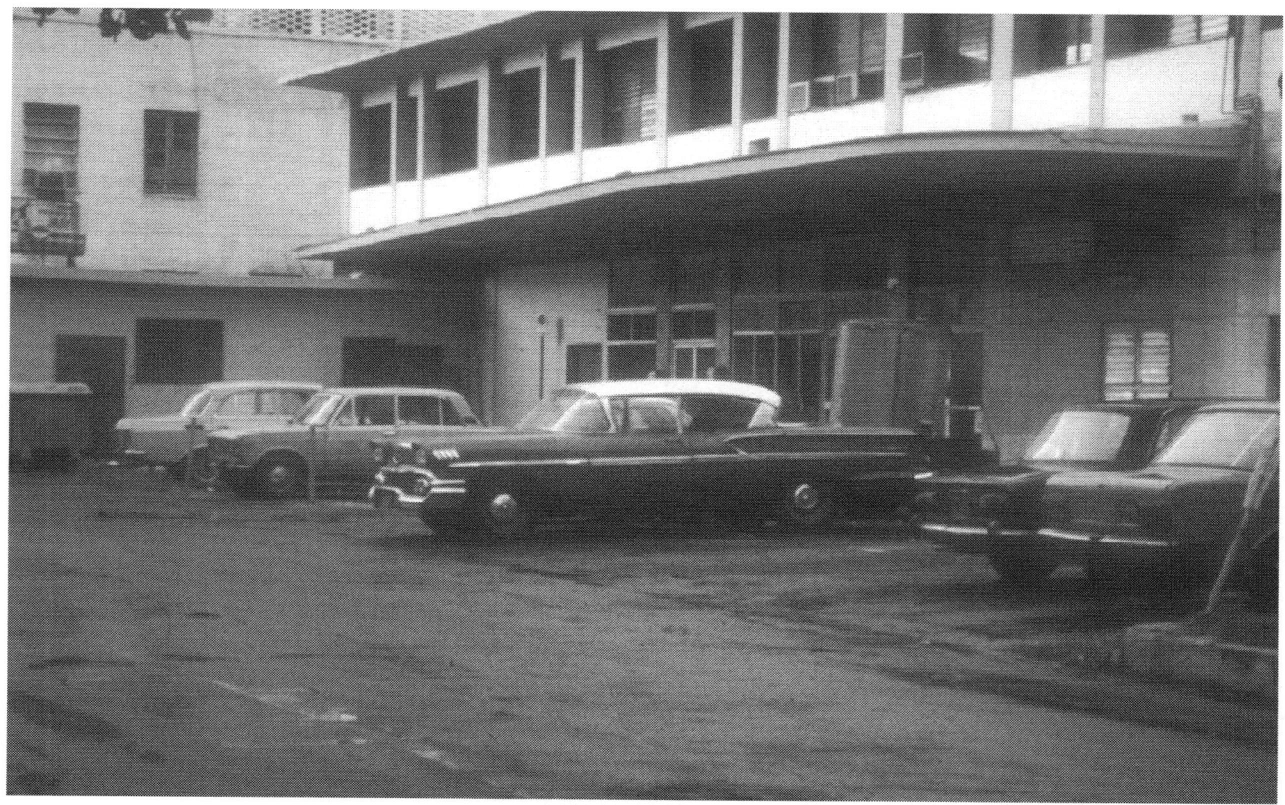

*Fig. 36.1 1958 Chevrolet, still running, surrounded by Russian Ladas, in front of Havana Children's Hospital.*

*Fig. 36.2 Tessier marveling at the length of the cigars in the "cave" of the Partegas factory, Havana.*

*Fig. 36.3 With our guide in the "cave" of the Partegas factory, Havana.*

*Fig. 36.4 In Havana's largest cigar shop, with purchases.*

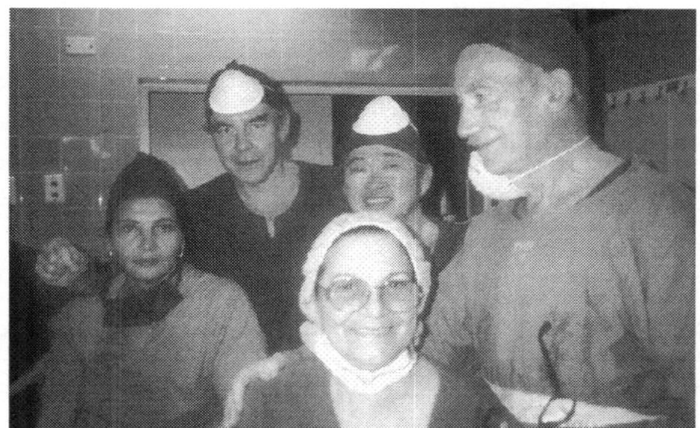

*Fig. 36.5 In the Children's Hospital, Havana. Tessier has his arm on the shoulder of their maxillofacial surgeon. Kawamoto and Wolfe are behind him.*

*Fig. 36.6 Tessier, oblivious to the Socialist jargon on the board behind him.*

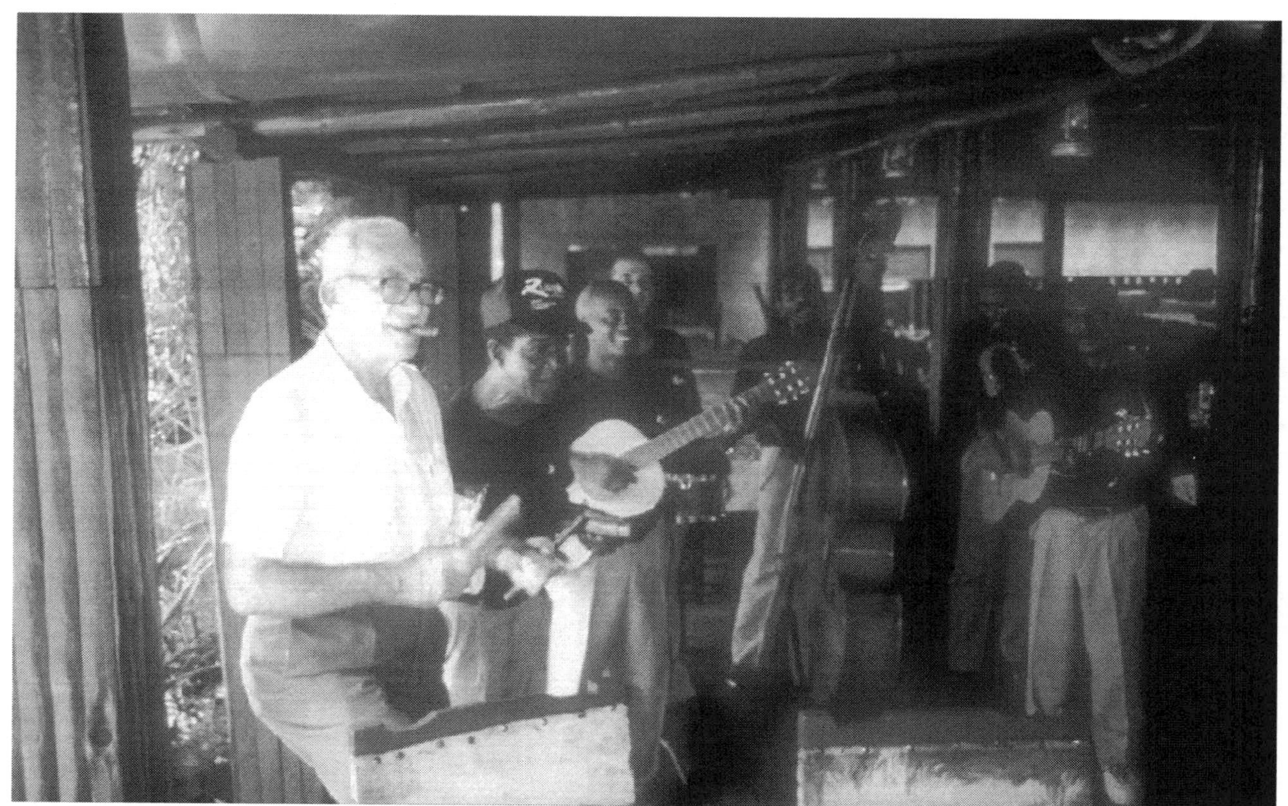

*Fig. 36.7 Tessier playing along with the band on "la clave."*

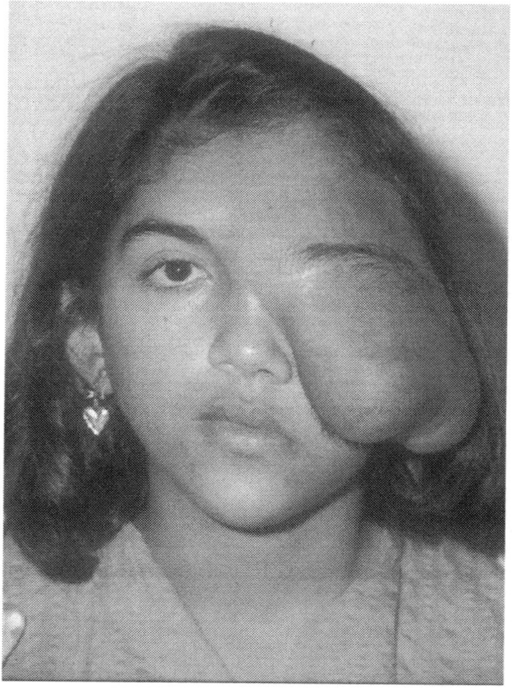

*Fig. 36.8 One of the patients we were asked to operate on.*

*Fig. 36.19 Shed for drying tobacco in Pinar del Rio, Cuba.*

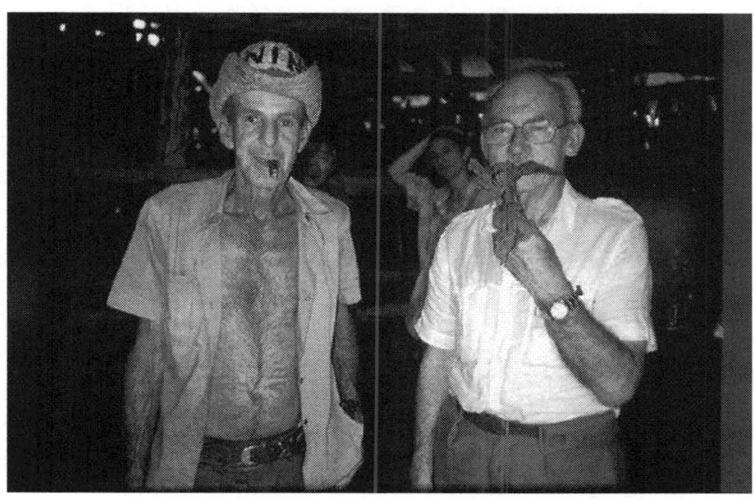

*Fig. 36.20 Tessier in a tobacco drying shed, Pinar del Rio.*

A cigar was a constant companion to Paul Tessier.

*Fig. 36.21 Tessier hidden behind a cloud of tobacco smoke with Serge Morax.*

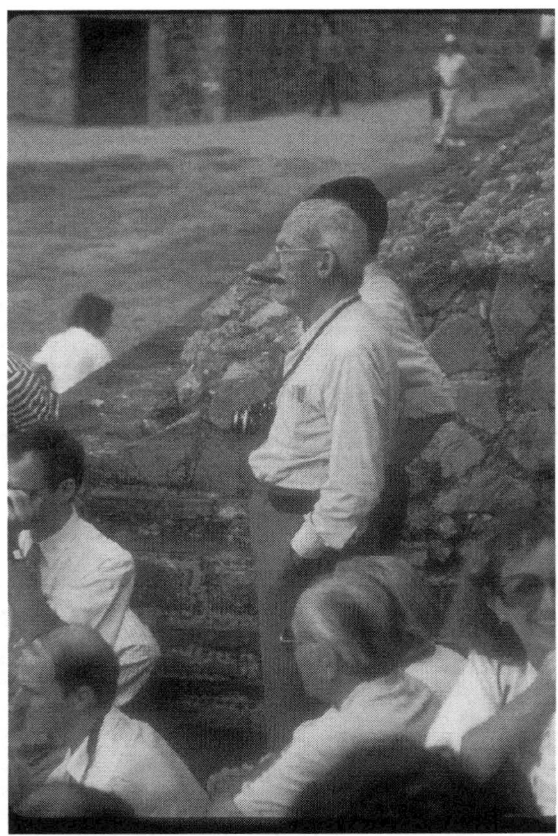

*Fig. 36.22 Meeting of The International Society of Craniofacial Surgery, Oaxaca, Mexico, 1993.*

*Fig. 36.23 Another picture taken at Oaxaca, with a Cohiba in his shirt pocket.*

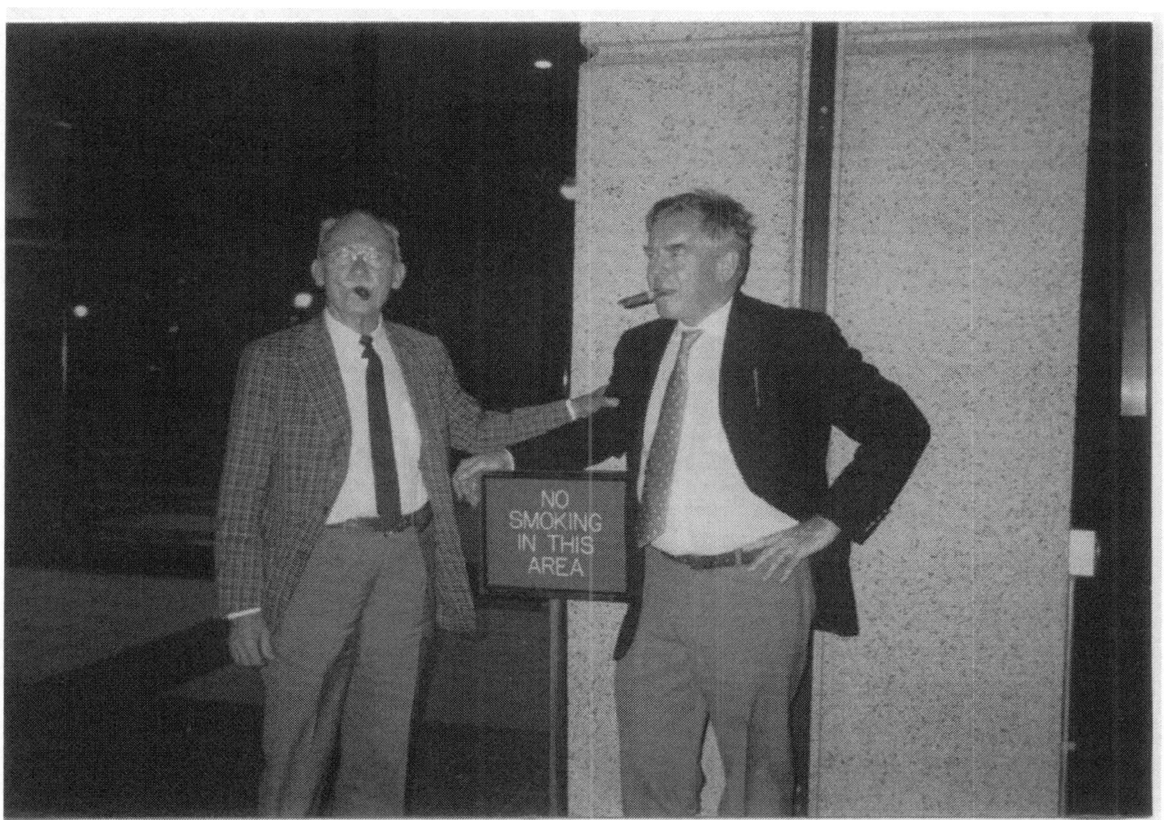


*Fig. 36.24 Scofflaws in Chicago, 2000.*

*Fig. 36.25 SAW, Tessier, and Henry Kawamoto during the "Tour de Bretagne"*

*Fig. 36.26 Making a point with a cigar.*

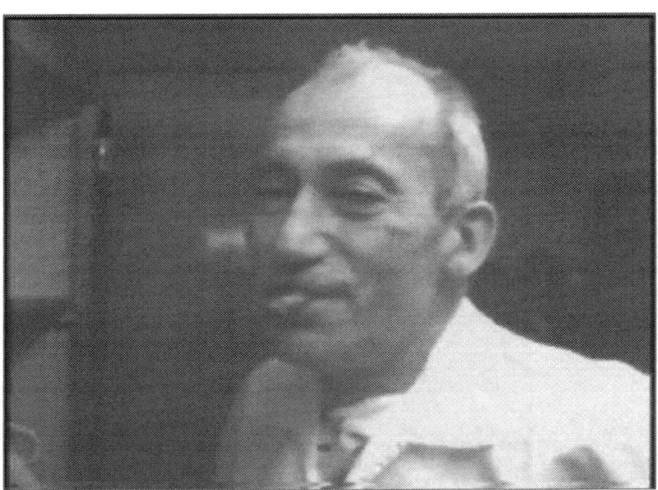

*Fig. 36.27 From a 1983 documentary on plastic surgery done for WGBH, Public Television in Boston, by Ted Begossian. Tessier is in the locker room between cases, taking a few puffs before heading back to surgery.*

Paul Tessier enjoyed a good cigar. A good cigar, in his opinion, could only be a Cuban cigar, and he bemoaned the fact that they were often not as good as he remembered they once had been.

In 1974–75, if one of us went to Switzerland and was near either Zurich or Geneva, it was *de rigeur* to stop off at the Davidoff tobacconist to pick up a box of *Château Lafite* or *Château Margaux*.

Zino Davidoff was a Russian who had opened a tobacco shop in Geneva and had had Lenin as one of his customers. He began his Chateau series in 1947 and, in 1969, was more or less given the pick of Cuban tobacco by the Cuban government. The cigars of that era were the best ones, according to Tessier. In 1990, Davidoff had a disagreement with the Cuban government and was no longer able to market Cuban tobaccos. The Cubans came up with their own brand, which they called Cohiba, and they also used other prerevolutionary names such as Hoyo de Monterey, Punch, Romeo y Julieta, and Partegas.

We were taken on a tour of the Partegas factory in Havana, arranged by the husband of my patient (the one who had come to Miami for treatment). We came to a very large room where there were perhaps a hundred men and women sitting at small workstations hand rolling cigars. The whole process was explained to us. At the front of the room, there was a raised area with a table. At the table sat the *Lector*—there was an old Cuban tradition of having someone read to the tobacco rollers from a book or newspaper, to educate them while they performed their somewhat monotonous work. One of the Cubans who was giving us our tour went up to the *Lector* and whispered something in his ear. The *Lector* stopped his reading, and announced to all of the cigar makers that there were some visitors present, from France, Los Angeles, and Miami, who had come to operate on Cuban children with facial malformations. Each cigar roller had at his or her workstation a semicircular knife called a *chuleta* that is used to cut the cigar. All one hundred workers applauded us in unison by banging their *chuletas* on the table. It was a touching moment.

In any event, we went then to a packaging room and saw that the same cigars (as the one we viewed in the Partegas factory) were being given Cohiba or other wrappers—so much for distinctiveness of the brands.

Many of us learned about the appreciation of cigars from Tessier. There should be a certain firmness when squeezed, yet some give. The cigar should not crackle when rolled between the fingers (too dry). And the aroma. *Savor.*

# Chapter 36

## "Tour de Bretagne."

Paul Tessier was enormously proud of "his Brittany," and had arranged tours lasting a week or longer for a number of his good friends, including Fred and Mary McCoy and Fernando and Leonore Ortiz-Monasterio. In the summer of 1997, he offered to take two of his American sons, Kawamoto and Wolfe (and their wives) on this same tour.

He had obviously spent a good deal of time arranging the itinerary—where we would stay every night, what we would visit, and were we would have lunch and dinner. Plus, he would bring along his notes and "grades"on previous meals and wines that he had had in these restaurants with Mireille.

He had been planning on renting a spacious car to drive us around, but he had forgotten that the Paris Air Show was taking place in June, so the largest car he could find was an Audi A4. It was quite a snug fit: either Henry or Tony was in the front seat, and Deirdre, Kathy, and the backseat male squeezed in rather tightly (along with whatever luggage could not be jammed into the trunk).

We stayed in a number of wonderful auberges, and had a tight itinerary, visiting Chartres, the Apocalypse tapestries in Angers, Mont. St. Michel, the areas by the sea where *fleur de sel* (sea salt) was harvested by drying in the sun, an area where electricity was generated by the tide, light houses, museums, small villages, and on and on. At each stop, he would buy a little book for us on the topic: light houses of Brittany, hydroelectric generation and the tides, the history of Mont. St. Michel.

But the important thing was the meals. We had long vinous lunches, and *Le Patron* insisted on doing all of the driving himself, at age 80. 170 km per hour is about 100 mph, and it seemed that this was about his average pace. HKK and SAW had their eyes shut during most of this because they were asleep, but the wives may have had them shut for another reason.

DOCTEUR PAUL TESSIER

25, BOULEVARD D'AUTEUIL
92100 BOULOGNE
TEL. (33-1) 46 04 61 60
FAX (33-1) 46 04 61 10

S. Anthony WOLFE, M.D.

Le 30 Avril 1997

Mon Cher Tony,

Merci de votre Fax du 28 Mai d'après lequel je suis heureux d'apprendre qu'Henry peut vraiment se joindre à nous à Paris dès le jeudi 12 Juin, mais plus probablement le vendredi 13 dans la journée, ce qui signifie dans la soirée.
Cela suffira et définitivement nous quitterons Paris tous ensemble le samedi 14 in early morning.

Les MAMIIANS devront donc quitter Miami le jeudi 12 pour arriver à Paris le vendredi 13 (comme Henry), mais le matin vers 10 H 30. Vous aurez votre chambre habituelle au stade Roland Garros. Nous récupérerons les MARBELLIENS là où ils auront couché.

Ma voiture est trop petite pour cinq personnes au cours d'un long voyage. Nous en louerons donc une deuxième.

Le T.T.S. "Tessier Tourning Service" s'occupera de toutes les réservations, excepté de celle du soleil.

Je ne connais rien aux "labial orthodontics" mais, dans ce cas, le terme anal orthodontics ne conviendrait-il pas mieux ?

La semaine dernière je vous ai renvoyé ma lettre de 1994 sur vos "orbito centriques". Ne vous fatiguez donc plus à la chercher dans les corbeilles à papier.

Toutes nos amitiés. A bientôt,

*Fig. 37.1 Letter from Tessier to author*

Dear Tony,

Thanks for your fax of 28 May, from which I was happy to learn that Henry can really join us in Paris on 12 June, but probably on Friday the 13th during the day, which means the evening.

That will be all right, and we will definitively leave Paris all together on Saturday the 14th in early morning.

The MIAMIANS should therefore leave Miami Thursday the 12th to arrive in Paris on Friday the 13th (like Henry), but in the morning near 10:30 am. You will have your usual room at the Roland Garros stadium. We will pick up the MARBELLIANS where they are staying.

My car is too small for 5 people and a long trip. We will rent another one.

The T.T.S. "Tessier Touring Service" will take care of all of the reservations, except for the sun.

Etc.

All the best,

Tessier

*Fig. 37.2 Tessier at the wheel after a two-bottle-of-wine lunch in Chartres, driving at a steady 130 kph Kathy Kawamoto's white-knuckled hand is visible on the left.*

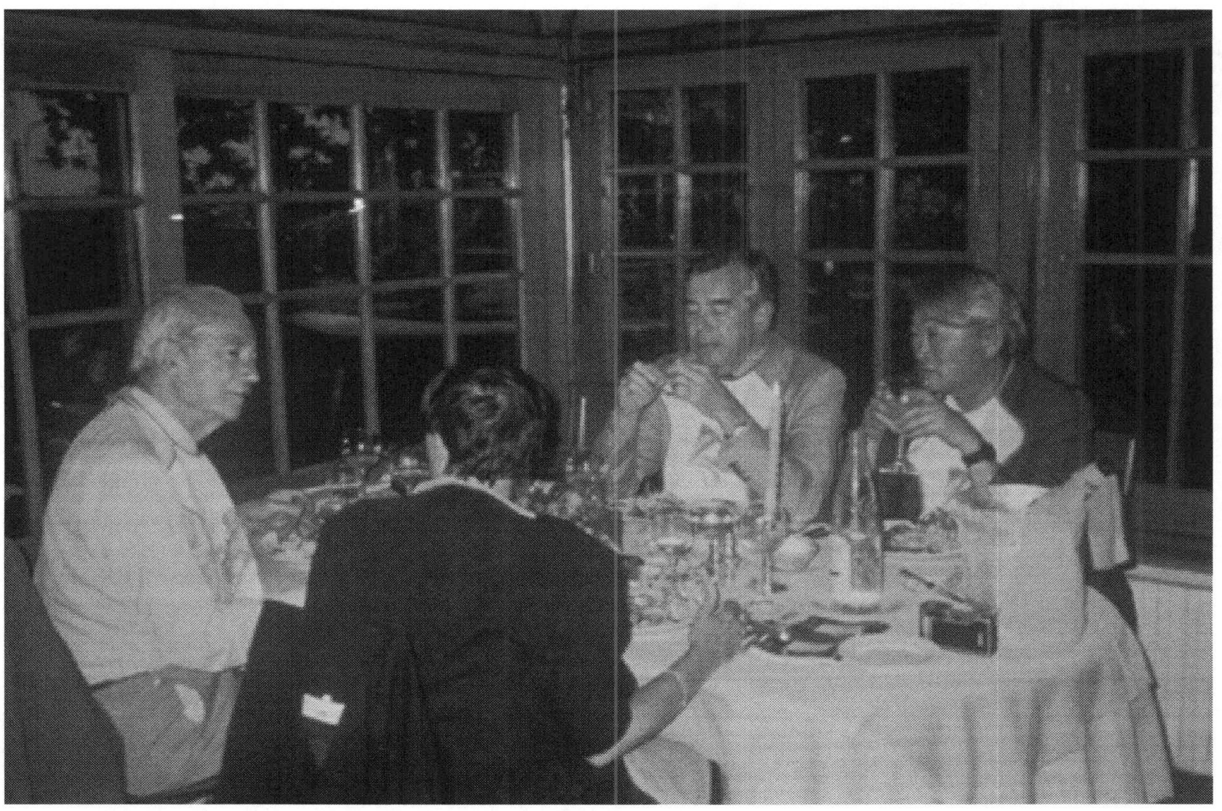

*Fig. 37.3 Dressed for lobster*

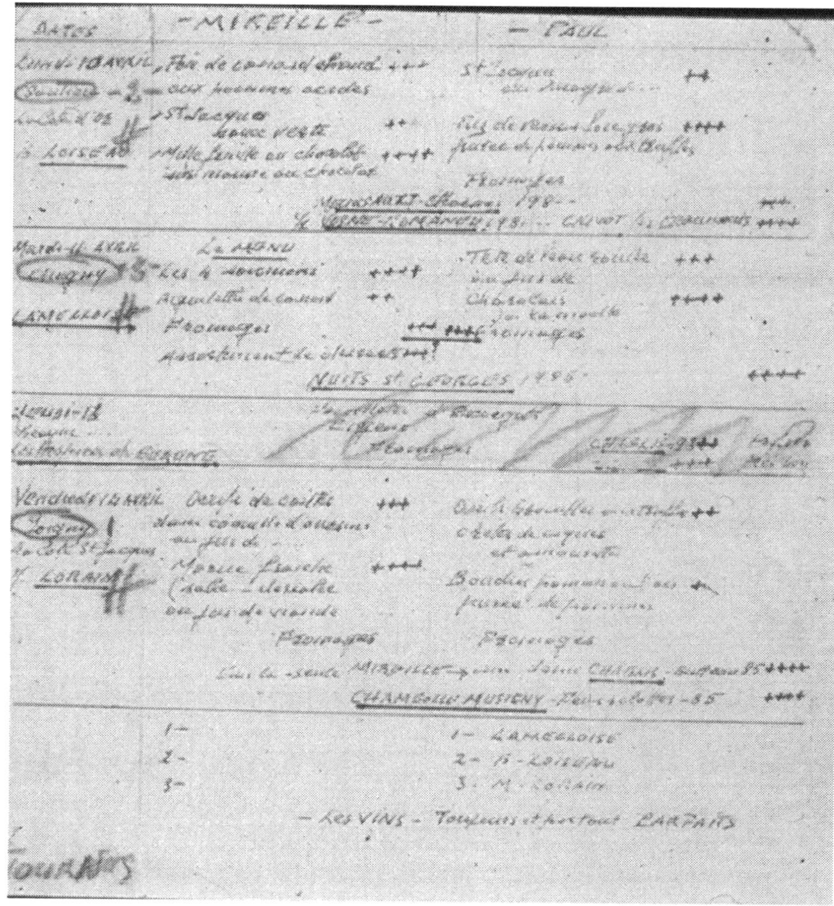

DATES — MIREILLE — — PAUL

NUITS St GEORGES 1986

1— LAMELOISE
2— B. LOISEAU
3— M. LORAIN

— LES VINS — Toujours et partout PARFAITS

*Fig. 37.4 This list is vintage Tessier. On a previous tour with Mireille, he rated the food and wines at every dinner along the way.*

*Fig. 37.5 Tessier waiting patiently on his buffoons (SAW and Henry Kawamoto).*

*Fig. 37.6 Tourists in Bretagne with their tour master (SAW and Henry Kawamoto)*

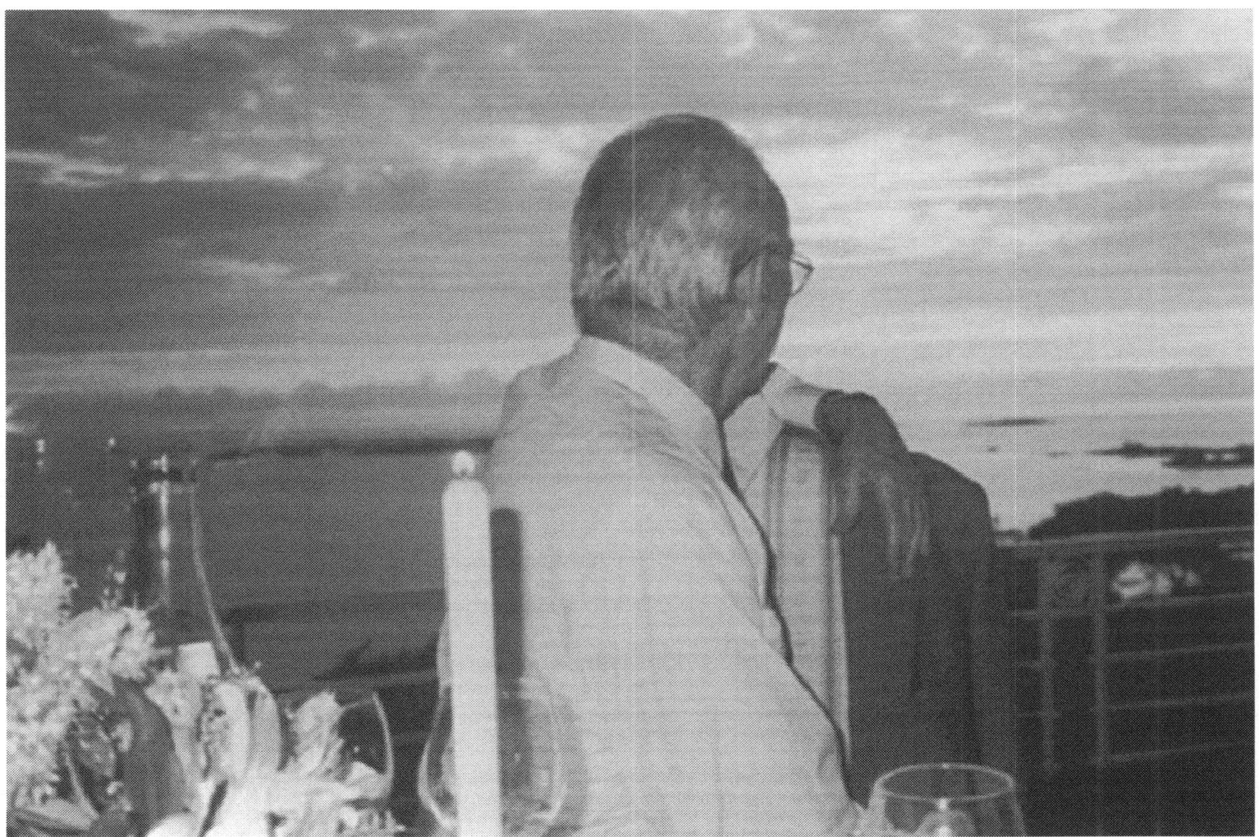

*Fig. 37.7 Tessier watching the sunset after a dinner on the terrace, St. Malo.*

*Fig. 37.8 A few minutes later.*

Henry Kawamoto took both of these pictures, and he was kind enough to send them to me. Seeing Paul Tessier in one picture and seeing him gone in the next is haunting. He is gone, but the candle still burns.

# Chapter 37

## Open Heart Surgery

Paul's mitral valve had most likely been damaged during his near fatal bout with typhoid fever in the early 1940s, and his cardiologist recommended that he have surgery to correct it. In January 2003, at age 85, he entered the George Pompidou Hospital in Paris and had a mitral valvuloplasty performed by Dr. Charpentier, who was seventy-five at the time (but he was the one who had developed the procedure). Another surgeon came in and performed a "pontage" (a coronary bypass graft). Tessier was fatalistic about having major surgery at this age, and he postponed the procedure until Jean-Paul could be back from his studies at Boston University.

*Fig. 38.1 Tessier in Héric, summer of 2003, six months after successful cardiac surgery.*

*Fig. 38.2 Tessier with Enzo, his Alsatian.*

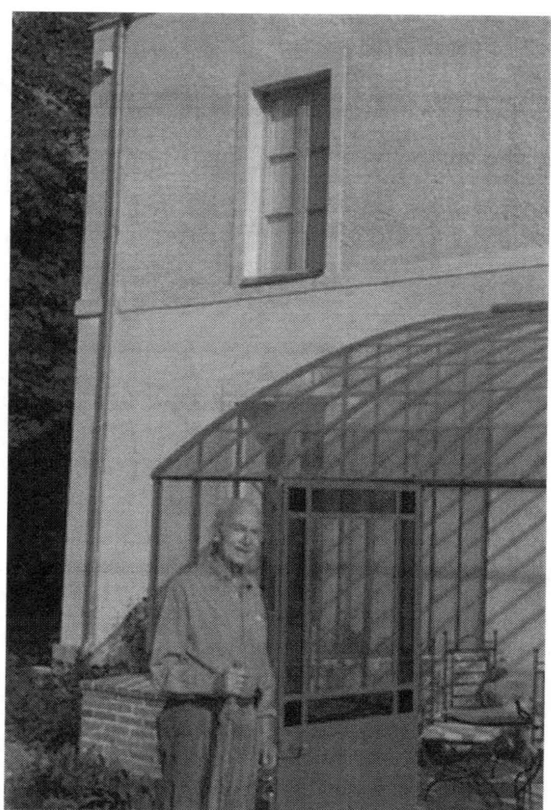

*Fig. 38.3 Tessier standing beneath the window of the room in Bonne Hygié in which he was born, eighty-six years before.*

# Chapter 38

## Chévalier de la Legion d'Honneur

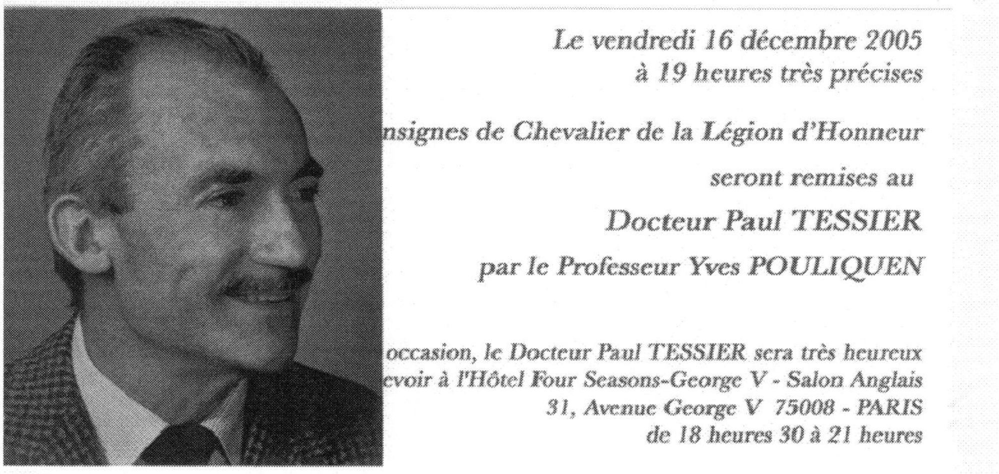

Le vendredi 16 décembre 2005
à 19 heures très précises

nsignes de Chevalier de la Légion d'Honneur
seront remises au
Docteur Paul TESSIER
par le Professeur Yves POULIQUEN

occasion, le Docteur Paul TESSIER sera très heureux
evoir à l'Hôtel Four Seasons-George V - Salon Anglais
31, Avenue George V 75008 - PARIS
de 18 heures 30 à 21 heures

*Fig. 39.1 Invitation to a ceremony awarding Tessier the Legion d'Honneur.*

Daniel Marchac, in fact, received the Legion d'Honneur before Tessier. He certainly made contributions to craniofacial surgery, but not anywhere near as many as Tessier. Marchac's wife's political connections with the Mitterand administration may have played a role in this outcome. In fact, when Tessier was nominated for the Nobel Prize, (by many, including laureate Joe Murray), the lukewarm feedback from his own countrymen is said to have put a kibosh on it. The reasons for this may be multiple but, in France, all power is concentrated in Paris, and the Parisians are notoriously snobby about people who are not from Paris. Tessier, although he had been chief of a service at Foch, was largely a force of his own, working outside of the French academic medical system. Nevertheless, the man from Héric finally received the highest recognition that his nation could bestow. The Legion d'Honneur is an award that was instituted by Napoleon Bonaparte, who regretted the fact that, after the Republicans had killed off the Bourbon regime, they had also eradicated all types of awards of merit.

*Fig. 39.2 Tessier arriving in a pink Cadillac, organized by Elizabeth.*

*Fig. 39.3 Tessier listening to Yves Pouliquen's speech.*

*Fig. 39.4 Chevalier de Legion d'Honneur, finally.*

*Fig. 39.5 Receiving congratulations from Professor Pouliquen.*

*Fig. 39.6 Grandson Gilles du Tertre, daughter Claude, Tessier, and son Jean-Paul.*

Francoise Firmin, Serge Morax, Hugo Obwegeser, and I were asked to say a few words after Tessier received his award. Tessier had given me a book about the French role in the American War of Independence and the Battle of Yorktown. There were several hundred French soldiers who died at Yorktown, and we never would have won had it not been for La Fayette, Rochambeau, and, particularly, Admiral de Grasse, who prevented the English fleet from coming to the aid of Cornwallis. I thanked Louis the Sixteenth for his help, and said that America might never have come to exist without the help of the French, and that I was glad we were able to pay them back by our participation in two world wars. There was a very long history of assistance extending in both directions across the Atlantic, and I said that I was most grateful for having been able to come to Paris to learn from the master.

*Fig. 39.8 Ceremony awarding the Legion d'Honneur in the Hotel Georges V. Tessier, Elizabeth Motel-Hecht, Alexander Stratadoukis (Athens), Nabil Hokayem (Beirut), and SAW. Elizabeth was largely responsible for arranging this reception, and she brought two elephant tusks to frame the speakers.*

*Fig. 39.9 The cover of a DVD that Elizabeth Motel-Hecht made for the Legion d'Honneur ceremony. The ceremony—and perhaps even the awarding of the prize itself—were orchestrated by Elizabeth.*

(Upper left: Gosti, who had made the large montage/sculpture of Tessier's old instruments, bent into fanciful shapes, and his wife. Also: Dr. Lekieffre, ophthalmologist from Lilles; Andrée Collesson and Tessier; pink Cadillac convertible that Elizabeth had arranged to have Tessier driven to the ceremony; Tessier, Elizabeth; and SAW. Second row, from the left: Alexander Stratadoukis of Athens and SAW with the Gosti sculpture behind them; Mme. Collesson and Snejina Freche; Yvon Raulo; LeKieffre and Tessier; Dr. Glicenstein; Gilbert Aiache, friend of Dr. Ohanna; and Carlo Cavina of Bologna. Third row, from the left: Tessier and Hans Peter Freihofer of Zurich then Nejmigen; Gilbert Ozun; Jean-François Tulasne; Chantal Guitton, nurse; Mme. Foste, secretary; Yves Polenquin; Mireille Tessier, Paul Tessier. Fourth row, from the left: Tessier, Dr. Ohanna; Freihofer; Dr. Duvanel; Beat Hammer of Berne; Dr. Besins of Paris; and Dr. Gross, internist in Paris. Bottom row, from the left: Paul Tessier; Mireille Tessier; Dr. and Mrs Robinson, United States; Polenquin and Tessier; Hugo Obwegeser, Zurich; Serge Morax, ophthalmologist, Paris.)

Elizabeth has written vertically: *Hommag au plus grand plasticien du XXieme siècle* (Homage to the greatest plastic surgeon of the twentieth century). I would say that this is not exageration.

# Chapter 39

## "Honoris Causa."

The Stryker Corporation was going to be holding their worldwide business meeting in London in March, 2006, and Andy Rogers of Stryker contacted Dr. Tessier to see whether a scientific meeting could be organized in his honor. Dr. Tessier was not certain whether he would be physically able to come, but he was *quite* certain that he did not want to have anything done with the organization of the meeting itself, and he suggested to Andy that he contact me to see whether I would be willing to put it together. I was happy to do so—especially when I heard that there would be some help. Impromed was an organization that helped put on medical meetings and provide CME credits; they were just down the street from Stryker in Kalamazoo, Michigan, and they had set up meetings for Stryker before. Suzanne Eggers founded Impromed, and she organized the meeting magnificently. (I asked for her help again a few year later when I had to put together the biennial meeting of the International Society of Craniofacial Surgery in Bahia, Brazil.)

Meetings of this sort—where all of the previous trainees of a professor are asked to give a presentation on his behalf, usually at his retirement—are usually called *Festschrifts*. But since Dr. Tessier was French, and particularly since he had spent some time as a prisoner of war in a German military hospital, I thought that perhaps another term might be appropriate. I decided upon "Honoris Causa," that is "For the Purpose of Conferring Esteem or Honor," a term with which honorary doctorates of science are often bestowed.

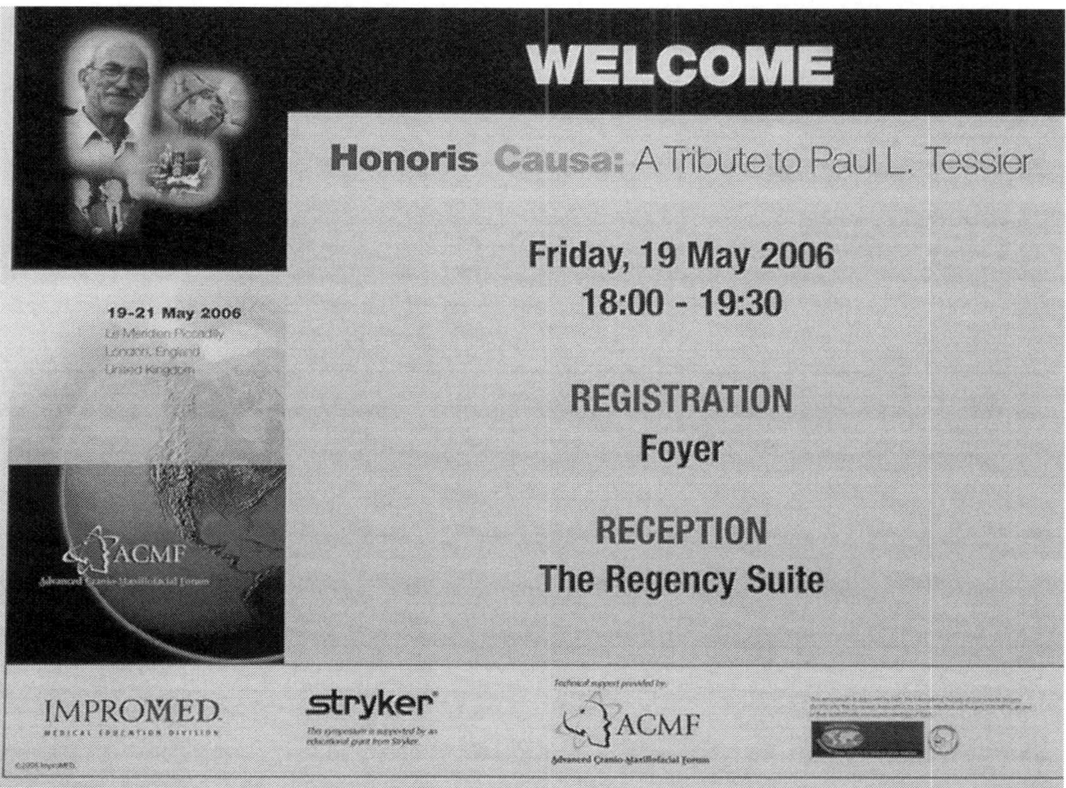


*Fig. 40.1 Sign in the Foyer of the Piccadilly Hotel.*

*Fig. 40.2 SAW, Andy Rogers of Stryker who was the impetus behind the meeting, and Tessier.*

We invited everyone who had spent a significant amount of time with Dr. Tessier as a trainee (and was still active in craniofacial surgery), as well as a few others who had been taking Dr. Tessier's principles into new areas and making major contributions (Paul Manson and Joe Gruss). Dr. Tessier's only input for the meeting was to approve the list of invitees. Most were able to come, except, alas, for Françoise Firmin, who had been closer to Tessier than anyone, but who had a family obligation that she could not alter.

Over the course of late 2005 and early 2006, I visited the Tessiers five or six times, staying for three to four days each time. There were a number of unfinished projects that he had hoped I would be able to get done. We had successfully finished the supplement for *Plastic and Reconstructive Surgery* entitled "Tools and Techniques for the Harvesting of Autogenous Bone Grafts," and there were other papers in various stages of completion: The Arrhinias (published now in *The Scandinavian Journal of Plastic Surgery,* after Dr. Tessier's death, unfortunately), The Barron-Tessier Flap (in press in *Annals of Plastic Surgery*), and the new version of his Cleft Classification, where he distinguished between clefts and ageneses (C.A.A.C.: The Classification of Ageneses and Clefts—published in an incomplete form in *The European Journal of Craniomaxillofacial Surgery).*

Most of the time (twelve to fourteen hours per day) that I was with the Tessiers, was spent in his small "archives" room, adjacent to his office/study. (See Chapter 30.) Here, he kept the medical records of most of his "significant" patients, the photographic negatives and 35 mm slides of all of his patients, most of his skull collection, and all of the drawings that Francine Gourdin and Merri Sheifflin had done over the years. I went through every chart, looked at every drawing, and pulled slides and negatives whenever pre-op and post-op results were available. I took these all back to Miami and had them scanned. I then put together a very large PowerPoint presentation of his entire career, from the early 1950s through the late 1990s. This presentation, entitled "London: Honoris Causa 2006, has been placed in the jacket at the back of this book along with my translation of the 1976 report to The French Society of Ophthalmology and several video clips of Dr. Tessier in 1983 and 2005.

Even a week before the meeting, we weren't sure whether he could come. His back bothered him a great deal, and he could only walk with a cane. Finally, he said that he would come, but he refused to fly (because airports were too much of a hassle, certainly not a fear of flying). So Stryker organized a car and driver to bring him, Mireille, and Laurence through the Chunnel. He enjoyed the meeting greatly, although it was evident that he was experiencing a lot of pain while traveling.

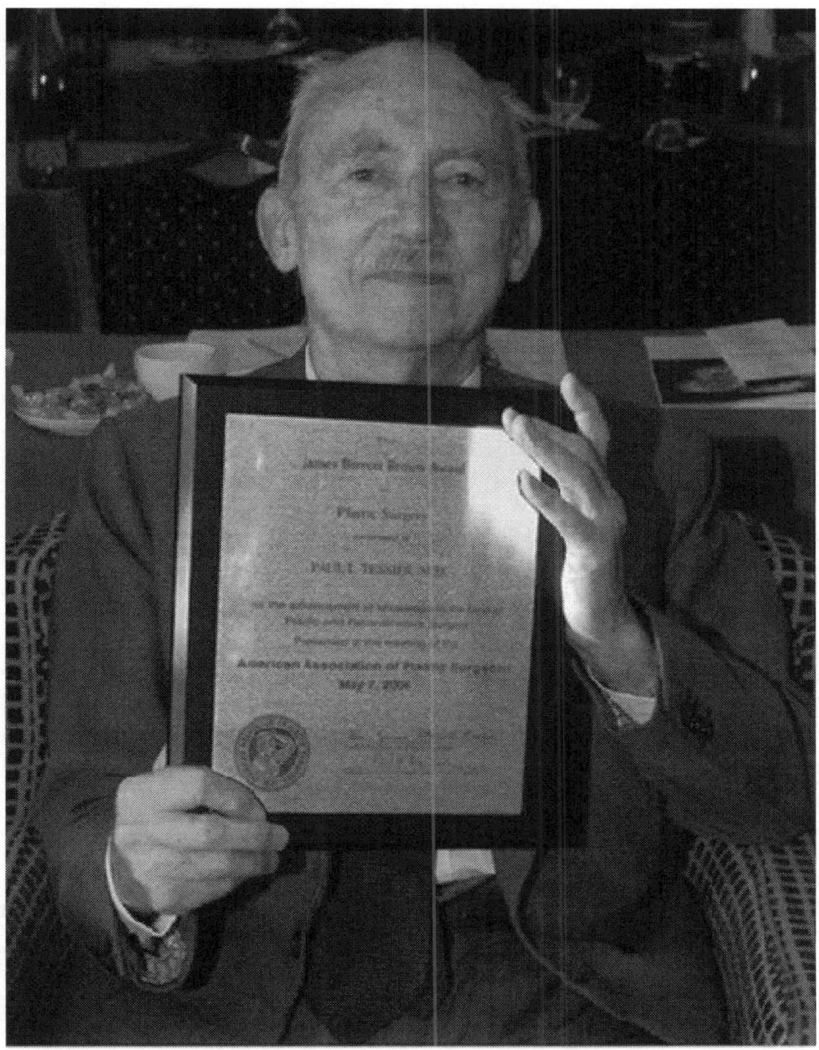

*Fig. 40.3 Tessier with his James Barrett Brown award, bestowed by Paul Manson, the outgoing president of The American Association of Plastic surgeons.*

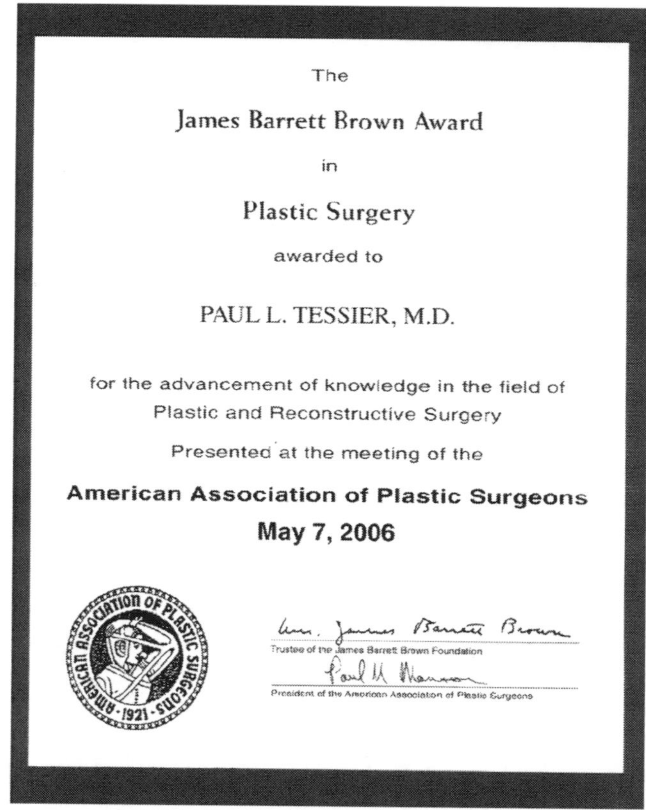

The

James Barrett Brown Award

in

Plastic Surgery

awarded to

PAUL L. TESSIER, M.D.

for the advancement of knowledge in the field of
Plastic and Reconstructive Surgery

Presented at the meeting of the

**American Association of Plastic Surgeons**

**May 7, 2006**

American Association of Plastic Surgeons · 1921 ·

Trustee of the James Barrett Brown Foundation

President of the American Association of Plastic Surgeons

*Fig. 40.4 The James Barrett Brown award is given every year for what the membership of The American Association of Plastic Surgeons considers the best paper to have appeared in Plastic and Reconstructive Surgery over the past year. This was the second time Dr. Tessier had won it; his paper on the Le Fort III-type osteotomy won in the 1970s.*

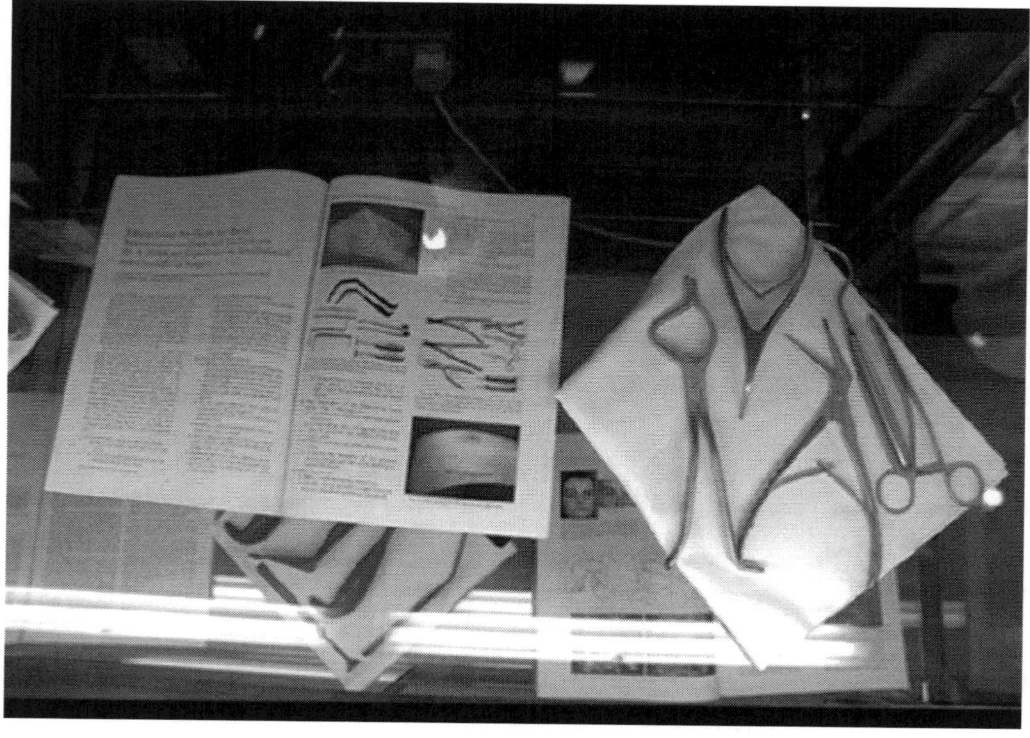

*Fig. 40.5 The PRS Supplement and some of the instruments designed by Dr. Tessier.*

*Fig. 40.6 Elizabeth Motel-Hecht, Dr. Tessier's instrumentiste (scrub nurse) who worked as hard as he did for twenty-five years.*

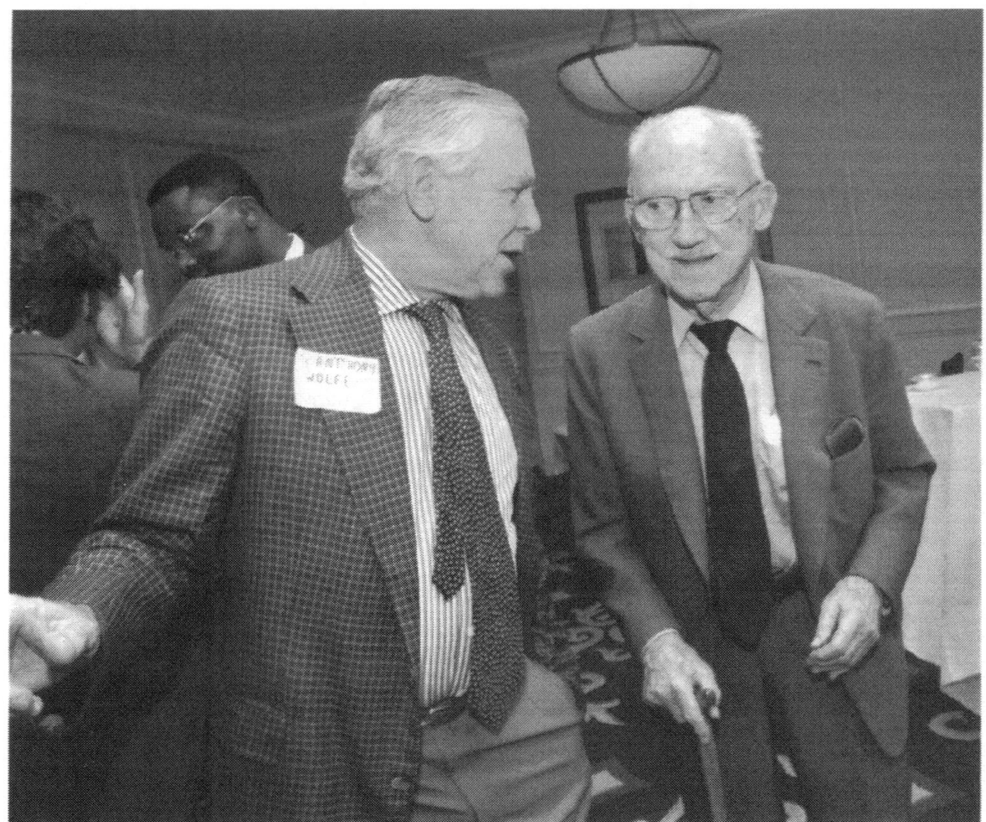

*Fig. 40.7 SAW and Tessier. I had learned to talk to the right ear.*

*Fig. 40.8 Tessier and Joe Murray (Nobel Prize winner in 1990 for his contributions to organ transplantation), reminiscing about old times.*

*Fig. 40.9 Joe Murray, Tessier, and Elizabeth in the front row.*

*Fig. 40.10 "Honoris Causa" participants. First row: Doug Ousterhout, Luigi Clauser, Nabile Hokayem, S. A. Wolfe, Steve Schendel, and Jean-François Tulasne. Second Row: Joe Gruss, Arlen Denny, Paul Manson, Barry Jones, McKay McKinnon, Darina Krastinova, Henry Kawamoto, Joe Murray, Paul Tessier, Elizabeth Motel-Hecht, Cornelius Klein , Beat Hammer, David Matthews, Jeff Posnick, and Richard Hayward.*

# Chapter 40

## A year of suffering

After returning to Paris from the 2006 Honoris Causa meeting in London, a fine tremor that Tessier had had for a year or two turned into full blown Parkinson's disease. This was treated with medication, but it seemed to flatten his affect. We looked into the possibility of minimally invasive neurosurgical ablation of the areas of the brain responsible for the Parkinson's, but he was deemed too old for this.

He went in to a rehabilitation center called La Porte Verte near Versailles, and Mireille visited him every day. I went with her for a visit and found him altered—as people often are when the L-Dopa dose gets titrated. He was not well. I had brought along as a present something that I knew he would like to see: the photographs and x-rays of a patient (unoperated) with total arrihinia. I had been working on his manuscript detailing his experience with over fifty cases of arrhinias, a number that dwarfed anything published elsewhere (this was finally published recently—unfortunately, after his death—in *The Scandinavian Journal of Plastic Surgery*).

I showed him the documents, and he pointed to the picture and said only one thing, "*Faites le bas*," that is, "Make it low." This is perhaps the key element in the treatment of an arrhinia: making the hole back to the pharynx through the curtain of skin over the upper lip. From his experience, making the hole low was the key to a good result. His mind was certainly all there.

On January 1, 2007, he tripped over his beloved Alsatian, Enzo, and Paul "hit the deck," landing on his hip and fracturing it. (One of the things that he told me about a year before this was that he was most afraid of falling.) He was taken to the Ambroise Paré Hospital in Boulogne, where the hip was pinned. He took one look at the x-ray and laughed, saying that it would not hold his hip in place for very long. He was right.

He then had a hip replacement at Clinique Bizet, and a post-operative infection developed. Six months later, in July, after the infection was thought to have been cleared up, he underwent a replacement of the hip prosthesis. Unfortunately, another chronic infection took hold, and he was not able to walk more than a few painful steps.

Mireille's mother Ginette had been staying with them with a chronic and terminal condition of her own. She bore her suffering without a complaint, and she died in October 2007, while Paul was hospitalized in Hôpital de la Croix de Saint Simon.

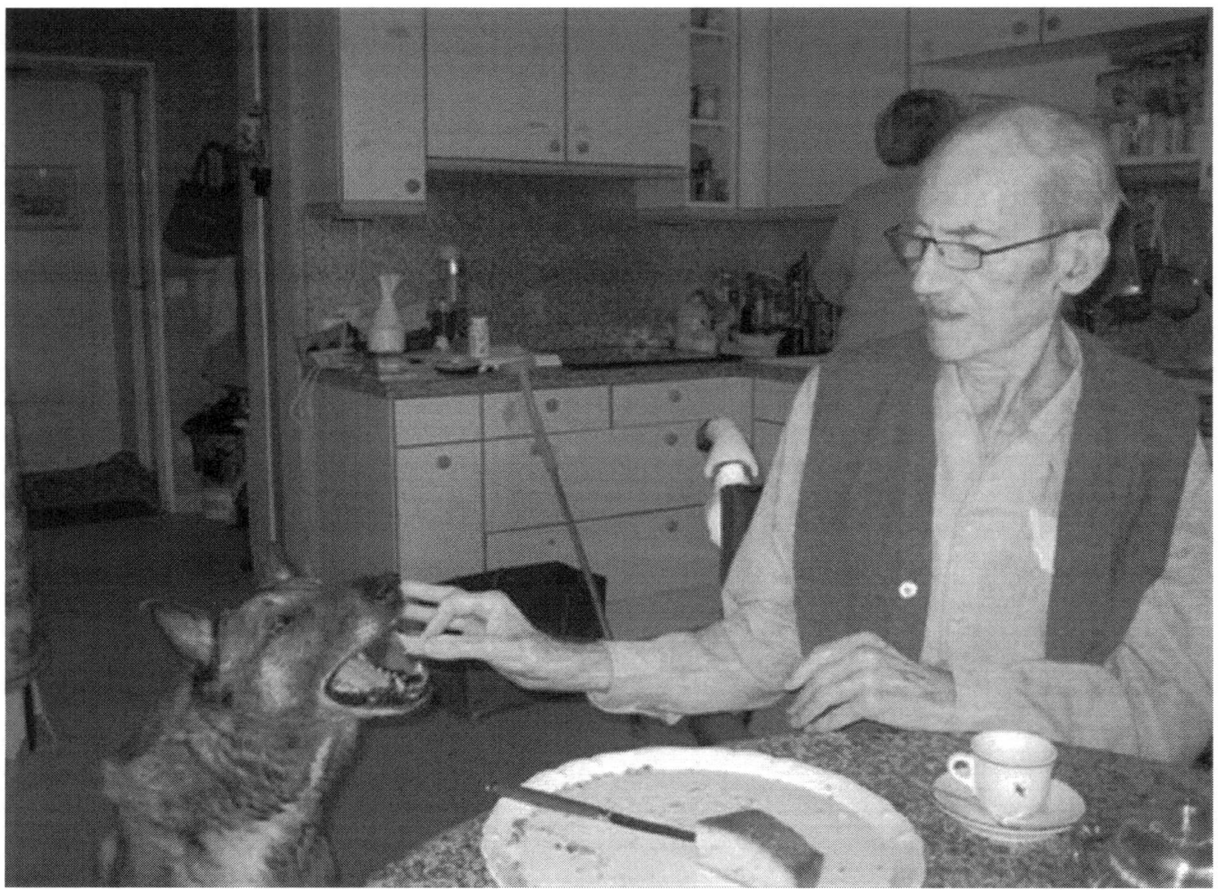

*Fig. 41.1 Paul and Enzo*

He continued to have difficulty writing due to the Parkinson's disease. Unfortunately, he had never used a Dictaphone—he always wrote his notes by hand, to be transcribed the next day by a secretary. I believe some of the letters that follow were dictated to his part-time secretary.

October 12, 2005

Mon cher Tony,

Je vous remercie de votre ponctualité. Les films, leurs « contact sheets » ; mes planches noires sont revenues .Leur rangement peut attendre votre retour. Je continue…

- La révision du texte est achevée, elle suivra après une nouvelle frappe.
- Les tableaux ne sont pas commencés ; ils sont plus importants que tout le reste

- D'autres images-probantes- ressortent de mes archives :tant mieux pour vous mais il faudra trier entre 2000 photos.
- Il y a davantage de résultats que je n'en escomptais en Décembre !!
- Je travaille, à mon rythme de solitaire total ; ne m'en demandez pas davantage.

Ne croyez surtout pas que les ARRHINIES effaceront le coup de pied au cul de TECHNIQUES and TOOLS donné par un butor. Les ARRHINIES ne seront plus jamais, jamais décrites ainsi en 2100 ( même quand le pétrole sera épuisé).laissez-moi faire ;relancez-moi parfois sur ce travail unique, long inique et inutile( contrairement à T.A.T)

Toutes mes amitiés .

P.S. David vient de m'envoyer le crâne stéréolithographié d'un T.AR de …6 ans. FORMIDABLE !!!Tout s'y trouve.
Malheureusement deux microphtalmies bilatérales et probablement pas fonctionnelles ( d'après les dimensions des orbites)

Dear Tony,

I thank you for your punctuality. The films, their "contact sheets," and my black sheets are returned. Putting them back in order can await your return. I continue:

- The revision of the text is done; it will follow after a new perusal
- The charts are not begun; they are more important that all the rest
- There are a lot more results than I had counted in December!!
- I am working at my rhythm of total solitude; don't ask more of me.

Above all, don't think that the ARRHINIAS will erase the kick in the ass given to the TECHNIQUES and TOOLS by an oaf. The ARRHINIAS will never, never be described even by 2100 (even when we have run out of oil), let me work, get me started again on this unique work, long, sinful and useless (contrary to the T.A.T.)

All my best,

P.S. David just sent me the stereolithographic skull of a T.A.R. [total arrhinia] of … 6 years of age. FORMIDABLE!!! I find everything there.

Unfortunately there are two bilateral micropthalmias, probably not functional (according to the dimensions of the orbits)

December 5, 2006

DOCTEUR PAUL TESSIER

26, BOULEVARD D'AUTEUIL
92100 BOULOGNE
TÉL. 01 46 04 61 60
46 04 01 10

5/28/07

Mon cher Tony,

Je vous remercie de l'affectueux message envoyé à Mireille et qui me concerne aussi. Comme toujours, ça a été un plaisir de vous avoir dans la maison travaillant dans VOTRE bureau. Qu'y avez-vous grappillé de nouveau ? Vous n'y avez pas tout exploré et vous pourrez encore vous distraire cet automne après votre présidence au Congres de Bahia. Vous avez laissé vierges dix sujets…

1- Les 14 Chapitres du livre préparé jusqu'en 1982 et prêts à partir chez l'éditeur.
2- 2-Une grosse liasse de feuilles de diapos pleine de Fentes et d'AGENESIES prêtes à vous servir pour VOTRE C.A.A.C (mais il n'y a pas les C.T correspondants)
3- 3-plusieurs liasses d'Esthétique qui ne sont pas tous indifférents.

Ailleurs j'ai retrouvé :

4- Le canthus externe,( totalement écrit en anglais)

5- Ma dermo mastopexie totalement écrite .Vous ne saviez pas que je me suis beaucoup intéressé aux seins (dont Françoise et Madeleine Lejour disaient qu'ils étaient les plus beaux du monde… ?)

6- La TMJ ankylosis ( à ma façon)

7- Une ébauche sur 7 cas (E.S.F)

8- Une nouvelle toute nouvelle approche de la D.O.G (intéressante me semble-t-il)

9- Vous pouvez aussi vous amuser sur mes 50 ou 70 crânes et leur trouver un riche acheteur(il y a deux cas dont je ne sais s'ils sont des Neandertal ou de grands primates actuels…)

Une autre fois vous pourrez vérifier comment les transferts de 50 ou 100 C.T ont été faits par nos radiologues (ERNEST et COQUILLE) d'analogique en numérique et s'ils vous semblent utilisables pour VOTRE C.A.A.C.
La prochaine fois nous ferons un livre avec tous ces matériaux.

Avec vos débauches de Londres je crains que vous n'ayez épuisé les trésors de publicité de STRYKER-LEIBINGER.

Aimez-vous bien votre Ambroise PARE .Y en a-t-il un autre à MIAMI ?

Toutes nos amitiés à vous à Derdree et vos six petits.

Dear Tony,

I thank you for your affectionate message sent to Mireille for me. As always, it was a pleasure to have you in the house working in YOUR office. What did you dredge up new? You have not explored everything and you can entertain yourself some more this autumn after your Presidency of the Meeting in Bahia. You have left virgin 10 subjects …

1- The 14 chapters of a book prepared in 1982, and ready to go to the editor [JIVAROS—I have only been able to locate one chapter of this, Plagiocephaly, which is in the Appendixes]

2- A big folder of slide jackets full of Clefts and AGENESES ready for you to use on YOUR C.A.A.C. (but the appropriate CT scans are not there)

3- Several folders of aesthetic cases which are not all uninteresting

<u>And then, I found:</u>

4- The lateral canthus (totally written in English)

5- My dermomastopexy totally written up. You didn't know that I am very interested in breasts (and Françoise and Madeleine Lejour said that the results were the most beautiful in the world ….?) [This is in press, in *Annals of Plastic Surgery]*

6- TMJ ankylosis (using my method) [David Matthews published this, in the *Annals* issue]

7- A start of 7 cases (of spheno-frontal encephalocoeles)

8- A new, completely new, approach to DOG [distraction osteogenesis](interesting, it seems to me)

9- You can amuse yourself with my 50 to 70 skulls and find a rich purchaser for them (there are two cases that I don't know if they are Neanderthals or currently existing grand primates)

Another time you can verify how the transfers of 50 to 100 CTs were done by our radiologists (ERNEST and COQUILLE) from analog to digital and if you think they can be used in YOUR C.A.A.C.

The next time we will make a book out of all of this material.

With the debauchery you arranged in London I fear that you haven't yet exhausted the great capacity for publicity of STRYKER-LEIBINGER.

Are you happy with your Ambroise PARÉ? Is there another one in MIAMI?

All our best to you and Deirdre and you six little ones.

6/14/2007

Mon cher Tony,
Merci de votre récente lettre datée du 27 mai.
Nous vous reverrons en Septembre après Bahia ou n'importe quand car ce sera toujours avec plaisir de notre part que voyons le grand Tony débouler dans la maison prêt à entreprendre ses excavations d'orpailleur dans les derniers filons du Klondik ou Guyane.

Nous aurons à entrevoir nos neufs projets de publication communes que je vous avez alignés dans ma lettre du 16 Mai.
Il y manque le muscle temporal la bonne à tout faire des reconstructions faciales depuis la lame criblée jusqu'à la mandibule .Voici un projet simple et facile à illustrer avec les diapos Per-Op.
Fernando doit nous rendre visite prochainement. Voici une bonne nouvelle ! En contrepartie votre lettre m'a noyé dans la tristesse !Ambroise PARE est bien à vous .Mais vous ne connaissez pas son caractére. En 1971 il a refusé de rester dans le prestigieux Smithunion Institute. Je crains que Boston lui soit fatal avec les pestilences qui y persistent toujours après le passage d'Erickson »It is time for you to stop operating »

Ambroise a été mon copain pendant 35 ans à Kléber et à Boulogne. Et pendant 35 ans il m'a toujours soufflé les bonnes choses y compris la voie cranienne Ambroise m'a quitté parceque je ne faisais plus rien mais il m'a souri quand je l'ai mis en boite pour Miami et j'ai compris qu'il voulait rester avec toute la famille pendant 35 ans. Faites leur toutes mes salutations.
Toutes mes amitiés à vous, à Derdree et à la brochette des six petits.

P.S Cette nuit AMBROISE est venu susurrer à ma bonne oreille : »Tu sais,Paul,je suis bien chez Tony et il a six petits enfants,l'un d'entre eux sera peut-être chirurgien alors je ferai son éducation

We will see you in September after Bahia or whenever since it is always a pleasure for us to have old Tony show up in the house ready to do his panning for gold in the last seams of the Klondike or the Guyana.

We will need to look over the nine projects for joint publication that I outlined for you in my letter of 16 May.

We should add the temporal muscle, good to use in all sorts of facial reconstructions from the cribriform plate to the mandible. Here is a simple project, easy to illustrate with pre-operative photos.

Fernando should be paying us a visit soon. That is some good news! In counterdistinction, your letter has left me awash in sadness! Ambroise PARÉ is in good hands with you. But you don't know his character. In 1971, he refused to stay in the prestigious Smithsonian Institute. I am afraid that Boston would be fatal for him with the pestilence that still persists there after the phrase of Erikson, "It is time for you to stop operating."

Ambroise has been my companion for 35 years at Kléber and Boulogne. And for 35 years he always whispered good things to me, including the cranial approach. Ambroise left me because I was not doing anything at all anymore, but he smiled at me when I put him in a box for Miami and I understood that he wanted to stay with the whole family for 35 years. Give them all my greetings. All my best to you, Deirdre, and the string of 6 little ones.

P.S. Tonight AMBROISE came and whispered in my good ear, "You know, Paul, I am happy with Tony, and there are six children, one of them will perhaps become a surgeon, and I will give him his education.

Dear Tony,

Your Christmas wishes arrived while I was still in the hospital. On my behalf, I send you all the best wishes of your old boss for you, for Deirdre, and for your escadron of children. Platoon or squadron? The names don't matter if all eight of you are in good health and of strong resistance.

Your wishes were touching also to Mireille, who has quite simply been extraordinary for the house (the SAPP), for our children, and for me, who have been more burdensome than demanding.

You have given me great pleasure in telling me that I have participated in your genetic patrimony in the form of ideas (rational) and also putting them into practice.

Have you found an editor enterprising enough to absorb the 50 arrhinias and the folder with the C.I.S.C. flap [B-T]? Are you interested in the dermo-mastopexy?

Given my state of exhaustion, I can't even envisage something simple on the description of the lateral canthus and its numerous abnormalities.

When are you coming to Paris? A room always awaits you.

My best to all of the WOLFES.

P.S. Now you have had experience with T-AR and H-AR [total and hemi arrnhinia]. The hole has been made. What is its diameter back to the pharynx?

These extraordinary letters show that, even though his body was giving up around him, Paul Tessier's mind, at age ninety, was as keen, analytical, and perceptive as ever. He showed an unfortunately unjustified hope that I would be able to finish a variety of the publications that he had in various forms of completion. Some I have done, and a few more I hope to finish. And I sincerely hope that there will be others to help mine the great amount of clinical material that he left behind.

2008 was a year of considerable suffering; his mind was totally intact, but he was essentially a prisoner in his own body. After the numerous problems with his hip replacement, which left him unable to walk, he lost a good deal of weight and experienced a sigmoid volvulus. This was reduced endoscopically under the direction of Francis Firmin at Clinique Bizet, but unfortunately recurred. Plus, there was some necrosis of the colon, which required an open resection, performed at Hôpital de la Croix de Saint Simon. Mireille and I came for a visit; she brought, as she had before, a picnic lunch, but he showed little appetite and only ate some grapefruit. He did recover from this well enough to return home, however.

# Chapter 41

## Final events

My correspondence with Paul Tessier from 1975 to 2008 was copious and regular. Whenever I came across an unusual case, I would send him a photo of the patient along with copies of the patient's CT scan. In the year before the London Honoris Causa meeting in 2006, I stayed with the Tessiers on many occasions as I went on a "rummaging mission" through his files.

He said that he was no longer physically able to do any work on a number of unfinished projects, and he hoped that I would carry on with that work. Among these projects were virtually finished papers on the arrhinias (congenital absence of half or all of the nose), the BT (Barron-Tessier, clavicular island) flap, the lateral canthus, sphenoethmoidal encephalocoeles, and the revised version of his classification of facial clefts. I blame myself for not finishing them more quickly so that he would have had the pleasure of seeing them in print. "The Arrhinias" has been published in *The Scandinavian Journal of Plastic Surgery* (most pediatric plastic surgeons will only see two or three of these in their careers; his experience with hemiarrhinia, total arrhinia, and hemiarrhinia with proboscis lateralis was over fifty cases); "The BT Flap" is in press for an edition of *Annals of Plastic Surgery* devoted to Dr. Tessier; the CAAC (Classification of Ageneses and Clefts), the rethought version of his 1976 Classification of Facial Clefts was published in an unfinished form in *The European Journal of Craniomaxillofacial Surgery.* The lateral canthus and the S. E. encephalocoeles are the most complicated and difficult to complete since they deal with his "impossible cases." Consequently, they remain on the back burner, but will be completed.

5/12/2008

Mon cher Tony,

Nous sommes heureux de savoir que vous passerez bientôt par Paris.

Je vous prie et ce bien sincèrement, de m'excuser de ne pas vous avoir encore proposé que nous soyons Co-auteurs dans les deux papiers que nous rédigeons.

L'un sur les Arrhinies l'autre sur l'ex BT Flap avec David Matthews. Il est même probable que vous-même ayez de très bons documents des cas postopératoires d'une part, des vues intra-buccales, du lambeau claviculaire en ilot et aussi des Arrhinies montrant l'essentiel du sujet: le trou central pour le passage de l'air.

Je suis tout à fait d'accord avec vous pour pressentir Eric Arnaud de centraliser en France la chirurgie orbito-crânienne.

C'Est-ce que je fais sans tarder.

A bientôt j'espère.

Toutes nos amitiés à vous et à Derdree.

Dated 5-12-08

Dear Tony,

We are happy that you will be passing through Paris soon.

I ask you, most sincerely, to forgive me for not having yet proposed that we be co-authors of the two papers that we are working on.

The one on the Arrhinias, and the other on the ex-BT flap with David Matthews. It is quite probable that you yourself have very good documents of post-operative cases on the one hand, intra-oral views of the clavicular island [flap] and also of the arrhinias showing the essential part of [the treatment] of the subject, the central hole for the passage of air.

I completely agree with you about having Eric Arnaud become the central figure in France in orbito-cranial surgery.

That is what I shall do without delay.

See you soon, I hope

All of our best wishes to you and Deirdre.

The above is the last letter that I have from Paul Tessier.

---

I had told Dr. Tessier on a number of occasions that I felt it would be good for Eric to come by the apartment to do as I had done, rummage through all of the records, find out what was there, and try to start deciphering and digesting. It would be much easier for Eric to do this since he lived in Paris, and I felt that he had the interest in orbital surgery and motivation to learn what he could from the master. I fault myself that I did not push for this earlier, but Eric was from another "school"—he was associated with Daniel Marchac, and I sensed that there might be some tension. Daniel and Paul Tessier had always had a cordial relationship, but I would not say it was a close one.

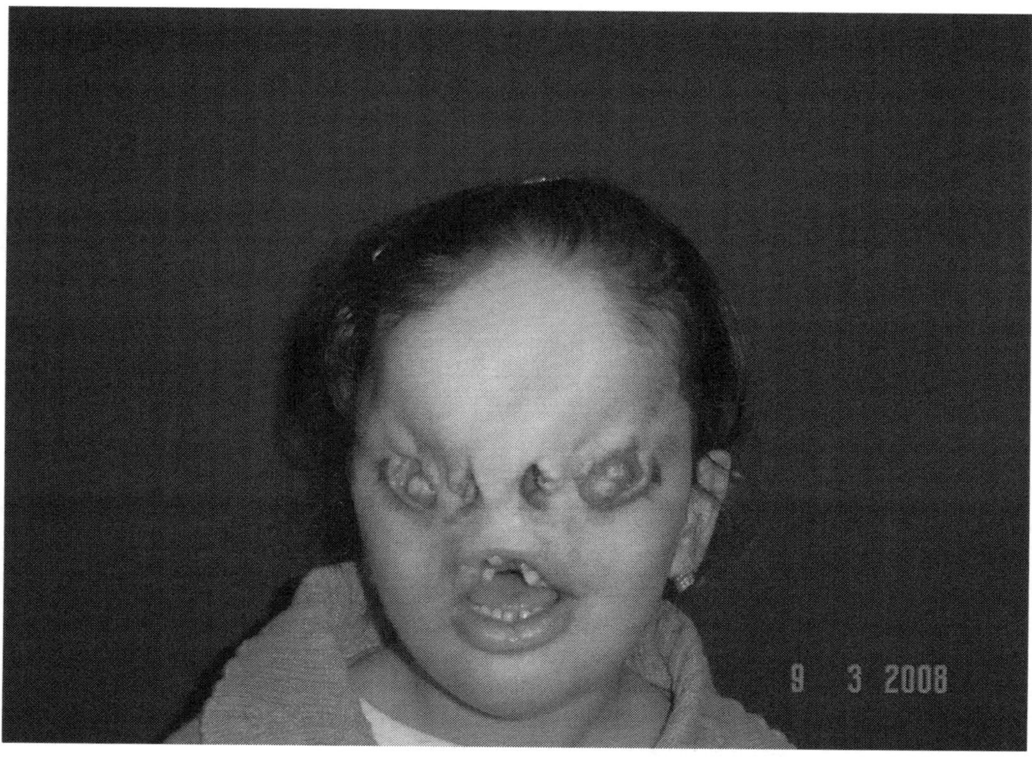


*Fig. 42.1 A case that Eric Arnaud took for consultation with Tessier, 8 May 2008.*

My dear Arnaud,

I thank you for the letter that you sent to Tony on the 28th of March.

As much as I can, I will try to help you use the enormous documentation of orbito-cranial surgery that Tony has taken several months to rummage through and sort out, but it will take several sessions to try to familiarize you with it all.

I thank you for the photographs and scans that you brought me of this <u>extreme case.</u> Concerning this case, I should like that we meet several times, because the multiple aspects of this case: palatal, maxillary, orbital, eyelid, nose and endocranial [aspect] cannot be resolved in several minutes.

Relating to this, I think that <u>right now</u> one should obtain *visual evoked potentials of the right eye.* That will determine everything to follow.

All the best,

*Fig. 42.2 Eric Arnaud, Oxford, U.K. October 2009.*

Then came an e-mail from Mireille:

**S. Anthony Wolfe M.D.**

| | |
|---|---|
| **From:** | mireille tessier [mireilletessierfr@yahoo.fr] |
| **Sent:** | Thursday, June 05, 2008 4:33 PM |
| **To:** | S. Anthony Wolfe M.D. |
| **Subject:** | RE: Dr. Tessier: Tribute possibility |

mon cher Tony,
J'ai une bientriste nouvelle à vous annoncer.Paul est décédé ce soir à 17h 30 à la Clinique Bizet ou on venait de le transporter pour des troubles intestinaux.Il a fait une fibrillation ventriculaire.Il est parti en 5 minutes.
Je lui avait montré votre lettre il avait l'intention de vous répondre il était d'accord pour Clauser mais il était ennuyé de lui nuire.
Je vous embrasse.
Mireille

June 5, 2008

Dear Tony,

I have very sad news to announce. Paul died this evening at 5:30 pm in the Clinique Bizet where he was taken for intestinal troubles. He had a ventricular fibrillation. He was gone in 5 minutes.

I had showed him your letter he intended to answer you he was in agreement concerning Dr. X but he didn't want to hurt him.

A hug,

Mireille.

Mme Mireille Tessier,
son épouse,
Claude Tessier,
Laurence Tessier,
Jean-Paul Tessier,
ses enfants,
et ses petits-enfants

ont la douleur de vous faire
part du décès du

**docteur Paul TESSIER**

chirurgien,
ancien chef de service
de chirurgie plastique
de l'hôpital Foch, à Suresnes,

docteur honoris causa
de l'université de Lund (Suède),
honorary fellow de l'American
college of surgeons,
honorary fellow du Royal
college of surgeons of England,
honorary fellow du Royal
college of surgeons
of Edinburgh,

chevalier
de la Légion d'honneur,
chevalier de l'ordre
du Mérite centrafricain,

survenu le 5 juin 2008, à Paris.

La cérémonie religieuse sera
célébrée le mardi 10 juin 2008,
à 10 heures, en la chapelle
de l'hôpital du Val-de-Grâce,
74, boulevard de Port Royal,
Paris (5$^{e}$).

L'inhumation aura lieu
au cimetière d'Heric
(Loire-Atlantique).

25, boulevard d'Auteuil,
92100 Boulogne.

This is the notice of Dr. Tessier's death that appeared in *Le Monde*, on June 6, 2008. I would suspect that he had something to do with its preparation. After noting his honorary degree from Lund, and honorary membership in the American, English, and Scottish colleges of surgeons, and his receipt of the Legion d'Honneur, it also includes his "Chevalier de l'ordre du Mérite of the Central African Republic." He most certainly in a droll fashion value this latter award as much as the others.

Many other obituaries appeared in the days to follow: *The Wall Street Journal, Lancet, British Medical Journal,* and the various ophthalmological and plastic surgery journals. Many of them had the day of his death stated incorrectly as the 6th or 7th of June. It was the 5th, about a month and a half short of his 91st birthday on August 1, 2008.

THE WALL STREET JOURNAL. Saturday/Sunday, June 28 - 29, 2008 A7

**REMEMBRANCES**

**PAUL TESSIER**
1917 — 2008

## *Pioneering Surgeon Found a Way to Rebuild Faces*

By Stephen Miller
And David Gauthier-Villars

Operating where few surgeons dared, Paul Tessier forged a medical specialty dedicated to giving his severely deformed and injured patients new faces.

Using innovative procedures and teams of specialists, he pioneered such techniques as going through the brain cavity to work on the face from behind, sometimes repositioning eye sockets and grafting bones.

"He showed the world that you can go through the intracranial route to the face," says Kenneth Salyer, founder of the International Craniofacial Institute in Dallas.

"He was the first one who had the gumption to do it when we shied away from it," says Donald Wood-Smith, chairman of the plastic-surgery department at the New York Eye & Ear Infirmary. "Now, we do it with impunity and don't think twice about it."

Not content with mere improvement, Dr. Tessier told his patients and students, "If it is not normal, it is not enough." He introduced his techniques

starting in the late 1960s. Today, there are more than 150 members of the International Society of Craniofacial Surgery, a group of doctors who address such problems as clefts that rend an entire face, gunshot wounds and conjoined twins connected at the head. Dr. Tessier's techniques allow all facial bones to be moved and modified at once. Sunken cheeks can be moved forward, chins reduced and the whole thing can be done without scarring by peeling the facial skin down from the hairline.

Typically, a craniofacial specialist is a qualified plastic surgeon who leads an operating team including brain surgeons, bone specialists and dentists. Most procedures—perhaps 80%—are performed on children with deformities. A half-million children world-wide are born each year with facial malformations but at least half receive no care, Dr. Salyer says.

"Craniofacial surgery is intensely collaborative," says S. Anthony Wolfe, a Miami craniofacial specialist who trained with Dr. Tessier in the mid-1970s.

Born in 1917 near Nantes, France, Dr. Tessier became a surgeon in 1943, after spending two years in a German prisoner-of-war camp. He joined the pediatric service at the Hôpital Foch in Paris in 1946, and received further training with British plastic-surgery pioneers Harold Gillies and Archibald McIndoe.

Frustrated at the limited treatment available to his most severely affected patients, he began experimenting on cadavers after work, investigating the complex bone structure of the face, which he learned to cut and reassemble like a jigsaw puzzle. Moving eye sockets meant he could fix congenital face asymmetry, a problem many victims say leaves them shunned by society.

"You see some of these patients," Dr. Wolfe says. "You can't believe what they've come through."

As word of his successes spread, young surgeons flocked to his operating theater and Dr. Tessier traveled abroad to lecture to doctors. Because sophisticated viewing systems such as magnetic resonance imaging weren't available, he turned to Michel Bourbon, a French sculptor, to prepare skulls showing malformations, interventions and results.

"Dr. Tessier traveled all over the world carrying my skulls in his suitcase," Mr. Bourbon says. "He loved holding a mold between his legs and cut into it to show the audience how he would do it on a real face."

A workaholic, Dr. Tessier was famed for his marathon operating sessions, and sometimes took on three patients at a time in parallel. He liked to take his recreation in big chunks, too. He trekked the Himalayas and went on African safaris, insisting on taking along a single gun-bearer instead of a whole retinue—in fairness to the elephants. He scuba dived with Jacques Cousteau, and he drove race cars under the name "Harry Covert"—French for green bean, perhaps a reference to his lanky frame.

After an operation, Dr. Wood-Smith says, he would head out to "one of the major Parisian restaurants and spend hours, eating, drinking and talking." He operated into his 80s and was still making contributions to the field up to his death June 6 in Paris at age 90.

His habitual answer to a challenge—"Pourquoi pas?," French for "Why not?"—became the International Society of Craniofacial Surgery's motto.

Dr. Tessier was awarded the Legion of Honor in 2005, and in 2000 was given the Jacobson Innovation Award by the American College of Surgeons.

*—Rhonda L. Rundle contributed to this article.*

# Chapter 42

## Funeral

I went with Mireille, Laurence and Françoise and Francis Firmin to see Paul in the funeral home before the casket was closed. There was quietness and seriousness in the presence of death. His arms were crossed over his chest, he was in a dark striped suit, white shirt without necktie, and wore the small red lapel strip indicating Chévalier de la Legion d'Honneur.

An officious woman from some French government agency bustled in, screwed the brass screws on the coffin shut, put hot wax over one of the screws and imprinted a seal with a small object that she produced from a leather sheath. The casket was made of blonde oak and brass finishings.

The funeral service followed at the Chapel of the Val de Grace Hospital, where he had been honored by The French Society of Maxillofacial Surgeons several years previously. Françoise Firmin spoke, Serge Morax, Laurence Tessier spoke, and I spoke. I can't recall precisely what I said, but in part it was that Paul Tessier was so far ahead of everyone else in his field, that he was all alone and had only himself to speak with.

With his body aboard we took the TGV (*train de grand vitesse*, that is, the high speed train) from the Gare de Monparnasse to Nantes. We went to Bonne Hygie, and then walked to the cemetery in Héric, a short walk down the street, through the small town.

The Mercedes Black Maria arrived, tall and glistening. Paul Tessier's spot was next to his sister Solange in the Clergeau family plot. But the wooden coffin was about two centimeters too long for the opening in the tomb. Multiple attempts were made to squeeze it in, but it would just not go. There was much consternation among the cemetery staff, many in reminiscent of "wife beater" undershirts,Marlon Brando in *A Streetcar Named Desire*. There were consultations and discussions. We suggested cutting back some of the stone to make the opening large enough. "Oh, no—French law strictly prohibits cutting anything in a cemetery," we were told.

What to do? Cut back the wooden coffin? Get a new one? The cemetery officials decided to check with the Mayor early in the next morning as to the proper course of action, and we would all reconvene mid-morning. In the meantime, Paul was parked overnight in a small shed.

When we returned in the morning, the various functionaries, having spoken to the Mayor, had managed to do the right thing and the opening in the tomb had enlarged the necessary 2 cm. The opening was just large enough now.

We all were in agreement that Paul Tessier would have found this to be hilarious. All through his professional career he had been stymied and frustrated by various elements of the French bureaucracy, and this was his final revenge.

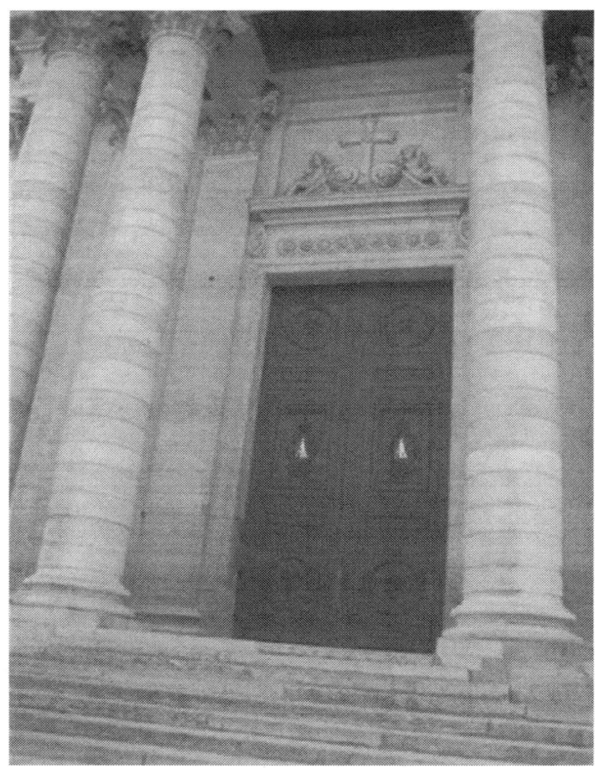

*Fig. 43.1 Chapel of Val de Grace Hospital, where the funeral ceremony was held, June 2008. The cobblestones beneath the steps were the same ones that Anne of Austria (1601–1666), mother of Louis XIV, walked over.*

*Fig. 43.2 Paul arrives.*

# Chapter 43

## Memorial Mass

There was a Memorial Mass on June 5, 2009, at the Val de Grace Chapel, one year after the death of Paul Tessier. Françoise Firmin and I read passages from the Bible: she had me read the one that started, "Moi, Jean" (I, John) since, she pointed out, it wouldn't make sense for her to say that as a woman. There were about a hundred people in attendance. In a light rain, after the ceremony, we went several blocks down the Rue St. Jacques to Merri Scheitlin's studio, where she hosted a wonderful reception.

Later that day we went on the T.G.V. (*Train de Grand Vitesse*) to Héric to visit the grave. Mireille, in the past year, had a new engraving created so that there was now a plot for the Tessier's and one for the Clergeau. We took some flowers that were in bloom at Bonne Hygie and placed them on the grave. Bonne Hygie was quiet and in pristine condition, and we all knew that Paul would have been pleased.

*Fig. 44.1 Plot of the Tessier's and Clergeaux, Héric cemetery, June 5, 2009.*

Paul Tessier, after a surgical career that spanned almost sixty years and was filled with a huge amount of operating, innovating, dreaming, categorizing, and pushing himself and his new specialty to their limits, now rests peacefully in his native land, in Héric, in "La Bretagne." His love for both was always evident. He was not really part of the Parisian medical establishment. He remained an outsider, although he was recognized for his unique abilities. Yes, he did head the plastic surgery unit at Hôpital Foch for a number of years, bringing it international acclaim, but Foch certainly did not treat him with any gratitude for his enormous contributions. He was respected by all of the younger plastic surgeons in France, but the ones of his own generation were at times jealous and spiteful. Although he was nominated for the Nobel Prize on a number of occasions, one of the things that may have blocked his getting it was that the Nobel committee always checks with sources in the country of the nominee, and a lukewarm response may have come from his colleagues in France.

Looking back at this point, there is not much question that he deserved the prize. Very few individuals have, by their independent and iconoclastic contributions, and their entirely new concepts, changed the way surgery is done. And there was a ripple effect, whereby the effects of his contributions were seen in many other specialties: neurosurgery, ophthalmology, head and neck Surgery, and traumatology.

Ambroise Paré, in the 1500s, altered surgery in the same fundamental way when he convinced the medical profession that patients with wounds—military or otherwise—did better when treated with soothing ointments than with cautery by means of a hot iron. I received one of my most prized possessions when I visited *Le Patron* during his last year of life. Inside one of the postal boxes (in his study) were all of the Gourdin drawings.

Mireille said, "Tony, this is a present for you." I opened it, and there was his copy of *Les Oeuvres d'Ambroise Paré*, dated 1585. There was an inscription on his stationery on the first page. It is hard to read, due to his tremor.

LES

OEVVRES

d'Ambroise Paré,

CONSEILLER, ET

PREMIER CHIRVR-

GIEN DV ROY,

A PARIS,

Chez Iacques du Puys.

1585.

*Fig. 44.3 Frontispiece of Paré's book, 1585.*

THE M.F.F. ADVANCEMENT

AND BIPARTITION

Since it's original description by Tessier, rehabilitation by Ortiz Monasterio, readoption by Tessier and modifications by Muhlbauer and Kawamoto, the monoblock Fronto-facial advancement (MFFA) has received mixed reviews. Some experienced craniofacial teams have tried the procedure, and advised against it on the basis of negative experiences encountered.
The autor has performed 26 MFFA in patients ranging from 9 months to 14 years of age, 11 of wich included facial bipartition, 21 were performed at the University of Miami, and 5 other Institutions. Complications included:
Deaths-1 (Caracas, due to late intraoperative aahytmia), Partial or complete division of nasotracheal tube (with good outcome)-2, Infections-0, CFS Leaks-0.
On the basis of this experience, the following conclusions are drawn: -MFFA is a safe procedure in non-shunted patients (and possibly in those with an anti-siphone device).
-Frontal advancement must not greatly outdistance alveolar advancement.
-Infants and young children more prone to airway problems. Experienced pediatric anesthesists and intensivists esencial.- Consider preliminary plating of zigomatico-maxillary suture in infants to prevent disjunction.
-Use oral intubation. Exact oclusal relationships uninpotant in view of expected eventual Le Fort I.
-Carnial basis treated with bone graft and large pericraneal patch in all cases.
-MFFA with facial bipartition is procedure of choice for Aperts, leading one to question the routine performance of frontal advancement in infant Aperts in absence of neurosurgical imperatives.

*Fig. 44.4 This must have been a transcription of my paper presented in Santiago, with enough serious typographical errors ("carnial basis" should say "cranial base"!) to lead me to think it was transcribed by a non-English speaker.*

NOTE N° .......

THE M.F.F. ADVANCEMENT
AND BIPARTITION

N° 79 - Santiago : Tony WOLFE

Voir aussi MARCHAC N° 41 - T.B.
Voir aussi WEXLER N° 39 - T.T.B. result

- Très bonne présentation, malheureusement raccourcie par le Chairman (I. MUNRO)
- Très, très bons résultats
- Des Apert remarquables
Enfin quelqu'un qui a compris et qui prend la suite.
Et cet acharnement a démontré l'antériorité
- "T" par la S.F.O., par le CARONNI

*Fig. 44.5 Tessier "grading."*

Dr. Tessier kept careful notes when he went to a meeting. And, in going through his papers, I found the abstract of the paper that I had given at the meeting of The International Society of Craniofacial Surgery in Santiago de Compostela, Spain. These are his notes that I found about my presentation—in short, my grade.

He writes: No. 79—Santiago: Tony WOLFE
See also Marchac No. 41—T.B. (*très bien*, very good)
See also Wexler No 39, T.T.B (very, very good) result

— Very good presentation, unfortunately cut short by the Chairman (I.Munro) [I was indeed cut off at 3 ½ minutes by the Session Chairman, who was Linton Whitaker, rather than Ian Munro. A possible explanations for this was that he could not read the clock, or, perhaps, he did not want me to be heard. In any event, the presentation was later published in *Plastic and Reconstructive Surgery* (with Glenn Morrison, neurosurgeon, and Sam Berkowitz, orthodontist, as coauthors) for all to see, and Dr. Tessier wrote the commentary on the paper, providing the best advice anywhere on how to safely perform a monobloc fronto-facial advancement].

— Very, very good results

— Some remarkable Aperts

Finally someone who has understood and is following
And obstinately showed the priority of the procedure

— "T" in the S.F.O., and The Carroni [SFO stands for Report to the French Society of Ophthalmology, and Carroni refers to the proceedings of the craniofacial meeting in Rome, 19__]

***That my teacher—and the man I most admired in surgery— gave me a good grade that I discovered only after his death was poignant indeed.***

# References

1 Tessier P Dysostoses cranio-faciales (Syndromes de Crouzon et d'Apert) Osteotomioes totales de la face 774-783 in Transactions of the Fourth international congress of Plastic and Reconstructive surgery, Rome , October 1967. Excerpta Medica, Amsterdam.

2 Gillies H and Harrison,Sh ( 1950) Operative correction by osteotomy of recessed malar maxillary compound in a case of oxycephaly. Br J Plast Surg; 3 : 123

3 Le Fort R Experimental study of fractures of the upper jaw (paper of 1901 translated by Paul Tessier ) (1972) Plast Reconstr Surg 50:497-506

4 Marchac D (1978) Radical forehead remodeling for craniostenosis. Plast Reconstr. Surg .61:823

5 Marchac D and Renier D ( 1982) Craniofacial surgery for craniosynsotosis .I vol 201 pages. Boston. Little, Brown and Company

6 Proceedings of the first International Congress of the ISCFS, D.Marchac, Ed. Ivol 495 p. Springer-Verlag,Berlin 1987.

7 Ortiz-Monasterio F, Fuente del Campo A,Carillo A( 1978) Advancement of the orbits and the mid face in one piece, combined with frontal repositioning, for the correction of Crouzon deformity. Plast reconstr Surg 61:507-516

8 Van der Meulen JC(1979) Medial Fasciotomy Br J Plast Surg .32: 339-342

9 McCarthy J G, Schreiber J , Karp N Thorne C H and Grayson B H (1992) Lengthening the human mandible by gradual distraction. Plast Reconstr; Surg 89: 1

10 Lauritzen C, Sugawara Y, Kocabalkan O and Olsson R (1998). Spring mediated dynamic cranio-facial reshaping. Case report Scand? J. Plast Reconstr Surg 32:331

# LIST OF PAUL TESSIER'S PUBLICATIONS/APPENDICES

Impressions d'Angleterre
(Revue d'Odontologie, de Stomatologie et Maxillo-faciale, 3rd Année, No. 1 Jan. 1947)

Traitemendte s et des Sequelles Mutilations de Traumatismos Nasales.
(Ouest-Medical, No. 9–10th année, May 10, 1957)

Radiodermites et Radionécroses de la Face.
(Extrait de l'Ouest-Médical, 10 année, No. 20, October 25, 1957)

Brulures et accidents de la route.
(Cahiers de traumatologie pratique No. 51, March 1958)

Traumatismes de la Face: et accidents de la route.
(Revue automobile médicale, No. 52, April 1958)

Les Brulures de la voie publique.
(Revue automobile médicale, No. 73, Nov. 10, 1959)

Considerations sur le développement de l'orbite; ses incidences sur la croissance faciale.
(Revue de Stomatologie, Paris, Tome: 63, 1965, No. 1-2, pp. 27–39)

La greffe dermique.

Procéré de protection cérébro-méningée et de blindage duremérien
(Annales de Chir. Plast. Vol. XII, No. 2, June 1967, pp. 93–102)

Osteotomies totales de la face. Syndrome de Crouzon. Syndrome d'Apert. Oxycéphalies. Scaphocéphalies. Turricéphalies.
(Annales de Chir. Plast. Vol. XII, No. 4, December 1967, pp. 273–286)

Chirurgie Esthétique
(Extrait de la Gazette Médicale de France, 1968 Nov; (28)

Colobomas: vertical and oblique complete facial clefts. Simultaneous operation of the eyelid, inner canthus, cheek, nose and lip orbitomaxillary bone graft.
(Panminerva Med. 1969 Mar; 11(3): 95–101)

Hypertelorism: cranio-naso-orbito-facial and subethoid osteotomy.
(Panminerva Med. 1969 Mar; 11(3): 102–16)

Faut-il opérer les méningiomes en plaque de l'aréte sphénoïdale?
(Minerva Neurochirurgica, Vol. 14, No. 4, Oct-December 1970, pp. 293–304)

Relationship of craniostenoses to craniofacial dysostoses, and to faciostenoses: a study with therapeutic implications.
(Plast Reconstr Surg. 1971 Sep; 48 (3): 224–37)

Total osteotomy of the middle third of the face for faciostenosis or for sequelae of Le Fort III fractures.
(Plast Reconstr Surg. 1971 Dec; 48(6): 533–541)

The definitive plastic surgical treatment of the severe facial deformities of craniofacial dysostosis, Crouzon's and Apert's diseases.
(Plast Reconstr Surg. 1971 Nov; 48(5): 419–42)

Traitement des dysmorphies facials propres aux dysostoses cranio-faciales (DCF). Maladies de Crouzon et d'Apert. Ostéotomie totale du massif facial. Déplacement sagittal du massif facial.
(Neuro-Chirurgie, Paris, tome 17, No. 4, pp. 295–322)

Le diadéme: nouveau fixateur facial universel à ancrage cranien.
(Annales de Chir. Plast. Vol. XVI, No. 1, 1971, pp. 12–20)

Chirurgie orbito-cranienne.
(Minerva Chirurgica Vol. 26, No. 16, 31 août 1971, pp. 878–904)

Total osteotomy of the middle third of the face for faciostenosis or for sequelae of LeFort III fractures.
(Plast Reconstr Surg. 1971 Dec; 48(6): 533–41)

Experimental study of fractures of the upper jaw.
(Plast Reconstr Surg. 1972 No; 50(5): 497–506

Les dislocations orbito-nasales. La canthopexie interne.
(Bulletins et Mémoires de la Société Française d'Ophtalmologie 85e année, 1972, pp. 636–654)

Les lacerations palpébrales. L'urgence en chirurgie palpébrale.
(Bulletins et Mémoires de la Société Française d'Ophtalmologie 85e année, 1972, pp. 423–432)

Experimental study of fractures of the upper jaw—Parts I and II.
(PRS Vol. 50, No. 5, 1972)

The classic reprint. Experimental study of fractures of the upper jaw. I and II.
(Plast Reconstr Surg. 1972 Nov; 50(5): 497–506 cont'd.)

The classic reprint: experimental study of fractures of the upper jaw. 3.
(Plast Reconstr Surg. 1972 Dec; 50(6): 600–7)

Orbital hypertelorism. I. Successive surgical attempts. Material and methods. Causes and mechanisms.
(Scand J Plast Reconstr Surg. 1972; 6 (2):135–55)

Commentary by Dr. Tessier on LeFort's Papers.
(Plast Reconstr Surg. 1972 Dec; 50(6): 605–606

The conjunctival approach to the orbital floor and maxilla in congenital malformation and trauma.
(J Maxillofac Surg. 1973 Mar;1(1):3–8)

Orbital hypertelorism. II. Definite treatment of orbital hypertelorism (OR.H.) by craniofacial or by extracranial osteotomies.
(Scand J Plast Reconstr Surg. 1973; 7(1):39–58)

Experiences in the treatment of orbital hypertelorism.
(Plast Reconstr Surg. 1974 Jan; 53(1): 1–18)

Orbital hypertelorism.
(Fortschr Kiefer Gesichtschir. 1974; 18: 14–27)

The anatomy of the external palpebral ligament in man.
(J Maxillofac Surg. 1976 Dec; 4(4):195–7)

Anatomical classification facial, craniofacial and laterofacial clefts.
(J Maxillofac Surg. 1976 Jun; 4(2):69–92)

Craniofacial reconstruction in patients with craniofacial malformations: The neurosurgical approach.
(Clin Neurosurg. 1977; 24: 642–52)

Sir Archibald McIndoe, C.B.E., F.R.C.S.
(Ann Plast Surg. 1979 Feb; 2 (2):167–75)

Craniospinal and cervicospinal malformations associated with maxillonasal dysostosis (Binder Syndrome).
(Head Neck Surg. 1980 Nov-Dec; 3(2): 123–31)

Clinical and radiologic aspects of maxillonasal dysostosis (Binder Syndrome).
(Head Neck Surg. 1980 Nov-Dec; 3(2): 105–22.)

Discussion: Chin advancement as an aid in correction of deformities of the mental and submental regions.
(Plast Reconstr Surg. 1981 May; 67(5): 630)

Compatibilité de la cranio-chirurgie premiére avec la chirurgie cranio-faciale seconde.
(Neurochirurgie, 1981, 27, pp. 103–113)

Aesthetic Aspects of Bone Grafting to the Face.
(Clinics in Plast. Surg., Vol. 8, No. 2, April 1981)

Closure of large cribiform defects with a forehead flap.
(J Maxillofac Surg. 1981 Feb; 9(1): 7–9)

Therapeutic aspects of maxillonasal dysostosis (Binder Syndrome).
(Head Neck Surg. 1981 Jan-Feb; 3 (3)207–15)

Analysis and late treatment of plagiocephaly. Unilateral coronal syostosis.
(Scan. J Plast Reconstr Surg. 1981; 15(3): 257–63)

Mandibulo-facial dysostosis. Analysis: principles of surgery.
(Scand J Plast Reconstr Surg. 1981;15(3): 251–6)

Fronto-facial advancement for Crouzon's and Apert's syndromes.
(Scand J Plast Reconstr Surg. 1981; 15(3): 245–50.

La transposition du muscle temporal dans l'orbite anophtalme.
(Anneles de Chir. Plast. 1982, Vol. XXVII, No. 3)

Inferior orbitotomy. A new approach to the orbital floor.
(Clin Plast Surg 1982 Oct; 9(4): 569–75)

Autogenous bone grafts taken from the calvarium for facial and cranial applications.
(Clin Plast Surg 1982 Oct; 9(4): 531–8)

Secondary repair of cleft lip deformity.
(Clin Plast Surg. 1984 Oct; 11 (4):747–60)

Experience in the treatment of orbital hypertelorism.
(Plast Reconstr Surg. 1984 Jan; 53(1): 1–18)

Sam Pruzansky as I remember him.
(J Craniofac Genet Dev. Biol. Suppl. 1985; 1: 19–21)

Lateral Canthoplasty to change the eye slant.
(Plast Reconstr Surg. 1985 Jan; 75(1): 10)

Maxillary growth following total septal resection in correction of orbital hypertelorism.
(Cleft Palate J. 1985 Dec; 23 Suppl 1: 27–39)

Complications of facial trauma: Principles of late reconstruction.
(Ann. Plast. Surg. 1986 Nov; 17 (5): 411–20)

Results of the Tessier integral procedure for correction of Treacher Collins syndrome.
(Cleft Palate J. 1986 Dec; 23 Suppl 1: 40–9)

Long-term results of LeFort III advancement in Crouzon's syndrome.
(Cleft Palate J. 1986 Dec; 23 Suppl 1: 102–9)

Three dimensional imaging in medicine. A critique by surgeons.
(Scand. J. Plast. Reconstr. Surg. 1986; 20 (1): 3–11)

A foreward in the form of a warning.
(Springer-Verlag Berlin Heidelberg, 1987)

An Interview with Paul Tessier conducted by Lars M. Vistnes, M.D.
(Ann. Plast. Surg. 1987 Apr: 18(4); 352–4)

Stability in correction of hypertelorbitism and Treacher Collins syndromes.
(Clinics in Plast. Surg. Vol. 16, No. 1, pp. 195–204, January 1989)

The monobloc frontofacial advancement: Do the pluses outweigh the minuses?
(Plast Reconstr Surg. 1993 May; 91(6): 988–989)

Complications associated with the harvesting of cranial bone grafts.
(Plast Reconstr Surg. 1995 Jan; (1): 14–20)

## BOOK CHAPTERS

Burns. Association "Les soins aux brules"; 1960-1969? (1 reel)

Surgical correction of craniofacial dysostosis. Audiovisual Concepts. 1974.

Symposium on Plastic Surgery in the orbital region: proceedings of the symposium of the Educational Foundation of the American Society of Plastic and Reconstructive Surgeons, Inc. held at Dallas, TX March 18–20, 1974. Mosby, London, 1976.

Chirurgie Plastique Orbito-Palpébrale. J. Rougier, P. Tessier, F. Hervouet, M. Woillez, M. Lekieffre and P. Derome. Masson, Paris, New York, Barcelone, Milan 1977.

"His methods and long term results of Bone Grafting of the nose in aesthetic containing the Craniofacial Skeleton." Editor Doug Ousterhout. (Little Brown & Co.) Boston, 1981: pp 257–292.

"Long Term Result of Nasal Bone Grafts," Esthetic Contouring of The Craniofacial Skeleton. Douglas Ousterhout, April 1991 (Lippincott, Williams & Wilkins).

"Modern Practice in Orthognathic and Reconstructive Surgery," Vol. 2. Chapter on Treacher Collins Franceschetti, Jean Francois-Tulane, and coauthor, Paul Tessier. William Bell, W.B. Saunders Co., July 1992.

Craniosynostosis: Diagnosis, Evaluation and Management, 2nd Ed. M. Michael Cohen and Ruth E. MacLean, April 6, 2000, Oxford: Oxford University Press.

Cirugia estetica del esqueleto facial. Editorial medica panamericana, 2005.

# Afterword

Héric's most famous citizen, and indeed one of Brittany's, became so perhaps because of Heric and Brittany. His love for both was always evident. He returned to the soil of his birth, and rests several hundred yards from the room in which he was born. In his time away from Héric—in Paris, in the United States, in Iran, and elsewhere—he became the best plastic surgeon of his age, and perhaps any age.

Why Paul Tessier turned out to be the surgeon that he did one cannot really say. He did not come from a medical family, but he had an internal drive to accomplish that may have been genetic. His determination to put things into the order that he wished, whether an enormously malformed child's faceor the workings of his service at Clinique Bélvèdere or his hunting trips to "*Secteur T*" was overwhelming. The demands on his family, his assistants, and his staff were great, but came nowhere near those he placed upon himself.

Those who were able to see him operate over the years often came away with the conviction that his will alone kept him going. Certainly his vast experience, extremely high standards, great technical ability, wide range of procedures (most of which he himself had developed),enormous energy and drive, and *will* "to have people, paticularly children, look *normal*" made him the surgeon he was. He helped innumerable patients and created a new surgical subspecialty.

What will be the future of the specialty that Dr. Tessier fathered? Between 1970 and 1995, probably around 75 young surgeons spent six months or more as assistants to Dr. Tessier: French, British, American, Brazilian, Swiss, Belgian, Spanish—and many more from Italy, Japan, and South America were there as visitors. It is hard to say how many of them are actually doing craniofacial surgery as the main part of their practice, but, in any event, coming after Tessier, they constitute the second generation of craniofacial surgeons. This second generation has trained a third generation, and perhaps worldwide there are several hundred plastic surgeons who will self-describe themselves as craniofacial surgeons. The International Society of Craniofacial Surgeons has about 150 members. There are between twenty andthirty centers around the world where training in craniofacial surgery is offered.

In some of these centers, the trainee will not see a monobloc frontofacial advancement, one of Dr. Tessier's favorite operations, because the craniofacial surgeon there does only Le Fort III-type advancements. In some of the centers that *do* perform monoblocs, they will all be done by distraction, in spite of the fact the Dr. Tessier's last *one hundred*_monoblocs without distraction had no significant complications. And the harvesting and use of autogenous bone grafts, because of which craniofacial surgery exists, may become a lost art. Increasingly, younger surgeons turn to titanium mesh and other alloplastic materials for orbital and cranial defects. And for the truly difficult cases, there already have been a few instances where facial transplantation is substituted for ability in classical reconstructive plastic surgery.

If the Specialty of craniofacial surgery is to continue, there will need to be at least a few surgeons willing to hold themselves rigorously to Tessier's principles. His papers and documents will hopefully be open to all who are interested. When a family brings a child with a major facial malformation to a plastic surgeon, the first question that they should ask is, "Do you know what Dr. Tessier did in cases like this?"

Will there be another surgeon capable of getting the results that Dr. Tessier obtained in his "impossible cases"? Certainly no plastic surgeon practicing in 2011 is capable of doing so. Will there be someone in the future who will have the experience, judgement, and technical ability to do so? One would hope so, but perhaps not. There was only one Leonardo da Vinci, and only one Mona Lisa … perhaps there will only be one man from Héric.

Paul Tessier has left us, but he lives on in the hearts and minds of those thousands of people—doctors and patients—who knew him. This picture was taken in the early 1980s by Jean-Claude de Wolf, partner-for-life of André Collesson, Dr. Tessier's nurse anesthetist for almost forty years. Jean Claude is one of France's foremost photographers, and he managed to take a picture that captures Paul Tessier better than any other; we see serenity, determination, strength, compassion, warmth, understanding, and a sense of humor and humanity all at once.

Made in the USA
Middletown, DE
14 July 2017